T5-CQC-555

THE
AMERICAN
LEGISLATIVE
PROCESS

Congress

and the States

William J. Keefe

UNIVERSITY OF PITTSBURGH

Morris S. Ogul

UNIVERSITY OF PITTSBURGH

Prentice-Hall, Inc., Englewood Cliffs, New Jersey

third edition

THE
AMERICAN
LEGISLATIVE
PROCESS

Congress

and the States

Library of Congress Cataloging in Publication Data

KEEFE, WILLIAM J
    The American legislative process.

    Includes bibliographical references.
    1.-Legislation—United States. 2.-Legislation—
United States—States. 3.-United States. Congress.
I. Ogul, Morris S.   joint author.
II. Title.
JK1001.K4 1972   328.73   72–1780
ISBN 0–13–028092–5

THE AMERICAN LEGISLATIVE PROCESS:
CONGRESS AND THE STATES,
Third Edition

William J. Keefe and Morris S. Ogul

Printed in the United States of America

10 9 8 7 6 5 4 3 2 1

PRENTICE-HALL INTERNATIONAL, INC., London
PRENTICE-HALL OF AUSTRALIA PTY. LTD., Sydney
PRENTICE-HALL OF CANADA LTD., Toronto
PRENTICE-HALL OF INDIA PRIVATE LIMITED, New Delhi
PRENTICE-HALL OF JAPAN, INC., Tokyo

to Martha and Eleanor

CONTENTS

part three

Legislatures,

Parties,

and Interests

part four

Interaction with

the Executive

and the Courts

TABLES

FIGURES

PREFACE

Once rather neglected in political science literature, research and writing about legislatures has increased dramatically in the past two decades. The upsurge partly reflects the centrality of the legislative process to the politics of democracy, especially as fresh questioning has arisen concerning the responsiveness of all American institutions to their publics. Two other developments help explain the increased attention given this subject. One has been the accessibility of legislators and legislative records to scholars. The other, perhaps more important, has been the inventiveness of researchers in applying sophisticated methodologies to the study of legislative processess and behavior. Whatever the complete explanation, the result has been the publication of a substantial and impressive literature. The need to take account of recent findings and trends is the principal justification for the preparation of this third edition.

At this point, no encompassing scheme for analyzing the legislative process seems to be sufficiently developed or supported to justify its exclusive adoption. In this respect, political scientists who engage in research in this field work under burdens shared by political scientists in all fields. Within this limitation, this book proposes to describe and analyze the American legislative process. We have sought to wring the most that we can from a variety of approaches to the study of legislative processes and problems and have drawn upon a wide-ranging assortment of studies—of legal, behavioral, normative, and historical dimensions. The only test invoked has been their apparent appropriateness to a better understanding of the behavior of legislators and the functioning of legislatures.

Three main assumptions continue to characterize this work. First, we believe that analysis is promoted when legislative institutions are viewed in relationship to larger environments and inclusive political systems. Accordingly, we have given the role of "outsiders"—parties, interest groups, chief executives, and courts—at least as much attention as the legislative institution itself. Second, we believe that a comprehensive study of the legislative process requires careful examination of state legislatures no less than of Congress. In each chapter, analysis moves between state and nation, depending upon the nature of the inquiry and the availability of data or interpretation. Third, we believe that legislative institutions and processes can be illuminated by stressing such aspects of legislative life as the roles, norms, and perceptions held by legislators.

Some account of the authors' perspectives may be of interest. Most important, we have tried to keep this volume from becoming disabled as a result of carrying a heavy load of our personal preferences and the incantations which they would tend to produce. Here and there a determined reader may encounter clues which suggest that the authors (a) hold a bias in favor of legislative institutions that are responsive to majority opinions and impulses in the institution and the electorate, (b) believe that American legislatures today are to be neither extolled nor disparaged in the abstract and that specific analysis should precede assessment, and (c) conclude that there is nothing inevitable about the present ordering of American legislatures, even though major change probably will be associated with major alterations in the broader political system. Given this primary assumption, our analysis inevitably moves toward ascertaining the relevance of contemporary trends in American society for the legislative process.

The basic structure of the book remains the same. The most extensive changes in this edition appear in the examination of reapportionment, legislative elections, the committee system and seniority, party and interest group behavior, and legislative reorganization and modernization.

A number of colleagues and friends have given us suggestions and assistance in the preparation of this book. For the first edition, James A. Robinson's comments were especially useful; for the third edition, Joseph Cooper's suggestions were similarly comprehensive and valuable. Others to be acknowledged for their contributions to one or more of the editions are Holbert N. Carroll, Edward F. Cooke, Charles S. Hyneman, Robert F. Karsch, Kathryn Keefe, Albert J. Ossman, and Rhoten A. Smith. Special acknowledgment is due Lynette Perkins for her research assistance for this edition. Martha Keefe typed a substantial portion of this revision. Finally, Roger Emblen and Helen S. Harris of Prentice-Hall contributed in a variety of ways to easing the problems that invariably accompany the authorship of a book.

Finally, a word is appropriate about the division of labor in the preparation of this edition. Chapters 1–10 and 14 were written by Mr. Keefe, while Chapters 11–13 were written by Mr. Ogul. Each author made numerous contributions to the other's work in order to develop an integrated book, one consistent in approach, content, and style.

W.J.K.
M.S.O.

Pittsburgh, Pennsylvania

ACKNOWLEDGMENTS

The authors wish to record their gratitude to those writers and publishers who gave us permission to quote from their works. Special thanks go to those university presses which have subscribed to the resolution on permissions. The following publishers have asked us to set forth their copyright notices: William Cary, "Pressure Groups and the Revenue Code: A Requiem in Honor of the Departing Uniformity of the Tax Laws," *Harvard Law Review,* LXVIII (March, 1955). Copyright © 1955 by the Harvard Law Review Association. Robert Luce, *Congress: An Explanation* (Cambridge, Mass.: Harvard University Press, Copyright © 1926, by The President and Fellows of Harvard College). Robert McCloskey, "Foreword: The Reapportionment Case," *Harvard Law Review,* LXXVI (November, 1962). Copyright © 1962 by the Harvard Law Review Association. Stanley Surrey, "The Congress and the Tax Lobbyist—How Special Tax Provisions Get Enacted," *Harvard Law Review,* LXX (May, 1957). Copyright © 1957 by the Harvard Law Review Association. V. Stanley Vardys, "Select Committees of the House of Representatives," *Midwest Journal of Political Science,* VI (August, 1962). Copyright © 1962 by the Wayne State University Press. Benjamin Fletcher Wright, ed., *The Federalist* (Cambridge, Mass.: Harvard University Press, Copyright © 1961, by The President and Fellows of Harvard College).

THE
AMERICAN
LEGISLATIVE
PROCESS

Congress

and the States

part one

Legislatures and Legislators in the Political System

I

THE LEGISLATIVE TASK

Complex social systems require institutions capable of establishing and maintaining the legal order, crystallizing and settling conflict, determining priorities, granting legitimacy to policies, and adapting existing rules of society to new conditions. These are tasks familiar to all democratic legislatures, though nowhere are they assigned exclusively to the legislature. The legislature comprises only part of the apparatus for making authoritative social decisions. In a variety of ways it shares power and responsibility with the chief executive, the courts, the bureaucracy, the political parties, and, in some cases, the public. Time, place, and leaders help shape the relations between the legislature and these separate centers of power. The legislature may choose to follow their lead, to join with them, to ignore them, to try to pit one against the other, or to struggle against them. On occasion the legislature wins ascendancy over competing branches and powers, due sometimes as much to their default as to its own leadership and determination.

An appraisal of the legislature that focuses on the institution as a separate legal entity may contribute to forming valid and useful distinctions, but it is certain to fall short of imparting a full sense of the character and the dimensions of the legislative process. The legislature does not and cannot maintain an independent group life. Instead, it is involved in an elaborate network of external relations, some of which it has designed and developed for its own purposes and others of which have been thrust upon it. Legislative oversight of the administrative branch, for example, is calculated to strengthen the position of the legislature and to help it secure from the bureaucracy certain attitudes and behavior perhaps best described as "responsible administration." On the other hand, executive initiative in the legislative process—an intrusion neither chosen by the legislature nor easily accepted by its members—often functions to stimulate the legislature to action, contributing to the development of new programs or to the abandonment or revision of old ones. For its success the legislature may be dependent on the collaboration of other institutions—for example, party, executive agency, or interest group. No legislature chooses independently all the roads it wants to go down, though it may be able to determine the speed at which it prefers to travel. About the same thing can be said for those institutions dependent in some way on the legislature or susceptible to its influence: the course of their affairs as well as their effectiveness may in large measure be attributable to steady legislative interest and backstopping.

3

4   The legislature is part of a larger political system. Its ability to act and to make its decisions stick is affected by the actions of other institutions and by the happenings and circumstances in the political process at large. Its linkages with other political institutions stand out clearly. No matter how specific the intent of the legislature, its decisions will require interpretation and implementation by executive officials; no matter how unambiguous its legislative purposes, its laws may come under review in the judicial process. In dealing with the executive branch and the courts, the legislature may have neither the first word, as represented in the origination of ideas for legislation, nor the last word, as represented in the determination of the constitutionality of its legislation. At mid-course, within the legislature the process of reconciling the demands of contesting groups and of choosing from among alternative courses of action may be as much the work of outsiders as of legislators.

Linkages between the legislature and the general political-constitutional system appear at numerous points and may have a decisive bearing on the behavior of legislators. The traditions and processes associated with elections and representation affect the kinds of people who are recruited as legislators, the conditions under which they hold office, the range of roles they select to play as members of the legislature, and the clienteles (organized private interests, the chief executive, the party, and others) to which they look for information, cues, instructions, or support. Members elected in districts or states of intense party competition may behave differently from members elected in districts or states of low or casual party competition. Legislators from marginal districts may emphasize certain roles in the legislature and ignore others; their voting behavior may show a special pattern in relation to their legislative party or to the positions of interest groups or the chief executive. The overall political-constitutional system may be designed to make it difficult for public sentiment to find its way intact to the legislature; it may be virtually impossible, for example, for one party to capture both houses of the legislature and the executive at the same time. Where arrangements rule out party control, party management of the legislature and party responsibility for a policy program are similarly ruled out.

In sum, the legislature is not an isolated institution. The struggle to gain the advantages it can allocate (or to avoid the penalties it can levy) takes place both inside and outside its walls. Eventually, conflicts are likely to be brought to the legislature because arrangements made outside are inconclusive, or precarious, or unsatisfactory, or because the legislature is in a position to contribute formulas for settlement and legitimacy to the provisions of settlement. The major decisions of the legislature ordinarily represent a temporary accommodation between private and public groups holding different objectives. As circumstances change and as elections upset old alliances and help to create new ones, consensus is impaired. A change in power relations gives rise to multiple demands that the legislature produce new settlements—"business as usual," whether in the way the legislature is organized (e.g., the power of a rules committee loosely tied to the leadership) or in the character of the policy output, may be entirely unsatisfactory to those newly come to power.

Briefly, these opening paragraphs have sought to show that the "legislative process" is much more than a legal system for taking inchoate ideas and fashioning them into firm statutes. The process is routine only when the questions are routine. Viewed more fundamentally, the legislative process will be seen as a major phase of the most wide-ranging struggles for political, economic, and social advantages. No understanding of the process will carry full meaning unless it takes into account the legislature's relationship to other central institutions and to environmental factors, including political parties, interest groups, constituencies, the executive, the judiciary, and the electoral-representative system. Within this book these matters receive noticeably more attention than those that might be described as uniquely legislative.

Discontent over the Legislature

Legislative assemblies have long been experiencing difficult days. Where totalitarian movements have been successful in gaining power, the independence and autonomy of legislatures have been diminished or lost altogether. Elsewhere, under democratic conditions, legislatures have declined in popular esteem, at times to the point of disrepute. American legislatures without exception no longer enjoy as great a measure of public confidence as was theirs in the early days of the republic. How great their fall from virtue has been is surely disputable, but there is no doubt that it has taken place.

The reasons that account for the decline of the legislature's prestige are more easily detected than weighed for significance. Discontent over the performance of the legislature appears to stem from a number of interrelated complaints. Briefly treated here and at length in later chapters, they look as follows:

The legislature is not sufficiently responsive to majority preferences either in the electorate or within the institution itself. Of all the charges laid against the legislature this one has been pressed most often and insistently. In the past, malapportionment has frequently been cited as a leading obstacle to majority rule in American legislatures. Majority sentiments in the electorate, according to this argument, have not easily made their way to the legislature because of a faulty system of representation in which rural and sparsely populated areas have held a disproportionate number of seats at the expense of populous urbanized areas. This imbalance allegedly has resulted in the formation of public policy inimical to the interests represented by urban legislators. Whatever the validity of this charge, the criticism it fosters will doubtless wane as more legislatures come into compliance with the equitable-apportionment doctrines laid down by the Supreme Court in the 1960s. Within the legislature the fragmentation of power due to the weakness of the parties, the independent position of committees, the custom of conferring committee chairmanships by order of seniority, and other rules and practices that enhance minority strength impede the effort to carry out popular mandates.

Legislative politics and public policy formation are dominated by organized special-interest groups. This assessment will be recognized as a variant of the first. It holds that the "public interest" is not often uppermost

6 in the minds of legislators bent on favoring (or placating) a multitude of pressure groups. When agricultural policy is under consideration, farmers' organizations arrive with drawn specifications; when labor-management legislation is at stake, labor and business organizations lock horns; when legislation to provide health care for the aged is introduced, the American Medical Association appears, ready to do battle with whatever advocates may be on the scene. To many observers the lesson has seemed evident that legislators do not make a careful distinction between the aims that serve private interests and those that serve public interests. All too frequently, in the view of some critics, public policy appears to meet only the claims and aspirations of the most organized elements of the population. E. E. Schattschneider writes:

> American government has grown great by meeting the demands made upon it. The catholicity and versatility of the governmental response to the demands made upon it seem at times to have been based on the assumption that all claims ought to be met regardless of their merits.... [Yet] sooner or later it becomes necessary...in any political system to *discriminate* among the demands. This involves the establishment of a public policy. No public policy could ever be the mere sum of the demands of the organized special interests. For one thing, the sum of the special interests, especially the organized special interests, is not equal to the total of all interests in the community, for there are vital common interests that cannot be organized by pressure groups. Government by organized special interests, without some kind of higher integration, must break down of its own weight.[1]

Legislatures have sometimes been tarnished by revelations concerning the power of interest groups in the legislative process. One should not forget, however, that legislators are parties as well as spectators to the clashes of interest groups; the legislator's personal welfare may be as much at stake as the welfare of any group when certain public policy questions come before the legislature. If the following account were true merely as an oddity, it would scarcely be worthy of mention. But the facts are otherwise: "conflict-of-interest"[2] cases occur with sufficient frequency to warrant their inclusion among the principal flaws of legislative institutions. Organized interest groups are often at the root of the controversy. Consider this account by an Illinois state senator of the regulation of the racing industry in that state:

> There are no regular lobbyists representing racing and parimutuel betting interests in Springfield. But several influential legislators, or members of their families, are stockholders in racetracks. On special guest nights, busloads

---

1 *Party Government* (New York: Holt, Rinehart & Winston, Inc., 1942), pp. 30–31.

2 In "conflict of interest" questions two interests come into play: "one is the interest of the government official (and of the public) in the proper administration of his office; the other is the official's interest in his private economic affairs. A conflict of interest exists whenever these two interests clash, or appear to clash." See Bayless Manning, "The Purity Potlatch: An Essay on Conflicts of Interest, American Government, and Moral Escalation," *Federal Bar Journal*, XXIV (Spring 1964), 239–56. Also see the discussion of conflict of interest in Daniel M. Berman, *In Congress Assembled* (New York: The Macmillan Company, 1964), Chapter 15.

of sympathetic legislators are driven to the tracks, given a lavish cocktail party and dinner, then escorted to reserved seats and provided with tips on likely winners on the day's card. At one track, important races are named in honor of individual legislators on these gala occasions. A notable racing enthusiast is the President Pro Tem of the Senate...whose family has long been registered with the State Racing Commission as track stockholders. [He] distributes fistfuls of season passes in the Senate chambers, and when racing bills are heard in committee he testifies for the industry. At one recent hearing, he was the only witness to oppose increasing taxes on winnings. Yet he prevailed.[3]

The legislature is seldom a force for innovation. This criticism rests on the belief that few if any significant changes are likely to result from a new session of the legislature. The caution and conservatism of the legislature, its unwillingness to experiment, and its inability to cast free from conventional ties very probably have served to stunt the interest of the public (or at least some sectors of it) in the institution and its policy processes. At times, change comes so haltingly as to be imperceptible. Temporization appears as policy. Duane Lockard has put the case this way:

> [Power in Congress is not] distributed in a neutral way; it favors the status quo. Congress is like the rest of American government: it is geared to grind slowly. Congress, through its formal rules and its informal practices, is an institution devoted inordinately to the prevention of action. Indeed it is so well equipped to stop legislation that even conservative interests at times have difficulty when they seek changes in the law. Usually conservatives need only to stop action to achieve at least their more limited goals, but liberal legislators, because they seek innovation more frequently, encounter obstruction from well-entrenched conservative opponents in addition to the usual difficulties in putting together majorities for their proposals.[4]

The same criticism has of course been raised concerning state legislatures: "If almost *anything* could happen when the legislature meets, isn't it likely that state governments would seem more important in the lives of their people?"[5]

Institutional arrangements in the legislature obscure the public's view of the decision-making process and, moreover, make it difficult to fix responsibility for actions taken by government. The legislature functions according to well-ordered routines, but even the most assiduous observer finds it baffling to follow the course of a bill through the legislative labyrinths. The haze that hangs over the lawmaking process is due chiefly to the complexity of rules of procedure, which opens up vast opportunities for maneuvering; the structure and design of legislative organization, which make the

---

[3] Paul Simon, "The Illinois Legislature: A Study in Corruption," *Harper's Magazine*, September 1964, p. 75.

[4] *The Perverted Priorities of American Politics* (New York: The Macmillan Company, 1971), p. 123.

[5] Karl A. Bosworth, "Lawmaking in State Governments," in *The Forty-eight States: Their Tasks as Policy Makers and Administrators* (New York: The American Assembly, Columbia University, 1955), p. 89.

8 institution vulnerable to minority domination; and the impotence of the party, which diminishes the possibility of holding an organized and highly visible group accountable for decisions.

Legislative proposals must surmount an extraordinary number of obstacles, some of which are imbedded in unlikely places. For example, a bill may be referred to a hostile committee and quietly pigeonholed, or it may never be placed on a committee agenda because of the chairman's opposition. Or, having passed through a standing committee, a bill may fail to win clearance from the rules committee and thereby be lost. A bill on the calendar may never be called up for consideration. A bill may be killed by recommitting it to committee "for further study" or emasculated by adopting an amendment which alters its purposes.

Why and how legislative decisions are taken are not easily discovered by outsiders. To the general public preoccupied with daily living, the design of the legislature appears to consist mainly of dark corners. As Dayton McKean, a political scientist and former New Jersey state legislator, writes:

> If a football game were played with four teams on the field at once, sometimes playing with one ball, sometimes with any number of balls which now and then they rained upon one another, the spectators would be no more confused about who fumbled than the voters may be about who was responsible for what happened (or failed to happen) at a legislative session. If now and then the captains of the four teams appointed conference committees, each of which took a ball into the fieldhouse for a while, later to emerge with the balls shortened, lengthened, painted another color, or deflated before they were put back in play, the spectators would stay away from the game in droves, as they stay away from legislative galleries.
>
> ...Difficult as it is for the voters to follow in their spare time what goes on in one legislative body, it is at least twice as difficult for them to follow what happens in (and between) two houses. The difficulty is greater when one party has a majority in one house, the other party in the other house; then each may blame the other for the record of the session, and the voters cannot confidently hold either party responsible.[6]

Many observers find the principal disabling feature of the legislature to be the weakness of the political parties. Their inability to close ranks and maintain cohesion on major legislation in Congress is well known. "Instead of a grand encounter between the rallied forces of the two great parties in House and Senate, the legislative battle often degenerates into scuffles and skirmishes among minority groups."[7] The chief consequence of having fragile parliamentary parties is that it becomes next to impossible to fix responsibility for the fate of most major legislation.

So vague and elastic is the concept of "responsibility" that almost anyone can be blamed or praised for a particular decision. On any given vote the press and commentators may supply one or more of these explanations: "the president failed to exert effective leadership"; "the House leadership erred in its calculations"; "the vote was a signal victory for the American

---

6 "The Politics of the States," in *The Forty-eight States*, p. 73.

7 James MacGregor Burns, *Congress on Trial* (New York: Harper & Row, Publishers, 1949), p. 35.

Farm Bureau Federation"; "the decision turned on the vote of the senator from West Virginia who was in the debt of the senator from Oklahoma"; "the loss has been attributed to the defection of several key Democrats"; "a biparty coalition won a narrow victory"; "the bill that emerged from the conference committee was accepted reluctantly by a House leadership anxious to adjourn"; and so on. In the absence of responsible parties the public lacks the means by which to hold the legislature as a whole accountable for its decisions.

Because of its natural conservatism, the legislature is capable of rapid response only in times of emergency. The legislature will respond to assuage a crisis, if it is sufficiently clear and compelling, only to slip back into the seesaw of stalemate or a preoccupation with minor problems and side issues. Those persistent problems that lack the element of exigency are ignored or demeaned.

As a way out of impasse, the chief executive may turn to manufacturing a serviceable crisis out of the material of foreign relations or of the economy, hopeful that the legislature can be induced to take action. But this is not easy to bring off. Is there a crisis today in civil rights? In agriculture? In education? In locating revenues for governmental functions? And what of the "natural" crisis, occasioned by sharp fluctuations in military, diplomatic, or economic patterns and relations? Have the public and its representatives become so inured to crisis that they fail to recognize its new dimensions? If Richard Neustadt is correct, the possibility for turning "conflict consensus" into a political opportunity for the president to spur Congress has been lessened. "We may have priced ourselves out of the market for 'productive' crises on the pattern Roosevelt knew—productive in the sense of strengthening his chances for sustained support *within* the system. Judging from the Fifties, neither limited war nor limited depression is productive in those terms."[8]

The legislature is populated by insecure and timorous men whose principal aim is to stay in office. This judgment has a wide currency and appears to be shared by all manner of critics, even two as unlike as C. Wright Mills and Walter Lippmann. Mills writes:

> Most professional politicians represent an astutely balanced variety of local interests, and such rather small freedom to act in political decisions as they have derives from precisely that fact: if they are fortunate they can juggle and play off their varied local interests against one another, but perhaps more frequently they come to straddle the issues in order to avoid decision. Protecting the interest of his electoral domain, the Congressman remains attentively loyal to his sovereign locality.[9]

And Lippmann observes:

> In government offices which are sensitive to the vehemence and passion of mass sentiment public men have no sure tenure. They are in effect perpetual office seekers, always on trial for their political lives, always required to court

8 *Presidential Power: The Politics of Leadership* (New York: John Wiley & Sons, Inc., 1960), p. 186.
9 *The Power Elite* (New York: Oxford University Press, 1959), p. 251.

their restless constituents. They are deprived of their independence. Democratic politicians rarely feel they can afford the luxury of telling the whole truth to the people.... With exceptions so rare that they are regarded as miracles and freaks of nature, successful democratic politicians are insecure and intimidated men. They advance politically only as they placate, appease, bribe, seduce, bamboozle, or otherwise manage to manipulate the demanding and threatening elements in their constituencies. The decisive consideration is not whether the proposition is good but whether it is popular—not whether it will work well and prove itself but whether the active talking constituents like it immediately. Politicians rationalize this servitude by saying that in a democracy public men are the servants of the people.[10]

The legislature is not sufficiently attentive to the need for developing and maintaining high standards of rectitude for its members. In the judgment of a host of critics, there is a dinginess about American legislatures that results from their tendency to overlook wrongdoings by members and their reluctance to adopt rigorous, enforceable codes of ethics. Prompted by a series of spectacular cases—the affairs of former Senate Democratic majority secretary Bobby Baker, Congressman Adam Clayton Powell, and Senator Thomas J. Dodd—Congress has recently turned its attention to the practices of its members. One result has been the creation of ethics committees in both houses—the Senate Select Committee on Standards of Conduct, formed in 1965, and the House Committee on Standards of Official Conduct, formed in 1967. As critics see the matter, the formation of ethical "watchdog" committees was a step in the right direction, but only the first step. Neither house, for example, has shown more than passing interest in the principal reform suggested to combat ethical lapses, which is to require members (and their employees) to put on public record a comprehensive statement concerning the sources of their wealth and their economic associations.[11] In the absence of a meaningful disclosure requirement, only the most blatant cases of conflict of interest are likely to come to the attention of the legislature, the press, and the public. Moreover, there is nothing in the brief history of Congress's ethics committees to suggest that they are anxious to investigate allegations of wrongdoing on the part of members.[12]

[10] *The Public Philosophy* (New York: The New American Library, 1956), p. 28.

[11] Under standards of conduct rules adopted in 1968, members of both houses are required to file financial reports each year. The reports are prepared in two parts, one to be made public and the other to remain confidential unless an official investigation is launched. Senate requirements are minimal. Each senator is required to disclose the source and amount of any honorarium of $300 or more, the source and amount of gifts of $50 or more, and the source, amount, and disposition of all political contributions. All other information concerning the senator's financial position —for example, income from business or law practice, interest in real or personal property, debts, loans, and so on—is placed in a confidential report filed with the comptroller general. Disclosure requirements in the House are more rigorous, though the financial details concerning members' assets or sources of income are also placed in the confidential category. For details concerning the financial disclosure requirements in each house, see the *Congressional Quarterly Weekly Report,* May 28, 1971, p. 1183.

[12] Robert Sherrill, "We Can't Depend on Congress to Keep Congress Honest," *New York Times Magazine,* July 19, 1970, pp. 5ff.

Such evidence as is available suggests that state legislatures are less likely than Congress to require members to adhere to stern codes of ethics. An extraordinary number of accounts have been published which suggest that state legislators are under the thumb of private interests and that they are careless in segregating their personal interests from their public responsibilities. Consider the following reports—of a party given by Harrah's Lake Tahoe gambling casino to welcome the Nevada legislature into session, of the commingling of public and private interests in the Florida legislature, and of "payoffs" in the Illinois legislature:

[Legislators, their wives, secretaries, and secretaries' boyfriends] were treated to an all-expenses-paid evening on the house, complete with dinner, champagne and entertainment by Robert Goulet. Nobody seemed to question the extending of such hospitality by a regulated industry to its regulators. Indeed, another such affair was scheduled for the following evening at The Nugget in Carson City.[13] [Nevada]

When the interests of the legislators are the same as those of big business and big industry, one must expect the state to wind up from time to time with a speaker of the House whose law partner may be registered as lobbyist for several different groups or a speaker who may have been hired as attorney for a controversial commission; or any number of powerful legislators who may be taking paychecks from agencies that must come to the legislature for appropriations, or from private banking and utility firms that wish to avoid further statutory restrictions. All this has been done quite openly.[14] [Florida]

Most of these [payoffs] are recorded as legal fees, public-relations services, or "campaign contributions," though a campaign may be months away. If questioned, the recipient simply denies that the payment had anything to do with legislative activity. This makes it technically legal. A somewhat smaller number of payoffs are not veiled at all; cold cash passes directly from one hand to the other....A few legislators go so far as to introduce some bills that are deliberately designed to shake down groups which oppose them and which pay to have them withdrawn. These bills are called "fetchers," and once their sponsors develop a lucrative field, they guard it jealously.[15] [Illinois]

Criticism of the organs of government is of course always in style, and critics are not always reasonable in the distinctions they make or fair in the illustrations they select. Accounts of the weaknesses or corruption of a few legislators, for example, will not support a case that the institution itself is corrupt. Yet whether the foregoing appraisals, taken as a whole, are convincing and square easily with the facts may be less important than that many estimable observers believe they are true. A little evidence goes a long way. Though not necessarily warranted, substantial dissatisfaction with

---

[13] James N. Miller, "Hamstrung Legislatures," *National Civic Review,* LIV (April 1965), 186.

[14] Robert Sherrill, "Florida's Legislature: The Pork Chop State of Mind," *Harper's Magazine,* November 1965, p. 86.

[15] Simon, *op. cit.,* pp. 74–75.

12 American legislatures is unquestionably present.[16] Above all else, what plagues the legislature is its failure to consolidate its earlier promise, to hold the public's confidence, especially the confidence of those people most attentive to the affairs of the legislature. And there is another point worth noting. The lament that "something is wrong with the legislature" is not simply the copyright of "liberals," though their voices are often heard. Even such a sturdy pillar of conservatism as the *Wall Street Journal* complains editorially of "the deterioration of Congress."[17]

The Functions of the Legislature

To begin the study of the legislature, we need to look at what it does. The functions of the legislature resemble the listings of a catalogue: no single, urgent theme ties them all together or dominates the rest; some represent a heavier investment than others; some appear as basic requirements, while others are simply the accretions that attach to a going institution. The hallmark of the legislature is of course its lawmaking function, and many pages of this book are concerned with how it carries this out. Yet lawmaking takes up only a portion of the legislature's time. The legislature is also engaged in three other *central* functions—checking the administration, providing political education for the public, and providing representation for several kinds of clientage; and two *minor* functions, described as the judicial function and the function of leadership selection. What the functions of the legislature depict, in short, is the contribution of the American representative assembly to the governing process.[18]

THE FUNCTION OF MAKING LAW

The principal legal task of the American legislature is to make law. The expansion of government services and functions, especially in recent decades, has contributed to an endless procession of ideas for laws. Legislation covers an immense ground: virtually any stray idea can gain some kind of hearing among legislators; virtually any proposal stands something of a chance of finding legislative expression. The instability of legislation differs only in degree from the instability of fashion and public taste. No statute is likely to settle a matter for all time; at best it can only temporarily conclude a problem. In all probability, subsequent legislatures will undo the statute,

---

16 See the evidence concerning Congress provided by Roger H. Davidson, David Kovenock, and Michael O'Leary, *Congress in Crisis: Politics and Congressional Reform* (Belmont, California: Wadsworth Publishing Company, 1966), Chapter 2. Perhaps of greatest significance is the fact that better-educated citizens rank among those most critical of Congress.

17 See an editorial by this title in the issue of March 13, 1962, the chief points of which are that Congress fails to rise above parochialism and that it "customarily accedes to the demands of pressure groups, whether those demands are formulated by the White House or its own members."

18 For further discussion of the functions of *state legislatures,* see William J. Keefe, *"The* Functions and Powers of the State Legislature," in *State Legislatures in American Politics,* ed. Alexander Heard (Englewood Cliffs, N.J.: Prentice-Hall, Inc., 1966), pp. 37–69.

rework it, perhaps remove it altogether. "Once begin the dance of legislation," wrote Woodrow Wilson, "and you must struggle through its mazes as best you can to its breathless end,—if any end there be."[19]

The widening of knowledge in science and social relations seems inevitably to foreshadow a greater burden for the legislature. It is obvious that tomorrow's legislature will run no risk of atrophy for lack of legislation to consider; rather it will be put to the test of coping with a body of requests and problems both more numerous and more complex than government has ever had to consider in the past. The increasingly heavy and the highly visible investment in lawmaking is not, of course, evidence that the legislature occupies a superior position among the branches of government. What it does signify is the close relationship between the growth in complexity of society and the resulting requirements for standard means of adjusting conflict and for new forms of social control.

A literal reading of the constitutional grants of power to the legislature discloses a minimum amount about the lawmaking process. The fact that the legislature is empowered to make laws does not mean that it initiates the ideas for legislation. Indeed, for the infusion of ideas and the origination of most legislation, the legislature is dependent upon familiar "outsiders"—the chief executive, administrative agencies, political interest groups, and various party agencies and party spokesmen. Most important among these "outside" interests is the chief executive: his ideas for legislation and the ideas of his advisers, set forth in "administration bills," regularly provide the major items on the legislature's agenda.[20] By and large, what the legislature brings to lawmaking is the power to represent the people and the authority to make social decisions; what it can leave is its distinctive imprint on the policies recommended by others. Neither in what it brings to the process of making law nor in what it leaves in public policy is its power trifling.

In its broadest sense, American lawmaking consists of finding major and marginal compromises to ideas advanced for legislation. The sifting and sorting of proposals accompanies the search for compromise—in caucus, in committee, on the floor, in negotiations with the executive, in confrontation with interest groups. The details of bills are filled in at many stages in the legislative process, though especially in committees. One can say that any proposal of consequence serves something of a probationary period; its ultimate fate depends on how well its advocates succeed in bringing additional supporters to its side. The task is not simply to beat the drums to excite one's followers but to neutralize outward and probable opponents and to convince the uncertain. The decisive support may come from one or more

[19] *Congressional Government* (New York: Meridian Books, 1956), p. 195. This work originally was published in 1885.

[20] It is tempting to exaggerate the argument of congressional passivity and executive initiative. Ralph K. Huitt writes: "[What] is easy to miss is the origin of many bills which in time pick up enough support to become 'Administration bills.' One or more members of Congress may have originated the idea and done all the spade work necessary to make it viable. One thinks of the lonely voice of George Norris in the 1920s calling for a Federal river project which became, in a different political climate, the Tennessee Valley Authority. Other crusades have taken less time to succeed. Area redevelopment and water pollution control are projects which began in Congress." "Congress, the Durable Partner," in *Lawmakers in a Changing World,* ed. Elke Frank (Englewood Cliffs, N.J.: Prentice-Hall, Inc., 1966), p. 17.

14 interest groups newly won over to the cause, perhaps from a newly invested and sympathetic committee chairman, perhaps from the chief executive who would incorporate the bill in "his" program.

The process of gaining converts to an idea, of strengthening a latent party position, or of putting together a winning coalition may and often does require more than a single session of the legislature. Today's opponents, under different circumstances (e.g., a new administration, the aftermath of a sweeping electoral decision), may be tomorrow's proponents or at least reluctant supporters. A considerable number of the major bills adopted at any session of any legislature have failed of passage in an earlier assembly. Ordinarily, where major change is involved, support is won gradually, perhaps accumulated over a number of sessions. Many proposals are given trial runs in the full knowledge that they have no chance of passage. But another day may bring another verdict. In the American political landscape, what is currently unconventional may yet become orthodox with the passage of time: in the formation of public policy the principal testing ground for orthodoxy is the legislature.

The overriding strategy in the advancement of legislation, from introduction to final vote, is to fashion a bill that can attract and consolidate the necessary support, preferably with a minimum of concessions to opponents. The process of winning support calls for tapering demands from the optimal down to the acceptable—ranging from what is most desirable to what, if necessary, will do—and it may begin as early as the initial drafting of the bill and run through to the final negotiations in a conference committee between the houses. The steady working of compromise and accommodation may lead to a curious assortment of provisions, most of which entered the bill as concessions to potential supporters; the end product may be a bill that no one, not even the original sponsor, really wants, or a bill that under the circumstances is the best possible. Getting a bill through the legislature requires ingenuity and leeway, and rare is the major proposal that ends up in law in the same form that it was introduced.

Legislative policies, few of which ever are totally new, derive from a vast array of factors. In the most general sense, a policy represents a response to some kind of problem, one acute enough to intrude on the well-being of a significant number of people and their organizations or on the well-being of the government itself, one conspicuous enough to draw the attention of at least some legislators. In a more specific sense, legislation is generated by apprehension, unrest, conflict, innovation, and events. Rarely, if ever, do policies spring full-blown from a theory of society.

Comprehensive federal pure food and drug laws came about as the result of the startling exposé of the practices of food and drug manufacturers and processors. More recently, internal security laws were the outgrowth of apprehension over the activities of American Communists; manpower retraining and area redevelopment legislation were thrust up as answers to new and special patterns of unemployment; legislation to provide for more rigorous control over the testing of drugs was passed in the wake of disclosures concerning the effects of thalidomide, a drug that caused numerous babies to be born malformed; the principal impetus to more liberal trade legislation was the development of the European Common Market; legislation to establish a system of communications satellites was passed shortly after the successful experiment with Telstar; and finally, supported by an unassailable rationale of public safety, the Minnesota House of Representatives not long ago passed a bill to make it a misdemeanor for any occupant of the front seat of a moving automobile "to put his or her arm around another person."[21] The list of legislation passed in response to the emergence of new problems or to the successful dramatization of old ones could be extended endlessly.

Legislation ultimately relates to people. Irrespective of the nature of group conflict that may be present, or of the policy field, or even of the extent of public awareness of their equity, the values and aspirations of certain popular segments inevitably are at stake in all significant legislation. "The truth is," one spokesman testified before a congressional committee, "that the affront and denials that this section, if enacted, would correct are intensely human and personal. The players in this drama of frustration and indignity are not commas or semicolons in a legislative thesis. They are people, human beings, citizens of the United States of America."[22]

Neither the wide perception of a social problem by legislators nor their recognition of a group's particular claims for governmental action is certain to lead to legislation. The chances for some form of legislative response increase when (1) influential pressure groups mobilize their members and seek a governmental solution; (2) the unorganized public becomes intensely concerned with the matter, as in the controversy over thalidomide, or conversely, is indifferent to the special measures sought by a pressure group; (3) the parties and powerful legislators take up the cudgels; and (4) the formation of strong counterpressures to defend the *status quo* fails to materialize. On occasion a number of major interest groups, the unorganized public, and party and legislative leaders act in concert to advance legislation. But more often than not, public opinion is inert and the parties are splintered. Under the circumstances the prudent legislator is inclined to take the path of least resistance, though it may seem to lead down a dark alley, and to vote for the best interests of organized pressures.

There are two special categories of lawmaking of constitutional origin. The first, involving the approval of treaties, is specified by the U.S. Constitution and technically brings only the upper house of Congress into the process. The second special category, the power to adopt constitutional amendments and thereby to alter the fundamental law, is a lawmaking function of both national and state legislatures.

The initiative in making foreign policy rests with the president. But the bare words of the Constitution afford only slight indication of Congress's prerogatives and opportunities for influencing presidential decisions and the broad thrust of foreign policy. And in recent years the significant increase in the number of international agreements and in the requirements for enabling legislation to carry broad policies into effect—both in large part a response

---

[21] As the measure left the House, there was at least some doubt as to whether a mother holding an infant would be permitted to ride in the front seat, although apparently this was not the problem which the legislation was designed to solve. *Washington Post,* May 13, 1963.

[22] This is taken from the testimony of the executive secretary of the NAACP, testifying before the Senate Commerce Committee on a Kennedy administration bill to ban discrimination in public facilities. *New York Times,* July 23, 1963.

16   to the challenge to the security of the nation posed by Communist powers—have greatly augmented the responsibilities of Congress in the field of foreign policy. "Foreign" and "domestic" policies, more or less distinct in an earlier period, have now become tightly joined in much of the major legislation of any Congress. Moreover, the House, though it has no constitutional role of advising and consenting to the ratification of treaties, is virtually as instrumental as the Senate in shaping foreign policy through the exercise of its ordinary lawmaking powers and especially through its influence on appropriations. By the same token, the treaty-making power of the Senate does not reveal much about the chamber's overall responsibilities in foreign policy; treaty-making, in fact, takes up but a small fraction of the time devoted to foreign policy questions. To quote Robert A. Dahl:

> American foreign policy rests on government loans and expenditures which require appropriations; on military aid, trade negotiations, resources control, which require enabling legislation; on the existence of military forces in readiness, which requires legislation and appropriations; and on the imminent possibility of war, which requires a Congress ready to accept the responsibility of war and beyond that a nation ready to accept wartime sacrifices.[23]

The other special lawmaking function entails the formulation and adoption of constitutional amendments. The process by which constitutions are amended includes two main stages: proposal and ratification.

Amendments to the U.S. Constitution may be proposed by a two-thirds vote of both houses of Congress on a joint resolution or by a national constitutional convention summoned by Congress in response to a petition adopted by two-thirds of the state legislatures. Amendment ratification may be secured in either of two ways: by adoption of the resolution by legislatures in three-fourths of the states or by constitutional conventions in three-fourths of the states. Only the first-mentioned method of proposing constitutional amendments, joint action by both houses, has been used. Only one amendment, the twenty-first, has been assented to by conventions held in the states; all the others have been ratified through the actions of state legislatures. Congress alone determines the method for ratification, and the president has no veto power over amendments.

The methods by which state constitutions are amended differ from those by which the national Constitution is amended, though in general the role of the legislature is the same. In all states except New Hampshire, which requires a constitutional convention to change the constitution, the legislature may propose amendments. Most commonly, a two-thirds vote of the elected members of each house is required to propose an amendment. Many states, however, require only a majority of the members; a few require a three-fifths vote. About one-third of the states require that a constitutional amendment be passed in two sessions of the legislature before being submitted to the voters. In Massachusetts, a proposed amendment must receive a majority of the vote of the members of both houses sitting in joint session. Except in Delaware, where the legislature acting alone is empowered to amend the constitution, all amendments proposed by the legislature must be

---

[23] *Congress and Foreign Policy* (New York: Harcourt, Brace & World, Inc., 1950), p. 105.

ratified by the electorate, ordinarily by a majority voting on the amendment. A few states—Minnesota, Mississippi, New Hampshire, Oklahoma, Tennessee, and Wyoming—require a majority of those voting in the election to approve the amendment. Hawaii is one of several states requiring a certain percentage of the electorate to participate in the election; its constitution specifies that the majority vote must constitute at least 35 percent of the total general election vote or 35 percent of the registered voters at a special election.

The most important difference between national and state practice in regard to the amending process is that the voters are directly involved in the ratification of state constitutional amendments but bypassed in the ratification of national amendments. Since amendments to the national constitution ordinarily are considered only by the state legislature, there is no opportunity for voters to vote directly on constitutional proposals. Few if any legislators will have been elected on the basis of how they stand on proposed amendments.

CHECKING THE ADMINISTRATION

The need to secure responsibility in government and to provide for the representation of the citizenry led to the creation of representative assemblies. An important point to remember, however, is that the legislature was not created to govern; this has been, rather, the responsibility of the executive power. It remains true, of course, that the legislature has a long-established concern with inquiring into administrative conduct and the exercise of administrative discretion under the acts of the legislature, as well as with ascertaining administrative compliance with legislative intent. In the usual phrasing, the legislature's supervisory role consists of questioning, reviewing and assessing, modifying, and rejecting policies of the administration.

The lawmaking prerogative of the legislature always has had the careful attention of legislators themselves—with good reason, of course, since this is the source of the institution's most important powers. In purely constitutional terms, the legislature's lawmaking power is as important today as ever in the past. Current experience shows, however, that much of the initiative and vigor in lawmaking is supplied by the chief executive. If the new balance in legislative-executive relations has been discouraging to legislators, it has also been instructive. Change invites reassessment. Executive leadership now tends to be accepted as inevitable in an increasingly complex and technical world.[24] Moreover, scarce resources, including time and power, require prudent handling. Hence many legislators, as well as many scholars, have come to see legislative surveillance of the administration as a means of

[24] The main dilemma of Congress, in the judgment of one group of scholars, is that it suffers a "severe information disadvantage" as compared to the executive. The formation of creative public policy depends on the gathering and analysis of enormous quantities of information, and in these tasks the executive is far more adept than Congress. See James A. Robinson, "Decision Making in Congress" in *Congress: The First Branch of Government,* ed. Alfred de Grazia (Washington, D.C.: The American Enterprise Institute for Public Policy Research, 1966), pp. 259–94; Kenneth Janda, "Information Systems for Congress," in *ibid.,* pp. 415–56; and Charles R. Dechert, "Availability of Information for Congressional Operations," in *ibid.,* pp. 167–211.

18   increasing the legislature's effectiveness.[25] Legislative oversight, as it is now called, serves as an instrument whereby the legislature can resist executive domination and strengthen its overall position in the constitutional system.

The legislature has several devices available for reviewing, influencing, and directing the administration. Legislation itself is an obvious technique of supervision: new laws can be put on the books and old laws revised with a view to changing administrative behavior. Probably the most formidable of its devices, however, is its power to appropriate funds for the conduct of government. The appropriations process is a continuing source of anxiety for administrators, for it is here that agencies can be disrupted and programs undone, chipped away, or discarded. In the final analysis, the direction and scope of government is determined by the amount of money made available for programs.

By itself the power of the purse does nothing to insure intelligent, effective control over agency expenditures. Indeed, this power is vulnerable to abuse, as when the legislature, lacking information, or else bent upon riding local hobbyhorses, or even out of sheer caprice, upsets and distorts the executive budget. Writing of Congress, Holbert Carroll sees the problem this way:

> ...Congress prefers to behave irresponsibly in dealing with fiscal matters. Congress prefers confusion. The Committees on Appropriations and Congress are not particularly interested in integrating their control over appropriations, in making more rational choices among alternatives, or in emphasis.... [Congress] prefers to use the budget for purposes of pre-audit, as an instrument of erratic control rather than as an instrument for the responsible allocation of limited resources.... Confusion, in addition, enables the members of Congress to mask their intrusions upon the executive budget to take care of politically pressing local needs, and pressure groups have more opportunities to get what they want when uncoordinated appropriation methods are employed.[26]

Constitutional requirements for legislative participation in the appointment process open up additional opportunities for checking and influencing the administration. At the national level, a great many appointments are made by the president alone, under authority given him by Congress, and still other lesser appointments are made by department heads. But major appointments, such as those of ambassadors, consuls, and judges, require Senate confirmation. The custom of "senatorial courtesy" prevails in the submission of names to the Senate for *certain* offices, such as those of district court judges and U.S. marshals. This custom dictates that prior to nominating a person for a position in a state the president will consult with the senators of that state, if members of his party, as to their choice for the position. Should the president ignore their wishes and submit a name objectionable to them, or simply fail to consult them, "senatorial courtesy" may

---

25 For development of this position, see Samuel P. Huntington, "Congressional Responses to the Twentieth Century," in *The Congress and America's Future,* ed. David B. Truman (Englewood Cliffs, N.J.: Prentice-Hall, Inc., 1965), pp. 5–31.

26 *The House of Representatives and Foreign Affairs* (Boston: Little, Brown and Company, 1966), pp. 207–8.

come into play, with the senators from that state contesting the nomination. Courteous to a fault, the rest of the Senate ordinarily joins them in opposition.

The state legislature may participate in the appointment process in two ways. First, some state constitutions or statutes provide for election of certain administrative officials by the legislature. For example, the Maine legislature elects the secretary of state, attorney general, treasurer, auditor, secretary of agriculture, and the members of the executive council. Second, as with national practice, state senates (occasionally councils or both houses) must approve executive nominations for high-level positions.

In general, the governor's power of appointment is more hemmed in than the president's. In a great many states he has to live with the fact that certain major administrative officers, such as the treasurer and the secretary of state, are popularly elected, and their independent status gives them control over appointments in their departments. And, both in appointments which the governor makes alone as well as in those which require senate confirmation, his power and options are circumscribed by political factors. There are state and local party leaders whose interests in jobs demand consideration, legislative leaders and factions to be mollified by patronage, key supporters of the governor's own campaign to be rewarded. In the politics of appointment, the governor's view is not unlike the president's.

The appointive power presents both opportunities and problems to the governor. The appointment that wins some friends loses others; rarely are there as many jobs as there are claimants, and never are there enough good ones. Rejected job-seekers and their sponsors, unfortunately, have long memories. Yet in many states, despite its unhappy side effects, the governor's appointive power (coupled with other forms of patronage at his disposal) is the key to securing enactment of his legislative program. In varying degrees and in sundry styles, patronage is used by all governors to win over legislators to their proposals, but it appears to be most important to governors in one-party states. In the absence of meaningful party programs and commitments, the governor and the legislature may have little in common, and "when the going gets rough, he cannot rely on party loyalty but must turn to patronage." Used promiscuously, patronage in a predominantly one-party state may corrupt the minority party. "The more patronage [minority party members] can get, the less incentive they have to gain majority status; the more often they support the governor, the fewer issues their party has for the next campaign."[27]

As a rule few nominations are rejected by the legislature. Legislators generally want to avoid the imputation of obstructionism; hence any warfare over nominations which may occur tends to be guerrilla rather than open in character. Where a two-thirds vote is required for confirmation, there is ample opportunity for the "out" party, if it holds a sufficient number of seats, to exact concessions from the governor. The price of confirming an administration nominee to the public utility commission may be the appointment of an "out" party member to the same or some other commission; to be sure that bargains are carried out, the nominations may be confirmed

---

27 Malcolm E. Jewell, *The State Legislature* (New York: Random House, Inc., 1962), pp. 126–27.

in tandem. It is not unusual in some states for the minority party in the senate to withhold the necessary votes for confirmation until agreements on certain legislation or appointments have been worked out. When confronted by a hostile senate, governors are likely to make good use of "recess" appointments—temporary appointments for the interim between sessions. This is not the handicap it might appear, since many legislatures are in session only a few months during the biennium.

Other legislative-executive encounters take place in committee hearings and investigations; these are treated elsewhere at length. Here it is sufficient to emphasize two things. First, these devices, especially investigations, are sometimes characterized by a doubtful blend of legitimate surveillance and the publicity aspirations of the investigator, notably the committee chairman. As such, inquiries sometimes lead to the embarrassing treatment of bureaucrats—a prospect unlikely to repel the typical legislator.[28] Second, hearings and investigations need to be seen as instruments in the struggle between the executive and legislative branches—as powerful deterrents to administrative waywardness and carelessness.

The proper limits of legislative intervention in administration affairs have long been a subject of debate. In some respects, this is a dispute between those who wish to strengthen the executive's hand and those who favor a strong legislature; in other respects, it is a dispute between liberals and conservatives. To some observers the main question concerns the legislature's suitability and capacity for the intelligent control of the administration: "Congress is the appropriate institution for representing the varied interests of the nation and for compromising differences so that broader purposes can be established through legislation. When congressmen take an active part in the superintendence of administrative agencies, they tend to bring into this branch of government values and standards that are more appropriate to representation than to administration."[29] Moreover, Congress as overseer of the administration collides with the theory of president as overseer. Be that as it may, Congress (or the state legislature, for that matter) is unlikely to resist using its influence to shape administrative conduct and decisions.

EDUCATING THE PUBLIC

A function of the legislature easily overlooked, though an exposition of it goes back at least as far as Walter Bagehot's classic analysis of the British House of Commons,[30] is the function of informing and instructing the public. "[Even] more important than legislation," wrote Woodrow Wilson in his volume on Congress, "is the instruction and guidance in political affairs which the people might receive from a body which kept all national

28 See Ralph K. Huitt, "The Congressional Committee: A Case Study," *American Political Science Review,* XLVIII (June 1954), 340–65, for examination of the conflict between legislator and bureaucrat in committee hearings.

29 Pendleton Herring, "Executive-Legislative Responsibilities," *American Political Science Review,* XXXVIII (December 1944), 1165. On this point, also see the evidence of Seymour Scher, "Congressional Committee Members as Independent Agency Overseers: A Case Study," *American Political Science Review,* LIV (December 1960), 911–20.

30 *The English Constitution* (first published in 1867), especially Chapter 6.

concerns suffused in a broad daylight of discussion."[31] Wilson thought that Congress had failed to meet this obligation, preferring instead to engross itself in matters of legislation—in adopting, amending, and revising laws. Few if any current writers argue that today's Congress provides significantly better or more extensive instruction for the public.

The opportunities for the legislature to teach the public things it needs to know are more circumscribed than might appear at first glance. In the first place, the structure of the American legislature inhibits the teaching function. By any reckoning, a large share of the crucial decisions of any session of any legislature are made in committee, yet neither committee discussions nor decisions are as well reported or appear as important (or are viewed as openly) as the affairs of the chamber itself—even though the chamber's role frequently consists simply of ratifying the actions (or acquiescing in the inactions) of sovereign committees. At the state level, reporting of committee activities in depth is virtually unknown; committee jurisdiction and power are both uncertain and unpredictable; committee votes are not readily available and sometimes not available at all; and committee records of any kind are all but nonexistent. The power of committees must be put down as a principal explanation for the failure of the legislature to highlight important matters of policy, to set forth alternatives in such a way as to make them intelligible to the public. If the public is an inattentive audience for legislative politics and, as a consequence, is unable to perceive the significance of decisions to be made, that is hardly surprising.

Another reason the legislature has been unable to master the teaching function lies in the volume and complexity of legislation itself. A sustained political exchange with and for the public over the purposes and meanings of policy, in the fashion of Wilson's dictum, is inordinately difficult under the press of hundreds and thousands of bills introduced each session. Informing the public of the choices available and making clear the stakes involved are tall requirements for a heavily burdened legislature. Indeed, the legislator faces a formidable task in instructing himself on legislation.

To these obstacles to communication between governors and governed must be added the demands of errand-running, the restless search for political security with constituents, the compulsion to campaign steadily for reelection—each urgency helping to shift legislative attention from the broad objective of educating the public to the more immediate and narrow objectives of getting the job done and retaining popular favor. It is no exaggeration to say that in the course of tending to the political shop, elaborate argument yields to expedient settlement, policy alternatives turn into slogans and issues, and conventional responses substitute for the effort to fathom and to explain the nagging problem or the new venture.[32] Out of such an

---

31 *Congressional Government,* p. 195.

32 Note these observations concerning the passage of the Atomic Energy Act of 1946, in which the principal issue before Congress was whether atomic energy should be under civilian or military control: "Several unique factors combined to deprive the legislator of his comfortable patterns for reaching policy decisions. He was not dealing with a recast of conventional controversy, a labor versus management or debt reduction versus public spending issue, on which his attitudes had long been fixed, his speeches ready at tongue, the public reception and opposition tactics already known. He could not judge by the people lined up on one or the other side, for traditional alignments were criss-crossed. Even commercial special interest groups were

22 uncertain mélange a program of public instruction is not easily fashioned.

There is some irony in the fact that two of the activities of Congress that are most demeaned, unlimited debate in the Senate and committee investigation, have as a leading purpose the instruction of the public. Though the argument may be regarded as simply a veneer, the typical band of filibusters justifies its action in terms of the need to alert and instruct the public:

> We are aware that during the last few months there has been a great public relations campaign in support of the immediate passage of the bill. All the stops of public relations have been pulled. Persuasive lobbying has occurred in many places. The real reason why so much pressure is being applied for the passage of the bill now on the part of some persons and some interests involved is that they feel—in fact, I think many of them know—that when the American people have had time to think over this proposal, they will take a different look at it; they will not be pleased, as they never have been in the history of the Nation with great, mammoth giveaways of the public domain, which is the treasure of the United States. . . .[33]

Filibustering ("prolonged debate," in the argot of sympathetic legislators) has a goal beyond the education of the public. For success it may require the collaboration of the public and its organized elements. The fact is that major legislation frequently makes no great stir. By delaying the vote on a proposal, opponents seek to win time and to gain new support for their cause. With time, friendly interest groups still on the fence may be induced to enter the fray, and there is always the hope that the publicity generated will rouse the wider public to write, wire, telephone, or visit their representatives. Whatever the disruptive effects of a filibuster, the issue over which it arises gains publicity far out of the ordinary, and the public presumably acquires better insight and an improved opportunity to register a claim in the matter.

The same service is performed by committee investigations. These inquiries serve a variety of purposes, including the important one of exposing the presence of problems and abuses in private groups and public agencies. "No aspect of congressional activity other than investigations is as capable

---

largely silent. In short, for most senators and many representatives, atomic energy legislation required an almost pure exercise of judgment. The very same factors also operated to induce a surprisingly wide expression of opinion by the public.

"The response of the Congress to this unparalleled necessity for original judgment was not one of imaginative suggestion. Rather, the reaction of many legislators was to escape the entire problem, one senator openly expressing a wish to dump all atomic energy knowledge into the ocean. Most, however, felt lost in a morass of technology, an attitude which appeared to survive the educational hearings. Hence the debates both in and out of Congress all too often exhibited a stubborn tendency to pose choices in terms of conventional opposites which bore little relation to the issues being decided." Byron S. Miller, "A Law is Passed—The Atomic Energy Act of 1946," *University of Chicago Law Review*, XV (Summer 1948), 799–800.

[33] These remarks were made by Senator Estes Kefauver (D., Tenn.), one of a small group of liberals who filibustered the communications satellite bill, a bill to establish a privately owned but government-regulated corporation to operate the system of global communications satellites. *Congressional Record*, 87th Cong., 2d sess., July 31, 1962, p. 14148. (Daily edition.)

of attracting the attention of the public and of the communications facilities that both direct and reflect public interest."[34] The impact on public awareness and attitudes made by certain congressional investigations—such as recent ones involving racketeering, improper activities in the labor and management field, monopolies, lobbying, loyalty and security, defense contracts, and administration malpractices—has been enormous. Irrespective of the motivations that underlie investigations, and they are doubtless diverse, congressmen recognize the extraordinary opportunities they offer for influencing public opinion. The standard justification for an investigation is the presumed need for new or remedial legislation; nonetheless, the informing function actuates many inquiries and at times is controlling. Moreover, publicity by itself may lead to the correcting of abuses, thereby allaying the need for legislation.

Teaching is a reciprocal act. It requires a public that is attentive to what is being taught, a legislature intent on making its instruction clear and effective. By and large, neither public nor legislature satisfies these requirements; typically, the public is passive and absorbed in daily living, while the legislature is immersed in the negotiations and details of lawmaking.

There is a final point to be made. Emphasis on the teaching or informing function may lead to overlooking the nature of the legislative *process,* at least insofar as the American legislature is concerned. "Legislation is not merely a matter of persuasion through eloquent speeches or of taking votes backed by a party majority. It is essentially a matter of making adjustments and regulating action so that anticipated desires may be met."[35]

THE FUNCTION OF REPRESENTING CONSTITUENTS, LOCALITIES, AND "INTERESTS"

"I learned soon after coming to Washington," a Missouri congressman reported, "that it was just as important to get a certain document for somebody back home as for some European diplomat—hell, *more* important, because that little guy back home votes."[36] Congressmen and state legislators alike spend much of their time running errands for constituents, answering their letters and telephone calls, interceding with administrative agencies on their behalf, and providing entertainment for them when they visit the capital. Probably no function of the legislator exacts a greater toll on his time and energy than the purely service activity he is expected to perform. In particular, members of the lower house, who must face the voters every second year, regard this service as a hedge against the future.[37]

[34] Francis E. Rourke, *Secrecy and Publicity: Dilemmas of Democracy* (Baltimore: Johns Hopkins Press, 1961), p. 118.

[35] Roland Young, "Woodrow Wilson's *Congressional Government* Reconsidered" in *The Philosophy and Policies of Woodrow Wilson,* ed. Earl Latham (Chicago: University of Chicago Press, 1958), p. 205.

[36] As quoted by Stephen K. Bailey, *Congress Makes a Law* (New York: Columbia University Press, 1950), p. 215.

[37] For the individual member, there are frequent conflicts between the roles he is expected to perform in the legislature and his career aspirations. Members are often torn between "doing their job" in the legislature and guarding their careers; success in meeting legislative expectations does not necessarily guarantee success in career terms. Joseph Cooper poses the problem this way: "Committee specialization

24   The fly in the ointment of errand- running is obvious: legislative matters too frequently are neglected because the member's time is preempted by his constituents' requests. For some legislators errand-running is a pretext for doing nothing with big problems. "There are congressmen elected year after year who never think of dissipating their energy on public affairs. They prefer to do a little service for a lot of people on a lot of little subjects, rather than try to engage in trying to do a big service out there in the void."[38]

Requests and complaints put to the legislator by constituents cover a wide sweep and have never excluded minor problems. The rule is that any request, no matter how improbable or zany, deserves a prompt and polite response: the constituent who writes his congressman learns by return mail of the pleasure with which his communication was received and of the careful consideration its contents merit. But there is an occasional legislator who violates this harmless folkway. To a constituent who complained that the taxpayers' money should not have been spent for the transportation to the United States of a horse given Mrs. John F. Kennedy, former Senator Stephen M. Young (D., Ohio) replied: "Dear Sir. Acknowledging your letter wherein you insult the wife of our President, am wondering why you need a horse when there is already one jackass at your address."[39] For the typical legislator running for reelection, replies of this sort are probably thin beginnings.

Catering to constituents is only part of the legislator's function in representation. He is also expected to be a guardian of district or state interests, a bidding which is demonstrated by the following colloquy in the U.S. Senate over the assignment of defense contracts:

> Mr. Lausche (D., Ohio): I do not know whether the Senators from the Midwest are familiar with the statement that was made [by the Secretary of Defense], that research and development contracts are not going to Illinois, Michigan, Indiana, and Ohio and other states in the Midwest because we do not have the brains. The Secretary...forgets that there has been a migration of scientists and a pirating of them from the Midwestern States by the States to which these grants have been made....

> Mr. Kuchel (R., Calif.):...I wonder whether the Senator from Ohio is accusing the Secretary of Defense and the Government of the United States of any fraud or chicanery or favoritism in the awarding of contracts....

> Mr. Lausche: I submit that it is *prima facie* wrong to have California, with

---

involves not only hard work but also narrowness and isolation from the public; constituent service involves not only time but also absorption in small problems and the assumption of a petitionary role with regard to the bureaucracy. Similarly, time spent out of Washington can be much more valuable to reelection or advancement to another position than time spent on committee work; a vote for district interests can be more valuable to career advancement than sustaining the party leadership's ability to aggregate majorities and produce necessary outputs." *The Origins of the Standing Committees and the Development of the Modern House* (Houston: Rice University Studies, 1970), p. 103.

   38 Walter Lippmann, *Public Opinion* (New York: The Macmillan Company, 1960), p. 247.

   39 *The Reporter,* August 16, 1962, p. 18.

perhaps 10 per cent of the population of the country, getting 24 per cent of the procurement contracts.

Mr. Kuchel: [The Senator from Ohio] has failed to answer my question whether the [Secretary of Defense], in the awarding of research and development contracts, is . . . guilty of any fraud or chicanery. . . .

Mr. Lausche: It is not necessary to prove fraud [or] chicanery. The fact is that contracts began going to California early. Money and equipment went there early. . . .

Mr. Humphrey (D., Minn.): . . . It seems to me the burden of proof is upon the Department of Defense. Senators cannot tell me that the great universities and technical laboratories [of the Midwest] have not something more to contribute than the Department of Defense has asked thus far.

Mr. Goldwater (R., Ariz.): . . . I rise to defend California, as I defend my own State and the rest of the West, when representatives of other States see the goose laying the golden eggs and want to get some of those for their own States. . . .

Mr. Lausche: The Senator from Ohio did not intend to cast any reflections upon California. The Senator from Ohio has been meticulous in his observance of the rule that he does not ask for Ohio anything that he would not be willing to have granted to another State. . . . But I do want to ask for Ohio what Ohio is justly entitled to. . . .

Mr. Kuchel: . . . All that the Senator from Ohio is doing is crying and whining and raising cain on this floor because he feels that the people of his state have been aggrieved.

Mr. Hart (D., Mich.): Mr. President, we have just now listened to one of the series of incidents which occur periodically in this Chamber in regard to who should get what, and under what rule. . . . [The Senate should give serious consideration] to a resolution which calls for the establishment of a Senate select committee to evaluate the economic impact of defense procurement. . . .[40]

It would be difficult to exaggerate the attention that many legislators devote to securing federal projects for their states and localities. Some state delegations, for example, have had an extraordinary capacity to influence the location of defense facilities—with all the attendant benefits that derive from such expenditures. Consider the observations of President Johnson when, late in his administration, he visited a Lockheed plant in Marietta, Georgia, for a ceremony unveiling a new cargo plane: "I would like to have you good folks of Georgia know that there are a lot of Marietta, Georgias scattered throughout our fifty states. All of them would like to have the pride that comes from this production. But all of them don't have the Georgia delegation."[41]

---

40 *Congressional Record,* 87th Cong., 2d sess., July 23, 1962, pp. 13536–39. (Daily edition.)
41 *Congressional Quarterly, Special Report, Weekly Report,* May 24, 1968, p. 1158, as quoted by John C. Donovan, *The Policy Makers* (New York: Pegasus, 1970), p. 142.

Viewed broadly, the legislator's representative role also encompasses the requirement of mobilizing popular consent for new public policies and maintaining consent for continuing policies. Legislators not only monitor the claims of their constituents, but also help to create conditions under which governments can better govern. Publics, like institutions, have their own inertia and intractability. When a government adopts significant new policies, the average citizen finds that his steadfast landmarks have moved. Old ways of doing things have been supplanted by new ways. New policies are often difficult to understand, and the citizen may have to consult new agencies as well. Uncertainty and frustration are therefore likely to accompany sharp departures in public policy. Consequently, from the standpoint of the government, there may be as great a need to gain understanding and political support for measures newly adopted as for those under consideration or those still on the drawing boards. The need to breathe new life into old policies also confronts all governments. The policy process, in other words, does not stop with the passage of a law. The complexities of modern government make it essential that continuing consultation and interchange occur between those who hold and exercise political power and those who are affected by it. The obligations that result for the representative are described by Congressman John Brademas (D., Ind.) :

> Many local leaders may not understand the purposes of the legislation or see its relevance to their communities. The Congressman or Senator, by organizing community conferences, mailing materials and in other ways, can supply important information, interpretation, justification and leadership to his constituency.... These activities of explaining, justifying, interpreting, interceding, all help, normally, to build acceptance for government policy, an essential process in democratic government....[42]

A final function of representation to be noted is not, in a strict sense, a legislative function but rather a legislative *party* function, well understood by members and carried on by them with singular resourcefulness. This is the function of using legislative power to advance or safeguard the interests of the party and its members.

In the classic model of party government, parties compete with one another for power, appealing to the electorate on the basis of principles and programs, with the victorious party pledged to translate its campaign commitments into public policy and a course of governmental action. In American practice the model is seldom if ever approximated even in two-party states because of the breakdown of party lines in the legislature; in one-party states the model bears no resemblance to the actual political process, unless we read "factions" to mean "parties."

Nevertheless, if not in their attitudes toward party programs and broad questions of public policy, legislators in at least one respect feel the pull of party loyalty. A fundamental function of the legislative party organization is to protect, solidify, and enhance the welfare of the organization, both in and out of the legislature. Legislative power offers an important means for transmitting benefits to the party organization, and on matters of organiza-

---

[42] Quoted by Samuel H. Beer, "The British Legislature and the Problem of Mobilizing Consent," in *Lawmakers in a Changing World,* pp. 45–46.

tional interest legislators ordinarily maintain a steady allegiance to their parties.

Consider the state legislature, where the quest for party advantage in legislation is perennial. The aims of party appear in legislative proposals and tactics designed to embarrass the administration, to convey special advantage through election law, to offset election defeats in city government, and to increase access to the fruits of government—patronage in all of its forms.

A favorite gambit of the "out" party to embarrass the administration is to sponsor dramatic pay-raise bills for state employees without, of course, providing for the increased funds required to meet the new salary scales. The onus for blocking such bills invariably is placed on the governor. The call for a committee investigation of the highway or the public welfare department can be another approach to harassing the governor and his party.

Revision of election law carries many opportunities for improving party fortunes. Reapportionment legislation is an obvious example. But there are also advantages to be won, for example, by changing local elections from nonpartisan to partisan (a change which Republican legislators in Illinois have long sought for the election of aldermen in Chicago, in the belief that party identification would assist their cause) or vice versa. Illinois Republicans have also attempted to remove the requirement that party challengers must reside in the precinct or ward in which they perform their functions, since they have long suspected that powerful Democratic ward organizations in Chicago control Republican watchers.

Many of the "rural-urban" disputes in the legislatures of northern states, in which rural Republicans control the legislature and Democrats control the major cities, are rooted in party interests. Republican legislators, mainly representative of rural and suburban areas, have no desire to see Democratic city administrations make good records or enjoy political security with their constituents. Suburban Republicans are especially sensitive to the politics of the nearby city and ordinarily have little difficulty in rallying the support of party colleagues who represent districts in the countryside. Where home rule is lacking, the legislature can place numerous impedimenta in the way of city administrations. It may turn a deaf ear to city requests for legislation to empower it to levy new or higher taxes; it may specify that the city real estate tax levy can be increased but that the additional revenue can be used only for the payment of salaries of firemen and policemen; it may require the city to pay several hundred dollars per year to each policeman and fireman to help them defray the costs of uniforms and other equipment; it may abolish a city department of public welfare and transfer its functions to a similar county agency, thereby shifting control over public assistance programs from one party to the other; it may transfer the power to appoint members of local redevelopment and housing authorities from the mayor to the governor. In sum, there are endless opportunities for the dominant party in the legislature to make harassing incursions into the government and politics of city administrations, and on legislative proposals which give advantage to one party and threaten the other each party exhibits a remarkable cohesiveness.

Occasionally, the function of representing organization interest leads both parties to a common position. The best example is found in the

28   preservation of patronage. When George Leader (D.), governor of Pennsylvania from 1954 to 1958, sought to give statutory civil service protection to ten thousand professional and technical positions, he encountered as much opposition from his own party as from the Republicans. "I refuse to believe ...that there is a job on this Hill or anywhere in this Commonwealth," stated the Senate Democratic floor leader, "that a Democrat cannot fill any more than I believe that there is a job in Washington that a good Republican cannot fill. There are Democratic engineers, Democratic doctors, and Democratic psychiatrists. If you want to give job security to them, all right, give it to them. I never have seen any party hire an engineer to do a psychiatric job."[43] Democrats and Republicans also joined efforts in a recent session of the Illinois legislature to exempt highway maintenance jobs from the personnel code on the grounds that the highway truck driver, who is often a precinct committeeman, "is the foundation of our political system." Parties as well as legislators look to legislation for the means of survival and increased security; the public either is unaware of the extent of maneuvering calculated to bolster party fortunes or else accepts it as legitimate practice.

THE JUDICIAL FUNCTION

Several powers lead to the legislature's assumption of functions that are authentically judicial in character, that is, that call for the legislative body to resolve disputes concerning individuals and to apply appropriate law to their cases. In this category are the functions of judging the election and qualifications of its members, punishing and expelling members for contempt or for disorderly behavior, and impeaching and removing from office members of the executive and judicial branches.

From a constitutional standpoint, the most important judicial function of the legislature involves the power to impeach and to remove officials. The impeachment process set forth in state constitutions closely resembles that found in the national Constitution. Under provisions in that Constitution, the House of Representatives may impeach ("indict") the "President, Vice-President, and all civil officers" accused of "treason, bribery or other high crimes and misdemeanors." Individuals impeached by the House must be tried by the Senate, with conviction and removal from office dependent upon a two-thirds vote of the members present. To date, only twelve officers have been subjected to impeachment trials, four of whom, all judges, were convicted and removed from office by the Senate. A few officials have resigned from office when threatened by impeachment. Impeachment proceedings are equally rare in the states, although some ten governors have been removed from office by such means, none in recent times.[44]

The impeachment process is more impressive in literary form than in practice. Already heavily burdened, legislatures are ill equipped to have impeachment proceedings thrust upon them. The U.S. Senate gave several months to the trial of President Andrew Johnson in 1868, but it is difficult to imagine that body finding time for such deliberations today. In the states,

---

[43] *Pennsylvania Legislative Journal,* March 12, 1957, p. 656.

[44] Charles R. Adrian, *State and Local Governments,* 2d ed. (New York: McGraw-Hill Book Company, Inc., 1967), p. 282.

where short legislative sessions are the rule, the time factor also influences the agenda. There are occasional reports of a state legislator calling for the impeachment of the governor, or of a congressman demanding the impeachment of a Supreme Court justice, but such threats are unconvincing and the grounds for the action often absurd. Although the typical demand for impeachment is couched in terms of malfeasance in office, more often than not the issue is an outgrowth of a policy or political dispute. In theory a classic power of the legislature, impeachment today is of slight significance, though not yet an anachronism.

THE FUNCTION OF LEADERSHIP SELECTION

Congress assumes certain functions of leadership selection under constitutional mandates. Under the terms of the Twelfth Amendment, the electoral vote of each state for president and vice-president is transmitted to the president of the Senate, who, in the presence of members of both houses, opens the certificates and counts the votes. Ordinarily this task is discharged perfunctorily, albeit with appropriate ceremony, since the winning candidates are known in a matter of hours or days after the polls have closed on election day. Occasionally, however, the electoral college has failed to produce its customary majority of votes for one of the party tickets. The Twelfth Amendment provides that if no candidate obtains a majority of the electoral votes, the choice of the president shall be made by the House of Representatives from among the three candidates having the largest number of electoral votes. Since 1804, when this amendment was adopted, the House has chosen one president, John Quincy Adams in 1824; in that year electoral votes were split among four presidential candidates.

The close election of 1876 between Rutherford B. Hayes and Samuel Tilden again brought Congress into the selection of the president. This came about when several southern states transmitted to Congress conflicting sets of electoral votes. To resolve the dispute over their validity, Congress created a commission of fifteen members, which ultimately awarded all of the contested votes, and thereby the election, to Hayes.

When selection of the president is thrown into the House, each state may cast one vote, and a majority is required for election. A shift of only a few states from the Democratic to the Republican or to the "states' rights" columns in the elections of 1948 and 1960 would have necessitated choice of the president and vice-president by Congress. To bring about such a situation was, in fact, the principal objective of the "Dixiecrat" movement in 1948, the leaders of which reasoned that if election of the president fell to the House, the southern states would hold a balance of power; not only could they exact concessions on civil rights legislation, but conceivably their candidate could emerge as the compromise choice among warring Democrats and Republicans. The continuing friction between the southern and northern wings of the Democratic party, which has led to southern defections and slates of unpledged electors in presidential elections, probably has increased the possibility of active congressional involvement in the selection of the president and vice-president.

If no vice-presidential candidate garners a majority of the electoral votes, a choice is made between the two top contenders by the Senate. Each

30 senator casts one vote, with a majority specified for election. Only once, in 1836, has the Senate chosen the vice-president.

The Constitution also devolves upon Congress the power to determine the order of presidential succession to be followed in the event that both the offices of the presidency and vice-presidency are vacant. Provisions for presidential succession have been changed several times since the early days of the republic. A statute enacted in 1947 shortly after Vice-President Truman was made president provides that the order of succession to the presidency, if both offices are vacant, shall be the Speaker of the House, the president *pro tem* of the Senate, and the secretaries of the executive departments, beginning with the Department of State. Following President Kennedy's death in 1963, new interest developed in the order of succession, due in part to the advanced age of Speaker John W. McCormack (D., Mass.).

Adoption of the Twenty-fifth Amendment to the Constitution in 1967 brought clarity to the question of presidential succession. Under its terms, the vice-president shall become president if the president dies, resigns, or is removed from office. Whenever a vacancy occurs in the office of vice-president, the president shall nominate a vice-president, subject to approval by a majority vote of both houses of Congress. Should a president conclude that he is unable to discharge the powers and duties of his office, he informs Congress, and the vice-president is empowered as acting president until the president is again able to assume his responsibilities. Other provisions of the amendment establish procedures to be followed in the event the president is unable to inform Congress of his disability or in the event there is disagreement over his ability to discharge the powers and duties of his office.

A Bill Becomes a Law

Skillful management of legislation in committee and on the floor at times appears as much an occult art as anything else. There are no certainties and few unbendable rules for putting together majorities at various stages. No one understands any better than a bill's sponsors and managers that its life en route to becoming a law is never safely predictable. Opportunities to delay and to kill proposals are built into virtually all points of the legislative compass.[45] Opportunities to change proposals in respects so fundamental as to destroy their original purposes are similarly numerous. And, of course, proposals may simply languish along the way, whether from the indifference of their sponsors, from the hopelessness of their cause, or from some other reason. No fact stands out more clearly than that it is

---

[45] See a discussion of the points of possible delay and defeat in the U.S. House of Representatives in Lewis A. Froman, Jr., *The Congressional Process: Strategies, Rules, and Procedures* (Boston: Little, Brown and Company, 1967), especially pp. 17–18. Delay may occur at any of a number of points (often by the action of less than a majority): subcommittee inaction in referring to a subcommittee; subcommittee inaction (prolonged hearings; refusal to report); committee inaction (prolonged hearings; refusal to report); Rules Committee inaction (refusal to schedule hearings; prolonged hearings; refusal to report); slowness in scheduling the bill; floor action (demanding full requirements of the rules)—reading of the journal, repeated quorum calls, refusing unanimous consent to dispense with further proceedings under the call of the roll, prolonging debate, and various points of order.

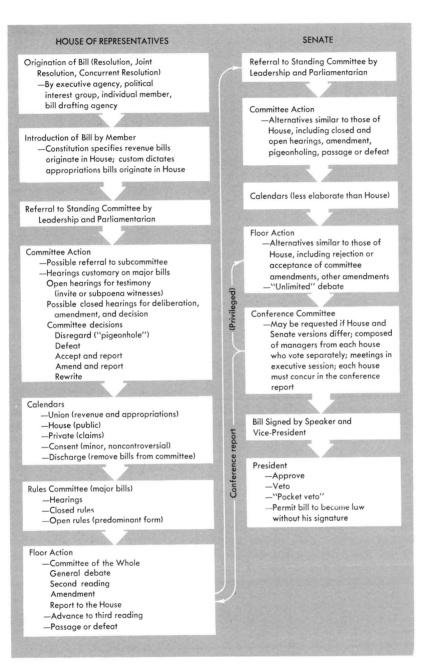

HOUSE OF REPRESENTATIVES

Origination of Bill (Resolution, Joint
  Resolution, Concurrent Resolution)
  —By executive agency, political
    interest group, individual member,
    bill drafting agency

Introduction of Bill by Member
  —Constitution specifies revenue bills
    originate in House; custom dictates
    appropriations bills originate in House

Referral to Standing Committee by
  Leadership and Parliamentarian

Committee Action
  —Possible referral to subcommittee
  —Hearings customary on major bills
    Open hearings for testimony
      (invite or subpoena witnesses)
    Possible closed hearings for deliberation,
      amendment, and decision
    Committee decisions
      Disregard ("pigeonhole")
      Defeat
      Accept and report
      Amend and report
      Rewrite

Calendars
  —Union (revenue and appropriations)
  —House (public)
  —Private (claims)
  —Consent (minor, noncontroversial)
  —Discharge (remove bills from committee)

Rules Committee (major bills)
  —Hearings
  —Closed rules
  —Open rules (predominant form)

Floor Action
  —Committee of the Whole
    General debate
    Second reading
    Amendment
    Report to the House
  —Advance to third reading
  —Passage or defeat

SENATE

Referral to Standing Committee by
  Leadership and Parliamentarian

Committee Action
  —Alternatives similar to those of
    House, including closed and
    open hearings, amendment,
    pigeonholing, passage or defeat

Calendars (less elaborate than House)

Floor Action
  —Alternatives similar to those of
    House, including rejection or
    acceptance of committee
    amendments, other amendments
  —"Unlimited" debate

Conference Committee
  —May be requested if House and
    Senate versions differ; composed
    of managers from each house
    who vote separately; meetings in
    executive session; each house
    must concur in the conference
    report

Bill Signed by Speaker and
  Vice-President

President
  —Approve
  —Veto
  —"Pocket veto"
  —Permit bill to become law
    without his signature

(Privileged)

Conference report

FIGURE 1 *A bill becomes a law: a generalized version.*

32 never easy to get fast results in the legislature; all of the important advantages rest with those who are in favor of minimal change, marking time, and the *status quo*.

Because the system is highly complex, as well as partially hidden from any public audience, the process by which a bill becomes a law in American legislatures is not only difficult to understand but also difficult to sketch without resort to numerous qualifications. The *obvious* features of the system, however, can be shown in a diagram, though care should be taken not to place too much weight on the structure. The process, except perhaps for routine measures, is not as symmetrical as Figure 1 shows. Nor do the arrows that mark the route fix all the stray possibilities whereby legislation is considered, shaped, or rejected. The contours of power and the structure of priorities that are natural to political institutions resist plotting on the diagram. Moreover, the diagram is silent as to the larger political system of which the legislature is a part and as to the extralegislative actors who press their claims insistently on the members and who are, in turn, influenced by the legislature's actions. The nature and impact of leadership, of legislative parties, and of formal rules of procedure all remain to be explored. Figure 1 thus may best be seen as representing in a general way the major stages and points of access in the legislative process (using Congress as an example); subsequent chapters seek to explain and place them in perspective.

2

LEGISLATIVE STRUCTURES
AND POWERS

No political system, least of all one that is democratic, is able to fix firmly and for all time the boundaries of the legislature's power. However great may be the power conferred upon the legislature, it is neither easily stored nor easily protected. In general, the legislature's claims to power are derived from a variety of closely linked factors, including the legal system and the prevailing ideology, the usages and precedents of history, the empowering responses of the people, the circumstances of the time, and the constitutional document with its allocation of formal powers.

In a constitutional order, governmental power is shared among several independent but interrelated branches—in the United States by the legislature, executive, and judiciary. In providing for the allocation of power among the divisions of government, no constitution is wholly neutral. Every constitution contains a series of judgments regarding the assignment of the major shares of power and responsibility. In purely *constitutional* terms, the American legislature is placed at the center of the political system, having been awarded the principal tasks of government and a major share of the powers presumed necessary to perform them.

Although this analysis begins with a discussion of the constitutional grant of powers to the legislature, it is important to remember that no written record is likely to provide precise statements as to where power lies, how it is managed, or for what purposes it is used. Constitution-makers, no matter how detailed their prescriptions, can do no more than sketch the contours of power. Power relationships among the branches of government and between the government and private power systems are both complicated and fluid; a written settlement is unable to protect power or to insure initiative. Finally, the outcomes of public policy skirmishes are affected as much by the power of particular men and the force of circumstance as by the broad language of the constitutional document.

This chapter seeks to point out how the legal-constitutional system establishes the legislature and charts its main tasks and how legal-constitutional arrangements affect the way the legislature goes about its business. In addition, it raises questions concerning the impact of legislative structure on public policy. Later chapters will consider the critical question of power

34 allocation within the legislative institution itself and its implications for policy ends.

The Constitutional Status of the American Legislature

CONGRESS

The constitutional primacy of the legislative branch is better illustrated by Congress than by the typical state legislature. Despite the principle of separation of powers and the network of checks and balances, the mission of government rests basically upon the broad decisions of Congress. In the catalogue of government functions it is Congress which determines the broad policies and creates the administrative organizations to execute them, which fashions standards for administrative action and for the appointment and removal of administrative officials, which appropriates funds for the support of governmental functions, and which, in varying degrees, supervises and reviews the work of administrative establishments. We need not now mull over the question whether Congress in fact is supreme (or ought to be), whether it carries on its tasks intelligently and responsibly or bungles them, whether it has a mind of its own or simply provides the arena in which organized interests monopolize the settlement of conflicts. The appropriate point is that the Constitution makes certain that decisions regarding the principal functions of government are entrusted to the representative assembly.

The central point of departure for exploring the status of Congress is Article I, Section 8, of the Constitution. This section provides a formal list of the powers of Congress; ranging the gamut, they include the power to lay and collect taxes, borrow money, regulate commerce, coin money, regulate standards of weights and measures, establish post offices, create courts, declare war, create an army and navy, provide for a militia, set up a government for the capital district, and adopt laws concerning bankruptcy, naturalization, patents, and copyrights.

These specified powers are known as *delegated* powers because they represent a delegation of authority by the people to the national government. In addition, the final clause in Section 8 of Article I confers upon Congress the power "to make all laws which shall be necessary and proper for carrying into execution the foregoing powers, and all other powers vested by this Constitution in the government of the United States, or in any department or officer thereof." This clause is the taproot of the doctrine of *implied* powers, an interpretation which holds that Congress has a broad authorization to use the means "necessary and proper" to carry into execution its delegated powers. As reasoned by Chief Justice Marshall in the case of *McCulloch* v. *Maryland* (1819) : "Let the end be legitimate, let it be within the scope of the constitution, and all means which are appropriate, which are plainly adapted to that end, which are not prohibited, but consist with the letter and spirit of the constitution, are constitutional."[1] A related, but

---

1 *McCulloch* v. *Maryland,* 4 Wheaton 316 (1819).

more abstruse or inferential, band of powers are termed *resulting* powers. A resulting power cannot be traced directly to a specific authorization in the Constitution but results, or is fairly deduced, from a circumstance in which certain delegated powers are associated.

Congress's legislative power, broad and inclusive as a result of numerous court decisions, is reinforced in still another clause in the Constitution which declares that the laws of Congress "made in pursuance" of the Constitution "shall be the supreme law of the land." The supremacy clause (Article VI, Section 2) has come to mean that state constitutions or laws in conflict with the national Constitution or the acts of Congress are null and void. Moreover, this clause not only makes federal enactments superior to those of the states, but it places upon state judges, no less than federal ones, the obligation to enforce their provisions. Disputes involving the supremacy clause occur in fields where federal and state governments exercise *concurrent* powers; that is, where both levels of government have interests and responsibilities.

The powers of Congress are extensive, but they are by no means unlimited. Several major restrictions may be noted. The powers conferred upon Congress may not be delegated by it to any other body or authority. The Supreme Court has insisted that, in formulating policy, Congress must adopt clear standards to guide the executive officials who will administer it. An act which grants too great a measure of discretion to the executive may be invalidated as an unconstitutional delegation of legislative power.[2] Nor can Congress delegate its power to the people in the form, say, of a nationwide referendum, though some states have made provision for direct legislation of this sort.

Because the lines separating legislative from judicial and executive functions are blurred and tenuous, occasional cases have arisen concerning congressional arrogation of executive and judicial powers. For example, an act of Congress requiring Senate agreement to the president's removal of certain executive officials has been held unconstitutional, since it represented legislative encroachment upon a purely executive power.[3]

Furthermore, congressional authority is contained by a number of constitutional provisions. First among them is the Tenth Amendment, stipulating that "powers not delegated to the United States by the Constitution, nor prohibited by it to the States, are reserved to the States respectively, or to the people." In addition, the Bill of Rights contains a wide range of prohibitions concerning civil liberties: Congress, for example, may not adopt laws respecting an establishment of religion; abridging freedom of speech, press, or assembly; depriving people of life, liberty, or property without due process of law; requiring excessive bail or denying trial by jury. And, finally, Article I, Section 9, specifically prohibits Congress from passing bills of attainder and ex post facto laws. None of these limitations, of course, represents an absolute standard, and the Supreme Court often has been involved in filling in their meanings and in judging the validity of congressional acts that touch upon them.

[2] *Panama Refining Co.* v. *Ryan,* 293 U.S. 388 (1935); *Schechter* v. *United States,* 295 U.S. 495 (1935).

[3] *Myers* v. *United States,* 272 U.S. 52 (1926).

By sketching in broad terms the division of powers between the national and state governments, the Tenth Amendment to the U.S. Constitution provides the basic formula for American federalism. Under its provisions, national powers are delegated while state powers are *reserved* or *residual;* specifically, powers not delegated to the national government or denied to the states are retained by the states and the people. Although some powers, a growing number in fact, are exercised concurrently by nation and state, the jurisdiction of state government is nonetheless very broad.

Because state powers are residual in character rather than simply enumerated, it is difficult to mark precisely the dimensions of state legislative authority. But it will help if several points are kept in mind. In the first place, the national Constitution places certain limitations upon the states. For example, Article I, Section 10, prohibits states from entering into treaties, from coining money, or from passing bills of attainder; in addition, it outlaws ex post facto laws and laws impairing the obligation of contracts. States may not levy import duties or enter into agreements or compacts with other states except with the consent of Congress. Moreover, the Fourteenth Amendment ("No State shall make or enforce any law which shall abridge the privileges and immunities of citizens of the United States; nor shall any State deprive any person of life, liberty, or property, without due process of law; nor deny to any person within its jurisdiction the equal protection of the laws."), as interpreted by the Supreme Court in recent decades, has served to place new and significant limitations upon state action. As a result of the Court's elaboration of the "due process" clause in this amendment, certain important protections guaranteed the citizen in the Bill of Rights against the national government now apply equally to state and local governments.

In the second place, many state constitutions divide power not only by parceling it among the three main branches of government but also by creating a number of independent and popularly elected officers, such as the attorney general, secretary of state, auditor of public accounts, treasurer, and superintendent of public instruction. Where these offices have certain constitutional powers and responsibilities, directly or by implication, the courts will invalidate legislative acts which diminish or restrict such authority.[4] Constitutional provisions regarding county government and municipal home rule place additional restrictions upon legislative power, though in most states very little authority is reserved for municipal governments, whose governing process is regulated in detail by state constitutional and statutory provisions.

The doctrine of "implied limitations" is a third factor affecting legislative power. As applied by some state courts, it means that legislative authority extends simply to the direct grants of power made by the constitution, and

[4] The fragmentation of power among several independent administrative officials also tends to stultify the governor's efforts to coordinate and to integrate the activities of the administrative branch. Because these statewide elective offices are independent sources of power, their occupants may be tempted to challenge the governor openly. Also, a good many campaigns for the governor's chair have begun in these elective offices.

therefore by implication the legislature's authority over other (nonspecified) activities is narrowed or denied. Judicial inference thus has sometimes made the presence of detailed constitutional grants to the legislature a limitation upon general legislative authority. "Under such circumstances the only way to restore the legislature's prerogative is to amend the constitution, specifically bestowing upon it the power denied by the courts."[5]

Highly specific constitutional restraints are the fourth, and most pervasive, means for whittling down legislative authority. Almost without exception, these detailed prohibitions are a product of the last half of the nineteenth century, having been written into constitutions in order to curb a variety of abuses then flourishing in the legislatures. Before examining the limitations introduced during this reform period, it will be instructive to glance backward at the early state constitutions, adopted at a time when legislatures and legislators ranked high in public esteem. James Willard Hurst comments on this early era of legislative supremacy:

> The early constitutions gave the legislature broad power. There they bore witness to its high public standing. The first state constitutions simply vested "legislative" power in described bodies. The grant implied the historic sweep of authority that [the English] Parliament had won, except as this was limited by vague implications to be drawn from the formal separation of powers among legislature, executive, and courts.
>
> ...Typically, the early constitution makers set no procedural requirements for the legislative process. They wrote a few declarations or limitations of substantive policy making. But these generally did no more than declare what contemporary opinion or community growth had already so deeply rooted as to require no constitutional sanction....[6]

The beginning of the end of legislative preeminence came with a series of disclosures of widespread graft and corruption in the legislatures during the early and middle years of the nineteenth century. Evidence that venality had uprooted the public trust appeared in state after state. Public funds were wasted recklessly, outright bribery of legislators was all too common, charters and contracts were granted to the highest bidders, spoils systems ran riot, and special legislation in the interest of a privileged few was distinguished by its prevalence. All in all, it would be difficult indeed to catalogue the variety of peculations, barefaced and ingenious, which colored this scandalous era.

Public anxiety over the pernicious operations of the legislature, if sometimes slow to be aroused, everywhere culminated in a demand for reform. Another look at the legislature's role was in order, and, in the process of review, belief grew that popular control might be made more effective and that corruption might be mitigated by placing rigorous constitutional shackles upon legislative action. One careful study of this period describes what took place during the reassessment of the legislature:

[5] Austin F. MacDonald, *State and Local Government in the United States* (New York: Thomas Y. Crowell Company, 1955), p. 139.

[6] *The Growth of American Law: The Law Makers* (Boston: Little, Brown & Company, 1950), p. 24.

Between 1864 and 1880, thirty-fiive new constitutions were adopted in nineteen states. Distrust of the legislature was the predominant characteristic of all of them. Records of these conventions contain pages on pages of vigorous denunciation of state legislatures by the most outstanding members of the conventions. In the constitutions they drafted, they sought to prevent a recurrence of the evils they denounced, by incorporating not only new proscriptions on what the legislature might do, but also extensive legislation regulating and controlling the new economic interests to which earlier legislators had fallen victim. Hence these constitutions added provisions defining and regulating railroads, business practices, trusts, monopolies and interlocking directorates, corporations, the marketing and watering of corporate securities, and the regulation of banking and financial institutions. New prohibitions on the passing of local and special legislation were added. By 1880 the pattern for state constitutions as legal codes, and as obstructions to the free exercise of legislative power, was clearly set.[7]

State constitutions bear a strong resemblance to each other in style, in length, in dogma, and especially in the battery of explicit limitations they fasten upon the legislative branch. A brief examination of these restrictions will help us to gauge further the range of legislative powers.[8]

In the first place, all state constitutions have limitations upon the legislature (and other branches) in the form of a bill of rights. Normally these rights are of the "inalienable" or "fundamental" variety found in the national Constitution, but this traditional statement has not sufficed in all states. The California Constitution, for example, gives the citizenry the "right" to fish upon and from public lands, while the Tennessee Constitution makes free navigation of the Mississippi an "inherent right" of the people. Some states have amended their constitutions in order to protect special economic and social rights—for instance, the right of labor to organize or, in other cases, not to organize (the "right to work"). Every constitutional settlement of a social or economic issue represents a further diminution of legislative power, a narrowing of alternatives for the representative assembly. Whatever the merits of the prevailing side in these social arguments, few if any students of government believe the constitution is a proper place for their enshrinement.

Second, state constitutions commonly prohibit the enactment of local or special legislation—bills which affect a single person, a single corporation, a single local government. Constitutional limitations upon special or local legislation, found in most states except some in New England and the South, were introduced to combat legislative preoccupation with dispensing favors to private individuals and organizations, launching special projects for particular localities, and interfering in local conditions. In some legislatures in the latter part of the nineteenth century perhaps half to three-quarters of all bills passed during a session were special acts. Not surprisingly, where special legislation was emphasized, less attention was given to public

7 Byron R. Abernethy, *Constitutional Limitations on the Legislature* (Lawrence: University of Kansas, Governmental Research Center, 1959), p. 15.

8 The following paragraphs on state legislative powers lean heavily upon Abernethy, *op. cit.,* especially Chapter 3.

business or to general priorities. When the states adopted constitutional provisions prohibiting special or local legislation, they specified that the legislature could pass only *general* laws, for example, those affecting not simply one local government but a whole class of local governments.

Much less private and local legislation is passed today than in the past, but the practice has not been eliminated by any means—even in states with lengthy lists of constitutional prohibitions. For example, where a multiple-category system for classifying local governments is used, the legislature has no difficulty in legislating for particular types of communities, perhaps for even a single political subdivision. Moreover, no extraordinary ingenuity is required to camouflage local and special legislation, making it appear to be general in scope. Finally, where state courts have not been rigorous in enforcing constitutional enjoiners concerning special legislation, the practice has flourished.

A third major category among constitutional restrictions involves the financial powers of the legislature, circumscribed in three principal ways in many states. The first limitation is placed on the taxing power; this may include provisions setting maximum tax rates, providing exemptions for certain kinds of institutions (e.g., educational, religious, and charitable), or requiring taxes to be uniform (the effect of which has been, often, to rule out *graduated* income, inheritance, and other taxes). Second, legislative fiscal authority also may be limited by imposing a state debt limit in the constitution. "These limitations on the authority of the legislature to borrow money are usually unrealistic. . . . They can become the refuge of legislators unwilling to act in the face of critical state problems. They have led to repeated amendments of state constitutions as the only way of achieving even a tardy remedy for critical financial problems of the state."[9] Third, some state constitutions carry provisions that earmark certain revenues for specific state functions, such as public education or highways. In thirty states, as of 1965, continuing or earmarked appropriations and special funds made up one-half or more of total expenditures; in a few states the proportion approached 90 percent, thereby giving the legislature control over a mere 10 percent of the state budget.[10] Earmarking may rest on either constitutional or statutory mandates. In either case it contributes to the erosion of the legislature's fiscal powers.

Fourth, state constitutions contain a variety of provisions concerning legislative procedure. Typical specifications in this mixed lot include such matters as requiring the reading of bills in full, requiring three readings of bills on separate days, requiring the legislature to keep and publish a journal, requiring a roll-call vote on final passage of bills, requiring bills to be limited to one subject (described in the title), defining a quorum, and setting the form which bills must follow. Plainly, not all these requirements are followed to the letter (e.g., reading of bills in full); certain restrictions are steadily ignored and others receive but token compliance.

Fifth, the habit of including large quantities of "statutory" law in con-

9 *Ibid.*, p. 56.
10 *State Expenditure Controls: An Evaluation* (New York: Tax Foundation, Inc., 1965), p. 74. See also *Earmarked State Taxes* (New York: Tax Foundation, Inc., 1965).

stitutions has served to enfeeble the legislature. Not only has this practice stretched the length of many state constitutions to the breaking point, but, more important, it has reduced the range of alternatives open to legislative majorities. In constitution after constitution, minute details govern corporate form and management (especially banks and railroads), public utilities, common carriers, toll bridges, judicial procedure, stock issues, compensation of public officers, control and management of schools, penalties for the misuse of public moneys, and so on. Of infinite variety and complexity, these provisions are generally anachronistic; worse still, they encumber the legislature unnecessarily and make it difficult for the legislature to respond rapidly to shifting circumstances and new problems. The "statutory" law of American state constitutions owes its place to the nineteenth-century era of corporate and legislative profligacy.

A sixth type of specific limitation results from provision in the constitution for the direct participation of voters in lawmaking. Present in one form or another in about one-third of the states, the two devices of direct legislation are the *initiative* and *referendum*.

The initiative consists of a procedure whereby a certain percentage of voters may by petition propose a law (or constitutional amendment) to be placed on the ballot for voter approval or rejection. Circumventing the legislature, the voters draft the proposal (in practice, a pressure group usually sparks interest in the idea and does the work), circulate petitions (to be signed normally by 5 to 10 percent of the registered voters), and campaign for its adoption. In certain states the legislature is given an opportunity to adopt the initiated measure, in which case no further step is required. Otherwise, voters may express themselves on the question in a coming election.

The referendum, an ancient device, has several variants. It provides for the submission of legislative and constitutional measures to the voters for their acceptance or rejection. In nearly all states a referendum is required to approve constitutional amendments; in many states it is required for bond issues and for changes in liquor regulations. In some states provision is made for optional referendums: questions are submitted to the voters on the judgment of the legislature. Where this option exists, there is a temptation for legislators to get out from under a nettling problem by calling for a referendum. Another variant of this device is known as the "protest" referendum; in states where it is authorized, voters have the power to prevent a measure already adopted by the legislature from taking effect. Petitions bearing the requisite number of signatures are filed with the proper state authority, and the question is then submitted to the voters. Should a sufficient vote (usually a majority) be cast against the enactment, it becomes null and void.

The argument over the initiative and referendum—valuable instruments of popular government in the opinion of some people and transparent nostrums in the opinion of others—has been carried on sporadically for over half a century. Much has been published about the details of these devices.[11]

11 For a broad survey of initiative and referendum, see Charles R. Adrian, *State and Local Governments* (New York: McGraw-Hill Book Company, Inc., 1960),

Our point will be confined simply to the view that they are cut out of the same cloth as other restrictions, that they encroach upon legislative authority, and that they occasionally lead to legislative timidity and irresponsibility. Manifestly, they add nothing to *legislative* initiative or autonomy.

LIMITATIONS ON THE LEGISLATURE
AND FEDERAL POWER

Taken together, the devices for containing the legislature introduced into state constitutions have had an exceptional impact on the capacity of the states to govern responsibly and effectively. "Hog-tied, drawn, and quartered" by old and outdated constitutions, many state governments today find it difficult to discharge their functions in such a way as is likely to restore public confidence.[12] It seems plain, as numerous writers have argued, that the failure of the states to come to terms with the formidable problems of the twentieth century has led to devolving new duties upon the federal government. This argument was stressed by the Commission on Intergovernmental Relations in its report to President Eisenhower in the mid-fifties:

> The success of our federal system...depends in large measure upon the performance of the States.... The strengthening of State and local governments is essentially a task for the States themselves.... [Many] State constitutions restrict the scope, effectiveness, and adaptability of State and local action. *These self-imposed constitutional limitations make it difficult for many States to perform all of the services their citizens require, and consequently have frequently been the underlying cause of State and municipal pleas for Federal assistance.*[13]

It is not true, of course, that the shortcomings of state governments today are attributable solely to the constitutional fetters placed on the legislature. Many factors are responsible, including the low visibility of state politics, malapportionment, unwholesome pressure politics, one-party political systems, diffusion of executive power, low salaries, inadequate research assistance for legislators, and monumental public apathy.

The root cause in the immobilization of state government, however, is the constitution. Under the circumstances, when the states seem unable (or unwilling) to find answers to the hard problems, the "states' rights" doctrine which is invoked appears to be no more than a handy myth to resist federal action. The dilemma of the states involves their capacity to act. It is unlikely that an awakening will take place in the states, or the flight of power to

---

pp. 151–54, and Jewell Cass Phillips, *State and Local Government in America* (New York: American Book Company, 1954), pp. 124–27.

12 James W. Fesler, "The Challenge to the States," in *The Forty-eight States: Their Tasks as Policy Makers and Administrators* (New York: The American Assembly, Columbia University, 1955), p. 8.

13 Commission on Intergovernmental Relations, *A Report to the President for Transmittal to the Congress* (June 1955), pp. 36–37 (emphasis added).

Washington be reversed, until state constitutions are reshaped to provide an appropriate legal framework for effective state action.

Organizing the Legislature

CONGRESS

The first task of Congress when it assembles in each odd-numbered year is to organize itself for the consideration of business. The way the chambers go about this differs to some extent because of differences between their election calendars. The Senate traditionally has been regarded as a "continuing body," since two-thirds of its membership carries over from Congress to Congress by virtue of incumbency. This "continuous" feature reduces most problems of organization to routine tasks. One question of organization, however, has become anything but routine: Do the rules of the Senate carry over intact from one Congress to the next? Or is each new Senate empowered to adopt its own rules by a majority vote? At the bottom of this argument is Rule 22, the "unlimited debate" rule which requires the agreement of two-thirds of the senators "present and voting" to terminate debate on legislation. Northern liberals in both parties have sought at the beginning of each new Congress to revise this rule by lowering the two-thirds requirement to three-fifths or to a majority, thereby making it easier to curb filibustering. They have claimed that the Senate is not a continuous body and that new rules may be adopted by a simple majority vote at the opening of any new Congress. Thus far their efforts have been unsuccessful.

After the Senate has attended to its organizational housekeeping, it is ready to proceed with the business of the session. It informs the House that it is assembled and ready to hear the president's annual message.

The ritual of organizing the House is more elaborate and time-consuming. It begins when the clerk of the preceding Congress calls the assembly to order and reads the names of the members who have been certified as elected. The next step is to call for the election of a Speaker, which follows after each party has made its nomination. The vote is taken and the defeated candidate escorts the newly elected Speaker to the chair where he is administered the oath of office. The other members-elect are then sworn in, except those whose election is under challenge. The majority party's candidates for the various offices of the chamber—clerk, sergeant-at-arms, doorkeeper, postmaster, and chaplain—are then presented, elected, and given the oath of office. The final step is the adoption of the rules of the chamber, normally identical to those which have previously been in force. The routine of organization is terminated, and the House apprises the Senate of its readiness to join with it for the purpose of hearing the president's message.

What has been described up to now is, as much as anything, the view from the galleries. The real work of organizing, the substance rather than the reflection, is a function of the party organizations, especially of the majority party. Preceding the formal organization of Congress, each party in each chamber caucuses to select its candidates for legislative offices— Speaker of the House, president *pro tem* of the Senate, floor leaders, and the whips. Selection of party leaders ordinarily is run through without much controversy, with party hierarchs from the previous Congress being returned to power as expected. As a rule, the caucus plays an important role in choosing leaders only when death, retirement, or election defeat has removed a member from the hierarchy; even then, the choice of a successor may be firmly settled well in advance of caucus action.[14] The official floor votes which follow simply ratify the decisions of the majority caucus in each house; party lines naturally are firm on votes to organize the chamber.

STATE LEGISLATURES

More by custom than by intent, or because problems of organization are everywhere about the same, the typical legislature goes through about the same motions as Congress in organizing for work. Hence, rather than to plow ground now familiar or to explore unique arrangements found here and there among the states, we may summarize state practice generally.

The critical factor in organizing the legislature in most states, as in Congress, is the majority party—with perhaps a considerable amount of nudging from an interested governor. It is the majority party—or at least a majority of the majority party—which makes the crucial decisions as to house and senate leadership, shapes the committee structure and the party ratio within the committees, appoints officers, reaffirms or transforms the rules, and settles the chamber into its job. The decisions that count usually have been taken before the session is convened, though it is by no means rare for intraparty conflict over the choice of the speaker, the president *pro tem,* or the majority or minority floor leaders to be settled after the session has begun—perhaps on the floor rather than in the caucuses.

In general, however, organizing the legislature is simple and mechanical, something which has to be gone through in order to get other things moving. New members are administered the oath of office, old members are welcomed back, election results are canvassed, quorums ascertained, nominating speeches are made, and elections concluded. Finally, amidst other festivities, a resolution is adopted appointing a committee "to wait upon his Excellency, the Governor, and inform him that the Senate [or House] is convened and organized and ready to receive any communication he may be pleased to make."

Presiding Officers

Political power in the legislature, its origins and dimensions, is neither easily identified nor easily evaluated. Elusive and transient, it may lie at one time with the presiding officers; at another time with committee chairmen,

---

[14] Studies of leadership selection in legislatures are scarce. See an analysis by Nelson W. Polsby of the struggle between Carl Albert of Oklahoma and Richard Bolling of Missouri to replace John McCormack as Democratic majority leader. "Two Strategies of Influence in the House of Representatives: Choosing a Majority Leader, 1962," in *New Perspectives on the House of Representatives,* ed. Robert L. Peabody and Nelson W. Polsby (Chicago: Rand McNally & Company, 1963), pp. 237–70. Also see an interesting account of the contest for the position of majority leader in the 92d Congress by Larry L. King, "The Road to Power in Congress," *Harper's Magazine,* June 1971, pp. 39–63.

44 a party caucus, or a nonparty bloc; and at still another time with the executive, an interest group, or an alliance of interest groups. It scarcely exaggerates the problem to say that where power starts and where it leaves off in the legislature, nobody knows. Formal and conventional powers—those made "legitimate" by constitutions, statutes, rules, or customs—are recognized without difficulty, however, and we shall examine certain of them here as they pertain to the role of the presiding officers.

CONGRESS

The Speaker of the U.S. House of Representatives, it may be said, wears two hats: he is the presiding officer of the chamber and, at the same time, the acknowledged leader of the majority party. Chosen by the majority party caucus and elected by a party-line vote on the floor, he will, normally, have become Speaker after a tour of party duty as floor leader. Inevitably he is an old hand in the House, though seniority is but one factor in his selection. Very few offices are as "permanent" as the Speaker's—once elected to it he has reason to expect reelection as long as he is in Congress, whenever his party holds a majority of the seats.[15] In his role as presiding officer, the Speaker interprets and enforces the rules of the chamber, recognizes members who wish to speak, calls for votes on questions, refers bills to committees, and appoints select and conference committee members. Though the Speaker's formal powers are no longer as awesome as in an earlier day (see Chapter 9), his influence is great, extending to and beyond the farthest reaches of Congress.

The position of presiding officer of the Senate, occupied by the vice-president, is something of an anomaly. Unlike the Speaker, the vice-president is not a member of the body over which he presides and he does not enter debate; he may vote only in case of a tie; strangest of all, as a result of his independent selection, he may be a member of the minority rather than of the majority party. Not surprisingly, therefore, the vice-president's legislative powers are neither important nor extensive; he is, pure and simple, a presiding officer. Such prestige as he gains, as well as the influence he wields, is derivative chiefly from his link to the White House. In addition, the majority party in the Senate honors one of its members by electing him

---

15 Like all good rules, this one has exceptions. Joseph Martin, Massachusetts Republican and for twenty years (1939–59) floor leader or Speaker of the House, lost his position by a narrow vote (74–70) in the 1959 Republican conference. Representative Charles A. Halleck of Indiana became the new GOP minority leader. Among the reasons for his loss, Martin cited the disastrous defeat of the Republican party in the 1958 congressional elections, encouragement given Halleck by the White House (especially by subordinates of President Eisenhower), and Vice-President Nixon's tacit approval of the Halleck challenge. Representative Martin's story of his denouement is told in his book, *My First Fifty Years in Politics* (New York: McGraw-Hill Book Company, Inc., 1960), Chapters 1 and 2. Another contest for minority leader took place in the Republican conference in 1965, and the vote again was close. By a margin of six votes (73–67), Gerald R. Ford, Jr., of Michigan defeated Halleck for the post. For accounts of events leading up to this struggle, and the struggle itself, see John Bibby and Roger Davidson, *On Capitol Hill: Studies in the Legislative Process* (New York: Holt, Rinehart & Winston, Inc., 1967), pp. 113–44, and Robert L. Peabody, *The Ford-Halleck Minority Leadership Contest, 1965* (New York: McGraw-Hill Book Company, Inc., 1966).

president *pro tempore,* in which role he presides in the absence of the president of the Senate (the vice-president). Usually the senior member of the majority party, the president *pro tem* acquires no distinctive power as a result of his selection.

STATE LEGISLATURES

In general, the presiding officers in the state legislatures have powers and duties similar to those of their counterparts in Congress, and they are selected in about the same fashion. The difference is one of degree. The speaker of the lower house at the state level usually has greater influence upon committee organization and legislation than does the Speaker of the U.S. House of Representatives. His authority in and out of the legislature is sufficient to rank him next to the governor in the list of leading state politicians.[16]

The presiding officer of the upper house in about three-quarters of the states is the lieutenant governor, elected at the same time as the governor by statewide vote. In contrast with the speaker, his powers are narrowly circumscribed; he does not take part in debate and has a vote only in the case of a tie. In about a third of the states he is given authority, nominal in most cases, to appoint standing committees. In sum, the net impact of the lieutenant governor upon senate decisions and state public policy is slight. Where state constitutions make no provision for this office, the senate selects a presiding officer from its membership. As in the case of the U.S. Senate, a president *pro tempore* is chosen; ordinarily he becomes the chief spokesman for the majority party in the chamber.

Rules of Procedure

A rudimentary requirement for any legislature is a set of formalized rules for governing the style and substance of internal organization, the choice of officers, and the mode of procedure to be followed by the assembly. The national Constitution provides that each house is free, with a few exceptions (e.g., the Constitution requires a journal to be kept), to draw up its own rules of procedure. Many state constitutions, as we have seen, specify in detail procedures to which the legislature is expected to adhere.

Evolving gradually over the years, rules have a tenacious quality and are neither easily nor frequently changed. The basic set of rules used by Congress, and to an extent by state legislatures as well, is found in *Jefferson's Manual of Parliamentary Practice.* The *Manual* is buttressed by a number of standing rules in each house of Congress.

Rules serve a multiplicity of purposes. They establish the order of business and provide for priorities and regularity in its consideration; they dilute opportunities for arbitrary and capricious treatment of the minority; they offer customary and traditional ways for settling disputes and for coming to decisions; and in their perpetuation from year to year and decade to decade, they impart continuity to the life of the chamber. Their essence is *systematization,* their major contribution *orderliness.*

---

[16] Chapter 9 explores the office of Speaker in greater detail.

46   Rules cover a vast and intricate variety of parliamentary conditions. Our purposes will be met here by revealing something of their character and scope; certain major rules, such as the discharge rule in the U.S. House of Representatives, are examined more fully in other chapters. Rules are designed to cover both routine and special questions which arise in the course of enacting legislation. Hence there are rules relating to the call of committees, quorums, recess and adjournment, calendars, appointment of conference committees, consideration of conference reports, offering of amendments, procedure in the committee of the whole, disposal of unfinished business, debate and its termination, consideration of veto messages, discharge of committees, and the readings to be given a bill. Formal rules are refined and elaborated by the rulings of the presiding officers.

Today's rules are the residue of earlier political settlements and as such are more than a means of facilitating and expediting the consideration of public business in a legislative body. They need to be understood in their *political* context, as instruments in the exercise of political power.[17] A good case can be made that the political function of rules is vastly more significant than the function of "regularizing" or "ordering" legislative processes.

Efforts to modernize legislative rules of procedure have resulted generally from two related complaints: (1) that many rules are tipped in favor of the minority, serving to put the majority in a legislative straitjacket, and (2) that many rules foster delay and inaction and tend to serve the interests of those who cling to the *status quo.*

The injustice of the rules has been a persistent lament in the U.S. Senate. Liberals, in particular, believe the rules are stacked against them. To quote Senator Hubert Humphrey (D., Minn.):

> Senators have long believed that their rules should be conservative, not creative; weapons for the defense of the minority rather than tools of the responsible majority; devices to promote local sovereignty rather than a more effective legislative system.... The rules of the Senate, as a continuing body, remain in force from Congress to Congress without reaffirmation.... The fact...that the Senate is governed by its old members under the seniority rule gives the conservatism of old age much influence.[18]

17 This point is well documented in a study by John Bibby and Roger Davidson of the passage of the Area Redevelopment Act during the Kennedy administration. They conclude that although rules influence legislative outcomes, they "are not independent of the power struggle that lies behind them. There is very little that the houses cannot do under the rules—so long as the action is backed up by votes and inclination. Yet votes and inclination are not easily obtained; and the rules persistently challenge the proponents of legislation to demonstrate that they have both resources at their command. Thus, there is little to prevent obstruction at every turn except the tacit premise that the business of the house must go on." In addition, their study points out that rules must be used with a degree of caution. "If they are re$_{\cdot}$:ted to indiscriminately or flagrantly, there is the risk that they will be redefined and the prerogative taken away or modified." *Op. cit.,* p. 217. See also Howard E. Shuman, "Senate Rules and the Civil Rights Bill," *American Political Science Review,* LI (December 1957), 955–75. On the contribution of the rules of Congress to irrational voting behavior in the amending process, see William H. Riker, "The Paradox of Voting and Congressional Rules for Voting on Amendments," *American Political Science Review,* LII (June 1958), 349–66.

18 "The Senate on Trial," *American Political Science Review,* XLIV (September 1950), 657.

As Lewis A. Froman has observed, there are important implications in the fact that the rules tend to favor those legislators who are more likely to resist change than to sponsor it:

> One is that those congressmen and senators who wish to change the *status quo* are forced, by the rules, to do a considerable amount of bargaining, not only on the differences which occur among themselves but also with those who favor the *status quo*. The alternative to bargaining will often be defeat, since those who wish to protect the *status quo* are often numerous, intense, and in strategic positions.
>
> A second implication of the fact that rules and procedures, generally speaking, favor those who prefer the *status quo* over change, has to do with attempts to change the "rules of the game." Looking at rules and procedures as not being neutral in the congressional contest, proposals to change the rules, in many cases, are attempts to change the ability of certain members, and hence certain interests, to prevail in future contests. In other words, changes in the rules may change the advantage of one group of players over others.
>
> In this sense, some rules changes redistribute power. Because this is so, certain proposals to change the rules are the most bitterly fought contests in congressional politics.[19]

Legislative rules are significant because the methods used to reach decisions often shape the decisions themselves; procedure and policy, in other words, are often interlaced. This fact accounts for the controversy inherent in all rules of procedure. Never wholly neutral, rules benefit some groups and disadvantage others. They are, commonly, one of the many faces of minority power.

The Legislative Body: Size, Terms of Members, and Sessions

SIZE

When the first Congress was called to order in 1789, there were eleven states in the Union and, therefore, twenty-two members in the Senate. The first House of Representatives had a total of sixty-five members. Both houses grew steadily in size until 1911 when the House membership was fixed by law at 435 and the Senate membership was set at ninety-six. With the admission of Hawaii and Alaska to statehood in the late 1950s, the Senate was increased to 100 members and the House, temporarily, to 437. Following the 1960 reapportionment of seats, the House reverted to its former population of 435.

Consensus on the proper size of state legislatures is very thin, for legislatures differ greatly in number of members. At the summit is New Hampshire with an immoderate total of 400 members in its lower house— a number nearly seventeen times as large as its upper house. By contrast,

---

[19] *The Congressional Process: Strategies, Rules and Procedures* (Boston: Little, Brown and Company, 1967), p. 191.

48 Delaware manages to draft its laws with a lower house of only thirty-nine members; Alaska and Nevada each has a lower house of forty members. About one-third of the states have lower houses which range between 100 and 124 members. Three other states with particularly large lower houses are Massachusetts (240), Pennsylvania (203), and Georgia (195). Following reapportionments in the mid-1960s, Connecticut's House dropped from 294 to 177 members, and Vermont's from 246 to 150.

Minnesota leads all state senates with sixty-seven members, followed by Illinois with fifty-eight, New York with fifty-seven, Georgia with fifty-six, and Montana with fifty-five. At the bottom of the order are Delaware with nineteen members and Nevada with twenty. Most commonly, state senates range between thirty and thirty-nine members. To argue that states sometimes have had an instinct for making novel arrangements in their legislative institutions is perhaps rash. What is plain, however, is that they have given no more than casual attention to the relationship between state population and the size of the legislature.

TERMS OF MEMBERS

Members of the lower house of Congress are elected for a two-year term of office, members of the upper house for a six-year term. Terms of legislative office in the states are variable. In thirty-nine states, senators serve a four-year period; in the remainder the term is two years. Lower house members in forty-five states hold office for two years; in four southern and border states—Alabama, Louisiana, Maryland, and Mississippi—the term is four years.

In about one-half of the states, senate terms are staggered; i.e., half of the membership comes up for election every two years. This contributes to continuity in the life of the chamber. Since legislation covers a broad band of complex affairs, it is useful to have a number of experienced lawmakers on hand; thus the provision for staggered terms has become a standard prescription for improving legislative organization. Obviously there is a case for staggered terms, though there is at least one reason for rejecting the principle or at least for viewing it as something less than an outright advantage. The flaw is that staggered terms contribute to the problem of divided party control in the legislature. The electorate is unable to effect a complete change in the makeup of the legislature at any one time. Although a party may win the governorship and the lower house handily, the senate often is beyond its reach due to staggered terms. The possibility of party rule and party responsibility, to an extent at least, is sometimes the price paid for the continuity fostered by staggered terms of office; whether it is worth it is open to question.

A major reason for the distress of legislatures, according to many observers, is the short two-year term of office provided for members of the lower house of Congress and for members of the lower houses of all but a few states. Legislators have no more than settled into their jobs before it is time to begin their campaigns for reelection. Not a few representatives from marginal districts yield to the pressure and engage in more or less continuous campaigning throughout their terms. A lengthened term of office

—four years, for example—undoubtedly would permit members to devote more time to public business. A four-year term might be especially advantageous for new legislators who must acquire experience in the lawmaking process before becoming valuable members of the legislature. A two-year term obviously does not provide much opportunity for seasoning.

The two-year term carries both electoral and policy consequences. From an electoral standpoint, its chief effect is in the realm of campaign costs. Most members find it very expensive to run for office every other year; indeed, in competitive districts it is not uncommon for each side to spend in excess of $100,000 in a campaign.[20] The policy consequences, as Charles O. Jones has noted, are also important:

> First, the President's party usually suffers losses at the mid-term election and he will, therefore, have less support for his program in Congress. Second, frequent campaigning does take time from other activities. Indeed, a few members find it necessary to run twice and sometimes three times (if there is a runoff primary) in one year to retain their seat. Third, House members' staffs tend to become very constituency-service oriented in their work and they, too, must divert some of their energies to campaigning. The result of frequent campaigning, it is argued, is a campaign-constituency orientation in the House of Representatives, particularly in election years, which has definite policy effects (though these cannot be measured with any degree of precision). It is also argued that controversial legislation is avoided during election years. While probably true in certain cases, it is difficult to demonstrate that this is a widespread phenomenon.[21]

The proposal for a four-year term for congressmen has often been discussed but seldom seriously considered. President Johnson's endorsement of the idea—proposing a four-year term with all House members to be elected at the same time as the president—was received with something less than unchecked enthusiasm in many quarters. Conservative newspapers and many members of Congress were fearful that four-year terms which coincided with presidential elections would erode the power of Congress, creating a permanent "coattail Congress." Some conservative newspapers found the plan acceptable if modified to provide for the election of *half* the House each two years; this arrangement, of course, would heighten the possibility of having a divided government, with the executive controlled by one party and the House by the other. Not the least of the reasons why prospects for a four-year House term appear to be remote is the opposition of many members of the Senate. A member of the House explains why:

> We will never get a four-year term. The Senate will never go along with the idea because senators will not want to have congressmen free to run against them without having to relinquish their House seats should they

---

[20] *Electing Congress: The Financial Dilemma* (New York: The Twentieth Century Fund, 1970), p. 8.

[21] *Every Second Year: Congressional Behavior and the Two-Year Term* (Washington, D.C.: The Brookings Institution, 1967), pp. 98–99.

lose. As it now stands, congressmen hesitate to risk everything by challenging a senator.[22]

CONGRESSIONAL SESSIONS

Several provisions in the Constitution relate to sessions of Congress. Article I, Section 4, requires Congress to "assemble at least once in every year." The Twentieth Amendment, ratified in 1933, provides that sessions shall begin at noon on January 3, unless otherwise provided. Article II, Section 3, gives the president authority to convene Congress on "extraordinary occasions," a power he has not hesitated to invoke in the past. The same section provides that should the houses be unable to agree on the time of adjournment, the president "may adjourn them to such time as he shall think proper. . . ." This latter power has never been used.

Each Congress covers a two-year period, with a new session beginning each January. Prior to World War II, sessions were relatively short, averaging, for example, only about 170 calendar days in the 1930s; as many as three or even four sessions might be convened in any Congress. The press of business in recent decades, however, has forced Congress to operate for longer periods—hence the typical Congress today has two sessions, each of which lasts the better part of the year. The "first" session of a new Congress begins in January of each odd-numbered year and the "second" session begins in January of the following (even-numbered) year. Special sessions are also numbered, though they are not likely to be held often in the future since Congress is now in regular session most of the time. The life of a bill is the life of a Congress; that is, bills introduced in the first session survive adjournment and may be taken up for action during the second session at the point where their consideration left off in the first session. A new Congress, of course, begins with the introduction of new bills.

STATE LEGISLATIVE SESSIONS

In the early state constitutions, drafted at a time when popular confidence in the legislative branch ran high, the legislatures occupied a strong and

---

[22] Charles L. Clapp, *The Congressman: His Work as He Sees It* (Washington, D.C.: The Brookings Institution, 1963), p. 330. The impact of a four-year term on the House would probably be substantial. One writer observes: "Since members would always run in Presidential years, it would accentuate the coattail effect that the top of the national ticket usually exerts. Individual Congressmen and Congressional candidates would become more dependent on the national party. In the same year as a Presidential campaign, the voters would be more likely to cross-examine Congressional candidates about their views on the national party platform and their agreement or disagreement with their party's national ticket. . . . A four-year term would eliminate the midterm election for the House, in which the party in power almost invariably loses seats. Since Presidents have enough trouble getting their programs through as it is, avoiding this drop in their political prestige at the midway point would represent clear gain for the White House." See William V. Shannon, "Reforming the House—A Four-Year Term," *New York Times Magazine,* January 10, 1965, p. 67. The truth of the matter is that no one really knows what the impact would be of a four-year term for representatives. At least a dozen different predictions have been made as to its consequences. Would Congress be more or less independent of the executive? The answer is by no means clear. See Nelson W. Polsby, "A Note on the President's Modest Proposal," *Public Administration Review,* XXVI (September 1966), 156–59.

central position. A vigorous legislature meeting annually, it was believed, would serve to stay the executive hand and to keep the assembly responsive to the electorate. Accordingly, few constitutional restrictions were placed upon the legislature, and it soon became the dominant voice of government. The scandals and venal acts of legislators in the mid-nineteenth century, however, led to the devitalization of its powers.

Popular confidence in the legislature gave way to popular obloquy. One manifestation of this was the substitution of biennial for annual sessions and the provision for rigorous limitation on the length of sessions. By the turn of the twentieth century, all but a handful of states had abandoned yearly meetings of the legislature. A legislature not in session could not very well get into new trouble. Moreover, an enfeebled legislature meeting infrequently and for short sessions was not as great a threat to the *status quo* and to the new men of vast economic power. This simple "solution" brought fundamental change to the political systems of the states.

The legacy of distrust continues to hang over many state legislatures today, as shown in Table 2.1, which presents in capsule form the principal data regarding legislative sessions. Despite a recent trend toward annual sessions, a substantial number of legislatures still assemble biennially. Constitutional limitations on the length of sessions continue to be the rule among the states, with a typical provision calling for regular sessions of no more than sixty calendar days. The Georgia Constitution stipulates that sessions shall not exceed forty *calendar* days, while the Alabama Constitution provides for a limitation of thirty-six *legislative* days. In addition, as Table 2.1

TABLE 2.1

Legislative Sessions in the States

	Years in Which Sessions Are Held		Limitations on Length of Regular Sessions		Special Sessions			
					Legislature May Call		Legislature May Determine Subject	
	Annual	Biennial	Yes	No	Yes	No	Yes	No
Number of States	36	14	29	21	18	32	30	20

SOURCE: *Book of the States, 1970–71* (Chicago: Council of State Governments, 1971), pp. 66–67, updated by data furnished by the Citizens Conference on State Legislatures, 1971.

shows, most legislatures are not given the power to call special sessions, and in twenty states the governor alone determines what subjects shall be taken up in special session. The broad picture is one of legislatures with modest control over their own existence, meeting infrequently, and conducting the public's business under oppressive limitations of time.

The Committee on Legislative Processes and Procedures of the Council of State Governments, in its 1946 report, argued that a major step toward the strengthening of state legislatures could be taken by removing restrictions upon the length of regular sessions:

Legislatures cannot properly fulfill their important functions without adequate time to dispose of the public questions before them. Restrictions on the length of sessions is one of several factors which today defeats the deliberative character of legislatures in many states. The effect of rigid constitutional restrictions is to increase the so-called legislative "jam" at the close of sessions in many states, and results in inadequate or no consideration for measures deserving of legislative attention. The volume and complexity of legislative business have constantly increased and constitutional or statutory measures which prevent the legislature from fulfilling its proper function cannot be held in the public interest, however appropriate the restrictions may have been when originally adopted.[23]

ANNUAL VS. BIENNIAL SESSIONS

Over the years a vast array of reforms and assorted palliatives have been suggested to ease the distress of the legislatures and to improve their effectiveness. With the possible exception of unicameralism, no reform has been pressed more persistently than the adoption of annual sessions. Several basic arguments have been adduced in favor of this change, based partly on the deficiencies of the biennial arrangement and partly on the outcomes anticipated from a shift to yearly meetings.

At the base of the argument is the belief that the biennial provision is anachronistic, wholly unsuitable for dealing with the complex and continuing problems which confront today's legislatures. The responsibilities of the legislature in mid-twentieth century have become so burdensome that they can no longer be discharged on an alternate-year basis. Congress has found it necessary to be in session most of the year, and the executive and judicial departments function more or less continuously at all levels of government. It is unrealistic to suppose, runs this familiar line of reasoning, that state business can be set aside for eighteen months or more while problems accumulate and programs deteriorate for want of legislative solutions. The matter is particularly acute where fiscal affairs are involved, since under a biennial arrangement the legislature must forecast income and expenditures well into the future.

Proponents of annual sessions call upon other arguments in support of the change. They contend that more frequent meetings may serve to raise the status of the legislature, thereby helping to check the flow of power to the executive branch. Moreover, they argue that continuing legislative oversight of the administration becomes feasible with annual sessions and that administrative accountability for the execution of legislative policies is more easily enforced. Another advantage they attach to annual sessions is that states may respond more rapidly to new federal laws which require state participation, as in the case of highway and social security programs. States which meet biennially may have to wait a year-and-a-half or longer before taking advantage of new or more elaborate federal programs. Finally, proponents of annual sessions cite the argument that the legislature cannot operate effectively in fits and starts, with biennial sessions followed all too often by special sessions. Annual sessions would serve to diminish the need for special sessions, and the policy-making process would be made more timely and orderly.

[23] *Our State Legislatures,* report of the Committee on Legislative Processes and Procedures (Chicago: Council of State Governments, 1946), p. 3.

Those who prefer the now traditional biennial session demur on most of the above points. They hold that the virtues of the annual session have been greatly exaggerated, that its flaws have not been understood. In the first place, there are already enough laws. Annual sessions inevitably will lead to the persistent advocacy of new legislation and to the adoption of meretricious policies; biennial sessions constitute a safeguard against precipitate and unseemly legislative action. Stability of policy is itself a mark of an orderly and effective legislature. Proponents of the biennial system also argue that yearly meetings of the legislature will contribute to legislative harassment of the administration and its agencies; although an annual session may help to put life back into the legislature, it might be expected to diminish administrative efficiency. The biennial system affords legislators more time to renew relations with constituents, to mend political fences, and to campaign for reelection. The interval between sessions also may be put to good advantage by individual legislators and interim study commissions, since there is never sufficient time during a session to study proposed legislation.

There is, finally, the matter of cost. Annual sessions inevitably lead to a spiraling of legislative costs, for the legislators and other assembly personnel are brought together twice as often. Other costs will become inflated, and perhaps legislative salaries will be increased. Moreover, new programs and new appropriations are likely to result; more expensive government is a natural consequence of annual sessions.

Advocates of annual sessions reject the argument of excessive expense in operating the legislature, pointing out that although state expenditures have climbed rapidly in recent decades, the percentage of legislative costs to the total budget is much smaller today than it was in the past. A study of the period 1927–32 revealed that legislative costs came to less than 1 percent of the total budget; follow-up investigations in 1948 and 1963 have shown a decrease in the proportion of funds allocated to legislative operations.[24] Given the magnitude of state government today, this view holds, there is no good reason to hope for economies simply by cutting legislative costs.

Unicameral or Bicameral Legislature?

Familiar and conventional political arrangements, no less than familiar and conventional ideas, have an extraordinary capacity for perpetuating themselves. Such is the case of bicameralism.

COLONIAL EXPERIENCE

The earliest colonial legislatures, developing out of stockholders' meetings, were unicameral in form. Deputies elected by the freemen of the towns and the appointed assistants of the colonial governors sat together in a single house. Conflict between these two groups was doubtless inevitable, leading to plans

[24] Belle Zeller, ed., *American State Legislatures* (New York: Thomas Y. Crowell Company, 1954), p. 93; *The New Jersey Legislature* (New Brunswick, N.J.: Rutgers University, Eagleton Institute of Politics, 1963), pp. 52A–53A.

54 for the creation of two chambers. First to adopt the bicameral form was the Massachusetts Bay Colony, when, in 1644, "following an acrid dispute between magistrates and Deputies over the case of Goody Sherman and her stray sow, the General Court separated into two co-equal Houses, the House of Assistants and the House of Deputies."[25] Many other colonies followed Massachusetts' lead, though the flight from unicameralism was not complete until the state of Vermont switched to a two-house legislature in 1836. Part of the stimulus to bicameralism in the states had come from the formation of a national legislature of two houses, replacing the single house under the Articles of Confederation.

THE ARGUMENT OVER VIRTUES

It is difficult to account for the acceptance of the bicameral idea today other than to note, as we have earlier, popular reluctance to abandon old moorings. Of the fifty states, only Nebraska, in 1934, has adopted the plan for a one-house legislature. Moreover, save in a few academic and reform circles, the debate over unicameralism vs. bicameralism is no longer very lively. Nevertheless, it may be useful to sketch briefly the principal claims made for each.

Bicameralism, its proponents have argued, "prevents hasty and careless legislation," "serves as a check against popular passions and impulses," "provides protection against corruption and the control of the legislature by special interest lobbies," "permits the use of a different basis of representation in the two houses," and represents "the traditional American form of legislature."[26]

On the whole, the arguments made by bicameralists have not been found convincing.[27] As much as anything, they appear to be rooted in a distrust of the legislature and the representative function. No evidence exists to suggest that bicameral legislatures prevent the passage of hasty and undesirable legislation—the principal claim made for the arrangement. In fact, an extraordinary number of bills move from one house to the other in the final days of the session, when the pressure of time often precludes anything more than superficial examination. Moreover, if the same party controls both houses, and a party matter is involved, the check supposedly given in the second house is unlikely to amount to much. Numerous studies have shown that a majority of the bills that clear one house go through the

25 Manual for the Massachusetts Constitutional Convention of 1917, p. 7, as quoted in Commonwealth of Massachusetts, *Report of the Special Commission on Legislative System and Procedure,* Senate Report no. 50, January 1, 1943 (Boston: Wright & Potter Printing Co., 1943), p. 94.

26 Zeller, *op. cit.,* pp. 51–56 *et passim.*

27 For an article which supports the "braking" function of bicameralism, see Frank E. Horack, Jr., "Bicameral Legislatures Are Effective," *State Government,* XIV (April 1941), 79–80, 96. But also see JeDon A. Emenhiser, "Sober Second Thought in the Utah Legislature: Toward a Theory of Inter-Chamber Relations," (Manuscript, Utah State University, 1965). This study finds slight evidence that the second chamber gives "sober second thought" to bills that have already passed the other house. Rather, what does emerge is that bills which pass both houses often have two things in common: early introduction and overwhelming passage in the initial chamber.

other without amendment, and far more bills are lost in the house of origin than in the second chamber. Finally, it is well to remember that the legislature has numerous other built-in safeguards against hasty and impulsive action—including intricate rules of procedure and an elaborate committee system. And in the background is the governor's veto power.

The other virtues claimed for bicameralism are hardly more impressive. Are lobbyists more powerful in a unicameral than in a bicameral legislature, their "corrupting" influence more pervasive in one house than in two? Although there is no way of proving this point one way or another, we have the argument of one authority, Roger V. Shumate, that lobbyists "will be less influential in a small body in which responsibility of individual members for passing or defeating bills can be more definitely fixed than under a system in which responsibility can be shunted back and forth from one house to the other...."[28] On this score, it should also be recognized that, since lobbyists often seek to block legislation rather than to advance it, bicameralism may afford new opportunities for defeating proposals.

The claim concerning the representative value of bicameralism requires a comment or two. At one time, state senators were chosen on a basis different from that of state representatives, with the upper house designed to represent an elite of property owners, the lower house to represent population. With one house "conservative" and the other "radical," a natural check, one upon another, would be present. In point of fact, it has been a long time since this concept held any significance. Today, senators and representatives are selected in the same way in all states. The qualifications for the state senate may differ from those of the house, and the senate term of office is usually longer than the house term, but the voters in all cases are the same. Moreover, the contention is spurious that any legislator today simply represents a district or area; rather he represents a heterogeneous grouping of voters, some of whom have augmented their power by membership in organized groups (including parties) whose constituencies extend far beyond the local legislative district.

The final assertion in support of bicameralism—that it is "American" and traditional while unicameralism is "foreign" and radical—needs little comment. Its fundamental flaw is that it is simply nonsense, plausible only to those who know nothing of colonial political organization or those who believe the Founding Fathers fashioned a political system without benefit of a glance at British or other European experience and theory.

Much of the literature concerned with legislative structure in the states comes down heavily on the side of unicameralism.[29] A survey of the case

---

[28] "The Nebraska Unicameral Legislature," *Western Political Quarterly,* V (September 1952), 510.

[29] There are a number of books and articles on the issue of bicameralism vs. unicameralism: C. A. Breckenridge, *One House for Two* (Washington: Public Affairs Press, 1958); Daniel B. Carroll, *The Unicameral Legislature in Vermont* (Burlington: University of Vermont Press, 1933); Mona Fletcher, "Bicameralism as Illustrated by the Nineteenth General Assembly of Ohio," *American Political Science Review,* XXXII (February 1938), 80–85; Jack W. Rodgers, "One House for 20 Years," *National Municipal Review,* XLVI (July 1957), 338–42, 347; John P. Senning, *The One-House Legislature* (New York: McGraw-Hill Book Company, Inc., 1937) and "Unicameralism Passes Test," *National Municipal Review,* XXXIII (July 1944), 60–65; Charles W. Shull, *American Experience with Unicameral Legislatures*

56 for this arrangement includes the claims that a single chamber "carries greater prestige...and hence attracts more outstanding and representative citizens," "is able to give more thorough consideration to proposed legislation than two chambers," eliminates "the jealousy, friction, and rivalry between the two houses," "facilitates the development of essential leadership...by concentrating such leadership in one place," "permits closer and more effective relations between the governor and the executive departments and the legislature," "reduces the power of special interest groups," "does away with the need for conference committees," "facilitates public reporting of the work of the legislature," reduces the cost of the legislature, and increases the possibility for fixing responsibility for legislative action.[30]

Notwithstanding the attractiveness of these assertions, for the most part their validity must be assumed; the "efficiency" of unicameralism, like the "Americanism" of bicameralism, is a difficult item to gauge. A fairly recent attempt to canvass the experience of the Nebraska legislature, for three decades the unicameral model, arrives at these conclusions: it has led to some saving in salary payments for legislators and in general legislative expense, to lengthened legislative sessions, to the introduction of fewer bills but the enactment of substantially more, to a decrease in the number of special sessions, to a more deliberate mode of procedure, and to an increase in the tenure of legislators. No evidence was found that unicameralism leads to the passage of hasty and ill-considered legislation. Whether legislators in the unicameral scheme are superior in talent, intellect, and moral caliber cannot be proved, nor can it be verified that the quality of legislation enacted by the "unicameral" is better than that enacted under the earlier bicameral legislatures. In sum, the unicameral experiment in Nebraska "has not fulfilled either the most optimistic hopes of its friends or the most pessimistic fears of its opponents. On the whole, however, it has given a good account of itself."[31]

Legislative Scheduling: The "Log Jam" in the States

The typical legislature operates at a bewildering pace in the closing days of the session. Few things are more common in the course of legislative affairs, especially in the states, than the last-minute rush to wind up business for another year or another biennium. It is not unusual to find as many as 50 percent of all bills passed during a session receiving final approval in the last week before adjournment.

(Detroit: Bureau of Government Research, 1937); O. Douglas Weeks, *Two Legislative Houses or One?* (Dallas, Texas: Arnold Foundation Studies, 1938); Charles B. Hagan, "The Bicameral Principle in State Legislatures," *Journal of Public Law,* no. 2 (1962), 310–27; Donald Janson, "The House Nebraska Built," *Harper's Magazine,* November 1964, pp. 124–30; Talbot D'Alemberte and Charles C. Fishburne, Jr., "The Unicameral Legislature," *University of Florida Law Review,* XVII (Winter 1964), 355–67; Demitrios M. Moschos and David L. Katsky, "Unicameralism and Bicameralism: History and Tradition," *Boston University Law Review,* XLV (Spring 1965), 250–70.

30 Zeller, *op. cit.,* pp. 57–58.
31 Shumate, "The Nebraska Unicameral Legislature," 504–12.

The closing rush in the legislature often has been criticized by close observers of the state scene. Major bills are voted "up or down" with but scant debate or explanation, perhaps none at all. Hastily drawn amendments wreak havoc with legislation that has been months in the making. Poorly drafted, ambiguous bills end up as state law, and a future legislature will be required to undo the damage.

REASONS FOR LOG JAM

Both institutional restrictions and political factors help account for the legislative log jam near the end of sessions. In the former category are such factors as: (1) the presence of sessional limitations which require an enormous quantity of public business to be transacted in a short space of time; (2) the absence of a consent calendar to facilitate consideration of minor, noncontroversial bills; (3) the existence of substantial disparities in committee workloads, contributing to log jams at the committee stage; (4) the absence of deadlines for the introduction of bills; (5) the shortage of staff assistance; and (6) the avalanche of proposals introduced each session.[32]

The log jam in state legislatures often is due mainly to political maneuvering. What separates legislative leaders from rank and file in the closing days of the session is that the leaders control the contingencies—they can cause things to happen if certain conditions are met. For example, leaders may find it expedient to stall the consideration of minor or noncontroversial bills until the major program bills have been voted upon. A member whose pet bill is pigeonholed in committee or lost on an overcrowded calendar knows the folkway well: if he votes against a major bill desired by the leadership, his own bill may never be moved toward passage. After the big bills have been brought to a vote, leaders clear the way for the rapid disposition of other bills. In some legislatures, control over the schedule is the principal weapon of discipline available to the leaders. Possibly no other wedge is so successful in wringing accommodations out of skeptical or stubborn opponents.

A second political factor that contributes to the closing rush involves logrolling—a mutual-assistance pact by which legislators combine to pass each other's bills. Often, logrolling alliances cannot be negotiated until a number of bills have been sidetracked, usually near the end of the session. When a number of legislators are involved and enough pressure has been built up, it is not overly difficult to form logrolling combinations sufficient to give proposals new momentum. In the practice of logrolling, what helps one legislator eventually helps all who join the club.

One final political factor that contributes to the problems of legislative scheduling needs identification. This is the budget bill—"key log in the jam." In state after state the budget bill is introduced long after the session has started; then begins a round of hearings marked by tedious negotiations between the parties, between the chambers, and between the legislature and the governor. Compromises are elusive, and the working out of amendments which will pull a majority vote takes time. The delay is thus considerable

---

[32] See Stanley Scott, ed., *Streamlining State Legislatures* (Berkeley: University of California, Bureau of Public Administration, 1956), p. 51.

58 and, while negotiations proceed, most of the other bills are left on the shelf. As is true of all good things, negotiations finally end. Sufficient support for the budget bill is won; legislators have been convinced, mollified, or dragooned, and the bill is cleared for passage. A quickening of the legislative tempo results, and the countless little bills clogging the calendars or bottled up in committee are rushed through to passage. Customarily, the legislature is now ready to adjourn *sine die*.

Critics who complain about the legislative log jam have a substantial argument. Especially deplorable is the hasty action often given major amendments introduced on the floor in the final days and hours of the session. It is also unfortunate that the log jam may lead to the legislature's forfeiture of the opportunity to override the governor's vetoes of bills passed immediately prior to adjournment.

Nevertheless, the broad indictment of the legislature for its failure to avoid the closing rush may exaggerate the dilemma. Last-minute voting on legislation is one thing, last-minute consideration of legislation is quite another. It is plainly not true that legislation voted upon in the tumult of the closing days has received no attention up to that point. Indeed, virtually all of the bills will have been studied in committee in earlier months at a time when the legislative pace was unhurried. And since legislative bodies customarily follow committee recommendations, whether made early or late in the session, there is no sure evidence that floor decisions would be markedly different if spaced more evenly throughout the session.

DEVICES FOR IMPROVING SCHEDULING

The states have experimented with several techniques designed to diminish the problem of the log jam. All but a handful of states have time limits on the introduction of bills. States may provide for the presession filing of bills. In Massachusetts, for example, bills must be introduced one month before the session opens. Some states employ terminal dates for the filing of bills during a session: e.g., Arkansas, none the last three days; Minnesota, ninetieth day; Nebraska, twentieth day; Wisconsin, fifty-first day. Another group of states regulates legislative scheduling by fixing a deadline at each session. Michigan seeks to avoid the end-of-session congestion by a series of deadlines for committee reports in the house of origin and in the second chamber. Generally, however, limitations tend to be deceptive, since usually they may be waived upon the vote of an extraordinary majority.

Illinois uses a device known as "clearing the calendar" to eliminate a large number of bills still pending late in the session. This procedure, ordinarily invoked with about two weeks of the session remaining, works in this way. A motion will be made to table all house bills still in house committees. Some days later, bills further along in the process—say, on second reading—will be tabled. Finally, a day before the end of the session, senate bills on third reading in the house will be tabled. A similar screening process takes place in the senate. Although the Illinois procedure helps to establish certain last-minute priorities, its main contribution may be simply to create an illusion of orderliness. Possibly that is better than nothing at all.

Provisions for prefiling and printing of bills, used in about one-half of the states, have been of some help in accelerating the legislative process in

the early weeks of the session and thereby diminishing the crush of legislation at the end. But their effect is to reduce the problem, not to eliminate
it. If prefiling is optional, legislators may ignore it. Moreover, major bills
are not often prefiled, since they tend to involve many legal and political
snarls which cannot be worked out until the session is well under way.
Finally, even though prefiling is permitted, many legislators prefer to postpone introduction of their pet bills until such time as the bills are likely to
attract maximum attention. All in all, political factors make up the principal
obstacles to improving legislative scheduling. Legislators themselves are not
greatly troubled by how the press and public view legislative behavior in the
tumultuous closing days of the session. By the time the next legislature is
ready to convene, most observers will have forgotten how the last one came
to a close.

Structure, Powers, and Policy

A knowledge of the legislature's legal-constitutional structure, its
formal powers, and its methods of organization and operation is basic to
understanding the legislative process. These "situational landmarks"[33]—the
major features of structure and organization—intrude on the behavior of
the legislators and affect the output and effectiveness of the legislature.
Furthermore, they offer certain analytical material useful in accounting for
the emergence and development of the legislature and are suggestive concerning the relationship between the legislature and the social system.

Yet there is much this body of information fails to disclose. Analysis
of the formal structural-organizational arrangements may be of but modest
value in accounting for action taken within the legislature; it provides no
certain assistance in locating power within the institution; it cannot show
how agents of parties and of private organizations influence decisions; and
it may be of only marginal help in explaining why legislators behave as they
do. Finally, it offers only vague clues concerning the biases of the institution
or the ways by which it maintains itself. We begin a more complete answer
to these questions by considering the theory and practice of representation
as it relates to the legislative system.

---

[33] The term is used in a study of the legislatures of California, New Jersey,
Ohio, and Tennessee. See John C. Wahlke, Heinz Eulau, William Buchanan, and
LeRoy Ferguson, *The Legislative System: Explorations in Legislative Behavior* (New
York: John Wiley & Sons, Inc., 1962).

3

REPRESENTATION
AND APPORTIONMENT

No popular precepts of democratic theory are rooted more firmly in American political thought and practice than that a legislator is expected to look continually to the people who elect him, to speak to their convictions and uncertainties, to protect their interests, and to defend his actions before them. The legislative process and the representative system are linked inseparably in all democratic political orders. Legislative action, whatever its form or significance, is the ultimate expression of the representative principle.

Representation leaves its stamp on the legislative process in several ways. In the first place, what the legislature does—the functions it emphasizes—is influenced by the way in which members perceive the job of representative—whether, for instance, they regard themselves as "constituency agents" or as "free agents." Second, the standard for evaluating legislatures which seems to have made the strongest impression on the public (and one recently adopted by the courts) is that of "representativeness"; the test of this criterion centers on the extent to which legislative districts contain approximately equal populations. Finally, a good indication of the significance of representation for the legislative process is that ideas concerning representation tend to shape a great many of the most familiar and important questions that are asked about legislators, legislatures, and legislation: How do legislators perceive their relationships to constituents? How do legislators' responses to constituents correspond to their responses to nation, state, or party? Are American legislatures responsive to and under the control of majorities? How does apportionment affect the distribution of power within legislatures? What are the consequences of apportionment arrangements for legislative action?

Political theory contains numerous inquiries directed to the nature and characteristics of representation; not surprisingly, there is no agreement as to its essential properties.[1] Alfred de Grazia defines representation as "a condition that exists when the characteristics and acts of one vested with public functions are in accord with the desires of one or more persons to

---

[1] Perhaps the best contemporary book on the general problem of representation is Hanna F. Pitkin, *The Concept of Representation* (Berkeley: University of California Press, 1967).

whom the functions have objective or subjective importance."[2] In these terms, the fundamental quality of representation is accord—between the representative and those who perceive him as "representative."

Representation may also be thought of as a process in which the attempt is made to prescribe continuing interaction between governors and governed. Representation is viewed as an offshoot of ideas concerning responsible government: those who hold political power are accountable to those in whose behalf they exercise it. "In modern parlance, responsible government and representative government have...almost come to be synonymous."[3] Elections, representation, and responsibility are all currents in the same stream. Electors choose those persons who will hold and use the community's power, and representation helps to endow the officeholder's decisions with legitimacy. Moreover, representatives must account for their actions when running for reelection; in some measure at least, representation makes it possible for the public to state and to enforce its preferences regarding public policy.

Historically, representation has had a unique relationship to legislative assemblies. Carl Friedrich writes:

> [Ever] since the sixteenth century legislation was believed to be the most striking manifestation of political and governmental power. Legislation entailed the making of rules binding upon the whole community.... [The] making of a rule presupposes that there is a series of events which have certain aspects in common. In other words, there must be a "normal" situation. This means that time is available for deliberation to determine what had best be done regarding such a situation. Representative, deliberative bodies require time, obviously, and therefore legislation seems to be peculiarly fitted for such bodies.[4]

There are three principal problems of representative theory: the first centers on the nature of the electorate—who participates, to what extent, and under what conditions; the second focuses on the nature of the relationships between representatives and constituents; the third is concerned with the system under which representatives are elected—this involves the central question of apportionment. The remainder of this chapter is devoted to exploring points two and three, beginning with a discussion of representative-constituency linkages.

Representatives and Represented

Whom does the representative represent—his immediate constituency, the nation, the state, his party, some special clientele? What forces intrude on the legislator's vote? Can the legislator be his own man or must he be somebody else's? If the member's constituents appear to hold a view opposite

---

[2] *Public and Republic* (New York: Alfred A. Knopf, Inc., 1951), p. 4.

[3] Carl J. Friedrich, *Constitutional Government and Democracy* (Boston: Ginn & Company, 1950), p. 264.

[4] *Ibid.*, pp. 268–69.

62 to his, must he square his position with theirs, at least at the stage of casting a vote? These questions point to the classic problem of representation: are representatives free to follow their own judgments on legislative matters or are they merely agents of their constituents? In actual practice, of course, the issue is neither simply nor sharply drawn. Other factors beside "constituency" and "personal judgment" require weighing. In some measure, the representative must assess his responsibility to his party, and it is also probable that he will need to consider the claims that organized interest groups have placed upon him. Each vote carries snares as well as opportunities, and the decision that satisfies one sector of his constituency may distress another.

REPRESENTATIVE AS AGENT OF CONSTITUENCY

The theory that representatives should serve manifestly as agents of their constituents, carefully mirroring their views, apparently stirs the hearts and influences the behavior of many American legislators. They see their job as that of advancing the cause of the people back home.[5] Lewis A. Dexter quotes a congressman explaining his vote on the Reciprocal Trade Extension Act of 1955:

> My first duty is to get reelected. I'm here to represent my district.... This is part of my actual belief as to the function of a congressman.... What is good for the majority of districts is good for the country. What snarls up the system is these so-called statesmen—congressmen who vote for what they think is the country's interest.... Let the senators do that.... They're paid to be statesmen; we [members of the House] aren't.[6]

Legislators believe their records are highly visible to their constituents. One way to increase their security, they believe, is to be certain that their records show that they have been attentive to constituency interests and effective in representing them. The point is made in these comments by an Illinois congressman requesting support for an amendment to appropriate $150,000 for studies of possible public works projects in his district:

> My people are up in arms. They want at least a study made of these problems. They do not mind me voting for worthy projects all over the United

---

[5] A recent study of a national population sample discloses that a large majority of the people (67 per cent) believe that the primary role of the congressman should be that of the "tribune"—specifically, that he should discover, reflect, or advocate the opinions and interests of his constituents. A majority of congressmen similarly emphasize this role. For an examination of the range of role prescriptions in the public's orientation toward legislators, see Roger H. Davidson, "Public Prescriptions for the Job of Congressman," *Midwest Journal of Political Science,* XIV (November 1970), 648–66.

[6] Quoted in Lewis A. Dexter, "The Representative and His District," in *New Perspectives on the House of Representatives,* ed. Robert L. Peabody and Nelson W. Polsby (Chicago: Rand McNally & Company, 1963), p. 6. See also R. Bauer, I. Pool, and L. Dexter, *American Business and Public Policy* (New York: Atherton Press, 1963), especially Part 5.

States, but I can tell you, I am not much to look at, and unless I get some money to be spent down in southern Illinois, to study some of these problems, you may not be seeing me here next year. I hope all of the Members will go along with me and vote for my amendment.[7]

REPRESENTATIVE AS FREE AGENT

The other leading theory of the role of the representative is that he should be unfettered by constituency directives and free to express his own views on matters of public policy. In the classic form of this theory at least, the legislator serves as a delegate from his district and, although he acknowledges the lines of responsibility to his constituents, he is not bound simply to reproduce their sentiments. The best-known interpretation of this position belongs to Edmund Burke who, following his election to the House of Commons in 1774, issued these remarkable instructions to his constituents of Bristol, England:

> Certainly, gentlemen, it ought to be the happiness and the glory of a repre-
> sentative, to live in the strictest union, the closest correspondence, and the
> most unreserved communication with his constituents. Their wishes ought to
> have great weight with him; their opinions high respect; their business un-
> remitted attention.... But his unbiased opinion, his mature judgment, his
> enlightened conscience, he ought not to sacrifice to you, to any man, or to
> any set of men living.... Your representative owes you, not his industry only,
> but his judgment; and he betrays, instead of serving you, if he sacrifices it to
> your opinion.... If government were a matter of will upon any side, yours,
> without question, ought to be superior. But government and legislation are
> matters of reason and judgment, and not of inclination; and what sort of
> reason is that in which the determination precedes the discussion, in which
> one set of men deliberate and another decide, and where those who form
> the conclusion are perhaps three hundred miles distant from those who hear
> the arguments?...Parliament is not a *congress* of ambassadors from different
> and hostile interests, which interests each must maintain, as an agent and
> advocate, against other agents and advocates; but Parliament is a *delibera-
> tive* assembly of *one* nation, with *one* interest, that of the whole —where not
> local purposes, not local prejudices, ought to guide, but the general good,
> resulting from the general reason of the whole. You choose a member,
> indeed; but when you have chosen him, he is not a member of Bristol,
> but he is a member of Parliament.[8]

American lawmakers also have spoken out in this fashion, and indeed the history of Congress is studded with examples of legislators who refused to sacrifice their judgment to appease their constituents. Among them is Senator Lucius Lamar of Mississippi, who opposed the Bland "free silver" act in 1878 even though he had explicit instructions from the Mississippi

[7] *Congressional Record,* May 22, 1956, p. 7862.
[8] Edmund Burke, *Works* (Boston: Little, Brown & Company, 1866), II, 95–96.

64 legislature to support the bill and to work for its passage.[9] He told the Senate:

> Mr. President: Between these resolutions and my convictions there is a great gulf. I cannot pass it.... Upon the youth of my state whom it has been my privilege to assist in education I have always endeavored to impress the belief that truth was better than falsehood, honesty better than policy, courage better than cowardice. Today my lessons confront me. Today I must be true or false, honest or cunning, faithful or unfaithful to my people. Even in this hour of their legislative displeasure and disapprobation, I cannot vote as these resolutions direct. My reasons for my vote shall be given to my people. Then it will be for them to determine if adherence to my honest convictions has disqualified me from representing them; whether a difference of opinion upon a difficult and complicated subject to which I have given patient, long-continued, conscientious study...is to separate us....[10]

EVALUATION OF THE REPRESENTATIVE'S ROLE

In the lore of political science as well as of everyday politics the belief is strong that legislators are heavily influenced by constituencies; in addition, at least among political scientists, the opinion is widespread that many of the difficulties of the political system are the result of the misplaced power of constituencies. For present purposes, the evaluation is less important than the evidence concerning representative-constituency relations. Does the search for political security require legislators to be submissive to the opinions of their constituents? Are all legislators equally oriented to defending constituency interests? Under what circumstances is constituency influence greatest?

One interpretation finds expression in the writing of Walter Lippmann, who contends that democratic politicians get ahead only if they are able to manage or mollify the interests in their constituencies.[11] On the other hand,

---

9 For an account of the doctrine of instructions—"the main avenue through which state legislatures pushed themselves into national affairs"—see William H. Riker, "The Senate and American Federalism," *American Political Science Review,* XLIX (June 1955), 452–69. Riker points out that, although state legislatures maintained the practice of instructing their senators until 1913, the doctrine had become enfeebled much earlier. By 1860, most senators tended to regard "instructions" merely as the expression of the legislature's opinion, and therefore not binding on them.

10 Quoted in John F. Kennedy, *Profiles in Courage* (New York: Harper & Row, Publishers, 1955), p. 171.

11 Walter Lippmann, *The Public Philosophy* (Boston: Little, Brown & Co., 1955), p. 27. The central thesis in Lippmann's book has considerable meaning for representation theory. It is that the relationship between the mass electorate and the government now suffers from a functional derangement. "The people have acquired power which they are incapable of exercising, and the governments they elect have lost powers which they must recover if they are to govern. What then are the true boundaries of the people's power? The answer cannot be simple. But for a rough beginning let us say that the people are able to give or to withhold their consent to being governed—their consent to what the government asks of them, proposes to them, and has done in the conduct of their affairs. They can elect the government. They can remove it. They can approve or disapprove its performance. But they cannot administer the government. They cannot themselves perform. They cannot normally initiate and propose the necessary legislation. A mass cannot govern" (p. 14).

there are at least some legislators who feel that they have substantial freedom of action, as these remarks by a congressman make plain:

> You know, I am sure you will find out a Congressman can do pretty much what he decides to do and he doesn't have to bother too much about criticism. I've seen plenty of cases since I've been up here where a guy will hold one economic or political position and get along all right; and then he'll die or resign and a guy comes in who holds quite a different...position and he gets along all right too. That's the fact of the matter.[12]

David Riesman takes something of a middle position. The fear of constituency sanctions does not explain why legislators strive to place themselves on the side of popular sentiment. Rather, political leaders "though considerably less complacent than their constituencies, nevertheless resemble them in fundamental perceptions, in lack of willingness to face alternatives, and in basic optimism." Moreover, he goes on to say, "they are themselves deceived by the feedback of their pronouncements and those of other issue makers."[13]

Several empirical investigations have sought to explain the role of the legislator as representative and the nature of the relationship between the legislator and his constituency. Studies of state legislators in four states—California, New Jersey, Ohio, and Tennessee—and of a sample of members of the U.S. House of Representatives disclose that representatives may adopt one of several role orientations. In the matter of representation *style,* legislators may see their role as that of *trustee* (the legislator who views himself as a free agent, free to use his own judgment in matters before the legislature); as that of *delegate* (the legislator who feels a need to consult his constituents, perhaps following their instructions even though they conflict with his personal judgment or principles); or as that of *politico* (the legislator who holds both the trustee and delegate orientations, alternating between them).[14]

In view of the usual notion that most lawmakers feel constrained to seek out and to respond to constituency opinions, the results of the studies

---

12 Quoted in Dexter, *op. cit.,* pp. 4–5. And, as Robert Dahl points out, congressmen enjoy the role of free agent. "They like to think of themselves as relying on their private preferences, which they call 'principles,' rather than on the 'dictates' of party leaders, or the party program, or pressure groups, or occasionally even constituents. They call this 'independence,' and 'independence' is highly regarded not only in Congress but evidently among the electorate." *Congress and Foreign Policy* (New York: Harcourt, Brace & World, Inc., 1950), p. 13.

13 "Private People and Public Policy," *Bulletin of the Atomic Scientists,* XV (May 1959), 204.

14 This discussion of representational-role orientations is based on two studies: John C. Wahlke, Heinz Eulau, William Buchanan, and LeRoy C. Ferguson, *The Legislative System: Explorations in Legislative Behavior* (New York: John Wiley & Sons, Inc., 1962), especially Chapters 12 and 13, and Roger H. Davidson, *The Role of the Congressman* (New York: Pegasus, 1969), pp. 110–42. For a study that finds a strong relationship between *prelegislative* life experiences (in particular, political experiences) and the representational roles assumed by freshman legislators in the state senate of California, see Charles G. Bell and Charles M. Price, "Pre-Legislative Sources of Representational Roles," *Midwest Journal of Political Science,* XIII (May 1969), 254–70.

TABLE 3.1

Legislators' Representational-Role Orientations

Role Orientation	Calif. N = 49	N.J. N = 54	Ohio N = 114	Tenn. N = 78	U.S. House N = 87
Trustee	55%	61%	56%	81%	28%
Politico	25	22	29	13	46
Delegate	20	17	15	6	23
Undetermined	0	0	0	0	3
Total	100%	100%	100%	100%	100%

SOURCES: John C. Wahlke, Heinz Eulau, William Buchanan, and LeRoy C. Ferguson, *The Legislative System: Explorations in Legislative Behavior* (New York: John Wiley & Sons, Inc., 1962), p. 281, and Roger H. Davidson, *The Role of the Congressman* (New York: Pegasus, 1969), p. 117.

are sharply surprising. Table 3.1 tells the story. Well over one-half of the state legislators (81 per cent of the respondents in Tennessee) held the trustee or free-agent orientation toward their role as representative. About one-quarter of the state legislators expressed their role orientation as that of a politico and, most interesting, only about one-seventh viewed their role as that of a delegate. The dominant role orientation for congressmen, on the other hand, was that of politico; nearly one-half of those members interviewed were grouped in this category. The trustee role orientation was held by 28 per cent of the congressional sample and the delegate conception by 23 per cent. The fact that so few state legislators and congressmen take the delegate role may be due mainly to the difficulties in learning what constituents want: one cannot be a delegate unless he understands what he has been delegated to do.[15]

In addition, legislators may perceive their role in terms of the foci of representation. By this we mean that legislators may be oriented primarily to the district, to the state, or to the district and state. Table 3.2 shows the areal-role orientation of the legislators in relation to the political character of their districts. Legislators from competitive districts plainly are more attentive to district interests and problems, while members from one-party districts are more likely to express concern over state programs and policies. What this indicates is that legislators most in jeopardy of losing office are

[15] A later study of Pennsylvania legislators by Frank J. Sorauf yields contradictory evidence on the constituency-vs.-judgment question. Only 31.1 per cent of the legislators stated unequivocally that they had assumed the role of "trustee," a much smaller proportion than in any of the four states. Why this should be true is not simple to document. Sorauf stresses the importance of "localism" in Pennsylvania politics. He believes that Pennsylvania legislators are more closely linked to their home communities than legislators in comparable states. This shows up in the importance of errand-running for constituents—a highly developed art among Pennsylvania legislators; it appears also in the attention that legislators give to satisfying local demands for state patronage—of which there is a great deal to pass around. The politics of reward and local interest are central to the job specification Pennsylvania legislators draw for themselves, which tends to make them "delegates" rather than "trustees" in representative role orientation. *Party and Representation* (New York: Atherton Press, 1963), pp. 123–24.

TABLE 3.2

Legislators' Areal-Role Orientations in Relation to the Political Character
of their Electoral Districts in Three States

Areal-Role Orientation	Political Character of District		
	Competitive N = 72	Semicompetitive N = 77	One-party N = 96
District	53%	48%	33%
District-State	28	34	33
State	19	18	34
Total	100%	100%	100%

SOURCE: Wahlke *et al.*, *op. cit.*, p. 292. The three states are California, New Jersey, and Ohio. "Not ascertained" respondents are omitted.

most likely to be sensitive to district stimuli, while legislators from safe districts have greater freedom to direct their attention to the wider problems of the state. The areal orientations of legislators are thus substantially influenced by the political character of the districts from which they are elected.[16]

Lewis Dexter has suggested that congressmen may enjoy substantial freedom from district pressures. Many of the policy questions that come before Congress do not have a direct impact on district interests. Moreover, a congressman trying to identify the prevailing view in his district on a particular issue, even such a major issue as reciprocal trade, may find this a difficult task, for there are few indices of community sentiment available to him. One consequence of this is that the views of men around the congressmen carry a great deal of weight. Dexter concludes that it is less a case of the individual congressman responding to the opinions of his constituents than it is of representing "what he hears from the district as he interprets it."[17]

An empirical study of representation by Warren Miller and Donald Stokes adds other evidence concerning constituency control over members of the U.S. House of Representatives.[18] Their study sought to investigate the extent of policy agreement between congressmen and their districts by comparing the policy preferences of constituents, as shown in interviews, with those of their respective congressmen, as revealed both by interviews and roll-call voting behavior. Covering a total of 116 congressional districts, the study tests policy agreement in three fields: social welfare, American involvement in foreign affairs, and federal civil rights programs on behalf of Negroes. On policy matters involving social welfare and civil rights, there

[16] At the congressional level it is equally clear that the factor of electoral uncertainty is a major explanation for the role orientations assumed by members. Trustees, for example, are more likely to be produced by safe districts than by marginal districts, while the reverse is true for delegates. Moreover, congressmen from safe districts are more likely to hold a national orientation while congressmen from marginal districts are more likely to be oriented toward district interests. See Davidson, *op. cit.,* pp. 121–28.

[17] Dexter, *op. cit.,* p. 12.

[18] "Constituency Influence in Congress," *American Political Science Review,* LVII (March 1963), 45–56.

68   is marked agreement between legislators and their districts, especially in the case of civil rights where congressmen tend to behave in the fashion of "instructed" delegates; on questions of foreign involvement, on the other hand, congressmen are inclined to follow the administration, irrespective of prevailing opinion in their districts.

Although the evidence of this study is firm that a district is able to influence its congressman on social welfare and civil rights legislation, there are few signs of meaningful communication between district and legislator. "The Representative has very imperfect information about the issue preferences of his constituency, and the constituency's awareness of the policy stands of the Representative ordinarily is slight." Yet the constituency's ignorance as to the specific positions of its congressman does not free him to vote as he pleases. In the first place, a great majority of congressmen *believe* that their records are essential for their reelection. Second, the fact that only a small number of constituents are informed about the record of their representative nevertheless can prove to be crucial in a close election— "the Congressman is a dealer in increments and margins." Third, voters may have acquired a general impression of the legislator's record, even though they know virtually nothing about its specific content. Finally, control results from the fact that the representative is always alert to potential sanctions by the constituency.[19]

At this point, studies of the linkages between legislators and constituencies produce only tentative inferences. The studies have not focused on precisely the same problems or utilized precisely the same methods. The study by Wahlke *et al.* discloses the prominence of the "trustee" role in the perceptions of state legislators; Dexter's interviews with congressmen lead him to believe that members have far more freedom of action than is commonly supposed, partly because they hear so little from their constituents; Miller and Stokes focus on constituency control and discover different relational patterns, dependent on the domain within which the issue arises (i.e., social welfare, civil rights, or foreign involvement). Although these studies do not add up to a body of related propositions concerning the representational roles of legislators, they suggest not only that there are several major options open to the legislator in choosing a role orientation but also that the orientation may be related to types of constituencies and types of issues.

The Representative System

There are three requisites to the formation of a representative system: a method by which representatives are chosen, an apportionment formula which provides for their assignment to constituencies, and a method for

---

[19] *Ibid.*, pp. 53–56, quotations on pp. 56 and 55, respectively. Constituency control or influence over legislators may derive from electing a legislator who shares the views of the constituents—in which case the legislator's policy preferences are directly related to those of his constituents—or from having a legislator who seeks to learn what the constituency wants in order to satisfy those elements which might otherwise turn him out of office—in which case the legislator's policies presumably relate to his perceptions of constituency objectives. This survey also reports that even

reapportionment as population changes occur. The first of these is met in the United States through an intricate election system based on mass suffrage. The second and third requirements are central to the focus of this chapter and necessitate extended and careful consideration.

CRITERIA FOR APPORTIONMENT

Apportionment is the act of forming constituencies or districts and allotting them units of representation. Alfred de Grazia identifies five possible criteria which can be employed in devising a method of apportionment. These are: (1) territorial surveys, (2) governmental boundaries, (3) official bodies, (4) functional divisions of the population, and (5) free population alignments. The fourth method, which never has been used in the United States, calls for the representation of certain nonterritorial functional interests of a social or economic character—as in the Chamber of Corporations created by the Fascist regime in Italy. The fifth method is central to proportional-representation schemes and has been used sparingly in the United States, principally in local elections. Method three, apportionment by official bodies, was used for the selection of United States senators until adoption of the Seventeenth Amendment in 1913. This amendment removed the choice of senators from state legislatures and vested the power in the people.[20]

The apportionment plan utilized most commonly is that of the territorial survey, which is designed to distribute the population into relatively equal, albeit artificial, districts. Analysis of population shifts is necessarily related to this method, since a new apportionment (i.e., reapportionment) must in some way take account of the movement of people in and out of areas. This problem will be discussed subsequently.

Governmental boundaries, the final criterion to be noted, figure in all schemes of apportionment. Precincts, wards, cities, counties, states, and the nation—the boundaries of each exist as a potential apportionment base. Some cities constitute their city councils through election of members from wards, and other cities provide for election of all councilmen at large. A group of wards may constitute a state legislative district and several counties may comprise a congressional district. Each state, of course, selects two United States senators from within its boundaries. In each case the unit of apportionment directly utilizes at least one formal governmental boundary.

The ideal apportionment based on territorial surveys would show districts equal to each other in population. To those people accustomed to the idea that one vote should equal one vote, such mathematical accuracy is appealing; it is also extraordinarily difficult to achieve. The current drive for equality in representation owes its momentum as well as its origins to the courts rather than to the legislatures. Undoubtedly, equal representation

---

among the *voting* sector of the public, only about one-half of the voters had read or heard something about either congressional candidate. "Information" usually consisted of nothing more than an evaluation such as "he's a good man." See pp. 50–51.

[20] This opening discussion of the criteria for apportionment is based on an analysis by Alfred de Grazia, "General Theory of Apportionment," *Law and Contemporary Problems*, XVII (Spring 1952), 256–67.

70   would have been attained long ago if it had not been inimical to other values bound into the apportionment system.

THE LEGAL FRAMEWORK FOR APPORTIONMENT: CONGRESS AND THE STATES

The apportionment of seats in the U.S. House of Representatives and in the state legislatures is affected by constitutional and statutory provisions on the one hand, and by court decisions on the other. Constitutions lay down the general guidelines for apportionment—for example, the maximum size of legislative assemblies is prescribed by the constitutions of the states— while statutes embody the decisions of a specific apportionment. Strictly speaking, apportionment combines two distinct processes, the allocation of seats to districts and the drawing of district lines. Under the federal system, the national government and the states cooperate in providing for the election of congressmen: the Bureau of the Census determines the number of seats to be awarded each state (apportionment), while the states perform the critical task of shaping congressional districts. The apportionment and districting of state legislative seats is formally a function of the legislature, though its discretion may be circumscribed by specific constitutional provisions or, as in recent years, by the courts.

The most important agency in the apportionment process in recent years has been the Supreme Court, supported by other federal and state courts. In 1962 the Court held in the Tennessee case, *Baker* v. *Carr,* that courts could hear suits brought by qualified voters to challenge legislative apportionments that failed to provide "equal protection of the laws" for all citizens.[21] Apportionment thus became a "justiciable" question. In a series of opinions two years later (the principal opinion appears in *Reynolds* v. *Sims*), the Court held that *both* houses of state legislatures must be apportioned on the basis of equality of population among districts.[22] In *Wesberry* v. *Sanders,* also in 1964, the Court declared that *congressional* districts must be composed of approximately the same number of people.[23] Although some legislatures were slow to comply with the Court's "one man–one vote" decisions, the great majority acted with dispatch. By the middle of 1964, therefore, the courts had come to play a critical role in the apportionment process. But this gets us somewhat ahead of the story.

The history of congressional apportionment begins with the Constitutional Convention in Philadelphia in 1787. The Convention settled a central question of apportionment when it approved the "Connecticut compromise," providing for equal representation of the states in the Senate and for representation on the basis of population in the House. Article 1, Section 2, of the Constitution specifically enjoined Congress to apportion representatives among the states according to population and to reapportion after each census. The Constitution made no mention of congressional districts, and in the early years many states chose to elect their congressmen at large.

For many years Congress took the easy way out in meeting the requirements for reapportionment: it simply chose to increase the size of the House.

21 369 U.S. 186 (1962).
22 377 U.S. 533 (1964).
23 376 U.S. 1 (1964).

Rapidly growing states could be awarded additional seats without penalizing the slowly growing states by cutting their quotas of seats. Finally, in 1911, Congress put a lid on its membership, setting it at 433, with the total to go to 435 upon the admittance of Arizona and New Mexico to the Union. When Hawaii and Alaska were admitted to statehood in 1959, the number was increased temporarily to 437; following the 1960 Census it returned to 435.

Congress took no action to infuse criteria for apportionment into law until 1842. Beginning with the apportionment act of that year and supplemented through the acts of 1862 and 1872, Congress set forth certain specifications for state redistricting; representatives should be elected from single-member districts, and such districts should be compact, contiguous, and, as nearly as possible, of equal population. Congress continued to impose these standards on the states in many subsequent acts, including the one adopted in 1911. However, these specifications were not included in the next apportionment act, thereby freeing state legislatures to draw congressional district lines to suit their purposes. Given this free rein, the boldness of their strokes as well as their ingenuity scarcely could be exaggerated.

When Congress failed to pass an apportionment act following the 1920 census, interest developed in a plan to provide a permanent solution to the problem. In 1929 Congress adopted an act providing for "automatic" reapportionment. Under the terms of this act, as later amended, a redistribution of seats takes place automatically after each decennial census, using the computation method of "equal proportions." The Bureau of the Census is charged with the responsibility of calculating the number of seats to be allotted each state; this information is then relayed to Congress by the president. The clerk of the House of Representatives must then notify the governor of each state as to the number of representatives allotted the state for the next session of Congress. With the apportionment function now largely the responsibility of executive authorities, Congress no longer is able to ignore the reapportionment obligation.

Since 1842 congressmen have been elected almost exclusively from single-member districts; state legislators, on the other hand, often are elected from multimember districts. A study by Maurice Klain published in 1955 disclosed that, contrary to the usual impression, less than one-fifth of the states elected all of their legislators from single-member districts, with 45.4 per cent of the members of the state lower houses elected from multimember districts.[24] Multimember districts continue to be widely utilized in the states. A 1967 survey disclosed that only fifteen of the lower houses and twenty-five of the state senates employed single-member districts exclusively. Two senates and three houses used only multimember districts, while the remainder used a mixed system. In recent years, larger states have been somewhat more disposed than smaller states to adopt the single-member district plan.[25] As

[24] "A New Look at the Constituencies: The Need for a Recount and a Reappraisal," *American Political Science Review*, XLIX (December 1955), 1105–19. Also see Howard D. Hamilton, "Legislative Constituencies: Single-Member Districts, Multi-Member Districts, and Floterial Districts," *Western Political Quarterly*, XX (June 1967), 321–40.

[25] William J. D. Boyd, "States Make Size, Electoral Changes," *National Civic Review*, LVII (February 1968), 94–97.

72 a result of recent Supreme Court decisions, to be considered subsequently, the future of multimember districts is in doubt, particularly when this arrangement manifestly discriminates against the election of black candidates for the legislature.

To state legislators faced with redistricting, one appeal of multimember districts is their simplicity: it is much easier, for example, to allocate an additional seat to a county than to divide the county into two districts. Another advantage of multimember districts is that they rule out gerrymandering *within* the districts, though of course any multimember district as a whole may serve gerrymandering purposes.

There are three main objections voiced to the use of multimember districts. The first is that some multimember districts have grown to an excessive size, making it difficult for voters to exercise intelligent choice. The second objection is that the majority party often wins all or virtually all of the seats in such districts, preventing the minority party from winning seats in proportion to its strength within the area. Finally, there is evidence that multimember districts in some states have made it difficult, if not impossible, for black citizens to elect black legislators; their votes are simply engulfed by those cast in the white community.

Prior to the court decisions of the last decade, a major obstacle to the development of equitable systems of legislative apportionment was the typical state constitution. As of 1960, for example, there were only ten states whose constitutions specified that representation in both houses should be based on population. It was common to find states in which area (e.g., town or county) representation counted fully as much as population in the allocation of legislative seats. Today, however, the picture has changed radically as a result of the *Reynolds* v. *Sims* decision. Apportionment provisions of state constitutions are invalid if they prohibit the legislature from basing district lines in both houses on population. Thus, states can no longer provide equal apportionment to each unit (e.g., town) or provide

TABLE 3.3

Year of Last State Legislative Apportionment Prior to Baker v. Carr (1962)

State	Year	State	Year
Vermont	1793	Wyoming	1931
Connecticut	S—1941; H—1876	Nebraska	1935
Delaware	1897	Rhode Island	1940
Alabama	1901	New Jersey	1941
Tennessee	1903	North Carolina	1941
Iowa	S—1911; H—1927	Kentucky	1942
New Hampshire	S—1915; H—1951	Maryland	1943
Mississippi	1916	Montana	1943
Indiana	1921	Florida	1945
Louisiana	1921	Kansas	S—1947; H—1945
Pennsylvania	S—1921; H—1953	Massachusetts	S—1948; H—1947
North Dakota	1931		

Source: Data from The Book of the States, 1962–63 (Chicago: The Council of State Governments, 1963), pp. 58–62.
Note: S = senate; H = house.

for representation of population in one house and representation of area in the other. The reapportionment cases represent a massive commitment to the principle of equality of representation for all citizens. State constitutions must now reflect this fact.

Though the record of Congress in discharging its limited reapportionment duties has not been exemplary, the records of the states have been infinitely worse. Table 3.3 shows the apportionment "history" of the worst offenders as of March 1962, immediately prior to *Baker* v. *Carr*, the Tennessee apportionment case in which the Supreme Court held that the validity of state legislative districts could be challenged under the Fourteenth Amendment.

In sum, nearly one-half of the states did not redistrict after the 1950 decennial census. Ten states had at least one house which had not been reapportioned since 1930; two states, Vermont and Delaware, had not reapportioned either house in the twentieth century. Vermont's last apportionment for its lower house had occurred in 1793, when it adopted its constitution.

The Malapportionment Issue

The role of the courts in the reapportionment cases can be better appreciated if the dimensions and characteristics of malapportionment prior to *Baker* are first understood. In retrospect, it appears that the failure of Congress and the great majority of state legislatures to deal with serious problems of malapportionment made judicial intervention inevitable.

CONGRESS

The assault upon the theory of representation according to population began in the Philadelphia Convention, when agreement was reached to allot each state two senators. Today, Alaska's population of 302,173 entitles it to two members of the Senate as surely as New York's 18,190,740 people entitle it to two. One student of apportionment wrote in the 1950s that "the distortions from the ideal of 'one man, one vote' are greater in the national upper house than in many state legislatures."[26] Be that as it may, equal representation of states in the Senate is such a conventional fact of civics, even though there may be no persuasive argument for it today, that it is rarely ever challenged.

The apportionment of the lower house of Congress, however, is entirely another matter. The fact that the Senate rests on an apportionment that bears no relationship to population is a good reason why the House should be apportioned so as to closely represent population distribution. It is plain that this was the intention of the members of the Philadelphia Convention, even though the Constitution does not contain an exact prescription for it.[27]

[26] Gordon E. Baker, *Rural Versus Urban Political Power: The Nature and Consequences of Unbalanced Representation* (New York: Doubleday & Company, Inc., 1955), p. 40.

[27] See Andrew Hacker, *Congressional Districting: The Issue of Equal Representation* (Washington, D.C.: The Brookings Institution, 1963), pp. 6–7.

TABLE 3.4

**Extremes in Congressional Districting: Population of Ten Largest Congressional
Districts Compared to Population of Smallest Districts Within Same States,
Including "Representation Weight" of Vote in Smallest Districts, 1962**

District	Population	Representation Weight	District	Population	Representation Weight
Texas (1957)			Indiana (1941)		
5th (Dallas)	951,527		11th (Indianapolis)	697,567	
4th	216,371	4.4	9th	290,596	2.4
Georgia (1931)			Michigan (1951)		
5th (Atlanta)	823,680		18th (suburban		
9th	272,154	3.0	Detroit)	690,259	
			11th	240,793	2.9
Michigan (1951)			Connecticut (1931)		
16th (Detroit,			1st (Hartford)	689,555	
Dearborn)	802,994		5th	318,942	2.2
12th	177,431	4.5			
Ohio (1951)			Texas (1957)		
3rd (Dayton)	726,156		20th (San Antonio)	687,151	
15th	236,288	3.1	1st	245,942	2.8
Maryland (1961)			Ohio (1951)		
5th (Baltimore)	711,045		12th (Columbus)	682,962	
1st	243,570	2.9	10th	274,441	2.5

SOURCE: The data on district populations are taken from *Congressional Redistricting: Impact
of the 1960 Census Reapportionment of House Seats*, Congressional Quarterly Special Report,
September 28, 1962, p. 1604. A comprehensive list on the same order may be found in
Andrew Hacker, *Congressional Districting* (Washington, D. C.: The Brookings Institution,
1963), p. 3.
NOTE: The year of the last congressional apportionment in each state is shown in parentheses.

Representation according to population means automatically that all citizens
will have votes of equal weight.

Table 3.4 shows the baleful facts of congressional maldistricting in
states containing the ten most populous districts in 1962, immediately prior
to the first of the major reapportionment decisions. Each of the ten districts
is compared to the smallest district (or districts, if the state had two districts
in the top ten) within the state. The relationship is pointed up by the
figure showing the "representation weight" accorded each resident in the
smaller districts. For example, each person in the sparsely populated 12th
congressional district in the upper peninsula of Michigan could be said to
have a vote that counted 4.5 times as much as the vote of each person
in the 16th district (assuming the same proportion of residents voted in
each district). Although each district elected a congressman, the Detroit
district had 4.5 times as many people within its boundaries. The difference
was almost as great between the 5th and 4th districts in Texas. A study
by Andrew Hacker revealed that of the forty-two states which then had
more than one congressional district, twenty-one had constituencies in which
the smallest district was less than one-half of the population of the largest

district, in effect making the vote of each resident of the smallest district at **75**
least twice as valuable as the vote of each resident of the largest district.[28]

THE STATE LEGISLATURES

With but few exceptions, in the halcyon "pre-*Baker*" days, the records of
the states in apportioning their own assemblies had little luster about them.
By and large, state legislative districts were even further removed from
population parity than congressional districts. How far the states had moved
away from the population factor in apportionment between 1910 and 1960
may be seen in Table 3.5 drawn from a study by David and Eisenberg. The

TABLE 3.5

**Relative Values of the Right to Vote for Representatives in State Legislatures—
National Averages and Averages for the Seven Largest States**

Population of County	1910	1930	1950	1960
	National Averages for All Fifty States			
Under 25,000	113%	131%	141%	171%
25,000 to 99,999	103	109	114	123
100,000 to 499,999	91	84	83	81
500,000 and over	81	74	78	76
	Averages for the Seven Largest States			
Under 25,000	116%	158%	165%	194%
25,000 to 99,999	111	134	139	155
100,000 to 499,999	99	93	99	100
500,000 and over	83	74	77	77

SOURCE: Paul T. David and Ralph Eisenberg, *Devaluation of the Urban and Suburban Vote*
(Charlottesville: University of Virginia, Bureau of Public Administration, 1961), p. 9.

table depicts the relative value of the vote (i.e., the voting power of the
individual resident) according to the size of the county in which it was cast,
combined for both chambers in all fifty states. Two central facts emerge
from this research: first, the votes of residents in the most populous counties
(500,000 or more people) counted for much less than the votes of residents
of rural counties (a condition true in 1910 as well as in 1960) and, second,
the gap between the voting power of urban and rural residents widened
steadily over the fifty-year period. Designating the average statewide value
of the vote as one, the 1910 resident of a county of 500,000 or more population had a vote with a value of 81 percent of the statewide norm, while
the vote of a resident of a county of 25,000 or fewer people was equal to
113 percent of the norm. By 1960, the large, urban-county vote was worth
only three-quarters (76 percent) of a vote, while the small-town or open-
country vote had climbed to a value of 171 percent of the norm. Another
way of describing the devaluation of the vote in populous counties is to
say that their vote in 1960 held less than one-half the voting power of the

28 *Ibid.*, p. 2.

76 rural vote, so far had representation gotten out of line with population in the election of state legislators.

THE GERRYMANDER

"First they took away some Democratic stuff, next they added more Democrats than they took away. And finally they gave him some new Republican stuff. But the net result was just a small Democratic gain, and the district's still safe for a Republican."[29] This description of a Pennsylvania congressional district after it had been refashioned by a Republican majority in the state legislature suggests the central characteristic of a gerrymander. No stratagem of American politics serves more unabashedly political aims than the gerrymander, a device employed by the dominant legislative party to maximize its strength and to minimize the strength of the minority party. State legislative majorities show remarkable ingenuity in laying out legislative districts that will lead to partisan advantage in elections.

To guide redistricting decisions, the majority party uses the statistics of past voting behavior of the state's political subdivisions. Under skillful hands, precinct and ward subdivisions can be spliced together in district designs calculated to produce the greatest number of legislative victories for the majority party. One technique is to *concentrate* the opposition party's voting strength in as few districts as possible, conceding the opposition these districts by wide margins but preventing it from winning other neighboring districts: the majority is always willing to forfeit one district if by doing so it can win three others. The other main technique calls for the majority to draw district lines in such a way as to *diffuse* the minority's strength, making it difficult for it to bring its popular support to bear effectively in the election. Skillful gerrymandering is likely to be worth a number of legislative seats to the architects of the district lines.

An immoderate emphasis upon party or area advantage is a characteristic of all gerrymanders. But not all gerrymanders are alike by any means. One type is the "silent" gerrymander, so designated because it exists as a result of legislative failure to bring forth a new apportionment act. Failure to reapportion has in fact been the principal cause of unequal representation. Until it was induced to reapportion in the mid-1960s, the Vermont legislature was a classic example of silent gerrymandering. Every town, irrespective of population, was given one representative in the lower house. This formula was pressed into the 1793 constitution and never revised. Accordingly, Victory, Vermont, with forty-six inhabitants, had representation equal to that of Burlington, with over 35,000 people. Silent gerrymanders are unlikely to be important sources of unequal representation in the future, since citizens of disadvantaged areas now have recourse to judicial relief.

The gerrymander which incites the most controversy stems from the deliberate manipulation of district lines by a legislative majority bent on serving its own interests, whether party or area. It is worth noting that states which redistrict fairly often may yet have notoriously gerrymandered districts; frequent redistricting offers no firm assurance of equitable redis-

[29] Chalmers Roberts, "The Donkey, The Elephant, and the Gerrymander," *The Reporter,* September 16, 1952, p. 30. See also Anthony Lewis, "On the Trail of the Fierce Gerrymander," *New York Times Magazine,* February 19, 1961, pp. 17ff.

tricting. Moreover, gerrymandering may be present even when all of the districts are about equal in population, since the lines may have been drawn in such a way as to make votes for the minority party less "effective," e.g., by compressing minority party strength into the fewest possible districts. The presence of legislators with a sharp sense of where the best opportunities lie for partisan gain, as well as the absence of rigorous legal requirements for equitable districting, has led to substantial experimentation with gerrymandering.

The majority party is not greatly concerned if it finds it necessary to create districts of bizarre dimensions. Neither, ordinarily, do party leaders lose sleep over the usual newspaper criticisms that attend the disclosure of gerrymandered districts. As one New York politico observed following the Supreme Court's decision holding unconstitutional the state's congressional districting plans: "Now it's just a question of slicing the salami, and the salami happens to be in our hands."[30] Whatever may be the explanation, reapportionment acts are not easily transformed into critical campaign issues.[31] And the votes the majority party loses because certain voters have been offended by gerrymandering practices are likely to be made up with some to spare by the votes it gains from using friendly territory to its best advantage. The practical aim of the party is to increase its security, and it resorts to gerrymandering to achieve this end.

A RANKING OF INTERESTS IN REAPPORTIONMENT

The preeminent characteristic of reapportionment is its political aspect. Political interests are served through reapportionment—but whose interests and in what ways? Why is the struggle over reapportionment so strenuous and the resolution of the problem so difficult? We begin to answer these questions when we recognize that apportionment legislation leads to a convergence of political pressures on the members. In an instructive study of Illinois redistricting, Steiner and Gove suggest that there are "informal limits" (as well as constitutional directives) that govern the formulation of redistricting bills. These are:

> (1) Individual preservation, the desire of each legislator to be in a "safe" district. (2) Mutual preservation, the willingness of members to cooperate with each other in protecting incumbents against potential challengers. (3) Political party preservation, the desire of the leaders of each political party organization to maximize its strength in the legislature. (4) Bloc preservation, the desire of members of voting blocs—whether based on geographic, economic, or ideological cohesion—to retain existing personnel and strength. Such blocs are often bipartisan, and their membership is relatively small.[32]

[30] As quoted in William J. D. Boyd, "High Court Voids States' Districts," *National Civic Review*, LVIII (May 1969), 211.

[31] For an exception to this "rule," see a study of congressional redistricting in Pennsylvania by Edward F. Cooke and William J. Keefe, "The Limits of Power in a Divided Government," in *The Politics of Reapportionment*, ed. Malcolm E. Jewell (New York: Atherton Press, 1962), especially pp. 158–61.

[32] Gilbert Y. Steiner and Samuel K. Gove, *The Legislature Redistricts Illinois* (Urbana: University of Illinois, Institute of Government and Public Affairs, 1956), p. 7.

78   The range of legislative choice in redistricting and the source of redistricting plans are more narrowly circumscribed than might appear at first glance. In Illinois, for example, two considerations were given top priority. The first was that reapportionment should be a legislative matter; the views of interested citizens, groups, and newspapers were neither sought nor welcomed. As one house member put it ingenuously: "Outsiders shouldn't stick their noses in and tell this committee how to reapportion the state. . . . Any man in this legislature who doesn't fight for his own district is a particular damn fool. I'm not for too many sitting members running against each other if we can work it out."[33] The second consideration, an offshoot of the first, was that the legislature had an obligation to safeguard the welfare of incumbent legislators, irrespective of party. In redistricting legislation, the authors conclude, "Neither party nor principle nor region are more important than a legislator's colleagues."[34]

All redistricting legislation carries risks for incumbents. But such legislation may be especially nettling to the members of Congress, who ordinarily find it more difficult than state legislators to defend their districts in a showdown over reapportionment. First of all, the congressman is not directly involved in making the decisions. Nor is he steadily on the scene; the state capital may be a long way from Washington. The views of the congressman may be solicited by a reapportionment committee of state legislators or perhaps by party leaders outside the legislature, and if the congressman's seniority record is impressive his district may go untouched. But the member who lacks friends in high places in the party organization or in the legislature may find his preferences ignored in order that other more powerful claims can be satisfied. To quote Malcolm Jewell, "A congressional reapportionment is an acid test of a Congressman's political strength among fellow politicians."[35]

The issue is critical when a state has lost seats in Congress. Congressional delegations hope that the legislature will change no more districts than absolutely necessary. But if several seats have been lost, a number of district lines may have to be moved about, though the rule of minimal change is observed as much as possible. In many cases the congressman occupies the uneasy role of just another spectator as state legislators and state party leaders tinker and toy with his district, balancing his convenience and welfare against the convenience and welfare of the party, other incumbents, and other regions, perhaps removing friendly blocs of voters in one area and adding hostile blocs in another. The lines that are drawn can remove him from office in one fell swoop. Understandably, from the vantage point of an incumbent, a congressional redistricting bill that serves generally his party's interest is not nearly so important as one that serves specifically his own interest. The congressman of one party ordinarily is quite willing to see the district of a congressman of the other party made more secure if, in the process, his own position can be made safer. The party, he feels, can take care of itself; and when his party fails to protect him, he looks for allies within the opposition party. In sum, everything about reapportion-

---

[33] Steiner and Gove, *op. cit.,* p. 17.
[34] *Ibid.,* pp. 31–32.
[35] Jewell, ed., *The Politics of Reapportionment,* p. 29.

ment, whether legislative or congressional, suggests the triumph of self-interest.

The Struggle for Equitable Apportionment

For decades equitable apportionment was something of an anomaly in American legislatures. Not until the 1960s did the outlook brighten for significant reapportionment at the congressional and legislative levels. Several reasons help explain why the principle of representation according to population was so late in visiting American legislatures.

In the first place, the public at large seems never to have mustered more than sporadic interest in the issue, perhaps because of its preoccupation with other, more tangible matters, or because of its conservative instincts, or simply because of its inertia and indifference. Understandably, the great majority of legislators never have been very responsive to the arguments for reapportionment. Finally, neither chief executives nor judges ordinarily have been inclined to risk involvement in a reapportionment dispute, to challenge legislatures on a matter which their memberships regarded as peculiarly within legislative jurisdiction. Over the years, the combination of these factors—indifferent public, self-interested legislators, cautious chief executives and judges—appeared to place out of reach the objective of winning political support for equitable districting. Accordingly, as the data of this chapter have shown, apportionment on the basis of rigorous population standards characterized very few legislatures at the opening of the 1960s.

JUDICIAL INTERVENTION

Past experience is not always a reliable guide, as shifting court doctrines testify. In 1946, the United States Supreme Court held in *Colegrove* v. *Green,* a case concerned with flagrant inequalities in the population of Illinois congressional districts (one district had nine times as many inhabitants as another), that apportionment was, for several reasons, a "political question," one which properly should be settled outside the judicial process. Arguing the majority position, Justice Frankfurter contended that "Courts ought not to enter this political thicket. The remedy for unfairness in districting is to secure state legislatures that will apportion properly, or to invoke the ample powers of Congress."[36] The suit was dismissed by a four-to-three decision. Although the *Colegrove* verdict technically left malapportionment undisturbed, the narrowness of the decision offered at least some prospect that no lasting precedent had been established.

In the late 1950s, a new phase of the struggle for equitable apportionment was opened by several state and federal courts. A federal district court in 1956 ordered at-large elections for the territorial legislature of Hawaii, which last had been reapportioned in 1901.[37] This sanction was never applied, however, because Congress was moved to draw new district

[36] 328 U.S. 549, at 556 (1946).
[37] *Dyer* v. *Kazuhisa Abe,* 138 F. Supp. 220 (1956).

80 lines. At least as important was the 1958 action of a federal district court involving the Minnesota legislature, which was then functioning under a 1913 apportionment act.[38] The defendants sought to have the case dismissed on the grounds of *Colegrove* v. *Green*. Instead, the court accepted jurisdiction, but stated that it would defer its decision until the next session of the legislature, a postponement which would give the lawmakers another chance to draw up a new apportionment act. The outcome was that the legislature heeded the court's advice and redistricted the state, in general submitting to the demands for population parity among districts. The upshot of these decisions, supported by several others by state courts, was that the judicial power came to be considered the principal hope for inducing reapportionment in the 1960s.

A court case involving the state of Tennessee finally led to a breakthrough in reapportionment. Despite a requirement in the Tennessee Constitution calling for decennial reapportionment, the legislature had not done the job for over sixty years; state legislative districts consequently were greatly out of line with population distribution. The vote of a resident of Moore County, for example, was worth nineteen times as much as the vote of a resident of populous Shelby County in the election of members of the lower house. Facts of this sort led a group of Nashville, Tennessee, voters to bring suit, contending that the 1901 apportionment act deprived them of equal protection of the laws, as guaranteed by the Fourteenth Amendment, and asking that the act be held unconstitutional and that subsequent elections be held on an at-large basis. The case was dismissed by a federal district court in 1959 on the ground that the case brought up a "political question" and that consequently the court lacked jurisdiction, as in *Colegrove* v. *Green*. The Supreme Court agreed to hear the case in 1961 and announced its decision in March 1962.

Baker v. *Carr*, the Tennessee reapportionment case, has been widely interpreted as a turning point in the struggle for equitable apportionment. By a vote of six to two, the Court held that the case was justiciable (that is, that a court might suitably consider a case involving this subject matter); that the federal courts had jurisdiction in the case; and that the plaintiffs had standing to challenge the act's constitutionality. Interestingly, in remanding the case to the district court for further consideration, the High Court did not offer any guidance in making its decisions nor propose any remedies. Instead, much of the majority opinion, written by Justice Brennan, centered on the question of whether reapportionment was a "political question" and thus beyond the reach of the Court.

Like many court decisions, *Baker* v. *Carr* answered some relevant questions and avoided some others. By making it clear that reapportionment was not a "political question," the majority opinion opened the possibility that judicial remedies could be proposed to correct inequitable districting arrangements. It served notice that citizens can seek judicial redress if they believe that apportionment debases the value of their votes, thereby depriving them of their right to "the equal protection of the laws" under the Fourteenth Amendment. In effect, the decision recognized that without outside help a majority within a state may be powerless to bring about

[38] *Magraw* v. *Donovan*, 163 F. Supp. 184 (1958).

changes in the apportionment system; many earlier state and federal court decisions had advised that relief from malapportionment could be won by the voting power and political effectiveness of an aroused and insistent citizenry. In essence, the outcome of *Baker* v. *Carr* indicated that the courts could provide a means by which underrepresented urban and suburban forces could gain a fair share of representation in state legislatures.

But there were many critical questions the *Baker* decision left dangling. (1) Did equal protection of the laws require *both* houses of the legislature to be apportioned on the basis of population? Since at that time approximately one-third of the states employed the so-called federal plan—one house based on population, the other based on a nonpopulation factor such as political subdivisions (e.g., counties)—the question obviously was of major significance. (2) At what point would divergence between population and representation become "invidious discrimination," hence prohibited by the equal protection of the laws clause? The *Baker* case provided no clues; in fact, the justices declined to say that apportionment must rest on districts of equal population. (3) If nonpopulation apportionment was produced by state *constitutional* provisions which discriminated against centers of population, were these arrangements incompatible with equal protection for all citizens? (4) How would gerrymandering be affected by the Court's equal-population doctrine? In *Gomillion* v. *Lightfoot*,[39] the Court held that an Alabama statute which set municipal boundaries in a way designed to deprive Negroes of their right to vote was in violation of the Fifteenth Amendment. Would a racial gerrymander differ from a party gerrymander? (5) And finally, how would *congressional* districts be affected by the judiciary's new role in the reapportionment struggle?

The impact of court decisions is never wholly evident in the short run. Yet, in *Baker* v. *Carr,* it is plain that the stage was set for a sustained attack on malapportionment. Subsequent cases yielded answers to some of the questions left unanswered in *Baker*. Thus, in February 1964, *congressional* districting finally became the subject of a Supreme Court ruling. In *Wesberry* v. *Sanders,* a Georgia case, the Court held that: "...the command of Art. 1, Section 2, that Representatives be chosen 'by the people of the several states,' means that as nearly as is practicable one man's vote in a congressional election is to be worth as much as another's."[40] Within four days of the Court's decision, the Georgia legislature had redrawn district lines; Atlanta was awarded a second congressional seat and other districts were brought more nearly in line with the equal-population doctrine. And it was not long before legislators in other states were queuing up to deal, in their fashion, with the new problem of congressional districting.

Additional reapportionment business came to state legislative agendas in June 1964. Then, in *Reynolds* v. *Sims,*[41] the Court ruled that *both houses* of state legislatures must be apportioned in accordance with population, thereby rejecting the "federal analogy" and extending the principle of "one

---

39 364 U.S. 399.

40 *Wesberry* v. *Sanders,* 376 U.S. 1 (1964).

41 377 U.S. 533 (1964). For a comprehensive examination of the *Baker* v. *Carr* and *Reynolds* v. *Sims* cases, see Richard C. Cortner, *The Apportionment Cases* (Knoxville: University of Tennessee Press, 1970).

82 man–one vote" which it had applied to congressional districts in *Wesberry.* In the case of *Lucas* v. *The Forty-fourth General Assembly of the State of Colorado,* announced on the same day, the Court ruled unconstitutional an apportionment plan which had been approved by the state's voters in 1962. This plan, which had been launched through the initiative process, fell before the Court because it failed to provide for apportionment in both houses on a population basis. "A citizen's constitutional rights can hardly be infringed," the Court declared, "simply because a majority of the people choose to do so."[42] Opinions in still other cases decided that day made it clear that state constitutional provisions that deny representation on a population basis are not sustainable under the equal protection clause.[43]

CONTINUING PROBLEMS

Although the Supreme Court has ruled out apportionment systems characterized by "invidious discrimination," it has declined to specify how much variation in district size is allowable. Lacking definite guidelines, lower courts have employed several different measures to evaluate state legislative apportionment. One method calculates "percentage deviation from the norm." If no district within a state contains a population of more than 15 percent *above* or *below* the ideal population per district (total state population divided by seats), the apportionment formula has frequently (though not invariably) satisfied the equal-protection test. On the other hand, apportionment plans in which deviation from the ideal has been greater than 15 percent regularly have been disapproved by the courts. Some courts have used the standard of "minimum control percentage" (the smallest population of a state that could elect a majority of one house) as a test of representative equality. The deviations permitted by the courts using this standard have varied from state to state; commonly, however, apportionment acts have been rejected if they would permit less than 45 percent of the population to elect a majority of legislators. Finally, many courts have used the "ratio of most populous to least populous district" as their standard; virtually all apportionments that have been approved have had ratios of less than two to one. Nevertheless, there have also been many apportionment plans rejected in which the population variance ratios were substantially less than two to one.[44]

In the case of congressional districting, two recent decisions indicate that the Supreme Court will tolerate virtually no population variation among districts. In *Kirkpatrick* v. *Preisler,* a congressional districting plan in Missouri was found wanting even though the maximum deviation from the norm was a mere 3 percent.[45] In *Wells* v. *Rockefeller,* a case involving congressional districts in New York, the Court nullified a districting plan

---

42 *Lucas* v. *The Forty-fourth General Assembly of the State of Colorado,* 377 U.S. 736–37.

43 *Maryland Committee for Fair Representation* v. *Tawes,* 377 U.S. 656 (1964); *Roman* v. *Sincock,* 377 U.S. 695 (1964).

44 Gordon E. Baker, "New District Criteria," *National Civic Review,* LVII (June 1968), 291–97.

45 89 S. Ct. 1225 (1969).

in which the maximum deviation from the norm was 6 percent.[46] The Court's position, disclosed in the Missouri case, holds that states must make "a good faith effort to achieve precise mathematical equality"; failing this, each population variance, "no matter how small," must be justified. The essence of the Court's position is that any districting plan that *can* be made more equitable *must* be made more equitable.[47]

The use of multimember districts for the election of state legislators is likely to continue to be a source of litigation. These districts have been challenged on the ground that they minimize or preclude the possibility that minorities can win representation in the legislature. Two cases involving the representation of black communities were decided by the Supreme Court in 1971. In the first case, *Connor* v. *Johnson,* the Court held in a six-to-three decision that the multimember district used in the election of twelve representatives and five senators in Hinds County, Mississippi, must be divided into single-member districts.[48] The effect of the Court's order was virtually to guarantee the election of several black candidates to the Mississippi legislature.

The Mississippi case did not, however, settle the question of multimember districts. In *Whitcomb* v. *Chavis,* a subsequent case involving the residents of a black community in Indianapolis, the Court held in a five-to-three decision that "experience and insight have not yet demonstrated that multimember districts are inherently invidious and violative of the Fourteenth Amendment."[49] Since the Democratic party in particular had regularly slated candidates from this black community, "the failure of the ghetto to have legislative seats in proportion to its population emerges more as a function of losing elections than of built-in bias against Negroes."[50] The salient factor thus appears to be the circumstances of a particular case. Overall, the Court has made it clear that "the challenger [must] carry the burden of proving that multimember districts unconstitutionally operate to dilute or cancel the voting strength of racial or political elements."[51]

Gerrymanders designed for partisan purposes have not been the subject of a Supreme Court ruling, despite the fact that "apart from malapportionment, the gerrymander is the device currently most destructive of fairness in the electoral process."[52] The Court understandably has been reluctant to become embroiled in this issue which has broad ramifications for the major party organizations. Nevertheless, it would be possible for the Court to develop guidelines to curb gerrymandering. By limiting the use of large multimember districts, for example, the Court could strike a blow against the "winner-take-all" election, with its tendency to inflate the representation of the majority party. Another guideline "would be to view a district system as suspect...whenever it is shown that the system consistently magnifies

[46] 89 S. Ct. 1234 (1969).

[47] See Robert G. Dixon, Jr., "One Man, One Vote—What Happens Next?" *National Civic Review,* LX (May 1971), 259–65.

[48] *Connor* v. *Johnson,* 91 S. Ct. 1760 (1971).

[49] *Whitcomb* v. *Chavis,* 91 S. Ct. 1858 (1971), at 1877.

[50] *Id.* at 1874.

[51] *Id.* at 1869. See also *Fortson* v. *Dorsey,* 379 U.S. 439 (1965).

[52] Robert B. McKay, *Reapportionment: The Law and Politics of Equal Representation* (New York: The Twentieth Century Fund, 1965), p. 255.

84 the legislative strength of one party far beyond its actual statewide voter strength."[53]

THE IMPACT OF THE REAPPORTIONMENT CASES

The permanent importance of the reapportionment cases—their bearing on structures of political power, political careers, and public policy—will be difficult to judge until the dust has settled from the massive changes that have occurred since 1962. Indeed, such an evaluation may always be hard to make. Those who have looked for the consequences flowing from reapportionment have found themselves in the midst of a jumble of crude facts, for the changes attributable to reapportionment have not been easy to sort out from those whose origins trace from other sources. Some results, of course, already stand out clearly. Nevertheless, the comments which follow should be considered with more than ordinary care, since the reapportionment story has not wholly unfolded.

Since the reapportionments of the middle and late 1960s, the greatest gains in representation have been achieved by the suburban areas of the nation. This development ranks among the principal outcomes of the reapportionment cases. As would be expected, the heaviest losses in seats have been suffered by rural areas. Big cities in some states have increased their representation, but not to as great a degree as their surrounding suburbs. In recent years, of course, suburbs have been at the center of population growth in all sections of the country, and thus the new apportionments which follow population have carried striking rewards for these areas. Many central cities, in contrast, have actually declined in population. No city today holds as much as 50 percent of the population of a state, nor is any city likely to achieve this. The long-time fear that reapportionment would bring big-city domination of the legislatures has proved to be groundless. Indeed, how large cities will fare in the reapportioned legislatures of many states may well depend on the response of the new suburban lawmakers. They will be in a stronger position than ever to advance or retard the multiple claims of the central cities, as well as to promote the welfare of their own districts. On certain kinds of issues, suburban legislators are likely to hold the balance of power in struggles between rural and big-city interests.

In conventional discourse on politics, reapportionment has often been celebrated as a way by which urban Democrats might wrest political power from rural Republicans—at least in the North. It was anticipated that if rural areas were cut back in representation, the populous urban areas would inevitably profit. Power would shift from rural to urban and, *pari passu,* from Republicans to Democrats. Today, this proposition warrants second thoughts. For one reason, Republicans have gained more than Democrats from the increase in representation awarded suburbs; rural Republicans have been replaced, to be sure, but often by suburban members of the same party. Moreover, taking the nation as a whole, the early evidence suggests

53 Robert G. Dixon, Jr., "Reapportionment Perspectives: What is Fair Representation?" *American Bar Association Journal,* LI, no. 319 (April 1965), reprinted in *Congressional Record,* 89th Cong., 1st sess., May 19, 1965, pp. 10601–4, at p. 10603.

that the strength of the two parties was not changed markedly by extensive reapportioning of the legislatures. Following the midterm elections of 1962, Republicans held 38.6 per cent of the seats in state legislatures. This figure dropped to 33 per cent after the Democratic landslide in 1964, but with their party's sharp comeback in 1966, Republican state legislators held 40.9 per cent of all legislative seats.[54] A later study of thirty-eight northern legislative chambers finds that reapportionment has led to a Democratic gain of about 2.9 per cent of the legislative seats.[55] In sum, for much of the nation, reapportionment appears to have had some effect on partisan divisions in the legislatures, but much less than was originally expected.

Yet national statistics often mask variations among the states. Several examples illustrate the varying effects of reapportionment. Prior to reapportionment, the Connecticut House of Representatives invariably was dominated by the Republican party. When representation of towns was supplanted by representation of population, the Democratic party promptly won control of both houses of the legislature. Similarly, the Republican party was never able to gain control of both houses of the Arizona legislature, irrespective of its state-wide strength, until reapportionment wiped out Democratic advantages. On a sectional basis, reapportionment appears to have bolstered Democratic fortunes in the East and Midwest while improving Republican prospects in the South and Southwest.[56] Interestingly, Republican growth in the South and Southwest has come principally from an increase in representation for Republican-dominated suburbs; their gains have come at the expense of rural Democratic strongholds.

The allocation of power *within* political parties is likely to be affected in those states where rural areas have lost a large number of seats from redistricting. It is a good guess that in the years to come many more legislative leaders in both parties will be drawn from urban and suburban areas. Suburban Republicans, long accustomed in many states to lodgment on the fringes of power, seem destined to replace some rural colleagues in elected leadership positions and in committee chairmanships. Over the long haul, the prospects are decidedly dim for what has come to be called "entrenched rural power" in the legislatures.

A variety of other developments have followed, or are likely to follow, in the wake of reapportionments. For one thing, many states have found it necessary to revise their constitutions in order to bring their apportionment articles into compliance with court rulings. The reapportionment rulings have also contributed, here and there, to a revival of interest in unicameralism—ostensibly because there is less reason to have two houses if both must be based on population. Whether this movement will get far off the ground, however, is doubtful at the least. Reapportionment has been accompanied in some states by a reduction in the size of the legislature; for example, the Connecticut House was reduced from 294 members to 177 and the Vermont House from 246 to 150. Another side effect in some states has been the election of an exceptionally large number of freshman

[54] William J. D. Boyd, "Little Effect Felt in Party Control," *National Civic Review,* LVI (February 1967), 95–96.

[55] Robert S. Erikson, "The Partisan Impact of State Legislative Reapportionment," *Midwest Journal of Political Science,* XV (February 1971), 57–71.

[56] Boyd, *op. cit.*

86 legislators. Very probably there will be some states in which the proportion of farm legislators will decline.

The loss of rural seats does not mean that a league of urban and suburban interests will dominate the state legislatures or Congress. Political interests are far too complex to be grouped neatly within geographic sectors or statistical abstractions. Neither urban nor suburban nor rural areas are now, or are likely to become, monolithic. Each houses a variety of interests; each is vulnerable to internal cleavages. An easing of rural power may mean only that no bloc will be sufficiently powerful, even when firmly united, to control legislative decisions. "With no segment of the population clearly dominant in the legislature," Royce Hanson has observed, "reapportionment [is] likely to produce a new pluralism in both legislative and electoral politics."[57]

Perhaps the most important question to be answered, and also the most difficult, is whether reapportionment has had a discernable effect on the public policy decisions of the legislatures. Most studies in the middle 1960s suggested that there was little or no relationship between malapportionment and public policy—that is, that fairly apportioned legislatures did not make significantly different policy choices than malapportioned legislatures.[58] Several recent studies, however, suggest this conclusion may be in error. There is growing evidence that important policy changes have accompanied reapportionment. Most notably, reapportionment has led to an increase in the amount of state aid made available to major cities and metropolitan areas.[59] If subsequent research confirms this finding, doubts as to the significance of reapportionment should fade. Few decisions that governments make are more important than those which involve the allocation of money.

RESPONSES TO THE REAPPORTIONMENT CASES

Not the least of the consequences of the reapportionment cases was their abrasive impact on relations between Congress and the Supreme Court. The announcement of *Reynolds* v. *Sims* in June 1964 touched off several major drives to blunt the effects of the Court's rulings. Initially, opponents rallied behind a House bill to remove state apportionment from the jurisdiction of federal courts. The bill passed the House easily, but was lost in the Senate. Attention then shifted to a Senate proposal, offered as a rider to a foreign aid bill, to delay imposition of the "one man–one vote" ruling for

[57] *The Political Thicket: Reapportionment and Constitutional Democracy* (Englewood Cliffs, N.J.: Prentice-Hall, Inc., 1966), p. 128.

[58] See Thomas R. Dye, *Politics, Economics, and the Public: Policy Outcomes in the American States* (Chicago: Rand McNally & Company, 1966), pp. 270–81; Richard I. Hofferbert, "The Relation Between Public Policy and Some Structural and Environmental Variables in the American States," *American Political Science Review*, LX (March 1966), 73–82; and Herbert Jacob, "The Consequences of Malapportionment: A Note of Caution," *Social Forces*, XLIII (December 1964), 256–61.

[59] See Roger Hanson, "The Policy Impact of Reapportionment," Annual Meeting of the Midwest Political Science Association, Chicago, April 29–May 1, 1971; H. George Frederickson and Yong Hyo Cho, "Sixties' Reapportionment: Is It Victory or Delusion?" *National Civic Review*, LX (February 1971), 73–85; and Ira Sharkansky, "Reapportionment and Roll Call Voting: The Case of the Georgia Legislature," *Southwestern Social Science Quarterly*, LI (June 1970), 129–37.

at least two years for all states, thereby making available more time to consider a constitutional amendment to reverse the decision in *Reynolds*. A filibuster by liberals contributed to the defeat of this proposal to stay proceedings.

The next round in the battle over reapportionment involved the so-called Dirksen amendment, a proposal to amend the Constitution to permit states to use factors other than population in the apportionment of one house of the legislature, provided such a plan was approved by the voters of the state. Strongly supported by such organizations as the Council of State Governments, the American Farm Bureau Federation, and the Chamber of Commerce of the United States, the amendment narrowly failed to receive a two-thirds vote in the Senate, and was lost. Having suffered these defeats at the congressional level, opponents of the equal-population doctrine turned their attention to the alternative method for amending the Constitution, as specified in Article V. Under its terms, Congress is directed to call a constitutional convention for proposing amendments upon receiving the applications of two-thirds (34) of the states.

The convention method of amending the Constitution has never been used, and thus there are no guidelines to shape the procedures and strategies of the participants. A great many states forwarded applications to Congress shortly after this campaign was begun, but legal uncertainties have clouded their actions. For example, can Congress be forced to call a convention, especially if it has doubts about the validity of some state applications? There is a strong likelihood that the applications of certain states would be challenged on the ground that they were approved by legislatures which were themselves malapportioned. Furthermore, the petitions passed by the legislatures have not been identical. There is a question of whether Congress can be limited to calling a convention to consider a single amendment, as the applications provide. Finally, the question has emerged as to whether a state legislature can withdraw the application submitted by a previous legislature; it is not improbable that a validly apportioned legislature might choose to withdraw an application that had been approved by a malapportioned legislature.[60] For reasons of this sort, there is no certainty that a convention will be called even though the necessary thirty-four states urge this course upon Congress. Despite this threat to the equal-population principle, time is on its side. The more states that bring their systems of representation into compliance with the reapportionment rulings, the less the likelihood that pressure can be sustained for reversing or otherwise modulating these extraordinary decisions.

"ONE MAN—ONE VOTE" AND THE LEGISLATURES

Under the aegis of the courts, the principle of representation according to population has rapidly become a reality in American legislatures. The sequence of events beginning with *Baker* v. *Carr* established three understandings concerning the apportionment of members of state legislatures and the lower house of Congress. The first is that the courts themselves are instruments for achieving the goal of fair representation. Second, no appor-

[60] See McKay, *op. cit.*, pp. 209–13.

88 tionment system is likely to survive judicial scrutiny unless it provides that all legislators will represent districts "as nearly of equal population as is practicable."[61] Both houses of bicameral state legislatures must meet this test, as must the U.S. House of Representatives. Third, gerrymanders designed to discriminate against Negroes contravene the Fifteenth Amendment of the U.S. Constitution and are therefore invalid. Moreover, multimember districts that minimize or cancel out black voting strength run a good risk of being held invalid.

Reapportionments pose problems and carry risks that are hard to calculate and hard to avoid. It is not surprising that legislators bridled at the prospect of having to untangle old apportionments and to fashion new ones. Their own careers were often threatened. Although some legislatures had to be dragooned into compliance with the reapportionment rulings, a surprising number acted with dispatch. When they have failed to act, districting plans often have been shaped by the courts themselves. Political historians may say that, considering the complexity of the problem, one of the remarkable features of the reapportionment era was the promptness with which legislatures came to terms with the unpleasant tasks placed upon them by the courts.

Although the barriers to fair representation have been breached, major reapportionment issues remain on the agenda. For some years to come, the courts will be pressed to refine the standards under which apportionment acts are to be evaluated and to bring consistency out of a welter of decisions by federal and state courts. Partisan gerrymandering is a problem that will not go away, however reluctant the Court may be to deal with its complexities. The use of multimember districts as a means of dissipating the strength of minority elements (racial or party) in state legislatures similarly has not been settled. In sum, neither the courts nor the legislatures have yet emerged from this political thicket.[62]

From among all the uncertainties produced in this struggle over political power and a principle of representation, one fact stands out above all others: great progress toward the goal of equalizing the voting power of all citizens was made in the 1960s. How this development ultimately will affect state and national political systems, political elites, and public policy is far from certain. Among scholars, few opinions concerning these matters show signs of hardening into dogma.

61 *Reynolds* v. *Sims,* 377 U.S. 577.

62 For a view that the Court never should have entered this thicket and that political scientists have been uncritical in their acceptance of the Court's social theory in the reapportionment cases (and served as propagandists for the decisions as well), see A. Spencer Hill, "The Reapportionment Decisions: A Return to Dogma," *Journal of Politics,* XXXI (February 1969), 186–213.

4

LEGISLATORS AND

THE ELECTORAL PROCESS

The systems used for choosing public officials in the United States call for an enormous investment of time, effort, and money. No other country so emphasizes its nomination and election devices. Rooted in law and in custom, American practices are exceedingly complex. Moreover, there are substantial differences between the states in their electoral arrangements and political cultures. This chapter sketches the main features of the political process leading to the election of state legislators and members of Congress. Three principal topics come under consideration: recruitment, nominations, and elections.

Recruitment of Legislators

The election of candidates to office is easily the most visible stage in the process of selecting political decision-makers. But it is not necessarily the most important stage. First, candidates must be recruited—that is, in some way induced to stand for office or else, in the case of multiple potential candidates, screened out.[1] Despite its significance, there is but little comprehensive evidence on legislative recruitment patterns; such evidence as exists deals mainly with state legislators in a small group of states.

[1] Although the discussion in this chapter relates only to legislators, the study of legislative recruitment is part of a general inquiry into how men and women gain entry into elective politics in the United States. One study has suggested five variables that are important in the recruitment process: (1) Certain personality traits are characteristic of elected officials, including a heightened need for prestige, power, and public deference. (2) Individuals having a "political personality" tend to gather in occupations that require them to play a brokerage role. (3) Brokerage occupations (e.g., lawyers, insurance salesmen, realtors) contribute a disproportionate number of elected officials. (4) "Brokers" enter elective politics by seeking offices whose esteem is compatible with their own social status. (5) The community's political structure is an important factor in the recruitment process. "In particular, where party organizations control nominations, only those brokers who have contact with the machine will enter politics. Where party control is weak, a random entry of brokers may be expected." See the development of this model by Herbert Jacob, "Initial Recruitment of Elected Officials in the U.S.—A Model," *Journal of Politics,* XXIV (November 1962), 703–16.

The most instructive studies of the career lines of state legislators suggest four principal conclusions concerning recruitment.[2] In the first place, the social characteristics of the constituency sharply constrict the list of potential candidates. Race, religion, ethnic, and national backgrounds tend to be "givens in the availability formulas to which candidates must conform." The mainstreams of American constituencies, rather than the eddies, give rise to the vast majority of legislative candidacies. The following observations by Frank Sorauf concerning the recruitment of Pennsylvania state legislators accurately reflect the norms of legislative constituencies throughout the country:

> The dominant values of the community result from its social characteristics, and these values are in turn imposed on all who would rise to positions of community leadership. The candidates for public office must reflect, at least in basic social affiliations, the constituency if they are to win its confidence and support. It is this fact rather than any systematic party policy that accounts, for instance, for the relation between Catholic candidates and the Democratic Party. The outsider, the stranger to the way of life of the community, stands little chance of breaking into any political elite. No matter how long he lives in the district, the atypical remains a newcomer. So the community stamps its image on its candidates for public office by demanding that they have absorbed the majority values from a background similar to that which predominates in the district.[3]

Second, many state legislators cannot stake a claim to previous government experience; for example, one-third to one-half of the members of the New Jersey, Ohio, California, and Tennessee legislatures in the 1957 sessions had been elected without serving in any other public office. An even larger proportion had made their way to the legislature without holding any party position along the way. Apprenticeship in lower office, an especially congenial idea in democratic theory, plainly is not essential for recruitment or election to the legislature; it occurs most frequently where competition between the parties is greatest.[4]

Third, there are a number of procedures by which candidates may launch their legislative careers. A study of Oregon state legislators by Lester Seligman describes four ways: conscription, self-recruitment, cooptation, and agency. Conscription of candidates ordinarily is associated with the minority party in districts where its prospects for victory in the general election are dim or nonexistent. Self-recruitment refers to those candidates who are self-starters, those who enter the contest without waiting for a nod

² Lester G. Seligman, "Political Recruitment and Party Structure: A Case Study," *American Political Science Review,* LV (March 1961), 77–86, and "A Prefatory Analysis of Leadership Selection in Oregon," *Western Political Quarterly,* XII (March 1959), 153–67; John C. Wahlke, Heinz Eulau, William Buchanan, and LeRoy C. Ferguson, *The Legislative System: Explorations in Legislative Behavior* (New York: John Wiley & Sons, Inc., 1962), Chapter 5; Frank J. Sorauf, *Party and Representation: Legislative Politics in Pennsylvania* (New York: Atherton Press, 1963), Chapter 5.

³ Sorauf, *op. cit.,* p. 89.

⁴ Wahlke *et al., op. cit.,* pp. 95–97.

from party officials. Cooptation describes a recruitment pattern in which party leaders seek out and persuade individuals who are not active party members to run for office; the candidate is often a well known person of high social status. The mechanism of agency refers to those candidacies generated by political interest groups, with a view to transforming "a lobbyist into a legislator without much apparent change in role."[5]

Fourth, the leading variable associated with legislative recruitment and career patterns appears to be the structure of party competition within the state or district. The study of Oregon legislators discloses, for example, that for the majority party in one-party areas, individuals and groups, rather than party officials, tend to instigate and promote candidates; conversely, the minority party officialdom in one-party areas often is required to conscript candidates. In competitive districts the "candidacy market place" is most open; here groups, factions, party officials, and the self-recruited vie with one another over nominations.[6]

While the parties in general play an insignificant role in the recruitment-selection process in Oregon, they occupy the center of the stage in Pennsylvania. In this state candidates for the legislature usually are induced to run for office by a party representative. Where the party is quite certain of victory, as the Democratic party is in many Philadelphia and Pittsburgh districts, Democratic leaders select candidates whose loyalty to the party is undoubted, often picking precinct or ward chairmen or individuals on the city or county payrolls. Where the minority party is weak, the local chairman will take almost anyone he can find, and he may be pressed to hand out a patronage job to the person who eventually agrees to make the race. In the rural and small-town districts of Pennsylvania, the parties look for candidates whose names add luster to the ticket, a quality found in the "right" name and family background, in important organizational affiliations, and in high social status. The emphatic point is that virtually everywhere in the state the parties dominate the process of picking men for legislative office; the party organizations in fact are the "nominators," and their influence is seldom diminished by the primary.[7]

The findings of the four-state study, *The Legislative System*, point to the critical impact of competition on recruitment. States with competitive political systems tend to produce legislators with a greater amount of prior governmental and party experience and those who perceive the party as sponsoring their careers and promoting their candidacies. "The better organized the party," the authors observe, "the more salient it is likely to be in legislators' careers and outlooks."[8]

In certain constituencies potential candidates jump at every opportunity to run for the legislature, while elsewhere party recruiters have to beat the bushes to flush out any sort of candidate. James D. Barber identifies three factors that appear to be related to the potential candidate's willingness to run and the readiness of recruiters to enlist him. These are *motivation, resources,* and *opportunity*—all interlinked. Motivation includes at least

---

5 Seligman, "Political Recruitment and Party Structure," 85–86.
6 *Ibid.,* 84.
7 Sorauf, *op. cit.,* pp. 107–20.
8 Wahlke *et al., op. cit.,* p. 120.

two elements: the potential candidate's personal needs that might be satisfied through political participation and his positive predisposition toward politics. Resources include such items as the candidate's skills, finances, and capacity to make time available for politics. Candidacies are generated when political opportunities become available; opportunity is governed to some significant extent by how recruiters evaluate the motives and resources of candidates. The kinds of candidates to whom recruiters devote a friendly ear undoubtedly vary from state to state and even from district to district. Everywhere, it would seem, the recruiter's test is political feasibility rather than any abstract standard. Finally, it should be remembered that candidates are not invariably recruited for their vote-getting power. Other considerations may loom more important:

> A candidate may be chosen because he will gain a substantial number of votes ("make a respectable showing"), add prestige to the party, work hard for other candidates, satisfy some important party faction, contribute money to the campaign, offer special skills useful in campaigning, be the best man for the job regardless of his actual chances, accept a nomination as reward for his past sacrifices for the party, take training in this campaign for one he may win later, or be sufficiently innocuous to leave a delicate intraparty balance undisturbed. Calculations along these dimensions will depend a great deal on the peculiarities of the political system within which the candidate is to be selected, including the community's population, stability, party balance, and political values.[9]

Further evidence on the significance of the political system for recruitment practices is available in a study of congressional districts in metropolitan Chicago. In the "inner city," dominated by the Democratic organization, long-time membership in the party organization is the principal factor in the recruitment of congressional candidates. The slating of candidates is controlled wholly by party leaders, although they may take into account the preferences of external groups such as unions and ethnic associations. Because a congressman has very little patronage to dole out and slight influence on local politics, the office is not highly valued or eagerly sought after. Other city, county, and statewide offices have greater visibility and are considered more important by the party organization. Democrats elected from "inner city" districts ordinarily come to Congress relatively late in life and are rarely "issue-oriented"; the office itself tends to be treated as a reward for faithful service to the party organization. In Congress, these members tend to be preoccupied with federal projects, concentrating their attention on rivers and harbors, highways, and housing. By contrast, in the suburban districts around Chicago, where the Republican party is safely ensconced and patronage is limited in quantity and effectiveness, congressional candidates tend to be younger, "issue-oriented" conservatives who have developed their own personal followings. On the evidence of this study of the Chicago metropolitan area, it seems clear that machine and nonmachine environments produce distinctly different kinds of congressmen,

9 James D. Barber, *The Lawmakers: Recruitment and Adaptation to Legislative Life* (New Haven: Yale University Press, 1965), pp. 10–15, quotation on p. 13.

and this in turn shapes the character of congressional representation for these districts.[10]

The Nominating Process

THE DIRECT PRIMARY

Most of the basic law governing nominations and elections for both state and federal office is written by the state legislature. Originally, nominations for office were private or party affairs, made by caucuses and conventions, unnoticed and unregulated by the legislature. Gradually states began to adopt laws prescribing a framework for the conduct of nominations; the trend toward more governmental regulation was sped along by several U.S. Supreme Court decisions concerning voting rights and corruption in primary elections. Today, nomination and election systems are regulated in detail by batteries of state laws and a few major acts of Congress.

Very early in the twentieth century, states began to adopt the direct primary for the nomination of state and local officials. The attractiveness of this method was attributable in large measure to popular disaffection with party conventions which were believed to be instruments easily manipulated by "bosses" and "special interests." Heightened popular control over government was required, ran the incantation of the Progressive era reformers, and the device best suited to assure it was the direct primary, which provided for an election to designate nominees for office. The reformist proposal shortly won statutory expression in many states, becoming in time the dominant method for making nominations; today it is used in all fifty states, although a few cling to the convention for selecting nominees for statewide office (e.g., governor and United States senator).

The installation of the direct primary ended the party organization's formal control over the choice of nominees; in practice, however, the primary has rarely been a major threat to a united organization. Through the use of preprimary endorsements, here and there countenanced by state law but practiced in any case, and through its campaign apparatus, the party organization usually manages to have selected the nominees it has earlier slated. Yet in states and localities where the parties are weak or rent by factions, legislative (and other) nominations may go to the individual who has managed to build a personal following, or who has spliced together factional support, or who has a name that sounds "right." The

---

10 Leo M. Snowiss, "Congressional Recruitment and Representation," *American Political Science Review*, LX (September 1966), 627–39. Snowiss also suggests that the recruitment pattern in the Chicago Democratic party helps to account for the high degree of voting cohesion found in the city's congressional delegation. However, a study of the voting behavior of the congressional delegations of cities with varying recruitment structures—Los Angeles, Detroit, New York City, and Chicago—fails to show that the Chicago delegation is any more cohesive than those of the other cities. The voting cohesion of big-city delegations in Congress may be more a function of constituency similarities than of recruitment patterns and processes. See Burton M. Atkins and Michael A. Baer, "The Effect of Recruitment Upon Metropolitan Voting Cohesion in the House of Representatives: A Research Note," *Journal of Politics,* XXXII (February 1970), 177–80.

94 crucial test simply may be his membership in a dominant religious or ethnic group. As V. O. Key's investigations have shown, a "bewildering variety of party structures exists behind the facade of the direct primary."[11] Nominations are made under circumstances that range from those where popular control is limited to mere ratification of the party organization's selections to those where the primary is a tumultuous free-for-all.

Several aspects of the direct primary may be observed. In the first place, primary elections in one-party states and districts, notably in the South, settle with finality the choice of legislators. Second, belying one critical assumption—that it would lead to greater competition for nominations—the primary has often been "deserted." Third, legislative nominations are made, by and large, under conditions of local autonomy; the choice of congressional nominees, for example, is seldom influenced by national party leaders.

PRIMARIES AND ONE-PARTYISM

In predominantly one-party constituencies, victory in the primary of the majority party is tantamount to election, resulting in keen competition for nominations. On the other hand, it is not unusual for the minority party in such circumstances to forfeit the election by failing to put up its own candidate or by offering only token opposition. Between 1920 and 1944, for example, over 40 per cent of the congressional elections in twelve southern states (the Confederacy plus Oklahoma) found the Democratic nominees unopposed by Republicans; in a heavy majority of the remaining elections, Republican strength was negligible.[12]

Although the Republican party has been more inclined to try its wings in presidential elections in the South since the Eisenhower victory in 1952, it still fails to contest many congressional elections. In 1958, for example, Republicans failed to nominate candidates in 70 per cent of the congressional districts in the twelve-state southern group. And although the party has nominated more candidates in recent years, it still had no nominees in about 40 per cent of the districts in 1962, 1966, and 1970. The explanation for these facts does not lie simply in the historic weakness of the Republican party in the South. Rather, it is probable that conservative southerners,

11 *Politics, Parties, and Pressure Groups* (New York: Thomas Y. Crowell Company, 1964), p. 377. Of related interest is the question of whether primary *electorates* are broadly representative of the entire following of the parties. There has long been a suspicion that primary voters differ sharply from their party as a whole in such matters as ideology, ethnic membership, religious affiliation, or socio-economic background. If this were true, it might be expected that the candidates who are nominated would tend to be unrepresentative of the party; this condition presumably would have substantial impact on the behavior of the party contingent in the legislature. Survey research data on primary voters in Wisconsin serve to discount this probability. Although each party's primary electorate in that state differs somewhat from the party following as a whole (e.g., better education and higher income), the differences are neither large nor greatly significant for the political process. Most important, the study indicates that very little difference exists between primary voters and general following in terms of their perceptions of ideological differences between the parties or their concern over state issues. See Austin Ranney and Leon D. Epstein, "The Two Electorates: Voters and Non-Voters in a Wisconsin Primary," *Journal of Politics,* XXVIII (August 1966), 598–616.

12 Cortez A. M. Ewing, *Congressional Elections, 1896–1944* (Norman: University of Oklahoma Press, 1947), p. 92.

who regularly vote Republican in presidential elections, see no reason to put up their own congressional candidates so long as their point of view is well represented by conservative Democrats, a group whose resistance to the programs of northern Democrats equals that of most Republicans. By contrast, Republican dominance in one-party areas is nowhere quite so unassailable, although there are certain constituencies in the Midwest and New England which scarcely give a second thought to the possibility of electing a Democrat.

COMPETITION IN PRIMARIES

In an important respect the theory of the direct primary collides with practice. This has not led to the primary's undoing, but it has diminished its significance. Though primary theory rests in part on the expectation that each primary election will produce a contest between two or more serious candidates, such competition frequently fails to appear. Rather, V. O. Key and others have shown that the incidence of primary contesting is related to the strength of the parties within districts.[13] In districts in which the Republican party is strong and victory in the general election seems assured, there often will be two or more candidates bidding for the party's nomination (unless an incumbent is running for renomination, a situation which tends to diminish opposition). On the other hand, to continue the example, in districts in which the Democratic party's prospects in the general election are slight, there is ordinarily much less interest in capturing the Democratic nomination, and hence there are fewer contests. In highly competitive districts there are likely to be contests in the primaries of both parties. This general pattern, with some exceptions, characterizes nominations for state legislative office and for Congress. Figure 2, drawn from Key's *American State Politics,* shows the presence of primary contests for the Missouri House of Representatives.

The relationship of the party system to the workings of the primary is perhaps best indicated by experience in southern states, where the primary is often *the* election. Here the primary most closely approximates the model drawn by its early advocates. Contests for nominations to Congress, even when incumbents are involved, occur in virtually all southern Democratic primaries. Run-off primaries—a second primary held if no candidate obtains a majority of the vote in the regular primary—are common throughout the South.

CONGRESSIONAL NOMINATIONS — CONVENTIONS AND PRIMARIES

The manner in which congressional nominations are made profoundly affects the American political system. Many political scientists argue, in fact, that the loose, decentralized character of the nominating process is the funda-

---

13 V. O. Key, Jr., *American State Politics: An Introduction* (New York: Alfred A. Knopf, Inc., 1956); William H. Standing and James A. Robinson, "Inter-Party Competition and Primary Contesting: The Case of Indiana," *American Political Science Review,* LII (December 1958), 1066–77; Malcolm E. Jewell, "Party and Primary Competition in Kentucky State Legislative Races," *Kentucky Law Journal,* XLVIII (Summer 1960), 517–35; Sorauf, *op. cit.,* pp. 110–18.

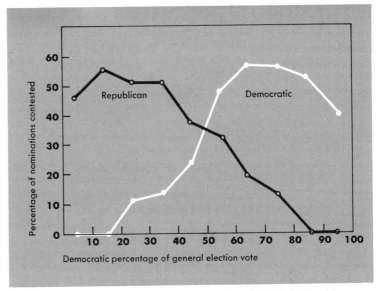

Source: V.O. Key, Jr., *American State Politics: An Introduction* (New York: Alfred A. Knopf, Inc., 1956), p. 173.

FIGURE 2 *Primary competition and the prospects for general election victory: relation between proportion of nominations contested and percentage of general election vote polled by Republican and Democratic Nominees for Missouri House of Representatives, 1942–1950*

mental cause for the derangement of power in congressional party organizations, manifested in the inability of the parties to maintain ranks on major policy matters.

The keys to congressional nominations are kept in the constituencies, where they are held at times by the public at large, at times by one or more powerful pressure groups, at times by a few local party leaders. The ultimate consequence of local control over nominations is that any brand of Democrat or Republican may be nominated and elected to Congress. With substitution of current issues for those of the 1920s, Senator William E. Borah's statement of the problem would be as appropriate today as it was then:

> Any man who can carry a Republican primary is a Republican. He might believe in free trade, in unconditional membership in the League of Nations, in states' rights, and in every policy that the Democratic party ever advocated; yet, if he carried his Republican primary, he would be a Republican. He might go to the other extreme and believe in the communistic state, in the dictatorship of the proletariat, in the abolition of private property, and in the extermination of the bourgeoisie; yet, if he carried his Republican primary, he would still be a Republican.[14]

14 Quoted in the report of the Committee on Political Parties of the American Political Science Association, *Toward a More Responsible Two-Party System* (New York: Holt, Rinehart & Winston, Inc., 1950), p. 27.

A few states have used state party conventions to make U.S. senatorial nominations. State conventions are similar in organization and mood to presidential nominating conventions. Some conventions are characterized by protracted negotiations and balloting before a nominee is selected, while in other cases leading party chieftains coalesce to pick the nominee in advance of the convention. Robert F. Kennedy's nomination by the New York State Democratic Convention in 1964 fits the latter category. Kennedy's campaign for the nomination was launched months in advance of the convention, when his supporters began to meet with Democratic party chairmen around the state. New York City leaders in particular were anxious to have Kennedy run for the Senate in the belief that his name on the ticket would help their local candidates. The Kennedy drive was bolstered by the fact that opponents could not agree on an alternative candidate—and to block a nomination it is necessary to have a candidate. In the weeks preceding the Albany convention, Kennedy received a steady stream of endorsements from key Democratic and Liberal party leaders. By the time Kennedy announced that he was entering the race for the Democratic senatorial nomination— several days before the convention was to open—his nomination was almost certainly in the bag. The convention held no surprises, and Kennedy received nearly 90 per cent of the delegate votes.

Senatorial nominations in convention states are won by candidates who are heavily endowed with political resources and who are determined to touch all bases within the party organization. When nominations are made by convention, the public is reduced to the role of spectator, and the campaign for the nomination focuses on party leaders. The formal nomination of Robert Kennedy in New York was the culmination of a long campaign to acquire endorsements by a variety of leading state politicians—"We had to be sure," as one Kennedy aide observed, "that this thing didn't look like a coup by the Irish Mafia."[15] The disarray of the Democratic organization in the state, the presence of intense factionalism within the party, the dearth of prominent alternative candidates, the appeal of Kennedy himself, and the knowledge that national and state party fortunes are often closely linked all contributed to the decision of New York Democrats to pick a nominee whose political experience had been gained almost exclusively outside their state.

The nomination of members of Congress by convention is exception to the general practice in the states. Most states provide for nomination through primary elections. Congressional primaries are not necessarily competitive, as may be seen in Table 4.1, which adds to the evidence offered in Figure 2. Primary contests for House seats are most likely to occur in those districts in which the victor will stand a good chance of winning the general election. A glance at the top line of the table reveals, for example, that the nominees in both parties tend to be unopposed (i.e., receiving 90–100 per cent of the vote) in those districts in which their chances for election in November (shown in the first column) are virtually nonexistent. Ordinarily, politicians do not struggle to win nominations that are unlikely to lead to public office. The reverse is true, as the bottom lines of the table show, in those districts in which nominations seem to lead directly to elec-

15 *New York Times,* August 26, 1964.

TABLE 4.1

Intraparty Competition for House Nominations and the Prospects of General Election Victory: Proportions of Nominees Winning Primaries Involving no Incumbents by Wide and by Narrow Margins Related to Subsequent General Election Vote, 1952–58

Candidates' Percentage of General Election Vote	Total Number of Primaries		Proportions of Candidates Nominated with Indicated Percentages of Primary Vote			
			Democratic		Republican	
	D	*R*	*Under 60 Per Cent*	*90–100 Per Cent*	*Under 60 Per Cent*	*90–100 Per Cent*
0–29	27	73	26%	74%	15%	68%
30–39	170	113	20	65	26	54
40–49	246	127	40	31	39	38
50–59	63	47	40	25	57	11
60–79	11	11	45	9	54	18
100	15	1	93	0	100	0

SOURCE: V. O. Key, Jr., *Politics, Parties, and Pressure Groups* (New York: Thomas Y. Crowell Company, 1964), p. 447.

tion. There is no surprise in this set of facts—the men and women who enter or stay out of primary races for Congress make their decisions on grounds that are grimly utilitarian.

The single theme explored above is less than a complete explanation for the presence or absence of competition in congressional primaries. Allowance must be made for two other factors. The first is that in some jurisdictions primary competition rarely occurs because the dominant party thoroughly controls access to office. Congressional nominees are "slated" by local party chieftains, and their endorsement is critical to nomination. Other potential candidates, deferring to the organization, bide their time, sometimes securing other appointments in return for their withdrawal from the congressional race. The second factor is that of incumbency. When a primary contest for a House seat fails to develop, even though the district is promising for that party, the explanation often lies in the fact that the incumbent is seeking renomination. Incumbency diminishes primary competition. The ability of incumbents to discourage candidates standing in the wings is not surprising. The longer a representative stays in office, the more time he has to establish personal followings among public, party, and interest group elements. Congressmen tend to feel that there is slight excuse for losing any election, so great are the advantages of incumbency—prestigious office, staff assistance, franking privilege, and numerous opportunities for distributing benefits to constituents and for attracting publicity both at home and in Washington.

Under certain circumstances, however, potential candidates all but queue up to challenge the incumbent. V. O. Key has pointed out that an aging representative is sometimes vulnerable to defeat by a younger candidate, as is a first-term representative who has not been in office sufficient time to solidify his position. A congressional redistricting which changes district lines significantly, thereby disrupting political followings, may lead to a primary challenge for the incumbent. Finally, in some states factional politics are both so vigorous and enduring that "sitting" representatives can expect to encounter a primary opponent almost every two years.[16] Hence, despite the advantages of incumbency, primary battles may have to be fought out from time to time. Even so, there is statistical comfort for representatives in knowing that very few incumbents, at least in the North, ever go down to defeat in *primary* elections.

The South is another matter. Not only are southern Democratic incumbents likely to encounter vigorous opposition in the primary, they run a fair chance of failing to win renomination. In primaries held over the period 1920–54, the chances were about one out of three that a southern senator bidding for renomination would be defeated. Incumbent senators from outside the South seeking renomination met defeat at a rate of fewer than one out of fifty (and a goodly number won without primary opposition).[17] Having won renomination, of course, the typical southern Democrat has slight cause to lose sleep over his Republican opposition in the general election. How long this will continue is problematic, for the once weak southern Republican organizations have shown new signs of life, as other data on congressional elections in this chapter will demonstrate.

NATIONAL PARTY AND CONGRESSIONAL NOMINATIONS

National party leaders are rarely involved in discussions with state and local party leaders over congressional nominations. By and large, the national party neither attempts to recruit candidates for congressional office nor intervenes in primary elections by backing one candidate over another. Experience has shown that national intervention in primaries is fraught with difficulties. President Franklin D. Roosevelt's attempt in 1938 to "purge" anti–New Deal incumbent Democrats—southerners in the main— by publicly supporting their primary opponents, ended in disaster, with nearly all of the victims singled out for elimination winning handily. A similar fate befell President Truman's efforts when he endorsed a candidate for the Senate in the 1950 Missouri Democratic primary. Although the presidential "purge" occasionally has met with success—Roosevelt, for example, initiated actions leading to the primary defeat of the Democratic chairman of the House Rules Committee in 1938—the overall record is marked mainly by failure.

Even though there are good grounds for claiming that national authorities have a legitimate interest in the nomination of congressional candidates, there are few signs today of national activity in the primaries. The usual denouement of the "purge" undoubtedly has produced a cautious attitude among national leaders, for the most part discouraging them from even such a mild form of intrusion as helping to recruit candidates when no incumbents are in the running. Congressional nominations are not regarded as much different from other nominations, and state and local political leaders show no enthusiasm for interference by Washington. For lack of a good alternative, Washington goes along with the folkway of local control.

---

16 Key, *Politics, Parties, and Pressure Groups,* pp. 451–52.
17 *Ibid.,* p. 441.

100   This awkward fact of American politics makes matters difficult for the party in Congress, for the presence of congressmen who are discovered locally and who owe virtually nothing to the national party confounds attempts to develop coherent party policies. Rampant parochialism, the frequent rupture of party lines, the evasion and confusion of national issues, and a possible loss of legislative talent—in the judgment of one school of writers—are the concomitants to the selection of congressional candidates on an almost exclusively local basis.

Congressional and Legislative Elections

CONGRESSIONAL ELECTIONS

Table 4.2 provides a point of departure for an examination of several features of congressional elections. The most important fact highlighted by the data is that a relatively small proportion of the elections finds one

TABLE 4.2

Marginal, Safer, and Uncontested Seats in Elections to U.S. House of Representatives and Senate, 1962–70, by Percentage of Total Seats

Election Margin	House					Senate				
	1962	*1964*	*1966*	*1968*	*1970*	*1962*	*1964*	*1966*	*1968*	*1970*
Marginal Seats (won by less than 55% of the vote)										
Democratic	10.4	14.2	7.6	10.6	6.0	33.3	26.5	20.6	21.2	21.2
Republican	8.0	11.3	9.4	6.0	6.5	15.4	17.7	8.8	27.3	21.2
Safer Seats (won by 55% or more of the vote)										
Democratic	38.9	44.9	39.3	37.0	42.1	28.2	50.0	20.6	30.3	45.5
Republican	31.9	20.6	32.9	36.3	34.2	20.5	2.9	41.2	15.1	12.0
Uncontested Seats	10.8	9.0	10.8	10.1	11.2	2.6	2.9	8.8	6.1	0.0
Total	100.0	100.0	100.0	100.0	100.0	100.0	100.0	100.0	100.0	100.0

SOURCE: Computed from data in *Congressional Quarterly Weekly Report,* supplement to issue of April 5, 1963; *1964 Congressional Quarterly Almanac,* pp. 1024–68; *Congressional Quarterly Weekly Report,* supplement to issue of May 12, 1967; *1969 Congressional Quarterly Almanac,* pp. 1202–38; and *Congressional Quarterly Weekly Report,* November 6, 1970, pp. 2771–78.

candidate narrowly edging out another. "Marginal" elections—those in which the winning candidate receives less than 55 percent of the vote— generally account for perhaps 35–45 percent of the Senate seats and from 15–20 percent of the House seats. In effect, this means that party fortunes in the House depend heavily on the outcome of elections in perhaps seventy to one hundred "marginal" districts.

In the other 300-plus House constituencies, victory is not greatly in doubt, though a landslide such as Roosevelt's in 1936 or Johnson's in 1964 is capable of upsetting allegiances of long standing. But many House and Senate seats are impervious to even the most sweeping national election tides. Moreover, Table 4.2 turns up a surprisingly large number of elections, especially in the House, in which candidates win without opposition—roughly 10 per cent of the seats in the elections between 1962 and 1970. There is nothing novel in the report that all but a handful of these elections took place in the South, where the Democratic party is the principal beneficiary.

Competition between the parties for congressional seats apparently has never been particularly high. In the great majority of districts the same party wins election after election. Table 4.3, the work of Charles O. Jones, shows

TABLE 4.3

Interparty Competition for Congressional Seats

Time Period	Percentage of Fluidity	Percentage of No-change Districts	Number of Changes
1914–26	11.8%	62.1%	308
1932–40	10.6	69.9	184
1942–50	11.9	74.0	199
1952–60	7.8	78.2	135

SOURCE: Charles O. Jones, "Inter-Party Competition for Congressional Seats," *Western Political Quarterly*, XVII (September 1964), 465.

the extent of interparty competition for congressional seats during four different intervals, beginning in 1914.[18] The table offers two measures of party competitiveness. One indicates whether there was any change in party control over the time period studied; for example, in the elections between 1952 and 1960, 78.2 per cent of all congressional districts were won by the same party. The second measure registers a "percentage of fluidity"—how many alterations were made in party control during any period. For example, in the House elections between 1952 and 1960, it would have been possible to have had 1,740 changes (435 $\times$ 4), an indication of perfect competitiveness. Actual changes numbered only 135, or 7.8 percent. Viewed broadly, the chances are that the same party will win five consecutive elections in about three-fourths of all congressional districts.

The main conclusion to be drawn from this study is that interparty competition for House seats has declined noticeably in the twentieth century, serving to make the House an increasingly stable body. But trends in competitiveness have not been uniform throughout the country. The Middle Atlantic, Central, Mountain, and Pacific regions have become less competitive in congressional elections in recent years. On the other hand, certain one-party areas have become significantly more competitive. Democratic strength, for example, has grown in New England and the West Central states, while Republican fortunes have greatly improved in the South. As Figure 3 shows, southern Democrats are now winning fewer congressional elections by default. Republicanism appears to be taking root in the states

[18] "Inter-Party Competition for Congressional Seats," *Western Political Quarterly*, XVII (September 1964), 461–76.

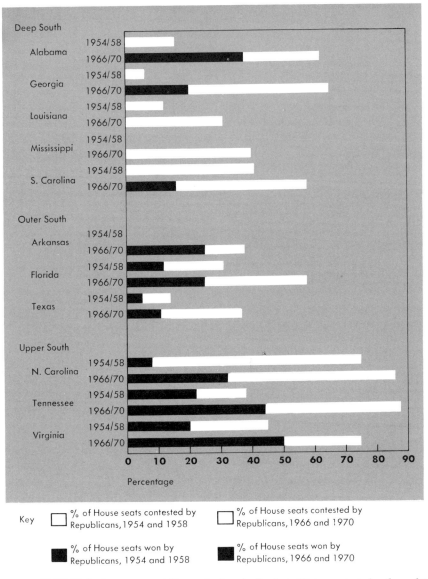

FIGURE 3 *Percentage of House elections in Southern States contested and won by Republicans, 1954–1958, 1966–1970.*

of the Deep South and is already significant in most of the states of the Upper South and Outer South. The southern Republican is less and less an anomaly. Although there were only eight southern Republican congressmen elected to the 86th Congress (1959–60), there were twenty-seven elected to the 92d Congress (1971–72).

Another way to explore competitiveness between parties is pictured in Figure 4. Developed by Joseph Schlesinger, this illustration employs two

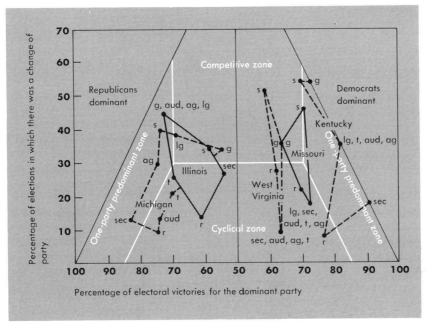

Office key

g: Governor
s: Senator
r: Congressmen
lg: Lieutenant governor
sec: Secretary of State
ag: Attorney general
aud: Auditor
t: Treasurer

". . . the more centrally located on the horizontal axis the more competitive an office was in over-all terms; the higher on the diagram the more rapid the rate of turnover; and correspondingly, the lower on the diagram an office falls, the longer the cycles of one-party control, regardless of the degree of over-all competition."

Source: Joseph A. Schlesinger, "The Structure of Competition for Office in the American States," *Behavioral Science*, V (July 1960), 203.

FIGURE 4 *Party competition for individual offices in selected states, 1914–58.*

measures of competitiveness: the horizontal axis depicts the extent to which the parties have divided control of each state office, while the vertical axis shows the rate of turnover in control of the office between the parties. The figure demonstrates convincingly that individual state offices vary sharply in competitiveness. Some offices regularly shift back and forth between the parties while others are controlled for long stretches of time by the same party. For the country as a whole, excluding southern states ordinarily dominated by the Democrats, the least competitive office has been that of congressman, the most competitive offices those of governor and senator.[19]

An important understanding is illuminated by this evidence: the American political party is a pastiche of disparate national, state, local, and personal organizations brought together for limited purposes. For reasons

[19] "The Structure of Competition for Office in the American States," *Behavioral Science*, V (July 1960), 197–210.

104   that are not easy to fathom, a party's candidates may run very well for some offices and very poorly for other offices—in election after election. The "structure of competition" for state and national offices is such that candidates are loosely affiliated with each other and with their parties. The dominant impression conveyed is that each candidate is on his own, a fact that requires him to develop his own campaign strategy, to siphon off financial support where he can find it, and to seize upon transitory circumstances to put together his own electoral majority. How the party as a whole fares in an election is not of first importance to the individual candidate; nor is it likely that party automatically will be of first importance once he has taken office. Following the evidence of this study, it seems plain that some major part of the explanation for party disunity in government, and perhaps especially in Congress, is found in the fragmentation of the electoral parties, marked by an inability of the parties to control a range of offices and by the necessity for candidates to develop their own personal organizations.

Once the relatively "permanent" character of the House is recognized, it is easy to understand why presidential legislative programs often encounter so much difficulty there. The popular impulses to which many congressmen must respond are far from identical to those which spur the president. Moreover, many congressmen have discovered how to maintain themselves securely in office, insulating their careers from national election tides and the vagaries of presidential elections. Presidents come and go, the House goes on and on.

CONGRESSMEN AND THE PRESIDENT'S
COATTAILS

The degree to which the voting strength of presidential candidates influences voting for congressional offices has long been a matter for speculation. Because the victorious presidential candidate ordinarily runs ahead of congressional candidates—by an average of 7.5 percent in elections between 1896 and 1948[20]—it often has been assumed that his popularity rubs off on his party's congressional candidates, swelling their votes and pulling some into office who might not make it on their own. Congressional candidates, in other words, "ride" into office on the president's "coattails."

Although undoubtedly there are elections in which certain congressional candidates profit from the vote-amassing ability of the presidential candidate, studies of the "coattail" factor suggest that the presidential candidate's influence is greatly exaggerated. In the first place, successful presidential candidates do not always run ahead of congressional candidates. In 1960, for example, John F. Kennedy trailed Democratic congressional candidates in 303 (69 per cent) of the 437 districts. Harry S. Truman won the presidency in 1948 with 49.4 percent of the total presidential vote, while Democratic congressional candidates obtained 52.5 percent of the total congressional vote.[21]

20 Malcolm Moos, *Politics, Presidents and Coattails* (Baltimore: Johns Hopkins Press, 1952), p. 12.
21 *Ibid.*, p. 13.

A second difficulty with the "coattail theory" is that it leans heavily on the assumption that if a presidential candidate leads the ticket, fellow party members running for Congress inevitably gain additional votes and thus are carried into office. But this is a tenuous assumption, as Malcolm Moos has shown, since ordinarily there is a much higher voting interest in the presidential contest; during the period 1920 to 1948, on an average only about ninety persons out of one hundred who voted for a presidential candidate cast a ballot for a congressional candidate.[22] The theory also suffers from those rare instances in which a president wins by a comfortable margin, as did Dwight Eisenhower in 1956, but fails to carry his party along to a House majority.

Third, the "coattail theory" ignores the losing presidential ticket. When the presidential candidate of the winning party does better than his congressional candidates, the presidential candidate of the losing party is bound to do worse than his congressional candidates.[23] Finally, there are a great many districts wholly dominated by one party; here the presidential race has negligible impact on the fortunes of congressional candidates.

In sum, the impact of the president's "coattails" is felt mainly in marginal districts. In these districts the presidential candidate's appeal may indeed be sufficient to assist his congressional running mates. Occasionally, of course, the "coattails" are reversed, with the congressional candidate running stronger than the head of the ticket.[24]

MIDTERM CONGRESSIONAL ELECTIONS

Off-year or midterm elections to Congress are characterized by two principal and consistent patterns. In the first place, voter participation declines precipitously in the absence of a presidential contest. Second, and of greater significance, the administration party at midterm nearly always loses seats in Congress, occasionally even its majority, such as in 1954 when House control shifted from the Republicans to the Democrats. Only once in the last century, in 1934, has the party in possession of the administration increased its representation at midterm. In 1962, the Kennedy administration won a startling "victory" by breaking even, losing four seats in the House and gaining four seats in the Senate. Four years later, in 1966, the Democrats suffered a sharp loss of forty-seven House seats; many Democratic candidates who had been pulled into Congress on President Johnson's "coattails" in

---

22 *Ibid.*, p. 17.

23 *Ibid.*, p. 122.

24 This discussion of the "coattail theory" hits only the most familiar facts. See Warren E. Miller, "Presidential Coattails: A Study of Political Myth and Methodology," *Public Opinion Quarterly,* XIX (Winter 1955–56), 353–68; and Charles Press, "Voting Statistics and Presidential Coattails," *American Political Science Review,* LII (December 1958), 1041–50. Press concludes that there is a national pattern to congressional races "and it tends to place limits on the vote a congressman can expect to attract in relation to that of the victorious presidential candidate of his party. Where the party is traditionally weak on the congressional level, the president will run ahead. Where the party is traditionally entrenched on the congressional level, congressional candidates will lead the president." In the 1956 election, for example, Republican congressional candidates began to lead President Eisenhower when they received about 60 percent of the vote. In several elections, the breaking point was encountered around 54 percent.

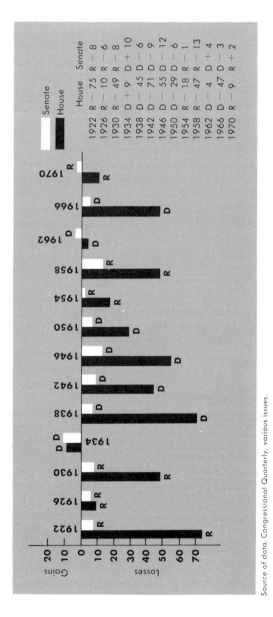

FIGURE 5 *Off-year gains and losses in Congress by the President's Party, 1922–1970.*

Source of data: Congressional Quarterly, various issues.

1964 lost out when their districts returned to normal at the next election. Finally, in 1970, a Republican gain of two seats in the Senate was offset by a loss of nine seats in the House. As would be expected, administration party losses are most likely to occur in marginal districts and states. Figure 5 shows the results of midterm elections from 1922 to 1970.

The rise and fall of party fortunes, in presidential and midterm elections, affects the parties alike. No president has reason to count on improving his party's congressional position at midterm; on the contrary, he has every reason to fear the worst. In the judgment of some observers, the midterm confrontation is a referendum on the administration's policies of the previous two years. But the picture lacks the president himself. Accordingly, party and administration performance as a whole cannot be brought into focus at midterm in the way that it can be in presidential elections. Midterm elections tend rather to focus on administration mistakes and on national policy as it intrudes on local interests. Although the midterm verdict culminates in "a broad decision in terms of party,"[25] ordinarily favorable to the "outs" and inimical to the "ins," it is fair to say that the general thrust of the administration party, its alternatives as against those of the opposition, is not highly visible to the multiple electorates bent on surveying policy as it affects their states or their districts. Midterm election results are loaded with imponderables; invariably, the data harbor a number of possible interpretations. Viewing the 1962 outcomes, the *Washington Post* had to settle for this enduring generalization: "The only conclusion that one can safely draw from American congressional elections is that the voters show a preference for the winners instead of for the losers."[26]

Midterm elections provide both a brake to the development of *national* leadership centering in the presidency and an invitation to jarring stalemate between president and Congress; at the same time, they make it difficult to develop a national party system broadly responsible to the total electorate. Whatever else may be said of them, midterm elections contribute heavily to the preservation of tenaciously decentralized political parties. Abandonment of the two-year term for House members in favor of a four-year term would strengthen national party leadership, especially if all senators were elected for the same period. Political scientists, who seldom are chary about recommending change, appear to support the four-year term for congressmen with great enthusiasm. But this prescription, like others involving major congressional reform, has won no authentic audience among either legislators or the public.

INCUMBENTS AND ELECTIONS

In traditional interpretation, the great divide in American political campaigns is the factor of incumbency. Potential candidates for Congress may grow restive as the years pass by and the old hands in Washington hang on,

---

[25] Key, *Politics, Parties, and Pressure Groups*, p. 616. See also Barbara Hinckley, "Interpreting House Midterm Elections: Toward a Measurement of the In-Party's 'Expected' Loss of Seats," *American Political Science Review*, LXI (September 1967), 694–700.

[26] *Washington Post*, November 5, 1962.

108 but there is not much they can do except wait for death, retirement, or a major redistricting act to provide an opening. The member of Congress who works at staying in office and utilizes the perquisites of his office fully is exceedingly difficult to defeat, even in a landslide election.[27] Some of the reasons for congressional longevity are made clear in these comments by a member of the House:

> I have the feeling that the most effective campaigning is done when no election is near. During the interval between elections you have to establish every personal contact you can, and you accomplish this through your mail as much as you do it by means of anything else. At the end of each session I take all the letters which have been received on legislative matters and write each person telling him how the legislative proposal in which he was interested stands.
>
> Personally, I will speak on any subject. I am not nonpartisan, but I talk on everything whether it deals with politics or not. Generally I speak at nonpolitical meetings. I read 48 weekly newspapers and clip every one of them myself. Whenever there is a particularly interesting item about anyone, that person gets a note from me. We also keep a complete list of the changes of officers in every organization in our district. Then when I am going into a town I know exactly who I would like to have at the meeting. I learned early that you had to make your way with Democrats as well as with Republicans. And you cannot let the matter of election go until the last minute. I budget 17 trips home each session and somehow I've never managed to go less than 21 times.[28]

To be sure, incumbency carries advantages. Among other things, an incumbent officeholder has a public record to which he can refer, visibility gained through previous public exposure, a position which enables him to help constituents with their problems, a staff and offices, and ordinarily good access to sources of campaign funds. Despite these obvious advantages to incumbency, however, it may not be the critical factor that conventional wisdom has made it. A recent study covering elections to the U.S. House of Representatives in northern states over an eight-year period (1952–60) finds that an incumbent gains only about 2 percent more of the two-party vote as a result of the incumbency factor. This increment, of course, *is* critical in close elections, but the fact is that relatively few House elections are "cliffhangers"; over the period of this study, for example, only 4 per cent of all northern incumbents who won reelection received less than 52

---

27 The member of Congress who loses touch with his constituency, however, is not invulnerable. The election defeat suffered by Senator Albert Gore (D., Tenn.) in 1970 fits this category. According to his aides, the principal reason for his loss was "his failure during his last term to mend the fences back home—with county chairmen, precinct workers, prominent supporters, and ordinary voters—and thereby cut down the resentment toward him that had obviously been building up over the years." See Richard Harris, "How the People Feel," *New Yorker*, July 10, 1971, pp. 34–54.

28 Quoted in Charles L. Clapp, *The Congressman: His Work as He Sees It* (Washington: The Brookings Institution, 1963), p. 332.

per cent of the two-party vote.[29] Incumbents are reelected to Congress in overwhelming numbers—typically over 90 percent of the incumbent congressmen on the ballot return to Washington after each election. But the major explanation for their success is not their incumbent status but rather the fact that they represent safe districts—districts that elect candidates of the same party year after year.

STATE LEGISLATIVE ELECTIONS

The broad facts concerning nominations and elections for most state legislatures appear to be about the same as for Congress. The important similarities are: first, that nominees are ordinarily slated by local party leaders and committees rather than by state leaders or committees; second, in nearly all cases formal nominations are made in primaries; third, incumbents are not often defeated in primary elections; fourth, state legislative districts are about as likely to be dominated by one party as are congressional districts; fifth, the crucial battles for control of the legislature in competitive states take place in a relatively small number of marginal districts; and sixth, the influence of the governor's "coattails" is felt mainly in marginal districts.

Legislative elections leave their imprint on state politics in many ways. One effect is especially important. A frequent outcome of state elections is that one party gains control of the governor's chair and the other party gains control of one or both houses of the legislature. Table 4.4, updating

TABLE 4.4

Incidence of Party Division (*Governor vs. Legislature*) in Competitive States, 1930–50, 1952–66, 1970

	1930–50 (32 States)		1952–66 (37 States)		1970 (37 States)	
	Number	%	Number	%	Number	%
Governor and majority in legislature not in same party	126	35.7	133	46.8	19	51.3
Governor and majority in legislature in same party	227	64.3	151	53.2	18	48.7
Total	353	100.0	284	100.0	37	100.0

SOURCES: The 1930–50 data are from V. O. Key, Jr., and Corinne Silverman, "Party and Separation of Powers: A Panorama of Practice in the States," in *Public Policy*, ed. Carl J. Friedrich and J. Kenneth Galbraith (Cambridge: Harvard University, Graduate School of Public Administration, 1954), p. 389.

NOTE: For the period 1930–50, fourteen states (mainly southern) are excluded because one party continuously held the governorship and both houses of the legislature. Similarly, for 1952–66 and 1970, the eleven states of the Confederacy are excluded, along with Minnesota and Nebraska, both of which have nonpartisan legislatures.

the findings of V. O. Key, Jr., and Corinne Silverman, shows the incidence of divided government in *competitive* states over a forty-year period. Although divided party control was substantial between 1930 and 1950, it has

[29] Robert S. Erikson, "The Advantage of Incumbency in Congressional Elections," *Polity*, III (Spring 1971), 395–405.

110 been even greater in recent years. Between 1952 and 1966, the chances were better than four out of ten that following each new state election the governor would be opposed by a majority of the opposite party in at least one of the two houses. Following the 1970 elections, over half of the states had divided governments. Democratic governors encountered this problem much more frequently than Republican governors in the 1930–50 period; in recent years both parties have been plagued about equally by this condition.

Disparities between party gubernatorial and legislative victories are due to a number of factors, including the election of legislature and executive for nonconcurrent terms, the use of staggered elections for upper and lower houses, and the separation of gubernatorial and presidential elections. The ability of some gubernatorial candidates to build nonparty personal followings by relying on their names, the media, and awesome campaign expenditures may be another explanation. Also, here and there, the distribution of safe legislative districts may give one party a distinct advantage over the other, irrespective of the gubernatorial election. Deliberate electoral preference for divided executive-legislative control is perhaps another factor. Whatever the reasons, divided government undoubtedly makes it difficult to fix responsibility for decisions on either party. At worst, it gives rise to deadlock and internecine warfare between the parties.

VACANCIES IN CONGRESS AND THE STATE LEGISLATURES

There are several methods for filling vacancies in legislative office due to the death, retirement, or (rarely) expulsion of members. The U.S. Constitution provides in the case of House vacancies that the governor of the affected state "shall issue writs of elections to fill such vacancies." In the case of the Senate, the Seventeenth Amendment stipulates that the governor "shall issue writs of election to fill such vacancies: provided, that the legislature of any state may empower the executive thereof to make temporary appointments until the people fill the vacancies by election as the legislature may direct."

House vacancies may be filled by calling for a special election, or the selection of a replacement may be put off until the next regular election. When a senatorial vacancy is filled by election, the senator chosen completes the term of the person he is replacing, instead of being elected to the usual six-year term. Unless a Senate vacancy occurs very close to an election, the governor ordinarily will appoint a new senator, who holds office until the next election. His appointment may rest on a clear understanding with party leaders in the state that he will serve only until the next election and not seek to win office in his own right: such appointments are no more than holding operations. There are also cases in which the governor himself resigns, having earlier made an arrangement to have his successor appoint him to fill the Senate vacancy. Perhaps stretching the bounds of propriety, two governors defeated at the polls in 1962 and 1963 resigned their offices before their terms expired and were appointed by their successors to the Senate; as it turned out, both were defeated in bids for election in 1964. Only rarely does a governor fail to appoint a member of his own political party to fill a vacancy, notwithstanding the party membership of the former senator.

Legislative vacancies occur far more frequently than might be imagined. From 1919 to 1965, 18 per cent of all Senate terms were not completed by the person elected to the office; on an average there were six vacancies during each Congress over this period. A large majority of these vacancies were filled by gubernatorial appointment, the rest by special election. The manner in which Senate vacancies are filled is obviously important, since the newly appointed senator has all the legal powers of any other senator. His appointment may affect the partisan division of the Senate, the outcomes of closely contested votes, and the politics of his home state. A good case can be made that popular control of government would be enhanced if state legislatures adopted laws to eliminate the governor's role in this process and to provide for special elections to fill vacancies.[30]

Vacancies in the state legislature are filled by holding special elections, by giving the power of appointment to the governor, or by empowering a local agency, such as a party committee, county commission, or county court to appoint replacements. It is not at all unusual for legislative vacancies to be left open until the next regular election, a practice which deprives certain districts of direct representation during the interval.

Elections and the Legislature

Decisions made at the recruitment and election stages of the American political process are as likely to shape legislative behavior as decisions made by legislators themselves once in office. The selection of legislators settles a great many matters in advance of sessions. Who runs, who wins, who loses—all help to form the boundaries within which the legislative process takes place.[31] The appearance of slack, options, or room for maneuver in the legislature may be more illusory than real. Recruitment determines whether the legislature will be populated by "lawmakers" or "spectators," by those who take their work seriously or by those who sit around watching others. The early decisions concerning who is to be recruited for legislative office are of critical importance because once members are established in office they are exceedingly difficult to dislodge. Old legislators may die, but they rarely fade away.

Similar observations may be made of legislative elections. They may

[30] These comments on Senate vacancies are based on an article by Alan L. Clem, "Popular Representation and Senate Vacancies," *Midwest Journal of Political Science,* X (February 1966), 52–77.

[31] There has been relatively little research on the losers in American political campaigns. For one such study (involving the 1964 congressional elections), see Jeff Fishel, "Party, Ideology, and the Congressional Challenger," *American Political Science Review,* LXIII (December 1969), 1213–32. For most districts, the study reports, it made no difference on the election outcome whether the nonincumbent candidate was conservative, middle-of-the-road, or liberal. Winners and losers were distributed about equally among nonincumbent candidates of all ideological persuasions. This study offers support for the generalization that electoral outcomes are principally influenced by constituency factors, in particular the pattern of party competition in each district.

112 constitute a sharp break with the past, and thereby contribute to different policy outcomes in the legislature, or they may duplicate the previous election, and thereby impose continuity on legislative decision-making. Losses by the president's party in off-year elections, for example, usually do more to define the character of congressional decisions (and executive-legislative relations) than any amount of resourcefulness on the part of legislative leaders of his party or of unity among the rank-and-file members. To a striking degree, legislative decisions are tailored to the measure of earlier election victories and losses.

Two concluding observations may help to fill out the argument. First, when legislators are largely on their own, as is the case generally in the American political system, there is scant reason to expect them to take cues from sources which have slight bearing on their careers. Some legislators live with risk and insecurity. Others thrive in safe districts. Party support is not necessarily critical to the careers of legislators from either marginal or safe districts. The independence of the American legislator is a fact of extraordinary significance for understanding the performance of legislative parties. More will be said about this in later chapters.

Second, when the composition of the legislature is remarkably *stable,* as in the case of Congress, there is scant reason to expect it to come forth with legislative proposals that depart sharply from previous settlements. Old policies have a tendency to look strictly modern to those who originally made them. Moreover, newcomers to the system, who might be more inclined to abandon past policies and practices, ordinarily lack the political resources to make their preferences count. Finally, what sometimes impresses outsiders as curious or irresolute legislative response to new demands or nagging problems may appear to legislators themselves as both appropriate and necessary. The stakes are rarely quite the same for nonmembers as for members. Largely left to their own devices, legislators stay in office by viewing large questions in parochial light and by making self-preservation their leading, if not their only, priority.

5

THE LEGISLATORS

To have great legislatures a nation or state must have greatly interested citizens, the most talented of whom are willing to run for office. Critics, whatever their preferences as to legislative design or function, seem to agree that the central element in the strength of any legislature is the quality of its members. The kinds of individuals who are being attracted to legislative service is one of the principal topics examined in this chapter. How they adapt to the legislature—the manner in which they relate to their offices and to legislative norms—is another. Whether they care to stay in office for any length of time, and are able to, is a third. Why they leave the legislature is a fourth. This chapter begins with an analysis of the backgrounds of American legislators. The pattern disclosed is much less variegated than might be expected.

Social and Occupational Backgrounds of American Legislators

Is the American legislature composed of men and women who represent a cross section of the American population? Who are the legislators who make our laws? What groups are "overrepresented" in the legislature? What groups are "underrepresented"? What conclusions can be drawn about the caliber of American legislators?

Political scientists and sociologists have published a number of studies of the social origins and occupational backgrounds of political decision-makers, a few of which have focused on legislators. Despite substantial gaps in factual knowledge about legislative personnel, as well as the presence of a number of special problems confronting such investigations, a certain degree of generalization about the individuals who serve as legislators is attainable.

(1) *Most legislators are drawn from a relatively narrow social base.* The most important fact emerging from studies of the social backgrounds of legislators is that a significant (and disproportionate) number come from middle- and upper-class environments. The legislature, it is apparent, is not a microcosm of the population at large. In the typical legislature no more than a handful of members come from the homes of wage-earners.

Evidence on this point is sufficient to puncture the myth that all American citizens have an equal chance to be elected to legislative office. In

114 his study of postwar senators (covering the years 1947–57), Donald R. Matthews found that 24 per cent of the senators' fathers were professional men, 35 per cent proprietors and officials, and 32 per cent farmers. Only 2 per cent of the senators were the sons of low-salaried workers; 5 per cent were the sons of industrial wage-earners; for 2 per cent the relevant facts were unknown.[1] Other studies of the membership of the lower house of Congress show a similar distribution.[2] An earlier investigation of the occupations of state legislators in thirteen states by Charles S. Hyneman established the fact that legislators are to a marked extent drawn from the more privileged classes.[3]

(2) *No single profile characterizes the political socialization of American legislators—that is, legislators acquire their political interests, values, and attitudes in a variety of ways and at different periods in their life cycles.* Although research on the political socialization of legislators is limited, several generalizations appear to be warranted. The first is that the initial political interest of legislators may be derived from a number of sources, including *primary groups* (e.g., family, friends), *political or civic participation* (e.g., school politics, activity in occupational groups), *public events and circumstances* (e.g., wars, elections, economic crises), *personal predispositions* (e.g., ambition, indignation, interest, sense of obligation), and *socio-economic beliefs*. Second, of those legislators who report that they became interested in politics at an early age, the socialization "agent" ordinarily responsible for this has been the family. The study of California, New Jersey, Ohio, and Tennessee state legislators shows, for example, a high proportion of members with relatives in politics—over 40 per cent in each of the states. Political interest becomes a natural out-growth of family associations and experiences—"I was born into a political family. . . . I grew up in politics." "I met lots of people in politics through my father." "People around home took their politics serious."[4]

A third generalization is that, notwithstanding the incidence and importance of preadult socialization, a surprising number of legislators become adults before they acquire an interest in politics. In the four-state study, nearly four out of every ten legislators indicated that their initial interest in public affairs occurred during adulthood. A more recent study of a group of seniority and elective leaders in Congress finds roughly the same proportion of members reporting that their first interest in politics came

[1] *U.S. Senators and Their World* (Chapel Hill: University of North Carolina Press, 1960), p. 20.

[2] Donald R. Matthews, *The Social Background of Political Decision-Makers* (New York: Random House, Inc., 1954), p. 23.

[3] "Who Makes Our Laws?" *Political Science Quarterly*, LV (December 1940), 556–81.

[4] John C. Wahlke, Heinz Eulau, William Buchanan, and LeRoy C. Ferguson, *The Legislative System: Explorations in Legislative Behavior* (New York: John Wiley & Sons, Inc., 1962), pp. 77–94, quotations on p. 83. Also see a study that analyzes the relation of family ties to the recruitment of members of Congress: Alfred B. Clubok, Norman M. Wilensky, and Forrest J. Berghorn, "Family Relationships, Congressional Recruitment, and Political Modernization," *Journal of Politics*, XXXI (November 1969), 1035–62. Factors associated with the recruitment of Iowa legislators are analyzed in Samuel C. Patterson and G. R. Boynton, "Legislative Recruitment in a Civic Culture," *Social Science Quarterly*, L (September 1969), 243–63.

relatively late—in college (or equivalent period) or after college.[5] Political socialization thus may occur at virtually any time in the life of the legislator. Finally, although preadult political socialization obviously has some bearing on adult attitudes and political behavior, an incumbent legislator's political behavior may not be affected significantly by the nature of his initial political socialization. Political socialization theory rests heavily on the idea that the attitudes, beliefs, and perceptions formed early in life fundamentally shape adult outlook and behavior. Wide-ranging evidence for this, however, is difficult to establish. Indeed, a recent study suggests that there may be no relationship between an individual's socialization into politics and his later orientations as a legislator. Specifically, no relationship appears to exist between a legislator's initial socialization and his legislative orientations toward his constituency ("representative role orientations"), toward interest groups ("group role orientation"), or toward performance of legislative duties ("purposive role orientation"). Legislators may recall their early introduction to politics vividly and enthusiastically, but these socialization experiences apparently have no distinctive impact on how they respond to their official duties. Their orientations are virtually the same as for those members whose socialization occurred as adults.[6]

(3) *In educational achievement, American legislators scarcely resemble their constituents.* According to the 1960 census, 16 per cent of the population twenty-five years old or over had attended college, 40 per cent had a grade school education or less. Isolated studies of the formal schooling of national and state legislators show a profile markedly different from that of the public. Among the postwar senators in Matthews' study, 84 per cent had attended college (24 per cent of the Democrats and 14 per cent of the Republicans who were graduated were members of Phi Beta Kappa); and only 1 per cent had terminated their education with grade school.[7] Of the same character, though less spectacular, is the record of educational attainment among state legislators. For example, between two-thirds and three-fourths of the lawmakers in recent sessions of the Missouri, Indiana, Iowa, and Illinois legislatures had attended college; over 50 per cent of the 1961 Indiana General Assembly were college graduates.[8]

[5] Allan Kornberg and Norman Thomas, "The Political Socialization of National Legislative Elites in the United States and Canada," *Journal of Politics,* XXVII (November 1965), 761–75. This study reports that law schools are among the principal agents of political socialization for members of Congress. "The dominance by lawyers of public offices involved in administering law in this country suggests that the embryo American legislative leader probably found himself in an environment in which politics and the political process were salient topics of conversation. He soon realized, or was made to realize, the possibilities inherent in combining a legal with a political career. Small wonder, then, that such a substantial proportion of American leaders recalled first becoming interested in politics while in law school" (p. 770).

[6] Kenneth Prewitt, Heinz Eulau, and Betty H. Zisk, "Political Socialization and Political Roles," *Public Opinion Quarterly,* XXX (Winter 1966–67), 569–82.

[7] See Matthews, *U.S. Senators and Their World,* p. 26.

[8] See Charles S. Hyneman and George W. Carey, "The Iowa Legislature: A General Description" (Manuscript, Indiana University, 1960); Don F. Hadwiger, "Representation in the Missouri General Assembly," *Missouri Law Review,* XXIV (April 1959), 183; K. Janda, H. Teune, M. Kahn, and W. Francis, *Legislative Politics in Indiana* (Bloomington: Indiana University, Bureau of Governmental Research, 1961), pp. 3–4.

116   These facts are not likely to cause anyone to demur. Their significance, however, may escape notice: they reveal more than a vagrant wisp of social class. The typical legislator is far from a typical citizen. Not only is his career launched from a more elevated social station than the typical citizen's, but it is also launched amid more of the social advantages conferred by education. Formal educational attainment thus appears as one of the central criteria in the winnowing-out process under which legislative candidates are recruited and elected. An invitation to legislative candidacy is not likely to come unbidden to those whose credentials fall short. Yet it would be interesting to know whether the educational attainments of candidates vary according to the intensity of party competition within districts. Possibly each party in one-party jurisdictions has less pressure on it to pick candidates with substantial formal education—the dominant party because its victory is assured, the minority party because its cause is hopeless. The minority party's election prospects, in fact, may be so dismal that its leaders consider it a profound advance if anyone can be induced to run under its banner.

(4) *The predominant occupations found among legislators are the professions, business, and farming.* We have already noted the prevalence of these occupations among the fathers of U.S. senators. Here we shall consider briefly the occupations of legislators themselves. Despite the fact that Congress is in session on virtually a year-round basis, many members are able to retain active affiliations with their professions or businesses. At the state level, where brief and biennial sessions are common, legislators find it relatively easy to hold other positions outside the legislature, including some which are political, such as jobs in city government.

The United States Senate presents the most striking example of the dominant representation of the professions in legislative assemblies. At the time of first election to the Senate, the Matthews' study discloses, 82 per cent of the senators were members of the professions—lawyers, teachers, journalists, professors, engineers, and the like. Fifteen per cent were proprietors and officials. Subsequent to their election, some switching of occupations occurred, resulting in a classification of the principal nonpolitical occupations of senators as 64 per cent professions, 29 per cent proprietors and officials, and 7 per cent farmers.

The conspicuous fact about the occupations of legislators in both Congress and the states is that lawyers are predominant. The legislature is not a sacred place to which only lawyers may repair, nor is it likely to become one, but the fact is that lawyers have somehow won a great advantage in the struggle for legislative office. How great this advantage is, especially at the national level, may be seen in the assorted statistics of Table 5.1.

Choosing the lawyer as legislator is a vogue of long standing; at the same time the "overrepresentation" of lawyers in assemblies has been a continuing object of critical comment, for although lawyers compose but a fraction of 1 per cent of the total labor force, ordinarily they occupy one-quarter to one-half or more of the legislative seats.

Several circumstances are associated with the emergence and development of the lawyer as policy-maker. In the first place, his profession, like that of the physician, outstrips most others in prestige—evidently an important factor both to party organizations in search of candidates and to voters in quest of representatives. Second, like all successful politicians, the lawyer

TABLE 5.1

Lawyers, Businessmen, and Farmers in Legislative Assemblies (Percentage)

	U.S. Senate, 1971	Arkansas, 1957–65	Colorado, 1957–66	Iowa, 1967	Minnesota, 1959		Mississippi, 1946–68		Oklahoma, 1967		Washington, 1941–51	
					H	S	H	S	H	S	H	S
Lawyers	66*	26	26	14	23	36	30		22	44	15	17
Businessmen	16	49	31	36	24	19	17		41	35	34	32
Farmers	7	13	13	33	31	25	38		21	6	19	20

SOURCES: Data for the U. S. Senate are from the *Congressional Quarterly Weekly Report*, January 15, 1971, pp. 127–28. State legislative data are from Donald T. Wells, "The Arkansas Legislature," in *Power in American State Legislatures*, ed. Alex B. Lacy, Jr., (New Orleans: Tulane University Press, 1967), p. 11; Victor S. Hjelm and Joseph P. Pisciotte, "Profiles and Careers of Colorado State Legislators," *Western Political Quarterly*, XXI (December 1968), 701; G. R. Boynton, Samuel C. Patterson, and Ronald D. Hedlund, "The Missing Links in Legislative Politics: Attentive Constituents," *Journal of Politics*, XXI (August 1969), 704; G. Theodore Mitau, *Politics in Minnesota* (Minneapolis: University of Minnesota Press, 1960), p. 58; C. N. Fortenberry and Edward H. Hobbs, "The Mississippi Legislature," in Lacy, ed., *op. cit.*, p. 92; John W. Wood, "The Oklahoma Legislature," in Lacy, ed., *op. cit.*, p. 145; and Paul Beckett and Celeste Sunderland, "Washington State's Lawmakers: Some Personnel Factors in the Washington Legislature," *Western Political Quarterly*, X (March 1959), 194–99.

NOTE: H = house; S = senate.

*All U. S. senators who list law as their occupation are counted here as lawyers; a few lawyer-senators also list business or farming as their occupation.

118 is an adroit broker of ideas as well as of interests. Legal training, if deficient and illiberal on some counts, is extraordinarily successful in assisting its recipients to master the intricacies of human relations, to excel in verbal exchange, to understand complex and technical information, and to employ varying tactics to seize advantage. These qualities of mind and make-up serve the legislator no less than the campaigner. Third, the lawyer, unlike the usual farmer, teacher, or mechanic, ordinarily finds it convenient to link his work to steady participation in politics; and political involvement may well bring an unearned increment by attracting, through publicity and social visibility, new clients and higher fees. Finally, while men in the workaday activities of other occupations stand on the outskirts of power, the lawyer, with his knowledge and skills, is automatically the representative of power:

> The attorney is the accepted agent of all politically effective groups of the American people. As the lawyer is habitually the representative of the grasping and abused in litigation, as he is increasingly the negotiator between businessmen with conflicting interests, as he is more and more the spokesman of individual and corporation in public relations—so is the lawyer today depended upon to represent citizens in the lawmaking body.[9]

For these and other reasons,[10] the lawyer has won a prominent place in the legislature. And from awareness of the lawyer's hegemony, it is a short and simple step to conclude that such "overmembership" has untoward consequences. It is said, for example, especially in the case of state legislatures, that only inferior lawyers become available for legislative service, since first-rate lawyers are unwilling to jeopardize lucrative practices for the small rewards and the vicissitudes of political life. Or one hears that lawyer-lawmakers, steeped in the study of precedent, tend instinctively to favor the conservative or traditional response to questions of social and economic policy. Finally, the imputation is made that lawyer-members come to wield great influence because they vote as a bloc, carefully advancing the welfare of the legal profession and the best interests of powerful economic groups with whom attorneys, by reason of function, are natural allies.

Despite the basic plausibility and attractiveness of these charges, they contain a fatal flaw, which is simply that no evidence exists to support them. A study by David R. Derge of the lawyer-members of the Illinois and Missouri legislatures finds these contentions to be bogus. Using the

9 Hyneman, "Who Makes Our Laws?," 569.

10 In some states urbanism (and the cultural and political factors associated with it) may contribute to the prominence of lawyers in the legislature. This appears to be the case in New York, where a large proportion of the lawyers in the legislature are elected from New York City. New York lawyer-legislators enter the legislature at an earlier age than nonlawyers and do not stay as long. Legislative service for the big-city lawyer is frequently a steppingstone to a higher public office, such as a judgeship in New York City. See the studies of Leonard I. Ruchelman, "Lawyers in the New York State Legislature: The Urban Factor," *Midwest Journal of Political Science,* X (November 1966), 484–97, and *Political Careers: Recruitment Through the Legislature* (Rutherford, N.J.: Fairleigh Dickinson University Press, 1970). Also consult Alan Fiellin, "Recruitment and Legislative Role Conceptions: A Conceptual Scheme and a Case Study," *Western Political Quarterly,* XX (June 1967), 271–87.

Martindale-Hubbell ratings of legal ability as a standard, he found that lawyer-legislators were "on the whole at least as good as, and sometimes superior to, their professional colleagues outside the assembly halls." An analysis of the voting behavior of lawyer and nonlawyer legislators on bills with a liberal-conservative cast (e.g., social and labor legislation) disclosed that lawyers were no more opposed to legislation benefiting the workingman than were nonlawyers. Indeed, the behavior of the two groups was quite similar; party membership provided the most significant difference. As to the charge that lawyers vote as a bloc—with high cohesion—analysis of contested roll-call votes revealed that lawyer solidarity is mainly a myth. (Other groups, including farmer-legislators, had higher indices of cohesion.) Nor did the investigation yield evidence to support the belief that lawyers are preoccupied with self-interest legislation designed to improve the general practice of law. Although the study is but a tentative probing of the charge that lawyers have something of a monopoly of power in the legislature and that they use their power to resist policy innovations, the findings ought to induce stock-taking among critics alarmed over the number of lawyers in the seats of power.[11]

Although the evidence is fragmentary, it appears that the two occupations most heavily represented in the legislature are those of business and law. It is common to find state legislatures in which over one-third of the members are businessmen; within this group, those engaged in the insurance business, real estate, and banking and investment are particularly numerous. In the less-urbanized states of the Midwest and South, legislators engaged in farming are likely to be about as numerous as those engaged in either business or law. Farmers, however, are not often elected to Congress.

In Congress, businessmen are second only to lawyers in number of seats held. Viewed from the standpoint of party, there are twice as many Republicans as Democrats with business backgrounds in the Senate. This circumstance is attributable in part to the Republican party's traditional association with the business community and in part to the nature of the constituencies from which businessmen are elected. Senators with business backgrounds are most frequently elected from mixed urban-rural states, which normally are Republican, and less frequently from predominantly urban or predominantly rural states. Hence, to some extent at least, the explanation for the large number of Republican senators drawn from the ranks of business lies in the rural-urban dimension in the states. It is interesting to find that the highly urbanized states thrust up almost as many Democrats as Republicans with backgrounds in business.[12]

It is beyond dispute that both lawyers and businessmen inhabit the legislatures to a degree well beyond that to which their numbers in the population would lay claim. Can the familiar charge of "overrepresentation" be assigned to the farmer-legislator as well? The truth of the matter is that in a number of legislatures farmers have less representation, based on their contribution to the population, than is their due. There are probably as

[11] David R. Derge, "The Lawyer as Decision-Maker in the American State Legislature," *Journal of Politics,* XXI (August 1959), 426–31. See also another study of lawyers by Joseph A. Schlesinger, "Lawyers and American Politics: A Clarified View," *Midwest Journal of Political Science,* I (May 1957), 26–39.

[12] Matthews, *U.S. Senators and Their World,* pp. 40–41.

120   many states in which actual farmer membership is less than an "ideal" allocation as there are states in which their membership is excessive. At the national level, a study of the hometowns of members of the 90th Congress shows significant *under*representation of rural, small-town America. A widespread belief to the contrary, the members of Congress are not simply a collection of "small-town boys."[13]

(5) *The typical American legislator is male, white, Protestant, and of Anglo-Saxon origin.* Although there are only a handful of studies of the racial, religious, and nationality backgrounds of legislators, such evidence as exists shows that certain groups are markedly overrepresented and that other groups are markedly underrepresented in American assemblies. In general, the usual minority groups—Negroes, Catholics, Jews, and southern Europeans—are elected to legislative office much less frequently than their proportions of the whole population would warrant.

The religious affiliation of members of Congress is a convenient starting point for this discussion. Denominations of high social status, such as Episcopalian and Presbyterian, regularly are overrepresented in the membership of Congress. Holding less than 3 percent of the church membership in the nation in 1971, Episcopalians constituted approximately 12 percent of the membership of the 92d Congress (1971–72). For Presbyterians, the percentages were 3.3 and 16. Methodists, with about 10 percent of the total church membership, made up 16 percent of the congressional membership. Overall, legislators belonging to Protestant denominations made up 75 percent of the membership of the 92d Congress. Reporting on church membership in 1971, the *Yearbook of American Churches* listed 54 per cent of the national church membership as Protestant.

Catholics and Jews, on the other hand, do not win seats in Congress in proportion to their numbers. With 37 percent of the church membership in 1971, Catholics accounted for 21 percent of the 92d Congress; Jews, representing 4.5 percent of the church membership of the nation, held 2.6 percent of the seats. Another aspect to the election of Catholics and Jews to Congress worth noting is their distribution by state and party. Nearly all Catholic and Jewish members are elected from northern industrial states, notably from the major cities where their numbers are substantial. Of the 101 Catholic members of the House, 58 were elected from six states: New York (14), Massachusetts (10), New Jersey (10), Illinois (9), Pennsylvania (8), and Ohio (7). Eight of the fourteen Jewish members of the House came from New York. Predictably, most Catholics (76 percent) and Jews (78 percent) in the 92d Congress were Democrats.

The evidence is firm that religious affiliation is a factor in the recruitment and election of legislative candidates. Year in and year out, Alabama, Mississippi, and South Carolina will send to Congress delegations largely composed of Baptists and Methodists; New York City will thrust up a delegation almost solidly Catholic and Jewish; Minnesota will have a significant number of Lutherans in its delegation; and the "silk-stocking" districts in urban and suburban areas will dispatch to Washington a large proportion of Episcopalians and Presbyterians. And, as one study has shown, when

---

[13] LeRoy N. Rieselbach, "Congressmen as 'Small Town Boys': A Research Note," *Midwest Journal of Political Science,* XIV (May 1970), 321–30.

new members appear to replace old, the chances are about four out of five that the successor will be of the same religious group (e.g., Protestant replacing Protestant) and about one out of four that the new congressman will represent the exact religious affiliation of the former member (e.g., Methodist replacing Methodist).[14]

By and large, Negroes have not won as much from politics as their numbers warrant. Discrimination diminishes their power. This is especially true in the holding of elective offices. Normally, predominantly Negro constituencies in northern core cities will elect Negro lawmakers, but because of the persistence of housing ghettoes, a densely populated Negro community is likely to be compressed into one, two, or a few legislative districts and usually into a single congressional district. Negro legislators, it is safe to say, are produced by an irreducible number of Negro districts. Populous Harlem in New York City was for years split into two congressional districts, serving to divide the Negro vote and thereby to prevent the election of a Negro congressman. At times, Negroes have been ignored as legislative candidates in districts in which their number is great because, in the words of white political leaders, "Negroes are not organized to win recognition."[15]

If Negroes were to gain representation in Congress equal to their proportion of the population, there would be fifty blacks in the House of Representatives and eleven in the Senate. In point of fact, however, only three blacks have ever been elected to the Senate, and Edward W. Brooke of Massachusetts, elected in 1966, was the first since 1881. In recent years, blacks have improved their position markedly in the lower house of Congress. In the 92d Congress (1971–72), for example, twelve blacks served in the House—the largest number ever elected to that chamber. Four states —California, Illinois, New York, and Michigan—had two black members each, while there were single black members from Maryland, Missouri, Ohio, and Pennsylvania. All the black congressmen were Democrats.

The story is roughly, though not precisely, the same in state assemblies. Although Negroes are underrepresented in nearly all of the state legislatures, significant gains have been made in recent years. As recently as 1960, there were only thirty-six black state legislators throughout the country. In 1970–71 there were 205 Negro members in forty-four state legislatures; the vast majority, of course, were "core-city" Democrats. In Ohio, as Table 5.2 shows, the proportion of blacks in the lower house exceeds the proportion of blacks in the population. The Missouri, Michigan, and Illinois legislatures do not lag far behind. Georgia leads all the southern states in the number of Negro legislators, although even in that case the number is small in proportion to the Negro population of the state. It remains true that in many states, in the North as well as the South, the underrepresentation or absence of Negroes in the legislature is an abrasive fact of life, one both understood and deplored by Negro political leaders and by the rank and file. If ticket-balancing were less the political imperative it is, if

---

[14] Madge M. McKinney, "Religion and Elections," *Public Opinion Quarterly,* VIII (Spring 1944), 110–14. The data on the religious affiliation of congressmen noted in this section appear in the *Congressional Quarterly Weekly Report,* week ending January 15, 1971, pp. 126–33.

[15] G. James Fleming, *An All-Negro Ticket in Baltimore* (New York: McGraw-Hill Book Company, Inc., Eagleton Institute Cases in Practical Politics, 1960), p. 3.

TABLE 5.2

Negro Membership in State Legislatures (Leading States), 1970–71

State	Lower Houses			Senates			Negro % of Total Population, 1970
	Total Members	Negro Members	Negro % of Total	Total Members	Negro Members	Negro % of Total	
Missouri	122	15	12.3	52	2	3.8	10.3
Ohio	99	11	11.1	33	2	6.1	9.1
Michigan	110	12	10.9	38	3	7.9	11.1
Maryland	142	15	10.6	43	4	9.3	17.8
Delaware	39	4	10.2	19	1	5.3	14.3
Illinois	177	16	9.0	58	4	6.9	12.8
New York	150	11	7.3	57	3	5.3	11.4
Georgia	195	13	6.7	56	2	3.6	26.0
California	80	5	6.3	40	1	2.5	6.5
Tennessee	99	6	6.1	33	2	6.1	16.0
New Jersey	80	4	5.0	40	0	0.0	10.7
Pennsylvania	203	10	4.9	50	2	4.0	8.6
Oklahoma	99	4	4.0	48	1	2.1	6.9
Connecticut	177	5	2.8	36	1	2.8	5.9

SOURCE: Data on Negro state legislators (as of December 1970) are from the *Congressional Quarterly—Current American Government,* Spring 1971, p. 27.

states were less urbanized than they are, Negro representation (and that of other minority groups) undoubtedly would be even further removed from parity. Over the long haul, legislative reapportionment and increased Negro voter registration are likely to contribute to the election of a larger number of Negro legislators.

Although more successful than Negroes in electing their number to legislative assemblies, national minorities also gain less than a full measure of "direct" representation. Partial corroboration for this statement is found in the number of foreign-born members elected to Congress. Between 1789 and 1949, 374 foreign-born men and women were elected to Congress out of a total of 9,618 individuals who sat in Congress, a percentage of 3.9.[16] Over most of this interval of better than a century-and-a-half, as much as 10–15 per cent of the population was born outside the United States.

First- or second-generation status is not, of course, everywhere a handicap to election to legislative office. In some states and in most of the major cities, certain congressional and state legislative seats are plainly earmarked by the political organizations for nationality occupancy, as others are reserved for blacks, Catholics, and Jews. In particular, the Democratic party has a close identification with ethnic groups. The Chicago delegations to Congress and to the Illinois legislature invariably contain a sizeable contingent of men and women of Irish, Italian, and Polish extraction, while Milwaukee

[16] The data on foreign-born congressmen are found in Murray G. Lawson, "The Foreign-Born in Congress, 1789–1949: A Statistical Summary," *American Political Science Review,* LI (December 1957), 1183–89.

political organizations are habitually alert to the need for fielding an array of legislative candidates of German and Polish ancestry. In Connecticut, Massachusetts, and Rhode Island, Irish and Italians are prominent among candidates for the legislature and for Congress. Providing for ethnic representation has long been a function of the political organizations in the major cities, one which they monitor with great care where national minorities are prominent.

Eventually a dominant "American" culture may dislodge the distinctive cultures of urban ethnic groups, making it less important for party managers to strive for balance in their slates of candidates. In the meantime, cultivation of ethnic groups by the party organizations appears not only in the best interests of the parties but also in the best interests of the groups themselves, seeking, as they do, to make their way to the centers of power. Whatever ethical questions it may seem to pose, "cultivation" is a two-way street, as well traveled and as well lighted on one side as the other.

Party managers and political organizations have assiduously suppressed the impulse to nominate women for legislative office. Normally, there are around fifteen women in both houses of Congress at any one time. Perhaps 40 per cent of this number will have been elected to serve out their husband's terms—a practice called "widow's succession." Most of the women who succeed to their husband's office serve only that term. In the fifty state legislatures at any one time there are usually about 250–350 women, perhaps 3 per cent of the total membership.[17] Although an increase in the number of women legislators is an agreeable idea to the unflagging supporters of equal rights for women, there is no reason to believe that an increase in their number would result in notably different legislation.

Briefly, what we have gained from the previous pages is this. No American legislature comes close to housing a cross section of the population it serves. The political system inevitably has built-in biases, numerous devices for the containment of minority-group aspirations for office and for the advancement of dominant segments of the population. Some groups win often, others lose often. Although the data on social-class attachments of legislators are fragmentary, they provide us with more than simple imaginings to support the view that national and state legislators speak mainly in the idiom and accents of the middle and upper classes.

The facts of social class in legislative representation, however, must be treated warily. They may conceal as much as they disclose and may invite misinterpretation. In the first place, they do not show that the legis-

17 Mary L. Worthman, "Political Role of American Women: A Study of Congresswomen" (Master's thesis, University of Wisconsin, 1966). This thesis indicates that congresswomen resemble congressmen in terms of education, occupation, and political background. They are somewhat more likely to come from "safe" districts and to follow party lines than congressmen. Between 1917 and 1964, seventy women served in Congress. A comprehensive description of these congresswomen is available in Emmy E. Werner, "Women in Congress: 1917–1964," *Western Political Quarterly*, XIX (March 1966), 16–30. In James D. Barber's fourfold typology of Connecticut legislators (Spectators, Advertisers, Reluctants, and Lawmakers), women constitute a disproportionate number of Spectators—"Typically a middle-aged, lower status housewife of modest achievements, limited skills, and restricted ambitions." *The Lawmakers: Recruitment and Adaptation to Legislative Life* (New Haven: Yale University Press, 1965), p. 214.

124 lature succumbs to upper-class pressures or that it is but a transmission belt for moving along benefits to privileged groups. Second, there is the matter of representing the interests of social groups as well as of representing the groups themselves. It is one thing to say that few men of working-class background ever make it to the legislature and quite another to say that the interests of the working class are treated unsympathetically by men not of this class. It is one thing to point to the ascendant position of the lawyer-legislator and quite another to say that he is preoccupied with improving the fortunes of the legal profession or any other special group.

Nevertheless, it is plain that for some groups, perhaps especially for Negroes, there are major grounds for distress over the failure of the political process to make room for them at the top. Every day public policies emerge that intrude on their interests and define their stake in society; yet their actual representation in positions of power is minimal or nonexistent. We might have greater confidence that value allocation by the legislature would approximate more nearly the interests of all segments of the public if the recruitment process produced a more nearly representative set of decision-makers.

At the least, this glance at the characteristics of American legislators ought to show sufficiently that they are not run-of-the-mill citizens. Their formal education, more than anything else, argues that they have had much better preparation for legislative service than the ordinary citizen.[18] But what no social background study has shown is whether they are usually men of integrity, men who reckon in terms of the general well-being of the social system, men in whom the public has reason to impart trust. Very little can be stated with certainty about the presence or absence of these qualities among the legislators as a whole. Nor, for that matter, can much be said with certainty about the presence or absence of these qualities among bankers, labor leaders, or college professors.

Legislative Experience: Tenure and Turnover

Although some differences between Congress and the typical state legislature are no more than minor subsurface variations, this is far from the case with respect to the tenure and turnover of their memberships. The membership of Congress is tenaciously stationary, while the membership of most state legislatures steadily undergoes major change.

CONGRESS

There are few if any fresh or effective formulas for wresting a seat from an incumbent member of Congress. Indeed, it is something of a novelty when significant numbers of incumbents lose in other than presidential landslide

[18] For a study that contrasts state legislators, attentive publics, and the general public in terms of their socio-economic status, political awareness, and political activity (in Iowa), see G. R. Boynton, Samuel C. Patterson, and Ronald D. Hedlund, "The Missing Links in Legislative Politics: Attentive Constituents," *Journal of Politics,* XXI (August 1969), 700–721.

elections. Accordingly, Congress has become an aging institution.[19] Trends which show the ratio of newcomers to old hands in the House of Representatives help to establish this point. When President McKinley took office the ratio of first- and second-term members to members in their tenth term or beyond was 34 to 1. The ratio was 25 to 1 when Woodrow Wilson became president, 6.3 to 1 when Franklin D. Roosevelt first took office, 3.3 to 1 at the time Dwight Eisenhower assumed the presidency, and 1.6 to 1 when John F. Kennedy was inaugurated. Congressmen have an awesome survival rate, as is shown in Table 5.3. In the 92d Congress, for example, the average member of the House had already served 5.9 *terms*, nearly twice as long as the average member elected to the 58th Congress. Moreover, there were eleven times as many members in the 92d Congress who had served ten or more terms as there were in the 58th Congress.

The broad significance of a high degree of congressional stability is difficult to establish. The fact is plain that contemporary Congresses are weighted heavily on the side of experience. Whether the current mixture of newcomers and veterans is more conducive to effective legislative performance than mixtures of half a century ago is impossible to say. Certain consequences of stability, however, can be identified. One is that the member of Congress today is more of a professional than the member elected around the turn of the century. His increased tenure affords him a much better opportunity to become familiar with legislative procedures and the multiple roles of the legislator. Second, the "survival" trend accentuates the importance of achieving seniority as a means of gaining influence in Congress, since it takes much longer to rise to a chairmanship in a veteran-dominated institution. (See Table 5.4.) Third, the increasing tenure of congressmen probably serves to strengthen the House's position in its relations with the Senate; House committee chairmen now have service records that are at least the equal of those of Senate chairmen. Finally, the power of the House *vis-à-vis* the executive would appear to be strengthened as a consequence of the growing tenure of members; presidents and bureaucrats alike must contend with committee chairmen who have accumulated singular experience in their special fields. The stability of congressional membership may be a partial explanation for the conflict that sometimes dominates executive-legislative relations. The time perspectives of the president and members of Congress are far from identical—the president, limited to two terms, is necessarily in a hurry to fashion a program, while veteran members of Congress from safe districts can afford to take their time. No one is ringing a bell for them—what is urgent for the president is not necessarily urgent for them.

[19] This discussion of congressional longevity relies mainly on the work of T. Richard Witmer, "The Aging of the House," *Political Science Quarterly,* LXXIX (December 1964), 526–41. For a study of contrasting career patterns in nineteenth- and twentieth-century Congresses, see H. Douglas Price, "The Congressional Career Then and Now," in *Congressional Behavior,* ed. Nelson W. Polsby (New York: Random House, Inc., 1971), pp. 14–27. Although Senate careers have not changed markedly over the last century, there has been a remarkable change in the House over that period. Two features in particular stand out. The typical House member today has a much longer career in the House than his nineteenth-century counterpart and, second, there is much less turnover in leadership ranks today than in the past.

TABLE 5.3

Distribution of Membership of the House of Representatives by Terms of Service

Congress	Terms of Service	Percentage of Members	Average Number of Terms of Service
92d	10 or more	20.0	5.9
(1971–72)	6–9	24.0	
	3–5	34.5	
	1–2	21.5	
		100.0	
	10 or more	17.3	
90th	6–9	20.7	
(1967–68)	3–5	33.2	5.5
	1–2	28.8	
		100.0	
	10 or more	17.0	
88th	6–9	28.7	
(1963–64)	3–5	26.5	5.7
	1–2	27.8	
		100.0	
	10 or more	11.1	
78th	6–9	16.6	
(1943–44)	3–5	36.9	4.4
	1–2	35.4	
		100.0	
	10 or more	4.2	
68th	6–9	16.0	
(1923–24)	3–5	35.9	3.6
	1–2	43.9	
		100.0	
	10 or more	1.8	
58th	6–9	11.4	
(1903–4)	3–5	38.2	3.1
	1–2	48.6	
		100.0	

SOURCE: Adapted from data in T. Richard Witmer, "The Aging of the House," *Political Science Quarterly,* LXXIX (December 1964), 538. Data calculated by author of article in 1971 for the 92d Congress.

The virtues of stability are often extolled, perhaps with good reason. Continuity, experience, expertise, and prudence—all are associated with a membership that continues relatively intact from Congress to Congress. But stability may also be seen in a light that illuminates its disadvantages. Somnolence sometimes settles over stable institutions. Opportunities for introducing major changes in policy or organization tend to be small, for changes often pose risks for the leadership, perhaps especially for committee chairmen. The price of continuity may be a low level of adaptability and a timidity toward experimentation. The ironic by-product of a stable institu-

TABLE 5.4

*Average Number of Terms of Service of House Chairmen and Ranking Majority
and Minority Members of Selected Committees*

Congress	Chairman		Ranking Majority Member		Ranking Minority Member	
	Dem.	Rep.	Dem.	Rep.	Dem.	Rep.
53d	6.8	—	4.6	—	—	6.4
54th	—	6.7	—	4.2	5.6	—
62d	7.4	—	6.6	—	—	10.1
66th	—	9.2	—	6.7	8.6	—
72d	10.8	—	8.6	—	—	10.6
80th	—	12.6	—	9.2	14.7	—
81st	15.6	—	10.0	—	—	12.1
83d	—	13.2	—	10.7	15.0	—
84th	14.5	—	10.9	—	—	14.2
88th	18.0	—	13.0	—	—	11.8
90th	16.6	—	12.9	—	—	9.5
92d	18.6	—	13.4	—	—	12.4

SOURCE: T. Richard Witmer, "The Aging of the House," *Political Science Quarterly*, LXXIX (December 1964), 533. Reprinted by permission of the *Political Science Quarterly*.
NOTE: Committees are Appropriations, Banking and Currency, Interstate and Foreign Commerce, Judiciary, Military Affairs, Naval Affairs, Rules, and Ways and Means. (In more recent Congresses the Armed Services Committee has been substituted for Military Affairs and Naval Affairs).

tion, made that way partly by the public itself, may be popular disaffection over the institution's reluctance or inability to come to terms with new demands and new conditions. Insofar as Congress is concerned, the evidence is less than persuasive on either side of the tenure-turnover equation.

IN THE STATES

Unlike the situation in Congress, a persistent condition of the American state legislature is a high rate of turnover among members. Among scholars, at least, there is widespread agreement that legislative turnover is excessive in many states and that greater membership stability would contribute to the strengthening of the institution. What are the advantages of having a significant number of incumbents returned to legislative office each election? One summary of the arguments holds that "it is only actual experience in a legislative body that enables a legislator to acquaint himself with the intricacies of governmental machinery, to permit him to exercise sound judgment . . . in respect to the improvement of public administration, to aid him in distinguishing between public interest and selfish demand, and to enable him to develop the facility for compromise and bargaining. . . . "[20]

Charles S. Hyneman, whose initial studies of legislative tenure and turnover posed the problem of legislative inexperience, observes:

[20] George S. Blair, "The Case for Cumulative Voting in Illinois," *Northwestern University Law Review*, XLVII (July–August 1952), 344–57, quotation on p. 353.

128   Each program of public policy must root itself in a mass of existing legislation; and each body of lawmakers, whether eager to push forward or concerned to preserve the *status quo*, will profit from a thorough acquaintance with the procedures and ways of the agencies, private and governmental, that put so much of legislative policy into execution. Old-timers in the legislature are more likely than newcomers to possess this needed familiarity with existing legislation and with the ways of these persons and groups that transform the black words of a statute into patterns of action.[21]

Although state legislatures are often charged with being invulnerable to change, the same cannot be said of their memberships. More than thirty years ago, Hyneman's survey of legislative tenure in about one-fifth of the states disclosed that men and women move in and out of legislative office with the regularity of a game of musical chairs. For example, at the time of the survey: (1) in all but one lower chamber (N.Y.) more than 25 per cent of the members were serving their first session in office; (2) turnover was especially high in the lower house, with a few states having 50–60 per cent freshman members each session; (3) on an average, 39.6 per cent of the members of lower houses and 20.3 per cent of the members of the senates were in their first legislative session; and (4) most significantly, members relinquished their seats much more often for reasons of voluntary retirement than as a result of defeats in primary or general elections. Turnover at the state legislative level continues to be high today, though not as high as it was the first half of the twentieth century.

The record shows that, in the main, membership instability is not to be charged to whimsical publics, to periodic election landslides that snap off legislative careers at an early stage, or to the character of the districts (e.g., about as many urban as rural legislators have short tenure in office). Hence what we need to account for is the high rate of voluntary withdrawals. One possibility is that legislators simply weary of the steady barrage of criticism leveled at them by constituents, pressure groups, and newspapers—and choose retirement:

> It's a big problem. It's a problem of time. Legislative duties are bad enough, but handshaking, dinners and speeches are the worst part. My phone rang 68 times yesterday. Politicians get a bad break from most newspapers and political scientists. A guy in his right mind wouldn't continue. I'm not going to worry if I get knocked out like these guys who make a complete career of it.[22]

Second, in some districts there are tacit agreements that seats in the legislature are to be rotated from county to county or from city to city, election after election; where this practice obtains, longevity is out of the question. "I'm running now, but I doubt that I'll do it again. They usually limit you to two terms. In such a large county it has to be spread around." Third, a fair number of legislators drop out of the legislature in order to run for

---

21 "Tenure and Turnover of Legislative Personnel," *The Annals,* CXCV (January 1938), 22.
22 This statement and those by state legislators in the following paragraph appear in John C. Wahlke *et al., op. cit.,* pp. 127–28.

other political offices. Fourth, there are doubtless a number of legislators who withdraw from office because they believe they have served long enough, or find the job too demanding, or are simply bored with it. The best explanation, however, is rooted in economics. According to Charles Hyneman, "the chief reason why legislators find one or two terms enough is a financial one; their experience proves what they already suspected—that it is money out of the pocket to serve in the legislature." Legislators' comments drawn from *The Legislative System* make the point clearly:

> I think it's time I devoted myself to my law practice. Being in the legislature has hurt my practice and cost me money. Also, I don't think anyone should make a career of serving in the legislature. You do your part and then make room for the next guy.

> Any way you look at it, the job means a sacrifice to you, your home, and your business. Most people don't realize that there are continual demands on your time outside the legislative sessions as well. I don't intend to make a career of politics.

> It depends on business. If it gets bad I won't be able to run. That's the way it is for a businessman. It's different for a lawyer. I can't depend on the pay up here. It doesn't even pay the food bill. I have four children. And the expenses are high, hotel bills and everything.

Although a number of states have increased legislative salaries and expense allowances, most states continue to pay inadequately. Burdened by low pay, high costs, and the frustrations of the job, members serve a brief tour of office and drop out.[23] Some will turn to positions in city and county governments where, perhaps surprisingly, salaries are usually more remunerative.

It may be that the presence of a large proportion of old hands in the legislature is something of a mixed blessing. Viewing politics "on the seamy side" in Rhode Island, Lockard remarks that "Experience for a legislator in some cases leads only to more refined means of bargaining and dealing for personally desired ends."[24] Even though this possibility has to be granted, the presumptions in favor of a legislative body of experienced members seem to be more persuasive.

Countless legislators have testified that it takes several sessions to gain familiarity with the legislative process and to come to terms with state problems: becoming an effective legislator is to some extent the result of

---

23 Heavy turnover in state legislatures is possibly less damaging than commonly supposed. New and less effective legislators are not expected to play a significant role in the legislative process. A study of the Michigan legislature concludes: "The structure of interpersonal relations within legislative systems functions to place legislators with high degrees of skill and conscientiousness in the center of the legislative system and to increase their influence, and to isolate legislators with low degrees of skill and conscientiousness on the periphery of the legislative system and to decrease their influence." Stephen V. Monsma, "Interpersonal Relations in the Legislative System: A Study of the 1964 Michigan House of Representatives," *Midwest Journal of Political Science,* X (August 1966), 363.

24 Duane Lockard, *New England State Politics* (Princeton: Princeton University Press, 1959), p. 220.

130 acquiring experience in lawmaking. If accumulated legislative experience is desirable, are there means by which it may be secured?

A response to the problem that is modest in scope, yet certain to make legislative service less transient, would be to lengthen the term of office of house members, perhaps to four years, as it is in most state senates where high turnover ordinarily is less of a problem. But change of this order does not come easily. When confronted with amendments to provide for four-year terms for house members, the typical response of voters has been to reject them.

Another estimate, supported mainly by intuition, grows out of the fact that state legislatures everywhere have failed to win any great measure of public confidence. Outstanding citizens are not apt to press impatiently for a seat in the legislature, or, if elected, to occupy it for long, if they find the institution feeble or unworthy, its powers and initiative shackled by ancient constitutions and outworn rules and procedures. We have argued earlier (Chapter 2) that the "bottoming-out" of the prestige decline of the state legislature is unlikely to occur so long as the popular view of the legislature remains one of suspicion or indifference. Under present circumstances, professionalization of the legislature, marked by the tendency of competent individuals to seek office and to invest many years in lawmaking, will be slow to develop.

The best short-run answer for breaking the turnover cycle lies, we believe, in what is by now a part of the "conventional wisdom" of political scientists. The tenet holds that a seat in the legislature may become a full-time career for members if they are given a salary that is more in line with those available in business and the professions. It is reasonable to suppose, though difficult to prove, that more lawmakers will be induced to stand for reelection and, equally important, to devote more time to public responsibilities than to outside economic interests (e.g., private law practice) if their income from public service is respectable. The difficulty in achieving a bold advance in legislative salaries is that, in the judgment of many legislators, the public is adamantly opposed to such action. At the least, legislators who must face the voters in another election *believe* that a "yea" vote on a pay-raise bill may lead to their defeat in the next election—such is the "conventional wisdom" of the wary legislator.[25]

Pay and Perquisites

IN THE STATES

State legislators traditionally have been among the lowest paid public officers found at any level of American government. Although in recent years many states have improved legislative salaries, the new pay levels, with some exceptions, tend to preserve the doubtful tradition that individuals should

---

[25] Very likely the best strategy for increasing legislative salaries is to link pay raises to legislative reform. This was done in a number of states in the middle and late 1960s. Apparently the public finds it easier to accept higher legislative salaries if there is evidence that the legislature is making an effort to strengthen its capabilities and modernize its procedures and practices.

not make legislative service a career. The idea of the citizen as part-time legislator has an uncommon virility in American politics; it helps sustain the practice of paying woefully inadequate salaries to legislators in many states.

Two basic salary-payment plans are used. The oldest method, which is still used in fourteen states, provides for payment on a *per diem* basis. More recently, states have adopted an annual salary plan, the method used presently in thirty-six states. In some states salaries are fixed wholly or in part by the constitution, making it a laborious task to effect changes. In Rhode Island, a state that sets salary in the constitution, citizens can point with pride to the fact that legislators are still paid the five dollars *per diem* begun in 1900. Substantially higher salaries are paid in those states in which compensation is set by statute rather than by constitution.

Of the thirty-six states that pay a fixed salary to legislators, California leads with *biennial* compensation of $48,950, followed by Michigan ($39,500), New York ($36,000), Illinois ($35,000), Florida ($33,600), Alaska ($32,300), Hawaii ($28,860), Maryland ($26,500), Massachusetts ($26,300), and Ohio ($25,500). At the bottom of the scale of states using the salary plan are New Hampshire ($200), West Virginia ($3,000), Arkansas ($3,600), Connecticut ($4,000), and Maine ($4,100). On the whole, legislators paid on a *per diem* basis fare much worse than those paid according to a salary plan. As of 1971, the average biennial compensation for all fifty states was $13,733. This sum, as in the case of individual states, represents "realized" compensation—that is, it includes salary, daily pay, *and* expense allowances.[26]

One need not believe that high salaries are a panacea for all the ills of the legislature to discover the inadequacy of salary provisions for state lawmakers. If here and there some state legislators are under the thumb of lobbyists who buy their meals and drinks or otherwise favor them, or of interest groups which place them on their payrolls in the interim between sessions, should such wayward confidence prove astonishing? If the legislatures are failing to attract individuals of unusual merit, if they are unable to retain most members for more than one or a few sessions, if they are low on imagination and seldom the authors of bold and original proposals— the familiar assertions—is there reason to believe that inadequate salaries have something to do with it? The burden of the evidence, it has seemed to many observers, warrants such an inference.

What constitutes a reasonable standard of remuneration for state legislators is difficult to decide for many reasons, not the least of which are the variations between the states in length and frequency of sessions and in the demands of the job during and between sessions. But this does not leave us without a solution. A general prescription would call for states to pay legislators salaries which meet "the cost of their election campaigns and [assure] them, during the period of their service, approximately the kind of living which they are confident they could win in other pursuits."[27] Beyond a doubt, a majority of states would fail this test.

[26] *Biennial Compensation of Legislators, 1971* (Kansas City, Mo.: Citizens Conference on State Legislatures, 1971).
[27] Hyneman, "Tenure and Turnover," 30.

Unlike many state legislatures that must seek popular approval of constitutional amendments to raise salaries, Congress is master of its own salary. And although low salary is not the same disabling feature in Congress that it is in state legislatures, a good case can be made that congressional pay is far from exceptional given the extraordinary costs confronting the typical member.

Congressional salaries have been raised three times since 1946, when the Legislative Reorganization Act was passed. That act provided for a salary of $12,500 for members. In 1955, following a report of a Commission on Judicial and Congressional Salaries, congressional salaries were raised to $22,500. They were raised again in 1964 to $30,000. Currently, a congressman's salary is $42,500, this figure having been adopted in 1969. The presiding officers—the Speaker of the House and the president of the Senate (the vice-president)—each receive a salary of $62,500. Members of Congress are also given sizeable allowances for staff assistance. The staff budgets for senators from larger states usually total several hundred thousand dollars.

Controversy occasionally swirls around congressional staffs because of the practice of some lawmakers in hiring relatives or political supporters for positions in their offices. The ugly charge of nepotism in Congress— favoring one's relatives for jobs—has often caught the attention of the American press. The most sensational case in recent years was that of Adam Clayton Powell, whose wife received a salary of over $20,000 a year even though she lived in Puerto Rico and did no work in his office. Nepotism cases often appear bizarre. An earlier investigation, in 1959, disclosed an imaginative first-term member of the House from Indiana who had put "both his wife and his front porch on the payroll." His wife was receiving more than $4,000 a year to run his home-district office located on his front porch, which in turn was being "rented" to the government for $100 a month. Of all the disclosures, however, the most incredible to the press concerned a freshman House member from Iowa who was paying his nineteen-year-old son, a prelaw student enrolled at a Washington university, in excess of $11,000 a year as a member of his staff. Apart from the usual justifications for his son's appointment, the congressman reported ingenuously that "Shirley Temple made $3,000 a week when she was seven years old."[28] Very little more could be said without being redundant.

The occasional flurries over nepotism and patronage appointments in congressional offices obscure for the public the importance and necessity of staff assistance. Congressmen would be hopelessly bogged down in trivia without assistants to relieve them of the multitude of routine tasks placed before them by constituents. Moreover, many staffs, especially in the Senate, are composed of individuals who bring exceptional qualifications to the job and specialized knowledge of political and legislative problems.[29]

28 *New York Times,* February 20 and 25, 1959.
29 Matthews distinguishes between two principal types of senatorial offices, one which is bureaucratic in organization, the other individualistic. In the former, "the senator has delegated considerable nonroutine responsibilities to his staff, establishing a fairly clearcut division of labor and chain of command. The administrative assistant is really a 'senator, junior grade.'. . ." The individualistic offices are " 'vest

In addition to raising congressional pay, the Legislative Reorganization Act of 1946 made provision for a retirement system. A member of Congress who elects to participate in the plan contributes 6 per cent of his annual salary to a retirement fund. At age sixty-two, provided he has served in Congress a minimum of six years, he may retire and draw a pension equal to $2\frac{1}{2}$ per cent of his annual salary multiplied by the number of years he has served. Although the retirement system provides comparatively generous allowances, it seems to have had no appreciable effect in inducing members of advanced age to retire from office.

One final perquisite of congressional office should be noted. This is the franking privilege, the right to send official mail postage-free. In practice, there are no limits on the use of the congressional frank, and some members of Congress employ it frequently to mail copies of their speeches and other literature to constituents, hopefully adding new life to their campaigns for reelection.

THE COSTS OF CONGRESSIONAL OFFICE

The annual salary of $42,500 paid to members of Congress looks better at a distance than it does close up—representatives and senators are subject to a great variety of special expenses that cut a heavy swath through their incomes. The great majority of members, for example, must maintain houses in their home states as well as in Washington. Social life is also expensive: there are countless constituents who must be entertained at lunch and at dinner, and endless social gatherings which legislators feel impelled to attend. Travel between Washington and home is extraordinarily expensive over the course of a year. Congressmen who live within a few hundred miles of Washington normally return home each weekend to make speeches and to settle political matters. Although congressional travel allowances have been raised significantly in recent years, they are still insufficient to cover the travel expenses of many members of Congress.

Finally, political expenses are exceptionally burdensome, especially for those members who represent competitive constituencies. Financial assistance from the party organizations and from private individuals is helpful but rarely adequate, and incumbents are often required to spend their own money to gain renomination and reelection. Here and there, congressmen not only raise their own campaign funds but are dragooned into making contributions to local party organizations as well, perhaps running to $1,000 —the donation expected of Democratic congressional candidates in Pittsburgh, for example. Cabell Phillips writes:

> Political expenses [of the lawmakers] do not end with elections. Members are expected to contribute generously to national and local party chests, to aid campaigns of their friends and party colleagues, to show up at the $100-a-plate fund raising dinners.... They must subscribe to the building fund for that new church, lodge hall or orphanage; buy tickets to the civic

---

pocket' operations in which the senator has delegated only routine tasks and in which the staff has little influence and less authority." *U.S. Senators and Their World,* pp. 83–84.

134   rallies and school plays; contribute prizes for the charity bazaars and bingo tournaments; buy space in countless programs and fraternal papers.[30]

Such reasons help explain why no member of Congress grows rich on his salary, why some go into debt, why others are driven into retirement, and why most feel the need to supplement congressional pay with outside income. The heavy cost of staying in office is one explanation for the persistence of the "Tuesday-through-Thursday Club"—those traveling lawmakers who depart Washington Thursday night and return Tuesday morning, using the interval not only to mend fences at home but also to practice law and to shore up business affairs. "Moonlighting" is as prevalent among members of Congress as it is among policemen, firemen, and high school teachers.

While many members continue their law practices and business operations, others turn to writing and lecturing to supplement their incomes.[31] A midwestern senator reported some years ago: "To do my duty as a Senator I have to go back home and talk to my people at least once a month. Each trip costs me from $200 to $250. But every time I go I have to scrounge the countryside like the Russian Army, making speeches and lectures along the way. I simply can't afford it out of my salary.[32]

The high cost of life in Congress leads occasionally to moral quandaries. Although it is not an altogether happy defense, legislators have sometimes justified nepotism on the ground that they could not make ends meet without a second member of the family on the payroll. Similarly, there are lawmakers who take private subsidies from supporters to defray political and personal expenses associated with officeholding. For example, responding to charges raised by newspaper columnists, the Senate Select Committee on Standards and Conduct carried out an investigation in 1967 which disclosed that Senator Thomas Dodd of Connecticut had obtained over $116,000 from "testimonials" held in his honor and that this money had been used for a variety of purposes, including such things as paying off federal tax debts, repaying loans, trips to the West Indies and London, and home improvements. After substantial debate, the Senate voted overwhelmingly to censure Dodd for having spent personally money which had been raised politically. This censure, sixth in the history of the Senate, in no way affected Dodd's legal status as a senator. Such losses as he suffered took place in the realm of political influence.

A similar controversy arose in the early 1950s when it was disclosed that Senator Richard Nixon of California had been subsidized by a group of California real estate, manufacturing, and oil interest representatives.

---

[30] "The High Cost of Our Low-Paid Congress," *New York Times Magazine,* February 24, 1952, p. 41.

[31] Prominent members of Congress can earn sizeable honoraria for speeches, public appearances, magazine articles, newspaper columns, and book royalties. The senators who led in honoraria income in 1970, for example, were Birch Bayh (D., Ind.), $44,331; Mark O. Hatfield (R., Ore.), $41,956; Edmund S. Muskie (D., Me.), $40,866; Abraham Ribicoff (D., Conn.), $37,800; and Barry Goldwater (R., Ariz.), $30,050. Most senators, of course, earn much less in honoraria. University speaking engagements are typically the most lucrative source of honoraria. See the *Congressional Quarterly Weekly Report,* May 28, 1971, pp. 1181–82.

[32] Quoted in Phillips, *op. cit.,* p. 7.

Receiving $18,000 in contributions during his term in the Senate, he explained that his expenses were "in excess of the amounts allowed under the law" and that private subsidies save the taxpayers' money. Whether this is sufficient justification is surely disputable, but it is not hard to agree with Mr. Nixon that lawyer-legislators who "take fat legal fees on the side" (from clients who may be in search of influence) are also faced with a moral issue of major proportions.

Privileges and Immunities

Buttressed by the Constitution and parliamentary conventions, members of Congress enjoy a considerable measure of freedom of speech as well as immunity from arrest. State legislators enjoy similar protection under state constitutions. The national Constitution provides in Article I, Section 6, that senators and representatives "shall in all cases, except treason, felony, and breach of the peace, be privileged from arrest during their attendance at the session of their respective Houses, and in going to and returning from the same; and for any speech or debate in either house, they shall not be questioned in any other place." The proviso granting immunity from arrest is not of major importance today. But the language concerning "speech or debate" is highly significant. In effect, this clause means that there are no formal limits to what a senator or representative may say in Congress (in committee as well as on the floor), no limits to charges he may choose to make, no danger of being sued for libel or slander for allegations he has made. Still another aspect to this constitutional grant was elaborated in 1966 when the Supreme Court ruled unanimously that the "speech or debate" clause prohibits the executive and judicial branches from inquiring into a congressman's official acts or the motives which support them. The Court reversed the conviction of a congressman who had accepted $500 to make a floor speech in support of savings and loan institutions; the congressman's assistance came at a time when several of these associations in his state had been indicted on mail fraud charges. The opinion in *U.S.* v. *Johnson* makes it clear that members of Congress enjoy wide-ranging protection from official inquiry concerning their remarks and behavior in Congress.[33]

The grounds for congressional immunity are broad, though, practically speaking, not incontestable. Protection of the speech of members of Congress is an indispensable condition if debate is to be meaningful and to roam freely over embarrassing and controversial matters. But, like other privileges, it may be twisted and abused. Safely within the congressional sanctuary, some few members of Congress have shockingly exploited their position, recklessly defaming the character of individuals by making wild and unsupportable charges. Such, in a nutshell, is the story of Joseph McCarthy's tumultuous years in the Senate seeking to uncover spies, intimidating the White House, and harassing any number of private citizens.

Although the citizen is unable to defend himself against a personal

---

[33] 383 U.S. 169 (1966). See also "The Bribed Congressman's Immunity from Prosecution," *Yale Law Journal*, LXXV (December 1965), 335–50.

136 attack by a member of Congress (made in Congress), each house may discipline a member for his remarks. The ultimate in discipline is expulsion, which requires a two-thirds vote of the membership. Rarely, however, is punishment of any sort meted out; an exception occurred in 1954 when Senator McCarthy was "condemned" for acting "contrary to Senatorial ethics," bringing the Senate "into dishonor and disrepute," obstructing its constitutional processes, and impairing its dignity. He was "condemned" (originally the resolution provided for "censure," presumably a stronger term) because, among other things, he had called an examination of his conduct by the Senate a "lynch party" and the select committee that carried on the investigation an "unwitting hand-maiden" and an "involuntary agent" of the Communist party. "Condemnation," of course, did not in any way alter McCarthy's formal powers as a senator nor diminish his "immunity," but it eliminated whatever influence he may have had at the time. His mistake, ironically, lay in flouting the Senate, its committee, and fellow members, not in his sustained and defamatory attacks upon private individuals.

Legislators' Adaptation to the Legislature

Legislators are recruited, nominated for office, and elected in a variety of ways.[34] In some jurisdictions, political parties are either the chief or the exclusive sponsor of legislative careers. Elsewhere, parties may count for little or nothing in generating candidacies. Where parties are weak, candidates may be "self-starters," launching their careers apparently on their own initiative. Candidates may be induced to run by former officeholders, friends and associates, or interest groups. Here and there factions appear among the explicit sponsors of legislative careers. A panoramic study of how individuals make their way out of private life or other public position and into the legislature would be certain to show a number of alternative routes or strategies available to candidates. Selection of an appropriate route to winning legislative office is perhaps the first critical decision that faces an aspiring candidate. His second critical decision, obviously of enduring significance for the legislature, involves "selection" of the role he will play in the system. Vastly different "models" are open to him.[35] How a legislator relates to his office and adapts to the legislative environment determines, in great part, the nature of his contribution to the work and effectiveness of the legislature.

A seminal study of the Connecticut legislature by James D. Barber identifies four major role orientations[36] among freshman legislators: Spec-

[34] For a recent study that examines the motivations in running for office of congressional challengers (nonincumbent candidates), see Jeff Fishel, "Ambition and the Political Vocation: Congressional Challengers in American Politics," *Journal of Politics,* XXXIII (February 1971), 25–56. The study produces a typology of congressional challengers based on their orientations toward politics and toward a political career.

[35] This discussion of legislators' adaptation to the legislature is based on Barber, *op. cit.* The statements by members are drawn from pp. 31, 69, 141, and 164–65.

[36] "Role orientation," as it is used here, refers to the kind of behavior that legislators themselves believe to be appropriate for fulfilling the duties of legislative

tator, Advertiser, Reluctant, and Lawmaker. Spectators do not come to terms with the matters that are central to the legislature. They attend sessions of the legislature regularly, listen to debate, but rarely participate. They like the idea of being in the legislature. Legislative activities, they find, are "tremendously interesting" and legislative service is "a wonderful experience." But they sit and watch. Although their role is passive, legislative service carries rewards for them, including recognition and prestige. These remarks by a Spectator invited to the Governor's Tea are instructive:

> We were very impressed. I mean you couldn't help but be impressed. It's a beautiful home. The Governor and his wife met us graciously and gave us the full roam of the house—"Go ahead, look at anything you want. Make yourself at home. We'll see you later on." And we wandered around. It's a beautiful home. Everything in it is beautiful. And, ah, then tea was served— so we had coffee (laughs). So we were sitting around, or standing there, and the Governor came by and he talked to everybody, and his wife talked with everybody. So—before that, we drove up in front of the house and a state trooper, there, he opened the car door. The passengers got out. I got out. The state trooper took the car, parked it for me. And, ah...so we had tea, and the Governor talked with us. His wife talked with us. And when it came time to leave, we departed. And again, why—a warm handshake. None of this fishy handshake, but a warm handshake. And, ah, they thanked us for coming—whereas normally we should have thanked them for being invited. They thanked us for coming. And we got out there, the state trooper, he opened the car door. And off we go. Well, as I say, we had a wonderful afternoon there. As I say, we were only there an hour, hour-and-a-half. It was very impressive. You couldn't help but be impressed. . . .

Advertisers, many of whom are ambitious young lawyers, view the legislature in the harsh light of personal opportunity. One of the main reasons that they decide to run for the legislature is that they may be able to use the office for their own advancement. The legislature is a good place to meet people, make contacts, and gain publicity. As legislators, they are active, aggressive, disdainful of other members, impatient, and often unhappy and frustrated over their inability to accomplish their objectives. Their stay in the legislature is likely to be brief. Motivation for legislative service is shown clearly in these comments by a legislator classified as an Advertiser:

> But—that's law—a lawyer cannot advertise. The only way that he can have people know that he is in existence is by going to this meeting, going to that meeting, joining that club, this club, becoming a member of the legislature—so that people know that there is such a person alive. And they figure that—"Oh, X, I heard of him. He's a lawyer. Good. I need a lawyer, I don't know one. I'll call him." Otherwise you're just in your cubbyhole waiting for someone to come in off the street. And it doesn't happen.

office. For a discussion of the difficulties involved in the use of role concepts and the development of a probability model, see Wayne L. Francis, "The Role Concept in Legislatures: A Probability Model and a Note on Cognitive Structure," *Journal of Politics*, XXVII (August 1965), 567–85.

Reluctants are in the legislature in spite of their attitudes toward it and the nagging problems of adjustment that confront them. These are legislators who are not really interested in politics and who were probably pressured into accepting the nomination by party leaders in their communities. Reluctants usually lack interest in political advancement, dislike political controversy, and are tempted to withdraw from legislative life. To avoid the "politics" and other unpleasant aspects of the legislature, Reluctants are likely to concentrate on mastering the formal rules and procedures that govern deliberation and decision-making. The chances are strong that they agreed to serve in the legislature out of a sense of duty:

> Well, of course, my father lived in this town all his life, and the town has been good to him and, well, he's been good to the town. And I thought to myself—of course, father's dead and all that—but I said to myself, Dad would say, "You've got the time, you ought to do it." So that's about the way I felt, that I was doing what was really set out for me to do, that I should do. I felt a, well, I felt duty bound to it, that's all. It wasn't a great hankering that I had. . . .

A legislature populated only by Spectators, Advertisers, and Reluctants would be a remarkably bland and unimaginative institution. Missing would be those legislators who carry the main burdens of the legislature: the Lawmakers. Legislators with this role orientation are highly interested in elective politics, hold positive sentiments toward the legislature, and take an active part in all phases of the legislative process. Deeply interested in issues and confident of their capacity to persuade others, their principal concern is to achieve concrete legislative results. Lawmakers recognize the need for compromise and bargaining and believe that the job of the legislator is to make decisions on bills. The key to understanding the Lawmaker is found in his concern over legislation. This is illustrated in the following comments by two members who were asked to rate their own performances:

> Well, I think I've done pretty well. For this reason, that I supported several issues. I served on two important committees, and I supported many main issues—when I say supported, I mean not only voted, but took an actual part in promoting and speaking for them. Appeared before many committees on subjects that were important to my constituents and to the projects that I mention. So I was successful in getting bills that our town needed, and also other bills.

> Well, I feel that I've done a big thing in being able to vote on the X bill. I think that was simply tremendous. And of course there are other bills in which I'm *very* interested. I introduced the bill for Y. And then the bill for Z will be heard tomorrow morning. That would be a big step forward.

Table 5.5, drawn from the Connecticut study, categorizes the four types of legislators according to their *activity* in the legislature (measured by bills introduced and participation in committee and floor discussions) and their *willingness to return* for at least three future sessions. Each variable provides evidence as to the manner in which the member relates to his office. Surprisingly, the variables are not correlated. Thus, the two types of

TABLE 5.5   *139*
Patterns of Adaptation among Legislators

		Activity	
		High	Low
Willingness to Return	⎧High	Lawmakers	Spectators
	⎩Low	Advertisers	Reluctants

SOURCE: James D. Barber, *The Lawmakers: Recruitment and Adaptation to Legislative Life* (New Haven: Yale University Press, 1965), p. 20.

legislators who are most active in the legislature—Lawmakers and Advertisers —differ sharply on the question of returning to the legislature for subsequent sessions. Similar mixing occurs among Lawmakers and Spectators, who differ strikingly in activity but agree in terms of willingness to stay in the legislature.

Legislatures are hospitable to almost all kinds of members. Apart from a few legal qualifications which candidates must meet, the only tests of entry are political, and these may be far from rigorous. Recruitment practices and "availability" criteria differ so widely that men and women with markedly different orientations wind up in the legislature—those who watch and applaud, those who advertise their wares, those who serve out of a sense of duty, and those who legislate. Each orientation, it may be argued, contributes something to either the work or the morale of the institution. Spectators, conciliatory and appreciative, doubtless help to reduce tension; Advertisers, aggressive and cynical, may help to illuminate issues and rationalize debate; Reluctants, motivated by a stern moral sense, work to keep "the rules of the game" observed and to keep conflict within tolerable limits. Whatever the occasional or special impacts these legislators may produce, however, it is the Lawmaker who supplies the central energy, ideas, and vision of the legislature. The permanent importance of the Lawmaker is that his work is located at the authentic center of the legislative process. Other roles, though functional for limited purposes, are peripheral.

Although hard evidence is lacking, it seems probable that these general role orientations are found in all state legislatures.[37] The types have an

37 Legislative role orientations may be considered in several ways. The authors of *The Legislative System* depict four major *purposive* role orientations: Ritualist, Tribune, Inventor, and Broker. The *Ritualist* is preoccupied with the same interests as the Reluctant, which is to say that he concentrates on mastering the rules of parliamentary procedure, stresses routine and formal decision-making, and virtually excludes power problems from consideration. The *Tribune* is the legislator who sees himself primarily as the agent of the people, obligated to discover popular needs and popular interests. The *Inventor* is the legislator who perceives himself as the initiator of policy, mainly concerned with devising solutions to current problems of public policy and anticipating future requirements. Finally, the role of *Broker* is to balance interests, arbitrate disputes, and search for solutions that accommodate the demands of multiple interests. In the four-state study (New Jersey, Ohio, California, and Tennessee), the purposive role encountered most frequently was that of Ritualist. The role of Broker, in some ways the most realistic role in contemporary political systems, was encountered least frequently in three out of the four states. The Broker role may not fit easily into a legislature in which party issues are often important and party lines typically firm. See Wahlke *et al., op. cit.,* pp. 249–58.

140   authentic ring for students of the legislative process. Perhaps the important question to be distilled from this analysis concerns the recruitment of legislators. There is no reason to believe that the present mixture of these four types in the legislatures is one of harmonious equilibrium or that it is conducive to effective legislative performance. Rather, it is a fair surmise that American legislatures today are overrepresented by legislators who opt for or sink into "secondary" roles, and underrepresented by legislators who fulfill the expectations of the Lawmaker role. The question, then, is whether there are ways by which Lawmakers can be identified and recruited.

Men and women who turn into effective legislators may always be in short supply, their recruitment at best uncertain. Endless statistics could be assembled to prove that business and the professions siphon off considerable talent that might otherwise be available for public office. This is one obstacle to the recruitment of more Lawmakers. A second is that not enough is known about the personal endowments of those individuals who become Lawmakers, and hence there is uncertainty as to the qualities to be sought after. On the basis of the Connecticut evidence, Barber believes that Lawmakers are characterized by a basic expectation of success, a strong and realistic sense of personal identity, a quest for personal goals, and a disposition to engage in cooperative efforts—confidence, recognition, achievement, and sharing.[38] A third obstacle is simply that there is no assurance that party recruiters regard the identification and selection of Lawmakers as a matter of high urgency; abundant evidence exists, in fact, to suggest that other "availability" criteria may outweigh that of "potential effectiveness as a legislator."

Yet assuming for the moment that some, perhaps many, party recruiters are interested in obtaining the best possible talent for the legislature, are there outward signs that provide clues as to potential Lawmakers? The Connecticut study shows that the prelegislative careers of Lawmakers are distinguished by *active* memberships in organizations, *persistent* involvement in organizational work, abiding interest in *political issues,* and a strong measure of *personal security.* In addition, their *careers* have been sufficiently successful that movement to the legislature is not merely an adventure for the purpose of rescuing a precarious business or profession. Whether, once recruited and elected, Lawmakers will make a career of legislative service appears to depend on the nature of the legislature and the nature of the job. For Lawmakers the preeminent requirement is that the legislature be engaged in important work and that the individual member be permitted to focus his energy and intelligence on the resolution of issues and the development of legislation.[39]

Legislators and Legislative Norms

All human institutions seek to maintain themselves and to guarantee their survival through establishing norms of conduct that apply to their members. These norms, folkways, or rules of the game govern a variety of

---

[38] Barber, *op. cit.,* pp. 251–54.
[39] *Ibid.,* pp. 256–57.

situations and practices, both prescribing and proscribing certain kinds of behavior. "For the legislator they set the approximate limits within which his discretionary behavior may take place."[40] They contribute to the continuity of the legislature and carry great significance for the established power structure, plainly helping to support it. The "unwritten rules" keep new members from breaking away from familiar and conventional ways of doing things and offer veteran members comfortable justifications for the way the system governs itself. To the extent that the norms are observed, they are a residual source of power for those members who receive advantage from a stable political institution. Some norms are deeply imbedded in the institution, affecting members' behavior in many significant ways. Other norms cover narrow ground and have slight significance for individual members. An erosion of norms may occur when the composition of a group changes drastically.[41] As would be expected, not all members of an institution regard the norms as presumptively valid and not all norms are perfectly observed. Violations may lead to the imposition of sanctions.

The most authoritative study of congressional norms has been done by Donald R. Matthews in *U.S. Senators and Their World*. Although this study examines only the Senate, there is abundant impressionistic evidence that House norms are distinctly similar. Matthews identifies six main "folkways" or norms: apprenticeship, legislative work, specialization, courtesy, reciprocity, and institutional patriotism.[42]

Congress has always had a large amount of enthusiasm for the idea that new members should serve an *apprenticeship* before entering fully into legislative activity. Although in recent years the apprenticeship norm has lost some of its force, it is far from being moribund. New members are regularly alerted to the demands of apprenticeship. The newcomer who enters debate too soon, speaks too often, and discusses too many subjects is likely to be criticized by other members. He is expected to be patient and not to become an active participant until he has something important to contribute. He is very likely to hear that "No congressman has ever been defeated by a speech he didn't make on the floor of the House."[43] Learning the rules and procedures, in the judgment of congressional leaders, is an important requirement for new members. John W. McCormack, former Speaker of the House, stated the matter this way:

> If I might make a suggestion to new members, going back myself thirty-five years when I came here as a new member, study the rules of the House of

---

[40] David B. Truman, *The Governmental Process* (New York: Alfred A. Knopf, Inc., 1951), pp. 348–49.

[41] See Meg Greenfield, "Uhuru Comes to the Senate," *The Reporter,* September 23, 1965, pp. 32–37, and Tom Wicker, "Winds of Change in the Senate," *New York Times Magazine,* September 12, 1965, pp. 52ff.

[42] *U.S. Senators and Their World,* pp. 92–117. For an analysis of the contributions of norms to legislative integration during the critical era immediately prior to the Civil War, see Dean L. Yarwood, "Norm Observance and Legislative Integration: The U.S. Senate in 1850 and 1860," *Social Science Quarterly,* LI (June 1970), 57–69.

[43] Quoted in Charles L. Clapp, *The Congressman: His Work as He Sees It* (Washington, D.C.: The Brookings Institution, 1963), pp. 126–27.

Representatives. That's the legislator's Bible. Study the interpretations of the rules as made by the various Speakers. Watch and study older members participating and putting into execution the rules. Learn from them through their experiences. It will be very, very helpful to you. . . . [Those congressmen] who devote themselves to [study] and become conversant with the rules of the House and the interpretation of the rules will . . . become model members of the House.[44]

Freshmen who grow impatient and flout the apprenticeship norm can easily get into difficulty with the leadership. Their influence may be significantly curtailed:

> The very ingredients which make you a powerful House leader are the ones which keep you from being a public leader. It is analogous to the fable that when you go over the wall you are speared; when you go underneath you end up with the fair lady. The yappers just won't get to be leaders. Take ———[a freshman] for example. He is a very able individual, but because he persists in getting on the floor and discussing the issues he'll never have any power around here. The structure of power in the House is based on quietude and getting along with the leadership. Freshmen who are vocal and want to exercise initiative and leadership are confined to the cellar, merely because they have been speaking too often.[45]

The way a freshman gets ahead is well understood. In the words of a new member of the House Appropriations Committee: "You have to sit in the back seat and edge up little by little."[46]

The apprenticeship folkway is especially oppressive for the congressman whose career begins at a late age. Thus a sixty-seven-year-old freshman announced in a recent Congress that he would not be a candidate for reelection, explaining that: "I could see I wasn't going to get any place. Nobody listens to what you have to say until you've been here 10 or 12 years. These old men have got everything so tied down you can't do anything. There are only about 40 out of the 435 members who call the shots. They're the committee chairmen and the ranking members and they're all around 70 or 80."[47]

A second folkway insists that members should give substantial attention to *legislative work,* even though much of it is tedious and politically unimportant. But someone has to do it, and members are expected to carry their fair share. Publicity is not something from which the average legislator shrinks, but the member who gets too much publicity, especially when it is gained at the expense of legislative work, is likely to suffer a loss of

---

[44] Quoted in Donald G. Tacheron and Morris K. Udall, *The Job of the Congressman,* 2nd ed. (Indianapolis: The Bobbs-Merrill Company, Inc., 1970), pp. 200–201.

[45] Clapp, *op. cit.,* p. 21.

[46] Quoted in Richard F. Fenno, "The House Appropriations Committee as a Political System: The Problem of Integration," *American Political Science Review,* LVI (June 1962), 318.

[47] *Washington Post,* April 3, 1964, as quoted by Nelson W. Polsby, *Congress and the Presidency,* 2nd ed. (Englewood Cliffs, N.J.: Prentice-Hall, Inc., 1971), p. 72.

esteem among his colleagues.[48] A former congressman points out that members sometimes ignore the fact that they have two constituencies—"the voters back home and the other members of the House.":

> There are three groups of members who either cannot or will not recognize their House constituency. The first group are the nonentities, the members who make no effort to acquire or exert influence in the House. They could be expected to have rather brief House careers, but some last a surprisingly long time. The second group are the demagogues. The term may be strong, but it is the one commonly applied in the House to the member who plays to the press gallery and the home folks on every possible occasion, in full knowledge that everything he says and does is recognized, and discounted, by his colleagues for exactly what it is. The third group who ignore the House constituency are the "pop-offs." Their behavior may occasionally be demagogic, but most of the time it is based on the sincere but greatly exaggerated notion that their colleagues and the world in general need their good advice. Their opinions are quite often sound, but because of their attitude, the "pop-offs" have no influence on the House at large.[49]

The norm of *specialization* serves to restrict the interests of members. The expectation is that members will concentrate on limited fields of legislation, ordinarily those which fall within their committee assignments or those which have major significance for their states or districts. The member who is an "expert" on everything is likely to be held in disdain. A congressman points out:

> If [a member] does speak when he is not on the committee concerned with the legislation, the subject matter should relate to a matter of vital importance to his district. Even if a man is exceptionally able there is resentment

[48] Members of the "Tuesday-to-Thursday Club" persistently violate the norm that each member of Congress should do his share of legislative work. These members commute back and forth between Washington and their homes, ordinarily spending only three days in Washington each week. From the standpoint of Congress as a whole, their behavior is "deviant." A state delegation that engages in this practice, however, has a different perspective. For the New York Democratic delegation, for example, the practice is regarded as appropriate and necessary. Spending substantial time in their home districts is seen by members as a political necessity if they are to be reelected or promoted to higher political office. In this sense, TTT membership is functional for the member's New York political career. But it is also probable that it is dysfunctional for his congressional career, since it represents an indifferent attitude toward legislative work. The result, for most New York members, appears to be a diminution in prestige and influence with House colleagues. See Alan Fiellin, "The Functions of Informal Groups in Legislative Institutions," *Journal of Politics,* XXIV (February 1962), 72–91. See also a related article by Fiellin, "The Group Life of a State Delegation in the House of Representatives," *Western Political Quarterly,* XXIII (June 1970), 305–20. For studies of informal groups at the state legislative level, see Charles M. Price and Charles G. Bell, "Socializing California Freshmen Assemblymen: The Role of Individuals and Legislative Sub-Groups," *Western Political Quarterly,* XXIII (March 1970), 166–79, and Stephen V. Monsma, "Integration and Goal Attainment as Functions of Informal Legislative Groups," *Western Political Quarterly,* XXII (March 1969), 19–28.

[49] Frank E. Smith, *Congressman from Mississippi* (New York: Pantheon Books, Inc., 1964), pp. 130–31.

if he seeks to be an expert on a matter not related to his district or his committee work. ———was one of the most able speakers on almost any subject that came up, and he usually spoke on every subject before us. Yet members resented the fact that he was in on every discussion.[50]

As members acquire increasing expertise in certain substantive fields, their stature rises among their colleagues. When education or social security or defense policies are under active consideration, they become the persons whom other legislators seek out for counsel. "[The] decision to specialize in some legislative field," a former member of Congress has written, "is automatic for the member who wants to exercise any influence. The members who are respected in the House are the men who do their committee chores and become able exponents of the legislative programs in which they have specialized."[51] The following comment by a congressman reveals the extent to which members are often dependent on the specialists:

> I'd say that not one per cent of the House knows anything about the work of the Defense Subcommittee, yet it involves crucial decisions. Only the written reports provide a clue to the real issues in much legislation, and they aren't particularly helpful in connection with the work of the Defense Subcommittee. In this business you've just got to trust your colleagues, especially when it comes to the committees on Ways and Means and Appropriations. The legislation with which those committees deal is so complicated and contains so many technical amendments that it is virtually impossible for the ordinary member to have any idea about what is going on. It is an unsatisfactory way to legislate, but unfortunately there is no alternative.[52]

Legislatures struggle over matters that count. The stakes are often massive—for parties, interest groups, executive, bureaucracy, and individual legislators. If it were not for the folkway of *courtesy,* conflict over major issues might easily extend beyond tolerable limits, jeopardizing the ability of members to work together in any fashion. The courtesy rule helps to keep political disagreements and personal aspirations from corroding relations between members.

> The selection of committee members and chairmen on the basis of their seniority neatly by-passes a potential cause of grave dissension in the Senate. The rules prohibit the questioning of a colleague's motives or the criticism of another state. All remarks made on the floor are, technically, addressed to the presiding officer, and this formality serves as a psychological barrier between antagonisms. Senators are expected to address each other not by name but by title.... Personal attacks, unnecessary unpleasantness, and pursuing a line of thought or action that might embarrass a colleague needlessly are all thought to be self-defeating—"After all, your enemies on one issue may be your friends on the next."[53]

50 Quoted in Clapp, *op. cit.,* p. 24.
51 Smith, *op. cit.,* p. 130.
52 Quoted in Clapp, *op. cit.,* p. 111.
53 Matthews, *op. cit.,* pp. 97–98.

The norm of *reciprocity* is an outgrowth of the need of both individual legislators and legislative blocs to aggregate support for their positions. Reciprocity activates the legislature, prompts members to examine problems from the vantage point of their colleagues, underlies bargains of all kinds, helps members to extricate bills from legislative bogs, and explains voting behavior on numerous proposals. Under the rule of reciprocity, members help each other with their problems—ordinarily the most significant exchange occurs in trading votes. Although this folkway is not perfectly observed by any means, there are numerous examples of its use every day legislatures meet:

> ————'s reclamation project carried by just a few votes. One thing that broke the liberal and big city line against it was the fact that all the boys who played poker and gin rummy with him voted for it. And they took some of the rest of us with them. They said he wasn't going to be so difficult in the future.[54]

> The gentleman and I have been seesawing back and forth on this committee for some time. He was chairman in the 80th Congress. I had the privilege of serving as chairman in the 81st and 82nd Congresses. Now he is back in the saddle. I can say that he has never failed to give me his utmost cooperation, and I have tried to give him the same cooperation during his service as chairman of this Committee. We seldom disagree, but we have found out that we can disagree without being disagreeable. Consequently, we have unusual harmony on this committee.[55]

> Over the years, House members come to know how most of the other members will react to any given issue, and it is natural that the closest relationships, working and personal, are developed among those men who face common problems and have compatible points of view. The influential member is not the man who limits himself to these natural associations; he is, rather, the man who takes time to study the problems of other groups of members, to seek among them the areas of compatible short-term interest, and who capitalizes on those interests by working with such groups in temporary alliances to mutual benefit.[56]

A final congressional norm is that of *institutional patriotism*. Members of Congress are expected to display conspicuous loyalty to the institution. In the eyes of the member, Congress is something of a cultural monument. Its traditions, its lore, its heroes, its personnel—all are beyond the ordinary, all deserve a special rhetoric, all are worthy of celebration. When thoroughly imbued with the norm, members see the institution and their colleagues as possessing exceptional qualities: "Nowhere else will you find such a ready appreciation of merit and character. In few gatherings of equal size is there so little jealousy and envy."[57] Some outsiders may be left with a touch of astonishment when they consider the virtues of Congress as portrayed by members. Consider the Senate: "the most remarkable group that I have

[54] Quoted in Clapp, *op. cit.,* p. 15.
[55] Quoted in Fenno, *op. cit.,* p. 319.
[56] Smith, *op. cit.,* p. 131.
[57] Quoted in Clapp, *op. cit.,* p. 16.

ever met anywhere," "the most able and intelligent body of men that it has been my fortune to meet," "the best men in political life today."[58] The member who is low in emotional attachment to Congress (or his house) and high in criticism of it sharply diminishes his chances for joining the "establishment" or gaining easy access to it.

Unwritten rules which govern the behavior of members are characteristic of all legislative institutions. They contribute to the overall effectiveness of the legislature by defining appropriate behavior, rewarding compliance, and diminishing opportunities and incentives for interpersonal conflict. Similarly, the existence of norms helps to make legislative relationships more predictable and to enhance the capacity of members to cooperate with one another. Although it is altogether unlikely that the norms that characterize Congress have identical importance in all state legislatures, there is no doubt that they are present and often significant. Other rules also apply. The four-state study (California, New Jersey, Ohio, and Tennessee) discloses that a large number of norms, or "rules of the game," are generally understood and accepted by members. Considering the states as a group, the most widely noted rules are that members should perform their obligations (i.e., keep their word, abide by commitments), respect other members' legislative rights, show impersonality in their legislative actions, exhibit self-restraint in debate, and observe common courtesies.[59]

INFLUENCES ON CONFORMITY

Although norms have a pervasive influence on legislative behavior, not all legislators observe them faithfully. In the U.S. Senate, for example, four factors appear to affect whether individual members will adhere to the norms: *previous training and experience, political ambitions, constituency problems,* and *political ideology.* Men with distinguished careers who enter the Senate relatively late in life (e.g., former governors) are among the members least likely to conform to the folkways, while former congressmen, state legislators, and judges show a high rate of conformity. Senators with strong ambitions for either the presidency or vice-presidency ordinarily rank low in conformity—understandably so, since they know that they are unlikely to make much progress toward their goals by deferring to such folkways as apprenticeship or specialization. In similar fashion, senators from large, complex, two-party states tend to grow impatient with the rules that impede their efforts to represent a multiplicity of interests and to make a record that is visible to their constituents. Finally, liberals often fail to follow the folkways, correctly perceiving that these norms are among the chief supports for the *status quo.*[60]

Legislators who bridle at the norms run the risk of alienating their colleagues and incurring sanctions. Study of the U.S. Senate shows that nonconformists are somewhat less likely to get their bills passed than conformists. Members also contend that nonconformists have trouble in securing favors for their states. Although evidence is elusive, there is a persistent belief that "mavericks" are often overlooked when assignments to "choice"

58 Quoted in Matthews, *op. cit.,* p. 102.
59 Wahlke *et al., op. cit.,* Chapter 7.
60 Matthews, *op. cit.,* pp. 102–14.

committees are made. Richard Fenno's study of the House Appropriations
Committee contains a graphic example of the treatment accorded a freshman member who neglected to observe the apprenticeship norm and tried
to ask "as many questions as the chairman" during subcommittee hearings.

> In the hearings, I have to wait sometimes nine or ten hours for a chance;
> and he hopes I'll get tired and stay home. I've had to wait till some pretty
> unreasonable hours. Once I've gotten the floor, though, I've been able to
> make a good case. Sometimes I've been the only person there.... He's all
> powerful. He's got all the power. He wouldn't think of taking me on a trip
> with him when he goes to hold hearings. Last year, he went to ———. He
> wouldn't give me a nudge there. And in the hearings, when I'm questioning
> a witness, he'll keep butting in so that my case won't appear to be too rosy.[61]

Potent sanctions also exist at the state level for the members who
violate the rules of the game. Table 5.6 summarizes the various types of

TABLE 5.6

Sanctions for Enforcing Rules of the Game Perceived by Legislators in Four States

	Proportion of Legislators Naming Each Sanction in			
Sanction	*Calif.* $N = 92$	*N.J.* $N = 74$	*Ohio* $N = 161$	*Tenn.* $N = 116$
Obstruction of his bills: abstain or vote against him; bottle up his bills in committee; amend his bills; pass them only if of major importance to general welfare.	55%	42%	57%	72%
Ostracism: give him the "silent treatment"; subtly reject him personally.	24	14	31	29
Mistrust: cross examine him on floor, in committee; don't put any trust in him.	34	14	25	12
Loss of political perquisites, inducements, and rewards: take away patronage, good committee assignments; report to constituents, local party organization.	15	9	19	4
Denial of special legislative privileges: denial of unanimous consent; otherwise delaying bills.	9	8	4	2
Reprimand: in caucus, in private.	—	12	—*	1
Overt demonstrations of displeasure: ridicule, hissing, laughter, etc.	3	1	2	3
Miscellaneous other sanctions.	5	12	—*	3
No sanctions perceived.	7	14	11	10

SOURCE: John C. Wahlke, Heinz Eulau, William Buchanan, and LeRoy C. Ferguson,
The Legislative System: Explorations in Legislative Behavior (New York: John Wiley & Sons,
Inc., 1962), p. 154. Percentages total more than 100 since most respondents named more
than one sanction.
*Less than 1%.

[61] Quoted in Fenno, *op. cit.,* p. 322.

148   sanction utilized in California, New Jersey, Ohio, and Tennessee. The sanction mentioned most frequently was "obstruction of a member's bills." Next most important was "ostracism" for the offending member. For the four states as a whole, only 7 per cent of the legislators interviewed were unable to perceive any sanction at all. Legislative norms at congressional and state levels are sufficiently pervasive and important to warrant expanded study. New research should help to unravel some of the remaining mysteries of legislative behavior.

Legislator and Legislature

Complaints against the legislature come together at two familiar locations. One stream of criticism, centering on the weaknesses in structure and organization of the legislature, finds fault with the fragmentation of legislative parties, with the fact of committee hegemony, and with all the institutional devices that divide power, smother majorities, and make it difficult to fix responsibility. This wide band of criticism not only finds that legislative structures are archaic or illogical, but also holds that they contribute heavily to deadlock and paralysis. "What kind of legislative body is it," asks Walter Lippmann concerning Congress, "that will not or cannot legislate?"[62]

By and large, Congress is faulted for its failure to organize itself—to organize its power—in a way that would permit it to act. The dominant position of its committees, the arbitrary rule of committee chairmen, the network of interlocking rules that immobilizes the decision-making process—these are among the structural-organizational attributes that expose Congress to a steady stream of criticism. For the most part, Congress goes unquestioned concerning the quality of its members, the exceptions being the occasional flurries over conflict-of-interest matters, the practice of nepotism, or the irresponsible behavior of its investigators.[63]

By contrast, the organizational logic of the state legislative process

62 *Pittsburgh Post Gazette,* July 6, 1963.

63 A recent study of Americans' attitudes toward government officials has shown that a large sector of the public has great respect for *federal appointees* (political executives), seeing them as "trusted leaders." Members of Congress are viewed in about the same light by the generally employed public. Elite segments of the public, however, evaluate federal appointees more favorably than they do congressmen. The differences are noticeable. For example, among college seniors, 85 per cent assess appointees favorably as compared with 65 per cent who assess congressmen this way. For graduate students, the percentages are 78 and 58; for college teachers, 76 and 54; for business executives, 71 and 48; and for federal executives, 82 and 72. Why elites and nonelites should differ in their appraisals of appointed and elected officials is not altogether clear. "It may be that the nonelites feel that their interests are viewed more sympathetically by the elected rather than the appointed. Possibly the elite segments personally identify more with appointees, whom they consider more elitist in composition. There seems to be a pattern of reasoning which holds that a highly placed appointed official has more virtue—perhaps because he was *selected* rather than *elected*—than does the Congressman." See M. Kent Jennings, Milton C. Cummings, Jr., and Franklin P. Kilpatrick, *Trusted Leaders: Perceptions of Appointed Federal Officials,* reprint 126 (Washington, D.C.: The Brookings Institution, 1967), pp. 379–80.

seldom attracts attention or comes under review. Though it is difficult to document, at least in any systematic way, popular uneasiness over state legislatures appears to derive from estimations of the quality of the men and women who serve as legislators. The belief that state legislatures are populated by mediocre men and women is an old complaint, at least as old as the allegations of venality among state legislators in the 'middle of the nineteenth century.

The criticisms of state legislators are more or less familiar to any newspaper reader: nominations for state legislative office all too often go to "party hacks" and to men too long accustomed to making their living from public jobs; legislative elections too frequently involve choices between greater and lesser evils; legislators and their parties are too devoted to individual, factional, or party gains; patronage is the *sine qua non* for holding office, and at those rare moments when legislators are not working to protect this interest, they are busy "playing politics" with the public's business; legislators are, on the one hand, subservient to local bosses and, on the other hand, vulnerable to the blandishments and the mischief of lobbyists; legislators are indifferent to their duties and attach the greatest urgency to their private and career interests outside the legislature; and election to legislative office becomes a sinecure for jobs well done in party vineyards, an advertisement for fledgling lawyers, or an interlude for some men of talent on the way up.[64] To sum up all the disparate accounts of legislative incompetence and waywardness, state legislatures are composed of too many men of second-rate ability, too many men anxious to serve the private interests of party, too many men actuated by base motives, too many men likely to be caught in this or that peccadillo. If this is not the public image of many legislators, then much of the discussion one hears about state legislators and much of the newspaper comment one reads about the institution and its members are simply unintelligible.

Does this appraisal—shared, it seems, about equally by the wider public, the various attentive publics, the press, and a good many of the press's political writers—have good standing in fact? Unfortunately, available data neither sustain nor invalidate these assessments, although the study of Connecticut legislators shows a large number of members (Spectators, Advertisers, and Reluctants) who are not seriously oriented to the main tasks of the legislature. What comprehensive data do show beyond any doubt is that the men and women who win seats in the legislature generally represent nonlegislative occupations of high social status and that they have attained a high level of formal education; on both counts they rank well above the voters who send them to office.[65] In these respects, then, they are

---

[64] For a study of Michigan state legislators that examines the relationship between political ambition and such factors as political socialization, personality traits, and legislative role orientations, see John W. Soule, "Future Political Ambitions and the Behavior of Incumbent State Legislators," *Midwest Journal of Political Science,* XIII (August 1969), 439–54.

[65] Far more is known about the social backgrounds of legislators than about their personalities. See John B. McConaughy, "Certain Personality Factors of State Legislators in South Carolina," *American Political Science Review,* XLIV (December 1950), 897–903, and also Arnold A. Rogow and Harold D. Lasswell, *Power, Corruption, and Rectitude* (Englewood Cliffs, N.J.: Prentice-Hall, Inc., 1963), especially Chapter 2.

anything but "representative"; in certain other respects, especially in religious and ethnic affiliations, they tend to resemble their constituents.

Yet the belief that many state legislators are men of modest talents, men not especially suited to meet the responsibilities of the legislature, has had a long life. If this evaluation is largely erroneous, as it could be, it is one that no legislature easily can afford; if this evaluation is largely accurate, as it could be, it is one that no political system easily can afford. Finally, if prevailing notions about state legislators could be shown to be accurate, they would lead to many salient questions about the public itself, since the typical legislator is in several major respects clearly superior to the voters who elect him.

part two

The Legislative Structure for Decision-Making

6

THE COMMITTEE SYSTEM

National and state constitutions vest supreme lawmaking power in the legislative branch of government. Such grants of legislative power are set down in broad terms and awarded to the representative body as a whole. Constitutions, however, cannot satisfactorily provide for the management or conservation of this power. In practice, legislative committees have come to occupy positions of great and often crucial importance in the American legislature's decision-making process.

This observation on committee power is far from new. Political scientists have long had a heavy intellectual investment in it, due in some part to its early sponsor. Writing near the end of the nineteenth century, Woodrow Wilson described the committees of Congress as "little legislatures," comprising a "disintegrate ministry." And although much has been written about Congress since *Congressional Government* was published in 1885, the newer evaluations of the committee system tend to be about the same as Wilson's assessments:

> The House sits, not for serious discussion, but to sanction the conclusions of its Committees as rapidly as possible. It legislates in its committee-rooms; not by the deliberation of majorities, but by the resolutions of specially-commissioned minorities; so that it is not far from the truth to say that Congress in session is Congress on public exhibition, whilst Congress in its committee-rooms is Congress at work.

> It would seem, therefore, that practically Congress, or at any rate the House of Representatives, delegates not only its legislative but also its deliberative functions to its Standing Committees. The little public debate that arises under the stringent and urgent rules of the House is formal rather than effective, and it is the discussions which take place in the Committees that give form to legislation.

> The privileges of the Standing Committees are the beginning and the end of the rules. Both the House of Representatives and the Senate conduct their business by what figuratively, but not inaccurately, might be called an odd device of *disintegration*. The House virtually both deliberates and legislates in small sections.[1]

1 These paragraphs are taken from Woodrow Wilson, *Congressional Government* (New York: Meridian Books, 1956 [first published 1885]), pp. 69, 71, and 62,

The Role of Committees

Tens of thousands of bills and resolutions are introduced in the fifty state legislatures each session[2] (probably nearly 100,000 in a biennium), and perhaps 20,000 during both sessions of Congress.[3] With a torrent of proposals flooding the legislatures each time they assemble, it is impossible for any chamber as a whole to consider all the individual measures put before it. Committee organization, a means for screening the legislature's business, has proved unavoidable.

The dominant characteristic of executive-legislative relations in the United States—a system of separated powers with relative independence for each—makes it unlikely that the committee system could have developed much differently than it did. In legal and formal terms, Congress is master of its own house; its committees are its creatures. Committees exercise those powers which Congress chooses to grant or to recognize. Over the years, however, there has been a steady accumulation of powers by the committees, and powers either developed upon the committees or quietly assumed by them have proved difficult to recapture. Thus, at times Congress seems to be very little more than the sum of its committees. What we have come to take as customary in this regard—the overriding power of committees—is in fact not typical of legislative experience elsewhere. In clear contrast is the position of committees in the British Parliament, where their powers are carefully circumscribed. As Herman Finer puts it:

---

respectively. One writer who points up the lack of research on committees, Ralph K. Huitt, argues that Wilson's insights on committees are quoted frequently today, not simply because of the wisdom of his analysis, but also because of the absence of other material from which to draw. Huitt is right, but the larder is growing. See his article, "The Congressional Committee: A Case Study," *American Political Science Review,* XLVIII (June 1954), 340–65. An excellent recent example of a committee-centered analysis of Congress is Richard F. Fenno, *The Power of the Purse: Appropriations Politics in Congress* (Boston: Little, Brown & Company, 1966). For a comprehensive analysis of committee organization, behavior, and influence in the congressional system, see William L. Morrow, *Congressional Committees* (New York: Charles Scribner's Sons, 1969).

2 Some legislatures are inordinately prolific. New York usually leads the pack: in its 1969 session, 12,913 bills were introduced, of which 1,523 were enacted into law. Other states which challenged New York's fecundity—enactments shown in parentheses—in 1969 sessions were Massachusetts with 7,314 (1,012); Connecticut, 5,900 (1,525); Minnesota, 5,776 (1,167); and Florida, 4,814 (1,680). As the figures on enactment show, however, an exceedingly large proportion of bills introduced in the legislatures are stillbirths. See *The Book of the States, 1970–71* (Chicago: Council of State Governments, 1971), pp. 80–81.

3 The number of proposals introduced in each Congress in the current era is much less than it was in the first decade of the twentieth century, Bertram Gross points out. "In part, the decline in the birth rate is probably due to the increasing ability of the administrative process to achieve objectives that formerly were sought more exclusively through legislation. The decline may also reflect a diminished number of private relief bills. A definitive explanation will not be possible until bills are counted in a manner that identifies both private relief bills and duplicate bills. Some observers have estimated that 40 per cent of all bills introduced represent duplications within and between houses and that, of the 60 per cent remaining, one quarter are private relief bills." *The Legislative Struggle: A Study in Social Combat* (New York: McGraw-Hill Book Company, Inc., 1953), p. 180.

The British Parliament differs from Congress in this one tremendous practical feature: *it is in the full assembly of the House, not in its committees, that the center of authority over political principle and action is located.* The House of Commons does not delegate to its committees the power of life and death over laws and the conduct of investigation as the House of Representatives and the Senate do. The principle of a bill, its main theory, the great lines of its enacting clauses, are decided by open debate in the House of Commons itself with the social passions, the party emotions, the flow of information and the contending interests, focussed in the one body open to the public view.[4]

The ascendant position which committees occupy in the American legislative process is not the result of the legislature's desire to divest itself of power, to relegate the crucial phase of decision-making to smaller units, to the "subsystem" as it might be called. Nor is committee power due simply to the prolonged neglect by the legislature of its internal processes. Many explanations for the prominence of committees are available. The volume of proposals introduced is an obvious reason—so great is it that consideration of each proposal by the entire assembly is impossible. A second reason grows out of the complexity of legislation. To the outsider, legislation may seem to flow placidly along, as Wilson observed; a closer look, however, shows this is not the case. Because it is complicated and almost invariably technical in detail, legislation demands a measure of expertise among those who consider it. Proposals need examination in light of existing statutes, details need to be fashioned, and estimates and decisions regarding the requirements for passage have to be made. To these tasks committees are able to bring specialization.

Many years of experience in considering a special brand of problem are wrapped up in a committee's members, especially in Congress. With committee experience comes the opportunity for specialization, which in turn contributes both to the member's and to the legislature's effectiveness—so runs a common string of assumptions. There may be nothing wrong with these assumptions, but two additional observations need to be made. The first is that years of legislative seasoning provide no guarantee of a member's expertise or effectiveness; its principal contribution simply may be to sharpen the legislator's instinct for conserving what is familiar and comfortable. And second, committees are composed of both "formal" and "efficient" parts. A committee's formal element is made up of the chairman and the party majority; a committee's efficient element is made up of the men who do the real work of the committee, who guide the hearings, who shape the amendments, and who chart the legislation when it is considered later on the floor. The formal and efficient parts of a committee do not necessarily coincide, though they may. Holbert Carroll, who makes this distinction, believes that the efficient element ordinarily is less than a majority of a congressional committee.[5] This suggests that the contribution of committees to specialization may be somewhat less than is usually presumed; neverthe-

---

[4] "Congressional Investigations: The British System," *University of Chicago Law Review,* XVIII (Spring 1951), 523. (Italics in original.)

[5] *The House of Representatives and Foreign Affairs* (Pittsburgh: University of Pittsburgh Press, 1966), pp. 27–29.

156 less, it is still considerable, and the norms of at least some committees insist that the members become specialists. Within the House Committee on Appropriations, for example, "respect, deference and power are earned through subcommittee activity and, hence to a degree, through specialization."[6]

A third reason which helps to account for the prominence of committees traces to the decentralization of American politics. The separation of powers, the difficulties that attend executive efforts to influence the legislature, the absence of a central agenda for the legislature, and the relative weakness of legislative party organizations—each of these contributes to the creation of a legislature with multiple and diffuse points of access. One specific outcome is a strong, sometimes independent, committee system. A fourth reason is that the committee process facilitates negotiation and logrolling. Congress turns most of its work over to committees, writes John Fischer, "simply because the committee room is the only place where it is possible to arrange a compromise acceptable to all major interests affected."[7]

Finally, though some lawmakers chafe under committee rule, it seems clear that most view sympathetically the role that committees have come to play in the legislative process. Committee chairmen, of course, have a stake in perpetuating the power of committees. Congressman Wilbur Mills, chairman of the House Committee on Ways and Means, defends committee influence in this way:

> I was always taught by Mr. Rayburn [long-time Speaker of the House] that our whole system was to settle disputes within the committees. It's just a waste of time to bring a bill out if you can't pass it. I just don't like to have a record vote for the sake of having a vote.[8]

Partially as the result of its concern to bring experience and specialization to the task of policy-making, Congress in recent years has made increased use of subcommittees—subsidiary units designed to handle legislation and

6 Richard F. Fenno, Jr., "The House Appropriations Committee as a Political System: The Problem of Integration," *American Political Science Review,* LVI (June 1962), 316. For an instructive analysis of specialization and expertise in the state legislature, see John C. Wahlke, Heinz Eulau, William Buchanan, and LeRoy C. Ferguson, *The Legislative System: Explorations in Legislative Behavior* (New York: John Wiley & Sons, Inc., 1962), pp. 193–215. The authors describe the development of an informal system of expertise which is characterized by "subject matter experts." Are these experts really experts? "The best answer to this question is in terms of the communication function performed by experts: they are sufficiently informed to be able to translate the arcana of a segment of society into terms that permit legislators, who after all are part-time officials, to estimate the relative merits and probable consequences of proposals. . . . The limiting factors on the development of genuine expertise are the inability of the legislature to recruit specialists in the fields where they are needed, to retain the ones it develops in view of the district system of elections and high turnover, and to get the ones it has into the right posts in face of partisanship, factionalism, and seniority" (p. 215).

7 "Unwritten Rules of American Politics," *Harper's Magazine,* November 1948, p. 31.

8 Julius Duscha, "The Most Important Man on Capitol Hill Today," *New York Times Magazine,* February 25, 1968, p. 76.

tasks, specific and customarily narrow in scope, passed on to it by the parent committee. In recent Congresses well over two hundred regular subcommittees have functioned, not counting many additional special and temporary subcommittees created to consider nominations or special bills. The membership of subcommittees varies from a majority of the parent committee to one or two members. Some committees, such as the Senate Committee on Foreign Relations and the House Committee on Foreign Affairs, have provided for their subcommittees to assume a consultative role, meeting often with officials in the State and Defense departments. To the specialists, to those with long experience and strategic assignment, enormous power accrues. An example is provided by the subcommittee system of the committees on appropriations, particularly the House group. Though it furnishes the ax, initially, and reports, finally, "the full committee is usually just the formal channel for the expression of the decisions of [its] subcommittees."[9]

As we have noted, congressional committees do not owe their formation to constitutional authorization: the Constitution is as unaware of their existence as it is unaware of political parties, the cabinet, and other central institutions which have developed over time. Similarly, the tasks assigned to committees and the powers accorded them have grown casually and more or less without plan. From time to time the parent bodies tinker with committee structure and organization; occasionally they deem it necessary to reduce the number of committees. But the changes made are minimal, seldom touching—and never dismantling—committee powers or functions. Committees are not simply conduits, natural passages through which legislation flows uneventfully and continuously. Apart from exercising what is often an imperious control over legislation, these subgroups discharge a number of other functions—some at least as important as "lawmaking," and frequently more spectacular and far-reaching.

The functions of committees, it is apparent, are the functions of the legislature itself. Whether we describe committees as "microcosms" of the assembly, as "little legislatures," or as something equally connotative, the important fact to recognize is their assimilation of the powers and duties given the larger houses. A committee's lawmaking function involves studying, sifting, sorting, drafting, and reporting legislation which has been referred to it. In their "executive" capacity, committees are concerned with matters of presidential nominations, treaties, and executive agreements. As investigative bodies, committees hold hearings, invite and subpoena witnesses to testify and to be interrogated, call for records, inquire into the operations of executive agencies and policies, and issue reports. Cast in the role of consultants, some committees meet and confer regularly with administration officials; among the committees dealing with foreign policy this attempt to improve executive-legislative relations is most highly developed. Finally, in a capacity of liaison, committees provide not only a link with the executive branch but, through hearings and other meetings, a bridge to public opinion, a point of access for groups and private individuals, and, in the case of the foreign relations committees, a forum for contact and consultation with visiting foreign officials.

9 Carroll, *The House of Representatives and Foreign Affairs,* p. 153. Also see Fenno, "The House Appropriations Committee," 316.

"Congress," Robert Luce wrote, "is not to any material extent an originating body" for legislation.[10] Neither, it can be quickly added, are its committees. Sometimes, of course, a proposal comes to life purely as a committee product, but that does not occur frequently. The customary response of committees is suggested in this evaluation:

> Occasionally, a committee may initiate a policy, refuse to approve one, or give it a quite different direction and momentum than those who framed it intended. In a broad sense, however, *the committees control policy mainly by a process of erosion.* They take the policy from the executive branch and modify it to suit the congressional temper. If the policy requires successive renewals of authority or funds, the erosion takes place over several years. The policy thereby acquires a congressional imprint.[11]

THE INDEPENDENCE OF COMMITTEES

The extent to which the committees of Congress are autonomous units, largely free from direction by their parent chambers, has long been a subject of discussion but only recently a subject of systematic analysis. In general, it seems likely that autonomy will vary among committees and that overall relationships between the chamber and any committee will be affected by the composition and leadership of each. More precise statements, however, can be made with respect to the appropriations committees of Congress.[12] Richard F. Fenno has found, for example, that House members have four expectations concerning the behavior of members of the Appropriations Committee. In the first place, this committee is expected to "follow consensus-building procedures"—that is, committee decisions are expected to represent the widest agreement possible among available alternatives. The House does not want to be confronted by a number of conflicts that the Appropriations Committee has been unable to solve. If the committee works diligently to gain a broadly based settlement, the chances are good that its recommendations will be accepted by the House. Second, the House expects that the Appropriations Committee will maintain the usual division of labor with other committees—specifically, that it will not *legislate* on appropriations bills, thereby encroaching on the powers of the substantive committees. Third, since the ability of the House to realize its lawmaking and oversight goals is dependent on relatively free access to information, members expect that the Appropriations Committee will utilize its resources to collect information from the executive branch and share it with the House as a whole. Fourth, members expect that the committee will observe the integrative House norms "which call for bargaining and compromise as methods of decision-making, reciprocity as a key to interpersonal relations, subject matter specialization as a key to intercommittee relations, consultation as a key to interparty relations, and seniority as a criterion for

---

[10] Reprinted by permission of the publishers from Robert Luce, *Congress: An Explanation* (Cambridge: Harvard University Press, Copyright 1926, by The President and Fellows of Harvard College), p. 1.

[11] Carroll, *op. cit.,* pp. 110–11 (emphasis added).

[12] This section is based on Richard F. Fenno, Jr., *The Power of the Purse: Appropriations Politics in Congress* (Boston: Little, Brown & Company, 1966). See especially Chapters 1 and 2.

distributing influence."[13] Conformity to these norms is thought by House leaders to be especially important for members of major committees, such as Appropriations; in filling vacancies on this committee party hierarchs look for members who are likely to observe the general integrative norms. To the extent that the committee adheres to these expectations, its autonomy is limited and its relationship to the House is basically dependent.

The failure of the Appropriations Committee to fulfill House expectations may culminate in the House's leveling sanctions against it. Several possible sanctions are available to the membership when "system-subsystem" conflict occurs. For one thing, the House may reduce the committee's jurisdiction, as it did in 1885 when it gave certain substantive committees control over appropriations for some executive departments—an arrangement that lasted until 1920. It is also possible for the House to circumvent the regular appropriations process, and thereby diminish the committee's influence. One way it may do this is to authorize an agency to borrow its funds directly from the Treasury; another way is to empower an agency to enter into contracts for goods prior to receiving appropriations for them. Grant-in-aid programs in which Congress agrees to match state contributions further constrict committee influence. (Liberals in both parties have been the main supporters of "backdoor spending" techniques, and thus the main opponents of the Appropriations Committee.) A second sanction open to the House involves the recruitment and selection of committee members. The appointment of new members can be used to select individuals who are likely to be more responsive to the expectations of the House. Moreover, the size of the committee and its majority-minority party ratio can be manipulated by the House as a means of bringing the committee into line.

A third sanction available to the House is highly visible: the House may accept, reject, or amend Appropriations Committee recommendations on the floor. Although the committee has had substantial success with its recommendations in recent years, the power of the House to upset committee decisions is always present—and occasionally demonstrated. In the fourth place, the House can reduce its dependence on the committee by requiring *annual* agency authorizations by the substantive committees. Appropriations must first be authorized. When an agency's appropriations are made under conditions of permanent authorization, only the Appropriations Committee is involved in yearly review of that agency's program. By contrast, an annual authorization procedure builds up a second group of subject matter experts—the members of the substantive committees—whose counsel then becomes available to House members. Understandably, members of the Appropriations Committee have shown slight enthusiasm over a recent tendency to institute annual authorization procedures, since this leads to a sharing of influence. A final sanction is that the House may change committee budgetary procedures in ways that will augment House influence as a whole in the appropriations process.

Study of the appropriations process indicates that the "whole" Congress is more than a passive spectator to the work of its committees. In both House and Senate there are clear-cut sets of expectations concerning the behavior of the appropriations committees. Behavior that fails to conform to these expectations may prompt the use of sanctions by the parent chamber.

---

13 *Ibid.*, p. 24.

160 The application of sanctions does not occur frequently, which is probably a strong indication that the membership as a whole is satisfied with committee performance. Whether the relationships that exist between the appropriations committees and their parent chambers are characteristic of relationships between other committees and the parent bodies remains to be discovered. Evidence is unavailable. But based on this study, it may be a good guess that relationships between committees and their parent chambers are at least more complicated than conventional interpretations—stressing committee independence and autonomy while ignoring chamber controls—have suggested.

The concern of this chapter, to this point, has been to introduce legislative committees by marking their principal characteristics, noting their activities, and suggesting the general dimensions of their authority. We can now turn to an examination of committee organization and the principal kinds of committees found in legislative bodies.

Kinds of Committees

STANDING COMMITTEES

Standing committees are the permanent units established in the rules of each house. They continue from one session to the next, though the parent house may of course choose to augment or decrease their number from time to time. Organized along policy lines, they are the real draft horses of the legislature, their power sufficient to prompt Woodrow Wilson to describe the American system as "a government by the Standing Committees of the Congress."[14] Their importance traces from the fact that all legislative measures, with but an occasional exception, are sent to appropriate standing committees for consideration.[15]

Standing or permanent committees have been used since the earliest Congresses, though in the formative years reliance was placed chiefly upon the select or special variety.[16] One early Congress created more than three hundred select committees to deal with *ad hoc* problems. To bring order and to save time, Congress soon turned to the further development of standing committees. During the 14th Congress (1816), for example, the Senate adopted a resolution which provided for the appointment of eleven additional standing committees each session, some of which, such as Foreign Relations, Finance, and the Judiciary, have continued to the present. Standing committees were also firmly established in the House by then, and before long each chamber had brought to life more permanent committees

14 Wilson, *op. cit.*, p. 56.

15 By comparison, standing committees in the British House of Commons have a much less significant role. They are clearly subordinate to the chamber—"the instrument and the handmaiden of the House of Commons designed to save its time," states Finer, "Congressional Investigations," p. 535. Their task is to refine legislation in its technical features, not to alter in any fundamental way its scope and purpose.

16 For a wide-ranging study tracing the development of standing committees in the U.S. House of Representatives, see Joseph Cooper, *The Origins of the Standing Committees and the Development of the Modern House* (Houston: Rice University Studies, 1970).

than in fact it knew what to do with. Occasionally it became necessary to weed out certain ones and to combine others, though evidence suggests that Congress was reluctant to make major cuts in committee numbers. Moreover, there were steady demands for new committees to deal with new problems, for example, at one point in history, for a Committee on Indian Depredations.

By 1913 there were seventy-three permanent committees in the Senate, almost one to a senator. Congress finally chose to do something about it, and eliminated a number of committees in 1921. Writing in 1926, Congressman Robert Luce described the situation: "In Congress the Senate has 34 committees, nearly all functioning, for it has reformed its organization. The House has 61, about two thirds of which get something to do, the rest being superfluities, sustained for ulterior but not altogether useless purposes. A score of the House Committees do nine tenths of the work."[17] In 1946 Congress made a concerted effort to rationalize the committee structure by passing the Legislative Reorganization Act, just about as well known under the names of its sponsors, Senator Robert M. La Follette, Jr., and Congressman Mike Monroney.

With the passage of this act Congress had, for the first time in over a century, organized itself in what appeared to be a reasonable number of standing committees. The House cut its roster of permanent committees from forty-eight to nineteen, the Senate from thirty-three to fifteen. Committees which had led a furtive, somnolent existence for decades were now merged with others or, in a few cases, abolished outright. Since 1946, only four new standing committees have been brought forward: Aeronautical and Space Sciences (Senate), Veterans' Affairs (Senate), Science and Astronautics (House), and Standards of Official Conduct (House). Hence the totals now read twenty-one for the House and seventeen for the Senate, as listed in Table 6.1.

It is an easy matter to authorize a new standing committee in Congress—all that is required is the adoption of a resolution. Many of the present standing committees trace their origin to select-committee status. One of the most spectacular, and manifestly among the most controversial, committees to be established in recent decades, shifting from select to standing status, was the House Un-American Activities Committee (HUAC), better known in its early years as the Dies committee and renamed in 1969 as the Internal Security Committee. Responding to the persistent agitation of Texas Congressman Martin Dies and others, the House in 1938 agreed to the formation of a temporary seven-member committee to investigate subversive or un-American propaganda, Fascist and Communist. This committee, whose life span was to have been seven months, became a permanent committee in 1945 in what Robert Carr describes as "one of the most remarkable procedural coups in modern Congressional history." Its transformation occurred on the opening day of the 79th Congress. The story began when the chairman of the Rules Committee made the customary motion that the House rules of the previous session be adopted.[18] Unexpectedly a Mississippi congressman offered an amendment to the resolution

---

17 Luce, *op. cit.,* p. 6.

18 This account is based largely on Robert K. Carr, *The House Committee on Un-American Activities, 1945–50* (Ithaca: Cornell University Press, 1952), pp. 19–20.

TABLE 6.1
Standing Committees of House and Senate

House	Senate
Agriculture	Aeronautical and Space Sciences
Appropriations	Agriculture and Forestry
Armed Services	Appropriations
Banking and Currency	Armed Services
District of Columbia	Banking, Housing and Urban Affairs
Education and Labor	Commerce
Foreign Affairs	District of Columbia
Government Operations	Finance
House Administration	Foreign Relations
Interior and Insular Affairs	Government Operations
Internal Security	Interior and Insular Affairs
Interstate and Foreign Commerce	Judiciary
Judiciary	Labor and Public Welfare
Merchant Marine and Fisheries	Post Office and Civil Service
Post Office and Civil Service	Public Works
Public Works	Rules and Administration
Rules	Veterans' Affairs
Science and Astronautics	
Standards of Official Conduct	
Veterans' Affairs	
Ways and Means	

to provide that the Un-American Activities Committee, which had been limping along in the preceding sessions, be made a standing committee. No alternative was present but to vote on the question on the floor then, since, technically, prior to the adoption of the rules, no committees were in existence. In a close vote, the amendment was accepted and the Un-American Activities Committee was given a long lease on life, probably for the reason that many members were reluctant to fasten on their public records a vote which might be interpreted as somehow "un-American."[19]

Presumably in quest of better organization and greater efficiency of operation, state legislatures have appropriated the formula fashioned in the

[19] HUAC comes under the review of the entire House each year at the stage of authorizing funds for its operations. In 1965, the annual authorization fight was enlivened by a motion to hold public hearings on the justification of funds for the committee. Not unexpectedly, the motion lost by a vote of 333 to 58. It is instructive to examine the variables that *tend* to be associated with opposition to HUAC. In the first place, nearly all the opponents of the committee are northern Democrats. Nonetheless, there are about twice as many northern Democrats who favor the committee as there are northern Democrats who oppose it. Among *northern Democrats,* what factors differentiate "pro-HUAC" members from "anti-HUAC" members? In general, "anti-HUAC" congressmen tend to come from urban districts with substantial foreign stock and ethnic concentrations (particularly Russian-American). As for the congressmen themselves, opponents of the committee are more likely to be Jews than Catholics or Protestants, to be better educated than supporters, to be lawyers rather than businessmen, to have more liberal voting records than supporters, to be nonleaders rather than leaders, and to rank lower in seniority than supporters. See Lewis A. Kaplan, "The House Un-American Activities Committee and its Opponents: A Study of Congressional Dissonance," *Journal of Politics,* XXX (August 1968), 647–71.

La Follette–Monroney act of 1946, that of reducing the number of standing committees. Despite the fact that committees once formed are difficult to uproot, the legislatures have been able to consolidate and eliminate an odd mélange of committees. How well they have succeeded in simplifying committee organization is shown in Table 6.2, taken from recent analyses

TABLE 6.2

Decrease in Number of Standing Committees in State Legislatures, 1946–69

Number of Standing Committees	Number of States in Each Range					
	House		Senate*		Joint	
	1946	*1969*	*1946*	*1969*	*1946†*	*1969‡*
10 or under	0	7	0	8	23	19
11–20	2	20	8	26	0	4
21–30	9	15	15	12	0	1
31–40	15	4	13	3	2	0
41–50	12	2	9	0	1	0
51–60	7	0	2	0	0	0
61–70	2	0	1	0	0	0

SOURCES: *The Book of the States, 1966–67* (Chicago: Council of State Governments, 1967), p. 68; *The Book of the States, 1970–71* (Chicago: Council of State Governments, 1971), p. 73.
* Nebraska is included only under "Senate."
† Excludes 22 states reporting no joint standing committees.
‡ Excludes 25 states reporting no joint standing committees.

in *The Book of the States*. What no analysis has shown, however, is whether a reduction in the number of committees contributes, either slightly or significantly, to the legislature's ability to maintain itself and to meet the demands that are made upon it. A generation of writers on the legislative process has become habituated to the notion that standing committee reduction is a good thing—but this is largely an article of faith.

In 1946 the median number of state house standing committees was thirty-nine; by 1969 the number had been reduced to eighteen. Comparable figures for state senates were thirty-one in 1946 and sixteen in 1969. Committee proliferation is best exhibited in Mississippi, which has forty-six standing committees in the house and forty in the senate, a total of eighty-six. Texas maintains a total of seventy-two committees, followed by North Carolina with sixty-seven, and Missouri with sixty-five.[20] About one-half of the states have more standing committees than Congress. Such vast redundancy obviously cannot be justified on the grounds that state legislation is more complex than national, necessitating greater specialization among committees. Nevertheless, it is difficult to bring about a consolidation of committees for the principal reason that the office of chairman, even of the lowliest committee, confers status upon its occupant. Committee chairmen are rarely in the vanguard of movements to rationalize the existing system. In addition, there is always a steady pressure to create new committees in order that chairmanships may be awarded deserving members of the party.

[20] *The Book of the States, 1970–71*, p. 73.

The tendency of legislatures to form a multitude of committees is not, by itself, any more a vice than getting along with a small number of committees is a virtue.[21] Yet this tendency does create a special problem, for the presence of numerous committees means that each legislator is given a heavy load of committee assignments. When C. I. Winslow made his pioneering study of state legislative committees in 1931, he found that the average senator held 7.6 committee assignments and the average representative 4.5. In Illinois, the average assignment for each senator was an incredible 18.5 committees, and senators from North Carolina, Pennsylvania, and Georgia were not far behind.[22]

Although there has been a notable reduction in committee assignments in recent years, there are still many state chambers (particularly senates) in which members serve on four or more committees. There is nothing mysterious about the consequences of multiple committee memberships: legislators are both overworked and underspecialized in the committees. Their plight is further aggravated by the impossibility of being in two or more places at the same time, since committee meetings are often scheduled simultaneously. Where legislators have numerous committee assignments, they are forced to be selective as to those committees in which they will be active members.

From the standpoint of number of committee assignments, national lawmakers find themselves in a better position than state lawmakers, but this has not always been true. Prior to the passage of the Legislative Reorganization Act of 1946, each senator held membership on an average of five standing committees, each representative on an average of two. Following passage of the act, with but a few exceptions, each senator was given a maximum of two committee assignments and each congressman was placed on only one. The trend since then has been for many members of the House to take on double committee assignments. As of 1965, 40 percent of the House members held two committee seats as compared with 11 percent in 1949. Single committee assignments continue to be the rule for members of such House committees as Appropriations, Ways and Means, Armed Services, Rules, and Agriculture.[23] Overall, the reduction of com-

---

[21] Discussing the Arizona legislature, Dean E. Mann argues that "the long-run impact of a large number of committees appears to be slight. The less important committees usually have little legislation referred to them, and their membership is usually made up of the least influential members of the legislature. On the other hand...the existence of a few decorative committees may have some positive benefits to the leadership. They may provide the means of casting into outer darkness certain mavericks who are out of favor with the leadership but who must be given some committee assignments. Moreover, these committees are useful in allowing the presiding officer to dole out favors in the form of chairmanships to certain members who may be flattered by the title, even though the chairmanships are meaningless in terms of power." "The Legislative Committee System in Arizona," *Western Political Quarterly,* XIV (December 1961), 925–41, quotation on p. 927.

[22] C. I. Winslow, *State Legislative Committees: A Study in Procedure* (Baltimore: Johns Hopkins Press, 1931), p. 37.

[23] Louis C. Gawthrop, "Changing Membership Patterns in House Committees," *American Political Science Review,* LX (June 1966), 366–73.

mittee assignments since the 1940s is somewhat deceptive, since subcommittees have been created in extraordinary number.

Further changes in committee assignments were made in the 1970 Legislative Reorganization Act. Under its terms, no senator is permitted to serve on more than one of the Armed Services, Appropriations, Finance, or Foreign Relations committees. In addition, the act limits senators to the chairmanship of one committee and one subcommittee of a major committee. However, these restrictions apply only to future assignments, not to positions held when the act was passed.

SELECT COMMITTEES

Select committees are limited, episodic bodies created by resolution for the purpose of undertaking a particular task, such as an investigation or study. Members ordinarily are appointed by the presiding officer, and when the committee has made its report to the chamber, it is disbanded. Although they resemble standing committees, and sometimes are transformed into them, they do not customarily originate legislation; for example, only two out of thirty-four select committees formed in the U.S. House of Representatives since passage of the 1946 Legislative Reorganization Act were given the power to report legislation.

Any one of several reasons may underlie the establishment of a select committee. In the House of Representatives they have been formed to accommodate interest groups wanting special attention given their claims, to reward a legislator by giving him the chairmanship of a committee, to evade the jurisdiction of a standing committee considered unsuitable for an assignment, and to undertake a particular task when two or more standing committees might contest jurisdiction in the matter. Select committees in the House generally have had slight influence on public policy. One study of House select committees established during six Congresses (80th–85th) concludes that a majority "did not perform as legislative committees but functioned as institutions for the self-education of the House and the education of American publics, and also as forums and service centers for interest groups that claimed to have inadequate access to the regular standing committees."[24]

JOINT COMMITTEES

Joint committees, formed through concurrent resolution or legislative act, get their names from the nature of their membership, since they are composed of legislators from each house. There are three principal subtypes: *conference* (which has the temporary status of a select committee), *select*

---

[24] See V. Stanley Vardys, "Select Committees of the House of Representatives," *Midwest Journal of Political Science,* VI (August 1962), 247–65, on which this discussion is based. The quotation appears on p. 265. See also articles by Roy Hamilton, "The Senate Select Committee on National Resources: An Ethical and Rational Criticism," *Natural Resources Journal,* II (April 1962), 45–54, and Dale Vinyard, "Congressional Committees on Small Business," *Midwest Journal of Political Science,* X (August 1966), 364–77.

166 (generally charged with very minor joint administrative functions),[25] and *standing*. Congress has made some use of joint standing committees, and in a few states—Connecticut, Maine, and Massachusetts—they constitute the predominant form of committee organization. Joint committees are used in twenty-one additional states, but their activities not only are limited but usually are of low urgency.

As of 1971 there were ten joint committees in Congress, probably the best known of which are the Joint Committee on Atomic Energy, the Joint Economic Committee, the Joint Committee on Reduction of Nonessential Federal Expenditures, and the Joint Committee on Internal Revenue Taxation. Most of the chairmen of joint committees happen to be senators, but this is the result of practice, not requirement. The only joint committee to which legislation is referred is the Joint Committee on Atomic Energy.

Joint committees traditionally have been prescribed as a means of achieving coordination in a bicameral legislative system. Some of the claims made for them are clearly verifiable, as the following list should indicate, while others rest chiefly upon the impressions offered by observers and legislators themselves. The advantages of joint committees, as estimated by the Committee on American Legislatures of the American Political Science Association, are that:

1. They avoid the necessity for dual consideration of bills, which is both time-consuming and expensive.
2. They provide the means for better coordination of the work of the two houses, avoiding much of the usual friction and misunderstanding.
3. They facilitate the expeditious consideration of legislation and afford some of the advantages of a unicameral legislature while retaining a bicameral system.
4. They provide, as a rule, for more thorough consideration of legislation and the better utilization of qualified staff than is possible with separate committees.
5. They reduce the use of companion bills, as well as the need for conference committees.[26]

CONFERENCE COMMITTEES

Among the run of joint committees, one kind in particular stands out—the conference committee. These committees, preeminent examples of committee power, hold the key to the fate of many major legislative proposals. Since committees of conference are more important in Congress than in the state legislatures, we begin discussion at the national level.

A conference committee is an *ad hoc* committee created to adjust differences between the chambers when a legislative proposal passes one house in one form and is amended in the other, with the second chamber

---

[25] Typical tasks of state joint select committees involve making the necessary arrangements for the inauguration of state officers-elect, escorting the governor to the chamber for his message to the assembly, or formulating joint rules for the two houses.

[26] Belle Zeller, ed., *American State Legislatures* (New York: Thomas Y. Crowell Company, 1954), pp. 100–101.

unwilling to recede from its amendment(s) and the originating house unwilling to accept the alteration. Since a bill or resolution cannot be transmitted to the executive unless it has passed both houses in identical form, in cases of interchamber disagreement a request for a conference committee may be made.

Conference committee members, termed managers or conferees, are appointed by the Speaker of the House and by the presiding officer of the Senate. The chairmen of the committees possessing jurisdiction over the bill normally will recommend the appointment of certain individuals. The principle of seniority may or may not be followed in selecting managers, though customarily each house will request the committee chairman and the ranking majority and minority members to serve. It is expected that the conferees will be prepared to represent the position of their respective houses in conference deliberations, but not to such a point that compromise is impossible. The following account of conference negotiations over appropriations shows the viewpoint of the House:

> The Appropriations Committee or, rather, a few of its members act as the spokesmen for the House in these negotiations. They are expected to drive as hard a bargain as possible on behalf of those provisions approved by the House. House expectations may be registered in different ways and with different degrees of intensity. In some instances the House may, by special roll call vote, "instruct" its conferees, i.e., bind them, to a certain position. Ordinary roll calls may also register House expectations. In these cases, the more lopsided the roll call votes the more firm is the House expectation that its position should be upheld. In other cases, individual Members will simply exhort the Committee to "stand hitched" or to "fight until the snow comes if necessary to maintain the position of the House in effecting reduction in these bills." The House expects, however, that the Committee will have to compromise if a bill is to be produced. They hope that Appropriations Committee conferees will draw upon a sufficient reservoir of institutional patriotism and skill to produce compromises which they can claim as "victories" over "the other body." But House members do not expect to fix the terms of the compromise themselves. Again, within certain guidelines, the specifics of decision-making are left to the Committee.[27]

The conference process calls for the appointment of between three and nine members in each house from the ranks of both parties; there is no requirement that each house appoint the same number of managers. A majority of the managers representing *each* house must agree to the conference report before it can be sent to the chambers.[28]

The houses may choose to instruct their managers or to grant them free rein—within the rules—to reach a compromise with conferees from the other house; in practice it makes little difference since the chambers actually do not insist on their instructions being followed. Conference committees

[27] Fenno, *The Power of the Purse*, p. 19.
[28] The discussion of conference committees in this section draws heavily upon the authoritative study by Gilbert Y. Steiner, *The Congressional Conference Committee, Seventieth to Eightieth Congresses* (Urbana: University of Illinois Press, 1951).

168 have been the object of persistent criticism over the years, the principal charge being that they exceed their authority, writing virtually new legislation rather than adjusting differences in the separate versions. If true, this becomes of crucial importance, since in each instance only a handful of legislators meeting in secret prepare the conference report; and reports brought back to each chamber commonly appear late in the session and, with time running out, usually are accepted.[29] The problem is magnified in the eyes of critics by the fact that nearly all major congressional measures wind up being routed through committees of conference.

Under congressional rules of procedure, conference committees are not expected to make any material change in the measure at issue, either by deleting provisions to which both houses have already agreed or by inserting new provisions. But this is a difficult provision to enforce. Note the problem when one house amends a proposal originating in the other house by striking out everything following the enacting clause and substituting provisions which make it an entirely new bill. The versions are now altogether different, permitting a conference committee to draft essentially a new bill. Gilbert Steiner's study of two decades of conference committee action, however, does not support the allegation that these committees are irresponsible or that they consistently flout the legal limits of their power. Out of fifty-six major pieces of legislation sent to conference committee between the 70th and 80th Congresses, he found only three cases in which completely new bills were produced by the committees. Of comparable interest is his analysis which shows that the House of Representatives had a greater impact than the Senate on the final versions of thirty-two out of fifty-six proposals. Senate influence was decisive in fifteen instances, and influence was about equal in the remaining nine. This finding contradicts the popular impression that the Senate's side usually wins out at the conference stage.[30]

The question of Senate and House influence in conference committees is not wholly settled. Although Steiner found that the influence of the House was predominant in *appropriations* conferences, a more recent study, covering the years 1947–62, finds that Senate conferees have tended to dominate decisions on appropriations. Of 331 appropriations conferences occurring during this period, the "dollar outcome" in the final bill was closer to the Senate version than the House version in 187 cases. House conferees won 101 times, and the two groups "split the difference" in forty-three cases. The Senate thus won almost twice as many contests in conference as the House. Several explanations for Senate dominance have been advanced. One is that the Senate tends to be the "high house"—that is, it usually comes to conference supporting higher appropriations than the House. When demands

[29] A study of five recent Congresses (86th through 90th) discloses that typically about one-quarter of all conference reports are submitted in the final calendar week preceding adjournment. Interestingly, not a single conference report brought to the floor in the final week of the *second* session of any of these Congresses was recommitted or rejected. Pressures to accept conference reports at this time are particularly acute since bills pending when Congress adjourns at the end of the second session are dead. See David L. Paletz, "Influence in Congress: An Analysis of the Conference Committee and its Procedures," Annual Meeting of the American Political Science Association, Los Angeles, September 8–12, 1970. This paper stresses manager influence and strategies in the conference process.

[30] Steiner, *op. cit.,* pp. 170–72.

for appropriations overcome sentiments for economy, as they often do, the Senate wins. Yet this explanation suffers from the fact that the Senate wins about as often when it supports the *lower* figure as when it supports the higher figure. Fenno believes that Senate influence is stronger in conference "because the Senate [Appropriations] Committee and its conferees draw more directly and more completely upon the support of their parent chamber than do the House [Appropriations] Committee and its conferees...." "When the Senate conferees go to the conference room," he writes, "they not only represent the Senate—they are the Senate. The position they defend will have been worked out with a maximum of participation by Senate members and will enjoy a maximum of support in that body." Chamber support for House conferees, in contrast, is more tenuous—one probable reason for this is that House members as a whole are not as "economy-minded" as the members of the Appropriations Committee. Given less than firm support by members of their own chamber, House conferees may be tempted to yield at critical junctures in conference negotiations.[31]

Whether the House or Senate "wins" in conference may well depend on the policy questions at stake. For example, John Manley has shown that the final settlements on tax and trade legislation tend to be closer to Senate versions than to House versions, while Social Security legislation is more likely to find the House getting its way. The study suggests that in the case of both tax and trade legislation, the Senate does better "because politically Senate decisions are more in line with the demands of interest groups, lobbyists, and constituents than House decisions." On the other hand, the House has tended to dominate Social Security legislation through its capacity to insist that such legislation be sound from an actuarial standpoint—i.e., that liberalized benefits be accompanied by increases in the Social Security tax and/or in the wage base subject to the tax.[32]

The "who wins–who loses" argument is invariably difficult to settle not only because of the complexity of legislation but because "the process is not a zero sum situation." Gains derived in one respect may be offset by losses in another:

> The overriding ethic of the conference committee is one of bargaining, give-and-take, compromise, swapping, horse-trading, conciliation, and malleability by all concerned. Firm positions are always taken, and always changed. Deadlocks rarely occur to the degree that the bill is killed. Someone gives

[31] Fenno, *The Power of the Purse,* Chapter 12, quotation on p. 669. In this discussion the dominance of the Senate refers only to *conference-committee decisions* and not to the appropriations process as a whole. Overall, the House wields far more influence on appropriations than does the Senate. Further evidence that in recent Congresses the Senate has had more success than the House in conference involving a wide range of legislation can be found in an article by David J. Vogler, "Patterns of One House Dominance in Congressional Conference Committees," *Midwest Journal of Political Science,* XIV (May 1970), 303–20. In a study of 596 conferences in five Congresses over a twenty-year period, Vogler found that of those conference outcomes marked by a "victory" for one or the other house, the House prevailed 35 per cent of the time as against 65 per cent for the Senate. This study should also be consulted for the identification of those House and Senate standing committees whose conference successes have been greatest over the years.

[32] *The Politics of Finance: The House Committee on Ways and Means* (Boston: Little, Brown & Company, 1970), pp. 269–94, quotation on p. 279.

a little, perhaps after an impressive walkout, in return for a little; compromise is the cardinal rule of conference committees. Small wonder that each side claims victory; because almost everyone does win—something, somehow, sometime.[33]

An ancient criticism of conference committees is that they are particularly vulnerable to the machinations of political interest groups. A small group of legislators conferring in private—not much imagination is required to see pressure groups lurking just out of sight, tugging strings to make certain that some provisions are included in the conference report and others excluded. This was a special theme sounded by George Norris, U.S. senator from Nebraska and a hardy advocate of unicameralism. How great lobby influence is at the conference stage remains unknown; all that can be stated with certainty is that the conference is a critical point in the evolution of legislative proposals and that lobbyists appreciate this fact as well as anyone. For those who like their politics laced with intrigue, the role of the lobby at this juncture in the process is interesting to imagine. Evidence, however, is fugitive.[34]

Very few state legislators have reason to lie awake nights lamenting the power of conference committees or their immoderate use, for as a rule they are neither very powerful nor used very often. Their influence occupies a threshold well below that of congressional conference committees, sometimes referred to as the "third house." States which use conference committees have adopted procedures similar to those of Congress: managers are appointed by the presiding officers, all meetings are conducted in secrecy, no witnesses may appear, reports require the independent approval of a majority of each house's managers, and each chamber must accept the report as a whole.

A study of several sessions of the Pennsylvania General Assembly shows that between 2 and 5 per cent of all bills passed are the products of conference committees; the legislation involved has often been of major significance.[35] In Wisconsin, conference committees do not loom very important, since normally one or the other of the houses will either agree to the change or else make it known that the differences are irreconcilable.[36] In North Carolina, conference committees seldom number more than a handful dur-

---

[33] *Ibid.,* p. 271.

[34] Not only private groups but party agencies and the administration ought to be viewed as "lobbies" for particular purposes. As an example, a controversy developed near the end of the 86th Congress when the secretary of defense attempted to influence House and Senate conferees meeting to reconcile differences on defense appropriations for the approaching fiscal year. Members of the conference committee reportedly were annoyed when the secretary, in a letter to the committee, did not limit himself to noting preferences between the House and Senate versions. Instead, he plumped for adoption of the administration plan, which was not fully represented in either version. This prompted one conferee to note that: "The purpose of the conference is to adjust differences between House and Senate and not between Congress and the Administration." *New York Times,* June 26, 1960, p. 1.

[35] Richard Lee Conaway, *The Legislative Process in Pennsylvania* (Master's thesis, University of Pittsburgh, 1958), pp. 196–99.

[36] *Securing Agreement on Legislation Between the Assembly and Senate in Wisconsin: The Conference Committee* (Madison: Wisconsin Legislative Reference Library, 1955), p. 1.

ing a session.[37] In Illinois, conference committees rarely are utilized because of the willingness of the house whose bill has been amended to accept the change made in the other chamber. Occasionally, of course, reconciliation of viewpoints is impossible, and bills die in conference.[38]

SUBCOMMITTEES

In some respects the most noteworthy development in committee organization and management in Congress has been the vigorous growth of subcommittees.[39] In 1946, shortly before adoption of the Legislative Reorganization Act which eliminated a number of standing committees, there were 180 subcommittees of all kinds in Congress; by the early 1970s the total had grown to a mixed lot of over 250. The typical senator today is likely to serve on at least six subcommittees while a representative may have two subcommittee assignments.

Among close observers of Congress there is no enthusiasm for the remarkable growth of the subcommittee system. Although numbers like these do not establish anything conclusively, they suggest to critics that power in Congress has become more fragmented, making the task of developing a coherent legislative program even more difficult. Be that as it may, what outsiders think of their parliamentary arrangements and habits is not often of great moment to the members of Congress. Moreover, congressmen may contend that the difficulties created by a large number of subcommittees do not outweigh their advantages. Among the latter, two claims in particular stand out: first, that an extensive subcommittee organization encourages increased specialization, thereby enlarging the effectiveness of the legislature as a whole; second, that the presence of many subcommittees permits younger members to play more prominent roles and to win recognition in a committee system ordinarily dominated by senior legislators. From the standpoint of political interest groups, an extensive subcommittee system is likely to be advantageous because it offers additional points of access in the legislative process.[40]

The crucial question concerning congressional subcommittees is their power *vis-à-vis* parent committees and chambers. By and large, there is no meaningful control over subcommittees by the parent chambers, and there is great variation from committee to committee. Subcommittees may be virtually autonomous. As one staff member has observed: "Given an active subcommittee chairman, working in a specialized field with a staff of his own, the parent committee can do no more than change the grammar of a

---

[37] Henry W. Lewis, *Legislative Committees in North Carolina* (Chapel Hill: University of North Carolina, Institute of Government, 1952), p. 54.

[38] Gilbert Y. Steiner and Samuel K. Gove, *Legislative Politics in Illinois* (Urbana: University of Illinois Press, 1960), p. 19.

[39] This discussion is based in large part on the work of George Goodwin, Jr., *The Little Legislatures: Committees of Congress* (Amherst: University of Massachusetts Press, 1970), especially pp. 45–63.

[40] Certain agencies in the executive branch also may profit from special clientele relations with subcommittees. For an account of the linkage between the military establishment and the appropriations subcommittees on defense (especially the House unit), a relationship that has substantially diminished the armed services committees' influence on military policy, see Bernard K. Gordon, "The Military Budget: Congressional Phase," *Journal of Politics*, XXIII (November 1961), 689–710.

172 subcommittee report."[41] In general, it appears that the extent to which subcommittees enjoy independent power is determined chiefly by the committee chairman's outlook and ideology. Ordinarily, a conservative chairman is reluctant to vest much authority in subcommittees (which might come under the influence of younger liberals); he may choose not to create subcommittees at all; if he finds it prudent to use them, he may seek to make their jurisdictions vague and indeterminate, perhaps simply by numbering them instead of assigning specific subjects to their attention.

The chairman's powers over subcommittees are impressive—including, usually, the prerogatives of creating the unit, establishing its size, naming the membership, specifying party ratios, making arrangements for staff and funds, and referring proposals to it. In committees in which power is decentralized, the subcommittee system is likely to have a life and style of its own, little regulated by the parent committee in matters of staff and operations. The House Committee on Government Operations tends to fit this model. Over the long run, centralized control over subcommittees by the chairman is likely to be eroded; whether further decentralization of power would prove salutary may depend on developments within the party organizations in Congress. Whatever the case, the question is important since subcommittee decisions often emerge as the ultimate judgments of Congress.

Committee Jurisdiction

The Legislative Reorganization Act of 1946 sought to simplify and improve the committee structure of Congress by reducing the number of committees and clarifying their jurisdictions, and there is widespread agreement among lawmakers and observers that this law has been beneficial. But organizational problems remain, and some undoubtedly can never be met fully. Among the nettling, recurring problems is that of committee jurisdiction over legislation. The dilemma is apparent in the nature of legislation itself, for very few measures are so simple as to deal with only one subject. Although the usual bill involves a number of complex and interrelated subjects, it is, as a rule, considered by a single standing committee, one relatively specialized at that. As a result, policy interrelationships may be missed, emerging policies may begin or come to work at cross purposes, and committees may wrangle with each other over the custody of measures and activities.

The problems resulting from committees working in relative isolation on complex and far-reaching legislation, if difficult to solve, are at least easy to see. One example is found in legislation affecting transportation. The Senate and House have parallel committees on public works, and each is assigned legislation that calls for the expenditure of funds for transportation, except for legislation on airports and highways which is referred to the committees on interstate and foreign commerce in both houses. Proposals which deal with the merchant marine are sent to the Senate Committee on Interstate and Foreign Commerce and the House Committee on Merchant Marine and Fisheries. Matters pertaining to inland waterways are expected

---

41 Quoted by Goodwin, *op. cit.,* p. 45.

to be sent, according to the rules, to the Senate and House committees on interstate and foreign commerce, but, at the same time, committees on public works in both houses are given jurisdiction over legislation relative to "rivers and harbors" and navigation. Not surprisingly, therefore, despite the enjoiner in the Transportation Act of 1940 for Congress to develop, coordinate, and preserve a "national transportation system by water, highway, and rail," legislation concerning these areas is considered piece by piece among separate committees. Hence it is difficult and perhaps impossible for Congress to act in terms of a total transportation problem.[42]

Even such a relatively narrow band of legislation as aid to education is affected by jurisdictional problems. Congressman Richard Bolling of Missouri, a long-time advocate of congressional reform, writes:

> Committee jurisdiction is now a maze that confounds even veteran members. For example, as many as eighteen committees have jurisdiction over one or more programs of aid to education. In any one Congress, only one-third to one-half of the education bills are referred to the Education and Labor Committee itself. Interstate and Foreign Commerce Committee, for an obscure historical reason, has jurisdiction over education bills affecting physicians and dentists; Veterans' Affairs over education programs for veterans; Armed Services over programs for servicemen and women; Ways and Means over legislation to give tax credits to parents with children in college; Banking and Currency has had bills relating to college classroom construction; and Science and Astronautics over science scholarships. The power and importance of a committee and its chairman can have an almost 1-to-1 relationship to its jurisdiction. Consequently, no matter how clear the need for rationalization in respect to jurisdictions, the *status quo* has sensitive, powerful allies outside the Congress. Inside, the condition persists by means of a mutual protection society. Members defend their own committee's entrenched preserve by telling the members of other committees, "You may be the 'victim' the next time."[43]

Committee jurisdiction has a substantial impact on the fate of legislation. Consider the matter of urban interests in Congress:

> House and Senate committee systems were hardly designed to promote rational, comprehensive consideration of federal policy for urban areas. Committees are organized largely on the basis of governmental functions, cutting across the concerns of area around which local governments are organized to tackle problems. [There are] six different House committees and six different Senate committees playing a central role in managing bills about urban problems. Not one of the committees demonstrates broad concern for urban dimensions of the issues before it. The closest to this ideal are probably the Housing subcommittees of the House and Senate Banking and Currency Committees, or perhaps the District of Columbia Committees

[42] Burton N. Behling, "Committee Organization of the Congress with Reference to Matters Affecting Transportation," in *Some Problems of Committee Jurisdiction,* S. Doc. no. 51, 82d Cong., 1st sess., July 1951, pp. 15–18.

[43] *Power in the House* (New York: E. P. Dutton & Co., Inc., 1968), pp. 262–63.

of the two Houses, but even here each pair of committees has its own special orientation, the former functional and the latter geographic.[44]

Any attempt to sketch the shape of committee coordination would be incomplete without reference to foreign affairs, since no field of congressional policy-making is more subject to the decisions of disparate, conflicting, and often competing units. Holbert Carroll writes of the problem in the House of Representatives:

> The Committee on Foreign Affairs now [i.e., in 1966] competes with eighteen other standing committees and miscellaneous select and special units for the foreign policy business of the House of Representatives. All of these committees are at least indirectly concerned with foreign affairs. More than half of them regularly consider important foreign policy matters, usually in jealous isolation from one another.

And again:

> At least twelve...standing committees of the House, as well as several special units that function intermittently, hold key pieces of the foreign economic jig saw puzzle. Like unwelcome ghosts, foreign economic policy considerations hover over committees working on seemingly "domestic" legislation such as price supports for farm products and the construction of public works. Only rarely has the House paused to survey objectives or goals or the relationships among the problems under consideration. Each committee, in response to the unique combination of pressures it feels, goes its own way.[45]

Occasionally, disputes erupt between committees over jurisdiction in particular investigations. For example, in the early 1960s, a Senate investigation of corruption among officials of the International Brotherhood of Teamsters was stalled as a result of jurisdictional conflict between the Permanent Subcommittee on Investigations and the Labor Committee. Labor leaders generally preferred the Labor Committee to assume jurisdiction, in the belief that unions might fare somewhat better in its more friendly environs. The permanent subcommittee's claim to jurisdiction was traced to the requirement that unions must submit annual financial statements to the Department of Labor, and such reports, numbering in the thousands each year, were examined rarely if at all by government agents. Since the permanent subcommittee's jurisdiction centers on investigation of inefficiency and malpractice in government agencies, it had at least a minimal claim to jurisdiction. The controversy eventually was stilled by the creation of a special committee, the Select Committee on Improper Activities in the Labor or Management Field, composed of four members from each committee. With this problem met, the formal investigation was begun.[46]

44 Frederic N. Cleaveland, *Congress and Urban Problems: Legislating for Urban Areas, reprint* 124 (Washington, D.C.: The Brookings Institution, 1967), p. 297.

45 Carroll, *op. cit.,* pp. 25–26 and 39.

46 See Robert F. Kennedy, *The Enemy Within* (New York: Harper & Row, Publishers, 1960), pp. 21–24.

Jurisdictional conflicts between the powerful House Appropriations Committee and the legislative (or substantive) committees occur with some frequency. Expenditures for governmental programs must first receive *authorization* by legislative committees, but money does not become available for programs until set forth in *appropriations* bills. The power of the Appropriations Committee and its subcommittees to influence programs, undoing earlier policy decisions, makes jurisdictional rivalries with the substantive committees inevitable. Moreover, the substantive committees object on jurisdictional grounds when the Appropriations Committee attaches conditions, or "legislates," in appropriations bills.

In general, committee jurisdictions are considerably more ambiguous in state legislatures than in Congress. Rules governing assignment of bills to state legislative committees are rarely detailed, and presiding officers (or committees on the assignment of bills) are likely to enjoy a large measure of discretion in bill referral.[47] The decision as to which committee a measure will be referred may well decide its fate. Thus, for example, the Illinois legislature was unable to pass a bill permitting the sale of precolored oleomargarine until the 1951 session when, abandoning precedent, the Speaker of the House referred the bill to the executive committee rather than the agricultural committee. The latter committee, a dominant voice of farm interests, had in previous sessions been able to protect the butter industry by refusing to send the oleo bill to the floor.

Practice and rules often conspire to define jurisdictions so broadly as to give a few committees a disproportionate share of the legislative workload. A statistical example drawn from a study of the New York Senate illustrates the problem. In one session, more than one-quarter of all bills were referred to two committees, judiciary and finance. The nine busiest committees averaged 176 bills per committee during the session, while the ten committees to which the fewest bills had been referred averaged but 11.6 bills per committee. Time for careful consideration obviously is short in those committees which process an unduly large number of measures.[48]

Since bills often involve the interests of two or more standing committees, jurisdictional squabbles inevitably arise. A partial solution, one which may soften conflicts, lies in promoting greater cooperation among committees. George Galloway recommends four methods by which this might be achieved: the formulation of parallel committees in the two chambers, interlocking memberships among committees with common concerns, simultaneous or consecutive reference of a bill to two or more appropriate committees, and increased utilization of joint committees and of joint staffing.[49]

Committee Members and Committee Chairmen

"Congress is an institution in which power and position are highly valued. Seniority is not only a rule governing committee chairmanships, it

[47] For the most part, however, bill referral is a perfunctory matter. As in the case of Congress, reference of bills is normally the task of the parliamentarian, his assistant, or clerks working in the offices of the presiding officers.

[48] Zeller, *op. cit.,* p. 99.

[49] *Some Problems of Committee Jurisdiction,* pp. 1–4.

176 is also a spirit pervading the total behavior."[50] There are few features of congressional life which elude a brush with seniority, extending as it does not only to the selection of committee chairmen but also at times to the assignment of members to committees and to the choice of subcommittee chairmen and conference committee members. "It affects the deference shown legislators on the floor, the assignment of office space, even invitations to dinner."[51] Before we consider the seniority system and its ramifications, however, an explanation of the methods for assigning members to committees is required.

THE MACHINERY OF CONGRESSIONAL COMMITTEE ASSIGNMENT

Not the least example of the proposition that the internal system of authority in Congress was never meant to be easily understood by the outsider is the manner in which committee assignments are made. Four techniques are used. In the House of Representatives the Democratic party gives the responsibility of distributing committee assignments to a committee-on-committees composed of the Democratic members of the Ways and Means Committee, the Speaker (when the party holds a majority), and the floor leader. Members of the Ways and Means Committee have been selected earlier by the party caucus,[52] and membership on the committee carries over from Congress to Congress. House Republicans employ a committee-on-committees to make the selections; each state which has a Republican representative is entitled to a seat on this committee, with each committee member permitted to cast as many votes as there are members in his state party delegation.

By and large, Democratic and Republican practices in making House committee assignments are about the same. The main difference is that the Republicans use a proportional voting system in the committee-on-committees, which augments the influence of states with large Republican delegations. If the Democrats were to adopt this plan, it would increase the influence of large northern, midwestern, and western states; such a plan would also collide with the southern power structure supported by seniority. Both the Republican and Democratic committees are dominated by senior members and are "virtually immune to immediate pressures brought about by electoral changes."[53]

Senate Republicans provide for the chairman of the Republican con-

---

[50] Ernest S. Griffith, *Congress: Its Contemporary Role* (New York: New York University Press, 1951), p. 19.

[51] George Goodwin, Jr., "The Seniority System in Congress," *American Political Science Review*, LIII (June 1959), 412.

[52] House committee appointments prior to 1910 were made by the Speaker. The power now rests with party leaders and committees-on-committees as a result of the successful "revolution of 1910" in which Speaker Joseph Cannon's formal powers were substantially diminished. Along with the power to appoint committee members, Cannon lost the right to select the chairmen.

[53] The discussion of committee assignment practices in the U.S. House of Representatives is based principally on research by Nicholas A. Masters, "Committee Assignments in the House of Representatives," *American Political Science Review*, LV (June 1961), 345–57, with quoted material drawn from pages 350 and 352.

ference to appoint the committee-on-committees, which in turn makes committee assignments. In the case of Senate Democrats, the floor leader appoints a steering committee to make the selections.

Because Congress devolves great power upon its committees, the mechanisms for making committee assignments take on great importance. Over the years liberal Democrats in the Senate have contended that the steering committee has tended to favor conservatives over liberals in the assignment of seats to preferred committees, thus leading to the maintenance of committees that lack geographical and ideological balance. Some evidence that this is true can be found in the fact that, taken as a group, the voting records of members of certain major Senate committees (e.g., Finance, Appropriations, Armed Services) rank among the most conservative in the chamber.[54] Whatever may be the full story, many party liberals believe that ideology is often the crucial variable in the assignment of members to key committees.

FACTORS IN ASSIGNMENT

Criteria invoked in making committee assignments are drawn from a surprisingly long list, including the principal items of party, seniority, geographical location, type of district represented, special competence and experience, personal preference and prestige, and ideology. In addition, getting along with party hierarchs may turn out to be a central "qualification," as this bit of doggerel out of the 1950s suggests:

> I love Speaker Rayburn, his heart is so warm,
> And if I love him he'll do me no harm.
> So I shan't sass the Speaker one little bitty,
> And then I'll wind up on a major committee.[55]

Many criticisms are laid at the door of the seniority system in Congress. Seniority, nevertheless, "has not been a controlling factor in the making of initial appointments and transfers, except among the Senate Republicans." In the 83d Congress, the "Johnson rule" was instituted under which each new Democratic member of the Senate is awarded at least one major committee assignment; hence membership on the important committees no longer falls automatically to those members with greatest seniority. In the past, Senate Republicans have attempted to make the appointment process

---

[54] Goodwin, *The Little Legislatures,* pp. 112-13. There is substantial reason to believe that, at least in the early 1960s, the conservative-dominated steering committee dealt harshly with the committee aspirations of those liberal Democrats who opposed the Senate "establishment" on certain key issues, particularly on resolutions to liberalize the cloture rule. Liberal Democrats who were willing to vote with conservatives against a more liberal cloture rule were much more likely to receive assignments to major committees than liberals who favored a change in this rule. For hard evidence on the steering committee's preference system during this period, see Wayne R. Swanson, "Committee Assignments and the Nonconformist Legislator: Democrats in the U.S. Senate," *Midwest Journal of Political Science,* XIII (February 1969), 84–94.

[55] These lines appeared initially in a column by Arthur Krock, *New York Times,* April 8, 1958, p. 28, and were also used by Goodwin. The discussion of the "Johnson rule" is based on Goodwin, "The Seniority System," p. 416.

178 wholly impersonal, to the point not only of measuring seniority but also of measuring previous government service. If the arithmetic of this method failed to provide an answer, the alphabetical position of the names was used. In 1959, George Goodwin notes, Senate Republicans moved toward an acceptance of the procedure used by the Democrats.[56]

The criteria used in making committee assignments vary somewhat from house to house and from committee to committee. A study of House committee assignments by Nicholas Masters shows that a member aspiring to a seat on an "exclusive" committee—Appropriations, Rules, or Ways and Means—is most likely to be selected if he represents a "safe" district (for the member, not necessarily for the party) in which constituency elements permit him substantial independence on policy matters, and if party leaders view his record as one of "legislative responsibility." Evidence as to the member's "responsibility" is of first importance. A "responsible" legislator, in the insider's view "is one whose ability, attitudes, and relationships with his colleagues serve to enhance the prestige and importance of the House of Representatives." He knows and observes the formal and informal rules of the House, has won a reputation for moderation in approach and for willingness to compromise, and apparently believes that Congress is not "the proper place to initiate drastic and rapid changes in the direction of public policy." A third factor for appointment to an exclusive committee involves geography. When a vacancy occurs on one of these committees, the appointee ordinarily is selected from the same state delegation as the member who previously held the seat.

The need to find "responsible" legislators to appoint to the House Appropriations Committee is illustrated in these comments by party "committee-makers":

> We want to know whether he has the ability and whether he will work and attend the meetings. That committee works very hard and has laborious hearings. There's a lot of detail work. The chairmen of those subcommittees want men on their subcommittees who will do the job.
> We don't just go by the fact that he's been elected. We go back in his community and we ask around. "Is he able? What's his background? Has he got the stuff to stand up under pressure? Or can he be gotten to by other interests?..." We make up a chart on his vote margin in past elections. If we put a man in from a close district, his committee assignment could defeat him in the next election. Maybe he couldn't stand up. We need someone who can do what he thinks best, who has the backing and whose district will say "We're with you no matter what you do up there."[57]

56 Goodwin, "The Seniority System," p. 416.
57 Fenno, *The Power of the Purse*, pp. 25–26. Selection criteria for members of the Senate Committee on Appropriations are similar. Fenno writes: "Insofar as they have a choice, Senate committee-makers would prefer to bring onto this important Committee Senators whom they believe are devoted to the Senate as an institution, to the protection of its influence, and to the preservation of its basic rules of the game. They want, in a word, the same kind of 'responsible legislator' that House committee-makers seek. They want an institutional insider rather than an outsider. And they want him for the same reasons—to ensure that the powerful Appropriations Committee, a citadel of institutional influence, be kept responsive to the other centers of influence in the chamber" (p. 527).

In making assignments to less prestigious committees, party leaders follow a general rule that appointments should help members to increase their security with their constituents.[58] Thus, for example, congressmen from rural areas hold a prior claim on the Agriculture Committee, while urban Democrats from districts with powerful labor organizations have a recognized claim on the Education and Labor Committee.

Certain committees receive special attention in the assignment process. The House Education and Labor Committee is composed chiefly of pro-labor Democrats and pro-management Republicans, an arrangement that inevitably produces controversy. The District of Columbia Committee, a relatively minor committee, attracts a number of southern congressmen bent on preventing the District from receiving home rule, one result of which would be to increase Negro influence in District politics.

When a committee vacancy appears, there are several steps normally taken to secure a replacement. The following account shows how the assignment process worked in filling a vacancy on the House Foreign Affairs Committee:

> Representatives from the region of the defeated committee member approached Democrats on the Ways and Means Committee to suggest the name of a replacement. The candidate's seniority in the House was adequate for assignment to an important committee. The ranking Democrat on the Foreign Affairs Committee was consulted, and the candidate was informally cleared as satisfactory to the formal party leaders. His foreign policy record was checked by some of the more careful Democrats on the Ways and Means Committee. Surviving these tests, the candidate was slated and elected to membership. . . .[59]

Party membership is naturally a factor in placing members on committees. In the case of most committees, as Roland Young has observed, the crucial matter is "party identity. . . not party regularity." To some extent, of course, members trace their fortunes to the party, but the party does not control their votes: "once appointed, a committee tends to have autonomous authority, fully subject to party influence but not to party discipline."[60] On the other hand, appointments to certain committees, such as the House Ways and Means Committee, seem to be heavily influenced by the factor of party regularity. In the words of a Republican member of Ways and Means:

> It's hard to generalize. There are a lot of factors—region, seniority. Then of course there are certain key issues that you want to be sure a member is pretty much a party-line type of member. You want to be sure that he

---

[58] There are exceptions to this rule, but few have ever appeared more unusual than the assignment of Shirley Chisholm, the first black woman to be elected to the House of Representatives, to the Committee on Agriculture. Her observation, made at the opening of the 91st Congress, is worth recording. "Apparently all they know about Brooklyn is that a tree grew there. I can think of no other reason for assigning me to the House Agriculture Committee." *Washington Post,* January 30, 1969, as quoted by Goodwin, *The Little Legislatures,* p. 78.

[59] Carroll, *op. cit.,* p. 29.

[60] Roland Young, *The American Congress* (New York: Harper & Row, Publishers, 1958), p. 61.

will go along with the party on certain things, you want to be sure he's safe on some things. On Ways and Means we get people who all fall within pretty much the same general philosophical area.[61]

The role of interest groups should not be overlooked in untangling the politics of committee assignment. Certain committees come close to being the captive of particular interests—organizational, sectional, or ideological. The agriculture committees in Congress rest firmly in the hands of legislators from the farm states, while the labor committees have a sizeable number of members from the urban, industrial states. The Senate Committee on Interior and Insular Affairs is as much as anything a caucus of westerners, and members of the Committee on the Judiciary in each house are all lawyers. Assignment to the House Committee on Ways and Means may depend upon the candidate having a sympathetic attitude toward the oil industry, in particular toward the oil depletion tax allowance.[62]

Finally, ideology is sometimes a potent factor in the allocation of committee seats. To return to the House Ways and Means Committee for an example, it seems clear that the Democratic leadership prefers to appoint liberal Democrats while the Republicans lean heavily to conservatives. A prominent Republican member of Ways and Means observes:

> Now when you get down to the individual, I think we want conservative people. And appropriately so. Taxes are not something that lends to experimentation. You want to go slow, you could knock the whole economy into a cocked hat with experimentation. So we put conservatives on and as a matter of fact this used to be true for the Democrats too. I think a Republican would have to be on the moderate side of conservatism and not on the liberal side of conservatism.[63]

So long as committees maintain their preeminent position in Congress, the methods for assigning seats will excite political controversy. At stake, ultimately, are important matters of public policy. Although Congress may occasionally tinker with the seniority rule, it would be surprising if it were sharply changed. As one student of Congress points out: "No wonder we hear so little about the shortcomings of the seniority system from congressmen. All congressmen are senior, more or less."[64]

COMMITTEE ASSIGNMENTS IN THE STATE LEGISLATURE

At the state level, a long tradition supports the prerogative of the Speaker to appoint committee members in the lower house. Party, political, factional,

---

[61] Quoted by Manley, *The Politics of Finance,* pp. 38–39.

[62] This orientation would seem to be less salient today than during the era when Sam Rayburn (D., Texas) served as Speaker of the House. In 1969, the Ways and Means Committee voted to cut the depletion allowance from $27\frac{1}{2}$ per cent to 20 per cent. Conventional wisdom asserts that, in addition to being "right" on oil, a Democratic member desiring appointment to this committee must be in favor of a liberal trade policy and (since 1960) pro-Medicare. For a wide-ranging analysis of the factors that influence appointment to this prestigious committee, see Manley, *op. cit.,* especially pp. 22–44.

[63] *Ibid.,* p. 40.

[64] John C. Donovan, *The Policy Makers* (New York: Pegasus, 1970), p. 61.

and personal considerations often circumscribe the speaker's selections, but only a handful of states provide for an alternative mode of selection or formally limit his discretion. To take several examples, a committee-on-committees may advise the speaker on appointments, as in the case of the New Mexico House of Representatives, or may recommend directly to the assembly, as in the case of Alaska. Rules of the Nebraska legislature provide simply that the committee-on-committees, which is elected by the legislature, shall select other committees.

Committee members in state senates are selected by three principal methods: through appointment by the president of the senate (the lieutenant governor), by the president *pro tem,* or by a committee-on-committees. About one-half of the states award this power to the president of the senate, even though, as an independently elected official, he may not be a member of the majority party in the senate. Another ten states use a committee-on-committees to make the selections, and all but a few of the remaining states vest this authority in the president *pro tem.* In the California Senate, appointments are made by the committee on rules. In general, the power of committee assignment in state upper houses is more broadly based than in the lower houses, where the Speaker's control is difficult to mistake.

The rules of the state chambers usually are silent regarding the factors to be taken into account in making committee assignments, but an exception or two may be worth noting. In California, senate rules stipulate that "seniority, preference, and experience" are to be taken into account in making appointments and that, so far as practicable, equal representation be accorded all parts of the state. The New Mexico Senate is the most insistent in its rules that seniority should be the principal consideration in making appointments: "Seniority of the members of the Senate shall prevail at all times in committee assignments, and chairmen of committees shall be appointed by request of the senior members." The seniority factor is strengthened through an accompanying provision that a three-fourths vote of the elected members is necessary to suspend the rule.[65]

The critical factors impinging on the choice of committee members and committee chairmen are not easily established, but it is obvious that the assignment process may be used to "stack" certain committees in the interests of factions, interest groups, and ideologies. A conservative leadership, for example, can use its influence to see to it that conservatives dominate certain key committees. Organized interest groups may enter the committee assignment process by pressing for the appointment of members who are disposed to favor their claims. It is common to find banking committees with a sizeable representation of bankers, insurance committees with a sizeable representation of insurancemen, and agriculture committees with a sizeable representation of farmers. Typically, the standing committees of the state legislatures are friendly environs for organized interests. What makes the politics of committee assignment important everywhere is that committee decisions usually are upheld on the floor.

The evidence concerning the extent to which committee assignments are made in response to pressures from outside the legislature is difficult

[65] This and the preceding paragraphs are based mainly on data drawn from *The Book of the States, 1966–67* (Chicago: Council of State Governments, 1967), p. 53.

182   to secure. But there is no reason to doubt that such pressures are exerted. A study of the Alabama legislature of some years ago reported that the governor was particularly interested in five major committees and often was able to name all the members of each. Appointments to lesser committees, on the other hand, were left to the leaders of the two houses.[66] How widespread this practice may be is conjectural, but it is a good guess that it is not uncommon in those states where the legislature customarily has been under the thumb of the governor.

THE COMMITTEE CASTE SYSTEM

A paramount fact about legislative committees is that there are major differences in their relative attractiveness and prestige. Some legislators serve their entire careers on the committees to which they were initially assigned. But it is far more common for members to transfer from one committee to another, moving from less prestigious to more prestigious assignments.[67] A study of committee transfers from the 81st through the 90th Congresses shows that the movement in and out of committees has a definite pattern; these transfers provide a good measure of the prestige of individual committees. The most and least attractive committees, as shown by their gains and losses through transfers, appear in Table 6.3.

TABLE 6.3

Relative Attractiveness of Congressional Committees

Senate		House	
Most Attractive	*Least Attractive*	*Most Attractive*	*Least Attractive*
Foreign Relations	District of Columbia	Rules	Veterans' Affairs
Finance	Post Office and Civil Service	Ways and Means	Post Office and Civil Service
Appropriations	Government Operations	Appropriations	Merchant Marine and Fisheries
Judiciary	Rules and Administration	Foreign Affairs	Banking and Currency
Armed Services	Public Works	Armed Services	Interior and Insular Affairs

SOURCE: George Goodwin, *The Little Legislatures: Committees of Congress* (Amherst: University of Massachusetts Press, 1970), pp. 114–15.

[66] Hallie Farmer, *The Legislative Process in Alabama* (University, Ala.: University of Alabama, Bureau of Public Administration, 1949), pp. 138–39.

[67] There are two principal reasons for seeking reassignment to a different committee: the prestige of the new committee and the opportunity it offers to provide constituency service. A study of committee reassignments in the U.S. House of Representatives covering the period 1947 to 1969 concludes that while both factors affect transfers, the more important is that of committee prestige. See Charles S. Bullock, "Correlates of Committee Transfers in the United States House of Representatives," Annual Meeting of the Midwest Political Science Association, April 29–May 1, 1971. Also see Charles Bullock and John Sprague, "A Research Note on the Committee Reassignments of Southern Democratic Congressmen," *Journal of Politics,* XXXI (May 1969), 493–512.

The prestige pattern is about the same in both houses. Committees with national-issue domains, such as Foreign Relations, Finance (Ways and Means in the House), Appropriations, and Rules (House) dominate the list of prestige committees, while the "housekeeping" committees (e.g., District of Columbia, Post Office and Civil Service) and certain "clientele" committees (e.g., Veterans' Affairs, Merchant Marine and Fisheries) bring up the rear.[68]

Prestige differentiation among committees contributes to several conditions. Newly elected legislators constitute a disproportionately heavy component in the less prestigious committees. Among these committees, "turnover is high, skill is lacking, and morale among members covetously eyeing other committee posts is frequently low." Party leaders gravitate toward the elite committees and avoid the less desirable ones. Good committee assignments are always in short supply. Members from highly competitive states (or districts in the case of the House), whose careers are threatened every election, find it difficult to gain chairmanships or senior positions on major committees. In sum, committee prestige is one of the main structural features of each house and an important clue to the distribution of power within the institution.[69]

SENIORITY IN CONGRESS

The seniority system in Congress is controversial because it is inextricably bound up with privilege and power. Although it confers both prestige and advantages on the individual members, its principal significance lies in its impact on public policy. The seniority system has never found expression in the rules of either house of Congress; yet its philosophy has been firmly embedded in legislative practice for well over a century. The form it assumes is simple and automatic, which in part explains its lasting power. When assigned to a committee, a member's name is placed at the bottom of his party's list. With reelection and the passage of time, his stake in the committee—his seniority—increases. Inevitably, death, retirement, and the vicissitudes of elections remove those members above him. The moment arrives in some session when his name rests at the top of his party's list for that committee. Should his party be in the majority at the time, the chairmanship is almost certain to be his. Having held a key to longevity, personal and political, he now holds a key to congressional power.

At the opening of the 92d Congress (1971), both parties in the House of Representatives agreed to modify their seniority rules to provide that seniority would not be the only factor taken into account in the selection of committee chairmen or ranking minority members. Under their new rule, House Republicans will now vote by secret ballot on whether to accept the nominations for chairman or ranking minority member made by their committee-on-committees. The Democratic rule provides that ten members can demand a caucus vote on their committee-on-committees' nomination

---

[68] Goodwin, *The Little Legislatures,* pp. 114–15. For another ranking of House committees, based on the percentage of members holding single committee assignments, see Gawthrop, "Changing Membership Patterns," pp. 366–73.

[69] Donald R. Matthews, *U.S. Senators and Their World* (Chapel Hill: University of North Carolina Press, 1960), pp. 148–52, quotation on p. 151.

184 for any chairmanship or on the seniority of any committee member. Should the caucus reject a nominee for committee chairman, the committee-on-committees is required to advance another name from the list of remaining committee members. Despite these changes in the House, the prospects are strong that seniority will continue to dominate the selection of chairmen.[70] The Senate continues to rely exclusively on seniority in the choice of committee leaders.

The seniority rule has been tested from time to time but seldom breached. One study notes that apparently there have been only five instances in the Senate in which the seniority rule was not followed in awarding committee chairmanships.[71] Similarly, as Figure 6 shows, the seniority practice has been violated in the House of Representatives only on rare occasions in recent years. In the 89th Congress two southern Democratic congressmen were stripped of their seniority ranking—one of them

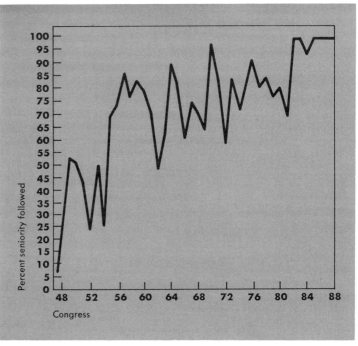

*Source: Nelson W. Polsby, Miriam Gallaher, and Barry S. Rundquist, "The Growth of the Seniority System in the U.S. House of Representatives," American Political Science Review, LXIII (September 1969), 793.

FIGURE 6   The growth of seniority: 1881–1963.* Percentage of committees on which seniority was followed in the selection of chairman, by Congress.

70 In the first test of their new rule in the 92d Congress, liberal Democrats failed by a caucus vote of 126 to 96 to remove the chairman of the District of Columbia Committee, Representative John L. McMillan of South Carolina. A second attempt to remove McMillan lost overwhelmingly in a vote on the House floor when Republicans declined to join forces with those Democrats opposing McMillan. "The Democrats ought to have the right to choose their own chairmen," contended the Republican minority leader. *New York Times,* February 5, 1971, p. 8.

71 Goodwin, "The Seniority System," p. 417.

had been in Congress twenty years and held the number-two position on
the Commerce Committee—for having bolted the party to support Barry
Goldwater for president. More significantly, in the 90th Congress Adam
Clayton Powell was deposed as chairman of the House Education and Labor
Committee by the Democratic caucus in order to discipline him for mis-
management of his committee's travel and staff funds. This preceded the
House move to bar him from membership, and was the first time a chairman
had been removed from his office since 1925.

If the office of committee chairman were meager in power and influence, few people would bother to argue over the manner in which men come
to this position. But the facts are that a chairman ordinarily wields an
assortment of wide-ranging powers. He may appoint subcommittees, decide
when to hold committee meetings, control the agenda, appoint staff members, and determine whether hearings will be held. Committee bills are
handled on the floor by the chairman, and he regularly sits on conference
committees when legislation from his committee is under consideration. Not
all congressional committees are wholly under the thumb of the chairman:
a former congressman has estimated that about two-thirds of the standing
committees are no longer subject to one-man rule. In committees that have
been "democratized," the chairman's role is more that of a presiding officer
who is expected to be responsive to the will of the committee.[72] Nevertheless, the powers of the chairman are great, if not abusive, in all committees.

In the "unreformed" committees of Congress, the chairman may kill
legislation in a variety of ways, all of which are related to inaction. He
may refuse to schedule hearings on a bill, "sit on it," or "carry it around in
his pocket"—to use the argot. Characteristically, chairmen of "unreformed"
committees do not appoint standing subcommittees, preferring to name
special subcommittees whose members can be more easily controlled. Moreover, they tend to rely heavily on closed-door or executive committee
meetings.

The power of committee chairmen—their critical impact on public
policy—prompts much of the controversy over seniority. Opponents of the
seniority system are able to muster an impressive arraignment of the practice.
Among their arguments are: (1) Seniority is incompatible with responsible
party government, since the party, rather than committee chairmen, should
be able to control the disposition of legislation.[73] (2) Adherence to the

[72] Stewart L. Udall, "A Defense of the Seniority System," *New York Times
Magazine,* January 13, 1957, p. 17.

[73] Given the lack of party responsibility, commonly said to characterize the
American political system, this argument in some measure is "academic." But it is
common to find the party *leadership* thwarted by a committee chairman of their own
party. The following account describes an attempt by the Senate Democratic leadership to have a displaced-persons bill reported out of the Judiciary Committee, which
was headed at the time by Senator McCarran, a Democrat from Nevada. McCarran
was invited to a meeting of the Senate Democratic Policy Committee, as it happened,
on his birthday. The floor leader notes the result: "We provided him with a huge
birthday cake, hoping that a birthday party might produce in the distinguished
Senator a mellow mood, and while in that mood he would consider this bill
(H.R. 4567).... The cake had no effect upon the Senator from Nevada whatever.
It was a large cake, too. I merely recite these facts to show that the Majority
Leader and the Democratic Policy Committee have not been derelict in their duty
in attempting to get a bill reported by the Senate Committee on the Judiciary"
(95 *C.R.* 14699). Quoted by Stephen K. Bailey and Howard D. Samuel, *Congress
at Work* (New York: Holt, Rinehart & Winston, Inc., 1952), p. 249.

seniority rule does not assure the appointment of chairmen of ability and special competence; similarly, it may stymie the advancement of promising younger men. (See Table 6.4 for the age distribution among chairmen). (3) Seniority tends to favor one-party areas, since the tenure of members coming from two-party constituencies is frequently short-lived; chairmen may represent a minority view within the party. (4) Once locked into power, a committee chairman is not easily removed, despite his inadequacy for the task.

TABLE 6.4

Age Distribution of Standing Committee Chairmen, 92d Congress (1971–72)

	Senate		House	
Age Group	*Number*	%	*Number*	%
Under 50	1	5.9	1	4.8
50–59	6	35.2	2	9.5
60–69	4	23.6	10	47.6
70–79	5	29.4	5	23.8
80–89	1	5.9	3	14.3
Total	17	100.0	21	100.0

SOURCE: U.S. Congress, *Congressional Directory*, 92d Cong., 2d sess., 1971.

Power in Congress flows to senior members. Safe districts produce them. When the Democratic party holds a majority in Congress, the dominance of southerners is unmistakable. The basis of southern power, however, is subject to conflicting interpretations. One, the so-called "insider's theory," holds that southerners place higher value on a congressional career than northerners. Accordingly, they stay in Congress longer, acquire seniority, and amass power. Northerners, on the other hand, are said to be more likely to give up their seats in Congress in favor of positions back home in state or local governments. Moreover, this "theory" holds that northerners do not use their seniority wisely, for they have a penchant for "committee-hopping," resulting in a diminution of their chances to gain chairmanships. The general thrust of the "insider's theory" is that southern power in Congress is due to *more* than the absence of party competition in the South. In counterpoise, the traditional or "textbook theory" holds that southern power traces directly from seniority, which in turn is the result of a lack of party competition in the South.

Each interpretation is plausible. Which is correct? A study by Wolfinger and Hollinger finds virtually no evidence to corroborate the "insider's theory." Congressmen elected from southern *safe* districts do not have any more seniority in Congress or in committees than congressmen from northern *safe* districts. Northern members are no more likely to "misuse" their seniority by "committee-hopping" than southern members. Finally, there is no evidence that northerners are more likely than southerners to desert Congress for other careers. Hence the explanation for southern power is not to be found in a superior dedication to legislative careers among southerners. Rather the explanation is simply that southerners have an advantage in chairmanships by virtue of the sheer volume of long-time, safe Democratic seats in the South. The "textbook theory" is essentially correct. Interestingly, the number of noncompetitive seats in the North has grown rapidly in recent years, especially in urban areas. In 1948, 33 percent of all safe Democratic seats were in the North, with the rest in the South. By 1958 the northern percentage was 46. Ten years later, following the 1968 presidential election, 52 percent of all safe Democratic seats were located in the North.[74] It seems clear that in the future northern Democrats, who have long felt disadvantaged by the linkage between seniority and congressional power, will be among the principal beneficiaries of the seniority rule.

If one looks for evidence of shortcomings in the seniority system and is not concerned to discover justifications, he is likely to end up viewing the system as unfair. Nevertheless, one of the criticisms of seniority can be validated: that some geographical areas have gained significantly more chairmanships than others. Table 6.5 shows the distribution of chairman-

TABLE 6.5

Distribution of Democratic Committee Chairmen and Republican Ranking Members by Geographic Region, 87th (1961–62) and 92d (1971–72) Congresses

	87th Congress		92nd Congress	
	% of Members	% of Chairmanships*	% of Members	% of Chairmanships*
HOUSE DEMOCRATS				
East	26	25	29	24
Midwest	19	10	22	19
South	42	60	34	43
West	13	5	15	14
SENATE DEMOCRATS				
East	14	0	18	12
Midwest	18	0	23	12
South	37	63	32	52
West	31	37	27	24
HOUSE REPUBLICANS				
East	35	40	27	24
Midwest	45	55	39	52
South	5	0	17	5
West	15	5	17	19
SENATE REPUBLICANS				
East	43	37	32	35
Midwest	34	50	25	29
South	6	0	18	18
West	17	13	25	18

NOTE: *East:* W. Va., Pa., Md., Del., N.J., N.Y., Conn., R.I., Mass., N.H., Vt., Maine. *Midwest:* N.D., S.D., Neb., Kan., Minn., Iowa, Mo., Ill., Mich., Ind., Ohio, Wis. *South:* Tex., Okla., Ark., La., Miss., Ala., Tenn., Ky., Ga., Fla., S.C., N.C., Va. *West:* N.M., Colo., Wyo., Mont., Ida., Utah, Ariz., Nev., Calif., Ore., Wash., Alaska, Hawaii.

* For the Republican party, in the minority in each Congress, the percentages are for ranking members.

[74] Raymond E. Wolfinger and Joan H. Hollinger, "Safe Seats, Seniority, and Power in Congress," in *Readings on Congress,* ed. Raymond E. Wolfinger (Englewood Cliffs, N.J.: Prentice-Hall Inc., 1971), p. 53.

188   ships in two Congresses, spaced ten years apart. Several understandings may be derived from it. First of all, the table shows plainly that the South has held a disproportionate number of chairmanships in the Democratic party while the Midwest has been similarly advantaged in the Republican party. Second, and often not understood, the preeminent position of southern Democrats and midwestern Republicans is due in considerable degree to the large number of members elected from these regions, not to the workings of the seniority system itself. Third, there has been a noticeable shift in the regional distribution of chairmanships and ranking members. The South and Midwest are not down and out by any means, but they have lost some of their edge in committee leadership positions. Overall, the table suggests that regional inequalities are on the wane.[75]

Seniority advantages some regions and disadvantages others.[76] In the short run, the South will continue to profit from the seniority system when the Democrats control Congress. It is thus important to examine the extent to which southern chairmen are representative of their party. A clue to this may be found in Figures 7 and 8, which show the voting behavior of Democratic committee chairmen in the 91st Congress on issues that brought together the "conservative coalition"—a majority of voting southern Democrats joined to a majority of voting Republicans in opposition to a majority of voting northern Democrats.[77] These scatter diagrams reveal that about one-half of the chairmen (nearly all southerners) were more inclined to join the conservative alliance than to stick with a majority of their own party. Another striking fact is that most of the chairmen in this wing are more conservative than the southern Democratic bloc as a whole. The pattern revealed in these figures would characterize most if not all Congresses of the past several decades.

Seniority thus poses serious problems for the congressional parties. Nevertheless, the issue may not be as clear-cut—the shortcomings of seniority so inordinate, the merits so few—as some critics have made out. Prudent reasons can be adduced for the retention of seniority, though they are likely to carry an odd ring for persons wholly attuned to majority rule democracy. Seniority does involve "gambler's chances," as Haynes remarked, but it also has a logic: "It usually brings to the headship of a committee a man who

[75] For a rigorous and wide-ranging study of the seniority system, see Barbara Hinckley, *The Seniority System in Congress* (Bloomington: Indiana University Press, 1971).

[76] Over the years a great many of the chairmen of congressional committees have come from small towns—places like Doddsville, Mississippi; Houma, Louisiana; Saxapahaw, North Carolina; Camden, Arkansas; Fayetteville, Arkansas; Kensett, Arkansas; Elkins, West Virginia; Winder, Georgia; and Huntsville, Alabama. This fact prompted Arthur Krock, long-time columnist for the *New York Times,* to argue that "the seniority system supplies the only remaining barrier in the Federal Government against its total capture by representatives of the urban population." "The Lords Proprietors of Congress," *New York Times Magazine,* January 22, 1967, p. 74.

[77] In the 91st Congress, for example, the coalition's stance was identified by opposition to the limitation of U.S. troop involvement in South Vietnam and Cambodia, expansion of the food stamp program, and deletion of funds for the supersonic transport plane; the coalition supported uniform expansion of school desegregation across the nation, expansion of the Safeguard Antiballistic Missile system, and a weakening of the Voting Rights Act of 1965. *Congressional Quarterly Weekly Report,* January 29, 1971, pp. 242–43.

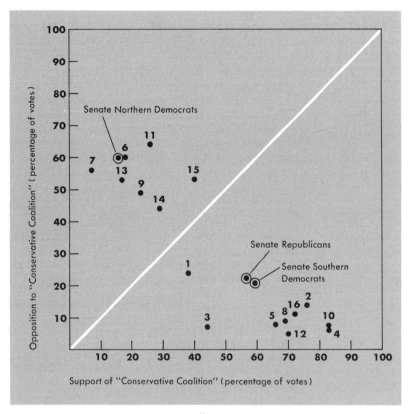

Key

Committee chairmen

1. Aeronautical and Space Sciences
2. Agriculture and Forestry
3. Appropriations
4. Armed Services
5. Banking and Currency
6. Commerce
7. District of Columbia
8. Finance

9. Foreign Relations
10. Government Operations
11. Interior and Insular Affairs
12. Judiciary
13. Labor and Public Welfare
14. Post Office and Civil Service
15. Public Works
16. Rules and Administration

FIGURE 7   Support of and opposition to "Conservative Coalition" by sixteen Democratic Senate Committee Chairmen and by Three Party Groups, 91st Congress (1969–70). (Failures to vote lower both support and opposition scores.) Source: Data from **Congressional Quarterly Weekly Report,** *January 29, 1971, pp. 242–45.*

has had many years of experience in handling the special problems in its domain."[78] Similarly, Congressman Emanuel Celler has argued that the seniority system "avoids the waste implicit in instability of committee composition and management."[79] Ex-Congressman Stewart Udall sees in senior-

---

[78] George H. Haynes, *The Senate of the United States* (Boston: Houghton Mifflin Company, 1938), I, 296–97.

[79] Emanuel Celler, "The Seniority Rule in Congress," *Western Political Quarterly,* XIV (March 1961), 164.

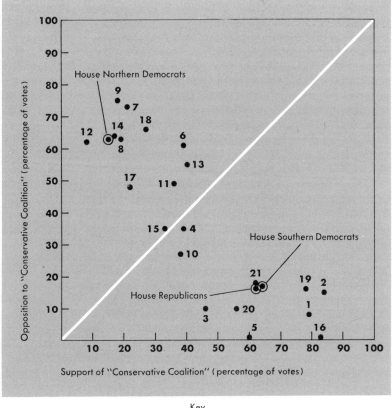

Key
Committee Chairmen

1. Agriculture	12. Judiciary
2. Appropriations	13. Merchant Marine and Fisheries
3. Armed Services	14. Post Office and Civil Service
4. Banking and Currency	15. Public Works
5. District of Columbia	16. Rules
6. Education and Labor	17. Science and Astronautics
7. Foreign Affairs	18. Standards of Official Conduct
8. Government Operations	19. Un-American Activities
9. House Administration	(Internal Security)
10. Interior and Insular Affairs	20. Veterans' Affairs
11. Interstate and Foreign Commerce	21. Ways and Means

FIGURE 8 Support of and opposition to "Conservative Coalition" by twenty-one Democratic House Committee Chairmen and by Three Party Groups, 91st Congress (1969–70). (Failures to vote lower both support and opposition scores.) Source: Data from **Congressional Quarterly Weekly Report,** *January 29, 1971, pp. 242–47.*

ity the advantage that it acts to "keep down the strife and politicking that otherwise would develop over vital committee assignments."[80] Since it eliminates intrigues and deals, "committees are able to get down to work im-

[80] Udall, *op. cit.,* p. 64. Udall advances several reasons for believing that the seniority problem is not nearly as serious as its critics contend: (1) the growth of

mediately, without having first to bind the wounds of disappointed aspirants
to leadership."[81] Moreover, the seniority system increases the attractiveness
of congressional service. Nelson W. Polsby writes:

> The House's major career incentive is the opportunity accorded a tenth
> to a fifth of its members to possess the substance of power in the form of
> a committee or sub-committee chairmanship or membership on a key com-
> mittee. At present seniority acts as a bulwark of this incentive system, by
> guaranteeing a form of job security at least within the division of labor
> of the organization. Without decentralization of power there would quite
> likely be no incentive for able men to stay in the House; without able men
> (there are few enough of these at any rate) there would be no expertise.
> Without subject-matter mastery, initiatives and modifications in public
> policy are capricious, responsive largely to prejudice, ineffective, and failing
> that, detrimental.[82]

Finally, it goes without saying that legislators who continue to be
reelected find it increasingly difficult to regard seniority as a problem to
which they should attend!

SENIORITY IN CONGRESS: PROPOSALS FOR REFORM

"I know not how better to describe our form of government in a single
phrase than by calling it a government by the chairmen of the Standing
Committees."[83] This appraisal by Woodrow Wilson, possibly as familiar as
any statement in his remarkable book, marks the distribution of power
within Congress almost, if not quite, as well today as it did in 1885. It is
the blunt fact of the chairman's powers, when combined with the seniority
system which elevates him to his position, that rankles so many observers
of Congress. One result is that there are few proposals for changing congressional practices that omit a plan to take the place of seniority.

Among the many proposals to diminish the seniority system are the
following: (1) rotation of the office of chairman every few years; (2)
automatic age limit of 70 years for chairmen; (3) authorization for committee members to choose one of their number as chairman; (4) authorization for each house to select the committee chairmen; (5) provision for
the choice of committee chairmen by the majority party caucus from a slate
composed of the three members with the greatest seniority on each committee; and (6) provision for the majority party to elect the chairmen and

---

standing subcommittees, which has made the chairman's control over the committee
more difficult; (2) an increase in successful uprisings against certain committee
chairmen; (3) introduction of the "Johnson rule"; (4) the impetus for committee reform generated by the Legislative Reorganization Act; and (5) an increase
in voluntary retirements of senior senators and representatives as a result of an
improved retirement system. (pp. 67–69).

81 Celler, *op. cit.,* p. 165.

82 "Strengthening Congress in National Policymaking," in *Congressional Behavior,* ed. Nelson W. Polsby (New York: Random House, 1971), pp. 6–7.

83 Wilson, *op. cit.,* p. 82.

192 for the minority party to elect its ranking members without reference to their seniority.

At the heart of the dispute over seniority, for many academic observers, is the issue of party responsibility for a legislative program. Can a party be held accountable if it cannot control the committees, if committees are simply the dominion of certain individuals or of small cliques? The 1950 report of the Committee on Political Parties of the American Political Science Association recognized the difficulty in changing the existing system and pointed out that "the problem is not one of abolishing seniority and then finding an alternative. It is one of mobilizing the power through which the party leadership can successfully use the seniority principle rather than have the seniority principle dominate Congress."[84] The committee's position was that:

> Advancement within a committee on the basis of seniority makes sense, other things being equal. But *it is not playing the game fairly for party members who oppose the commitments in their party's platform to rely on seniority to carry them into committee chairmanships. Party leaders have compelling reason to prevent such a member from becoming chairman—and they are entirely free so to exert their influence.*[85]

In arguing the case for clear-cut party control over the committee structure, the committee offered these recommendations: (1) Competence and party loyalty ought to be weighed more heavily than seniority in assigning members to major committees. (2) The party leadership committees in each chamber should draw up the slates of committee assignments and submit them to the appropriate party caucuses for evaluation. (A variation of this is now used in the House of Representatives.) (3) Committee assignments should be reviewed periodically—at least every two years—by the appropriate party caucuses. (4) The majority party should always hold a comfortable margin of seats on each committee, thus reducing the power of the individual majority party member and increasing the responsibility of the party as a collectivity.[86]

The seniority tradition is firmly fixed in Congress, and many members have a big stake in its preservation. Withal, the skepticism of critics does not much trouble the seniority leaders of Congress. Nonetheless, there are two possibilities of promise for attacking the seniority problem. One calls for vesting more power in committee majorities, perhaps through the development of rules of procedure that diminish the opportunity for arbitrary action by the chairman. To some extent, this development is now under way. The other possibility for transformation is through the electoral process, by changing the composition of Congress. This would accompany the extension of competitive party politics throughout the country. With the erosion of one-party control, the main drawback to the seniority system

---

84 *Toward a More Responsible Two-Party System* (New York: Holt, Rinehart & Winston, Inc., 1950), pp. 61–62.

85 *Ibid.,* p. 62. (Emphasis in original.)

86 *Ibid.,* pp. 62–63.

would be eliminated; it is, after all, the ties between one-party domination in states and districts, the undisturbed tenure of their legislators, and the powers of the chairman that make seniority an issue.

SENIORITY IN THE STATE LEGISLATURES

Seniority does not reign in the states as firmly as it does in Congress, and apparently it never has. On the basis of scattered studies and informed judgments,[87] it is evident that seniority is simply one factor among several in the selection of committee members *and* committee chairmen. In the Illinois legislature, for example:

> Committee chairmen...are not chosen in accord with any regularly established practice, although, other things being equal, the incumbent can usually expect reappointment. In at least one recent session, however, an influential veteran of fourteen sessions was without a chairmanship, a House member serving his second term became chairman of an important committee, and a senator was refused reappointment as head of a committee by way of discipline for lack of party regularity.[88]

Similarly, in Michigan, although most members of the major committees rank high in terms of legislative experience, seniority is not supreme. The Speaker of the House and the committee-on-committees of the Senate "quite frequently appoint new members to important committees, and they sometimes appoint a person as chairman of an influential committee with little regard for seniority."[89] In the Texas House, over a period of twenty-six years, only 11 per cent of the committee chairmen had served on their committees two or more sessions.[90] In Mississippi, veteran members appear to be given preference in the assignment of chairmanships, but there is no established seniority rule.[91] Hyneman and Carey have shown that seniority counts for little in assigning committee chairmanships in the Iowa legislature, where a chairman rarely heads the same committee for more than two consecutive sessions. Commonly, a man will serve on half-a-dozen committees in one session and four or five different ones the following session. Previous service on a committee as a factor in determining the chairmanship seems virtually an exception in the Iowa scheme. Of this practice the authors say:

[87] See Karl A. Bosworth, "Law Making in State Governments," in *The Forty-eight States: Their Tasks as Policy Makers and Administrators,* prepared for the American Assembly (New York: Columbia University, Graduate School of Business, 1955), p. 104; and Malcolm E. Jewell, *The State Legislature: Politics and Practice* (New York: Random House, 1962), pp. 81–82.

[88] Steiner and Gove, *op. cit.,* pp. 14–15.

[89] Robert G. Scigliano, *Michigan Legislative Report, 1954* (East Lansing: Michigan State University, Governmental Research Bureau, 1955), p. 17.

[90] William E. Oden, "Tenure and Turnover of Recent Texas Legislatures," *Southwestern Social Science Quarterly,* XLV (March 1965), 371–74.

[91] C. N. Fortenberry and Edward H. Hobbs, "The Mississippi Legislature," in *Power in American State Legislatures,* ed. Alex B. Lacy, Jr. (New Orleans: Tulane University Press, 1967), p. 82.

By adopting a practice which resembles a game of musical chairs, the Iowa House and Senate no doubt avoid many disadvantages which the two chambers of Congress suffer because of their practices of fixed committee assignments and rise to chairmanships by seniority. But whatever is gained by avoiding these disadvantages is undoubtedly largely offset by failure to capitalize on specialized experience. Members of the Iowa House and Senate do not stay on the same committees long enough to permit each committee to have a nucleus of men who have had several sessions of experience in dealing with the kind of legislation which, session after session, will come before that committee.[92]

Where the seniority factor is unstressed, and where political competition is volatile, committee chairmanships may be up for grabs. This is a natural condition in those states which give the speaker free rein in appointing chairmen. Candidates for the office of Speaker find committee chairmanships attractive bait to offer in return for promises of support when the legislature convenes. The winning candidate thus makes his appointments in keeping with the arrangements worked out during his campaign for the office.[93]

Despite the absence of a large reservoir of studies covering practices in other states, it is still much better than a guess to say that state legislatures in general do not attach great importance to seniority. A questionnaire survey conducted by the American Political Science Association received estimates that seniority was a prominent factor in the selection of committee chairmen in fourteen senates and twelve houses and was not important in twenty-three senates and thirty-six houses.[94]

Committee chairmen in state legislatures ordinarily are not as powerful as committee chairmen in Congress. If the powers of the chairman were more formidable, undoubtedly there would be a greater insistence that seniority should be the principal consideration in making appointments. The position of the chairman in the Illinois legislature would seem to be broadly representative of most states: "Committee appointments, and particularly appointments to committee chairmanships, are valuable as indications of confidence by legislative leaders. Virtually no actual legislative power attaches to a chairmanship, but legislators regard chairmen of particular committees as part of an influential circle. Being a chairman is not a source of

---

92 Charles S. Hyneman and George W. Carey, "The Iowa Legislature: A General Description" (Manuscript, Indiana University, 1956), p. 22. Statistical data on this point cover the period 1937–53.

93 On the use of this strategy in Wisconsin, see Douglas C. Chaffey, "The Institutionalization of State Legislatures: A Comparative Study," *Western Political Quarterly,* XXIII (March 1970), 184–88; and in Illinois, Thomas Littlewood, *Bipartisan Coalition in Illinois* (New York: McGraw-Hill Book Company, Inc., Eagleton Institute Cases in Practical Politics, 1962), p. 22. In a bitter struggle for the Illinois House speakership in 1959, committee chairmanships became a major object of barter. With the help of Republican votes, a downstate Democrat won out over a Chicago Democrat. The new Speaker explained his decisions on committee chairmen in this way: "I appointed chairmen on the basis of loyalty and ability. My friends stayed with me and I rewarded them."

94 Zeller, *op. cit.,* p. 197.

power, but being designated a chairman very well may be a source of informal power."[95]

Committee Staffs

CONGRESS

The enormous volume of work set before committees, the quest for technical knowledge, and the pressure of time have combined to crystallize the need for professional staffs to serve committees. This development was a long time in the making, however, and in fact it was not until the turn of the twentieth century that specific funds were set aside for staffs for the standing committees. Congress placed the employment of committee personnel on a firmer basis in 1924.[96] Finally, in the La Follette-Monroney act of 1946, professional staffs came of age, with provision made for the employment of up to four staff members and six clerks by each standing committee of Congress. Certain committees, most notably the appropriations committees, were empowered to appoint larger staffs.

The size of committee staffs has grown steadily over the years. A survey taken in the 90th Congress revealed that there were a total of 1,083 staff members assigned to the standing committees and their subcommittees, the number about equally divided between the Senate and the House. The largest committee staffs were those of the Senate Judiciary Committee, with a total of 150, and the House Government Operations Committee, with a total of 54; special permission of their chambers was required to enlarge their staffs beyond the allotted total. Some committees, such as the House Rules Committee and the Senate Agriculture Committee, carried fewer staff members than authorized.[97]

The central reason for creating professional staffs was to free committees from excessive reliance on research studies produced by executive agencies. "For Congress to function as a coequal partner with the executive in the legislative process," Gladys Kammerer observed, it was essential "that Congress empower itself to obtain its own independent staff services and that it pay adequately for them."[98] Competent professional staffing in the legislative branch becomes especially important in the American form of government, characterized as it is by a system of separated powers and by legislative party organizations whose most conspicuous feature is their fragility. Needing information and expert counsel, an independent legislature had to look to its own devices, which in this case led to the development of expanded staff services.

The augmentation of the staff function since 1946 has not altogether met the pristine purposes of that year's Legislative Reorganization Act,

---

[95] Steiner and Gove, *op. cit.,* p. 82.

[96] George B. Galloway, *The Legislative Process in Congress* (New York: Thomas Y. Crowell Company, 1953), p. 410.

[97] Goodwin, *The Little Legislatures,* p. 145.

[98] "The Record of Congress in Committee Staffing," *American Political Science Review,* XLV (December 1951), 1126.

196 although improvements in the caliber of staff members and in the quality of their work have been substantial. Congressional committee staffs are good, bad, and in-between, just as committee chairmen are—and the quality of the two are probably related. A competent professional staff can improve the general efficiency and quality of the legislative process through a variety of contributions: by collecting, winnowing, and analyzing data, by identifying problems of relevance for members and suggesting alternative courses of action, and by preparing studies and committee reports on legislation.[99] Responsible committee decisions and imaginative legislation usually rest on a foundation of intelligent staff work. Ernest Griffith writes that "the enlargement and strengthening of the staffs of Congress have in fact been a major factor in arresting and probably reversing a trend that had set in in the United States as well as in every other industrialized nation. This is the trend in the direction of the ascendancy or even the virtually complete dominance of the bureaucracy over the legislative branch through the former's near-monopoly of the facts and the technical and specialized competence on the basis of which decisions are ultimately made."[100]

In the estimation of most observers, Congress is still understaffed, and this may be especially true with respect to the foreign policy committees. While information and intelligence resources have increased steadily in the executive branch, Senator Hubert Humphrey has contended, there is "a concurrent scarcity of vigorous and continuing *countervailing expertise*" in Congress. "Without competent independent sources of fact and wisdom [Congress] cannot make discriminating judgments between alternative programs and proposals. Faced with an impressive case by the Administration, and unarmed with counter facts and arguments, even a conscientious Senator sometimes vacillates between giving a grudging consent and opposing for the sake of opposing." This imbalance, he observed, "constitutes a serious threat to the integrity of the Legislative Branch." With more adequate staffing of the Senate Foreign Relations Committee, the House Foreign Affairs Committee, and the Foreign Affairs Division of the Legislative Reference Service, Congress could better provide initiative in policy-making and more effective surveillance over the executive branch.[101]

A minority opinion on the need for bigger and better staffs emerges in the views of Dean Acheson, secretary of state in the Truman administration, who wrote that Congress will begin to exercise intelligent review of the activities of the executive branch when its members

> have time to inform themselves and to think. It does not call for large staffs and extensive organization, but it cannot be done by men who spend the hours, when their chambers are not meeting, in going from one com-

[99] See an essay by David E. Price that distinguishes between two types of staff aides: "professionals" and "policy entrepreneurs." While "professional" staff aides are distinguished by "neutral competence," "policy entrepreneurs" are inclined to use their positions to advance their own policy preferences, even though this requires them to play a political role in the committee. Both staff orientations, the author contends, are essential. "Professionals and 'Entrepreneurs': Staff Orientations and Policy Making on Three Senate Committees," *Journal of Politics,* XXXIII (May 1971), 316–36.

[100] Griffith, *op. cit.,* pp. 74–75.

[101] "The Senate in Foreign Policy," *Foreign Affairs,* XXXVII (July 1959), 534.

mittee meeting to another.... It is an interesting fact that those members of the Washington community who notoriously do their own thinking and their own work—our judges—have the smallest staffs and lead the most quiet lives.[102]

Despite its contributions and potential, the professional staff is not a remedy for all the problems which beset committees in search of information and intelligent counsel. Bertram Gross lists a number of fallacies regarding professional staffing in Congress. In the first place, it is impossible for staffs to meet the complete needs of members of Congress, for notwithstanding improved staff services, Congress continues to require and to use the assistance of executive agencies and private organizations. Second, increased congressional staff assistance has not been able to offset the influence of executive officials and private groups. Third, an increase in staff has not been accompanied by a significant decrease in the work load of members of Congress. A good staff uncovers "new problems, new opportunities, and new challenges"—the net result of which may be to expand the responsibilities of the conscientious legislator.[103] Finally, pockets of resistance to professional staffing have developed. Chairmen may see their staffs as competitors; they may not know how to use a staff properly; they may regard policy alternatives advanced by the staff as deficient in political terms. On occasion, a change in committee leadership may bring about an entirely new staff.

STAFFS AND POLITICS

A troublesome point at times is the relationship between staff members and the minority party members of the committee. This association easily falls short of connubial bliss. An extreme example of estrangement occurred in the case of the Permanent Subcommittee on Investigations in the heyday of Senator Joseph McCarthy's investigations. The subcommittee staff was chosen personally by McCarthy and assigned as he saw fit, prompting the Democratic subcommittee members to resign in protest; since this was no ordinary committee, as Richard Rovere points out, their action had little effect—at least not at that moment.[104] This example, if spectacular, is not unique. Staff members are appointed by the majority party, often simply by the chairman acting on his own. The staff, in some cases, may become the voice of a narrow partisan cause or of a special view or, at worst, a staging

---

[102] *A Citizen Looks at Congress* (New York: Harper & Row, Publishers, 1956), pp. 122–23.

[103] Gross, *op. cit.*, pp. 421–22. Also see Norman Meller, "Legislative Staff Services: Toxin, Specific, or Placebo for the Legislature's Ills," *Western Political Quarterly*, XX (June 1967), 381–89.

[104] *Senator Joe McCarthy* (New York: Harcourt, Brace & World, Inc., 1959), pp. 218–19. The staff issue presented a good opportunity for protest—obviously there were other aspects of Senator McCarthy's methods that contributed to the resignations. Probably no committee staff ever has been so controversial as the one assembled by McCarthy. Along with J. B. Matthews, who made a spectacular charge of subversion among the Protestant clergy, the committee employed Roy M. Cohn and G. David Schine in major staff positions, Cohn as chief counsel. Their exploits at home and abroad, made possible by Senator McCarthy's delegation of authority to them, contributed directly to the army-McCarthy imbroglio and to the eventual condemnation of McCarthy by the Senate.

198   point for the spoils system. This particular pitfall is recognized in the *Toward a More Responsible Two-Party System* report; it argues that in the interest of effective party operation, minority members of the committee should have access to staff assistance, since neither the Legislative Reference Service nor the Library of Congress are adequate substitutes. Moreover, a sharp turnover in personnel as a result of a change in power can be avoided if the staff accommodates itself to minority as well as majority needs.[105]

Under the terms of the 1946 Legislative Reorganization Act, appointments to committee staffs were to be made without regard to political affiliation. Some committees have followed this enjoiner, but many others have not. Probably the best examples of highly professional, nonpartisan staffs are those of the House Foreign Affairs Committee and the Senate Foreign Relations Committee. At the other extremes are the House Agriculture Committee and the House Education and Labor Committee—two committees which have developed highly partisan staffs. Where staffs are strongly oriented to partisan demands, minority members of the committee may have to depend on a single staff member for assistance, intrastaff cooperation tends to be minimal, and minority staff members may be prevented from using committee files and other office facilities. There are apparently more partisan than nonpartisan staffs in Congress. Not surprisingly, partisan staffs tend to develop in those committees characterized by major ideological conflicts among members. The partisan role of committee staffs is a natural outgrowth of the staff selection process. As long as staff members owe their loyalty to the committee chairman or ranking minority member, their own security is likely to require them to adopt a partisan orientation toward committee business. The existence of partisan staffs is a recognition of at least two facts—that public policy alternatives are often laden with significance for the parties and that there is a need for different kinds of experts.[106]

All varieties of staff involvement appear in committee work and in committee politics:

> In some cases staff members make a valiant effort to stand apart from the legislative struggle and provide objective assistance to both sides. When this

---

[105] *Toward a More Responsible Two-Party System*, pp. 63–64. On the question of whether certain staff members should be "earmarked" for the minority, see Kenneth Kofmehl, *Professional Staffs of Congress* (Lafayette, Ind.: Purdue University Studies, 1962), Chapter 4. Congressman Richard Bolling's observations on partisan staffing are instructive: "The committees need full and factual information. There is a view that this may be provided by creation of a nonpartisan staff at the service of members of both parties. Committee work, however, with its jockeying for partisan advantage, does not lend itself to this antiseptic situation, even with the best of intentions. The minority party is slighted. Its busy members do not have available, at the committee level, adequate numbers of professionally trained people who share the same angle of political vision. Policy is made, in large part, on political differences. Real policy differences require sound information. The bipartisan policy unanimity of the promilitary Armed Services Committee is just as destructive to the making of creative policy as is the shrill divisiveness characterizing the splintered Education and Labor Committee." *Power in the House*, p. 264.

[106] James D. Cochrane, "Partisan Aspects of Congressional Committee Staffing," *Western Political Quarterly*, XVII (June 1964), 338–48. See also Samuel C. Patterson, "The Professional Staffs of Congressional Committees," *Administrative Science Quarterly*, XV (March 1970), 22–37.

happens, they pass into the background whenever a really "hot" issue comes up. The genuine staff work, which is necessarily controversial, is thereby left to the staffs of executive agencies and private organizations. In other cases, staff members are required to take sides or do so of their own choosing. When this happens the more imaginative ones are in a better position to mobilize and direct the staff operations of friendly agencies and organizations. The others tend to serve as transmission belts—with some leeway for initiative and judgment—between members of Congress and noncongressional groups.[107]

A recurrent plaint is that staffs have encroached upon the members' role in policy-making. The staff contribution to shaping committee positions and legislation, it is argued, has thrust it forward as virtual spokesman for committee members. The problem this creates can be estimated from the following critical paragraphs found in the individual views appended to a Senate Judiciary Committee report on juvenile delinquency. Contending that the report should be described as a "staff study" rather than as a report of the committee itself, two minority members state:

> Staff help is indispensable. It is skilled and experienced in its specialty. It knows what to look for, where to find it, and how to reduce the information collected to usable form.
>
> But it also has its own jurisdiction in which to work and limitations which should be observed. Its province is investigation and the assembling of source material. At this point it is normal procedure for members of the subcommittee to familiarize themselves with the subject and source material at hand. In this manner they will be able to direct, if not actually produce, the end product and especially that portion of it which contains general policy, conclusions, and recommendations.... The instant report follows an all too common pattern for investigative activities by this body. It embraces the practice of abdicating committee responsibility and relying totally upon a professional staff which, however competent and authoritative, lacks certain basic qualifications. It is not composed of elected representatives of the people who are the true policy-deciding officials.[108]

The role which a committee staff assumes in the formation of public policy is affected by several considerations. A study by John Manley of the Joint Committee on Internal Revenue Taxation discloses four principal variables that shape staff influence in this committee. Of leading importance is the subject matter handled by the committee. "As the complexity of decisions facing legislators increases so too does the likelihood that the staff will exert influence on the outcomes." Second, staff influence tends to be constricted on those issues that are important to a large number of participants. A third factor involves the personal relations between the staff and leading committee members. Finally, the influence of the staff will depend on the extent to which staff judgments are congruent with the judgments of the committee majority. Although staff experts undoubtedly play an important

[107] Gross, *op. cit.,* pp. 282–83.
[108] Senate Committee on the Judiciary, *Juvenile Delinquency,* Senate report no. 1593, 86th Cong., 2d sess., 1960 (Washington, D.C.: Government Printing Office, 1960), pp. 127–28.

200   role in the legislative process, on the whole "they take more cues from the formal policy-makers than they give."[109]

What kinds of people compose a committee staff? The answer is, all kinds, but many share a common background in law. A survey taken in Congress a few years after the passage of the 1946 reorganization act disclosed that approximately one-half of the professional staff members were lawyers. Another one-sixth were social scientists.[110] Many committee aides have earlier held appointments in the executive branch, where their work was about the same as their committee work.[111]

The predominance of lawyers among committee staff aides has been viewed skeptically at times, especially by social scientists. Gladys Kammerer, for example, has contended that "the great danger in overemphasis of legal training for professional committee work is that lawyers are too seldom exposed in their training to social, economic, and political problems. They bring to committee work the same narrow, technical, legalistic background already characteristic of so many legislators."[112] On the other hand, another student of congressional staffing, Kenneth Kofmehl, argues that a legal education has a number of advantages: It encourages the staff member "to adopt a client-counsel attitude. It equips him to be a generalist. It is helpful in preparing bill analyses, briefs, opinions, and other legal memoranda.... It is very useful in handling casework and other kinds of legislative oversight duties involving technical points of law...and is an asset in dealing with ...liaison officials...that are lawyers. The committees operate in a legal context."[113]

The suggestion is made from time to time that coordination among committees could be improved through cooperation between the committees' professional staffs. Coordination has a particular value in areas such as foreign affairs, likely to be touched by the activities of a number of committees. The record of communication and cooperation between professional staffs, however, is not impressive, though a few conspicuous examples may be found in each congressional session. One explanation for the lack of comity is that:

> Cooperation between the staffs of the committees is deterred by the same obstacles that discourage other cooperative arrangements between committees. The professional and non-professional staff employees often share the same jurisdictional jealousies as the men they serve.... Occasionally, factual information is exchanged for use in studies and reports. Staff politics is as complex as committee politics. Even if inclined to cooperate with the staff of another committee, a staff may be restrained by the hostility of its committee to even mild collaboration. Thus, in some situations, cooperation between staffs must proceed covertly, or not at all.[114]

109 "Congressional Staff and Public Policy-Making: The Joint Committee on Internal Revenue Taxation," *Journal of Politics,* XXX (November 1968), 1046–67, quotations on pp. 1066 and 1067.

110 Kammerer, *op. cit.,* p. 1130.

111 Kofmehl, *op. cit.,* p. 83. For examination of hiring and firing practices of committee aides, see Chapter 5.

112 Kammerer, *op. cit.,* p. 1130.

113 Kofmehl, *op. cit.,* pp. 85–86.

114 Carroll, *op. cit.,* pp. 230–31.

Congress makes limited use of joint staffs, such as the one which serves the Joint Committee on Internal Revenue Taxation. The tax technicians comprising the joint staff also aid the House Ways and Means Committee and the Senate Finance Committee. Congressmen are greatly dependent upon the recommendations of the joint staff, particularly its chief, because of the complexity of tax policies. Representing congressional interests, which in turn tend to center on helping interest groups to secure special tax provisions, the chief of staff is often the principal opponent of the Treasury Department in the tax committees. With experts in dispute on both sides of the issue—the chief of staff and the Treasury—it is not too difficult for the congressman to justify his decision, which often is in favor of the pressure group.[115]

IN THE STATES

A leading priority in the current drive to revitalize state legislatures has been the development of professional staffs. All but a few states now have legislative reference services or legislative councils, and committee members may turn to them for assistance.[116] But in the committees themselves, where the need for information and counsel is steady and insistent, the staff idea has only recently begun to take hold. Standing committees now have access to research and technical assistance in about three-fourths of the states.[117] Even here the service is often incomplete, with staff aid available only to certain major committees, such as finance, appropriations, and judiciary. Legislative indifference is not so great in the case of secretarial and stenographic assistance; in most states these services are now available to all committees.

The principal consequence of limited professional staffing for committees is that they are obliged to look elsewhere for information and assistance. If the committee's work is important enough, if a critical matter is at hand, ready aid becomes available—from executive agencies affected by committee decisions and from political interest groups whose welfare is at stake. Surprisingly, a few states rely exclusively on executive agencies for the staff assistance necessary in budget review.

The capacity of legislatures to make intelligent, independent judgments is sharply influenced by the presence of expert staff assistance. A study of the Wisconsin legislature has shown that the addition of research analysts to each party caucus in the Assembly and Senate has had notable effects on legislative decision-making, integration, and performance. Among the consequences have been a strengthening of the caucus system at the expense of the committees, a greater visibility for legislative party leaders, a growth in party cohesiveness and in interparty conflict, and a new capacity for the

[115] Stanley S. Surrey, "The Congress and the Tax Lobbyist—How Special Tax Provisions Get Enacted," *Harvard Law Review,* LXX (May 1957), 1166–70.

[116] For an account of the development and activities of research and service agencies linked to the state legislature, see William J. Siffin, *The Legislative Council in the American States* (Bloomington: Indiana University Press, 1959). Also consult Alan Rosenthal, "The Effectiveness of Legislative Study and Interim Work," *State Government,* XLIV (Spring 1971), 93–101.

[117] *Staff and Services for State Legislatures* (New York: National Municipal League, 1968), p. 20.

development of legislative alternatives to executive proposals and for legislative control of the administration.[118]

The need for staff support in the state legislatures is every bit as important as it is in Congress. Staff support systems, including assistance for individual members, are highly developed in only a handful of states—California, Florida, and Hawaii stand out in this respect.[119] Elsewhere, advances are being made, but change comes slowly. Staffing is a crucial matter in the development and maintenance of legislative autonomy. Where the legislature must rely on outside forces for information and assistance, it loses control over its own activities. The net result is a loss of independence.

[118] Alan Rosenthal, "An Analysis of Institutional Effects: Staffing Legislative Parties in Wisconsin," *Journal of Politics,* **XXXII** (August 1970), 531–62.

[119] *Report on an Evaluation of the 50 State Legislatures* (Kansas City, Mo.: Citizens Conference on State Legislatures, 1971), p. 16.

7

COMMITTEES AT WORK

Congress and state legislatures are beset by much the same irritation: a nagging doubt as to their self-sufficiency. The reasons for this are many and complex, ranging from those that reflect problems largely internal to any legislature to those that arise from the pressure of external agencies and events. Public policy today is complicated beyond comparison; it changes at a rate that tends to make last year's information inappropriate to this year's understanding; it grows steadily as a result of the new ventures of government; it suffers from contingencies policy-makers can never fully estimate; and it imposes a heavy burden on the legislator who attempts to meet his responsibilities conscientiously.

The growing complexity of public policy has not made the legislature obsolete, but it has made its tasks extraordinarily difficult. Troublesome as this may be, it is not the only big problem that weighs on the legislature. Of at least equal significance is the fact that the legislature has lost some measure of autonomy and substantial initiative. The chief executive and the bureaucracy,[1] outsiders in the legislative system, have gained in both respects and often are the dominant forces in the legislative struggle itself.

If legislators are restive over how well they are doing their jobs, this is linked as much as anything to their perceptions of the advantages held by the executive branch.[2] The legislator is a generalist; his frequent antagonist, the bureaucrat, is a specialist. In the legislator's view, the executive branch is a vast organization, geared to efficient collection of facts and served by an immense battery of experts.[3] By comparison, legislative access

[1] See Peter Woll, *American Bureaucracy* (New York: W. W. Norton & Company, Inc., 1963).

[2] There are, to be sure, exceptions to these large and general observations. Consider the House Appropriations Committee's perception of its significance in the legislative system: "The Committee's view begins with the pre-eminence of the House...in appropriations affairs. It moves easily to the conviction that, as the efficient part of the House in this matter, the Constitution has endowed it with special obligations and special prerogatives. It ends in the view that the Committee on Appropriations, far from being merely one among many units in a complicated legislative-executive system, is *the* most important, most responsible unit in the whole appropriations process." Richard F. Fenno, Jr., "The House Appropriations Committee as a Political System: The Problem of Integration," *American Political Science Review*, LVI (June 1962), 311.

[3] There is a sea full of examples of this point in the statements made by representatives and senators. A statement by former Senator Thomas Hennings to

204 to specialized knowledge appears limited and episodic—too frequently, legislative decisions seem to be based on fragmentary evidence, supplied by outsiders at that.[4]

The principal, though not the only response of the legislature to these circumstances has been to try to expand its own resources.[5] This is shown by the steady concern of some legislators with attempts to augment and enhance the staff contribution to members and to the committee system. It is also manifested, especially in Congress, by a preoccupation with collecting data, expert opinions, and all variety of information appropriate to policy-making and to strengthening the legislature's position. Writes Douglass Cater:

> The quest for knowledge has become a new way of life for the ambitious members of Congress. As soon as seniority gives him a crack at a subcommittee chairmanship he is off. The competition for budgetary allocations to conduct hearings is as fierce as the old-time scraps over patronage. Hardpressed staff directors vie to produce superior rosters of experts who can be lured from the universities and laboratories to serve as witnesses. The more highbrow among the hearings have taken on attributes of graduate seminars.[6]

The committee is the principal agency of the legislature for gathering information and the principal instrument by which the legislature can defend and maintain itself in struggles with the chief executive and the bureaucracy. "A committee is commissioned not to instruct the public, but

---

the acting director of the International Cooperation Administration, who was testifying before the Hennings committee, will serve our purpose. Senator Hennings: "I think you are asked superficial questions by rustics like ourselves who do not quite understand the more ethereal and erudite things. On some of these things, you gentlemen in the executive branch have the advantage. You become specialists. We are spread pretty thin, you know. . . . I think that many of the things that plague us are [due to] lack of full information. . . . Can we get down to the basic proposition, how thoroughly has all this been checked? I can't help but feel myself sometimes when I vote for appropriations I am taking so much on faith." *Hearings on Executive Privilege and Freedom of Information* before the Subcommittee on Constitutional Rights of the Senate Committee on the Judiciary, 86th Cong., 1st sess., 1959, pp. 357–58.

4 Though it cannot be proven, there is a good argument that Congress today is more introspective, more concerned with its internal policy-making processes than ever before. Indeed, so concerned is Congress to secure relevant data and expert analysis that it has taken to contracting for studies by various private research agencies, usually university-centered. This has led to a curious but not unexpected result in some cases. As one writer sees it: "The trouble is that Congress lacks the capacity to assimilate this outpouring of the experts. The reports multiply and gather dust. The congressman grows fretful or, worse, he becomes cynical, hemmed in by his expanding library of unread paperback tomes." Douglass Cater, "The Lonely Men on Capitol Hill," *The Reporter,* October 15, 1959, p. 25.

5 A less happy response is that some legislators, seeking to avoid the responsibility of intelligent choice among complex alternatives, have become, for all intents and purposes, simply "case-takers" or "errand-runners" for demanding constituents. They keep busy by doing favors, justifying their preoccupation as the obligation of the representative, while policy matters swirl over their heads.

6 Cater, *op. cit.,* p. 24.

to instruct and guide the House."[7] A major technique for carrying out this task is the hearing.

Committee Hearings

The practice of committee hearings is associated historically with the right of citizens to petition Parliament, either in support of or in opposition to a proposed action. In the English experience, limits were clearly defined. In assessing the value of *public* measures, Parliament became the sole judge, and citizen opinions were neither sought nor entertained except when measures were thought to have adverse consequences for private rights and interests. The principal opportunity for witnesses to appear before committees developed in the case of private bills, those involving the claims of individuals, companies, or local authorities.

American experience with hearings has been mixed. Writing in the 1920s, Robert Luce observed that "on this side of the water it has generally been held that no right exists in any case, whether public or private."[8] Many state legislatures make only limited use of hearings. Congress, however, has long been inclined to open its doors to nonmembers and in recent years has actively solicited their testimony. David Truman writes that the development of the public hearing in the United States, in the period since 1900, "was a consequence of the proliferation of interest groups and of the challenge to established interests that their claims constituted."[9] Today few major bills emerge from congressional committees without having proceeded through the hearing stage. Whether viewed as a right, a privilege, a political stratagem, or simply as happenstance, the hearing process is now securely lodged in congressional practice.

THE FUNCTIONS OF HEARINGS

The advantages of legislative hearings, particularly the public (or open) variety, are steadily extolled by American legislators. Hearings, their litany insists, present an opportunity to "get at the facts," to "hear all sides" (and "interested parties"), to educate the member to the provisions of a bill and their probable consequences, and to inform the representative as to the "wishes of the people." In sum, the public face of hearings, the one immediately described by legislators, shows the lawmaker educating and warming himself in the glow of the active citizen's opinions and intelligence. The only trouble with this description is that it does not completely square with the facts.

David Truman describes the functions or purposes of public hearings as three in number. The initial purpose, defined by the glossy accounts above,

7 Woodrow Wilson, *Congressional Government* (New York: Meridian Books, 1956 [first published 1885]), p. 71.

8 Robert Luce, *Legislative Procedure* (Boston: Houghton Mifflin Company, 1922), p. 143. The preceding paragraph is based on Luce's work.

9 David Truman, *The Governmental Process* (New York: Alfred A. Knopf, Inc., 1953), p. 373.

206 is to provide "a means of transmitting information, both technical and political, from various actual and potential interest groups to the committee." The second function "is as a propaganda channel through which a public may be extended and its segments partially consolidated or reinforced." Third, public hearings serve "to provide a quasi-ritualistic means of adjusting group conflicts and relieving disturbances through a safety valve."[10]

Purposes two and three rank well above one in importance. If the principal purpose of hearings were to transmit information to committee members, the major groups would make better use of expert staff personnel as witnesses, because they are better equipped to testify on technical points. The fact is that organizations tend to use ("parade" may be a better word) their most distinguished members as spokesmen, men whose names command committee respect and newspaper print. The very appearance of the representative "is a subtle reminder that it might cost precious votes or support in the next campaign if the measure under consideration is not dealt with 'properly.' "[11] The propaganda function is achieved through coverage by the news media, including television and motion pictures. "At some points in the development of a measure, in fact, the primary purpose of hearings lies in their propaganda value."[12]

The "safety-valve" function involves a further dimension of committee hearings. Legislators recognize its utility, though they do not publicize it. Even witnesses may understand this function, as shown in the statement by a South Carolina attorney testifying on civil rights legislation: "I appreciate the fact that you have been sitting all day, but I have come about 500 miles to get something off my chest and I hope you gentlemen will let me do it."[13] "In my own opinion," wrote Luce, "not the least, and perhaps the greatest, of the advantages of public committee hearings is their service as a safety-valve. If the wild reformer, the crank, can but be heard, he is often content and thereafter for a while will do little mischief. Bottle him up and he will explode."[14]

The traditional interpretation described the committee member as an impartial judge, charged with studying the facts, listening, weighing the evidence submitted by contesting parties, and deciding the case. The committee member's standards, so this interpretation held, were those of the "public interest," and his role was that of guardian. A much newer generalization has it that the member himself may be a willing and active participant in the political struggle, with interests far from neutral.

Ralph Huitt examines the suitability of these generalizations in explaining the behavior of members of the Senate Committee on Banking and Currency in 1946 hearings on the question of extending price controls, an explosive controversy in which the leading antagonists were the NAM and the CIO among the organized interest groups, and the Republican senators and the administration among the officialdom. The study's findings accent

---

10 *Ibid.,* p. 372.

11 Julius Cohen, "Hearing on a Bill: Legislative Folklore?" *Minnesota Law Review,* XXXVII (December 1952), 39.

12 Truman, *op. cit.,* pp. 373–74.

13 *Hearings on Civil Rights—1957* before the Subcommittee on Constitutional Rights of the Committee on the Judiciary, Senate, 85th Cong., 1st sess., 1957, p. 727.

14 Luce, *op. cit.,* p. 146.

the political function of hearings: (1) Committee members tended to identify with particular interest groups—the supporters of price control with the administration, labor spokesmen, and the National Farmers Union; the opponents with the NAM, the American Farm Bureau Federation, and other business groups. (2) "Each group [of senators] seemed to come into the hearings with a ready-made frame of reference. Facts which were compatible were filled into it; facts which were not compatible, even when elaborately documented, were discounted, not perceived, or ignored." (3) "The members of this Committee did not sit as legislative judges to discover an abstract general interest, nor did they seem concerned with presenting a balanced debate for public consideration. On the contrary, most of them did take sides."[15] In a word, most of the members were involved in the price-control squabble as participants. The likelihood is great that this behavior is characteristic, especially in the case of legislation having major socioeconomic implications.[16]

TESTIMONY AND INTERROGATION OF WITNESSES

A committee witness begins his presentation by reading or summarizing a statement of his views. As a rule, committee members appear more interested in questioning the witness than in listening to him read a statement. "We just hope the witness will keep in mind that there are many more witnesses to be heard and much of the testimony is cumulative," the chairman is likely to caution. As a result, formal statements tend to be brief, merely recording the salient points of the written statement which will be incorporated into the record. A surprisingly large amount of testimony is taken with only a small contingent of the committee members present. This may be partly attributable to the fact that the committee is concerned with simply going through the motions of hearing out witnesses, but it also occurs because other activities contest for the members' time. Important witnesses—cabinet members, governors, the heads of major pressure groups—are likely to attract a full complement of committee members.

Testimony given in committee ranges widely. At times it has a distinctly authentic ring, with witnesses introducing new and relevant information, identifying clearly the positions of their organizations, and helping to bring the issue into sharp focus. But there is no avoiding the fact that much of what is said in formal statements and in response to questioning is designed mainly to win propaganda advantage, to intensify old loyalties, and to fill

[15] "The Congressional Committee: A Case Study," *American Political Science Review*, XLVIII (June 1954), quotations from pp. 354 and 365. Additional support for Huitt's interpretation of the character and functions of hearings appears in a study of hearings conducted by subcommittees of the Senate Committee on Labor and Public Welfare and the House Committee on Education and Labor. See an article by Paul Lutzker, "The Behavior of Congressmen in a Committee Setting: A Research Report," *Journal of Politics*, XXXI (February 1969), 140–66.

[16] On this point, also consult Seymour Scher, "Congressional Committee Members as Independent Agency Overseers: A Case Study," *American Political Science Review*, LIV (December 1960), 911–20. This study of the House Education and Labor Committee as it reviewed the actions of the National Labor Relations Board discloses the steady involvement of congressmen in helping witnesses adversely affected by NLRB actions to develop their arguments against the agency's trial examiners.

208 out the record. This cuts both ways: legislators often are just as anxious as witnesses to establish their orthodoxy. They can be of immense help to a witness or they can go a long way toward making his committee appearance uncomfortable, even unpleasant. A witness who can claim a personal friend, or whose organization has gained a sympathetic ear among the members, starts with an advantage worth having, irrespective of the legislation under consideration. If he gets into a jam, there is someone to help extricate him.[17] The value of friendly committee members to a witness is shown in Elias Huzar's description of relations between military spokesmen and the Appropriations Committee at the hearings stage:

> Since its budget estimates are defended by the men who spend the appropriations, it is of great importance to the War Department [now the Defense Department] that these officers should be able to make friends with members of the subcommittees on military appropriations and to influence them favorably. Good relations with the Congressmen reduce time-consuming and possibly embarrassing probing into the estimates and increase the prospects that Congress will appropriate the funds the Department requests.... Although professional soldiers, who constitute the bulk of the Department's witnesses, are sometimes said to be poor pleaders, very few of the Military Establishment's representatives have lacked "the gift of tongues." However, if they should falter and be at a loss for words, the budget officers of the Department and its bureaus are at hand to help them out. Occasionally, also, a member of the subcommittee comes to their assistance—and sometimes his questions suggest that he has been primed on what to ask in order to give the Department's representative a chance to make the case he wants to prove.[18]

The committee reception to a witness, on the other hand, may try the patience of the witness and fray the nerves of some committee members.[19] Questioning by a hostile committee member is apt to be prolonged, dilatory, and involved, and to call for specific data the witness is unlikely to have.

---

[17] An observation by William Benton, former senator from Connecticut, is apropos here: "I think a man must work in Washington for some time, possibly even serve in the Senate itself, in order to discover how terribly important one single Senator is. I remember when I left the State Department to go back to Connecticut, I told my friends that I would never again take an administrative job in Washington unless I felt I owned a piece of one Senator. To an administrative officer, one Senator who knows him and is friendly to him, and has an interest in what he is trying to do, can make all the difference between his success and his failure. ... If he has one Senator who is prepared to get up and defend him, and stand up for him, other members of the Senate are far more cautious, and far slower to go after him or to attack him, are far more careful to get the facts and to avoid possible injustice." *Hearings on the Organization and Operation of Congress* before the Senate Committee on Expenditures in the Executive Departments, 82d Cong., 1st sess., 1951, p. 32.

[18] Elias Huzar, *The Purse and the Sword: Control of the Army by Congress Through Military Appropriations, 1933–1950* (Ithaca, N.Y.: Cornell University Press, 1950), p. 74.

[19] The army-McCarthy hearings in 1954 ran for thirty-five days, took up 187 hours of television time, and were watched by an estimated 20 million people. Richard Rovere describes them as "ordeal, combat, theater, duel, confession, catharsis [and] the testing of wills...." *Senator Joe McCarthy* (New York: Harcourt, Brace & World, Inc., 1959), p. 208.

Stated and repeated answers rarely satisfy. Doggedness, sometimes brusqueness, and a mixture of irony and humor may serve to keep the witness off balance. The following snapshot of an interrogation of the attorney general by a southern senator provides a good illustration:

> Senator Ervin. Mr. Attorney General, this provision of the subcommittee print which is unnumbered provides that whenever two or more persons shall knowingly in concert commit or attempt to commit violence upon any person, because of his race, color, creed, national origin, ancestry, language, religion, such persons shall constitute a lynch mob within the meaning of this title, and it provides for their punishment.
>
> I give you a hypothetical case. There was a Presbyterian and a Methodist down in North Carolina who got to arguing about the Presbyterian doctrine of predestination, and like all religious arguments the longer it lasted the more wrathful they became. Now it happened that the Methodist had a brother standing by, and finally the Methodist said, "Well, I will admit that there may be something in the doctrine of predestination. I think the Presbyterians are predestined to go to hell." Then the Presbyterian said to the Methodist, "Well, I would rather be a Presbyterian and know I am going to hell than to be a Methodist and not know where in the hell I am going." Now thereupon the Methodist brother who was standing by said, "Knock the devil out of him," and the Methodist hit the Presbyterian and knocked him down.
>
> Now under this bill those two Methodists would constitute a lynch mob, would they not, because that violence arose out of their creed?
>
> Mr. Brownell. I can't imagine a Methodist doing that, Senator. [*Laughter.*]
>
> Senator Ervin. I will ask you to imagine that these were North Carolina Methodists.... Now under this bill those two Methodists would be a lynch mob, would they not?
>
> Mr. Brownell. I think I had better consult my pastor on that....[20]

An often dominant impression conveyed by hearings is that witnesses are questioned in such a way as to elicit statements which buttress the views of one or more members of the committee. Committee members may help a witness plead a point of view. Although the following exchange, which occurred in hearings on an open-housing bill in the 89th Congress, may not find a niche in the enduring literature of the legislative process, it amply illustrates the point. The witness is the president of a real estate association and the interrogator is a southern senator:

> Senator Ervin. I want to commend you on the excellence of your statement, and to say that I agree with everything you have said.... Can you see any way that a person of intellectual integrity can say that an amendment which merely prohibits State action can be used as a basis of legislation to prohibit individual action?
>
> Mr. Smith. No, sir; I cannot.
>
> Senator Ervin. And with reference to the commerce clause, can you imagine anything or any kind of property that is more local in nature than real estate?
>
> Mr. Smith. No, sir.

[20] *Hearings on Civil Rights—1957,* pp. 21–22.

Senator Ervin. Did you ever see any real estate moving across State lines?

Mr. Smith. Not since I have been in the business, sir.

Senator Ervin. Take this case. If a widow were to rent one room in her private dwelling house, a person that she didn't want to rent to could force her to let him occupy that room. Can you see any interstate commerce in compelling a widow to do that with respect to a private dwelling house?

Mr. Smith. No, sir; we cannot.

Senator Ervin. Don't you believe that, if people are to be truly free, that they must have the right to make their own decisions independent of government dictation?

Mr. Smith. We feel that they should have absolute right; yes, sir.

Senator Ervin. I read an editorial the other day that said you could not secure freedom for some people by taking freedom away from all people. Isn't that exactly what title IV would do?

Mr. Smith. We feel it does just that, sir; yes, sir.

Senator Ervin. [Do] you not believe that people of a particular race or particular religion naturally prefer to associate together rather than with people of other races and other religions? Isn't that sort of a natural thing?

Mr. Smith. Yes, it is.

Senator Ervin. That you have observed.

Mr. Smith. Very much so.

Senator Ervin. I certainly agree with the observations you have made. . . .[21]

WITNESSES AT COMMITTEE HEARINGS

From what ranks are congressional committee witnesses drawn? No general answer to this question is available, since the character of the legislation is the governing factor. Sometimes the contingent of witnesses represents a quite narrow sector of society. At the hearings on legislative reorganization in the 89th Congress, the great bulk of the witnesses were members of Congress and political scientists. Among a small number of interest groups offering testimony were several veterans' organizations, the Americans for Democratic Action, the Americans for Constitutional Action, the National Committee to Abolish the House Un-American Activities Committee, and the National Committee for an Effective Congress. Also in the 89th Congress, the witnesses at the well publicized hearings on U.S. policy with respect to mainland China were drawn almost exclusively from the academic world. Major legislation will invariably call forth witnesses from three main sources: the administration, Congress, and private organizations. There is nothing in the rules of either house which insists that committees must listen to the arguments of all prospective witnesses; yet it is a rare instance in which a representative of any organized group is denied an opportunity to appear and testify.[22] The doors are, of course, virtually wide open to legislators and administration officials.

[21] *Hearings on Civil Rights—1966,* before the Subcommittee on Constitutional Rights of the Senate Committee on the Judiciary, 89th Cong., 2d sess., 1966, pp. 941–42.

[22] Any person can ask to appear before a committee, and there is a good chance that he will be heard. As a result, hearings on major legislation are usually under the pressure of too many witnesses and too little time. Minor witnesses are

An example of the types of witnesses who appear before committees is available in the 1966 Senate hearings on civil rights legislation. In the course of twenty-two days, or parts thereof, a considerable number of governmental and private witnesses gave testimony, including seven senators, one congressman, ten clerks of U.S. district courts, one governor and various other state government officials, several law professors and lawyers, the representatives of some thirty-two private organizations (mainly real estate associations opposed to the "open-housing" title in the bill), and several individuals apparently representing no one other than themselves. In addition, several other senators and congressmen, twenty-three chief judges of U.S. district courts, ten governors, twelve state attorneys general, and many private organizations submitted written statements for the record. Hearings on civil rights legislation invariably attract as witnesses a great many government officials, state as well as national.[23]

EXECUTIVE SESSIONS

Testimony is sometimes taken in executive or closed session. There are three principal justifications for proceeding with hearings behind closed doors. In the first place, the information to be disclosed may be of such a nature that it should not be released to the public—for example, certain military, diplomatic, and scientific data. In the second place, witnesses are more likely to be forthright when testifying under conditions of relative secrecy. And third, legislators have less opportunity to use the hearing to win publicity, a similar obstacle to witnesses who are inclined to lay a dramatic or meretricious case before the press.

The congressional route to classified information in the executive branch is through closed hearings, permitting greater freedom of testimony for government witnesses. A common practice is to ask each witness to review his testimony in order to make as much of it as possible available for public inspection. Given the complex regulations regarding publication of executive

---

regularly cautioned by the committee chairman to make their presentations brief and to the point, but often this is to no avail. Even brief statements may prompt lengthy cross examinations. The following exchange between the Washington Director of the NAACP and the chairman of the Subcommittee on Constitutional Rights, which was holding hearings on civil rights legislation, shows the problem:

> Mr. Mitchell. In this situation, Mr. Chairman, Mr. Courts here is a man who was shot in Mississippi because he was seeking the right to vote. He has come to Washington for a chance to tell the Senate of the United States what his problem is. Mr. Austin T. Walden, a respected lawyer in Georgia, has come up to tell about his problem. The Reverend Dr. Borders, who is pastor of one of the largest churches in the city of Atlanta, has come to tell how he as a clergyman was arrested simply because he was riding on a bus.
>
> Senator Hennings. Mr. Mitchell, in no derogation of your assembled witnesses, I would say if the Attorney General of the United States were sitting here, or indeed the President, we would have no way of just going on and on and on and on because this sort of thing requires examination. . . . I am sure the committee would like to accommodate all witnesses, but there are only 24 hours in a day.

(About two weeks later the witnesses were heard.) *Hearings on Civil Rights—1957,* pp. 275–76.

[23] *Hearings on Civil Rights—1966.*

212 information, this often is a frustrating task; not surprisingly, there may be disagreement between legislators and administrators concerning what information may safely be released.

CONGRESSIONAL COMMITTEES AND EXECUTIVE PRIVILEGE

The quest of Congress for information sometimes is thwarted by the doctrine of executive privilege, with committees usually at the center of the controversy. Briefly, this doctrine asserts that executive officials, at their discretion, have a right to withhold information from Congress when they believe that disclosure would not serve the national interest. The doctrine, which has been invoked by presidents on numerous occasions, was defined and justified by President Eisenhower in this way:

> [Under] the historic doctrine of the separation of powers between the three great branches of our Government, the executive has a recognized constitutional duty and power with respect to the disclosure of information, documents, and other material relating to its operations. The President has throughout our history, in compliance with his duty in this regard, withheld information when he found that the disclosure of what was sought would be incompatible with the national interest. It is essential to effective administration that employees of the executive branch be in a position to be fully candid in advising with each other on official matters, and that the broadest range of individual opinions and advice be available in the formulation of decisions and policy.... The disclosure of conversations, communications, or documents...can accordingly tend to impair essential reporting and decision-making processes, and such disclosure has therefore been forbidden in the past, as contrary to the national interest....[24]

Executive privilege nettles and disrupts Congress for several basic reasons, all involving the legislature's own "institutional self-interest."[25] For Congress to carry out its varied responsibilities, it often requires documents that rest in executive hands. Numerous cases arose during the 1940s and 1950s—involving, for example, loyalty-security files, foreign-aid programs, and weapons systems—in which the president and his subordinates used the privilege of secrecy to deny congressional requests for information. At times quarrels over executive privilege mask a basic struggle for ascendancy, as shown by these comments of a former senator:

> [None] of us was born yesterday. We all know the technique, very common on Capitol Hill, of stridently demanding information when what we really want is to influence a course of action. A part of the game is to disclaim the true intent and to wax indignant when challenged. It is also a part of

---

24 This statement is taken from a letter from President Eisenhower to Senator Mansfield, refusing to make available an ICA evaluation of the Vietnam program requested by the Committee on Foreign Relations. *Withholding of Information from the Congress,* a survey by the Subcommittee on Constitutional Rights of the Committee on the Judiciary, Committee Print, 86th Cong., 2d sess., 1961, pp. 20–21.

25 Francis E. Rourke, "Administrative Secrecy: A Congressional Dilemma," *American Political Science Review,* LIV (September 1960), 684. Also see his book, *Secrecy and Publicity* (Baltimore: Johns Hopkins Press, 1961).

the game for the people on whom the demand is made to pretend that they do not understand the true import of the demand. All of this is a stylized performance in the never-ending tug-of-war between the legislative and executive branches.[26]

What irritates members of Congress above all else is the belief that administrative secrecy is a pretext for concealing irregularities and incompetence. Many members believe that bureaucrats have an instinct for the suppression of information, regardless of its importance. The press is just as devoted as Congress to breaking down secrecy, since it affects the well-being of the industry itself.[27]

Sporadic conflict over the issue—safeguarding information in the public interest versus Congress's or the people's "right to know"—is likely to continue. A high point of executive-legislative conflict was reached during the Eisenhower administration when his attorney general developed the interpretation that executive privilege provides for "uncontrolled discretion" to withhold information. Numerous cases of executive withholdings occurred during this period, causing substantial conflict between the branches. The Kennedy and Johnson administrations took a different tack. With only one exception, Congress was given complete access to executive information during the Kennedy administration. President Johnson continued this policy, much to the approval of Congress. Curtailment of the claims of executive privilege in these administrations may have been due to the legislative experience of both presidents. Despite recent practice, however, there is no reason to believe that future presidents will hesitate to invoke the executive privilege doctrine. The doctrine is unusually alluring—at least to executive eyes.[28]

As it stands now, each branch is vague about the limits of its powers—to withhold on one side, to inquire on the other. It can be argued that this ambivalent status, which favors the executive branch, is generally satisfactory:

(1) There is little reason to believe that, in practice, the lack of an absolute power to compel the executive to produce information appreciably handicaps

[26] Robert Kramer and Herbert Marcuse, "Executive Privilege—A Study of the Period 1953–1960," *George Washington Law Review,* XXIX (April–June 1961), 623–717, 827–916, quotation on 717.

[27] The seriousness with which the press assays the "extreme secrecy doctrine" can be estimated in the following two articles: Clark Mollenhoff, "Executive Privilege—A Problem for Press and Bar: A Journalist's View," pp. 135–45, and J. R. Wiggins, "Government Operations and the Public's Right to Know," pp. 167–89, both in *Hearings on Executive Privilege.* In practical terms, the problem is that "the ability of the press to penetrate executive agencies is pretty much contingent on the power of congressional committees to penetrate these agencies. . . . I've heard of a few hardy journalists who feel they can pry loose sufficient information without any aid from Congress," writes Mollenhoff, but ". . . most realists will admit that their own effectiveness in getting information of any unfavorable character is pretty closely tied to the power of Congress to move in and document the case" (p. 135). Also see his book, *Washington Cover-Up* (Garden City, N.Y.: Doubleday & Company, Inc., 1962).

[28] This paragraph is based mainly on Raoul Berger, "Executive Privilege v. Congressional Inquiry," *UCLA Law Review,* XII (August 1965), 1044–1364, reproduced in *Hearings on the Organization of Congress* before the Joint Committee on the Organization of the Congress, 89th Cong., 2d sess., 1966. References are to pages 1045, 1320, and 1360.

Congress in the exercise of its legislative function. (2) Congress may not be a safe repository for sensitive information: there can be no guarantee that information coming into the hands of Congress or the whole membership of one of its main committees will long remain silent. (3) There are serious weaknesses in the assumption...that public policy ought to draw a sharp distinction between "military and diplomatic secrets" on the one hand and all other types of official information on the other, giving Congress free access to the latter. In the first place, the line is by no means easy to draw....[29]

There are counterarguments, however, that are equally compelling: "Nothing could be more axiomatic for a democracy than the principle of exposing the processes of government to relentless public criticism and scrutiny."[30] Moreover, congressional investigation is "the surest guard...against corruption and bureaucratic waste, inefficiency and rigidity."[31]

To an important extent, administrative secrecy exists because the road has been cleared for it by Congress itself. Although Congress has adopted certain laws to increase the disclosure of information, such as the freedom-of-information bill in the 85th Congress, it has passed many other bills that offer firm support for administrative secrecy. Moreover, the claim for publicizing executive records would seem more persuasive if congressional committees had a better record in disclosing their own decision-making processes and records. Table 7.1 testifies that the inclination to secrecy is not unique to the executive branch.[32]

In theory, the answer to the problem of making classified information available to the Congress is to hold hearings in executive session; in practice, this solution is far from satisfactory, since it is difficult to prevent "leaks" of committee discussions. It is one thing to strive for secrecy and quite another to achieve it, as these remarks by a former congressman show:

...We say that the information may not get out. I have been in public life for a long time.... If you are in a conference with over two or three people, no matter how sincere they may be, if the subject matter of the conference has to do with some matter or information which is secret and other information that is not secret, then after days go by, your recollection becomes dim as to what is secret and what is not secret.... Then it is only a short

29 Joseph Bishop, "The Executive's Right of Privacy: An Unresolved Constitutional Question," *Yale Law Journal*, LXVI (February 1957), 486–87. In addition, for the congressional point of view in the controversy, see Berger, *op. cit.*, and Philip R. Collins, "The Power of Congressional Committees of Investigation to Obtain Information from the Executive Branch: The Argument for the Legislative Branch," *Georgetown Law Journal*, XXXIX (May 1951), 563–98; and for the executive's side, see Kramer and Marcuse, *op. cit.*, and Richard P. Milloy, "The Power of the Executive to Withhold Information from Congressional Investigating Committees," *Georgetown Law Journal*, XLIII (June 1955), 643–60.

30 Rourke, *op. cit.*, p. 691.

31 Berger, *op. cit.*, p. 1360, quoting Wyzanski, "Standards for Congressional Investigations," *Record of N.Y.C.B.A.*, III (1948), 103.

32 The Legislative Reorganization Act of 1970 carries a provision that all committee hearings shall be open to the public unless a committee majority votes to close them. It remains to be seen whether the number of closed sessions will now decline significantly.

TABLE 7.1

The Use of Executive Sessions by Congressional Committees, 1953–70

Year	Total Meetings	Number Closed	% Closed
1953	2,640	892	35
1954	3,002	1,243	41
1955	2,940	1,055	36
1956	3,120	1,130	36
1957	2,517	854	34
1958	3,472	1,167	34
1959	3,152	940	30
1960	2,424	840	35
1961	3,159	1,109	35
1962	2,929	991	34
1963	3,868	1,463	38
1964	2,393	763	32
1965	3,608	1,242	34
1966	3,869	1,626	42
1967	4,412	1,716	39
1968	3,080	1,328	43
1969	4,029	1,470	36
1970	4,506	1,865	41
Total	59,415	21,989	37

SOURCE: *Congressional Quarterly Weekly Report*, February 12, 1971, p. 387. Reprinted by permission of the Congressional Quarterly Service.

NOTE: The committees that usually lead in proportion of closed meetings are Armed Services and Foreign Relations in the Senate, and Appropriations, Agriculture, Ways and Means, and Armed Services in the House.

time before the information begins to seep out over your radio and through your news commentators.[33]

HEARINGS IN THE STATE LEGISLATURES

Unlike Congress, whose attachment to the use of hearings is only slightly less than to the flag, most state legislative committees are both inclined and geared to act on measures without bothering to gather testimony. Apart from a few states which make considerable use of the device, public hearings are regarded either as rarities or as a special treatment to be accorded only major or controversial bills. Dayton McKean's description of the significance of hearings in the New Jersey legislature, in broad lines, apparently represents the situation in a majority of the states:

> The only committees in the legislature of New Jersey which have hearings during every session are the two committees on appropriations which hold joint hearings on the appropriation bill. There is no rule regarding hearings; they are held if there seems to be sufficient public demand and if the leader-

[33] Remarks of Representative Sasscer of Maryland, 94 *Cong. Rec.* 5724 (1948), quoted in Milloy, *op. cit.*, p. 658.

ship of the majority party wants to have them held. Aside from the regular hearings held by the committees on appropriations, not more than ten are held in most sessions.... Probably the chief reason for the paucity of hearings is that the members of committees begrudge the time which must be taken from their businesses, and, in addition, there is the general feeling among the legislators that hearings are futile, for the party leaders will do as they please about a bill no matter what comes out at a hearing, unless there is some great public clamor, for or against.[34]

State legislators, no less than members of Congress, realize that few if any votes are switched as a result of public hearings. As Hallie Farmer notes of Alabama legislators, many of them admit privately "that for influencing legislation such hearings are quite useless"—even though, of course, "they listen to the performance very patiently."[35] And in North Carolina, "except for budget measures, full-scale public hearings are held on only a small percentage of the bills introduced."[36] In Illinois, "elaborate committee presentations are rarely developed for the purpose of influencing committee votes. The more important the bill, the more likely it is that the voting pattern is predetermined. The presentation is designed to afford a justification for votes."[37]

Public hearings in the state legislatures are likely to be spectacular, boisterous, and entertaining, and indeed traveling circuses would be hard put to compete with some of them. Let a state legislature schedule a hearing on a bill to license chiropractors and hundreds of them will be in attendance, conveniently, because the annual convention happened to be held in the state capital the week of the hearing. Let a joint committee on sports and physical fitness schedule hearings to consider fitness programs, and among those present to "testify" will be a representative of a physical culture studio, clad appropriately in a black leotard, to demonstrate "body rhythms" for attentive committee members. And should a bill to furnish medical schools with unclaimed dogs and cats for research be up for a hearing, it is a foregone conclusion that dog and cat lovers from hundreds of miles around will be there, carrying gory, colored photographs of vivisections and testifying, among other things, that dog spelled backwards is "God."

Few people who watched the legislatures in the 1950s will ever forget the titanic battles waged in public hearings to permit the sale of precolored oleomargarine. Seldom have so many owed so much to so few as to the heroic housewives who, under the kindly eyes of the soybean farmers and the big oleo manufacturers, happily splattered oleo throughout the state committee rooms of the nation as they demonstrated the tedious method by which it is hand-colored. Last to drop the bar against precolored oleo was Wisconsin (in 1967), a legislature which has always had an abnormal affinity

[34] *Pressures on the Legislature of New Jersey* (New York: Columbia University Press, 1938), p. 47.

[35] *The Legislative Process in Alabama* (University: University of Alabama, Bureau of Public Administration, 1949), p. 158.

[36] Henry W. Lewis, *Legislative Committees in North Carolina* (Chapel Hill: University of North Carolina, Institute of Government, 1952), p. 36.

[37] Gilbert Y. Steiner and Samuel K. Gove, *Legislative Politics in Illinois* (Urbana: University of Illinois Press, 1960), p. 83.

for butter and cheese, not to mention a good many legislators from dairy counties.

EVALUATION OF COMMITTEE HEARINGS

No student of the legislature describes committee hearings as models of efficiency or of objectivity. The assessment usually is just the reverse. The most serious charges deal with problems of misinformation, unrepresentative opinions, bias, and staging. Robert Luce, for example, evaluated committee hearings in the Massachusetts legislature in this way:

> The value of the opinion brought out by hearings is as uncertain as that of the information. The opinion is the more dangerous, for misinformation can be corrected, but there is no test for opinion. Ponder it for a moment, and you will see the risk in drawing inference as to the opinion of two million or so of adult human beings in a State like Massachusetts, from the views expressed by five or fifty persons in a committee room. It may be said that these are the persons most interested, which may or may not be true. Unfortunately the persons attending are usually extremists, biased, uncompromising. Therefore no cautious legislator refrains from having at hand, metaphorically speaking, a bag of salt from which he may take many grains when he listens to speakers addressing a committee. The most to be said for opinion so furnished is that it may help.[38]

Julius Cohen attacks committee hearings on many points, but perhaps his sharpest criticism is reserved for the committee staff, among whose tasks, he says, "critical investigation" is not numbered. The political dimensions of committee hearings may be revealed as clearly by the behavior of the staff as by that of the members themselves. The job of committee aides may be:

> ...the delicate one of slanting the hearing, of manipulating the hearing machinery in such a way that a previous commitment on a bill would be made to appear as a decision reached by rational, detached deliberation.... This the staff can do by several means: by inviting the strongest, most persuasive witnesses to testify on behalf of the measure, by endeavoring to limit the number of strong opposition witnesses to a minimum; by asking "proper" questions of "friendly" witnesses and embarrassing ones of witnesses who are "unfriendly"; by arranging to close the hearing at a propitious time; by writing a report which brings out the best features of the testimony in favor of the bill and the most unfavorable features of that offered by the opposition; by subduing or discarding facts which do not fit the pattern of preconceived notions, opinions, or prejudices. In addition, the bill might be given the "killed-with-kindness" treatment—that is, given so lengthy a hearing that no time is left prior to adjournment to consider the measure on the House or Senate floor, thus assuring its defeat.[39]

[38] Luce, *op. cit.,* pp. 145–46.
[39] Cohen, *op. cit.,* p. 38.

It is not unfair to characterize Congress as preoccupied with the hearings process. Outside critics are persistent in questioning this activity which consumes inordinate time, harasses legislators, and yields an uncertain product. Nevertheless, this is not the full story. It is true, if hackneyed, that there is educational value to hearings—if not consistently to the legislators, at least to sectors within the public which follow the well-reported hearings on major bills. Quite apart from the intrinsic value of information conveyed by interest groups, an important function of instruction is served. Whether the testimony of interest-group representatives or administration spokesmen is partisan, factual, or superficial, is not the main point. Hearings may be justified in terms of the American publics which look to group testimony both for policy cues and for an extension of their own outlooks—hearings may be considered a useful stage in the representative process.

A defense can also be constructed from evidence concerning hearings on the programs of administrative agencies. A study of congressional review of price-control legislation contends: "The possibility of a public hearing before a committee of Congress is not only a protection to all individuals dealing with the agency but leads to sounder standards and greater attention to facts in arriving at an agency conclusion. Without such criticism, agency action would become more arbitrary and the discipline within the agency itself would deteriorate."[40]

No critic contends that all hearings are a waste of time. Some hearings cover an immense ground, yielding data and opinions of significance. And as to interrogations, if they are sometimes banal, niggling, and obsessively partisan, they are also, in counterpoise, sometimes illuminating and productive. Major policies occasionally trace their origin directly to the explorations of hearings, and important problems may be brought to the attention of the press and the public. Whatever the verdict on hearings, they represent an ambitious attempt to blend the legislature's requirements for information with the member's and party's requirements for influence and advantage.

Investigating Committees

Congress, wrote Woodrow Wilson in 1885, "may easily be too diligent in legislation. It often overdoes that business."[41] "What is quite as indispensable as the debate of problems of legislation," he contended, "is the debate of all matters of administration." Moreover:

> It is the proper duty of a representative body to look diligently into every affair of government and to talk much about what it sees. It is meant to be the eyes and the voice, and to embody the wisdom and will of its constituents. Unless Congress have and use every means of acquainting itself with the acts and the disposition of the administrative agents of the government, the country must be helpless to learn how it is being served; and unless Congress both scrutinize these things and sift them by every form

[40] William C. Burt and William F. Kennedy, "Congressional Review of Price Control," *University of Pennsylvania Law Review,* CI (November 1952), 333.
[41] Wilson, *op. cit.,* p. 199.

of discussion, the country must remain in embarrassing, crippling ignorance of the very affairs which it is most important that it should understand and direct. *The informing function of Congress should be preferred even to its legislative function.*[42]

The instrument for looking "into every affair of government" is the legislative committee. To conduct an investigation, Congress may create a special committee or entrust the task to one of its standing committees (or subcommittees). One major aim of the Legislative Reorganization Act of 1946 was to cut back the number of legislative committees, and accordingly, since passage of the act, more and more investigations have been conducted by standing committees, though Congress still continues to form some special (or select) investigating committees. A central feature of the special committee is that the member who comes up with the plan for an investigation is named chairman of the investigating committee. This practice has the advantage of circumventing the seniority rule by giving newer members a chance to head a committee. But it also raises a serious question: Can the member who found reason for the investigation, and succeeded in convincing the chamber to launch it, conduct the investigation fairly and remain impartial as to its outcome? Undoubtedly the temptation to vindicate the need for the investigation is strong.

There is no precise accounting of the number of investigations that have been held since the initial one in 1792—the House investigation concerned with General St. Clair's abortive campaign against the Indians. As of the early 1950s, over six hundred investigations had been held.[43] It is probable that considerably more investigations have been conducted in the last two decades than in all previous Congresses put together.

Evidence on the growth of the investigatory function appears in the increasingly large sums of money made available for investigations. In the 90th Congress (1967–68), for example, congressional committees (standing, select, and special) were *authorized* to spend nearly $22 million on investi-

---

[42] *Ibid.,* p. 198 (emphasis added).

[43] This is the informed estimate of M. Nelson McGeary, who has researched the question as thoroughly as anyone. See his book, *The Development of Congressional Investigative Power* (New York: Columbia University Press, 1940), and also his summary article, "Congressional Investigations: Historical Development," *University of Chicago Law Review,* XVIII (Spring 1951), 425–39. The general discussion of investigating committees in this section relies heavily on McGeary's work; Robert K. Carr's *The House Committee on UnAmerican Activities, 1945–50* (Ithaca, N.Y.: Cornell University Press, 1952); Harold W. Chase, "Improving Congressional Investigations: A No-Progress Report," *Temple Law Quarterly,* XXX (Winter 1957), 126–55; and Edward J. Heubel, "Congressional Resistance to Reform: The House Adopts a Code for Investigating Committees," *Midwest Journal of Political Science,* I (November 1957), 313–29. Space is too brief to note the many other excellent studies in book and article form, except: Robert F. Kennedy, *The Enemy Within* (New York: Harper & Row, Publishers, 1960), an account by the former counsel to the McClellan committee during its investigation of crime and corrupt practices within the leadership of certain labor unions; the examination of the history, uses, and abuses of investigating committees by Telford Taylor, *Grand Inquest: The Story of Congressional Investigations* (New York: Simon and Schuster, Inc., 1955), and by Alan Barth, *Government by Investigation* (New York: Viking Press, Inc., 1955); and the indignant and still interesting essays by Elmer Davis, *But We Were Born Free* (Indianapolis: Bobbs-Merrill Company, Inc., 1954).

220 gations—about three times as much as was authorized in the 84th Congress (1955–56). Senate committees regularly spend more than House committees, though the difference between the chambers is not as great as in the past. The committee that regularly outspends all others on investigations is the Senate Judiciary Committee. Ordinarily next in line is the Senate Committee on Government Operations.[44]

LEGISLATIVE INVESTIGATIONS AND THE COURTS

The power of Congress to conduct investigations was well established before it was ever examined carefully by the judiciary. In the early decades of the national government, the House authorized many more investigations than the Senate. The Senate's initial investigation was approved in 1818; its initial investigation specifically designed as an aid to legislating did not take place until 1859, when it set out to learn the facts "attending the late invasion and seizure of the armory and arsenal at Harper's Ferry." By this time congressional investigations had become commonplace. Congress was using its power to compel witnesses to testify and to produce their records; witnesses who refused to cooperate were cited for contempt and, on occasion, committed to jail. Although there were occasional disputes in Congress over the wisdom of certain inquiries, few if any members questioned the legislature's power to authorize investigations.[45]

In 1881, however, the scope of the investigative power was whittled down by the Supreme Court. In the case of *Kilbourn* v. *Thompson,* the Court upbraided Congress for having confined Kilbourn to jail following his refusal to produce papers concerning the bankruptcy of Jay Cooke & Co. The investigation was held improper on several counts: the resolution authorizing the investigation was indefinite, the House had undertaken a "clearly judicial" function, and the inquiry was not directly concerned with producing information relevant to the function of legislating.[46] The lasting significance of the *Kilbourn* case was that it brought the Supreme Court directly into the controversy over congressional investigations; its immediate impact was to throw into doubt the dimensions of the investigative power. Nonetheless, Congress, not extraordinarily impressed, continued its investigations in about the same fashion as before.

The right of Congress to investigate was given firm legal support in 1927 by the Supreme Court in *McGrain* v. *Daugherty,* a case arising out of an investigation of the administration of the Department of Justice. The Court held unanimously that Congress had the power to investigate in order to secure information relevant to its lawmaking function:

> We are of opinion that the power of inquiry—with process to enforce it—is an essential and appropriate auxiliary to the legislative function. . . .
>
> A legislative body cannot legislate wisely or effectively in the absence of information respecting the conditions which the legislation is intended to

44 For data on committee investigation funds for several Congresses, see the *Congressional Quarterly Weekly Report,* July 4, 1969, p. 1197. It should be noted that not all the funds authorized for investigations are necessarily spent.

45 McGeary, "Congressional Investigations," 425–27.

46 *Kilbourn* v. *Thompson,* 103 U.S. 168, 190 (1881).

affect or change; and where the legislative body does not itself possess the requisite information—which not infrequently is true—recourse must be had to others who do possess it.[47]

A 1957 case involving the House Committee on Un-American Activities, *Watkins* v. *United States*,[48] renewed the challenge to congressional investigations launched in *Kilbourn*. In this case the Court refused to uphold a conviction of a witness who had declined to answer questions about individuals he believed were no longer associated with the Communist party. Although the Court recognized the importance and the sweep of the investigatory power of Congress, it held that the power was not without limits: "There is no general authority to expose the private affairs of individuals without justification in terms of the functions of the Congress. . . . No inquiry is an end in itself; it must be related to, and in furtherance of, a legitimate task of the Congress."[49]

A decision on the same day concerned the conviction of Paul Sweezy by a New Hampshire court.[50] The New Hampshire state legislature had empowered the attorney general of the state to investigate subversive activities and persons, and in the course of the investigation Sweezy was summoned to appear before the attorney general and to answer questions concerning a lecture he had given at the University of New Hampshire. His refusal to answer the questions led to his citation for contempt, and, as in the *Watkins* case, the Supreme Court set aside the conviction.

The 1957 decisions established the fact that witnesses could not be punished for contempt unless the *pertinency* of questions asked them was unmistakably clear and the inquiry itself was related to a valid legislative purpose; moreover, the Court ruled in the *Watkins* case that a committee's jurisdiction must be spelled out in detail sufficient to permit a witness to judge whether questions put to him were pertinent. The *Watkins* case was especially notable for its sharp censure of the investigatory practices of the House Un-American Activities Committee.

The immediate reaction to these decisions by most observers was that the Court had put a tight rein on investigating committees. This evaluation soon was proven erroneous. In 1959 a sharply divided Court upheld the contempt conviction of Lloyd Barenblatt, a former college professor, who refused to state before a subcommittee of the House Un-American Activities Committee whether he was or ever had been a Communist party member. Barenblatt contended that the committee's authority for the investigation was vague, that the pertinency of the questions asked him was not made clear, and that the First Amendment supported his refusal to answer the questions. The Court held that the committee had been duly authorized and that the relevance of the questions had been established. Coming to the constitutional issue, the Court invoked the "balance-of-interest" test and concluded that "the balance between the individual and the governmental interest. . . must be struck in favor of the latter. . . ."[51]

[47] *McGrain* v. *Daugherty,* 273 U.S. 135, 174–75 (1927).
[48] 354 U.S. 178 (1957).
[49] *Id.,* at 187.
[50] *Sweezy* v. *New Hampshire,* 354 U.S. 234 (1957).
[51] *Barenblatt* v. *United States,* 360 U.S. 109, at 134.

In 1961, again dividing five to four, the Court upheld the House Un-American Activities Committee and its procedures in two cases in which outspoken critics of the committee had been cited for contempt.[52] Both witnesses had refused to answer questions concerning possible Communist party membership, contending that the questions asked were not pertinent and that the inquiry did not serve a valid legislative purpose. The Court ruled otherwise.

Later cases involving investigating committees have yielded decisions based on fairly narrow grounds. By a five-to-two vote in 1962, in *Russell* v. *United States,* the Court set aside the convictions of six men who had declined to answer questions concerning Communist associations which had been asked by subcommittees of the House Committee on Un-American Activities and the Senate Internal Security Subcommittee. The Court held that the indictments against the men were "defective in failing to identify the subject which was under inquiry at the time of the defendants' alleged default or refusal to answer."[53] Henceforth, indictments for contempt of Congress must show specifically the subject of the committee investigation; it is not sufficient simply to state that the questions asked witnesses were "pertinent" to the inquiry. In 1963 the Court held, by a five-to-four vote, that a state legislative investigating committee must have hard evidence concerning Communist infiltration of an organization before it can ask questions of its members. In this case, *Gibson* v. *Florida Legislative Investigation Committee,* the Court reversed the contempt conviction of the president of the Miami branch of the NAACP, who had refused to provide information to a state investigating committee concerning the membership of the local NAACP organization.[54] The Court held that the contempt conviction violated the free speech and free association provisions of the First and Fourteenth Amendments, since evidence was insufficient to show a substantial connection between the local branch of this organization and Communist activities. In *Yellin* v. *United States* (1963), the Court again split five to four, while reversing the conviction of a witness who had refused to answer questions asked him by the House Committee on Un-American Activities. The witness, Edward Yellin, had challenged his conviction on the ground that the committee had violated one of its own rules when it failed to consider his request to be heard in executive session before being questioned in a public hearing. The rule provides that "if a majority of the Committee or Subcommittee...believes that the interrogation of a witness in a public hearing might endanger national security or *unjustly injure his reputation,* or the reputation of other individuals, the Committee shall interrogate such witness in an Executive Session for the purpose of determining the necessity or advisability of conducting such interrogation thereafter in a public hearing."[55] The committee's failure to observe this rule led the Court to upset the conviction.

In recent years there have been two unsuccessful challenges to the constitutionality of HUAC (now HISC) on the grounds that its investiga-

[52] *Braden* v. *United States,* 365 U.S. 431 (1961); *Wilkinson* v. *United States,* 365 U.S. 399 (1961).

[53] *Russell* v. *United States,* 369 U.S. 749 (1962).

[54] *Gibson* v. *Florida Legislative Investigation Committee,* 372 U.S. 539 (1963).

[55] *Yellin* v. *United States,* 374 U.S. 109 (1963).

tions violate the First Amendment guarantee of free speech. In *Krebs* v. **223**
Ashbrook (1967), a federal district court in the District of Columbia held
that it lacked jurisdiction to rule on the question, since HUAC was established by a House rule (XI) and not by an act of Congress.[56] In *Stamler* v.
Willis (1968), a federal district court in Chicago dismissed another suit
challenging the constitutionality of HUAC, holding that Article I, Section
6 of the Constitution protects members through its stipulation that "for any
speech or debate in either House, they shall not be questioned in any other
place."[57]

The upshot of the Court's decisions in the 1950s and 1960s is not
altogether clear. The Court continues to insist that the investigative power
is not unlimited and that certain committee procedures must be followed.
Yet it is also apparent that the limits of this power are very wide. A declaration of purpose, either in the authorizing resolution or in the statements of
the committee chairman or committee members, may serve to put an investigation in the clear as far as the Court is concerned. "Exposure for exposure's
sake," if ruled out in those terms, may not be ruled out in practice. Beyond
this, it is clear that the Court recognizes a necessity for investigations and
is reluctant to interfere with them.

PURPOSES OF CONGRESSIONAL INVESTIGATIONS

There are four widely accepted purposes for investigations.[58] In the first
place, Congress can investigate for the purpose of securing information
relevant to its responsibility for the enactment of legislation. This power is
implied by the specific grants of power awarded to the legislature by the
Constitution, "and each time that Congress' power of legislation is broadened, it follows that the power of investigation is similarly expanded."[59]
Second, Congress can investigate the management of executive departments,
and it has done this persistently from the earliest administrations. The legitimacy of these inquiries was made clear in *McGrain* v. *Daugherty* and
reaffirmed in *Watkins* v. *United States.*

The need for Congress to inform the public is the third reason
advanced in support of investigations—a justification that seems presumptively valid. Robert Carr observes that the Supreme Court never has specifically upheld this use, but there is probably no necessity that it do so, since
any investigation for the purpose of informing the public would not be
"utterly devoid of legislative possibilities."[60] Senator William Fulbright notes
that congressional investigations sometimes result "only in public disclosure—
or exposure. When this is the case, the results may be regarded as an appeal
to public opinion, an invitation to the people to say whether or not they
discern the need for legislation which the legislators themselves have not yet
seen fit to enact."[61] Alan Barth argues, however, that to expose a problem

---

[56] *Krebs* v. *Ashbrook,* 275 F. Supp. 111 (D.C. 1967).
[57] *Stamler* v. *Willis,* 287 F. Supp. 734 (N.D. Ill. 1968).
[58] These are categories used by Chase, *op. cit.,* 138–44.
[59] McGeary, "Congressional Investigations," 435.
[60] Carr, *op. cit.,* p. 411.
[61] "Congressional Investigations: Significance for the Legislative Process," *University of Chicago Law Review,* XVIII (Spring 1951), 443–44.

224 and to invite public attention through congressional investigation is one thing, to harass and to malign individuals is quite another. He writes:

> Congress does not need to expose individuals in order to expose the dimensions of the Communist problem. To compel men to confess beliefs and associations which will subject them to odium neither serves any legitimate congressional purpose nor comports with the American tradition of respect for privacy, heterodoxy, and conscience. This kind of investigation by an official governmental body can have no other purpose than to compel conformity, and no other consequence than to inhibit independence of thought and expression. The punishment of men for beliefs and associations must be no less repugnant to the Constitution of the United States when it is done by congressional investigation than when it is done by congressional legislation.[62]

The fourth purpose of investigations is to permit Congress to resolve questions concerning its membership. This authority stems directly from Article I of the Constitution, which makes each house "the judge of the Elections, Returns and Qualifications of its own members. . . ." For example, congressional committees have investigated campaign expenditures in congressional elections, attempts to influence improperly or illegally a member of the legislature (e.g., the oil and gas lobby investigation in 1956), and a senator's use of political contributions to pay personal bills (the case of Senator Thomas Dodd in 1967).

ABUSES OF THE INVESTIGATIVE POWER

Congressional investigations are designed as well for other less accepted, if widely recognized, purposes. These include investigations to gain an end which could not be achieved through legislation, to punish witnesses by subjecting them to public censure and ridicule, to gain personal publicity, to aid executive agencies such as the FBI, and to usurp executive functions, as in the case of Senator Joseph McCarthy's negotiations with Greek shipowners calling for them to suspend trade with North Korea, Communist China, and the Soviet Union.[63]

The need for reform is manifest to most observers—but not to most members of Congress. Abuses of the investigative power, numerous and flagrant in the case of a few committees, have had a deleterious impact on the prestige of Congress. William S. White has written, for example:

> Whatever may be said only with many qualifications there is one thing that can be said for certain. It is that generally speaking the Senate's investigations have unquestionably hurt more than helped its reputation, entirely apart from all questions of the usefulness or the lack of usefulness of the inquiries that it has made. . . . [No] other activity, with the possible exception of the filibuster, has tended more often, justifiably or not, to bring the place into disrepute.[64]

62 Barth, *op. cit.*, p. 23.
63 Chase, *op. cit.*, 144–47.
64 *Citadel: The Story of the U.S. Senate* (New York: Harper & Row, Publishers, 1956), p. 228.

The principal abuse occurs in the treatment of committee witnesses. Evaluating the House Committee on Un-American Activities, Robert Carr writes:

> Perhaps the most serious shortcoming in the committee's record is the way in which it has always insisted upon *personalizing* its undertakings. This tendency has created an exceedingly serious threat to the Anglo-American concept of criminal justice. . . . It is quite clear from the six-year record of the committee between 1945 and 1950 that one of its leading purposes has been to demonstrate the "guilt" of certain persons for offenses not always defined in the law and to see them punished in the sense of the destruction of their reputations and the loss of their means of livelihood.[65]

Although HUAC no longer dominates the headlines, its actions continue to provoke controversy. Recently, for example, it has investigated the SDS, the Black Panthers, and alleged "radicals" earning fees on the college lecture circuit. Among critics, the belief persists that the committee is more concerned with the pillorying of individuals than with serving valid legislative purposes.[66] Theodore Lowi observes:

> [The basic technique of HUAC] is the public interrogation of hostile witnesses. Once the witness refuses to testify, the committee counsel or one of the members proceeds to ask a series of undocumented questions which, when left unanswered by the hostile witness, suggests guilt on unspecified but vaguely menacing evils. Moreover, most of the questions concern themselves with alleged acts and associations of many years previous. Thus, the committee seems to concern itself not with "clear and present danger" but with danger clearly past.[67]

The familiar questions concerning congressional investigating committees are perhaps the most difficult to answer: How are committees that abuse witnesses, ignore their legal rights, and expose them to social obloquy to be restrained?[68] What is to prevent inquiries from becoming "fishing

---

65 Carr, *op. cit.,* p. 452.

66 Partial evidence on this score is that from 1945 to 1970, only six HUAC bills were enacted into law. Of the six, the best known are the Internal Security Act of 1950 and the Communist Control Act of 1954. *Congressional Quarterly Weekly Report,* April 24, 1970, p. 1130.

67 "The Wheel of Panic," *The Nation,* May 19, 1969, p. 626.

68 Few investigating committees overlook the extraordinary possibilities for gaining publicity. The most virulent form of publicity-seeking is suggested by the following memorandum circulated quietly to members of a House committee investigating the Federal Communications Commission in 1943. This is how a committee can maximize its publicity potential, reads the memorandum: (1) "Decide what you want the newspapers to hit hardest and then shape each hearing so that the main point becomes the vortex of the testimony. Once that vortex is reached, *adjourn.* (2) In handling press releases, first put a release date on them, reading something like this: 'For release at 10:00 A.M. EST July 6,' etc. If you do this, you can give releases out as much as 24 hours in advance, thus enabling reporters to study them and write better stories. (3) Limit the number of people authorized to speak for the committee, to give out press releases or to provide the press with information to the *fewest number possible.* It plugs leaks and helps preserve the concentration of purpose. (4) Do not permit distractions to occur, such as extraneous fusses with would-be

226   expeditions" into the personal affairs of individuals or the activities of government agencies?

The answer provided by the courts is that the public should look to Congress for elimination of these abuses. The courts assert that this is a legislative responsibility, with solutions to be worked out by the legislature itself. For many reasons, however, reform has been slow in coming about. In the first place, Congress is not inclined to view the courts as accredited spokesmen for congressional responsibilities. And second, it is difficult to get agreement in Congress as to what, if any, controls are required: what to one observer appears as an improper and unwarranted intrusion on the affairs of individuals or of executive agencies may seem to another person to be safely compatible with valid legislative purpose. A third reason is offered by Dean Acheson, secretary of state in the Truman administration and a man whose views on congressional investigations fall well short of enthusiastic endorsement. Discussing relations between Congress and the executive branch, he writes: "The virus of busyness [in Congress] has bitten deep. Impulses born of parochial interests at stake, of personal ambition, of partisan maneuver, all make for interference with administration and the attempt to control it. They are hard to resist in favor of more plain and unspectacular courses."[69] In a word, investigations offer unrivaled opportunities for political advantage and publicity—resources not easily ignored by elected officials of any kind.

REFORMING INVESTIGATING COMMITTEES

A literature of extensive proportions indicting investigating committees and offering prescriptions for their reform (occasionally calling for their dismantling) was produced in the 1950s. The prescriptions were not always as appropriate as the diagnosis, but they were offered in great number and covered the entire sweep of investigating committees' activities. Much of the criticism tended to converge on the central point of adopting codes of fair conduct for the treatment of witnesses before committees.

Out of this discussion came the first code governing committee investigations. Adopted by the New York legislature in 1954, the code contained

---

witnesses, which might provide news that would bury the testimony which you want featured. (5) Do not space hearings more than 24 or 48 hours apart when on a controversial subject. This gives *the opposition* too much opportunity to make all kinds of counter-charges and replies by issuing statements to the newspapers. [Emphasis added.] (6) Don't ever be afraid to recess a hearing even for five minutes, so that you keep the proceedings completely in control so far as creating news is concerned. (7) *And this is most important:* don't let the hearings or the evidence ever descend to the plane of a personal fight between the Committee Chairman and the head of the agency being investigated. The high plane of a duly-authorized Committee of the House of Representatives *examining* the operations of an Agency of the Executive Branch for constructive purposes should be maintained at all costs." These "rules" were fashioned by a former reporter for the International News Service and subsequently an employee of the Republican National Committee. Quoted by Douglass Cater, *The Fourth Branch of Government* (Boston: Houghton Mifflin Company, 1959), pp. 58–59. Note rule 5, which regards witnesses and others being investigated as "the opposition."

69 *A Citizen Looks at Congress* (New York: Harper & Row, Publishers, 1957), pp. 123–24.

a number of safeguards for witnesses—providing that they should be apprised of the nature of the investigation, be given the right to counsel, and be permitted to file a sworn statement for the record. In addition, the law gave the counsel the right to submit questions to hostile witnesses; a witness's testimony was to be made available; one-man investigating committees were eliminated; a majority of the committee was required to release testimony taken in secret; and a person whose name was defamed in testimony was given the right to be heard before the committee or to submit a sworn statement.[70]

In 1955 the U.S. House of Representatives finally settled for a mild code of fair procedure, but one more in the nature of a limited reorganization than a basic reform. The lack of vigorous support from organized groups, as well as the desire of congressional leaders to protect the *status quo,* made it impossible to achieve profound changes.[71] Under the terms of the Legislative Reorganization Act of 1970, Senate committees are now required to adopt and publish rules of procedure.[72]

Among other things, the House code prohibits one-man investigations, permits witnesses to have a counsel to advise them, provides for taking testimony in executive session under certain circumstances (and preserves such testimony from being made public without the committee's consent), and gives the committee discretion to permit witnesses to submit written statements for the record. Nevertheless, critics contend this is not an impressive reform. The code's principal deficiencies are that too few aspects of committee affairs require *majority* approval and that it lacks any meaningful techniques for enforcement—such as, for example, providing for court action in the case of rules infractions or giving the House a clear-cut responsibility for supervising its investigating committees. During hearings on the proposed legislative reorganization act in the 89th Congress, a spokesman for the American Civil Liberties Union recommended that an enforcement agency be established in Congress and given the "power to censure offending Congressmen or Senators, the power to recommend an official apology to an individual wrongly accused or mistreated by an investigating committee, or the power to award money damages to victims of investigatory committee abuse."[73]

A code of fair procedure, desirable as it may seem, is not a panacea— the House Committee on Un-American Activities, as controversial for its practices as any committee has ever been, adopted a voluntary code in 1954. The difficulty is that:

> . . . rules and regulations can do very little to cure the major faults that exist in Congressional committees. What rule can you pass to prevent a Congressman or Senator or counsel from asking an unfair question? What regulation

70 Chase, *op. cit.,* p. 127.

71 This discussion of the House code derives from Heubel, *op. cit.,* pp. 327–29.

72 One explanation for the reluctance of Congress to adopt a standard procedural code for committees is that such procedures, even though imposed by Congress itself, might contribute to control by the judiciary. Congress obviously wants to avoid this possibility. "Congressional Investigations: Their Effect on a Witness' Right to a Fair Trial," *Alabama Law Review,* XXII (Summer 1970), 563.

73 *Hearings on the Organization of Congress* before the Joint Committee on the Organization of Congress, 89th Cong., 1st sess., 1965, pp. 2024–25.

can you write to prevent a committee member from yelling at or browbeating a witness? To set up a system under which all questions are cleared with the chairman, as though he were a judge, would not only be too cumbersome but completely unacceptable to individual committee members. Furthermore, the fault with many investigating committees has been their chairman.[74]

The standard by which to measure the worth of investigations is not easily determined, but obviously it is not to be found in the extravagant and reckless behavior of a few aggressive investigators.[75] It is important to remember that only a few congressional investigating committees have been abusive in their activities. Unfortunately, their actions often have obscured the fair and responsible behavior of other committees. The Senate War Investigating Committee, headed by Senator Harry S. Truman during World War II, made a brilliant record in helping to eliminate inefficiency and bottlenecks in the nation's war production. The McClellan committee's investigation in 1957 of corruption and improper activities in certain labor unions, despite an occasional sensational flair, illuminated an enormously important problem. A long list of other useful investigating committees could be compiled.[76]

STATE LEGISLATURE INVESTIGATING COMMITTEES

In general, our previous judgment regarding the use of hearings by state legislatures applies equally well to investigating committees, for the states devote less energy and resources to investigations than Congress does. No argument exists as to whether state legislatures possess the investigative power; clearly they do, deriving it from the implied and auxiliary power to gather information held relevant to the enactment of future legislation. State investigating committees may be created by statute, joint resolution, or the resolution of one house. Ordinarily, committees that are intended to function in the interim between sessions are created by statute.

The legislative council movement in the states, beginning with Kansas in 1933, to some extent has diminished the need for regular investigating committees and interim committees. The powers of legislative councils vary from state to state, but all are concerned with research and data collection in aid of lawmaking. Councils in a few states have been armed with the subpoena power. Legislatures set down specific problems for investigation

---

[74] Kennedy, *op. cit.,* p. 309.

[75] For a provocative article which supports the use of investigations as *political* instruments, see Frank C. Newman, "The Supreme Court, Congressional Investigations, and Influence Peddling," *New York University Law Review,* XXXIII (June 1958), 796–810. Newman defends these theses: "(1) Opinions of the Supreme Court do not imply that flamboyant investigations of federal agencies are improper. (2) Not even the most extreme reforms proposed for investigating committees would immunize a government official from harm to his reputation. (3) If we demand that congressmen use only the 'nice guy' approach in investigating the bureaucracy, then, maladministration and the need for reform of administration will often go unexposed. (4) We *can* legislate morals, significantly" (p. 797).

[76] A considerably stronger case for congressional investigations, particularly of the executive branch, may be found in James Burnham, *Congress and the American Tradition* (Chicago: Henry Regnery Company, 1959). See particularly Chapters 16 and 17.

by the councils, with instructions to report back their findings, sometimes with accompanying recommendations. Rather than attempt an investigation itself, a legislature may request the governor to make an inquiry into a particular agency. Occasionally, a legislature will memorialize Congress to investigate a matter whose ramifications touch the interests of the state.

State legislative investigations are justified on the same grounds as congressional investigations: to secure information needed for the enactment of legislation, to inquire into the management of administrative agencies, to inform the public, and to examine the qualifications of members of the legislature. The activities of state investigating committees are comparable to those of congressional committees. They hold hearings, take testimony, issue subpoenas commanding the presence of persons and the production of books, papers, and records, administer oaths, and report to the parent body their findings together with recommendations for remedial legislation.

Almost any incident or rumor is likely to spur a resolution to create a special investigating committee. A turnpike attendant treats a patron discourteously and the act is witnessed by a legislator; he immediately introduces a resolution to investigate the personnel policies of the turnpike commission. A sportsman's club in a rural district tells its representative that rabbits imported from out of state to replenish the native stock are carriers of communicable diseases, and he promptly calls for an investigating committee to learn the facts. The committee on fisheries may be asked to investigate the reason for the decline in the sale of fishing licenses. A special committee may be set up to inquire into the adequacy of measures for protection of school children against fire. Negro lawmakers may contend that a hotel in the capital city has discriminatory practices and request a committee of their fellow legislators to investigate. A rumor circulates that peculiar circumstances surround a pardon made by the governor, and a committee is formed to investigate the incident, and probably the board of pardons as well.

The investigations that count involve highly political subjects rather than the communicable diseases of out-of-state rabbits or the ennui of fishermen. An investigation handled skillfully, with "proper" attention to the potential of publicity, may be worth a good many thousands of votes in the next election. In the 1950s not many northern state legislatures could resist the temptation to form an investigating committee to look for Communists in the cities and in the universities, and in a few states their activities became almost as well known as those of Senator McCarthy's committee. Two kinds of investigations are especially commonplace. The first is an inquiry into the administration of election laws and alleged examples of vote frauds, which almost invariably makes the big cities the object of investigation. The second, doubtless more prevalent, is an investigation of state agencies and the management of state institutions of one type or another.[77] Many begin with a rumor elevated to the initial "whereas" of a

---

[77] The political leverage inherent in investigations of state institutions is quietly recognized by the rules of some state legislative houses. Thus, a Florida House rule specifies: "No member living in any county in which any state institution is located shall be appointed a member of any select committee to visit such institution for the purpose of investigating and reporting its conditions and needs."

230 resolution for an investigating committee. The highway and public welfare departments, both major spending agencies, are great favorites for investigating committees.

Obviously, it is hazardous to ascribe motives to the investigators, but it is very difficult to escape the impression that partisan advantage, the desire to harass and embarrass the governor and perhaps to wring an accommodation from him, is at the root of many investigations. On the other hand, however, it is true that the public interest is sometimes served equally with the party interest. Even so, state investigating committees often seem to be merely instruments of harassment, or as Walter Lippmann said of congressional investigating committees in 1922, "legalized atrocities."

Committee Decisions

A preoccupation with committee hearings obscures the fact that the significant decisions in congressional committees and in the committees of many state legislatures are made following hearings in *executive,* or non-public, sessions. Important and informal, these "mark-up" sessions permit the members to work out compromises that will improve the legislation's prospects on the floor. Though firmly rooted in a majority of American legislatures, the committee practice of deliberating and voting in executive session is often the object of strictures. Holding that it is an undemocratic practice, Harvey Walker has contended: "Those who have an interest in the legislation have a right to know just what is said about it by each member of the committee and just how each member votes. The power of committees to pigeonhole bills, coupled with secret sessions, enables sinister interests to work their will unseen."[78] Robert Luce, contrariwise, argued that "the ignorance of the public about [what transpires in executive sessions] is one of the causes of its usefulness. Behind closed doors nobody can talk to the galleries or the newspaper reporters. . . . Another reason is that publicity would lessen the chance for the concessions, the compromises, without which wise legislation cannot in practice be secured."[79]

COMMITTEE REPORTS

It is a fact of legislative life that not all bills become law. Those that fail— and normally these comprise a majority in any session of any legislature— often meet their demise in committee. Bills seldom die as a result of wounds inflicted in battle. Instead, they die of neglect, because nobody, or at least not very many, cared sufficiently one way or another. Among the tidy-minded in committees, the proper thing called for in the case of unwanted bills is euthanasia, followed by silent interment. Except for its possible impact upon the sponsor and maybe a friend of the idea here and there in the assembly, the whole operation is rather painless. If this description is too extravagant, the process at least is quite simple: committees eliminate far more bills by ignoring them than by voting them down.

[78] *The Legislative Process* (New York: Ronald Press Company, 1948), p. 244.
[79] *Congress—An Explanation* (Cambridge: Harvard University Press, 1926), pp. 12–13.

In thirteen states, however, committees are required to report out to the floor all bills referred to them, although this requirement may receive only technical compliance. Congress and the rest of the states are not hobbled by this provision and, consequently, are able to eliminate a large number of proposals simply by pigeonholing them. Between 80 and 90 per cent of all bills introduced in Congress die in committees without action having been taken on them, a proportion unquestionably much higher than found in the state legislatures. In the absence of a large number of studies, it is risky to generalize regarding the extent of pigeonholing in those legislatures where it is permitted. The great majority of bills lost in committee die in the house of origin; those that clear one house have a good chance of getting out of committee in the second house.

On the basis of scattered studies, it would be a fair guess that in most states between 20 and 35 per cent of all bills referred to committees are never reported out. In a few states the proportion is as high as 40 to 50 per cent, in other states as low as 10 per cent. Many legislatures have committees informally known as "graveyard" or "pickling" committees—those which suppress an abnormally high proportion of the bills referred to them. McKean writes of the New Jersey legislature: "If a bill on some general matter is sent to the judiciary committee, it is understood that party leaders are not opposed to it, but if it is sent to the committee on miscellaneous business, 'the graveyard,' it is usually dead for the session. This committee is generally made up of men who come from some sure counties so that they are less susceptible than other members to group pressure."[80]

In some states, it is clear, committee decisions are largely perfunctory. Pennsylvania provides an example. In this state the authentic center of decision-making is the party caucus. To quote the House majority leader, "What takes place on the floor is a postscript. By then everything has been decided [in caucus] and we know what the vote will be." A Pennsylvania state senator makes a related point: "We'll call a committee meeting, walk off the floor for a few minutes and then return and report out a dozen bills. It's a sham, and everybody knows it."[81]

There are three principal courses of action open to a committee in deciding the fate of a proposal, apart from the pigeonholing option already mentioned. Committees may report a bill: (1) as committed with a recommendation that it pass; (2) together with committee amendments, with the recommendation that it pass; (3) with the recommendation that it "do not pass." In addition, committees sometimes recommend that the chamber adopt a committee substitute in place of the original proposal. Finally, provisions may exist for reporting a measure without a recommendation of any sort. The latter alternative is used on very rare occasions by Congress and the states and comes close to being an adverse report.

The usual response of state legislative committees, except where rules require them to report all bills, is either to report a bill with a "do pass" recommendation or to make no report at all. In most states there is infrequent resort to the "do not pass" recommendation, probably in less than 5 per cent of all referrals. Some chambers avoid it entirely. It is much easier

---

[80] McKean, *op. cit.,* p. 50.

[81] Jack H. Morris, "A State Legislature is Not Always a Model of Ideal Government," *Wall Street Journal,* July 28, 1971, p. 16.

232 simply to keep an unwanted bill bottled up in committee, thereby serving the same purpose and diminishing the likelihood of controversy. While legislators do not shrink from controversy, neither as a rule do they promote it if an alternative is available. Nevertheless, an adverse report occasionally is brought out, and a bill so recommended limps onto the floor more dead than alive. The sponsor may move that the house nonconcur in the committee report, but it is unusual for the motion to be adopted.

It is a curious fact that in many state legislatures a favorable committee recommendation may not at all represent the sense of the committee members; indeed, a majority of the members may be plainly opposed to a measure to which "do pass" is affixed. This action occurs because committees are hesitant to take on the responsibility for weeding out bills. A sponsor may contend that in the interest of "fair play" his bill should be permitted to go before the chamber as a whole, and members who intend to oppose it on the floor may agree and recommend accordingly. Legislatures may have a tradition of letting bills slide out of committee despite the presence of strong opposition to them. A legislator who works hard enough has a good chance of moving his bill to the floor, even though it has no chance of acceptance by the chamber. There is nothing unusual about hearing committee members say, "I'll vote to send it out but I reserve the right to help vote it down on the floor."

The height of committee detachment, of unwillingness to kill a bill, is the occasional practice of reporting out two diametrically opposed bills, such as gasoline tax bills with vastly different apportionment formulas, each carrying a recommendation of "do pass." Action of this type usually placates those sponsors who might lose in committee and helps to avoid committee wrangles; unfortunately, it also adds new work and new problems to an already heavily burdened chamber. A former Speaker of the Illinois House of Representatives illustrates the problem: "I think we would be able to conduct more business more efficiently if the committees would find a bad bill bad and say so at the committee level."[82]

Committees devote considerable time to considering amendments to bills, some of which have emerged from the hearings. Amendments may include only slight changes or be so extensive as to involve a substitution for the original measure. As a general rule, amendments, if not emasculatory, are best accepted at the committee stage because if proposed and adopted on the floor they may stimulate the introduction of other amendments which would imperil the bill's purpose.[83] A great many amendments are proposed at the floor stage, even though the chambers are generally chary about accepting amendments which have not been given prior committee study. Committee amendments must be accepted by the parent chamber, but this is usually not a major problem since the houses tend to defer to the decisions of their committees.

---

82 Quoted in Steiner and Gove, *op. cit.,* p. 62.

83 Bills subjected to major alterations in committee often become "clean bills" before submission to the floor. This procedure involves incorporating committee amendments into the original bill and treating the product as a brand new bill to the point of giving it a new number. The advantage of this is that the alterations become a fundamental part of the bill and are no longer treated as amendments. Hence, they are not considered separately on the floor.

Although a proposal may not have clear sailing once out of committee, it has at least surmounted the major obstacle in the legislative process. This is notably true of Congress, where possibly nine out of ten bills die in committee. A bill which emerges from a state legislative committee is very likely to be passed by the chamber. Scattered studies suggest that between 65 and 85 per cent of favorable committee reports are accepted on the floor in the house of origin.[84] Having survived committee action in one house, a bill is not likely to be lost in a committee of the second chamber; those that do fail often are identical to bills already passed by that chamber. In short, committee action in American legislative bodies may well be crucial. Plainly, committees do more than advise and recommend to their parent chamber; instead, their decisions tend to be the eventual decisions of the body itself.[85]

The reports of congressional committees are substantially more elaborate and possess a greater utility than those of the states. Whereas a state legislative committee will simply record its decision, which constitutes a recommendation to the body, a congressional committee will submit a written explanation of the bill and a justification for the recommendation. Evidence considered by the committee in arriving at its decision is summarized and evaluated. Some reports go into extraordinary detail in recapitulating facts and opinions brought out in the committee's study of the proposal, including the arguments that may prove useful on the floor. Reports also may serve as campaign documents. "Individual views" of committee members are sometimes appended to the body of a report. The position of members not in accord with the majority may be submitted separately in the form of a minority report.[86] Congress has put increasing emphasis upon committee record-keeping and instructive reporting, much of it as a result of the Legislative Reorganization Act of 1946.

State legislative committees operate under a number of handicaps, some of which are self-imposed, and all of which tend to drain off their efficiency. In the first place, there is a shortage of trained staff members; in many cases, committees carry a heavy work load without staff assistance in any form. Second, committees are generally so numerous and individual assignments so heavy that even the most conscientious committee member

84 See C. I. Winslow, *State Legislative Committees* (Baltimore: Johns Hopkins Press, 1931), p. 112; Robert F. Karsch, *The Standing Committees of the Missouri General Assembly* (Columbia: University of Missouri, Bureau of Governmental Research, 1959), pp. 30–31; George A. Bell and Evelyn L. Wentworth, *The Legislative Process in Maryland* (College Park: University of Maryland, Bureau of Governmental Research, 1958).

85 There are obvious differences between states in the extent to which members expect their chambers to uphold committee recommendations. In the Montana House, for example, committees have substantial autonomy and their recommendations carry great weight on the floor; in the Wisconsin Assembly, by contrast, there is less deference paid to committee recommendations, particularly when party leaders detect partisan implications in the legislation at hand. Independent, powerful committees appear to be largely incompatible with a strong party caucus system. See Douglas C. Chaffey, "The Institutionalization of State Legislatures: A Comparative Study," *Western Political Quarterly*, XXIII (March 1970), 191–92.

86 Dissenting reports are not frequently issued. One study shows them occurring on about 5 per cent of all reports. Their appearance is usually the result of conflict between the parties in committee. George Goodwin, Jr., *The Little Legislatures: Committees of Congress* (Amherst: University of Massachusetts Press, 1970), p. 170.

234 finds it difficult to keep abreast of his work. Committee members come late to meetings and leave early, not for lack of interest but for lack of time; there are always other things they should be doing and other meetings they should be attending; there is scarcely any relaxation from the pressures of constituents and lobbyists.

Quorums are difficult to get and to hold. It is common, if incongruous, to find committees searching for a place to hold their meetings; all too often there are not enough rooms to go around. Committee meetings shift from room to room from week to week. A committee may even assemble in the gallery of the chamber. Meetings are called at short notice, and it may not be unusual for members to have to resort to newspapers for information concerning time and place. And while no state may suffer from all these shortcomings, most endure some. Poor facilities and indifferent practice undermine legislative efficiency.

Committee Integration and Power

COMMITTEE-FLOOR RELATIONS

The factors which affect the capacity of committees to maintain themselves and to achieve influence in the legislative system are not fully known. At both state legislature and congressional levels, however, it is plain that some committees have more success than others in securing floor approval of their recommendations. A study of the U.S. Senate by Donald Matthews reports that the high-prestige committees—Foreign Relations, Appropriations, Finance, and Armed Services—have been most successful with their measures on the floor. These prestigious committees also tend to have a high level of unity. Evidence that prestige and unity are distinct variables, however, appears in the fact that some Senate committees characterized by a high level of cohesiveness, comparable to that of the prestige committees, nevertheless have fared badly with their proposals on the floor. The contribution of committee unity, as shown in *floor* voting, is nonetheless impressive for all committees: "[If] a motion had the support of more than 80 per cent of the reporting committee's members, it passed the Senate every time. If from 60 to 79 per cent of the committee favored it in their roll call voting, it passed nine times out of ten." When a committee's cohesion fell below 60 per cent, its effectiveness on the floor dropped sharply.[87]

The pattern of committee success is somewhat different in the House. A study by James Dyson and John Soule of roll-call votes over a ten-year period shows that, by and large, prestige committees are no more likely to achieve success on the floor than unattractive committees; nor, for that matter, are they notable for their integration or nonpartisanship. Those committees with the highest rates of floor success tend to be characterized by minimal partisanship and a high level of integration (as judged by the voting behavior of committee members on the floor).[88]

[87] *U.S. Senators and Their World* (Chapel Hill: University of North Carolina Press, 1960), pp. 168–69.

[88] "Congressional Committee Behavior on Roll Call Votes: The U.S. House of Representatives, 1955–64," *Midwest Journal of Political Science*, XIV (November 1970), 626–47.

The success of the House Appropriations Committee on the floor, according to Richard Fenno, is due to its capacity to maintain a high degree of internal unity.[89] Despite the exceptionally controversial nature of the Appropriations Committee's work, its recommendations have met with substantial success on the floor. Table 7.2 tells a major part of the story.

TABLE 7.2

House Action on Appropriations Committee Recommendations—
36 Bureaus, 1947 to 1962

	Number of Decisions	% of Decisions
Accept Committee Recommendations	517	89.9
Decrease Committee Recommendations	30	5.2
Increase Committee Recommendations	28	4.9
Total	575	100.0

SOURCE: Richard F Fenno, Jr., *The Power of the Purse: Appropriations Politics in Congress* (Boston: Little, Brown & Company, 1966), p. 450

Over a sixteen-year period, nearly 90 per cent of the Appropriations Committee's funding recommendations for thirty-six bureaus were accepted by the House without change. On an average, only about one floor amendment was adopted per every eight bureaus per year. Notwithstanding the pressures for increased expenditures among program-minded congressmen and pressures for decreased expenditures among economy-minded congressmen, surprisingly little floor conflict has occurred over the committee's recommendations. It is apparent that the committee meets the House's expectations, and the end result is committee success on the floor.

If the key to the House Appropriations Committee's success is found in committee integration, how is this achieved? The answer is complex. Viewed broadly, it is that within the committee there is marked consensus concerning committee goals, tasks, norms, and roles. Veterans and newcomers, Democrats and Republicans, members of one kind or another—all share (or through socialization come to share) a remarkable consensus on the goals or tasks of the committee: to *protect the power of the purse* (the principal legislative power, in the view of members), to *guard the federal treasury* against raids by "spenders," to *reduce budget estimates* by paring "fat," "padding," "pork," and "oleaginous substance" ("There isn't a budget that can't be cut 10 per cent immediately"), and to *serve member constituency interests* (a subordinate goal since it is likely to clash with the budget-cutting tasks committee members are expected to perform). There is similarly wide agreement on the norms which prescribe the role of committee and subcommittee members: *hard work, specialization, reciprocity, subcommittee unity, compromise, minimal partisanship,* and *apprenticeship.* Several of these norms are illustrated in the following comments by Committee members:

[89] This paragraph and the following two are based on the work of Richard F. Fenno, Jr., *The Power of the Purse: Appropriations Politics in Congress* (Boston: Little, Brown & Company, 1966). See especially Chapters 2–5 and 9. The quotes by congressmen are drawn from pages 162–65.

Specialization: During the six years he has been on the subcommittee we have turned over the job of looking after the health of Indians to him and he has really done a job. We never question his position when it comes to the health of the Indians, because we know he has looked into it thoroughly. The committee has also turned over the job of looking after the Bureau of Mines to the gentleman from Pennsylvania. He spends a lot of time on that.

Compromise: If there's agreement, we go right along. If there's a controversy, we put the item aside and go on. Then after a day or two, we may have a list of ten controversial items. We give and take and pound them down until we get agreement.

Minimal Partisanship: Usually we come to an agreement and compromise things out. Most subcommittee reports are unanimous reports. I never saw a unanimous report on anything in my last committee. I guess you could say there's a lot less partisanship on Appropriations.

Still other conditions help to facilitate unity within the House Appropriations Committee. Among them is the fact that committee members themselves attach high value to internal integration. Moreover, members chosen for this committee are those who perform well in legislative give-and-take and are flexible and cooperative—members whose style is that of the "responsible legislator." An unusually stable membership, including the top leadership as well as the rank and file, also serves integrative purposes. Finally, the committee has a strong attractiveness for members, a fact likely to promote acceptance of integrative norms. Influence, prestige, information, and involvement—all these rewards and more are conferred by membership on the committee. In sum, a variety of inducements and the presence of broad consensus as to goals and norms contribute to committee integration, which in turn contributes to the success of committee recommendations on the floor. Other House committees unable to manage conflict and rent by sharp cleavages doubtless confront far more opposition on the floor. Unity at the committee level, however it may be derived, maximizes committee influence in the legislative system as a whole.[90]

COMMITTEE LEADERS AND PARTY LEADERS

Another way to evaluate committee influence is to examine relations between committee leaders and party leaders. David Truman's book, *The Congressional Party,* a study that focuses on legislative party leadership in the 81st Congress, questions the hoary interpretation of legislative politics which stresses the primacy of standing committees and their chairmen. One phase of his inquiry is especially important. Within each legislative party, Truman points out, there are two sets of leaders: "elective leaders" and

[90] For an analysis of the House Ways and Means Committee, which is also characterized by a high degree of integration, see John F. Manley, "The House Committee on Ways and Means: Conflict Management in a Congressional Committee," *American Political Science Review,* LIX (December 1965), 927–39.

"seniority leaders." The first set, which includes the floor leaders, traces its position to election by the party caucus or conference, and the second set, composed of committee chairmen and ranking minority members, comes to its position through continuous tenure on a committee. In Woodrow Wilson's analysis, the committee chairmen were the principal custodians of congressional power, and since they were independent of one another ("the dissociated heads of. . . little legislatures"), often suspicious and hostile, there was slight opportunity to develop unified leadership within the legislative party. In this study of the roll-call votes of the 81st Congress, Truman accumulates evidence that suggests power and influence have in some degree moved away from the committee chairmen and come to rest with the elected leaders of the legislative parties.[91]

The study discloses that chairmen do not vote in concert: "Even more than the elective leaders, especially among the Democrats [Senate committee chairmen] appear as individuals, acting in response to variations in personal ideology, region, or constituency rather than to the demands of a collective leadership role." The same behavior appeared in the floor voting of the House committee chairmen. Wilson's assessment of the independent bent of chairmen remains appropriate today.[92]

A more important matter, however, concerns the relationship between the seniority leaders and their respective floor leaders. Agreement between them at the roll-call stage obviously is not always present. When they differ on a vote, whose position usually prevails—the committee chairman's or the floor leader's? Truman's data show that the floor leader is usually on the winning side, especially in the case of the majority leader. On questions in which the committee chairmen voted opposite the leader, members of the chairman's own committee voted more frequently with the leader than with the chairman. This would appear to be a critical test of influence. The floor leaders, Truman states, "were not at the mercy of the seniority leaders and they did, with varying degrees of effectiveness, act as if they were the trustees of the party's record."[93] This held true in both houses.

The data on the voting structure of the parties in the 81st Congress suggest that the "formal" and the "real" leadership of the party coincide much of the time. Whether the role of the committee chairman is as critical as was made out by Wilson, subsequently to be chiseled in stone by other writers, is now brought into question by Truman's data. At least there is room for doubt when analysis is confined to the *voting* stage on the floor. These data do not show how successful committee chairmen are in preventing legislation desired by elective leaders from getting to the floor. In any case, current explanations of committee power need to take increased account of the relations, both of conflict and of accommodation, between the seniority leaders and the elected leaders.

Much else could be said about committees in relation to legislative leadership, political interest groups, and the bureaucracy. We shall return to these topics in later chapters.

---

[91] *The Congressional Party* (New York: John Wiley & Sons, Inc., 1959), p. 99.
[92] *Ibid.*, p. 134.
[93] *Ibid.*, p. 246. For an analysis of the voting relationship between committee chairmen and the floor leader in the Senate, see particularly pp. 139–44, and for the House, pp. 239–44.

238   Following committee action, measures proceed to the floor for decision. The flow of legislation from the committees to the floor, unlike water over the dam, is neither steady nor predictable. The next chapter begins with an analysis of how the flow is regulated, how the floor may attempt to control its committees, and the way in which proposed legislation is scheduled for consideration by the parent chamber.

8

DEBATE AND DECISION-MAKING
ON THE FLOOR

The decisions of Congress are not often independent of the decisions of its committees. By and large, legislation that provokes a stir in committee provokes a stir on the floor; legislation that escapes controversy in committee escapes controversy on the floor. Although the public gaze fastens on the floor of the House or Senate, where talk ranges and final decisions are made, the assembly's deliberations often engage only the alternatives defined and narrowed by committee analysis and decision. At times, floor action consists of no more than the ratification of decisions put together by committee majorities. The legislature is not immobilized by the preferences and power of its committees, but it is steadily and strongly influenced by them.

First among all congressional committees in the authority to frame the dimensions of floor discussion and action is the Rules Committee of the House of Representatives. An analysis of its role follows a brief description of the House calendar system.

From Committee to Floor

THE CALENDARS

Bills which succeed in running the committee gauntlet are reported to the floor and placed on a calendar. The most complex calendar arrangement is that of the U.S. House of Representatives, which has five distinct calendars: union, House, private, consent, and discharge. The union calendar receives bills which provide for revenue or appropriations, while the remaining public bills go to the House calendar. Bills of a private character (e.g., an individual's claim against the government) are placed on the private calendar and considered on the first and third Tuesdays of each month. The consent calendar, as its name suggests, is for the purpose of expediting disposition of minor, unopposed bills which have appeared on the union or House calendars; it is taken up twice a month on the first and third Mon-

240 days.[1] The discharge calendar, taken up on the second and fourth Mondays, lists motions to "discharge" bills from committees. Also, in a procedure designed to expedite floor action, bills which are not highly controversial may be called up and considered by unanimous consent.

Two additional provisions in the House scheduling system require comment. Under the first of these, the District of Columbia day, the second and fourth Mondays in each month are set aside for the consideration of measures called up by the Committee on the District of Columbia. The committee determines the order in which it wishes to present bills. The second special day is Calendar Wednesday, which permits standing committees to call up for immediate floor consideration proposals listed on the House or union calendars that have been sidetracked for lack of privileged status or a special rule of the Rules Committee. Privileged bills, such as appropriations, are not eligible for action on Calendar Wednesday.

THE RULES COMMITTEE OF THE HOUSE
OF REPRESENTATIVES

The calendars, though not without use, tell very little about the order in which bills are brought before the House. There are two main reasons for this. First, certain bills from a few committees, Appropriations and Ways and Means among others, are accorded privileged status and can be reported at any time for prompt consideration; this also applies to conference-committee bills and measures vetoed by the president. Second, the Rules Committee has the authority to regulate the flow of legislation from the standing committees to the floor and to prescribe the conditions under which it will be considered.

The power of the Rules Committee, its impact on legislative committees, and the influence it has come to wield over the chamber itself have at certain times been of critical significance. The base of its power has not always been the same, but it has played an important role in the House since the days of Speaker Thomas B. Reed of Maine in 1890. "Czar" Reed was succeeded by Charles Crisp, an aggressive Georgian who piled new and greater powers on the Rules Committee. The zenith of Rules Committee power was reached under the speakership of Joseph G. Cannon of Illinois shortly after the turn of the century.

In the heyday of Reed and Cannon, the Rules Committee was a powerful instrument for control of the House and its agenda. "The right of the minority," Speaker Reed is reported to have lectured House Democrats,

---

[1] Measures on the consent calendar are passed by unanimous consent and without debate, unless objection is raised, after they have been on the calendar for three days. If objection is made to a bill, it is carried over to another consent calendar day, and if objected to again by as many as three members, it is removed from the calendar for the duration of that session. To facilitate the screening of the many proposals placed on the consent calendar, each party appoints three official objectors whose task is to examine the proposals listed on the calendar, noting any which they believe should receive more careful consideration. A bill removed from the consent calendar does not lose its position on either the House or Union calendars.

"is to draw its salaries and its function is to make a quorum."[2] As Speaker and as chairman of the Rules Committee, Cannon used the full power of the offices to determine which proposals would be enacted and which defeated. Eventually, his heavy-handed rule got him into trouble. A successful revolt against "Cannonism" in 1910–11, directed by insurgent Senator George W. Norris of Nebraska, sharply constricted the Speaker's powers and removed him from his position as chairman of the Rules Committee.

There are two things of main significance in this episode of "revolution." The first is that the revolutionaries did not touch the powers of the Rules Committee itself. The second is that their action severed the link between the committee and the elected leadership of the House. Comparing the Cannon regime with its successors, Luce argued that "the most striking difference between the old and the new methods is that, whereas leadership was then in the open, it is now under cover. Then the Speaker was the recognized centre of authority. Now nobody knows who in the last resort decides."[3]

The 1910–11 revolution laid the groundwork for the Rules Committee to establish itself as an *independent* center of power. From the late 1930s until the 1960s, many House sessions (especially in the later years) were dominated by a conservative coalition of southern Democrats and northern Republicans which held sway in the Rules Committee, making many critical decisions and at times holding the assembly in "parliamentary thralldom," as one critic has put it.[4] Throughout this period, members from urban, industrial states of the North, East, and West were underrepresented on the Rules Committee; their power was slight even when one of their number, such as Adolph Sabath of Illinois, held the chairmanship. The ruling coalition on the committee was sometimes in harmony with the House leadership and sometimes indifferent to it; at times it could be moved aside when Speaker Sam Rayburn secured the vote of a moderate Republican member; rarely was the committee sympathetic to the legislative requests of the president. Year in and year out, its hue was distinctly conservative, irrespective of significant changes in the House membership produced by elections.

The Rules Committee's composition and its relationship to the elected leadership are important because of the extraordinary array of powers it possesses. What are these powers which at times have made the committee—specifically, a majority of its members—a virtual oligarchy? To begin with, we need to point out that the committee does not control all bills and resolutions reported from the legislative committees. The great majority of measures brought to the floor each session of Congress are mainly free from controversy and are handled in routine fashion by any of several devices, such as the consent or private calendars; the Rules Committee takes no part in their disposition. Perhaps one hundred bills and resolutions each

[2] Hubert Bruce Fuller, *The Speakers of the House* (Boston: Little, Brown, & Company, 1909), p. 231.

[3] Robert Luce, *Congress: An Explanation* (Cambridge: Harvard University Press, 1926), p. 117.

[4] Tom Wicker, "Again That Roadblock in Congress," *New York Times Magazine,* August 7, 1960, p. 14.

session are sufficiently important and controversial to warrant at least a moderate amount of debate on the House floor. Of this number slightly more than one-half ordinarily will be considered under special resolutions adopted by the Rules Committee.[5]

The Rules Committee lays out the central paths which the House takes by controlling its agenda. Favorable action on a bill by a legislative committee is but the initial step toward passage. Committee reports which lack privileged status require a rule from the Rules Committee in order to be brought to the floor for consideration, and ordinarily these rules are accepted by the floor, a majority vote being required. The effect of this is to give the committee substantial control over the major items on the agenda.

The Rules Committee grants four kinds of rules. Most legislation scheduled by the committee moves to the floor under open rules which permit the House to amend measures sent out by the standing committees. Less commonly, the committee will send measures to the floor under closed rules which limit the alternatives open to the members. A closed rule may prohibit amendments altogether or permit only certain amendments, such as those offered by the legislative committee which handled the measure. During the period 1939 to 1956, the House adopted sixty-five closed rules as compared with 886 open rules. Closed rules more often involve controversial matters than open rules, and they also tend to accompany legislation that would be especially vulnerable to "special interest" amendments on the floor. A third type of rule is for the purpose of waiving points of order against the provisions of a particular bill. For example, although House rules prohibit the Appropriations Committee from including legislation in a general appropriations bill, the Rules Committee may grant a rule waiving all points of order against the measure. Rules granted for this purpose are not common— forty-seven were adopted by the House between 1939 and 1956. The fourth type of rule is employed for the purpose of arranging a conference between the Senate and the House when they have passed legislation in different versions.[6]

Not all requests by committees for rules are granted, and the refusal of the Rules Committee to give a bill a "green light" to the floor is often sufficient to kill it for the session. The committee may stipulate when a bill is to be brought up for consideration and how much time is to be set aside for debate (usually one or two hours); it may provide for the floor consideration of a bill that has not been approved by a legislative committee, but this is rare; it may insist that a certain amendment be made to a measure as the price for getting a right of way to the floor; it may clear

---

5 James A. Robinson, "The Role of the Rules Committee in Arranging the Program of the U.S. House of Representatives," *Western Political Quarterly,* XII (September 1959), 653. See also his analysis of the principal variables affecting Rules Committee decisions in "Decision Making in the House Rules Committee," *Administrative Science Quarterly,* III (June 1958), 73–86, and a study by Lewis A. Froman, Jr., *The Congressional Process: Strategies, Rules, and Procedures* (Boston: Little, Brown & Company, 1967), especially pp. 52–61.

6 James A. Robinson, "The Role of the Rules Committee in Regulating Debate in the U.S. House of Representatives," *Midwest Journal of Political Science,* V (February 1961), 59–69. Also see an article by John C. Blydenburgh, "The Closed Rule and the Paradox of Voting," *Journal of Politics,* XXXIII (February 1971), 57–71.

one bill as payment for the demise of another. Through its power to withhold bills from floor action as well as its ability to bargain for the inclusion or deletion of particular provisions, the committee tends to become the final arbiter of content on certain bills, often major ones, a role well beyond that of a "traffic cop" regulating the legislative schedule.[7]

Nonetheless, as a former chairman of this committee has argued, the Rules Committee's control over legislation should be kept in perspective. Howard Smith (D., Va.), perhaps the best known and most powerful Rules Committee chairman in history, put the matter this way:

> Remember there are 15,000 bills that are introduced in the House every Congress. The weeding process begins with the legislative committees, and they weed out, and then the Rules Committee weeds out, and after we get through weeding out sometimes the Speaker weeds out and won't call up a bill that we have introduced. So there is a lot of weeding out that is done, and I think that the Rules Committee only does a fair share of it. When the chips are down, we refuse rules on very, very few bills.[8]

The Rules Committee may block bills short of floor consideration in two ways, either by denying committee requests for hearings on their bills and resolutions or by refusing to grant rules after hearings. The committee is more likely to refuse to hold hearings than to deny a rule following hearings. From the 87th through the 90th Congresses, the committee refused to hold hearings on 159 bills, an average of forty bills per Congress. At the same time, the committee declined to grant rules to twenty-eight bills on which hearings were held—an average of seven per Congress. Not all of the measures which failed to secure hearings were lost, since some moved to the floor via unanimous consent or suspension of the rules procedures. The number of bills effectively bottled up by the committee averaged twenty-eight per Congress over the period studied.[9]

Because actions of the Rules Committee occasionally provoke great controversy, it is easy to lose sight of the fact that the majority of bills stymied by the committee are not of major significance. The truth of the matter is that among those bills that fail to clear the committee there are more that deal with matters of secondary importance (e.g., development of recreational areas or historic sites, copyright law, rural electrification financing, bank holding companies) than those that deal with major national problems or central items in the president's program (e.g., civil rights, aid

---

[7] Until the 89th Congress, when a rules change was made, the House could be prevented from entering into conference committee negotiations with the Senate to work out a compromise bill, since a single objection on the floor to a conference was sufficient to give the Rules Committee possession of the bill. Accordingly, many bills that had already passed the House again came under the jurisdiction of the Rules Committee. Under the new rule, a bill can be sent to conference by a majority vote of the membership.

[8] *Christian Science Monitor,* December 21, 1966, p. 3.

[9] Douglas M. Fox and Charles H. Clapp, "The House Rules Committee's Agenda-Setting Function, 1961–68," *Journal of Politics,* XXXII (May 1970), 440–43. Also see their article, "The House Rules Committee and the Programs of the Kennedy and Johnson Administrations," *Midwest Journal of Political Science,* XIV (November 1970), 667–72.

244 to education, model cities). That this is statistically true, however, is of slight moment when the Rules Committee, seemingly oblivious to strong pressures within the House and the nation, prevents major legislation from reaching the floor.

It should be emphasized that there are no statistics to show how frequently the Rules Committee has been able to insist on certain provisions being eliminated, revised, or added to measures as a condition for clearing them for floor consideration. That legislative committees find it expedient to accept Rules Committee intrusions is a well-worn assertion.

A final observation on the role of the Rules Committee is that its influence is essentially *negative:* it can help to defend the *status quo* (especially against liberal attempts to adopt new domestic welfare policies) much more effectively than it can act to bring forth changes in existing policies. It is, in sum, less awesome than often pictured. To quote James Robinson:

> The least controversial measures can be passed under unanimous consent, suspension of the rules, or special legislative days. The most controversial, including those which affect large numbers of people in important ways—e.g., tax bills and civil rights proposals—can usually be brought to the floor, albeit with delay, by a determined majority leadership or a determined House majority. It is on the middle level of importance and controversy that the Committee is likely to escape public notice and external pressure.[10]

CONTROVERSY OVER THE RULES COMMITTEE

Opposition to the Rules Committee flares when major legislation is obstructed by committee decisions, though only occasionally does it reach the proportions of revolt. In 1949, the House adopted the so-called twenty-one-day rule to curb the power of the Rules Committee. The rule provided that any measure held by the committee for a period of twenty-one days could be brought to the floor by request of the chairman of the legislative committee that had reported the bill. Under the twenty-one-day rule, eight measures were brought to the House floor in the 81st Congress; seven of them passed, including bills outlawing the poll tax and providing for statehood for Alaska and Hawaii. The rule survived only one Congress, being abolished in 1951 by a coalition of Republicans and southern Democrats.

A similar rule was adopted in 1965, at the opening of the 89th Congress, over the strong opposition of a majority of Republicans and southern Democrats. The main difference between the 1965 rule and the 1951 rule was that the 1951 version had made it mandatory for the Speaker to recognize the chairman invoking the twenty-one-day rule; the 1965 provision left recognition to the Speaker's discretion. The twenty-one-day rule was used six times during 1965 to pry bills out of the Rules Committee; four of the six bills brought to the floor under this procedure eventually were enacted into law, including a bill to increase federal pay and a bill to authorize a

---

10 From *The House Rules Committee* by James A. Robinson, copyright © 1963 by The Bobbs-Merrill Company, Inc., reprinted by permission of the publishers. Also see Robert L. Peabody, "The Enlarged Rules Committee," in *New Perspectives on the House of Representatives,* ed. Robert L. Peabody and Nelson W. Polsby (Chicago: Rand McNally & Company, 1963), pp. 129–64.

Foundation on the Arts and Humanities. The rule was used twice in 1966, on a civil rights bill and a bill to raise postage rates. The postage rate bill was enacted into law, but the civil rights bill fell victim to a filibuster in the Senate. In addition, the threat to employ the twenty-one-day rule was apparently sufficient to prompt the Rules Committee to release several other bills it would have preferred to block.[11] Bolstered by the arrival of a large number of freshman Republican members in the 90th Congress, the conservative coalition promptly eliminated the twenty-one-day rule, again restoring power to the Rules Committee. The parallel between 1951 and 1967 was striking.[12] The precarious life of the twenty-one-day rule is evidence not only of its effectiveness but also of the continuing power of the conservative coalition. An additional explanation may be, simply, that some members do not want to weaken the Rules Committee because it affords them greater leeway: they can profess to support a measure which they privately oppose, secure in the knowledge that the committee will keep it bottled up.

The most serious challenge to the Rules Committee in recent decades occurred in 1961, following the election of John F. Kennedy to the presidency. In the preceding Congress the coalition had become increasingly militant in its conservatism. In the judgment of House liberals, presidential advisers, and Speaker Rayburn, it was imperative that the conservative hold on the committee be broken. After exploring a number of alternatives, a decision was made to try to change the composition of the committee by enlarging its membership from twelve to fifteen. To make a long and bitter story short, following exceptional efforts by the Speaker and last-minute telephone calls by the president and members of his cabinet to unsteady or doubtful supporters, the resolution to enlarge the committee was adopted by a vote of 217–212. The Speaker's support included about one-third of the southern Democrats, all but one of the northern and western Democrats, and twenty-two liberal Republicans. "Judge" Smith secured the votes of the rest of the southerners and those of 148 Republicans. The appointment of new Democratic members loyal to the Speaker then proceeded as planned.[13]

The significance of the 1961 decision is that it upset the main structure of coalition power in the House, at the same time joining a Rules Committee majority to Speaker Rayburn and the Kennedy administration. Equally important, neither the committee's jurisdiction nor its powers were impaired in the slightest—what it could do before the vote it could do after. Although liberal elements found the Rules Committee much less troublesome after the change, their expectations were not met altogether. Late in the first session of the 87th Congress a major administration bill providing aid for public

---

[11] *Congressional Quarterly Weekly Report,* October 28, 1966, pp. 2621–22.

[12] *Ibid.,* January 13, 1967, pp. 38–39.

[13] There is a strong parallel between the curbing of Judge Smith in 1961 and the overthrow of Speaker Joseph Cannon in 1910. Each case involved a House reaction against "excessive leadership." Both men had grown out of touch with elements of their "procedural majorities"—those members who provide the support necessary to organize the House and maintain that organization. The manner in which they had exercised power, ignoring constraints and the bargaining behavior expected of leaders, led to their undoing and the development of procedural changes designed to prevent such independent rule. For analysis of these themes, see Charles O. Jones, "Joseph G. Cannon and Howard W. Smith: An Essay on the Limits of Leadership in the House of Representatives," *Journal of Politics,* **XXX** (August 1968), 617–46.

246 schools died in the Rules Committee by an eight-to-seven vote—a northern Democrat, dedicated to aid for parochial schools, joined the conservative coalition to kill the bill, giving rise to the observation that "the 'unholy alliance" has got religion."[14]

The power of the Rules Committee was cut back again in the 89th Congress, with the adoption of a new twenty-one-day rule. But this experiment lasted only two years—until the convocation of the 90th Congress. Liberals, fearful of a revival of the conservative coalition in the Rules Committee, lost another battle in the 90th Congress when their proposal to enlarge the Rules Committee to seventeen members, adding the majority and minority leaders as *chairman* and *ranking member,* failed to win support. Conceived by the Democratic Study Group, a liberal group of some 140 House Democrats, the plan was designed to make the Rules Committee "an effective arm of the leadership." Had the DSG proposal been adopted, Congressman William Colmer (who replaced Howard Smith as senior member following Smith's primary defeat in 1966) would have been denied the chairmanship and given the position of vice-chairman. When the plan failed, Colmer became chairman, and the matter was settled temporarily.

Still another effort to curb the Rules Committee occurred at the opening of the 92d Congress, when a proposal was made to institute a thirty-one-day rule. Under this plan, a chairman would have a ten-day "grace period" to request the Rules Committee to report a rule on a specific bill. If the rule were not awarded within twenty-one days following the request, the Speaker would be empowered to recognize the committee chairman for the purpose of gaining floor consideration on the bill. Despite the approval by the Democratic caucus and the support of Speaker Carl Albert, the proposal was handily defeated by a coalition of Republicans and southern Democrats.[15] New struggles over the Rules Committee, its composition, and its powers can be anticipated in future Congresses.

In its fully developed form, the dilemma surrounding the Rules Committee concerns the question of who shall rule, not whether such rule is essential. A basic requirement for any legislative chamber is a system for channeling its affairs, for controlling the legislative program. Who is to control the Rules Committee? There has not been a *formal* link between the committee and the majority leadership since the 1910–11 revolution, and from this divorce results the single most important fact about the committee: it is not a completely reliable instrument of the majority party and it bears no formal responsibility to elected party leaders. The judgments of a majority of its members as to the priorities of policies may or may not coincide with those of majority party leaders, most rank-and-file members, or the president. The 1961 "face-lifting" did not alter this fact. Discussing his legislative program two years later, President Kennedy remarked. "The

14 Hugh Douglas Price, "Race, Religion, and the Rules Committee: The Kennedy Aid-to-Education Bills," in *The Uses of Power,* ed. Alan F. Westin (New York: Harcourt, Brace & World, Inc., 1962), p. 64.

15 *Congressional Quarterly Weekly Report,* January 29, 1971, 258. During the debate on the thirty-one-day proposal, the chairman of the Rules Committee, William Colmer, observed: "the language of this resolution...provides for what I consider the liquidation of the Rules Committee." It would, he said, "turn the clock back 60 years" and give the Speaker "czar-like" power.

only thing that has ever concerned me is whether the Rules Committee of the House of Representatives will release it for a vote."[16]

Some years ago Stephen K. Bailey set the problem in these terms:

> Unfortunately, many liberals in Congress think the answer to existing minority rule is anarchy. They dislike the Rules Committee not only because it is conservative but because it *rules*. With this in mind, liberals are busily working out devices to cut the power of the Rules Committee. But what is wrong with the Rules Committee is not that it rules, but that it rules irresponsibly, and for minority interests.
>
> The ultimate cure is not to make it easier for temporary coalitions of Congressmen to break the power of the Rules Committee. Nor is the answer to strengthen the Rules Committee as an instrument of bipartisan coalition in the Congress. The only answer that squares with majority rule and political responsibility is to make the Rules Committee an instrument of the majority party. This means the abolition of the Rules Committee in its present form, and its reconstitution as a majority policy committee under the chairmanship of the Speaker. Policy committee members would, of course, be chosen by caucus.[17]

THE DISCHARGE RULE AND CALENDAR WEDNESDAY

The parliamentary weapons that House members may call upon in attempting to bring obdurate committees to heel are not impressive. There are two principal means by which the floor can gain possession of a measure pigeon-holed in a legislative committee or sidetracked by the Rules Committee: the discharge rule and Calendar Wednesday.

The discharge rule was adopted in 1910 when the House was warring with Speaker Cannon and the Rules Committee. Floyd Riddick records that the rule has been changed half a dozen times since first adopted, with each party at intervals having shaped it to its purposes.[18] The present provision, adopted in the 74th Congress (1935), enables a majority of the members of the House (218) to compel a committee to release its hold on a bill or resolution and to send it to the floor. The liberal rule in the 72d Congress (1931) required only 145 signatures. Discharge days occur on the second and fourth Mondays. Discharge petitions can be readied after a bill has been in a legislative committee for thirty days or after a resolution has been held up by the Rules Committee for seven days. Motions to discharge bills must be listed on the calendar seven days before they can be brought up for consideration, an interval which permits committees to report bills likely to be pried out from under them by the House. Simply because a majority of the members have signed a discharge petition, however, does not insure the bill's removal from committee; it must be accepted by a majority vote on the floor when the formal motion is offered.

[16] *Washington Post,* April 26, 1963.

[17] "Congress and Majority Rule: House Rules Committee," *The New Republic,* January 5, 1959, p. 8.

[18] *The U.S. Congress: Organization and Procedure* (Manassas, Va.: National Capitol Publishers, Inc., 1949), p. 237.

The history of this rule is not marked by significant successes. In the thirty-year period between 1935 and 1965, nearly three hundred discharge petitions were filed (an average of about eighteen per Congress), but only twenty gained sufficient signatures to warrant a place on the discharge calendar. Seventeen of the twenty measures passed the House, but only two eventually became law, the Wage and Hour Act of 1938 and the Federal Pay Raise Act of 1960. Fewer discharge petitions are filed today than in the past—during the 1960s the number ordinarily averaged around six per Congress.[19] In practical terms, this rule holds little hope for frustrated House members attempting to wrest a measure out of committee. It is a small-caliber "gun behind the door" whose presence may spur the search for a compromise solution which can be brought to the floor.

Calendar Wednesday, in use since 1909, is simple in form but has been difficult to invoke in practice. It may be used to call up nonprivileged bills or those denied a rule by the Rules Committee. Under its terms, each Wednesday is to be set aside for calling the role of the standing committees, in alphabetical order, with each committee permitted to bring forth any bill it has earlier reported which lacks privileged status. In earlier years, a number of successive Calendar Wednesdays might be taken up with the consideration of a single bill brought before the House. Progress down the alphabetical list of committees was slow, and an entire session could go by without reaching all the committees. Eventually, this problem was met through a limitation of debate to two hours on any measure called up on Calendar Wednesday, permitting more committees to get their turn. Nevertheless, Calendar Wednesday is cumbersome and largely ineffective. Theoretically, minorities are protected under this rule by the requirement that a two-thirds vote is needed to set aside this procedure. In practice, however, it is common for the majority leader to request each week that Calendar Wednesday for the following week be dispensed with, and this motion is usually accepted by the House. Since 1950, Calendar Wednesday has been used effectively only twice to bring measures to the floor.

SUSPENSION OF THE RULES

Another way of bringing (noncontroversial) bills and resolutions before the House for consideration is to suspend the rules, which requires a two-thirds vote for adoption. This procedure can be utilized two days each month, on the first and third Mondays, and also during the last six days of a session. Under its terms, the motions of individuals are given preference on the first Monday and those of committees on the second. This method of getting a vote on a bill, while it eludes the control of the Rules Committee over bills on the calendars, vests great authority in the Speaker, whose power to recognize members desiring to make such motions is complete. If the motion secures a two-thirds vote, the rules are suspended and the bill is passed at one and the same time. Under this procedure, debate is limited to forty minutes and no amendments are in order. Suspension of the rules is not a

---

[19] *Congressional Quarterly Almanac*, XXI (1965), 617.

frequent practice, and as the Rules Committee gained prominence this method declined.

Like the House, the Senate permits its committees to throttle measures by not reporting them to the floor, and its pigeonholes are fully as crammed as those of the lower chamber. A conspicuous difference between the two bodies, however, lies in the function of screening bills and resolutions for floor consideration. In the House this power rests formally (and much of the time, actually) with the Rules Committee, while in the Senate it is held by the majority floor leader and the majority policy committee.[20] The policy committees occasionally are compared to the House Rules Committee in terms of their role in scheduling legislation, but, as Hugh Bone points out, the comparison leaves something to be desired. "The latter enjoys the status of a standing committee with authority to issue specific rules, impose limitations, and bottle up measures; none of these powers are possessed by the policy bodies. Scheduling in the real sense...involves discussion of strategy, decision as to sequence, consideration of timing." Actually, the decisions as to which measures shall be called up for floor consideration in the Senate are made by the majority party leadership. "Quite often the floor leader simply brings in a legislative agenda for the ensuing week and asks the policy group if it has any questions. Members may then ask to have certain items included."[21]

The differences between Senate and House practices are apparent. The legislative program in the Senate is controlled more firmly by the elected majority party leaders; lines of responsibility, consequently, are fairly clear. This, of itself, however, does not assure majority party members a significant role in shaping the program.

The procedure of the Senate in considering legislation is both simple and casual in comparison with that of the House. With its much smaller size, it finds slight need for rigidly defined schedules such as both guide and limit the activities of the House. The Senate has but two calendars and no system of special days. Bills and resolutions reported from committee are routed to the calendar of business, while treaties and nominations go to the executive calendar. Much of the Senate's important work is accomplished under an arrangement of unanimous consent. This agreement, subject to the veto of any member, limits the time to be allotted for debate and sets the time for voting. Except in the instance of a highly controversial measure, a unanimous consent agreement is easy to obtain, and in recent decades the Senate has made increasing use of the rule. "While the Senate passes some legislation only after debate is exhausted," states Roland Young, "it passes other legislation in a very brief time by the unanimous consent of the members. Unanimous consent allows the Senate to spend large amounts of time on what may interest it at the moment; it allows it to pass much legislation in

---

[20] See Chapter 9 for a discussion of the policy committees.
[21] Hugh A. Bone, "An Introduction to the Senate Policy Committees," *American Political Science Review,* L (June 1956), 349–50.

250 a very small amount of time; and it allows individual Senators to secure favors—such as agreeing to recommendations for appointments—from their colleagues."[22]

SCHEDULING THE LEGISLATIVE PROGRAM
IN THE STATE LEGISLATURES

Most state legislative houses employ only a single calendar on which all bills ready for floor action are listed. Bills and resolutions are segregated into classes on the calendar, such as "House Bills—second reading," "Senate Bills —third reading," and "Consideration Postponed." The order in which measures are listed is not altogether a reliable guide as to when they will be brought before the chamber, although it is more reliable than in Congress. Proposals of meager consequence are mixed in with those of major importance on most legislative calendars. Hence it becomes necessary to single out the measures whose importance warrants privileged action, irrespective of order of arrival on the calendar. This is a function of the majority party leadership, though it is impossible to generalize safely as to the way in which decisions are taken. In those legislatures with a tradition of strong caucus action, the legislative program is shaped by the majority party caucus. In Connecticut, possessor of strong legislative party organizations, the party imprint on the program is substantial:

> In the daily caucus—to which is normally devoted far more time than that spent on the floor of the Senate—the procedure is to review the day's calendar of bills and to come to agreement on the party stand on all bills. All senators attend their respective caucuses, as do the state chairmen of the parties. Each senator is responsible for the bills being reported out of his committees (those over which he is Senate chairman). As the list of bills is read off by the majority leader, the senator from whose committee the bill came will briefly outline its intent and implications. This may be only a cursory comment on insignificant bills or a lengthy analysis in other cases. Discussion among the senators as to the bill and the appropriate position for the party to take on it may occupy minutes or hours. By custom any senator may by simple request have any bill held over for consideration another day.[23]

The Connecticut practice, however, is apparently not typical of most states. According to a study some years ago by a committee of the American Political Science Association, in only one-quarter of the states were majority caucuses powerful agencies for the control of the legislative program.[24] Where the party is an effective instrument, party leadership necessarily assumes the function of scheduling, the essence of which is to single out those bills it will support and those it will oppose. In states in which parties are weak, control over the agenda may rest with calendar committees, rules com-

[22] *This Is Congress* (New York: Alfred A. Knopf, Inc., 1943), p. 142.
[23] Duane Lockard, *New England State Politics* (Princeton: Princeton University Press, 1959), p. 282.
[24] Belle Zeller, ed., *American State Legislatures* (New York: Thomas Y. Crowell Company, 1954), p. 194.

mittees, factions, or a leadership that pays slight attention to partisan considerations.

In legislative houses in which the rules committee bears an important responsibility for scheduling legislation, it ordinarily derives its power from its role as a party agency, as a steering committee for the majority party leadership and caucus. A common arrangement provides for the Speaker of the house to serve as chairman of the rules committee and to appoint its members. The number of members on the committee ordinarily is quite limited, and some states emphasize its party function by stipulating that appointees be drawn exclusively from the majority party.

The significance and the functions of the rules committee vary from legislature to legislature. It is doubtful, however, whether any rules committee at the state level matches in power its counterpart in the lower house of Congress. Ordinarily, rules committees in the state legislatures either deal with miscellaneous "housekeeping" matters of secondary importance or become screening agencies for legislation only in the turbulent closing days of the session. The latter function is common. With the calendars bulging with measures whose priority is ambiguous and the session rapidly coming to an end, most state houses use the rules committee (or create a special sifting committee) to identify those measures to be given floor consideration and those to be consigned to the waste basket. At this juncture, the rules committee, operating under the direction of the majority leadership, has enormous power over the fate of bills. Since legislatures pass an inordinate number of proposals the last week of the session, particularly on the last day, the sifting committee may gain a decisive voice in molding the legislature's record.

The power to discharge bills from committees, customarily present in the rules of state legislative houses, is not in practice very useful in diminishing committee control over legislation. In the states, unlike Congress, it is an easy matter to gain a vote on a discharge resolution since usually a handful of legislators is sufficient to file a motion and to bring it to a vote, whereas in Congress a majority of the total membership is required. Yet the net result is about the same. One survey found that the discharge rule was ineffective or infrequently employed in at least one-half of the houses.[25] Even this appraisal may exaggerate the potency of the rule in the states. Individual studies show that, except in those states where committees must report all bills by a certain date or automatically lose them, there are few instances in which they lose control of measures referred to them. Bottled up in committee, a controversial bill stays bottled up.

In the vigorous two-party states, the principal function of the discharge rule is to permit the minority party to place its position on a bill or resolution on record in a formal floor vote. Discharge resolutions often become party issues, and when party lines hold, as they invariably do on matters of this sort, the motions are lost. Thus, this rule has utility as a campaign weapon, a technique for recording party policy and principle. Even here, however, the issue may be blurred or blunted, since in opposing a discharge motion the majority leadership usually contends that the vote is not on the substance of the bill but on the issue of protecting orderly procedures and

[25] *Ibid.*, p .198.

preventing committee powers from becoming enfeebled. A discharge resolution is also a handy device for mollifying a lobby group whose measure is tied up in committee, for it demonstrates that something is being done, even though it usually comes to naught.

The Amending Process

An amendment is a proposal to make a change in a bill, resolution, or motion under consideration. In addition, existing law is changed through passage of "amendatory" bills. The legislative process contains several junctures at which measures may be amended: in committee, on second reading, in the committee of the whole, or on third reading. Committee amendments are actually more in the nature of recommendations, since they do not become a part of the bill until adopted by the house to which they have been reported. Amendment of bills and resolutions on third reading, preceding the vote on passage, is comparatively rare and, where permitted, may require the unanimous consent of the membership or other special action. The amending process is most important in committee, on second reading, or—in those legislatures which make extensive use of the device—in the committee of the whole.

The crucial vote in the history of many measures occurs not on final passage but on amendment. Major bills typically will invite tens of amendments, many of which will be offered in committee, with others to follow on the floor. Normally, the chairman of the committee reporting the bill will manage it when it reaches the floor. While it is hazardous to predict the fate of a bill on the floor, an influential chairman and a powerful and respected committee ordinarily can withstand the onslaught of amendments which would significantly alter their measure.

A good example of a committee's power to resist floor amendments, even in the face of pressure exerted by the president and party leaders, is shown in House action on a foreign-aid bill some years ago. The plea of the chairman of the House Committee on Foreign Affairs, which had cut more than a billion dollars from the program, went as follows:

> Here they are, the former Speaker of the House and the present Speaker of the House, who have said time after time how they loved this House and how they would fight to preserve the integrity of this House, leading this fight to repudiate what a committee, an arm of this House has done.
>
> ...Instead of building up the prestige of this House and its committee today, I feel that our leaders are contributing to the tearing down of that prestige because they are surrendering to the executive department. In this I hope the membership here will not follow them.[26]

The House upheld its committee and the cuts were not restored. Committees short on prestige or unrepresentative of the chamber's outlook are not likely to fare so well.

Amendments are not always what they seem. They represent ways both

---

[26] *Congressional Record*, CII (June 7, 1956), 9830–31. As quoted by Holbert Carroll, *The House of Representatives and Foreign Affairs* (Pittsburgh: University of Pittsburgh Press, 1966), p. 334.

of perfecting bills and of undermining them. Weeks and months of study and planning may precede their introduction, or, in the case of occasional floor amendments, only a few minutes. The alterations they impose may be so slight as to involve nothing much more than a change in language, or so drastic as to effect total substitution. Sponsors may number one or a dozen or more, perhaps representing both parties, and may include members who fully intend to vote for the bill on final passage and those who intend to oppose it. Every now and then a bill is amended to such an extent that the sponsor is forced to vote against his "own" bill. The reverse of this is the sponsor who is willing to accept virtually any alterations in order to get his bill passed, unmindful of the changing substance of his proposal.

Despite the frequency with which amendments are offered on the floor, the amending process is not wide open. The Rules Committee of the U.S. House of Representatives, as we have seen, may bring out a "gag rule" providing that amendments may be introduced only by members from the committee which handled the bill, acting with the consent of a majority of the committee. Tax legislation in the House is customarily brought to the floor under such a closed rule. Since they circumscribe the range of choice on the floor, closed rules often are opposed as undemocratic; yet their existence is recognition of the fact that a single amendment, perhaps innocuous to all appearances, can easily mangle a bill. Carelessly written amendments passed in haste are a similar peril to measures. Thus, in the 86th Congress, Representative Frank Smith of Mississippi introduced a sixty-two-word amendment to a minimum-wage bill, which, following a one-minute explanation, was adopted by a voice vote. A day later it was discovered that the amendment's language served to exclude 14 million out of 24 million workers who were then covered by the wage-and-hour act. The way it happened, Representative Smith explained, was:

> I picked up a piece of paper on the [House] floor and wrote it out quickly in order to get it in the bill and exempt those agricultural workers who have been exempt but now are being ruled into wage-hour provisions by the wage-hour administrator. The House Labor Committee knew what I was trying to do, but I just didn't get the right language. Maybe I should have let a lobbyist write it.[27]

The House finally discovered its mistake, but the error was sufficient to jeopardize the bill's chances for passage.

A favorite gambit in attacking a bill is to "perfect" or amend it to death. Under this plan, amendment after amendment is submitted to the bill, ostensibly to make it a "better" bill. With each amendment a new group can be antagonized and brought into opposition to the bill. Nor is it very difficult to make a bill unworkable, even ridiculous. Thus the president of the Illinois Retail Merchants Association succeeded in getting a committee in the Illinois House to adopt an amendment to a minimum-wage bill, a measure he vigorously opposed, setting up a $500,000 fund to be used in enforcement of the law. This move was calculated to stimulate new opposition to the bill.[28] A variation on this strategy was used in Connecticut when

[27] *New York Times,* July 4, 1960, p. 4.
[28] *Chicago Sun-Times,* April 10, 1957, p. 35.

254 a primary bill was before the legislature. It came a cropper, however, as Lockard explains:

> Probably the law would never have passed, however, had it not been for the misfiring of the "improve-it-to-death" weapon. This technique involves the amendment of a bill in one chamber so as to "improve" it (by making its restrictions more rigorous or its terms more inclusive), always in the hope that the other side will not accept the changes. Then the last side to pass the bill can piously point to their "record" of having passed the "best" bill which the other chamber defeated. In just this manner the primary bill made five trips between the two Houses before it was passed in the same form by both.[29]

Crippling amendments, extreme in scope, were offered to the Atomic Energy Act of 1946. They included provisions to require the death penalty for violation of secrecy stipulations and to provide for FBI investigation of the "character and associations" of all employees and contractors involved in the program, each of which would add an additional weight to the bill.[30] A final example of this common practice appears in the struggle to prevent repeal of prohibition in Oklahoma, where "dry" leaders in the lower house almost succeeded in amending a repeal referendum, hoping to kill it by adding a provision which put the state itself into the liquor-store business.[31] Many a bill has been put to death by a carefully drawn and skillfully maneuvered amendment.

A recurrent and vexatious problem posed for sponsors is to determine when to accept amendments and when to resist them. An effective floor manager needs to be able to anticipate, and incorporate if possible, those amendments likely to pull a majority vote, since a defeat on one amendment sometimes leads to an avalanche of additional amendments, each one difficult to overcome. New support for a measure or consolidation of initial strength is often to be won by the prudent acceptance of an amendment—a "sweetener," as it is sometimes called. Usually a "sweetener" amendment provides for the exclusion of some group from the provisions of a bill, such as exempting a certain group of workers from coverage under minimum-wage legislation. Moreover, good strategy may at times dictate the acceptance of an amendment even though the sponsor has the votes to defeat it, Roland Young suggests, "for in the long run the friendship and good will of the opposition may be more valuable than securing a legislative victory...."[32]

Amendments whose chances on the floor are nonexistent nevertheless are often introduced as a means of recording a personal or party position on a bill. This is illustrated in the following remarks by the Democratic minority leader in the Pennsylvania Senate at the time a sales tax bill was under consideration.

29 Lockard, *op. cit.*, p. 284.
30 Byron S. Miller, "A Law is Passed—The Atomic Energy Act of 1946," *University of Chicago Law Review*, XV (Summer 1948), 815.
31 Robert S. Walker and Samuel C. Patterson, *Oklahoma Goes Wet: The Repeal of Prohibition* (New York: McGraw-Hill Book Company, Inc., Eagleton Cases in Practical Politics, 1960), p. 17.
32 *The American Congress* (New York: Harper & Row, Publishers, 1958), p. 143.

[If] the gentlemen will tell me that they are not intending to take any amendments offered today, we will go through the motion of presenting the amendments to make the record clear and let it [rest] at that stage. If the amendments that we are offering are not to be considered on the basis of the merits of them, then we will offer the amendments, have them voted down by the Republican side and, at least, make the record for the future.[33]

An additional quirk of the amending process requires discussion: the legislative rider. As its name hints, it refers to an irrelevant amendment—one which is tacked onto a bill which is well on its way to passage. Unlikely to make it on its own for one reason or another, the amendment rides into law as a part of another measure. Typically, a rider is attached to an appropriation bill, and there is good reason for this choice. The chief executive who lacks the item veto—as do about a dozen governors and the president—must accept the whole bill, including the rider, or accept none of it. In the case of a rider attached to an agency appropriation bill, enormous pressures are generated to accept the bill, rider and all, rather than to jeopardize a program. Under such circumstances, it is an unusual chief executive who thinks twice about rejecting the bill, despite a repugnant and irrelevant rider.

Congress, of course, is mindful of the abuses associated with riders, and the House in particular is likely to quash an amendment which is not germane to a bill under consideration. The temptation to resort to a rider is strong, however, when no other possibility seems likely to succeed. The chief offender tends to be the Senate, even though it attempted to reform itself in 1946 by outlawing riders attached to appropriations bills. Budget bills for the District of Columbia regularly have served as vehicles for riders. The Fair Trade Act, nationwide in scope, was hooked onto a District of Columbia bill and accepted reluctantly by President Roosevelt in order not to hamstring the municipal government of Washington, D.C.[34] Riders are likely to be resisted, however, if their adoption may appear to imperil the legislation at hand. Thus, in 1971, the Senate defeated a rider to the 18-year-old voting rights amendment that would have granted the District of Columbia full voting representation in Congress; a number of senators who favored D.C. representation opposed the rider in the belief that its inclusion would jeopardize the amendment. The familiar interpretation of riders characterizes them as evasive, underhanded, and, in degree, even dangerous; however that may be, Congress has given its tacit consent to their use, a point readily verified in roll-call votes.

Debate

THE UNITED STATES SENATE

In the traditions of the Senate, no rule or practice has seemed more firmly rooted or drawn more discussion, much of it contentious, than that of "unlimited" debate. The tradition insists on the right to free and unlimited

---

[33] *Pennsylvania Legislative Journal,* March 19, 1957, p. 782.
[34] Estes Kefauver and Jack Levin, *A Twentieth-Century Congress* (New York: Duell, Sloan & Pearce, 1957), pp. 53–55.

debate for members, even at the cost of freedom to act and to govern. The extreme of unlimited debate is the filibuster. This term refers to the tactical efforts employed by a minority to prevent the majority from making a decision. Its essence is obstruction, its tactics dilatory. Weapons are also available in the parliamentary arsenal to slow down action. Quorum calls are a particularly handy weapon of obstruction, as are amendments introduced in great quantity.

The "rule" of unlimited debate in the Senate has not always been a fixture in the chamber's practice; in the formative years of the government it posed only an occasional problem. The first rules adopted by the Senate made provision for the "previous question," requiring only a majority vote to bring debate to an end and to effect a vote. Shortly after the turn of the nineteenth century, Senate rules were revamped and the previous-question provision was dropped. Free and unfettered debate thus became a possibility from that time onward, although it did not emerge as a major issue until 1841 when Henry Clay found his fiscal bills thwarted by a Democratic filibuster. Clay sought to have the Senate adopt the hour rule for limiting debate, an innovation in the House at the time, but his efforts were unproductive. A few more attempts were made to limit Senate debate in the late decades of the nineteenth century, but none was successful in the slightest and few were considered even seriously.[35] Throughout this period (indeed to the present day), the Senate rules carried the admonition: "No one is to speak impertinently, or beside the question, superfluously or tediously." But virtually all members on occasion did, and filibusters grew in volume and disputatiousness. Slowly the lines were being drawn for a battle over talk in the Senate.

Prefaced by preliminary sparring in the first decade of the twentieth century, the main battle over unlimited debate was fought in 1917. At stake was President Wilson's proposal to arm merchant ships. The bill passed the House handily but ran into opposition and a well-organized filibuster in the Senate. Stymied by the filibuster of a hostile band of eleven senators, President Wilson strongly attacked the Senate. It is, he said, "the only legislative body in the world which cannot act when its majority is ready for action. A little group of willful men, representing no opinion but their own, have rendered the great government of the United States helpless and contemptible." The way out of this impasse, President Wilson continued, "is that the rules of the Senate shall be so altered that it can act. The country can be relied on to draw the moral. I believe that the Senate can be relied on to supply the means of action and save the country from disaster."[36]

With a large majority of the Senate in favor of the president's recommendation to arm merchant ships, and with public resentment against the filibusterers running high, the Senate moved to adopt its first cloture rule since 1789. Less than a week following Wilson's statement, it had fashioned a rule to limit debate, but its concession was one of expediency and of little consequence. Henceforth, the new rule (rule 22) provided, debate could be brought to an end when certain conditions were met: (1) sixteen senators

[35] Lindsay Rogers, *The American Senate* (New York: Appleton-Century-Crofts, Inc., 1931), pp. 165–67.

[36] Quoted in George H. Haynes, *The Senate of the United States* (Boston: Houghton Mifflin Company, 1938), p. 403.

must sign and present a petition calling for termination of debate, (2) a period of two days should elapse prior to a vote, and (3) two-thirds of the senators *voting* would have to agree that further debate on the question be foreclosed. Having adopted the motion, no senator could speak more than one hour on the measure, dilatory motions and amendments were ruled out, and points of order would be decided without debate. Debate ended following the last one-hour presentation.

In theory, the Senate had now fastened a shackle on its right to talk, but, in fact, nothing of the sort had happened. The proof lies in the record. Between 1917 and 1949, nineteen cloture motions were filed, but only four, all coming in the first ten years of the rule, were approved by the requisite two-thirds vote. In 1948, rule 22 became further enfeebled when Senator Arthur Vandenberg (R., Mich.), acting as president *pro tem,* ruled that cloture could not be applied to a *motion* to call up a measure, only to the measure itself. Under this ruling, a group bent on filibustering a bill need only launch its drive earlier, on the motion to call up a bill, and the Senate would be powerless to invoke even its mild cloture provision.

In 1949 there were further efforts to liberalize the cloture rule. The first step was taken by the Senate Rules Committee, which recommended that rule 22 be amended to provide that all matters brought before the Senate, including the troublesome motions, be made subject to cloture. The intent of the change was to undo the damage done by the Vandenberg ruling. Adding irony to injustice, at least as the liberals saw it, the motion to take up the proposed amendment to the rules became the focus of a new southern filibuster. After many days of desultory argument, Vice-President Barkley sought to break the obstruction by ruling that a motion to consider a measure was covered by the cloture rule quite as fully as a measure itself, a reversal of the Vandenberg position. In an extremely close vote, a coalition of southern Democrats and northern Republicans overturned the Barkley holding, and the filibuster droned on. Then, having thwarted the efforts of the Rules Committee and the majority leadership, the coalition produced its own version of a cloture rule. It was adopted by a vote of 63–23.

The coalition's "compromise" rule was, in fact, no compromise at all. Although it provided that motions and other pending business would be subject to cloture, which had been the immediate objective of the liberals, it tightened up other requirements. Two important changes were introduced.

The first provided that the two-thirds requirement for closing debate be based on *total membership* rather than on those present and voting, which at that time would require sixty-four votes. A senator absent from the chamber would in effect represent a negative vote on cloture. The second alteration, at least as significant, provided that cloture would not apply to any motion to consider a change of rules; a motion to take up such a resolution would thus become an invitation to filibuster. Plainly, the 1949 amendment strengthened the conservative hand in the Senate.

During the 1950s, pressure grew steadily for a change in rule 22. Efforts to adopt a new rule were unsuccessful until the "liberal tide" running in the 1958 congressional elections brought a new group of Democratic senators to Washington. Well before the Senate convened in 1959, some members were demanding that a new cloture rule be passed, and it became apparent that strong pressure for a change would be exerted. The anti-

258 filibuster bloc based its strategy on the holding that each new Senate has the right to adopt new rules by a simple majority vote. Their new rules would, of course, include an amended rule 22. Conservative opponents, mainly southerners, were equally insistent that the Senate is "a continuing body," since two-thirds of its membership carries over to each new Congress. If the membership carries over, their argument ran, the rules of the preceding Congress similarly carry over, and hence a motion to adopt a new set of rules would not be in order.

The outcome of the 1959 hassle was unsatisfactory to the antifilibuster forces. The liberal position that each Senate may alter its rules at the beginning of a new Congress was handily defeated. The Senate then rejected the principal reform proposal, authored by Senator Paul Douglas (D., Ill.), which provided that cloture could be imposed by a two-thirds majority of those present and voting after two days of debate, or by a simple majority after fifteen days of debate. It also rejected a plan by Senator Thruston Morton (R., Ky.) under which debate could be halted by a three-fifths majority of those present and voting.

The issue was settled, if only temporarily, by the acceptance of a plan advanced by Democratic majority leader Lyndon Johnson. The Johnson plan of 1959 became the Senate's third cloture rule of the twentieth century, its fourth in history. Passed by a vote of 72–22, with the hard core of Democratic and Republican liberals as well as a few southerners (for different reasons) opposed to it, the amended rule bore a close resemblance to the 1917 rule. It carries three provisions: (1) as in the 1917 rule, two-thirds of the senators *present and voting* may now order cloture, (2) cloture may be brought to bear on motions to change the rules, thereby removing the "perpetuity" feature of the 1949 amendment, and (3) the Senate is designated as "a continuing body," which means that its rules carry over from one session to the next. The first two provisions make it slightly easier to break a filibuster, while the last, a concession to the South, will impede efforts to gain a more liberal cloture rule. This is true because the key to the strategy of the antifilibuster group is the interpretation that the Senate is not a continuing body and is, therefore, free to adopt new rules by *majority* vote at the opening of any Congress. Efforts to fashion a new cloture rule have occurred at the opening of each new Congress since the Johnson proposal was adopted, but each time the bipartisan liberal bloc has lost. During Senate consideration of the proposed legislative reorganization act of 1967, an unsuccessful attempt was made to repeal rule 22 and to substitute a provision empowering a majority to close debate after fifteen hours of debate on a motion or amendment, or after fifteen days on a measure. Many senators who earlier had supported efforts to modify rule 22 opposed this amendment on the ground that its adoption would jeopardize passage of the reorganization bill itself.[37]

RECENT CLOTURE VOTES

For the first time in thirty-five years and the fifth time in history, the Senate in 1962 adopted a cloture motion, by a vote of 63–27. At stake was a bill to

---

[37] *Congressional Record,* 90th Cong., 1st sess., March 2, 1967, pp. 2989–92. (Daily edition.)

establish a private corporation to develop, launch, and manage communications satellites such as Telstar. Opponents of the bill, a small band of liberal Democrats, contended that the bill was a "monstrous giveaway" (since private industry would benefit from the extensive research and development already financed by the government), that the corporation would be dominated by the American Telephone and Telegraph Company, and that a better solution would be government leasing or ownership. Two weeks after the liberals' filibuster began, the cloture motion was adopted.

Among those senators who have opposed attempts to curtail debate in the past, unlimited debate often has been justified as a principle of governing designed to protect *any* minority and to give each member the full opportunity to have his say. In the language of its traditional supporters, unlimited debate was not simply a parliamentary safeguard but also something of a moral principle, sustained by a validity that could not be compromised. What the remarkable cloture vote in 1962 demonstrates more clearly than anything else is that for many senators unlimited debate is much less a "principle" than a weapon. Whether unlimited debate is a good thing seems to depend mainly on whose chestnuts are in the fire.

The best evidence for this interpretation is the vote itself, in which all groups compromised something. Most noteworthy was the behavior of Republicans and certain southern Democrats. Republican members, who in the past consistently had favored unlimited speech when the issue was civil rights (citing grounds of "principle" rather than policy), voted to curtail it when the issue was one of private ownership versus government ownership. Similarly, five southern Democrats who had always opposed cloture were conspicuously absent at the time of the roll call, making it easier to secure the necessary two-thirds vote; their absence, like the new-found Republican support for cloture, was critical. Another mixed group of senators, hoping to cast their votes on "principle," abstained from voting until the outcome was certain. Finally, a number of liberals exposed themselves to charges of compromise by using the filibuster weapon they had criticized in the past.

The 1962 cloture decision demonstrated that the Senate can break a filibuster if it is determined to do so. One southern senator remarked at the time that the vote was like "getting olives out of the bottle—after the first the rest come easy." Two years later, in 1964, the Senate for the first time in history adopted a cloture motion to limit debate on a civil rights bill. The vote came after a seventy-five-day filibuster, the longest since the cloture rule was adopted in 1917. In 1965 a cloture motion was adopted on another civil rights bill, the Voting Rights Act. Most recently, cloture was successful in 1968 on an open-housing bill and in 1971 on a bill to extend the draft. Between 1917 and 1972, of fifty-eight cloture votes taken, only nine were adopted.[38] Despite the several successes of recent years, opponents of rule 22 continue to press insistently for its modification.

EVALUATING UNLIMITED DEBATE

Many famous filibusters have caught the attention of the nation, particularly those which involved spectacular achievements in individual endurance. In

[38] See a listing of cloture votes in the *Congressional Quarterly Weekly Report,* September 25, 1971, p. 1975

the *tour de force* class are Robert La Follette's eighteen-hour speech against a currency bill in 1908, Huey Long's wild and irrelevant filibuster of over fifteen hours in 1935 on the National Recovery Administration, Wayne Morse's speech of twenty-two hours and twenty-six minutes on the offshore oil bill in 1953, and J. Strom Thurmond's record-making denunciation (twenty-four hours and eighteen minutes) of a civil rights bill in 1957.[39] Long's speech, which was sometimes germane to the subject, is best remembered for the recipes he gave for southern style cooking and "pot-likker." Morse's and Thurmond's talks, on the other hand, stayed surprisingly close to the subject.

While one-man filibusters are effective in dramatizing an issue and focusing public attention on Washington, they rarely accomplish very much. Far more significant is the effort of a team of senators intent on bringing the legislative process to a halt unless their demands are met, which usually means the abandonment of a bill. With proper attention to organization, a determined, cohesive, and resourceful group can keep the Senate at a standstill for weeks on end, as southern members have done when civil rights legislation has been called up. Often as effective as a filibuster in frustrating majority intentions is the threat to start one. If made near the end of the session—when work is piled high on members' desks and the chamber is driving for adjournment—it may force the majority to drop an "offensive" bill in order not to jeopardize other proposals.

The durability of rule 22, Raymond Wolfinger has argued, is due largely to the fact that filibusters are likely to occur on only a narrow range of issues. Indeed, for the most part, filibusters have been reserved for civil rights legislation. Evidence on this point appears in Table 8.1, which shows that the issues at stake in seven of the nine *conservative* filibusters between 1953 and 1968 involved civil rights. Of similar interest, the table also reveals that the prospects are strong that a filibuster will be broken if the president lends his influence to the antifilibuster forces. So much has been written about the evils of filibustering that it is easy to miss the point that from the end of World War II until 1964 "only one civil rights bill was killed chiefly by unlimited debate, the anti–poll tax bill of 1946. During the Eisenhower and Kennedy Administrations no civil rights filibuster was strongly opposed by the leadership of either party or by the Executive Branch, and no cloture vote won even a simple majority."[40]

Although evidence accumulates year after year that a majority of the Senate either likes rule 22 or at least is prepared to live with it, the issue continues to excite controversy. The principle of unlimited debate finds a good many supporters, not all of whom, by any means, are southerners. How is it viewed? What can be said for it? What are its dangers? The answers are

[39] For the first time in his Senate career, Senator Thurmond voted for cloture in 1971 on a draft extension bill. "I still support the right of unlimited debate," he said. "It is essential to protect the rights of minority views." His vote for cloture on the draft bill, he told the Senate, was based "on the ground of national security." Six other southern senators who had never supported a cloture motion also voted for it on this issue. *New York Times,* June 24, 1971, p. 8.

[40] Raymond E. Wolfinger, "Filibusters: Majority Rule, Presidential Leadership, and Senate Norms," in *Readings on Congress,* ed. Raymond E. Wolfinger (Englewood Cliffs, N.J.: Prentice-Hall, Inc., 1971), pp. 286–305, quotation on pp. 300–301.

TABLE 8.1

Conservative Filibusters Against Liberal Legislation, 1953–68

Year	Bill	Cloture Vote	Votes Needed for Cloture	Presidential Pressure	Cloture Imposed
1960	Civil Rights	42–53	64	low	no
1962	Restrict Literacy Tests	43–53	64	low	no
1964	Civil Rights	71–29	67	high	yes
1965	Voting Rights	70–30	67	high	yes
1965	Repeal Section 14(b)*	45–47	62	low	no
1966	Repeal Section 14(b)*	51–48	66	low	no
1966	Civil Rights	54–42	64	high	no
1966	D.C. Home Rule	41–37	52	low	no
1968	Open Housing	65–32	65	high	yes

Source: Raymond E. Wolfinger, "Filibusters: Majority Rule, Presidential Leadership, and Senate Norms," in *Readings on Congress*, ed. Raymond E. Wolfinger (Englewood Cliffs, N.J.: Prentice-Hall, Inc., 1971), p. 296.

Note: Data covers only filibusters on which a cloture petition was filed and excludes nonlegislative issues such as rules reform and the Fortas confirmation.

*Section 14(b) of the Taft-Hartley Act permits states to adopt right-to-work laws.

a matter of opinion, as the following appraisals show:

Estes Kefauver and Jack Levin: It is a privilege that leads to prostitution of the vital deliberative function and results in spectacular filibusters that at times have brought the entire legislative machinery of the Congress to a complete halt.[41]

William S. White: [Those] who mock the Institution, and demand of it "speed" and yet more speed and "efficiency" and yet more efficiency, might remember that there is altogether a good deal of both at present in American life. For illustration, those who denounce the filibuster against, say, the compulsory civil rights program, might recall that the weapon has more than one blade and that today's pleading minority could become tomorrow's arrogant majority.[42]

James M. Burns: That a handful of men can deadlock our legislative machinery is one of the marvels of American government. But considering the power of minority groups in Congress, it is hardly surprising that the filibuster and other devices, buttressed by elaborate parliamentary rules, are still used to obstruct the majority. For those devices are the logical extension —although to a new height of absurdity—of the instruments of minority control. . . .[43]

Lindsay Rogers: Advocates of restrictions on debate rest their case on the clichés of democracy, and transform government by a majority from an imperfect device into an eternal principle. They completely overlook the

[41] Kefauver and Levin, *op. cit.*, p. 33.

[42] *Citadel* (New York: Harper & Row, Publishers, 1956), p. 19.

[43] Burns, *Congress on Trial* (New York: Harper & Row, Publishers, 1949), p. 61.

fact that even if filibustering minorities kill some meritorious legislation and treaties, the price will be a small one to pay for retaining some measure of legislative control of the executive.[44]

Robert Luce: Many of the wise men who have served in the Senate have come to believe...that it is important that there should be one place in the legislative journey where the opportunity for discussion is unfettered. They have found that this has not in the end prevented any decisions persistently wanted by the people, but on the other hand has stood in the way of much action that the country has come to conclude would have been unwise.[45]

Howard E. Shuman: Some [writers] like *New York Times* correspondent William S. White in his book on the Senate, *Citadel,* have argued that unlimited debate is needed to protect minority rights and prevent a ruthless temporary majority from acting too fast. If our states had unitary systems; if urban groups were fairly represented in their legislatures; if seats in the House of Representatives were not gerrymandered; if the Senate were based on population; if there were no system of checks and balances; if the seniority system did not exist; and if committees and their chairmen were more representative; then a good case might be made for unlimited debate. But in existing circumstances fears of a ruthless temporary majority are wholly unfounded. The real problem is the opposite—the power of permanent, regional minorities.[46]

Senator J. W. Fulbright: Some issues—such as civil rights and war-making power—arise in our kind of governmental community that need time for delay and consideration so that a compromise can be worked out. A simple majority...should not have the right to impose a decision on a significant minority.... We have to be extremely careful not to give up what few powers the legislative branch has, and to resist this enormous increase in the power of the executive, and to keep balance within our constitutional system. To that end I think rule 22 is an extremely important element.[47]

Washington Post *editorial:* In many respects the filibuster is the most intolerable carryover from an easy-going and uncomplicated past. As it now operates, it only prevents Congress from getting its work done. Again and again it results in minority decisions because a few senators can kill vital measures by long-windedness. Unlimited debate has become only another name for frustration and defeat of the will of the majority. It is an undemocratic practice which threatens to drag our entire system into disrepute.[48]

The search for a formula with which to break the hold of filibustering takes place with the approach of each new Congress. Securing a practical cloture rule has been difficult for a variety of reasons. One is the sheer problem of altering any major rule of the chamber. The Senate, like many other legislative bodies, always has been reluctant to modify its historic ways—

44 Rogers, *op. cit.,* p. 6.
45 Luce, *op. cit.,* pp. 24–25.
46 "What's the Matter with Congress?" *The New Republic,* April 1, 1957, p. 16.
47 *Congressional Quarterly Weekly Report,* February 19, 1971, p. 416, and March 5, 1971, p. 510.
48 *Washington Post,* January 7, 1971.

not simply because they are "historic," of course, but because they are congenial to established power arrangements.[49] A second reason is that unlimited debate has had special and traditional significance for the Senate: this is perhaps its most distinguishing characteristic. In no legislative body anywhere has the right to talk been so fully or so zealously guarded. Third, unlimited debate and civil rights legislation are now so intimately joined that any move to liberalize the cloture rule is viewed by southerners as a precursor to new civil rights legislation. In previous eras liberals made fully as much use of the filibuster as did conservatives; today the weapon is employed mainly by conservatives whose center of strength is the South. There is a final explanation to the lasting power of the filibuster which runs like this: some senators who do not approve of the interests which presently are served by the filibuster nevertheless are reluctant to see it checked, thereby eliminating any future possibility that they themselves might use it. To add a footnote to this, it is a well-recorded fact that certain senators who have condemned the practice of filibustering later have found occasion to engage in it.

Southern power and unlimited debate in the Senate are tightly linked and widely acknowledged. A parry and riposte between Senator Sam Ervin of North Carolina and former Illinois Senator Paul Douglas suggests how it all came about:

> Senator Ervin. It takes 34 Senators to prevent cloture under existing rules of the Senate. Unfortunately for the country we have only 22 Senators from the South when none of us secede from the Confederacy.
>
> Senator Douglas. May I say I don't wish to get into a prolonged discussion on this point, but I have always noticed a close degree of cohesion of the Senators from south of the Mason-Dixon line, whereas those of us from other sections of the country are more dispersed. I remember how Cortez took Mexico, I think, and Pizarro took Peru with very small groups, because they were united and the others were diffused. Sometimes I think that this is what has happened after the late unpleasantness—that the South has taken possession of the legislative branch of both House and Senate. And I may say as individual gentlemen you are very fine.
>
> Senator Ervin. In other words, you love us individually but sometimes you deplore our actions collectively.
>
> Senator Douglas. I think the Senate is the South's revenge for Appomattox.[50]

THE U.S. HOUSE OF REPRESENTATIVES

In their treatment of time the House and the Senate are wholly unlike. On the one hand is the Senate, casual in its rules and concerned with maintaining its tradition of free and unlimited debate; in counterpoise is the House, brisk and punctilious toward its legislative schedule with its rigid system for processing legislation. It is this difference, more than anything

---

[49] See Joseph S. Clark, *The Senate Establishment* (New York: Hill and Wang, 1963).

[50] *Hearings on Civil Rights—1957* before the Subcommittee on Constitutional Rights of the Committee on the Judiciary, Senate, 85th Cong., 1st sess., 1957, p. 114.

else, which distinguishes the procedures of the two chambers. Legislation may be held back in the House, it is true, but as a result of committee action or inaction, not as the consequence of a slowdown on the floor. Measures which reach the floor of the House shortly meet their fate, for there is very little opportunity to defer action or obstruct decisions.

A number of House rules combine to place restrictions on debate and to limit the possibilities for rear-guard delaying tactics. Major legislation normally comes to the floor by a special order of the Rules Committee specifying the time to be allocated to the measure. Special rules look like this:

> *Resolved,* That upon the adoption of this resolution it shall be in order to move that the House resolve itself into the Committee of the Whole House on the State of the Union for the consideration of the bill (H.R. 7435) to reauthorize construction by the Secretary of the Interior of Farwell unit, Nebraska, of the Missouri River Basin project. After general debate, which shall be confined to the bill, and shall continue not to exceed one hour, to be equally divided and controlled by the chairman and ranking minority member of the Committee on Interior and Insular Affairs, the bill shall be read for amendment under the five-minute rule. At the conclusion of the consideration of the bill for amendment, the Committee shall rise and report the bill to the House with such amendments as may have been adopted, and the previous question shall be considered as ordered on the bill and amendments thereto to final passage without intervening motion except one motion to recommit.

By adopting the resolution, the House approves the terms under which the measure will be considered.

House debate is abridged in yet other ways. Unless exception is made, "general debate" on a measure by an individual member is confined to one hour. Under "suspension of the rules," a period of forty minutes is set aside for debate. The "five-minute" rule in committee of the whole restricts a member to a five-minute presentation on an amendment, unless consent is given for a brief extension of time.[51] The formal technique for cutting off debate in the House is to move the "previous question," a highly privileged motion. In use since 1811, the previous question permits a majority of those voting to end debate, after which the House advances immediately to a vote on the pending matter. The previous question is used to close debate on amendments and on final passage of a measure.

Opportunities to delay action on the floor of the House of Representatives are not as numerous today as they were in an earlier era, and neither are the parliamentary means as potent. An effective device to forestall action formerly used by members called for them to remain silent when a quorum call was held, and without a quorum the chamber was powerless to act. This

---

[51] A member who wishes to secure the floor for five minutes to discuss a section of a bill may utilize a *pro forma* amendment, a parliamentary move under which he can record his views. Thus a member will rise and say, "I move to strike out the last word," after which he is permitted to talk for five minutes. Normally, an opponent will then obtain the floor by stating, "I rise in opposition to the *pro forma* amendment," and deliver a five-minute talk. The *pro forma* amendment is a device for entering debate and has no substantive significance.

practice was broken in 1890 when Speaker Thomas Reed, over the vigorous objections of the Democrats, began to count as present any members who sat silent in their seats.[52] His practice was later made a part of the House rules. Also contributing to the death knell of filibustering in the House was the innovation during Reed's tenure that dilatory motions would not be entertained by the Speaker. By then, the "country at large, and the leaders of both parties, had wearied of the spectacle of a minority, of even a single member, defying the majority and effectively blocking legislation, and they were united in the belief that a radical reform must be brought about."[53] The rigorous and controversial "Reed rules" achieved such reform; at the same time, they laid the groundwork for a major shift in power to the Speaker.

Prior to the Legislative Reorganization Act of 1970, any individual member of the House could insist that the *Journal* be read in full—a tactic designed to delay proceedings or possibly to force action on some measure. Under the new rules, the *Journal* is to be read only if ordered by the Speaker or by a majority of the members present.

While filibustering is not unknown in the House today, it is but a slim shadow of its former self. Bent on delaying a vote, members can still resort to quorum calls and demand roll-call votes; they can offer amendments designed to stall proceedings; they can seek a recess or attempt to adjourn the chamber. Such efforts, however, are of minimal avail. Delay is brief and inconclusive, and soon the House is back on schedule.

THE NATURE AND FUNCTION OF DEBATE IN CONGRESS

In the judgment of a number of critics, debate in the Senate is superior to debate in the House. Whenever it is suggested that meaningful controls should be placed on Senate debate to curb filibustering, for example, the response is likely to be a variation of Lindsay Rogers's view that the Senate would "gradually sink to the level of the House of Representatives where there is less deliberation and debate than in any other legislative assembly."[54] As to the character of debate in the House, a former congressman writes: "While short tenure limits the foresight of the House, the unwieldy size of the body has muted its voice. As in most large assemblies, debate in the House is controlled to the point where much of the discussion is not debate at all but a series of set speeches."[55]

From knowledge of the "unlimited speech" tradition in the Senate, it is a natural step to conclude that debate ranges more freely and that questions of public policy are explored more fully there than in the House. Although this may indeed be true, rigorous supporting evidence is hard to find. There is a great deal of talk in each house, but there is very little "debate"—in the sense of direct and immediate confrontations over issues between adversaries—in either house. Like the House, the Senate devotes

---

[52] For a colorful description of the tempest occasioned by Reed's ruling on this and other filibustering practices, see Fuller, *op. cit.*, pp. 218–32.

[53] *Ibid.*, p. 230.

[54] Rogers, *op. cit.*, p. 6.

[55] Stewart L. Udall, "A Congressman Defends the House," *New York Times Magazine,* January 12, 1958, p. 69.

266 substantial time not to "debate" but to set speeches, and these often are poorly attended, indifferently received, and frequently interrupted. Moreover, much time is given over to questioning, often only for the purpose of assisting the speaker to emphasize a point. Colloquies on the floor may be helpful, informative, humorous, or caustic, but most do not impart a strong sense of "debate." The following examples show certain dimensions—of humor and acrimony—on the Senate floor.

> Mr. Dirksen. Mr. President, I do not know what impeachments have to do with satellites. I do not know why we have to go back to 1867.
>
> That reminds me of a story. A man went into a restaurant, sat down, and asked "What kind of soup do you have?"
>
> The waiter replied, "Oxtail."
>
> The customer said, "Oh, why go back that far?" [Laughter.]
>
> We are dealing with satellites now.
>
> Mr. Morse. Mr. President, will the Senator from Illinois yield?[56]
>
> .   .   .
>
> Mr. Lausche. (D., Ohio) Mr. President, I heard the comment made by the Senator from Tennessee that the question of aggression is one of doubt, and that it might well be said that the United States is the aggressor.
>
> Mr. Gore. (D., Tenn.) Mr. President, will the Senator yield?
>
> Mr. Lausche. I yield.
>
> Mr. Gore. I said aggression might be subject to debate. I did not say "it might well be said." I indicated that some people might say it.
>
> Mr. Lausche. Does the Senator make the statement that the United States is the aggressor?
>
> Mr. Mansfield. (D., Mont.) No, the Senator was just citing a hypothetical case.
>
> Mr. Lausche. Let the Senator speak for himself.
>
> Mr. Gore. The Senator from Tennessee does not propose to permit the Senator from Ohio to put words in his mouth, and then be interrogated thereon. If I have a statement to make, I shall make it without the assistance of inquiry from the Senator from Ohio.
>
> Mr. Lausche. My position is that the North Vietnamese are the aggressors, and I should like to ask the Senator from Tennessee whether he is, either expressly or impliedly, stating that the United States is the aggressor.
>
> Mr. Gore. Mr. President, in the first place, it is contrary to the rules of the Senate for one Senator, having the floor, to interrogate another Senator who has not the floor.
>
> Mr. Mansfield. The Senator is correct.
>
> Mr. Gore. I resent the Senator from Ohio undertaking to place in the mouth of the Senator from Tennessee statements which he did not make, and then

[56] *Congressional Record,* 87th Cong., 2d sess., July 31, 1962, p. 14133. (**Daily** edition.)

proposing to ask him questions as if he had made such statements or intended so to state.

Mr. Lausche. Mr. President, if I am out of order, I will withdraw the question.

The Presiding Officer. The Senator's time has expired. Who yields time?[57]

Senate debate, writes Donald Matthews, ordinarily "lacks drama and excitement. Since most members have already made up their minds, the audience is pitifully small and often inattentive. Moreover, the senators tend to listen to the speakers with whom they agree and to absent themselves when the opposition takes the floor. The debate is not sharply focused but skips from one subject to the next in an apparently chaotic manner. 'I wonder,' one old reporter once said, 'if in the whole history of the Senate two speeches in a row ever were made on the same subject.' "[58]

Whatever impressions congressional debate may convey, it serves several distinct purposes. One function of floor talk is to help supporters of a bill communicate with one another: "Floor statements are often the quickest and most effective methods of passing the word around among other members of Congress, strengthening the cohesiveness of a group or fanning the enthusiasm of supporters." Strong speeches may also win additional votes. There are usually some members who are undecided on major bills, and "a well-oriented speech or series of speeches can often directly influence fence sitters to jump in one direction or another." Speeches may serve a strategy of delaying the vote, permitting leaders to bargain for additional support. Finally, floor talk can be useful in establishing a record for future campaigns, and it may even be consulted by the courts later as evidence of "congressional intent."[59]

THE MEMBER IN DEBATE

Not all members of a legislative body share equally in debate any more than all share equally in influence within the chamber or within their party. Party leaders, committee chairmen, and ranking members set the style and contribute a disproportionate share of the talk in the state legislatures and in Congress. They focus the debate on a measure and pick the principal speakers to be heard. The scheduling of speakers is most complete in the U.S. House of Representatives, though floor participation is ordered in some respects in all legislatures.

The practices and circumstances that affect and sometimes govern the participation of members in debate are not easily perceived by the casual observer. Legislative folkways, or traditional norms of conduct, Matthews has shown, tend to mold the interests, outlook, and behavior of members of the U.S. Senate. Many of these important, but unwritten, rules of Senate

---

[57] *Congressional Record,* 90th Cong., 1st sess., March 15, 1967, p. 3842. (Daily edition.)

[58] *U.S. Senators and Their World* (Chapel Hill: University of North Carolina Press, 1960), p. 246.

[59] Bertram Gross, *The Legislative Struggle: A Study in Social Combat* (New York: McGraw-Hill Book Company, Inc., 1953), pp. 366–67.

268 behavior relate to the participation of members in floor activity. Thus, for example, freshman senators are expected to serve an "unobtrusive apprenticeship" before engaging fully in the activities of the chamber, particularly in its debate. One long-time member of the "club" tells a story about a newcomer to the Senate who failed to observe this norm:

> When I came to the Senate, I sat next to Senator Borah. A few months later, he had a birthday. A number of the older men got up and made brief, laudatory speeches about it. Borah was pleased. Then a freshman senator— one who had only been in the chamber three or four months—got to his feet and started a similar eulogy. He was an excellent speaker. But between each of his laudatory references to Borah, Borah loudly whispered, "That son-of-a-bitch, that son-of-a-bitch." He didn't dislike the speaker personally. He just didn't feel that he should speak so soon.[60]

Other folkways relating to debate exact similar observance from senators. A personal attack by one senator upon another, though not unknown, is uncommon. Relations between members in public debate are impersonal, enforced through the rule that remarks be addressed to the presiding officer and not to any member. By observing this and related rules of courtesy, senators believe that partisanship can be kept within bounds, cooperation made possible, and disruptive personal enmities kept from developing. Another norm dictates that senators specialize in certain fields of legislation, and the senator who ranges the gamut of legislative affairs may find his influence diminished even where his recognized competence is embraced.[61]

Folkways are a potent force in shaping total Senate outlook. Nevertheless, not all senators observe them equally, for there are nonconformists in the Senate as elsewhere. Certain characteristics set mavericks apart from their colleagues. Ex-governors, especially those who represent large states, find it difficult to observe the folkway that members should not "talk too much." "The greater a man's pre-Senate accomplishments (either in or out of politics) and the greater his age at election, the less likely he is to conform."[62] Active presidential aspirants in the Senate tend to disregard the rule that senators should maintain a high degree of specialization in legislation; their political ambitions impel them to become speechmakers on a variety of subjects. A senator who comes from a competitive two-party or large state is likely to be a nonconformist in two important respects: customarily he takes a more vigorous role in debate and speaks on a greater variety of subjects than his colleagues from smaller or less competitive states. Finally, an ideological factor is associated with nonconformity: liberal members speak far more frequently on the Senate floor than do moderates or conservatives; they also are less inclined to observe the enjoiner to specialize.

The importance of this evidence is that conformity is related to the

---

[60] Quoted by Donald R. Matthews, "The Folkways of the United States Senate: Conformity to Group Norms and Legislative Effectiveness," *American Political Science Review*, LIII (December 1959), 1066. The discussion of Senate norms respecting debate is based on this article.

[61] *Ibid.*, pp. 1067–71.

[62] *Ibid.*, p. 1079.

"legislative effectiveness" of the members. The "effective" senators, defined as those who are most successful in getting their bills passed, are distinguished by their adherence to the unwritten code of the Senate. They abide by apprenticeship rules and treat their colleagues with deference. Their policy interests are narrow and particularistic, and their contribution to debate is measured and infrequent. The nonconformists, pictured in the previous paragraph, are least "effective" in the Senate. To the senator who hopes to gain influence and esteem within the Senate and who seeks acceptance as a full-fledged member of the "club," outward conformity to the norms of the chamber is important and usually vital.

No extended argument is required to make the point that the Senate, like other human groups, has a set of fairly well-defined norms of behavior and that these are generally understood and widely shared by the members. There is also abundant evidence that the members most influential within the Senate ordinarily conform to the norms and, moreover, are chary of colleagues who do not. Ralph Huitt questions, however, whether "legislative effectiveness" can be defined in terms of "the ability to get one's bills passed." He suggests that the "Outsider" in the Senate—the member who ignores or flouts the institutional norms and who scores low on the test of "legislative effectiveness"—may meet other tests of effectiveness which are fully as important. One additional test might be the member's ability to get reelected; another might be his capacity to initiate and dramatize ideas, or to win a national audience, or to sharpen conflict and contribute to its resolution.

In Huitt's judgment, the Outsider plays a role which the Senate accepts as "legitimate"; contrary to the "spirit of accommodation" that characterizes the "Senate type," the Outsider "is notable for his determination to speak out whenever he pleases on whatever subject he chooses without regard to whether he can get any vote but his own." Rather than take his cues from the "Man of Accommodation," the Outsider looks to "his constituents and to his ideological allies across the nation. . . ." Models for today's Outsider are such former members as Robert M. La Follette of Wisconsin and George W. Norris of Nebraska.[63] In answer, Matthews argues that "the existence of systematic deviations from these norms by a few senators is consistent with a widespread recognition of them." In the norms of the Senate, the Outsider's behavior is merely tolerated—which the courtesy folkway specifies—rather than regarded as legitimate. "The Outsiders themselves," he writes, "seem to have a lurking doubt of the legitimacy of their own behavior."[64]

[63] "The Outsider in the Senate: An Alternative Role," *American Political Science Review,* LV (September 1961), 566–75, quotations from p. 571.

[64] See Matthews, "Can the 'Outsider's' Role be Legitimate?" *American Political Science Review,* LV (December 1961), 882–83; and Huitt, "On Norms, Roles and Folkways," *American Political Science Review,* LVI (March 1962), 142. The articles by Matthews and Huitt, backed up by rebuttals that venture through the intricacies of role theory and neglected thickets of prostitution (the fallen lady: legitimate or deviant role?), are uniquely interesting and instructive. Our discussion simply skims off parts of each, mainly for the purpose of examining expectations and behavior concerning the member's participation in debate. For a study of the norms of behavior and of deviant roles in the Wisconsin legislature, see Samuel C. Patterson, "The Role of the Deviant in the State Legislative System: The Wisconsin Assembly," *Western Political Quarterly,* XIV (June 1961), 460–72.

"Debate" in the states, as in Congress, is no longer a feature of the legislative process; and oratory, in the full sense of the word, is conspicuously absent. Legislative talk is composed almost entirely of "set" speeches and interrogation—of the sponsor or, if a party measure, the majority or minority floor leaders. The following colloquy illustrates a typical "debate" in the legislatures. Perhaps the facts of the matter are more difficult to establish than is ordinarily the case, but the approach is representative:

> The Speaker. Will the gentleman from Dauphin, Mr. Hocker, permit himself to be interrogated?
>
> Mr. Hocker. I shall, Mr. Speaker.
>
> Mr. Petrosky. Mr. Speaker, does the gentleman have information as to what type of highway these bridges will join?
>
> Mr. Hocker. Mr. Speaker, there are main highways on both sides of the Susquehanna River north and south. Any place they put these bridges in the area designated will connect main arteries.
>
> Mr. Petrosky. My specific question was, what type highway is it? Is it a Federal aid interstate, Federal aid primary, Federal aid secondary?
>
> Mr. Hocker. They are state highways, Mr. Speaker, that were in business before we got crazy about Federal this and Federal that.
>
> Mr. Petrosky. They are 100 per cent state highways?
>
> Mr. Hocker. Yes, sir, I am told they are.
>
> Mr. Petrosky. I thank the gentleman.
>
> Mr. Hocker. And I think they are primary highways, Mr. Petrosky.
>
> Mr. Petrosky. They are primary highways?
>
> Mr. Hocker. I think they are.
>
> Mr. Petrosky. Federal aid primary highways?
>
> Mr. Hocker. No, not Federal aid highways. These roads were built long before we depended on the Federal government to build highways in Pennsylvania.
>
> Mr. Petrosky. Are they in any category of highways for which we receive Federal aid?
>
> Mr. Hocker. Mr. Speaker, I do not think they are. I say I do not think they are. If they are, it is unbeknown to me.
>
> Mr. Petrosky. I thank the gentleman, Mr. Speaker.... This is a dangerous precedent. It has a tendency to move toward logrolling with the Highway Department projects.... I assure every Member of the House, if you pass one highway bridge project here making it mandatory for that project to be installed, then I believe every bridge project in each individual legislative district will have to be treated the same way.[65]

[65] *Pennsylvania House Legislative Journal,* May 27, 1957, p. 2190.

The impact of floor talk on members is not easily estimated. Many bills, it should be noted, are voted upon with virtually no floor discussion, in effect making the committees' deliberations and decisions final. When debate takes place, do speeches change the voting intentions of members or simply buttress the views of believers? Legislators themselves usually argue that few votes are won or lost as a consequence of floor arguments.

What has been said about the functions of debate in Congress applies equally to the state legislature. Moreover, floor debate in the legislature, as well as in Congress, is highly useful in advancing personal interests and objectives: it is a good way for members to persuade colleagues of their competence in a public policy field; it enables them to affirm a personal position or to support or back off from a party position; it presents an opportunity to gain publicity, to consolidate old support, and perhaps to attract new followers; and it permits members to marshal evidence useful in campaigns for reelection.

Although legislators contend that floor speeches do not often sway votes, they do admit that members with expert knowledge have a continuing influence on the membership. Each chamber has its battery of experts—on school legislation, banks, insurance companies, conservation, agriculture, fish and game, mental health, and other fields. When issues are of low urgency to party or factional groupings and when they do not intrude on special constituency interests, members are inclined to take their cues from other legislators whose special competence is recognized. Possibly, as one analysis shows, the expert's influence on other members is greater in the early stages, when bills are shaped and considered in committee, than "after an issue has been recognized as controversial, differences structured and sides chosen."[66]

Specialization is essential, but its impact is lessened by certain circumstances, including the increasing complexity of legislation—expert knowledge is also vulnerable to obsolescence—and the extravagant volume in which it is introduced. Overworked and understaffed—these are the recurrent complaints of members who attempt to make discriminating judgments on legislation. A former state senator, who also holds credentials as a political scientist, describes the difficulties he encountered in Connecticut:

In the 1955 session of the Connecticut General Assembly we considered no fewer than 3,600 bills. I undertook to read every one of them as they came from the printers but soon had to give it up. Later I tried to read the bills with favorable committee reports. Finally, in the end-of-session rush, not even that was always possible. All this work has to be done within five months. Constitutionally, the session must end when five months have elapsed.... I had no office staff and indeed no office except for a corner in my hallway at home, where unsorted and unfiled letters, brochures, notes, and thousands of bills constantly threatened to bury my children under a

[66] William Buchanan, Heinz Eulau, LeRoy C. Ferguson, and John C. Wahlke, "The Legislator as Specialist," *Western Political Quarterly*, XIII (September 1960), 649. This observation is made specifically with reference to the California legislature. For a study of factors that shape state legislators' influence (in the Indiana Senate), see Wayne L. Francis, "Influence and Interaction in a State Legislative Body," *American Political Science Review*, LVI (December 1962), 953–60.

paper cascade. It is the same way with most other state legislators. We are on our own, and you get worse laws as a result.[67]

Where there are legislatures there are filibusters, but they are one thing in the U.S. Senate and quite another in the legislatures of the states. Lengthy filibusters in the states are almost unknown, and the little ones, if they occur at all, invariably develop in the final days or hours of the session. The rules of most state legislatures, notably those of the lower houses, are well fashioned to guard against prolixity. With the exception of Vermont, all lower houses authorize use of the previous question to cut off debate. And better than two-thirds of the state senates can call upon this motion to effect cloture.[68] Many states have supplementary cloture rules to go along with the previous question, and a few maintain a practice of setting the time for a vote.

Participation in debate is further controlled by rules, present in all but a handful of chambers, which limit the number of times and the number of minutes a member may speak without leave of the floor. The typical provision in state senates is for two speeches on a given issue without additional permission, with Maine and New Jersey providing their senators a generous three. Senators in Arkansas, Indiana, and Missouri must do the best they can on one speech on a single issue. Substantially more rigorous in limiting debate are the rules of the lower houses, particularly in confining the length of the member's remarks. In the California lower chamber, for example, a member may speak but one time on an issue and for no longer than five minutes' duration unless given leave. Florida legislators in both houses may speak twice on an issue, up to thirty minutes on each occasion. Least restrictive in their rules limiting talk are Colorado and South Carolina, where senators may speak for a period of two hours on an issue.[69] The point is that there are few opportunities for state legislators to make either immoderate incursions upon the time of their colleagues or rapacious demands by threatening a filibuster.

What has been said up to now does not mean that determined minorities have no weapons at hand to snag proceedings. But the weapons are small-gauge, and timing is most important. Hence most filibusters in the states occur in the waning days or hours of the session. Tactics designed to impede majority action are about the same everywhere; as a rule, their effect is to delay decision, not to postpone it indefinitely. Roll calls, whether to establish the presence of a quorum or to settle another procedural question, can and are used to serve a dilatory objective. The demand that the journal of the previous day be read in full, instead of dispensing with the requirement in the customary fashion, may be used to hold up proceedings. More effective as a weapon of the minority is the right to insist that all rules be strictly followed, including the reading of bills in their entirety. This latter filibustering device occasionally has been broken by hiring a battery of clerks to read different sections of a bill simultaneously, resulting in a cacophony of sounds wholly unintelligible to anyone. Finally, as in Congress, a bill may be filibustered by offering numerous amendments and then debating each one as long

[67] Duane Lockard, "The Tribulations of a State Senator," *The Reporter,* May 17, 1956, p. 27.

[68] Zeller, *op. cit.,* pp. 112–14.

[69] *Ibid.*

as time permits. In sum, dilatoriness is a conventional weapon of the minority everywhere; its effectiveness varies from legislature to legislature, depending upon the willingness of the majority to acquiesce.

RECORDING DEBATE

An account of debate in Congress which aims to be "substantially a verbatim report of proceedings" is recorded each day in the *Congressional Record.* Bound volumes appear on a semimonthly basis. Actually the *Record* extends well beyond the debate of the day, since it also contains a wide variety of other materials, some valuable and some not, in its appendix and daily digest. The panorama of members' interests is revealed in the appendix, for virtually anything that comes to their attention, and meets with their approval, is apt to wind up as an entry in its pages. Speeches, articles, and editorial comment—typically, coincidental with the sponsoring member's views—appear in quantities guaranteed to discourage the most avid reader of congressional fare. As a current index to Congress, the daily digest is highly valuable. Appearing as the final section of each issue of the *Record,* it summarizes and reports the principal activities of Congress and is particularly useful for its record of committee work.

Although congressional debate is recorded in full, a good deal of its original purity has been lost by the time it appears in the cold pages of the *Record.* Its transformation in the course of moving from floor to printed page often has been an issue.[70] Two things happen to it en route. In the first place, both houses permit members to revise their remarks before being printed, and although such revision is not supposed to alter the substance of statements, it is often so extensive that floor statements become unrecognizable in print. "This privilege has been abused to the extent that even in a colloquy which has occurred in debate the remarks of one of the debaters has been so changed as to render meaningless the printed remarks of his opponent which remain unrevised."[71] Adulteration of the transcript takes place in yet another way, by the House practice of authorizing its members to "extend" their remarks. What occurs is that a member gaining the floor will speak for perhaps a minute, or possibly five, and then seek the consent of the House to have his remarks entered in full in the *Record* ("leave to print" is the argot of the request). The House readily assents, thereby creating doubt as to what was said on the floor. Thus, as it goes into the *Record,* House debate is a curious mélange of the opening lines of many speeches never heard on the floor, coupled with revised, sometimes totally new, remarks. Senate debate in the *Record,* by contrast, is closer to what actually was said on the floor, if for no other reason than that an individual senator has a greater allotment of floor time and can ordinarily deliver his speech in full. Nevertheless, members in both houses rearrange the facts and rewrite bits of historical record.

[70] See an article by Howard N. Mantel, "The Congressional Record: Fact or Fiction of the Legislative Process," *Western Political Quarterly,* XII (December 1959), 981–95; and Richard Neuberger, "The Congressional Record Is Not a Record," *New York Times Magazine,* April 20, 1958, pp. 14ff.

[71] Statement by Representative Curtis of Missouri, *Congressional Record,* CIV (1958), 6594, quoted by Mantel, *op. cit.,* p. 983.

274

Preservation of legislative debate in the states is for the most part absent, haphazard, or incomplete. Stenographic or tape recording of debate is complete or relatively so, in only ten states: Connecticut, Maine, Nebraska, Nevada, New York, Pennsylvania, Tennessee, Utah, Vermont, and West Virginia. One or both chambers in six additional states—Hawaii, Louisiana, Michigan, New Hampshire, North Dakota, and Washington—record speeches in part or upon request.[72] Failure to record debate or, in some cases, to publish it after it has been recorded, is unfortunate for many reasons, two of which should be noted here. In the first place, transcripts of debate not only serve an informational function for the public, newspapers, and scholars, but also contribute to a healthy measure of political control. Recorded speeches are likely to keep legislative talk more responsible and to discourage the use of bogus data in debate. The record of deliberations, the ways in which decisions were reached, and the votes themselves become a part of the public domain, open to study and evaluation. In the second place, recorded debate may be used to help clarify legislative intent at the time the measure was passed. In the interpretation of statutes, courts will sometimes turn to the legislative history of an act to seek the meaning of certain language or to learn the intention of the majority which passed it. This source of information obviously is not available where debate goes unrecorded.

Casting the Vote

The legislative act of casting a vote is not taken lightly, at least where major legislation is at stake.[73]A permanent record, hardened, irretrievable, available for public inspection—these are the qualities of the vote. Of all the facts that might be recorded about voting, none seems more necessary to emphasize than its complexity. A vote on a major measure is rarely made easy for the legislator; reasons for voting "yea" shade into those for voting "nay." Robert Luce, with experience in both a state legislature and Congress, describes the matrix of influences which shape voting:

> Assuming that it is best for constituents to be informed of each act of their representatives, yet it is far from certain that records of roll-calls disclose the votes adequately or that they accurately inform. There are such things as half truths, and often the record of a vote is in effect a half truth. Often it fails to show the real nature of the matter decided. Titles of bills are necessarily brief and rarely tell the whole story. Again and again a legislator will sympathize with a measure, will desire what its title purports to give, and

[72] *The Book of the States, 1970–71* (Chicago: Council of State Governments, 1971), pp. 70–72.

[73] Voting on obscure and special bills is another matter. In the 1971 session of the Texas House, a resolution was passed unanimously commemorating Albert DeSalvo for "noted activities and unconventional techniques involving population control and applied psychology," serving to make him "an acknowledged leader in his field." DeSalvo, better known as the "Boston Strangler," is now serving a life sentence for armed robbery and assault. The resolution was introduced simply to establish the point that legislators know little or nothing about the minor legislation on which they vote. *Time,* April 12, 1971, p. 12.

yet be compelled to vote against it because he knows it is improperly drawn or because he thinks it will not accomplish its ostensible purpose or because it will also accomplish some other purpose of more harm than enough to offset the good. Every legislator has seen a wise bill, for which he has voted at one stage, ruined by amendments at the next, forcing him to reverse his vote. Or again the time may not be ripe for the measure; or some other step ought to be taken first; or a measure may be undesirable unless some other measure goes with it. Any one of a score of perfectly legitimate reasons the public will never know may lead a conscientious and honorable lawmaker to record his vote in a way that will put him in a false light, and may bring him political ruin.[74]

T. V. Smith points to the problem for the legislator of understanding the dimensions of a vote:

The predicament of the legislator is that every vote is a dozen votes upon as many issues all wrapped up together, tied in a verbal package, and given a single number of this bill or that. To decide what issue of the many hidden in each bill one wants to vote upon is delicate, but to make certain that the vote will be actually on that rather than upon another issue is indelicate presumption.[75]

Legislatures have devised a variety of voting methods: *viva voce,* division, tellers (including recorded tellers), and roll calls (or yeas and nays). The first three methods have in common the fact that no formal record is made of the votes of individual members, though sharp-eyed observers can gain a fair impression of supporters and opponents when division or tellers are used. Under *viva voce,* the chair simply calls for a voice vote of yeas and nays, and then estimates which chorus constitutes the prevailing side. A close voice vote may lead to utilizing one of the other methods. A division vote is held by having members rise and be counted, first those in favor and then those in opposition. Vote by teller, such as used by the U.S. House of Representatives, requires the members to pass down the center aisle and be counted, the yeas first and then the nays. In each case, it is the outcome or total vote that counts, and the chamber makes no record of individual positions. Under the Legislative Reorganization Act of 1970, provision was made for recording teller votes if demanded by twenty members. The effect of this reform will be to give greater visibility to members' votes at the crucial stage of amending legislation.

The U.S. House of Representatives makes use of all four methods, and the Senate uses all but tellers. The typical vote in each house is the voice vote, though customarily this is reserved for less important, less controversial measures. A division vote may be requested by a single member. One-fifth of a quorum may demand a roll-call vote in either house, except in the House committee of the whole, which accelerates deliberations by using only the first three methods.

[74] Robert Luce, *Legislative Procedure* (Boston: Houghton Mifflin Company, 1922), p. 361.
[75] "Custom, Gossip, Legislation," *Social Forces,* XVI (October 1937), 31.

The success of party leaders in convincing members to follow their lead may depend on the voting method which is used. On votes which are not highly visible to the public, the press, or others—as in the case of committee voting and division and voice voting on the floor—party leaders can often count on a high measure of support from rank-and-file members. "Division and voice voting, because they happen so quickly, and because few members may be on the floor, or know the nature of the choice being made, are very often simply party votes. Many members scurry from the cloakrooms to the floor to vote in support of their party's side, as defined at the moment by the majority and minority floor managers from the substantive committee in charge of the bill." Roll-call votes on final passage of controversial bills, however, are another matter. Members cannot quietly go along with the party, relatively assured that their votes are hidden from critical eyes. A roll-call vote is the most visible vote of all, and visibility tends to attenuate the influence of party leaders and to strengthen the hand of those opposed to the leadership. A southern Democratic congressman, for example, may be able to support his party leadership on a civil rights bill at the committee stage, whereas to do so on the floor would certainly jeopardize his career.[76]

Both houses of Congress make use of voting "pairs," a form of proxy voting for the record. Under this practice, a member who cannot be present for a roll-call vote, or simply wants to avoid it, agrees to "pair" with another member on the question, one to be recorded as voting for and the other against. Pairs may also be "general" in character, which means that the arrangement holds until the two members agree to cancel it. A convenient device when members find it necessary to be absent at the time a vote is scheduled, "pairing" is also a means of dodging a controversial vote. The votes of pairs are not counted in the official tally, serving nothing more than to identify the intentions of the contracting members. Pairs are often arranged simply by having the clerks match names, with no overtures between individual members having preceded the coupling. "The system is for the most part farcical. ... The assumption is that every vote is a party vote, and that every absentee if present would vote with the leaders of his party, both of which things are far from true. Therefore the printed list has no real significance."[77] The practice of pairing has been used in the state legislatures but is unimportant today.

The business at hand determines the voting requirements in Congress. In most cases the vote demanded is a majority of a quorum. Interestingly, in the House committee of the whole, where numerous major decisions are taken and where a quorum is but 100 members, amendments can be adopted or defeated by as few as fifty-one votes. Some matters require extraordinary majorities, as in the case of the two-thirds vote needed in both houses to override a veto and the two-thirds vote in the Senate to ratify a treaty. In yet other cases, as we have seen earlier, unanimous consent is a prerequisite for taking a particular action.

The number of votes needed to pass a bill in the legislature varies some-

---

[76] Lewis A. Froman, Jr., and Randall B. Ripley, "Conditions for Party Leadership: The Case of the House Democrats," *American Political Science Review,* LIX (March 1965), 52–63, quotation on p. 60.

[77] Luce, *Legislative Procedure,* p. 381.

what from state to state. About two-thirds of the states require a majority of the members elected, while most of the rest call for a simple majority of those present and voting. The requirement of a "constitutional majority"— majority of the members elected—has come to present a convenient and evasive way of killing a bill without going on record against it. An absent or nonvoting member becomes in effect an opponent of the bill; if enough members decline to vote, the bill is certain to fail. The individual legislator can, if he chooses, argue that he was meeting with constituents, or that he did not hear the bell, or that he was otherwise detained. Legislative devices for evasion, for escaping pressures and avoiding records, are numerous; most of them are maintained by plausible, if not altogether convincing, reasons.

Commonly, the states require extraordinary majorities, perhaps two-thirds of all members elected, in order to override vetoes and to pass emergency legislation or special kinds of appropriation measures. In about one-quarter of the states, constitutional provisions require a roll-call vote on the final passage of all measures; in contrast, Congress frequently passes bills by voice vote. Even in those states where this requirement is absent, it is usually a simple matter to demand a roll call on final passage—only a few members needing to make the request. The average state legislature conducts many hundred more roll-call votes than Congress does.

The Multiple Points of Decision-Making

A principal theme of this and other chapters is that there are multiple points in the legislative process where critical decisions are fashioned. Frequently, they are made in the standing committees, with or without direction or approval by party leaders; at other times, they are made in screening committees such as the Rules Committee of the U.S. House of Representatives, similarly with no assurance that accredited party spokesmen will share the committee's valuations; here and there, the chief decisions are taken in party caucuses and later ratified at appropriate stages of the legislative process; on occasion, decisions are shaped outside the legislature, in the councils of interest groups, and subsequently made authoritative through the public processes of the legislature; and decisions are also the product of negotiation and settlement on the floor of the legislature itself.

No fact about the legislature is more commonplace than that committees play a role of decisive importance. In Congress, committee independence is often very great—at times certain committees virtually seem to have broken away from the legislature as a whole. The evidence of committee hegemony contributes to responses of two main kinds: the first, reformist in intent, argues for correcting the proportions of committee and of floor power (e.g., by strengthening central party agencies, institutionalizing majority rule in the committee system, using devices such as the twenty-one-day rule); the second, though carrying no proposals for reform, sees the legislature as dominated by an elite which makes the critical decisions behind closed doors—in consequence, interpreting the most public phases of the legislature (e.g., debate and roll-call voting) as mainly pretense, not to be taken seriously, and as fair game for debunking.

278   The fact is that all stages of the legislative process engage members in the processes of compromising competing interests and resolving conflict. It is a good hypothesis that the more controversial an issue, the more likelihood that the processes of legislative bargaining and adjustment will be exposed to public view. Where the stakes are large, the contestants vocal and insistent, and a test of strength desired, it is difficult to keep the attentive public from getting frequent clear views of the struggle. In addition, the more the burden of decisions can be transferred to the floor, the greater the likelihood that larger portions of the public will be attracted by the contagiousness of conflict and stimulated to become involved in its resolution.[78]

[78] On the strategy for expanding and managing conflict in politics, see E. E. Schattschneider, *The Semisovereign People* (New York: Holt, Rinehart & Winston, Inc., 1960), especially Chapters 1 and 4.

part three

Legislatures, Parties, and Interests

9

POLITICAL PARTIES AND
THE LEGISLATIVE PROCESS

The stark fact about American legislatures is that total power is seldom, if ever, concentrated in any quarter. This is the chief truth to be known about the legislative process, and if it is well understood, a lot of other things may be safely forgotten. A certain quantity of political power, variable according to men and circumstance, is lodged within each of the legislature's principal parts. Committees, committee chairmen, seniority leaders in general, officers of the chambers, sectional and ideological spokesmen, and agencies of the parties cooperate and compete with one another in the exercise of legislative power. Executive agencies and private organizations, from vantage points within and without the legislature, contribute varying measures of content and thrust to legislative decisions. On occasions more rare, the court slips into the struggle as acts of the legislature fall under its scrutiny. In a word, numerous centers of power in and out of the legislature negotiate for the right to have a say on public policy.

Although party leaders strive steadily to unite their memberships on policy and tactical matters and to assert the primacy of party claims over those of constituency or interest groups, their efforts are often vitiated. This happens because the power of the legislative party organization, like power within the formal apparatus of the legislature, is fragmented and elusive. One way of sketching the party condition is to examine the ideological cleavages that impair party unity, which we shall undertake to do later in the chapter. Another way is to describe the functional divisions within the parties —that is, the offices and agencies which comprise the legislative party organization.

At a minimum our analysis should disclose that the edifice of party-in-the-legislature generally is not imposing and that there are major obstacles to developing a conception of party responsibility for a legislative program. Some of the evidence supplied in this chapter concerning the location and the use of power in the legislature—as in the argument over the presence of a southern Democrat–northern Republican "coalition" in Congress—is no more than circumstantial. Fortunately, however, circumstantial evidence is often sufficient to establish a point.

Legislative Party Organization

PARTY CONFERENCES

One of the oldest agencies of party is the legislative party caucus or conference. In theory, the caucus is regarded as the central agency for the
selection of party leaders and for the development and promotion of party
policy. But, in this instance, theory is an inadequate guide to practice. In
most of today's legislatures the tasks of the caucus are few and seldom of
more than routine significance. Membership in one or the other of the party
conferences is automatic for the party member upon election to the legislature.

The high point of caucus power in Congress was reached in the second
decade of the twentieth century. The earlier eras of Reed and Cannon saw
the House so dominated by the Speaker—through his control of the Rules
Committee—that the majority caucus had no independent voice. Following
the Speaker's loss of power in the 1910–11 revolution, the majority party
caucus waxed strong, and during the Wilson administration was notably
effective. Loyalty to the party was expected, binding caucuses were frequent,
and steady efforts were made to translate party platforms into congressional
programs. After World War I, the power of the caucus dropped sharply, due
mainly to the growing unpopularity of its compulsory features.

While the role of the caucus in Congress is now confined mainly to the
selection of party leaders at the beginning of the session, there are state legislatures where party caucuses are called on a daily or weekly basis to consider
legislation and to define party programs. Connecticut is a good example of
a state with a virile caucus system. Duane Lockard reports that the daily
senate caucus "is the scene of some protracted disputes and debates on bills,
but when the senators leave their caucus to come to the floor it is rare
indeed for the disputes of the inner chamber to be brought out in Senate
debate and rarer still for members to desert in a roll call."[1] According to a
survey conducted in the mid-fifties, only about one-quarter of the state legislatures have strong majority party caucuses or conferences.[2] In about the
same number of states—especially those dominated by one party—majority
caucuses are nonexistent. Minority party caucuses are found in about one-
half of the states but as a rule do not function actively.

Even in states where the caucus is an important party instrument, its
decisions usually are not binding on the member, who may claim that the
proposed action would run counter to the best interest of his district or that
it would contravene a pledge he has made to constituents. Having been
shorn of its coercive powers, the caucus functions now mainly as an agency
to facilitate discussion, accommodation, and compromise among party members.

[1] Duane Lockard, *New England State Politics* (Princeton: Princeton University
Press, 1959), p. 281.
[2] Belle Zeller, ed., *American State Legislatures* (New York: Thomas Y. Crowell
Company, 1954), pp. 194–97.

The need for greater party responsibility in legislative chambers has been a persistent theme in the literature of political science during the last two decades.[3] Legislative party organization should be tightened up, runs this view, in order that the majority party can be held accountable for the conduct of government, especially for the formulation of public policy. Invariably, proposals directed toward the reform of Congress have included steps to be taken to shore up the party leadership committees. The Joint Committee on the Organization of Congress in its 1946 report recommended the creation of policy committees "to formulate over-all legislative policy of the two parties."[4] Subsequently, the provision was placed in the La Follette–Monroney reorganization bill and accepted by the Senate, only to be stricken in the House. In an independent action in 1947, the Senate set up its own policy committees. Two years later House Republicans converted their steering committee into a policy committee.[5] The opposition of Speaker Sam Rayburn to the formation of a policy committee for House Democrats doomed the plan to failure.

There are about as many differences as similarities in the organization and performance of the two policy committees in the Senate. The Republican policy committee was launched with a membership of nine; by 1955 it had grown to twenty-three, when all Republicans up for reelection were made members. Currently there are fifteen members, some of whom are *ex officio* while the rest are elected by the Republican conference. The Democratic policy committee is composed of ten members, chosen by the floor leader. Except for the *ex officio* members, senators on the Republican committee hold their positions for two-year periods. Members of the Democratic body hold indefinite appointments, apparently as long as they continue to serve in the Senate.

The most important difference between the parties is that the Republicans have sought to institutionalize their committee while the Democrats have made theirs an instrument of personal leadership. The Republican policy committee operates under a set of responsibilities enumerated by the Republican conference; in contrast, the Democratic policy body has functioned much of the time according to the preferences and outlook of the floor leader. The influence of any Democratic leader will depend, of course,

---

[3] This section is based principally on three studies. The ground-breaker of the three is Hugh A. Bone's "An Introduction to the Senate Policy Committees," *American Political Science Review,* L (June 1956), 339–59. The other two are Malcolm E. Jewell, "The Senate Republican Policy Committee and Foreign Policy," *Western Political Quarterly,* XII (December 1959), 966–80, and Ralph K. Huitt, "Democratic Party Leadership in the Senate," *American Political Science Review,* LV (June 1961), 333–44. Another discussion of the committees is available in Hugh A. Bone, *Party Committees and National Politics* (Seattle: University of Washington Press, 1958), Chapter 6.

[4] *Report of the Joint Committee on the Organization of Congress,* 79th Cong., 2d sess., Senate Report no. 1011, March 4, 1946, p. 12.

[5] See Charles O. Jones, *Party and Policy-Making: The House Republican Policy Committee* (New Brunswick, N.J.: Rutgers University Press, 1964). As of 1971, there were twenty-seven members of the House Republican Policy Committee.

284 on such factors as his personality, skill, and steady support within the party. When Lyndon Johnson served as Democratic floor leader (and as policy committee chairman) during the Eisenhower administration, he chose men who were compatible and who represented independent centers of power within the legislative party—men whom "he would have to deal with if there had been no policy committee...."[6] Republican reliance on election of members, on a chairman independent of the floor leader, and on written specifications have given its committee a distinctly different character from its Democratic counterpart.

A review of the experience of the Senate policy committees since 1947 is not reassuring to those who hoped these agencies might serve to enhance party responsibility in Congress. The name "policy committee" itself is illusory. "They have never been 'policy' bodies, in the sense of considering and investigating alternatives of public policy, and they have never put forth an over-all congressional party program. The committees do not assume leadership in drawing up a general legislative program...and only rarely have the committees labeled their decisions as 'party policies.'"[7] Issues seldom are resolved by votes being taken, and decisions are never binding.

Uncertainty over the functions the policy committees should perform has been present since their inception. An excerpt from a debate over appropriations for the committees makes the point:

> Mr. Proxmire.... The reason why I raise this objection at this time is that ...we are now appropriating 20 times as much [for the policy committees] as was originally appropriated by Congress only 15 years ago. These committees serve none of the functions for which they were set up—none of them.... I hope the leadership on both sides will explain why it is necessary to have this big increase....
>
> Mr. Dirksen. The item as it pertains to the policy staff on the Republican side is necessary.... Never has the minority had the benefit of so much excellent and scholarly work from its policy staff as it has now.... The results of the staff work are available to every Member on the minority side. The staff has developed monographs; it has done work on the Appropriations Committee.
>
> Mr. Proxmire.... I have always felt that Senate committees should be well staffed. [I would] support any request for a more adequate staff for the minority on standing committees. But the policy committees, which are supposed to work on party policy, belong to the parties. It is not at all clear to me what they do.... [The need for more staff experts on the Appropriations Committee] is not a justification for increasing the staffs of the Republican and Democratic policy committees....
>
> Mr. Pastore.... As the Senator from Illinois has pointed out, the minority must rely more on its staff because it does not have a comparable number of staff members on the various committees. We on the majority side are better staffed...and therefore do not have to rely to the same extent upon

---

6 Huitt, *op. cit.*, 342.
7 Bone, "Introduction," 352.

our policy committee. But it is true that once funds are provided to one side, they must also be provided to the other side.[8]

In the view of former Democratic floor leader Johnson, neither the policy committee nor the party conference should make policy—this responsibility belongs to the standing committees. Members should make their influence felt "in committees of which they are members.... If they cannot get a majority vote there, how do they expect me to get a majority vote out here?"[9]

The permanent importance of the policy committees is that they have served as forums for discussion, compromise, and communication. To a marked extent in the Senate, they have assumed the functions of the party conferences. The staff of the Republican committee has been utilized for research purposes by Republican members. In a general way, both committees have participated in preparing the legislative schedule and in monitoring the calendar. Issues likely to divide the party have been skirted by the committees or approached in such a manner as to alleviate a threatening party crisis. During his years as Democratic floor leader, Lyndon Johnson sought to use the policy committee to diminish factional antagonisms and to lay the groundwork for greater party unity.

The failure of the policy committees to fulfill the expectations of those who have sought a more meaningful party performance in Congress is not hard to explain. At bottom, the dilemma is based on a conflict between irreconcilables. The stark simplicity of the plan—a centralized party body to shape legislative policy—could not overcome the many problems that have repeatedly confounded attempts to gather and store legislative power in a central place. A policy committee worthy of its name necessarily would intrude upon the traditional arrangements of power and authority. Inevitably, seniority leaders would be forced to relinquish some share of their considerable power over legislation, for an independent committee system and central party leadership are incompatible. Correspondingly, individual power, carefully nurtured, negotiated, and encrusted by time, would be threatened by the party. There is nothing novel in the finding that powerful men in Congress greatly prefer the customary allocation of prerogatives. Moreover, those outside Congress who secure policy advantages from existing legislative arrangements obviously have an aversion to change.

The policy committees have not provided a significant departure from the past because they could not go to the root of the problem, party disunity, nor, as Ralph Huitt has argued, could they accommodate the relationship between the individual member and his constituency. Many lawmakers have cultivated "careers of dissidence." Closely attuned to the interests and aspirations of their constituents, they know that what counts is pleasing the voters who elect them, not satisfying a legislative party agency.[10] Moreover, the party is unable to exert effective discipline over them. "The American legislator," Clinton Rossiter wrote, "is uniquely on his own, and he lives and dies polit-

---

[8] *Congressional Record,* 87th Cong., 2d sess., August 2, 1962, pp. 14404–5.

[9] *Ibid.,* 86th Cong., 2d sess., May 28, 1959, p. 9260, as quoted in Huitt, *op. cit.,* 343.

[10] Huitt, *op. cit.,* 335.

286 ically through the display of talents more numerous and more demanding than party regularity. He must therefore make his own adjustment among the forces that play upon him, even if this means defiance of his party's leadership."[11]

THE FLOOR LEADERS

The chief spokesmen of the parties in the legislature are the floor leaders. Majority and minority floor leaders are chosen by party caucuses in each house. Customarily, the majority leaders have greater influence in the legislature than anyone save the Speaker of the House.[12]

The role of the majority leader is much easier to describe than are the elements which combine to shape his influence. His task, in general, is to plan the work of his chamber, which he does as leader of the majority party. Depending upon his skills, personality, and support, he may have a decisive voice in formulating the legislative program as well as in steering it through the house. In the course of developing and scheduling the legislative program, the majority leader works closely with committee chairmen and other key leaders in his party. His relations with the committees are basic: "You must understand why the committee took certain actions and why certain judgments were formed," stated Lyndon Johnson. Or, as Mike Mansfield, his successor, has said: "I'm not the leader, really. They don't do what I tell them. I do what they tell me.... The brains are in the committees." Effective leadership grows out of continuing communication between the majority leader and the rest of his party; he must be especially sensitive to the interests of those who hold power in their own right. The importance of keeping the lines of communication open can scarcely be exaggerated, for certain kinds of intelligence can keep the majority leader from being caught on the short end of a floor vote:

> First, you must know what is in the bill. Second, you must understand how it is related to the various states and the various personalities in the Senate. And, third, you have to be sure that it will command the respect of a majority.[13]

The floor leader has few formal powers. David Truman observes that the leader must construct his influence out of "fragments of power":[14] his

[11] *Parties and Politics in America* (Ithaca, N.Y.: Cornell University Press, 1960), p. 22.

[12] The point may be argued. At intervals in the history of the U.S. House of Representatives, the chairman of the Rules Committee has appeared not only more important than the majority leader but fully the equal of the Speaker himself. The generalization is much less arguable when speaking of the state legislatures.

[13] The statements by Lyndon Johnson in this section appear in "Leadership: An Interview with Senator Lyndon Johnson," *U.S. News and World Report,* June 27, 1960, p. 90. Of formal powers attached to the office of the majority leader, Johnson lists only the "power of recognition"—i.e., the right to be recognized first by the vice-president. See Huitt's analysis of Senator Johnson's leadership, *op. cit.,* 337–44. For the Mansfield statement, see Russell Baker, *New York Times,* July 17, 1961, as quoted by James A. Robinson, *Congress and Foreign Policy-Making* (Homewood, Ill.: Dorsey Press, 1962), pp. 215–16.

[14] David Truman, *The Congressional Party* (New York: John Wiley & Sons, Inc., 1959), pp. 104–5. A study of leadership strategies in the Connecticut legislature,

influence over committee assignments, his ability to help members with their special projects, his control over the legislative schedule, his role as leader in debate, his ties to the administration if his party is in control, his links to the leadership of the other chamber, his skill as a parliamentarian, his position as party spokesman through the media of communication.

What makes the post of floor leader so important is that it is located at the center of things in the legislature. Only the floor leader can gather together the partial powers scattered throughout the legislature and forge them into an instrument of leadership. By using his powers skillfully and judiciously, he can hold them intact. "The only real power available to the leader is the power of persuasion," Lyndon Johnson, an extraordinarily effective Senate leader, once observed. "There is no patronage; no power to discipline; no authority to fire Senators like a President can fire his members of Cabinet." When he was criticized by some Democratic senators for not providing more vigorous leadership, Mike Mansfield offered this analysis of the role of the majority leader:

> Most recently, I believe I have been accused of acting as though I were the President of a high school sorority. I do not think I regard the Democratic Conference as a sorority. Nor do I regard it, may I say, as a boy scout troop to be led by a scoutmaster. The leadership, as I view it, is an instrument of the Conference and the Senate as a whole, not the other way around. And so long as I remain as leader I shall not be blustered, badgered or bluffed into reversing that order.[15]

As interpreted by Johnson and Mansfield, the leader's task is to serve as an intermediary within the legislative party organization.

Members' expectations regarding the role of the floor leader, especially in his relationship to the chief executive, present another perspective of the office. Writing of the U.S. Senate, William S. White contends that while there is no unified view of what a leader is or what he ought to do, "there is general agreement on what he is *not* and what he ought *not* to do." In the first place, except in extraordinary circumstances, the Senate expects that its floor leader, if a member of the party of the president, "will not so much represent the President as the Senate itself." Second, if the floor leader is a member of the party that lost the presidency, he should "represent not so

---

where party organizations are powerful, emphasizes that leaders normally rely on persuasion rather than command to maintain party cohesion. At other times, however, an appearance of persuasion may be sufficient to satisfy members. The relationship is complex. James D. Barber writes: "Persuasion legitimizes pressure. As long as the leader-follower relationship can be perceived as a situation in which the leader furnishes information, seasoned judgment, and technical guidance, members are inclined to accept instruction. . . . The reality of being bossed can be borne by many legislators who find the appearance of it unendurable." In their use of patronage and pressure, leaders manipulate the expectations of members. The leader strives to convince members "(a) that he has unquestioned control over the distribution of political rewards and punishments, and (b) that he is sure to distribute these rewards and punishments in such a way as to maximize party voting. But members are left uncertain as to precisely how and, especially, *when* such 'pressure' will be applied." See Barber, "Leadership Strategies for Legislative Party Cohesion," *Journal of Politics,* XXVIII (May 1966), 347–67, quotations on pp. 365 and 353–54.

[15] *New York Times,* January 1, 1967.

288   much that party as the Senate itself." Finally, the floor leader should "consider himself primarily the spokesman for a group in the *Senate* and not so much for any group in the country or any non-Senatorial political organism whatever, not excluding the Republican and Democratic National Committee organizations."[16] The floor leader's "constituency," in this view, is the "institution" itself: it, not the president, provides the cues for its leaders; its prerogatives, not the president's, must be protected. The effective leader, then, is one who puts first things first: the interests of the senatorial group.

David Truman offers a counterinterpretation which asserts that a relatively close tie between the majority leader and the administration, far from being an incubus, is a condition associated with effective leadership. He holds that "elective leaders are, and probably must be, both the President's leaders and the party's leaders. . . . [In] order to be fully effective as leaders of the Congressional parties, they must above all be effective spokesmen for the President; or at least, excepting the most unusual circumstances, they must appear to be his spokesmen." Evidence pointing to this conclusion lies in the roll-call behavior of majority leaders on administration support votes. In the 81st Congress, Truman shows, the Senate Democratic majority leader opposed the administration position fewer times than any other member. Similarly, the Democratic majority leader in the House was not recorded in opposition to the administration on a single roll call out of 129 classed as administration support votes. On seven votes he was recorded as "absent"— apparently a deliberate action on his part to avoid open opposition to the administration.[17] Doubtless, the role of the majority leader varies according to occupant and to circumstances, but these data argue that the president's impact upon the leader is substantial.

The floor leader must be a "middleman in the sense of a broker."[18] Prominent identification with an extreme bloc within the party, Truman hypothesizes concerning Congress, is likely to jeopardize the leader's effectiveness. Leaders' voting records generally locate them close to the center of the legislative party. Moreover, members on the ideological edges of the party structure are virtually disqualified for the position as leader, since problems of communication, difficult at best, might prove insurmountable if the leader were drawn from the extreme reaches of the party.[19] Location within the party, as well as relative skills and personality, is thus a factor affecting choice of the floor leader.[20]

<hr/>

[16] *Citadel* (New York: Harper & Row, Publishers, 1956), p. 96.

[17] Truman, *op. cit.,* pp. 110–11. The quotation is drawn from p. 298.

[18] For evaluation of the "middleman" requirement in the Senate and House, see Truman, *op. cit.,* especially pp. 106–16 and 205–8.

[19]   For corroboration of this finding in recent Congresses, see Barbara Hinckley, "Congressional Leadership Selection and Support: A Comparative Analysis," *Journal of Politics,* XXXII (May 1970), 268–87.

[20] The "middleman" role of the floor leader—his tendency to locate near the center of his party structure—may or may not apply generally to the state legislatures. Duncan MacRae's study of the Massachusetts legislature, though not focused directly on the problem examined by Truman, helps to illuminate factors that bear on the choice of legislative leaders. In one session of the legislature he found that the principal leaders in each party (all members of rules and ways and means committees from the majority party, including the Speaker and majority leader) tended to hold the most extreme identification within their parties on a "liberalism-conservatism"

Another element in the legislative party structure is the whip organization. A whip is chosen by the party caucus (or floor leader) in each house. While the "organization" is both simple and informal in the state legislatures— usually consisting of a single member—it is fairly elaborate in Congress, especially in the House. Organized in Congress around 1900, the whip system provides a communications network for the party membership. The whip is expected to keep in touch with all members of the party—to find out what, if anything, is troubling them; to discover their voting intentions; to relay information from party leaders; to round them up when a vote is being taken; and, in the case of the administration party, to apply pressure on members to support the president's program. The large size of the U.S. House of Representatives necessitates appointment of numerous assistant whips, who are selected to provide regional representation.

When a crucial vote on a major administration bill is scheduled, the whip's office is likely to go all out to insure maximum attendance of party members known to be friendly to the bill. Telegrams and telephone calls will be made to members, urging them to be on the floor when the vote is to be taken. Efforts will be undertaken to persuade members at home in their districts to return to Washington. The effectiveness of the whip organization depends ultimately on the quality of the information which it collects concerning the preferences and intentions of members.[21] One assistant whip has noted:

> On some whip checks where we have asked people how they will vote, we ask what their objection is if they indicate opposition to a bill the leadership wants. If you can determine that there are enough members objecting to one feature of the bill and that elimination of that feature might move the bill, it can be a very valuable piece of intelligence.[22]

The main source of intelligence is the poll, which the whip's office conducts if the leadership decides one is required. Randall Ripley's study of the whip system has shown that these polls are remarkably accurate. Their principal value is that they help the leadership decide where to apply pressure. On the basis of poll information, wavering members may be brought

---

scale (Democratic leaders with "liberalism," Republican leaders with "conservatism"). In other sessions the tendency for the Democrats to select their leaders in terms of their "liberalism" was not evident. Republican leaders, in contrast, were much more "conservative" than their party colleagues in all sessions examined. Democratic leaders exhibited considerably more "organization loyalty" ("measures involving the disposition of power or resources between the two parties, or of measures involving the allocation of praise or blame on a partisan basis") than Republican leaders. See MacRae, "Roll Call Votes and Leadership," *Public Opinion Quarterly,* XX (Fall 1956), 543–58.

[21] See Randall B. Ripley, "The Party Whip Organizations in the United States House of Representatives," *American Political Science Review,* LVIII (September 1964), 561–76.

[22] Quoted in Charles L. Clapp, *The Congressman: His Work as He Sees It* (Washington, D.C.: The Brookings Institution, 1963), p. 303.

290   back into line and some opponents may even be converted to the leadership's position.[23]

The significance of the whip organizations doubtless varies according to the style and preferences of the leadership. At times the whip organizations (particularly in the Democratic party) "are at the core of party activity" and "the focus of a corporate or collegial leadership in the House." Some speakers and floor leaders, on the other hand, have made limited use of the whip organization. In general, those leaders with fewer resources have tended to augment the role of the whip.[24] Where party languishes, of course, whips function indifferently and sporadically.

THE HOUSE DEMOCRATIC STUDY GROUP

Another party group active in Congress is the House Democratic Study Group, a loosely knit organization formed in 1959 by the liberal bloc in the Democratic delegation. As described by one DSG member, the group is composed of one-third "organization-oriented, machine-type Democrats" and two-thirds "knee-jerk, issue-oriented liberals."[25] Composed of about 140 members, the DSG is organized to the point of possessing elected officers, a whip system, a full-time professional staff member, and a campaign fund-raising unit. One of its principal functions is to conduct research on policy questions of interest to its members. Perhaps the most concretely issue-oriented body in Congress, the DSG was formed in order to press for certain major pieces of legislation, including civil rights, area redevelopment, comprehensive medical care for the aged, federal aid to education, and a higher minimum wage with expanded coverage. Functioning as a counterbloc to the powerful southern wing of the party, the study group has gained success through its strategy of keeping pressure on party leaders. On occasion, it has used the discharge rule and Calendar Wednesday to challenge the conservative coalition. At the opening of the 87th Congress the study group was in the forefront of a successful drive to curb the power of the conservative coalition which had long dominated the Rules Committee. In the 89th Congress the DSG led the drive to strip two southern Democrats of their seniority for having supported the Republican candidate for president in 1964. And in both the 88th and 89th Congresses the study group played a critical role in the passage of major civil rights acts. DSG leaders consult with party leaders on major matters and are careful to keep their group

[23] Ripley, *op. cit.*, pp. 572–73. "There are several reasons for a member's making an inaccurate report of his position. He might want to avoid leadership pressure by not alerting anyone to his opposition. He might be annoyed at the inconvenience of repeatedly reporting his position. Finally, he might use the report of opposition as a bargaining device" (p. 572). Some House members are highly critical of the whip organizations, contending that they do not fully perform the "informing" function. These members tend to see their organization as "a group of poll takers." Or, in the words of one congressman, "All they do is call up and say we should be on the floor." Clapp, *op. cit.*, p. 302.

[24] Ripley, *op. cit.*, pp. 574–75. For a study of the whip system in the Senate, see Walter J. Oleszek, "Party Whips in the United States Senate," *Journal of Politics,* XXXIII (November 1971), 955–79.

[25] *Current American Government* (Washington, D.C.: Congressional Quarterly, Inc., 1971), p. 107.

from being stigmatized as "insurgent." The group appears to have won the tacit approval of the formal party leadership.[26]

THE SPEAKER IN CONGRESS

The development of the office of Speaker of the U.S. House of Representatives provides good evidence of the growing "institutionalization" of that chamber.[27] In earlier times, it was not uncommon for men who had served only one or two terms in the House to rise to the speakership. Henry Clay, for example, was elected Speaker at the age of 34, a mere eight months after he was first elected to the House. His rapid rise to power was by no means unusual, as Figure 9 shows. A typical Speaker during the nineteenth century would have served six years in the House before his election to the speakership; by contrast, during the twentieth century he would have served a remarkable twenty-six years prior to his election. The speakership, it is plain,

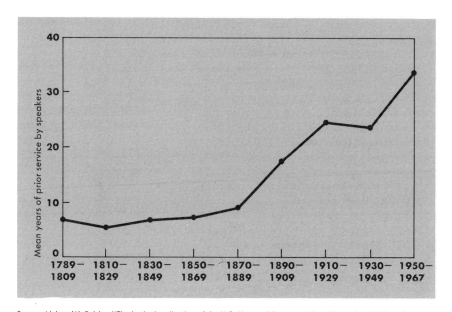

Source: Nelson W. Polsby, "The Institutionalization of the U.S. House of Representatives," American Political Science Review, LXII (March 1968), 149.

FIGURE 9 *Mean years served in Congress before first becoming speaker by 20-year intervals.*

[26] See Kenneth Kofmehl, "The House Democratic Study Group: The Institutionalization of a Voting Bloc," *Western Political Quarterly,* XVII (June 1964), 256–72, and Paul Duke and Arnold B. Sawsilak, "The 'Group' That Runs the House," *The Reporter,* May 20, 1965, pp. 29–31.

[27] To say that the House has become more "institutionalized" means that it has become "perceptibly more bounded, more complex, and more universalistic and automatic in its internal decision making." For an analysis of specific characteristics of institutionalization in the House, see Nelson W. Polsby, "The Institutionalization of the U.S. House of Representatives," *American Political Science Review,* LXII (March 1968), 144–68. Quotation drawn from p. 145.

292   has become a "singular occupational specialty." Many prominent congressmen doubtless aspire to the office, but it is open only rarely and then only to those men who have amassed great seniority.

There have been times in the history of Congress, such as in the first decade of the twentieth century, when the Speaker of the House has appeared virtually as powerful as the president. His primacy in House affairs came about not by original design but with time, circumstance, and the contributions of men who held the office. The first Speaker of the House was hardly more than a presiding officer and a moderator of debate; in no way was the office distinguished as a source of independent power. Gradually, however, the Speaker accumulated powers, first that of appointing committee members. More important, with the development of distinct legislative parties, the Speaker became more and more a party leader, a role firmly established during the tenure of Henry Clay, six times elected to the office.

By the turn of the twentieth century, the Speaker's powers were almost complete, his hegemony virtually unchallenged. His power of recognition was unlimited; he appointed committee members as he saw fit and named committee chairmen; the Rules Committee, of which he was chairman, had become his personal domain; he interpreted House rules according to his and his party's interests; he entertained such motions as suited his aims. The architects of this structure of power were many, though Speakers Reed and Cannon are singled out for special acknowledgment. Eventually, Cannon's overweening exercise of power led to the office's undoing. Democrats and dissident Republicans joined forces in 1910, under the leadership of George W. Norris, to shear the prerogatives of Speaker Cannon. "It was 'Uncle Joe' Cannon's economic and social philosophy that first aroused the western Congressmen against his autocracy. The question of power in itself did not greatly excite the average Congressman; but power exercised for reactionary economic and social ends seemed downright pernicious."[28]

The 1910–11 imbroglio ended with the Speaker's powers diminished in three important respects. His power to appoint members and chairmen of standing committees was eliminated, his position on the Rules Committee was taken away, and his power over the recognition of members was cut back. As a result of this upheaval, a number of individuals got keys to the House leadership: the committee chairmen, the Rules Committee, the seniority leaders, and the sectional spokesmen. The imprint of the "revolution" remains highly visible: at that time a drastic expedient to curb autocratic rule, its legacy for today's House is an arrangement of fragmented power, a built-in bias toward the *status quo,* and an illusory scheme of responsibility for the legislative program.[29]

[28] Kenneth Hechler, *Insurgency: Personalities and Politics of the Taft Era* (New York: Columbia University Press, 1940), p. 31.

[29] "What progressively replaced party rule through party control mechanisms [in the years following the 1910–11 revolution] was a highly pragmatic approach to assembling the majorities needed to pass party bills and a highly permissive, personal, and informal leadership style. These combined with increased party fractionalization and the rise again to dominance of attitudes that accorded primacy to the individual member and scorned party discipline as rank coercion resulted in the modern or contemporary House of Speakers Rayburn and McCormack (1940–1970). In this House party remains the basis of organization and the most cohesive force. But it provides no basis for strict control of the body.... As a result, the leadership must construct its majorities anew from issue to issue through bargaining, appealing to party loyalty, bringing the President's influence to bear, and exploiting both the

Despite the extraordinary loss of power in the 1910–11 revolution, the **293**
Speaker remains the most influential official in Congress. A former incumbent, Joseph W. Martin (R., Mass.), Speaker during the 80th (1947–48) and 83rd (1953–54) Congresses, reviews what has happened to the office:

During the half-century since that revolt against Cannon's rule Speakers have succeeded in rebuilding a great deal of the power that "Uncle Joe" lost. While the committee on committees may formally select members for committees, for example, the Speaker does in fact exercise a strong influence over these choices from among the ranks of his own party. Thus members must look to him for a chance of advancement. In the four years that I served as Speaker no Republican went on an important committee without my approval. In the case of select committees created for certain limited but important tasks the Speaker does appoint the members from his own party. The Speaker is in a position to expedite or delay legislation and to encourage or shut off debate. Another element that goes to make up his authority is his power of recognition. Merely by ignoring a member he can deprive him of the floor. I believe, however, that many tend to exaggerate this power. In order to maintain his effectiveness a Speaker has to be fair. He is no longer a Reed or a Cannon. His rulings can be overturned by the House.

The thing that makes the Speaker's influence greater in a way than it used to be is the much broader role the House plays in the government than it did in Cannon's day. Until World War II, for example, the House had scant voice in foreign affairs, as contrasted with the Senate, which has the constitutional responsibility for ratifying treaties. In the postwar world, however, United States foreign policy has rested on programs which... require large sums of money. Since the Constitution provides that all appropriations must originate in the House, the House has come to have a large influence over the scope and nature of these instrumentalities of foreign policy. As the role of the House has grown, the Speaker's influence has increased.[30]

---

credits it has amassed from past favors and hopes for future rewards." Joseph Cooper, *The Origins of the Standing Committees and the Development of the Modern House* (Houston: Rice University Studies, 1970), p. 120.

[30] Joe Martin, *My First Fifty Years in Politics* (New York: McGraw-Hill Book Company, Inc., 1960), pp. 181–82. The observations of Randall Ripley on the influence of the Speaker help to fill out the argument. Ripley writes: "[The Speaker's] personal traits influence his ability to deal with members of his party. The one constant element is the importance of his showing trust in and respect for individual members of his party. A smile or nod of the head from the Speaker can bolster a member's ego and lead him to seek further evidence of favor. Being out of favor hurts the individual's pride, and may be noticed by his colleagues. Most Speakers have had an instinct for knowing their loyal followers on legislative matters. Others have either kept records themselves or made frequent use of whip polls and official records to inform themselves about the relative loyalty of their members. Speakers have been able to convey critical information to members on a person-to-person basis, often with the help of the Parliamentarian. They have also encouraged their floor leaders and whip organizations to become collectors and purveyors of information on a larger scale. Particularly useful to a number of Speakers has been an informal gathering of intimates and friends of both parties to discuss the course of business in the House. Through such discussions, Speakers have been able to keep themselves informed of developments in the House and, at the same time, convey their desires to other members invited to attend." *Party Leaders in the House of Representatives* (Washington, D.C.: The Brookings Institution, 1967), pp. 23–24.

294   The principal challenge to the Speaker's leadership in recent decades has come from the Rules Committee. Former Speaker Martin described this relationship:

> An effective Speaker needs to hold the good will of members of the Rules Committee, which controls the flow of legislation to the floor. I never had any trouble on this score, partly perhaps because I had been a member of that committee since before most of the members then sitting ever came to Congress.[31]

The relationship between the Rules Committee and the Speaker (representing the administration) became a major issue in the first session of Congress following the 1960 presidential election. With President Kennedy's legislative program threatened by a biparty conservative bloc in the Rules Committee, the House, by a close vote of 217–212, accepted Speaker Sam Rayburn's plan to break the coalition's rule by enlarging the committee's membership from twelve to fifteen, adding two Democrats and one Republican. Appointment of the new Democratic members, of moderate to liberal persuasion and loyal to Speaker Rayburn, resulted in a transfer of control over the committee majority from the leader of the conservative coalition, Chairman Howard Smith of Virginia, to the Speaker and the administration. Rather than a "reform" of the committee, diminishing its powers, this action constituted a shift in command—the net impact being to augment the Speaker's influence.

The long-run consequence of this political settlement are problematical. Changes will occur as new men enter the elite of the lower house and as circumstances shift. In general, however, the Speaker's position may be summarized as follows. He now shares power once lodged almost exclusively within his office. Although he continues to control the parliamentary machinery much as before, his direct influence upon legislation is no longer as great as in the era of Cannon. On occasion, the dominant voice of the House and principal custodian of its powers has been neither the Speaker nor the party he leads but the chairman of the Rules Committee, speaking for a majority of its members. Finally, we must reckon with the fact that policy is shaped through negotiations between competing centers of influence, resulting in a condition in which party considerations are often of slight moment and party leaders are largely without real power.

THE SPEAKER IN THE STATE LEGISLATURE

In the typical state government the Speaker's powers are very great, second only to those of the governor. Although state legislatures often have emulated congressional organization and style, there has been no counterpart in the states to the 1910 revolution in the U.S. House of Representatives. Ties between the Speaker and the committee system, wrenched in the national House during the revolt against Cannonism, are firm in the states—thus helping to centralize decision-making. For example, in all but a handful of states the Speaker continues to be responsible for committee appointments, naming the members of standing committees as well as members of special, select, and conference committees. His influence in the committee structure

---

[31] *Ibid.*

is reinforced through his power to name committee chairmen in a great many states. As one might expect, chairmen often feel it is necessary to take their cues on legislation from the Speaker, as is made clear in these comments by a chairman in the New York Assembly:

> A chairman has to vote with [the Speaker] if he wants to be sure he's going to stay a chairman. We have a race problem at home and I'd like to vote with the Republicans—80 per cent of the Democrats feel the same way— but I know what I have to do. [The Speaker] didn't say a word to me, but he could take my committee away.[32]

The Speaker is frequently a member of the committee on rules—which often plays a critical role near the end of the session in screening proposals— and he may be an *ex officio* member of all committees. Ordinarily, the Speaker does not take an active part in committee deliberations, though his presence may be felt. When he does appear at committee meetings, it may be a good sign that the administration is unusually interested in a bill up for consideration.

The Speaker is the principal leader and grand strategist of the major- ity party in the lower house. Both the majority and minority party caucuses nominate candidates for the office (as well as for other positions), but or- dinarily this is only a perfunctory gesture by the minority, since it will not have the votes to elect its candidate. Following the floor vote, the majority's candidate is declared Speaker, the minority moves to make it unanimous, and the minority's candidate for Speaker becomes his party's floor leader— such is the public record of Speaker selection in the typical legislature. But politics is rarely so bland. This account tells too little about how the Speaker in fact is chosen and, moreover, ignores the occasions when the minority party enters the fray and is able to determine the outcome.

When the same party controls both administration and house, the Speaker is often the governor's man. In theory the house is free to choose its leadership as it pleases, in practice it often defers to the wishes of the governor. Obviously, there are states where executive "interference" would be resented, and there are governors who are reluctant to risk a quarrel with legislators over a charge of aggrandizement. Nonetheless, if the governor hopes to play a key role in fashioning the legislative program and if condi- tions are propitious for such action, he is unlikely to resist an opportunity to offer his own candidate for presiding officer.[33] To some extent at least, this is a matter of self-defense: a hostile Speaker has a vast array of powers which can be employed to hamstring the administration's legislative program. A friendly Speaker, on the other hand, can do much to facilitate passage of the governor's bills.

The voice of the minority party may ring the loudest in the choice of

---

[32] Richard Reeves, "The Other Half of the State Government," *New York Times Magazine*, April 2, 1967, pp. 89–90.

[33] The governor's concern with legislative organization may extend beyond the speakership, to the choice of floor leader, whip, and, not uncommonly, committee chairmen. On the general subject, see Coleman B. Ransone, Jr., *The Office of Governor in the United States* (University, Ala.: University of Alabama Press, 1956), pp. 202–4.

the Speaker. Although there is only one case in the history of Congress when a Speaker was chosen by a combination of majority and minority votes (the 4th Congress in 1795), a number of states can point to such incidents. When the majority party cannot settle upon a single candidate in caucus, the door is opened for the minority to have its say. In the 1959 session of the Illinois legislature, a bitter, drawn-out fight between Chicago and downstate Democrats over which area was to secure the speakership finally was settled when the Republican delegation, after casting a first vote for its own candidate, broke the impasse by voting unanimously for the downstate Democrat. The Republican party's decision to become involved in the majority's quarrel and to support the downstater was made by the governor, a Republican. The downstate winner helped his cause further by the judicious bargaining of committee chairmanships.[34] In similar fashion, a protracted struggle among New York Democrats over the post of Speaker in the 1965 session was settled when the Republican governor succeeded in convincing Republican members to plump for one of the Democratic candidates. Later in the session, the Speaker delivered the necessary Democratic votes for a state sales tax which the governor had wanted.[35] Although the commingling of parties in this way strikes a dissonant note for advocates of "party responsibility," an aggressive governor is likely to see the matter otherwise. The main difference between successful and unsuccessful governors often appears to be the ability to seize upon transitory circumstances (including power struggles in the opposition party) to advance the administration's legislative program.

As in Congress, the Speaker in state legislatures engages only rarely in floor debate. On those few occasions when he does take the floor, it is usually to defend an administrative action or to support a major administration bill. His floor appearance is not a casual decision. By not "going to the well too often" he can command greater attention for his views and preserve to some degree the "principle" that the Speaker serves the pleasure of the whole House and is not merely the leader of the majority party.[36]

In summary, the Speaker's influence in the states is compounded of numerous elements. In the first place, he is the guardian of party fortunes and policies. Second, he is charged with many official duties, nearly all of which hold implications for the party interest. Thus, typically, he appoints the members of standing, special, and conference committees; he chairs the rules committee; he refers bills to committee; he presides over house sessions, decides points of order, recognizes members, and puts questions to a vote; he has it within his power to assist a member with a "pet" bill or to sandbag

[34] Thomas Littlewood, *Bipartisan Coalition in Illinois* (New York: McGraw-Hill Book Company, Inc., 1960).

[35] Reeves, *op. cit.*, p. 85.

[36] A former Speaker of the Pennsylvania House of Representatives, Hiram Andrews, in his valedictory remarks to the body, stressed this point: "I do not think I will go down the years as a strong Speaker, because I have not endeavored to control the action of the Democratic Caucus by any power the Speaker may have, I have not endeavored to control the action of any committee by and through the powers the Speaker might exercise and I have not endeavored to control the action of this House by arbitrary action, or by arbitrary rulings. I have not regarded, and perhaps in this I have been remiss, the Speakership as purely a partisan office. I have considered myself responsible to see to it that the rules and regulations of this House, its traditions, were respected. I have tried to keep my parliamentary rulings in line with that thought." *Pennsylvania Legislative Journal*, May 22, 1956, p. 8390.

it; he can ease the way for new members or ignore them; he can advance the legislative careers of members or throw up roadblocks before them. All these prerogatives contribute to a network of influence. And, finally, if the Speaker has the strong support of the governor, if he meets with him regularly and is privy to administration plans and secrets, new measures of power and influence come his way. Of all the legislative posts, the one most sought after is the speakership.

CHANGE IN PARTY LEADERSHIP

The selection of legislative leaders has great significance for the distribution of power and the representation of interests in legislatures. When a change occurs in a leadership position, some members (and the constellation of interests they represent) gain influence in the system while others lose ground. About the same thing may be said for public policy—a change in leadership may improve the prospects for the passage of some legislation and dim the prospects for the passage of other legislation. Although some concern for continuity is imposed on new legislative leaders, they nevertheless have enormous opportunities to influence the careers of other members and the course of public policy. Under the circumstances, it is surprising that political scientists have given so little systematic attention to change in the composition of legislative party elites.

A conspicuous exception to this observation is a study by Robert Peabody of change in party leadership in the U.S. House of Representatives in the six Congresses between 1955 and 1966.[37] A change in party leadership may result from *interparty turnover* (i.e., the minority, through an election, displaces the majority), *intraparty change* (new leaders supplant old leaders in the same party), or *institutional reform* (powers of an existing office are altered or a new position is created). As would be expected, most leaders continue in their posts from Congress to Congress. When changes occur, the most common method is that of intraparty change.

Intraparty change, according to Peabody, may take any of five forms: (1) routine advancement, (2) appointment or emergence of a consensus choice, (3) open competition, (4) challenge to the heir apparent, and (5) revolt or its aftermath. Routine advancement occurs when the ranking and "logical" successor moves into a vacated position, as in the traditional practice of elevating the majority leader to fill a vacancy in the office of Speaker. When there is no pattern of succession (e.g., in the appointment of whips), contests may be avoided through the emergence of a consensus choice. Open competition occurs in still other cases when a vacancy has appeared and a succession pattern has not yet developed (e.g., in the selection of the chairman of the Republican Congressional Campaign Committee and the chairman of the Republican Conference). Under the fourth type of intraparty change, the heir apparent to an office may be challenged by dissident elements within the party. Finally, the most intense intraparty struggles occur when no vacancy exists, opposition is present, and the incumbent is deter-

---

[37] The analysis in this section is based on an article by Robert L. Peabody, "Party Leadership Change in the United States House of Representatives," *American Political Science Review,* LXI (September 1967), 675–93.

298   mined to retain his office. In this category are such recent cases as the Halleck-Martin struggle over the post of Republican minority leader in 1959 and the Ford-Halleck contest over the same position in 1965. In each instance the challenger defeated the incumbent by a very narrow margin.

In recent years, the two House legislative parties have had sharply different patterns of leadership change. Most of the Democratic changes since the mid-1950s have been brought about without contests.[38] By contrast, changes in the Republican leadership have tended to be the product of strenuous, sometimes acrimonious, intraparty struggles. The real and imagined ills of Republican House members have made the legislative life of a Republican leader precarious indeed. A skillful leader, of course, may be able to assuage the anxieties of restive members or otherwise deflect their opposition. But this is far from easy to do, especially in the case of leaders of the minority party. Their opponents can capitalize upon the usual discontents that visit minority party members (e.g., less desirable committee assignments, frequent disappointments in committee and floor actions) or upon election defeats to argue the need for a change in leadership. It is interesting to find that Halleck's defeat of Martin in 1959 and Ford's defeat of Halleck in 1965 both followed major election debacles suffered by the Republican party, which lost a net of forty-seven House seats in 1958 and thirty-eight in 1964. The fact that junior members composed a large proportion of the Republican membership in the Congresses following these elections probably contributed to the pressure for change.

CONDITIONS FOR PARTY LEADERSHIP

At times it appears as if the only thing that some congressional Democrats have in common with other congressional Democrats (and some congressional Republicans with other congressional Republicans) is the same language.[39] Each congressional party is a bundle of interests, orientations, and

---

[38] The tendency of House Democrats to select their leaders without contests did not hold in the election of the party's nominee for majority leader in the 92d Congress. Hale Boggs, House whip, was eventually elected by the Democratic caucus. Morris Udall, his principal opponent, observed following his defeat: "The leadership ladder bit—tradition, promotion, seniority—was stronger medicine than I originally thought. This House apparently just insists on people getting in line, serving time. Boggs knew this, and exploited the sentiment very effectively. . . . In the South, the Boggs people put the heat on recalcitrants through lobbyists for various industries: oil, tobacco, textiles, and so on. They snatched six or eight votes from me there. He played the freshmen like a virtuoso: he could pass out more goodies than I. The big-city boys came to him through a combination of his contacts with mayors and other politicians I didn't know externally. . . . Boggs had people all over Washington —lawyers and lobbyists and bureaucrats—dating back to the New Deal, and almost all of them knew somebody to pressure for him." See an interesting account of this drawn-out struggle in Larry L. King, "The Road to Power in Congress," *Harper's Magazine,* June 1971, pp. 39–63, quotation on p. 62.

[39] This and the following paragraph are based mainly on an article by Lewis A. Froman and Randall B. Ripley, "Conditions for Party Leadership: The Case of the House Democrats," *American Political Science Review,* LIX (March 1965), 52–63. Also see an instructive analysis of how majority parties in both houses of Congress have performed under a variety of conditions (e.g., president and congressional majority of same party, president of one party and congressional majority of other party) in Randall B. Ripley, *Majority Party Leadership in Congress* (Boston: Little,

ideologies. On certain kinds of issues party lines are likely to bend or break while bipartisan coalitions perform as if they had been empowered as the majority. As a result of intraparty cleavages and the resultant decentralization of power in Congress, party leaders rarely find it an easy matter to assemble their troops behind them when major legislation is at stake.

Whether a legislative party is an empty promise or a cohesive unit depends on a number of conditions. Research by Lewis Froman and Randall Ripley helps to identify the conditions under which party leadership is likely to be relatively strong or relatively weak, and party members relatively responsive or relatively indifferent to the call of party. Their study of the Democratic leadership in the House of Representatives describes six conditions that bear on the success of party leaders: the commitment, knowledge, and activity of the leadership; the nature of the issue (procedural or substantive); the visibility of the issue; the visibility of the action; the existence of constituency pressures; and the activity of state delegations. In general, the prospects that the leadership will prevail are best when the principal leaders are active and in agreement, when the issue is seen as procedural rather than substantive, when the visibility of the issue and of the action to be taken is low, when constituency opposition is slight, and when the state delegations are not involved in bargaining for specific provisions. As a rule, members prefer to support their party, and they will do so if they believe that their careers will not be jeopardized.[40] The less visible the issue and the action to be taken on it, the easier it is for members to go along with the leadership. The stern test of leadership comes when the party's interest appears to be incompatible with the constituency interests of members—and the matter at stake is highly visible to press and public.

Party Influence on Legislation

Popular political thought seldom has taken account of the virtues of party or of the potential of party government. The vices of party, by contrast, are persistently deplored; it is not too much to say that American parties have grown up in an atmosphere of general hostility.[41] Independence from party, in the public mind, appears often to be the mark of a good man, the justifiable claim of a good legislator. Yet there is little evidence to suggest that the

---

Brown & Company, 1968). For a study that examines the influence of state legislative leaders on the voting behavior of members (in Iowa), see Harlan Hahn, "Leadership Perceptions and Voting Behavior in a One-Party Legislative Body," *Journal of Politics,* XXXII (February 1970), 140–55.

40 A recent study by David M. Olson based on interviews of congressmen and local party leaders bears on this point. He finds that while most congressmen prefer to support their party's position on policy questions, very few feel much "obligation" to do so. Moreover, when party and district positions are in conflict, most congressmen will "vote" their district. The congressman's willingness to side with district interests is not, for the most part, a function of communication with local party leaders. Indeed, the typical congressman hears very little from party leaders in his district. See *The Congressman and His Party* (Manuscript, University of Georgia, 1971), especially Chapters 5 and 6.

41 See E. E. Schattschneider, *Party Government* (New York: Holt, Rinehart & Winston, Inc., 1942), especially Chapter 1.

300 obloquy which hangs over the party system is the result of a careful assessment of the workings of political parties or of their contributions to representative government. One point of departure in assaying the importance of parties is to evaluate their role and potential in the legislative process.

PARTY VOTING IN CONGRESS

In the ritual and practices of Congress, as of nearly all American legislatures, the party can perform a variety of functions. In varying degrees and with varying success, the parties organize the legislature, select the leadership, shape the ground rules for negotiation and decision-making, rationalize the conduct of legislative business, monitor the activities of the executive branch, and assist in familiarizing the public with the work of government. The parties' tasks in representative government are formidable and their functions indispensable.

One phase of the party role in the legislative process is especially vague: the direct contribution of the party to shaping legislation. The parliamentary machinery is, of course, controlled by majority party members. But to what extent does legislation bear the imprint of party *qua* party, to what extent is it simply the product of transient nonparty majorities or of persistent coalitions? Do the parties present genuine policy alternatives in Congress— i.e., do the parties differ? Can the voting behavior of a Republican congressman be distinguished from that of a Democratic congressman, the voting behavior of a Republican senator from that of a Democratic senator? How much party responsibility for a legislative program do we want? How much do we now have? If party performance falls short, is it reasonable to expect otherwise—given the milieu in which parties function?

Satisfactory answers to these questions are hard to determine, even though an impressive number of studies of legislative parties have been made in the last half-century, particularly in the last two decades. At the risk of exacerbating the problem of understanding, let us have a good look at the relationship between party and public policy. Our analysis leans on a variety of studies.

There are two principal views of the *raison d'être* of political parties. The first argues that parties have ideological roots and that principle undergirds their organization. In the classic definition of Edmund Burke, "Party is a body of men united, for promulgating by their joint endeavors the national interest, upon some particular principle in which they are all agreed."[42] The other view finds party preoccupation with winning elections as the fundamental basis of organization. James Bryce put it this way:

> [Legislation] is not one of the chief aims of party, and many important measures have no party character. [The] chief purpose [of political parties] is to capture, and hold when captured, the machinery, legislative and administrative, of the legal government established by the constitution.[43]

[42] *The Works of Edmund Burke* (London: G. Bell and Sons, Ltd., 1897), I, 375.

[43] *Modern Democracies* (New York: The Macmillan Company, 1927), II, 42–43.

Conflicting claims such as those of Burke and Bryce have often been investigated. The pioneering study traces to A. Lawrence Lowell, who, in 1901, published *The Influence of Party upon Legislation in England and America*.[44] Lowell assumed that the main test of party influence lay in the behavior of party members on roll-call votes. He defined a "party vote" as one in which 90 per cent of the voting membership of one party was opposed to 90 per cent of the voting membership of the other party. His analysis disclosed that party rivalry of this order was much less in evidence in Congress than in the British House of Commons in the nineteenth century. Legislative proposals before Congress were not frequently passed or lost in "party votes." The "influence" of party upon legislation in the state legislatures was even less than in Congress. Party affiliation, it was plain to Lowell, did not often affect the deliberations of American legislators, and party lines were not often drawn.

Party voting in Congress was reexamined by Julius Turner in 1951. Using Lowell's "90 percent versus 90 percent" test, he found that in various congressional sessions between 1921 and 1948 about 17 percent of the roll-call votes in the House were "party votes."[45] An updating of this study by Edward Schneier finds that in a number of House sessions since 1950, between 2 and 8 percent of all roll-call votes have been "party votes." How this compares with party behavior in the British House of Commons—the model used in the argument for disciplined, responsible parties—is shown in Table 9.1. Not only is party voting found much less frequently in the House of Representatives than in the House of Commons, but it has declined markedly over the years. There are few hints in this statistical picture which point to the development of cohesive and responsible congressional parties.[46]

That the congressional parties function only sporadically as cohesive units has been documented sufficiently to put the matter to rest. More important in any case is the question of party differences over legislation. What policy matters are at stake when "party votes" (or approximations) do develop?

Conflict between the parties has cropped up consistently on legislation involving the tariff, agriculture, labor, business, and social welfare legislation, and on a variety of subjects where the issue is one of government versus private action. The parties' orientations have been plain for some time: (1) Democrats have persistently favored a low tariff, Republicans a high one. "When the tariff is considered, most Democrats unite against most Republicans as a matter of principle." (2) Where agricultural problems have arisen, Democrats ordinarily have argued that the federal government should assume responsibility for the development of programs (e.g., price supports, food

[44] *Annual Report of the American Historical Association for 1901* (Washington, 1902), I, 321–543.

[45] Julius Turner, *Party and Constituency: Pressures on Congress* (Baltimore: Johns Hopkins Press, 1951), p. 23.

[46] The "90% vs. 90%" definition of party voting is obviously quite rigorous. If the standard is relaxed to "50% vs. 50%," the picture is much different. In typical sessions during the 1950s and 1960s, party *majorities* were arrayed against each other on about half of the roll-call votes. See Schneier's revised edition of Turner's *Party and Constituency: Pressures on Congress* (Baltimore: Johns Hopkins Press, 1970), p. 17.

TABLE 9.1

Party Unity as Reflected in Proportion of Party Votes Cast in Selected Twentieth-Century Legislative Sessions, Great Britain and The United States

Britain, Commons		United States, House	
Year	*% Party Votes*	*Year*	*% Party Votes*
1924–25	94.4	1921	28.6
1926	94.8	1928	7.1
1927	96.4	1930–31	31.0
1928	93.6	1933	22.5
		1937	11.8
		1944	10.7
		1945	17.5
		1946	10.5
		1947	15.1
		1948	16.4
		1950	6.4
		1953	7.0
		1959	8.0
		1963	7.6
		1964	6.2
		1965	2.8
		1966	1.6
		1967	3.3

SOURCE: Julius Turner, *Party and Constituency: Pressures on Congress* (Baltimore: Johns Hopkins Press, 1951), p. 24. Data for years since 1950 appear in the revised edition of this volume (Baltimore: Johns Hopkins Press, 1970), prepared by Edward V. Schneier, Jr. (p. 17).

stamps) to assist the farmer, while Republicans ordinarily have offered an alternative of free enterprise in agriculture and, therefore, have opposed the development or extension of federal programs. (3) Democrats have been steadily more vigorous than Republicans in their support of government action to assist labor and low-income groups—through support of health and welfare programs, programs to raise the living standards of union members, and defense of collective bargaining. (4) In contrast, Republicans have been consistently more sympathetic than Democrats to the interests of business. (5) In general, Democrats have been more inclined to call for government action to remedy domestic problems or to launch new projects (e.g., aid to education, antipoverty programs, medical care) than have Republicans. Where a choice is posed between government involvement or private action, a larger or a smaller federal role, party lines have tended to form rapidly, with the Republicans moving strongly to the defense of private means and a limited federal role.[47]

Differences between the parties on foreign policy have been notable during certain periods and scarcely distinguishable during others. Robert Dahl's study of congressional voting on foreign policy between 1933 and 1948 disclosed substantial differences between Republicans and Democrats. Democratic lawmakers tended to give strong support to international organizations,

[47] This paragraph is based largely on Schneier, *op. cit.*, pp. 41–106. The quotation is drawn from the original Turner volume, p. 68.

domestic economic mobilization, military appropriations, selective service, foreign aid, and tariff reduction. Republicans, heavily committed to neutrality and "isolation," took counterpositions. "Internationalist" Democrats versus "isolationist" Republicans—a convenient stereotype for decades—had considerable meaning during this interval.[48] The lines were blurred somewhat during the early years of the Eisenhower administration, though the principal opponents of his foreign policy were usually "isolationists" in his own party. Democrats, by contrast, gave considerable support to Eisenhower's foreign policy requests. Although there have not been sharp differences between the parties on foreign policy questions in recent years, it continues to be true that Democrats are more inclined than Republicans to support internationalist and pro-foreign-aid positions.[49]

Analysis of congressional voting on foreign-aid legislation provides good evidence of how voting patterns shift over time. In the 1940s the principal cleavage on foreign aid occurred between Democrats and Republicans. As party conflict over foreign aid declined in the 1950s, other variables came to be associated with voting on this legislation. Most recently, LeRoy Rieselbach has shown, the principal supporters of foreign aid in the House have come from urban, coastal, high ethnic, high education, and high socio-economic status districts; in counterpoise, the main opponents have come from rural, southern, low ethnic, low education, and low socio-economic status districts. In a word, constituency characteristics now provide a better explanation than party affiliation for congressional voting on foreign aid.[50]

Voting on labor and social welfare legislation in Congress shows two distinct patterns. First, it is plain that this legislation produces significant cleavages within each party. Second, party disunity is not so serious that it blots out the major differences between the parties on "liberal-labor" legislation.

A fair test of party differences is available in the voting behavior of senators on legislative questions of concern to the AFL-CIO. Figure 10 shows the range of opinion in the Senate on issues covering a long span of years. Each issue, in the view of the AFL-CIO, has a "right" and a "wrong" side. A senator voting "right" in the 91st Congress, for example, would have voted in favor of liberalization of the filibuster rule, increased appropriations for urban renewal, an increase in personal income-tax exemption, unemployment insurance coverage for migrant farm workers, and federal grants for health facilities; in turn he would have voted against "freedom-of-choice" plans in school desegregation, weakening of the Voting Rights Act of 1965, an open shop for the postal service, and a gubernatorial veto power over legal service projects for the poor.

Despite the absence of high cohesion within each party, real differences between the parties are unmistakable. Figure 10 shows that 71 percent of the votes cast by Democratic senators were in support of the "liberal-labor" point of view, as contrasted with 33 percent of the votes cast by Republican

---

[48] Robert Dahl, *Congress and Foreign Policy* (New York: Harcourt, Brace & World, Inc., 1950), especially pp. 187–97.

[49] Schneier, *op. cit.*, p. 66.

[50] "The Demography of the Congressional Vote on Foreign Aid, 1939–1958," *American Political Science Review*, LVIII (September 1964), 587. Also see his book, *The Roots of Isolationism* (Indianapolis: Bobbs-Merrill Company, 1966).

304   senators. The congressional parties plainly do not look at the country in the same way when it comes to legislation of this sort,[51] although the fact is obscured partially by the behavior of a conservative band within the Democratic party and a liberal band within the Republican party.

The most noticeable division appears in Democratic ranks, making it tempting to generalize that northern (nonsouthern) Democrats are the liberals of the party while southern Democrats are the conservatives. But this masks as well as explains, as Figure 10, showing the behavior of individual senators lodged in the wings of their groups, should demonstrate. It will readily be seen that northern Senators Hart and Muskie, for example, have more in common with Senator Harris of Oklahoma than with Senator Bible

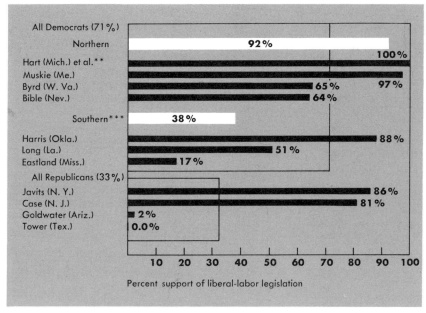

*This graph was prepared from data reported in the AFL-CIO News, August 29, 1970. This issue, which focuses on the 91st Congress, also carries the cumulative voting record of each member since taking office.

**Other Democrats with "perfect" cumulative voting records, as judged by the AFL-CIO, were Cranston (Calif.), Hughes (Iowa), Kennedy (Mass.), Mondale (Minn.), Eagleton (Mo.), Pell (R. I.), and Nelson (Wis.).

***Ala., Ark., Fla., Ga., La., Miss., N. C., Okla., S. C., Tenn., Tex., and Va. All non-southern Democrats are classified as "northern."

FIGURE 10   Democratic and Republican support of key liberal-labor legislation, cumulative voting records of individual members through 91st Congress, by section, U.S. Senate.*

[51] Another analysis by the *Congressional Quarterly* confirms the difference between the parties. Using key roll-call votes on legislation that would *enlarge federal responsibilities* (e.g., Social Security, teacher corps, unemployment compensation, open housing, public works, aid to education, minimum wage, rent supplements, government financing of election campaigns), the *CQ* studies throughout the 1960s show the Democrats to be far more likely to vote in favor of a larger federal role than the Republicans. See, for example, the *Congressional Quarterly 1962 Almanac,* p. 717, the *Weekly Report,* October 23, 1964, p. 2549, and the *Weekly Report,* February 10, 1967, p. 212.

of Nevada. Within the southern contingent, there is a considerable difference in the voting records of Harris, at the liberal end, and Eastland, at the
conservative end. And although Senators Eastland, Goldwater, and Tower
are not all members of the same party, there is not much difference in their
voting records on labor and social welfare legislation. The most that can be
said is that the center of Democratic liberalism is located in the North, but
not all northern Democrats are equally liberal, while the center of Democratic conservatism is located in the South, but not all southern Democrats
are equally conservative. Party life is about the same in the House (Figure
11).

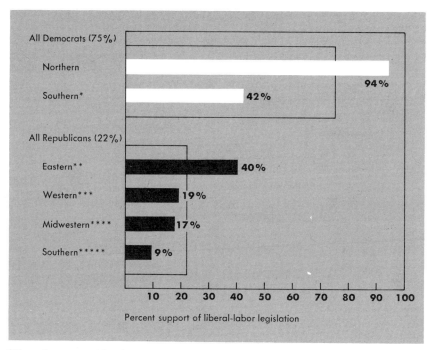

Percent support of liberal-labor legislation

*This graph was prepared from data reported in the AFL-CIO News, August 29, 1970. This issue, which focuses on the
91st Congress, also carries the cumulative voting record of each member since taking office.

*Ala., Ark., Fla., Ga., La., Miss., N. C., Okla., S. C., Tenn., Tex., and Va. All non-southern Democrats are classified as
"northern."
**Conn., Del., Md., Mass., N. H., N. J., N. Y., Pa., and Vt.
***Alas., Ariz., Calif., Colo., Ida., N. M., Ore., Utah, Wash., and Wyo.
****Ill., Ind., Iowa, Kans., Mich., Minn., Mo., Neb., N. D., Ohio, S. D., and Wis.
*****Ala., Ark., Fla., Ga., Ky., N. C., Okla., S. C., Tenn., Tex., and Va.

FIGURE 11 *Democratic and Republican support of key liberal-labor legislation,
cumulative voting records of individual members through 91st Congress, by section, U.S.
House of Representatives.**

People who like their party politics neat and logical will be offended by
similar scattering within Republican ranks. Senators such as Javits of New
York or Case of New Jersey are more frequently aligned with northern
Democrats on "liberal-labor" legislation than with members of their own

306   party such as Tower of Texas. And there are other cases. Nonetheless, when all the exceptions are listed, totaled, and explained, there are still important differences between the parties. Over the years a majority of the Democratic party has been determined to chart a liberal course for the federal government on labor and social legislation, while a majority of the Republican party has been equally insistent in posing a conservative alternative. The latter choice has varied with circumstances—a smaller expenditure for the same program, a project of more modest proportions, state rather than fed-

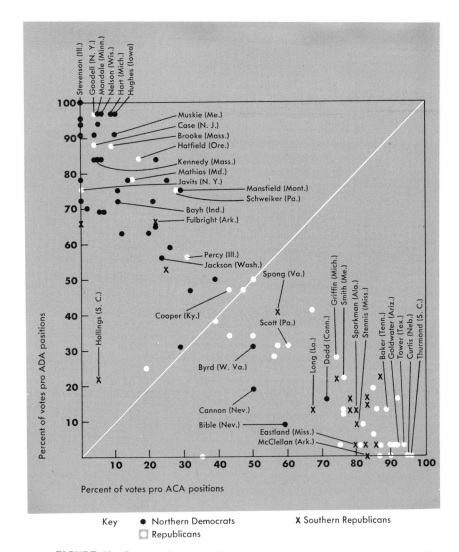

FIGURE 12 *Support of positions held by Americans for Democratic Action and by Americans for Constitutional Action by each senator, in percentages, 91st Congress 2nd Session. (Data are drawn from the* **Congressional Quarterly Weekly Report,** *April 16, 1971, p. 865.*

eral responsibility, defense of the rights of property as against those of labor unions and workers.[52]

Figure 12 offers another approach to the problem of disentangling party voting in Congress. It shows the voting record of each senator in the 91st Congress (2d session) on issues of key importance to two political interest groups at opposite ends of the ideological spectrum—the liberal Americans for Democratic Action and the conservative Americans for Constitutional Action. A strong majority of northern Democrats supports issues that are consonant with the philosophy of the ADA, while a similar group of Republicans votes in accordance with positions adopted by the ACA.[53] Of equal interest, over three times as many southern Democrats are on the ACA side of the diagram as are on the ADA side. The distribution of senators in this figure comes close to being an inherited pattern: *mutatis mutandis,* this figure could easily depict any Congress from the late 1930s up to the present.[54]

PARTY FRAGMENTATION AND INTERPARTY
COALITIONS IN CONGRESS

The burden of the previous pages has been to mark the policy positions which differentiate the parties in Congress. It should be clear by now that the congressional parties are by no means "Tweedledum and Tweedledee"; that, despite the indifferent success which characterizes some party efforts, there are still important policy distinctions between the two groups. No claim has been made, of course, that party performance in Congress is either "dis-

[52] David Mayhew's study of party loyalty among congressmen describes the Democratic party as a party of "inclusive" compromise and the Republican party as a party of "exclusive" compromise. His study of voting alignments in the postwar House of Representatives (1947–62) shows that the program of the Democratic party was regularly fashioned by splicing together the specific programs of various elements of the party—farm, city, labor, and western. By and large, the demands of these interests could be met through federal aid programs; the function of the House Democratic leadership became that of working out the "inclusive" compromises (intraparty accommodations) that would permit all Democrats to back the programs of Democrats with specific interests. The Republican party, by contrast, behaved as a party of "exclusive" compromise. *"Whenever possible,* most Republican congressmen opposed federal spending programs and championed policies favored by business. Thus, whereas 'interested' minorities in the Democratic party typically supported each other's programs, each 'interested' minority in the Republican party stood alone. The Republican leadership responded to the legislative demands of each minority by mobilizing the rest of the party to oppose them." See Mayhew's book, *Party Loyalty Among Congressmen: The Difference Between Democrats and Republicans, 1947–1962* (Cambridge: Harvard University Press, 1966), especially Chapter 6 (quotation on p. 155).

[53] For a listing of the issues on which these scores are based, see the *Congressional Quarterly Weekly Report,* April 16, 1971, pp. 868–71. They include such matters as foreign aid, crime control, "no-knock" warrants, aid to education, school bussing, school desegregation, equal employment opportunity, child nutrition programs, foreign military sales, debt-limit increase, deployment of the Safeguard ABM system, abolition of the electoral college, and manpower training.

[54] For a study of legislative voting blocs in the U.S. Senate, emphasizing voting in different policy areas, see Alan L. Clem, "Variations in Voting Blocs Across Policy Fields: Pair Agreement Scores in the 1967 U.S. Senate," *Western Political Quarterly,* XXIII (September 1970), 530–51.

308 ciplined" or "responsible," in the usual sense of these words; indeed, it is quite obvious that antithetical views are present within each party.

At this point, therefore, it is appropriate to examine the party fabric for snags and tears. Finding them is no problem; the difficulty comes with mending.

Table 9.2 provides strong evidence of the failure of party unity among congressional Democrats in a number of recent sessions.[55] It is a bleak

TABLE 9.2

Northern vs. Southern Democrats in Congress

Year	Total Roll-Call Votes, Both Chambers	North-South Democratic Splits*	% of Splits
1957	207	64	31
1958	293	84	29
1959	302	83	27
1960	300	119	40
1961	320	107	33
1962	348	74	21
1963	348	84	24
1964	308	75	24
1965	459	160	35
1966	428	124	29
1967	560	148	26
1968	514	173	34
1969	422	153	36
1970	684	233	34

SOURCE: *Congressional Quarterly Weekly Report,* January 29, 1971, p. 254. Reprinted by permission of the Congressional Quarterly Service.
* A majority of voting southern Democrats opposed to a majority of voting northern Democrats.

picture for those who believe that party loyalty should weigh heavily in the deliberations of members. In seven of these sessions, a majority of southern Democrats opposed a majority of "northern" (all other) Democrats on over 30 percent of the roll-call votes. The conflicts which split the party during this period were roughly the same from session to session. In 1970, party splits developed on such issues as school desegregation, voting rights, equal-employment enforcement, Social Security, family assistance, right to work, school lunch programs, import quotas, and foreign military sales.[56] The general outlook of southern legislators, it is clear, is one of staunch conserva-

[55] Although conflict between northern and southern Democrats registers frequently on floor votes, it is not necessarily significant in all committees. A study by James T. Murphy shows that the norm of partisanship has a profound impact on party solidarity in the House Public Works Committee. Rarely do southern and northern Democrats on the committee differ on committee bills, although, once on the floor, the same bills commonly provoke disagreement between these wings. "Partisanship, Party Conflict and Cooperation in House Public Works Committee Decision-Making," Annual Meeting of the American Political Science Association, Washington, D.C., 1968 (as revised in 1971).

[56] *Congressional Quarterly Weekly Report,* January 29, 1971, p. 253.

tism—based on states' rights, resistance to certain kinds of federal spending programs, pro-business commitments, and fiscal "integrity." Among major interest groups, organized labor in particular has felt the cold hand of the southern contingent in Congress.[57]

The main paths along which Congress moves are not always staked out by the majority party or by a majority of the majority party, as Table 9.3 readily verifies. Two facts in particular emerge. The first is that Republicans and southern Democrats (at least a majority of each) have progressed from furtive courtship to virtual wedlock. At the least, to continue the metaphor, amatory adventures across party lines occur with considerable frequency. In recent Congresses the coalition has appeared on one-sixth to one-fourth of all roll-call votes. And, second, not only do these groups get on well together, but their efforts have proved notably effective.[58] This untidy combination, as the party-government school instinctively views it, won about six of every ten roll-call battles in the 86th and 87th Congresses, five of ten in the 88th Congress, four of ten in the 89th Congress (a Congress in which there were more Democrats than at any time since 1936), and nearly seven of every ten in the 90th and 91st Congresses. The coalition is fused on about the same issues that split southern from northern Democrats.[59]

---

[57] Basic explanations for the conservatism of southern congressmen appear in V. O. Key, Jr., *Public Opinion and American Democracy* (New York: Alfred A. Knopf, Inc., 1961), pp. 100–105, and George Robert Boynton, "Southern Conservatism: Constituency Opinion and Congressional Voting," *Public Opinion Quarterly,* XXIX (Summer 1965), 259–69. Abbreviated, their conclusions are: (1) the conservative bent of southern congressmen is not derived from a dominant conservative strain in the population; (2) the active electorate of the South contains a disproportionate number of middle-class elements; (3) although the southern population as a whole is only slightly more conservative than the nation as a whole, southern Democratic identifiers are much more conservative than Democratic identifiers in the nation as a whole; and (4) the southern political activists who communicate attitudes of the electorate to congressmen are more conservative than the relatively inactive members of the electorate.

[58] John C. Donovan makes an interesting observation about power within the coalition and the coalition's accountability to the public: "Republicans in Congress provide most of 'the troops' in the conservative coalition while the southern Democrats have developed most of the 'generals.' If the aim of most Congressional Republicans since 1938 has been to limit the effectiveness of activist Presidents, it may very well be that the partnership with the southern oligarchs better serves their purposes than would outright Republican control. This way it is almost impossible for the ordinary American citizen to have any clear notion as to who is responsible for public policy." *The Policy Makers* (New York: Pegasus, 1970), p. 68.

[59] Wilfred E. Binkley's view of the coalition, set down in the middle 1940s, is worth quoting: "Here is a congressional bloc not to be explained by any resort to the dogma of original sin. It is motivated as normally as any sectional group at any time in American history. The assumption that Republican congressmen combine with anti-administration Democrats merely to embarrass the administration constitutes a misconception of the nature of our representative system. These coalition congressmen, whether Democrats or Republicans, represent the dominant social forces, that is to say, the most influential interests in their predominantly rural districts. By and large theirs is an anti-metropolitan ideology induced by a phobia of our American Babylons with their slums and laboring masses organized in unions that exert pressures at the polls through political action committees." *President and Congress* (New York: Alfred A. Knopf, Inc., 1947), p. 276. For a study of the origins of the coalition, see James T. Patterson, "A Conservative Coalition Forms in Congress, 1933–1939," *Journal of American History,* LII (June-March 1965–66), 757–72.

TABLE 9.3

Successes of the Conservative Coalition, 86th–91st Congresses

Congress	Total Roll-Call Votes	Number of Coalition Roll Calls*	% of Coalition Roll Calls	Coalition Victories†	% of Coalition Victories
86th					
Both chambers	602	116	19	74	64
Senate	422	86	20	57	66
House	180	30	17	17	57
87th					
Both chambers	668	138	21	79	57
Senate	428	99	23	55	56
House	240	39	16	24	61
88th					
Both chambers	766	121	16	61	50
Senate	534	94	18	43	46
House	232	27	12	18	67
89th					
Both chambers	887	219	25	85	39
Senate	493	131	27	60	46
House	394	88	22	25	28
90th					
Both chambers	1,074	231	22	156	68
Senate	596	126	21	86	68
House	478	105	22	70	67
91st					
Both chambers	1,106	265	24	178	67
Senate	663	176	26	115	65
House	443	89	21	63	71

SOURCES: *1961 Congressional Quarterly Almanac*, p. 642; *1963 Congressional Quarterly Almanac*, p. 740; *1965 Congressional Quarterly Almanac*, p. 1085; and the *Congressional Quarterly Weekly Report*, December 30, 1966, p. 3080; reprinted by permission of the Congressional Quarterly Service. Data for 90th and 91st Congresses furnished by Richard N. Billings, executive editor of the Congressional Quarterly.
* A "coalition roll call" is defined as any roll call in which a majority of voting southern Democrats and a majority of voting Republicans are opposed to a majority of voting northern Democrats. The southern wing of the Democratic party is defined as those legislators from Ala., Ark., Fla., Ga., Ky., La., Miss., N.C., Okla., S.C., Tenn., Texas, and Va. Members from all other states are considered "northern."
† Defined as the number of roll-call victories achieved by the coalition when there are divisions between the coalition and northern Democrats.

Support for the conservative coalition is especially notable among congressmen linked to rural, small-town America. Table 9.4 shows the degree of support given the conservative coalition by three party groups (northern Democrats, southern Democrats, and Republicans), broken down in terms of the members' birthplaces and residences. Within each group, congressmen who were born *and* now reside in rural areas or small towns are more likely to vote in league with the conservative coalition than those lawmakers who were born *and* reside in more urban areas. Whether due to the process of political socialization or to other factors, it is clear that Democrats and Republicans from small towns or open-country districts are much more in-

TABLE 9.4

Birthplace and Hometown in Relation to Support for the Conservative Coalition,
U.S. House of Representatives, 90th Congress

Birthplace and Hometown	Northern Democrats	Southern Democrats	Republicans
Both rural, small-town (under 10,000)	29.9 (20)	69.6 (28)	75.0 (35)
One rural, small-town; one urban*	14.3 (43)	64.3 (47)	70.8 (82)
Both urban (10,000 and over)	8.4 (78)	49.6 (23)	63.3 (68)

SOURCE: LeRoy N. Rieselbach, "Congressmen as 'Small Town Boys': A Research Note," *Midwest Journal of Political Science,* XIV (May 1970), 327.
NOTE: Each entry depicts the mean percentage of support given the conservative coalition by each party group; the number of cases is shown in parentheses.
* "One rural, small-town; one urban" refers to those representatives with either rural, small-town birthplace *or* residence. (See the footnote to the previous table for a definition of the conservative coalition.)

clined to support the parochial or conservative side of public policy questions than their party colleagues who come from larger cities.[60]

Over the years the southern Democrat–Republican coalition—a pastiche of ideology, convenience, and expediency—has had an extraordinary impact on the formation of public policy in Congress. The success of this group has been due not only to its substantial cohesiveness in floor voting but also to the power of Democratic committee chairmen who have been aligned with it. While the seniority system has been among the principal supports of coalition power in the past, it probably will not be as important to the coalition in the future. A quiet but spectacular change has occurred in the pattern of Democratic safe seats in Congress, as shown in Table 9.5, the work of Raymond Wolfinger and Joan Hollinger. The number of northern noncompetitive districts has grown markedly since the middle 1950s; over half of all safe seats in the House are now held by northern Democrats, most of whom represent *urban* districts. In the years to come, some of these districts undoubtedly will produce Democratic committee chairmen. And as the South loses committee chairmanships to the North, its power in Congress will almost certainly decline. Moreover, the chances will be heightened that congressional support for the legislative programs of Democratic presidents will increase.

THE CONGRESSMAN AND HIS PARTY

Table 9.6 shows the range of attitudes of a large sample of congressmen toward political parties. Several findings are worth noting. Only a small proportion of congressmen question the legitimacy of political parties—a mere 10 percent of the respondents agree with the proposition that it would be better if congressmen were elected without party labels. On the other

[60] LeRoy N. Rieselbach, "Congressmen as 'Small Town Boys': A Research Note," *Midwest Journal of Political Science,* XIV (May 1970), 321–30.

TABLE 9.5

TABLE 9.5

Congressional Seats Won by Democrats by at Least 65 Percent
of the Two-Party Vote, by Year and Region, 1946–68

	North				South				Total Seats Won by 65% or More		Total Democratic Seats Won
	Urban		Rural		Urban		Rural				
Year	No.	%	No.	%	No.	%	No.	%	No.	%	
1946	16	15	7	6	11	10	76	69	110	100	188
1948	31	23	14	10	12	9	78	58	135	100	263
1950	25	19	13	10	12	9	79	61	129	99*	235
1952	24	20	4	3	12	10	78	66	118	99*	213
1954	40	28	14	10	9	6	79	56	142	100	232
1956	32	26	8	7	13	11	68	56	121	100	234
1958	61	35	20	11	20	11	75	43	176	100	283
1960	57	36	12	8	19	12	70	44	158	100	260
1962	53	39	10	7	10	7	64	47	137	100	259
1964	81	49	25	15	12	7	48	29	166	100	294

	Combined Northern				Combined Southern						
	No.		%		No.		%				
1966	66		53		59		47		125	100	248
1968	61		52		57		48		118	100	243

SOURCE: Raymond E. Wolfinger and Joan Hollinger, "Safe Seats, Seniority, and Power in Congress," in *Readings on Congress,* ed. Raymond E. Wolfinger (Englewood Cliffs, N.J.: Prentice-Hall, Inc., 1971), p. 53.
* Does not sum to 100 because of rounding.

TABLE 9.6

Attitudes of Congressmen Toward Political Parties

	Agree	Tend to Agree	Unde- cided	Tend to Disagree	Dis- agree	No Answer
"The best interests of the people would be better served if congressmen were elected without party labels."	7%	3%	3%	14%	70%	2%
"Under our form of government, every individual should take an interest in government directly, not through a political party."	17%	12%	5%	20%	46%	1%
"If a bill is important for his party's record, a member should vote with his party even if it costs him some support in his district."	9%	26%	7%	15%	37%	6%
"The two parties should take clear-cut, opposing stands on more of the important and controversial issues."	17%	28%	3%	16%	35%	1%

SOURCE: Roger H. Davidson, *The Role of the Congressman* (New York: Pegasus, 1969), p. 145.

hand, when more rigorous tests of party support are invoked, pro-party responses decline sharply. Over one-half of the congressmen (52 percent) oppose the idea that a member should support his party "even if it costs him some support in his district." Finally, those congressmen who believe that the parties should take clear-cut, opposing stands on issues are slightly less numerous than those congressmen who oppose this idea. "The picture that emerges from these responses," writes Roger Davidson, "is one of overwhelming support for the norm of party activity but considerable disagreement over the degree of loyalty that party membership should imply."[61]

A closer look at those congressmen who are most and least loyal to their parties (as revealed by their responses to the items in Table 9.6) discloses several interesting characteristics. "Loyalists" and "Mavericks" can, in general, be distinguished on several counts:

Loyalists	*Mavericks*
Leaders	Nonleaders
First-term members	Senior members
Members from marginal districts	Members from safe districts

This categorization, of course, represents only central tendencies. There are some high-seniority members who rank high in party loyalty (perhaps because they are also in the leadership network) as well as some members from marginal districts who resist the claims of party. Nevertheless, the general pattern appears clear: the incidence of party-centered roles varies according to leader-nonleader status, length of time in the House, and the competitive character of the district.[62]

TWO OR FOUR PARTIES?

The American party system provides a good illustration of the proposition that it is just about as difficult to abandon ideas concerning an institution as it is to abandon the institution itself. Conventional interpretation reassures us that our politics is of the common two-party variety, consisting of Republicans and Democrats. But there is a good deal of evidence that, at least at points in the political process, the two parties have been undermined by other persistent combinations. James Burns argues that we should accept the fact that, in practice and where it counts, we have a "four-party" sys-

[61] *The Role of the Congressman* (New York: Pegasus, 1969), p. 149.

[62] *Ibid,* pp. 149–60. Davidson explains the attitudes of the senior congressman toward political parties in this way: "With one or more re-election campaigns under his belt, he can view his career with somewhat more confidence. He has developed his own style of maintaining rapport with his constituents—sometimes by carving out a position distinct from that of his national party. His independence is encouraged by the fact that he is more likely than his freshman colleagues to represent a safe district. Within the House of Representatives, the veteran Congressman is less apt to need the services provided by the party organization: His committee assignment is usually fixed, and he has developed a network of informal communications with House colleagues who can supply him with the information he needs" (p. 153).

314 tem.[63] The main lines of his argument can be noted without going into a detailed analysis.[64]

The American "four-party" system consists of two presidential and two congressional parties: Presidential Democrats, Presidential Republicans, Congressional Democrats, and Congressional Republicans. On a left-right, liberal-conservative continuum, they line up in the order listed, though some overlap is, of course, inevitable. Congressional Democrats like Adlai Stevenson, III, of Illinois and Philip Hart of Michigan, among others, are "members" in good standing of the Democratic Presidential party; and Congressional Republicans like Clifford Case of New Jersey and Jacob Javits of New York, among others, belong to the Republican Presidential party. But the main divisions are intact.

The distinguishing mark of the "parties" is policy. *Both* presidential parties are more liberal and more internationalist than *either* congressional party. "They are separate parties in that each has its own ideology, organization, and leadership. In political outlook, the Congressional Republican party slants sharply to the right, and the Congressional Democrats lean almost as far in that direction." Control of the national committees and national conventions has enabled both presidential parties to choose liberal candidates for the presidency; the congressional parties acquiesce because they cannot do otherwise and, moreover, a liberal presidential candidate helps them in the battle for a congressional majority. Elections, therefore, decide "what kind of liberals will run the White House and what kind of conservatives will run Congress."[65]

Frustration and stalemate often accompany intraparty cleavages. Examples abound in recent decades. President Kennedy's relations with the 87th and 88th Congresses, for example, were characterized as much by deadlock as by anything else. Numerous presidential bills dealing with domestic matters were defeated by the "congressional" parties, especially in the House. (See "coalition victories" in Table 9.3) Toward the end of this administration, the president's foreign policy measures also came under heavy attack, and sharp cuts were made in the foreign-aid program. Persistent conflict between "presidential" liberals and "congressional" conservatives stands as one of the principal characteristics of the thirty-five-month presidency of John F. Kennedy.

[63] The "four-party" system appears to be more nearly "factional" than "party" in character. It might be said that on legislation having clearly defined "liberal" and "conservative" dimensions, there are two empirical parties in Congress: the conservative coalition (southern Democrats and northern Republicans) and the "liberal" coalition (mainly northern Democrats plus a small group of northern Republicans). But there are exceptions, since some southern Democrats are usually in the liberal coalition and some northern Democrats are usually in the conservative coalition.

[64] The theme of an American "multiparty" system is found in several articles. See James M. Burns, "America's 'Four-Party' System," *New York Times Magazine,* August 5, 1956; "Two-Party Stalemate: The Crisis in Our Politics," *Atlantic Monthly,* February 1960, pp. 37–41; "White House vs. Congress," *Atlantic Monthly,* March 1960, pp. 65–69; "Memo to the Next President," *Atlantic Monthly,* April 1960, pp. 64–68. The most complete analysis of the four-party system, coalition politics, and the consequences of these arrangements for the government and the people is Burns, *The Deadlock of Democracy* (Englewood Cliffs, N.J.: Prentice-Hall, Inc., 1963).

[65] Burns, "White House vs. Congress," pp. 65–66.

Nevertheless, deadlock between the branches is not inevitable and conservatives do not always get their way in Congress. The 89th Congress, for example, was as responsive to the initiatives of President Johnson as the previous one had been unresponsive to those of President Kennedy. Some major share of the explanation for President Johnson's considerable success with his legislative program lies in the fact that the Democratic House plurality in the 89th Congress was almost twice as great as that in the 88th Congress.[66] The many new Democratic congressmen elected in Johnson's landslide victory over Goldwater gave overwhelming support to the president's program, and "coalition victories" dropped sharply in the House (Table 9.3). But the coalition's eclipse was brief. The severe losses by the Democrats in the 1966 congressional elections, dropping forty-seven seats in the House, was followed by a revival of the conservative coalition in the 90th Congress. Among the coalition's first acts was the elimination of the twenty-one-day rule that had been in force the previous two years. The coalition's successes continued to be high during the Nixon administration.

Democratic liberals, especially in Congress, have long been apprehensive over the schism in their party. Former Senator Paul Douglas of Illinois, a long-time foe of the southern Democrat–Republican coalition, once described the dilemma of northern Democrats in this way:

> The States which run the Democratic Party in the Senate are not the States which can carry a presidential election. The presidential elections are decided in the States which are on the outside looking in, so far as the organization of the Senate is concerned. And, indeed, it has been the election of Senators from these large industrial States which has given us the balance of power— not merely the balance of power, but the preponderance of the power in the Senate itself as well as in the House. We carried the House, and largely carried the Senate, because those of us who come from the industrial States advanced, generally, a declaration in favor of civil rights, a declaration in favor of liberal tax policy, a declaration to protect consumers of gas and oil, a declaration for liberal labor legislation, and so forth.
>
> The voters, believing what we have advocated will happen, elect us to the Senate and to the House.... Then we come to Washington and find that the machinery of the Senate, under the seniority system, is controlled by those who represent the localities where the predominant opinion is very different from ours. Very frankly, we go through a process of frustration. Not only do we go through a process of frustration, but the folks back home somehow feel they have been shortchanged.
>
> I am perfectly frank to say I do not know how long the Democratic Party can continue with this situation. We know it exists. I submit we should do something about it. One way we can do something about it is to make our

---

[66] See a study which suggests that the growth in support of President Johnson's legislative program in the 89th Congress was due principally to the substantially altered composition of the newly elected Congress—marked by the election of fifty-nine new northern Democrats—rather than to any change in congressional attitudes consistent with a mandate theory. Marvin G. Weinbaum and Dennis R. Judd, "In Search of a Mandated Congress," *Midwest Journal of Political Science,* XIV (May 1970), 276–302.

governing bodies, whether they be the conference, the policy committee, or the steering committee, truly representative. . . .[67]

PARTY VOTING IN THE STATES

Party politics in the legislatures varies in form and intensity from state to state. The dimensions of party conflict and of party differences are not easily compared or contrasted. The reasons for this are several and varied. To begin with, there are wide differences in party competition among the states. There are southern states where Republican politicians come in contact with the legislature only by visiting the state capital and northern states where Democratic legislators have a status only a notch above that of interloper—so dominant are the major parties in their localities. Under conditions of one-party rule, factions lay plans and struggle for ascendancy somewhat in the fashion of political parties, and perform some of their functions as well,[68] but all this bears only a dim resemblance to the idea of responsible party government.

In two states, Nebraska and Minnesota, state legislators are elected on ballots shorn of party designations. Although this leads to a nominal "non-partisanship," other group commitments tend to take the place of the parties. In Minnesota, the House and Senate each have Liberal and Conservative caucuses which function in a party capacity, nominating candidates for the principal offices, controlling committee chairmanships, and otherwise directing the affairs of the legislature. The presence of party is felt in the open attachment of most Liberals to the Democratic-Farmer-Labor party and of many Conservatives to the Republican party. Proving further that party spirit cannot be legislated away, Liberal and Conservative caucus ("party") lines can be distinguished on certain types of roll-call votes.

A second obstacle to generalization about state legislative parties is that they function in disparate environs and under variable conventions. In no two states is rural-urban cleavage of the same intensity and scope, a factor which plainly has a bearing on party behavior. In addition, the way in which legislators are chosen, their tenure and turnover, the power customarily accorded party leaders and the criteria which govern their selection, the existence and utilization of party agencies like the caucus, and the persis-

---

[67] *Congressional Record,* 86th Congress, 1st sess., March 9, 1959, 3195–99, as found in Francis M. Carney and H. Frank Way, Jr., *Politics 1960* (San Francisco: Wadsworth Publishing Company, 1960), p. 33.

[68] For a discussion of the nature of factions in southern states, see V. O. Key, Jr., *Southern Politics* (New York: Alfred A. Knopf, Inc., 1949). See also Malcolm B. Parsons, "Quasi-Partisan Conflict in a One-Party Legislative System: The Florida Senate, 1947–1961," *American Political Science Review,* LVI (September 1962), 605–14. Parsons' study shows a persistent struggle between northern and southern factions in the state over committee positions and control of the office of president of the senate as well as over a variety of policy questions. Not all one-party legislatures are beset by significant factionalism, however. In Oklahoma, for example, where factions are not important, legislators appear to respond to diverse pressures, depending on the subject matter of the legislation. The rural-urban character of the legislator's district appears to influence voting behavior on certain issues; on other issues the competitiveness of the district is associated with particular responses; on still other issues socio-economic status of the member's constituents may be the controlling factor. For an account of this, see Samuel C. Patterson, "Dimensions of Voting Behavior in a One-Party State Legislature," *Public Opinion Quarterly,* XXVI (Summer 1962), 185–200.

tence of cohesive elements within each party vary from state to state. Finally, just as party structures differ throughout the country, the legal-constitutional systems within which party processes are carried on differ from state to state.

Comparative analysis of state legislative parties is hindered most of all, however, by "the problem," the variable practice with respect to roll-call votes in the legislatures. Where variations are significant, roll-call data are not altogether comparable. In most studies of legislative party behavior, roll calls have been the unit of analysis. In some states, however, such as Connecticut and Massachusetts, roll-call votes are not required for the passage of bills; as a result, they are not frequently taken. In most states, roll calls are mandatory on the passage of bills, whether controversy is present or not; in these states a thousand or more record votes may be taken during a session. Evaluation of the dimensions of "party voting" is obviously difficult where voting requirements are substantially different. And this is only one of many problems which beset roll-call vote studies.

Despite the obstacles to systematic comparison of the role of political parties in fifty state capitals, the general contour of party behavior can be sketched.[69]

[69] A variety of approaches to the study of legislative party behavior in the states have been used. Not all of the conclusions coincide neatly with the interpretations of these paragraphs. The controversy is not so much over the facts as over the way in which they should be handled. For a book-length study of party behavior in the California legislature, see William Buchanan, *Legislative Partisanship: The Deviant Case of California* (Berkeley: University of California Press, 1963). See Thomas J. Anton, "The Legislature, Politics, and Public Policy, 1959," *Rutgers Law Review,* XIV (Winter 1960), 269–89—on the New Jersey legislature; Robert W. Becker, Frieda L. Foote, Mathias Lubega, and Stephen V. Monsma, "Correlates of Legislative Voting: Michigan House of Representatives, 1954–1961," *Midwest Journal of Political Science,* VI (November 1962), 384–96; Thomas A. Flinn, "The Outline of Ohio Politics," *Western Political Quarterly,* XIII (September 1960), 702–21, and "Party Responsibility in the States: Some Causal Factors," *American Political Science Review,* LVIII (March 1964), 60–71; Malcolm E. Jewell, "Party Voting in American State Legislatures," *American Political Science Review,* XLIX (September 1955), 773–91; William J. Keefe, "Party Government and Lawmaking in the Illinois General Assembly," *Northwestern University Law Review,* XLVII (March 1952), 55–71, and "Parties, Partisanship, and Public Policy in the Pennsylvania Legislature," *American Political Science Review,* XLVIII (June 1954), 450–64, and "Comparative Study of the Role of Political Parties in State Legislatures," *Western Political Quarterly,* IX (September 1956), 726–42; W. Duane Lockard, "Legislative Politics in Connecticut," *American Political Science Review,* XLVIII (March 1954), 166–73, and *New England State Politics,* pp. 70–72, 116–17, 152–56, 212–17, 277–85; Robert H. Salisbury, "Missouri Politics and State Political Systems," in *Research Papers 1958* (Columbia, Mo.: Bureau of Government Research, 1959), pp. 9–24; George D. Young, "The Role of Political Parties in the Missouri House of Representatives," (Ph.D. thesis, University of Missouri, 1958); Zeller, *op. cit.,* pp. 189–213; James Herndon, "Patterns of Roll Call Voting in the 1963 North Dakota Legislative Assembly" (Manuscript, University of North Dakota, 1965); and Charles W. Wiggins, "Party Politics in the Iowa Legislature," *Midwest Journal of Political Science,* XI (February 1967), 86–97. Hugh L. LeBlanc, "Voting in State Senates: Party and Constituency Influences," *Midwest Journal of Political Science,* XIII (February, 1969), 33–57. For a general survey of the relevant literature, see Norman Meller, "Legislative Behavior Research," *Western Political Quarterly,* XIII (March 1960), 131–53, and "Legislative Behavior Research Revisited: A Review of Five Years' Publications," *Western Political Quarterly,* XVIII (December 1965), 776–93; and Morris S. Ogul, "Research on the Legislative Process in Congress," in *The Legislative Process in Congress and the States* (University Park: Pennsylvania State University, Institute of Public Administration, 1961), pp. 13–23.

318

1. The model of a responsible two-party system—disciplined and unified parties presenting genuine policy alternatives—is met more nearly in certain northern state legislatures than in Congress. New York, Connecticut, Massachusetts, Rhode Island, and Pennsylvania all have considerably more "party voting" than is found in the usual state legislature. These states are distinguished by a high degree of urbanization, impressive industrialization, and competitive two-party systems. In states where rural-urban cleavage tends to coincide with major party divisions (rural Republicans versus urban Democrats), it is predictable (a good bet, at least) that conflict between the parties will be fairly frequent and sometimes intense.[70] In contrast, party voting appears to be found much less frequently in rural, less populous states.[71]

2. As in Congress, party battles in the legislatures are episodic. A great deal of legislative business is transacted with a minimum of controversy. General concensus at the roll-call stage is common, and in many legislatures well over one-half of the roll-call votes are unanimous. Legislation having a major impact upon conditions of private and public life within the state—involving schools, governmental organization, constitutional reform, state services, and other areas—is often shaped and adopted in actions in which the parties either are in general agreement or have taken no stands. This is true even in states where substantial disagreement between the parties is found, as in Pennsylvania. A conception of party which includes the notion that Democrats spend most of their time quarreling or bargaining with Republicans (and vice versa) over legislation is a gross distortion of reality, with perhaps the exception of a state or two.

3. Party unity fluctuates from issue to issue: party lines are firm on some

[70] Politicians and political scientists have long adjusted to the idea that rural-urban conflict is important and persistent in the typical state legislature. In the literature of political science this theme is something of an "authorized version" in descriptions of the legislative struggle. An examination of roll-call voting behavior in the Illinois and Missouri legislatures, however, leads David R. Derge to these conclusions: (1) "Nonmetropolitan legislators seldom vote together with high cohesion against metropolitan legislators; (2) The metropolitan legislators usually do not vote together with high cohesion; and (3) Metropolitan legislators are usually on the prevailing side when they do vote together with high cohesion." "Rural-urban" conflict in many northern states, studies such as this have shown, is very likely to revolve around battles between a rural-based Republican party and an urban-based Democratic party. The problem is one of proportions: how much conflict is due to rural-urban differences, how much to party differences? Evidence seems to point mainly to party. Whatever the appropriate terminology, there is no doubt that in many states big cities have suffered at the hands of rural and open-country legislators, mainly Republican, and suburban legislators, also mainly Republican. Derge is surely correct that "the city's bitterest opponents in the legislature are political enemies from within its own walls, and those camped in adjoining suburban areas." "Metropolitan and Outstate Alignments in Illinois and Missouri Legislative Delegations," *American Political Science Review*, LII (December 1958), 1051–65, quoted material on p. 1065. For a criticism of Derge's study, using data drawn from the New Jersey lower house, see Richard T. Frost, "On Derge's Metropolitan and Outstate Legislative Delegations," *American Political Science Review*, LIII (September 1959), 792–95; and for a rejoinder, see Derge, "On the Use of Roll-Call Analysis: A Reply to R. T. Frost," *American Political Science Review*, LIII (December 1959), 1097–99.

[71] On this point, see Jewell, "Party Voting," 784.

kinds of questions, rarely visible on others, and, despite the appeals of party leaders, usually collapse on still other kinds.[72]

4. It seems safe to say that in most states parties stay in business by being flexible as to policies. They veer and tack as electoral winds dictate.

5. There is apparently no counterpart in the state legislatures to the conservative coalition of Republicans and southern Democrats which sometimes dominates Congress. Party lines are crossed in the states, to be sure, but the biparty combinations appear to lack the spirit and continuity of the congressional prototype.

6. In northern states distinguished by rigorous party competition in the legislatures, party lines are highly visible on liberal-conservative issues. The Democratic party ordinarily originates and lends considerable support to legislation favorable to the interests of labor, minorities, and low-income groups (e.g., employer-liability laws, disability benefits, unemployment compensation, fair employment practices, public accommodation, open housing, and public housing).[73] The Republican party generally is concerned with fostering the interests of the business community, and this objective is likely to take the form of resisting legislation backed by organized labor or of blocking new regulation of business. In addition, Republican legislators usually are more anxious than Democrats to devise state tax structures which are favorable to the interests of industry. Health and welfare legislation usually finds the Democratic party in the forefront to liberalize benefits or to extend state services; Republicans tend to view these questions in a fiscal context, which typically means a cautious approach to new expenditures. In a word, socio-economic-class legislation often serves as a rallying point for each party.

7. Party conflict often is generated on issues of narrow partisan interest. In one sense, the party organizations perform essentially as interest groups, seeking to strengthen their hand in state politics and to thwart actions which would place them at a disadvantage. The welfare and survival of the party is a persistent theme in both legislation and legislative maneuvers. Accordingly, conflict is common on patronage and appointments,

---

[72] The factor of majority size, according to one strand of coalition theory, affects the cohesiveness of legislative parties. In large majorities, the theory holds, there is less incentive to solve internal conflicts in an amicable fashion because the threat of the opposing coalition is so slight. Rent by intraparty struggles, the capacity of a large majority to govern is diminished. A test of this theory over a large number of sessions of the Indiana House of Representatives, however, finds no corroboration for it. Quite the contrary, the greater the size of the majority party, the greater its success in winning roll-call votes. Studies of many other legislatures, of course, would be required before confirming or rejecting this theory. See David W. Moore, "Legislative Effectiveness and Majority Party Size: A Test in the Indiana House," *Journal of Politics,* XXXI (November 1969), 1063–79. For exposition of the theory, see William H. Riker, *The Theory of Political Coalitions* (New Haven: Yale University Press, 1962).

[73] Party differences clearly are important on some kinds of policy questions. A recent study discloses that over the period 1945–64, civil rights legislation was three times as likely to be passed when the legislature and governorship were under the control of the Democrats than when they were under the control of the Republicans or subject to split control. See Robert S. Erikson, "The Relationship Between Party Control and Civil Rights Legislation in the American States," *Western Political Quarterly,* XXIV (February 1971), 178–82.

320　　organizational and procedural matters in the legislatures, election law
(especially reapportionment), bills and resolutions designed to embarrass
the state administration, and measures to increase state control over
municipal governments (especially where the state legislature is controlled by the Republicans and the big-city administrations are controlled
by the Democrats). In sum, organizational party interest[74] cuts through
a variety of public policy questions, and its presence is felt even though
dissimulated in debate.

CONSTITUENCIES AND LIBERAL-CONSERVATIVE
VOTING RECORDS

Political outlook in the legislature is a function of party and section, as the
previous pages have shown, and also of constituency. In general, less head-
way has been made in evaluating the impact of constituency conditions on
legislative voting than in analyzing the significance of the party factor. Here
we shall be concerned briefly with examining the relationship between a high
or low degree of party competition in constituencies and the voting behavior
of party members in the legislature. We shall have to be content with sketching the shape of the problem, since evidence is too scarce to support general
propositions.

An interpretation of American politics made familiar by Schattschneider is that a two-party system tends to produce moderate parties. "A
large party must be supported by a great variety of interests sufficiently tole-
rant of each other to collaborate, held together by compromise and concession, and the discovery of certain common interests. . . ."[75] Moderation results
from the quest for a majority, since neither party can make exceptional concessions to any interest without antagonizing a counterinterest. The corollary
to this is that each party contains representatives whose voting records range
the length of the liberal-conservative scale. This interpretation has been put
to empirical test several times in studies of Congress and state legislatures.

A study of the U.S. House of Representatives by Samuel Huntington
disclosed that members coming from marginal (or closely contested) districts presented the most marked differences in liberalism and conservatism:
i.e., Republicans from districts where party competition was rigorous had a
relatively low index of liberalism on House roll-call votes, while Democrats
from comparable districts had a very high index of liberalism. In terms of
election margins, the parties were most evenly balanced in urban congressional districts, which in turn were the districts characterized by the greatest
ideological cleavage between the parties. In rural areas, where "one-party"
constituencies were predominant, election margins were widest and the ideological differences between the parties were smallest. Huntington hypothesized that increasing urbanization will lead to the development of sharper
differences between the parties. "The parties will strive to win not by

---

[74] For a consideration of legislators' allegiance to the party on matters relating
to the organization's welfare, see Duncan MacRae, Jr., "The Role of the State
Legislator in Massachusetts," *American Sociological Review*, XIX (April 1954),
185–94.

[75] Schattschneider, *op. cit.*, p. 85.

converting their opponents but by effectively mobilizing their own supporters, *not by extending their appeal but by intensifying it.*"[76] Attractive as the Huntington theory may appear to advocates of party responsibility, a more recent study by Wayne Shannon of the 86th and 87th Congresses finds little support for it. Rather it appears that there is at best only a thin association between the competitiveness of the congressman's district and his policy choices in Congress. To the extent that there is a relationship at all, it is that congressmen from close districts are most likely to deviate *toward* the policy position of the opposition party. The relationship between competitiveness and policy choice probably varies considerably over time. Further research on Congress will be required before more definitive statements can be made concerning the impact of electoral marginality on roll-call voting.[77]

Close elections and sharp ideological divisions between the parties are unrelated in the Massachusetts legislature. Duncan MacRae found that legislators from competitive districts were those most likely to cross party lines on socioeconomic-class legislation (e.g., labor, taxes, old-age assistance, public works). Legislators from safe districts, on the other hand, tended to be party regulars, Republicans as "conservatives," Democrats as "liberals." In other words, members from competitive districts were most likely to vote in about the same way, irrespective of their party affiliations.[78] These findings are consonant with the view that sees the parties appealing to a broad range of social interests. In contrast to the Massachusetts study, a study of the Ohio legislature found only a slight relationship between the legislators' electoral margins and their loyalty to their parties.[79] The one conclusion that emerges is that research on a number of states will be required in order to understand the relationship between electoral insecurity (or security) and party loyalty.

MacRae's study is also instructive for its analysis of the relationship between the socio-economic character of districts and the voting behavior of legislators. Using voting data on socio-economic-class legislation—e.g., labor, taxation, public works—MacRae found that House members rep-

[76] "A Revised Theory of American Party Politics," *American Political Science Review,* XLIV (September 1950), 669–77 (quotation on 677). (Emphasis added.) The liberalism-conservatism index was fashioned from issues singled out by the CIO and the *New Republic,* and covered such matters as labor relations, price control, agriculture, public power, civil rights, taxes, Social Security, monopoly, housing, and foreign affairs.

[77] *Party, Constituency and Congressional Voting* (Baton Rouge: Louisiana State University Press, 1968), pp. 166–70.

[78] "The Relation Between Roll-Call Votes and Constituencies in the Massachusetts House of Representatives," *American Political Science Review,* XLVI (December 1952), 1046–55. The findings of three later studies are in general agreement with those of MacRae. See Thomas R. Dye, "A Comparison of Constituency Influences in the Upper and Lower Chambers of a State Legislature," *Western Political Quarterly,* XIV (June 1961), 473–80; and Pertti Pesonen, "Close and Safe State Elections in Massachusetts," *Midwest Journal of Political Science,* VII (February 1963), 54–70. Dye's study focuses on the 1957 session of the Pennsylvania legislature. In Wisconsin those legislators who play a role of "maverick" and are least inclined to take cues from the party tend to be representatives of closely contested districts. See Samuel C. Patterson, "The Role of the Deviant in the State Legislative System: The Wisconsin Assembly," *Western Political Quarterly,* XIV (June 1961), 460–72.

[79] Flinn, "Party Responsibility," 67.

322   resenting districts typical of their party (based on a home-ownership index:
Democrats, low owner-occupancy; Republicans, high owner-occupancy) were
more loyal to their party than members representing districts atypical of their
party. "Democrats from high owner-occupancy districts tend on the average
to vote more like Republicans, and the Republicans from low owner-occupancy districts tend to vote more like Democrats."[80]

The liberal-conservative differences between Democrats and Republicans are due in some degree to the differences in the kinds of constituencies
they represent. Constituency differences between the parties are as noticeable
at the congressional as at the state level. Northern Democrats tend to be
elected to Congress from districts having certain pronounced characteristics:
lower owner-occupancy of dwellings, higher proportion of nonwhite population, higher population density, and higher percentage of urban population.
Northern Republicans tend to be elected from districts whose characteristics
are the opposite. Table 9.7, taken from Lewis Froman's study, makes the
point clearly.

TABLE 9.7

Comparison between Northern Democrats and Northern Republicans on Mean
Average Values of Four Constituency Variables

	Average Owner-occupied (%)	*Average Nonwhite* (%)	*Average Population Per Sq. Mile* (No.)	*Average Urban** (%)
Northern Democrats	55.5	13.6	26,697	74.5
Northern Republicans	67.1	3.8	5,040	65.3

SOURCE: Lewis A. Froman, Jr., "Inter-Party Constituency Differences and Congressional
Voting Behavior," *American Political Science Review*, LVII (March, 1963), 59. Data compiled
from the *Congressional District Data Book, Districts of the 87th Congress* (Washington, D.C.:
Bureau of the Census, 1961), and the *Congressional Quarterly Weekly Report*, February 23,
1962.
* "Urban is census definition, 1960.

Northern Democratic congressmen ordinarily win out in districts whose
characteristics make "liberalism" an appropriate guide to their voting behavior; their Republican counterparts ordinarily come from districts where
"conservatism" is an equally appropriate response. The critical fact is that
northern Democrats who represent districts with "conservative" characteristics (e.g., higher owner-occupancy and small nonwhite population) most
frequently vote with conservative forces in Congress, while Republicans who
represent districts with "liberal" characteristics most frequently vote liberal
positions.[81] In sum, this evidence gives merit to the argument that liberal-

80 MacRae, *op. cit.*, p. 1051.
81 Lewis A. Froman, Jr., "Inter-Party Constituency Differences and Congressional Voting Behavior," *American Political Science Review*, LVII (March 1963),
57–61. Another study by David Mayhew offers additional evidence for this point.
Over the period 1947–62, Republican *city* congressmen who represented districts
characterized by low ownership occupancy were more inclined to vote with the
Democratic party on housing issues than their colleagues who represented districts

ism-conservatism differences between northern congressmen may not be so much a function of party as an expression of constituency priorities that stem from economic and demographic variables.[82]

The act of voting is influenced by a number of pressures that converge on the legislator. In some degree, each legislator sorts out and evaluates the significance of these pressures, perhaps weighing or balancing them against his personal attitudes. Although the central factors influencing voting are well known, new theoretical and empirical work is required if we are to make noticeably more precise statements about the *comparative* impact of factors described as uniquely of party, constituency, organized interest, or personal origins.

PARTY AND SEPARATION OF POWERS

Effective performance by the parties, as collectivities, is hindered not only by ideological cleavages within their ranks but also by the institutional arrangements within which the parties must function. Theoretically, the majority party acts to mesh or harmonize the operations of the executive and legislative branches, permitting a common party approach to the fashioning of public policy. The one requirement essential to this function is that "electoral procedures and representative systems be so constructed that candidates of either party may capture both executive and legislature."[83] Where one

---

with more homeowners. Those city Republicans who remained loyal to their party often had short careers in Congress; they failed to recognize that "one of the best ways for a Republican to construct a safe seat in a city area was to vote with the Democrats on city questions." *Op. cit.,* p. 78. See also a study of the impact of constituency demographic and electoral characteristics on the voting habits of southern Democratic House members by Thomas A. Flinn and Harold L. Wolman. Their study discloses a strong relationship between certain demographic characteristics of constituencies and constituency electoral behavior (support of Kennedy in 1960 election, opposition to Dixiecrats in 1948), on the one hand, and support of the Kennedy program and a larger federal role in the 88th Congress, on the other hand. "Constituency and Roll Call Voting: The Case of Southern Democratic Congressmen," *Midwest Journal of Political Science,* X (May 1966), 192–99. See a somewhat similar study by Loren K. Waldman, "Liberalism of Congressmen and the Presidential Vote in Their Districts," *Midwest Journal of Political Science,* XI (February 1967), 73–85.

82 This generalization, like many others involving legislative voting, is not ready to be set into concrete. A study of Congress over the period 1953–62 finds that party differences over public policy questions (especially government-and-the-economy issues) cannot be attributed simply to differences in the types of constituencies which elect Democrats and Republicans. When the constituency factor is held constant, Democratic members of the House still vote consistently more liberal than Republican members. This characterizes the voting of representatives from both "swing" and "safe" districts. See Clarence N. Stone, "Issue Cleavage Between Democrats and Republicans in the U.S. House of Representatives," *Journal of Public Law,* XIV, no. 2 (1965), 343–58.

83 This section is based on a study by V. O. Key, Jr., and Corinne Silverman, "Party and Separation of Powers: A Panorama of Practice in the States," in *Public Policy,* ed. Carl J. Friedrich and J. Kenneth Galbraith (Cambridge: Harvard University, Graduate School of Public Administration, 1954), pp. 382–412 (quotation on p. 403). This study excludes the twelve one-party Democratic states of the South, the heavily Republican states of Vermont and New Hampshire, and the states of Nebraska and Minnesota with their nonpartisan legislatures.

324 party controls the executive branch and the other party controls one or both houses of the legislative branch, no opportunity exists for a party to bridge the gap created by the separation of powers. Ordinarily, indeed, the breach is widened.

Divided party control is a typical condition in many of the northern states (see Table 4.4, p. 109). Malapportionment has sometimes contributed to this. It also may be due to the weakness of the minority party's organization, which prevents it from competing vigorously in all legislative districts: "Long nourished only by the prospect of defeat, it has neither the candidates nor the campaign resources—to say nothing of a frequent lack of will—to command support at the grass roots commensurate with its gubernatorial vote." Other factors which contribute to party divisions between the executive and the legislature are staggered and nonconcurrent terms of office (e.g., four-year term for governor, two-year term for lower house) and the separation of gubernatorial and presidential elections, an arrangement which serves to shield state politics from national trends. Finally, on some occasions voters appear to make a deliberate choice to give the governorship to one party and the legislature to the other. V. O. Key and Corinne Silverman conclude that institutional arrangements and electoral procedures in the states "have been more or less deliberately designed to frustrate popular majorities."[84]

Divided government has been a persistent problem at the national level as well. During six of his eight years in office, President Eisenhower was confronted by a Congress controlled by the Democratic party. The elections of 1968 and 1970 dealt a similar fate to President Nixon. In sum, only one-half of the elections from 1952 to 1970 resulted in control of both houses of Congress and the presidency by the same party.

The significance of this is easily apparent by now. The prospects for party government—in the sense that the electorate makes a decision to give the reins of government to one of the parties and to hold it responsible for the conduct of affairs—are severely diminished when the system makes it virtually impossible for one party to win control of both the executive and legislative branches at the same time.

American Parties: Diagnosis and Prescription

RESPONSIBLE PARTIES IN THE LEGISLATURE

Dissatisfaction over the arrangement of power in Congress and concern over the inability of the parties to legislate have been central themes in the burgeoning literature of American party politics. A spate of books and articles on political parties, their performance and their potentialities, has been written recently, serving, in the literature at least, to mark their coming of age. Most of the commentary, but not all, has been critical of party performance, especially in the legislative process. The new literature of protest, coupled with rejoinders to it, has been concerned chiefly with congressional parties.

---

[84] *Ibid.*, p. 398.

Since the issue is roughly the same in many states, no license is needed to apply it to American legislatures generally. Here we shall use the language and example of Congress.

At dead center in the controversy over American parties is the issue of an "effective" or "responsible" party system. The 1950 Report of the Committee on Political Parties of the American Political Science Association, which sparked the debate over the role that parties should assume in a democratic government, held that American parties were "unable to reach and pursue responsible decisions." When the party system fails to chart the course of government, the result is irresponsibility, vacillation, and drift. The model party system which the committee had in mind is suggested in several statements taken from the report:

> An effective party system requires, first, that the parties are able to bring forth programs to which they commit themselves and, second, that the parties possess sufficient internal cohesion to carry out these programs.

> The fundamental requirement [in making the parties accountable to the public] is a two-party system in which the opposition party acts as the critic of the party in power, developing, defining and presenting the policy alternatives which are necessary for a true choice in reaching public decisions.

> A stronger party system is less likely to give cause for the deterioration and confusion of purposes which sometimes passes for compromise but is really an unjustifiable surrender to narrow interests. Compromise among interests is compatible with the aims of a free society only when the terms of reference reflect an openly acknowledged concept of the public interest. There is every reason to insist that the parties be held accountable to the public for the compromises they accept.[85]

The report contains a comprehensive series of proposals designed to help achieve a more responsible party system, covering national party organization, intraparty democracy, party platforms, political participation, and party organization in Congress. Although the proposals tend to come together in a common stream, we shall consider only those directly related to the composition and structure of Congress.

Party unity in Congress is fundamentally impaired, the report contends, because national party leaders have neglected congressional nominations and elections. "Above all, the basis of party operations in Congress is laid in the election process." National party leaders have a legitimate interest in discussing congressional nominations with local party leaders in an effort to winnow out prospective candidates who are likely to oppose the main

---

[85] *Toward a More Responsible Two-Party System,* published as a supplement to the *American Political Science Review,* XLIV (September 1950). The statements are taken from 17, 18, and 20, respectively (italics omitted). The importance of congressional nominations is discussed on 24, 56–57; the election of party leaders, 57–59; leadership committees, 59–60; party caucuses, 60–61; seniority, 61–63; legislative schedule and debate, 64–65. These subjects are discussed in subsequent paragraphs.

326 "planks" in the party's program. If the national parties are unable to control the use of their party labels, candidates with all manner of policy views are likely to become party nominees; the result, inevitably, is that the congressional parties encounter great difficulty in seeking to unify their memberships on policy matters of major importance.

Congressional party organizations are weak and ineffective not for lack of proper structure, the committee stated, but for lack of use. Improvement lies in revitalizing party instruments. Increased emphasis should be placed upon meetings between the president and the "Big Four" of Congress—both majority leaders, the Speaker, and the vice-president—when all belong to the same party. Election of party leaders in Congress should be preceded by "broad consultation throughout the national leadership."

Party leadership in Congress is diffused and ambiguous. A single leadership committee for each party and each house, supplanting the policy and steering committees, should be created. Elected by party members and subjected to a vote of confidence every two years, the committees would be responsible for placing proposals before the rank and file, keeping a rein on the legislative schedule, and otherwise managing party affairs. House and Senate leadership committees of each party would need to meet together regularly, and the four leadership groups might be brought together on specific occasions—perhaps to consider the president's principal messages.

Party caucuses (or conferences) should meet more frequently, and their functions should be augmented. If party principles and program are at stake, caucus decisions should be binding. "Rewarding party loyalty is a proper way of fostering party unity...[and] *when members of Congress disregard a caucus decision taken in furtherance of national party policy, they should expect disapproval.*" Members who often flout party decisions should expect their transgressions to cost them patronage and better committee assignments.

The seniority principle should be made to work in harness with the party system. Party leaders should exert their influence to keep a member who is hostile toward party aims from becoming a committee chairman. Committee assignments should be recommended by the party leadership committees to the party caucuses for approval or modification; moreover, committee assignments should be reviewed at least every two years. "Personal competence and party loyalty should be valued more highly than seniority in assigning members to such major committees as those dealing with fiscal policy and foreign affairs."

Finally, the party leadership committee should control the legislative schedule. More responsible party control could be achieved if the power to steer legislation were removed from the House Rules Committee and awarded to the leadership committee of the majority party. A majority vote in the Senate should be sufficient to end debate on all matters.

The party-responsibility model[86] offered by the Committee on Political

---

[86] For an analysis of the development of this concept and its key features, see Austin Ranney, *The Doctrine of Responsible Party Government* (Urbana: University of Illinois Press, 1954). The best known *exponent* of the doctrine is E. E. Schattschneider. See his *Party Government,* and *The Struggle for Party Government* (College Park: University of Maryland Press, 1948).

Parties has been warmly praised in some quarters and vigorously criticized in others. Analysis of the debate is quite beyond the scope of this chapter, especially since we have been concerned with only one section of the report, that which relates to party organization in Congress. The main objections to the report, however, need to be indicated.

On the whole, critics of the report have been more concerned with the broad implications of making the party system more centralized and disciplined than with the specific proposals offered by the committee. A brief condensation of the criticisms would show that one or more writers believe that the committee underestimated present party responsibility in Congress, that certain proposals are unrealistic given the cultural and social milieu in which the parties function, that the party system might be further debilitated were the report followed, that the committee failed to recognize the virtues of the present decentralized system, and that major renovation of the party system cannot be undertaken unless other basic constitutional changes are first instituted. In general, critics feel that the cost of responsible party government is too high a price to pay. Whether it is or not can be better judged after the evidence and arguments have been evaluated first-hand.[87]

CHANGE IN THE PARTY SYSTEM

Old ideas die hard, and social blueprints are not easily transformed into social facts. No matter how the model of party responsibility is evaluated, it is plain that small progress has been made toward its achievement. It is just as apparent that most people and most politicians are both accustomed to, and satisfied with, the present proportions of party, sectional, and pressure interests that dominate Congress. Moreover, the attitudes of people and politicians toward state legislatures seem to be cut out of the same cloth. In a word, outside of the pressure of a limited audience there is no persistent and widespread demand for party reform, whether bold or modest. But this is not the entire story.

To be sure, there are no grounds for open optimism regarding party

---

[87] For exposition and argument, see Hugh A. Bone, Inc., 1971), *American Politics and the Party System* (New York: McGraw-Hill Book Company, Inc., 1971), pp. 15–23; William Goodman, "How Much Political Party Centralization Do We Want?" *Journal of Politics,* XIII (November 1951), 536–61, and *The Two-Party System in the United States* (Princeton; D. Van Nostrand Co., Inc., 1964), pp. 621–54; Ivan Hinderaker, *Party Politics* (New York: Holt, Rinehart & Winston, Inc., 1956), pp. 599–675; Austin Ranney, "Toward a More Responsible Two-Party System: A Commentary," *American Political Science Review,* XLV (June 1951), 488–99, and *Democracy and the American Party System* (New York: Harcourt, Brace & World, Inc., 1956), pp. 525–33; Murray S. Stedman, Jr., and Herbert Sonthoff, "Party Responsibility—A Critical Inquiry," *Western Political Quarterly,* IV (September 1951), 454–68; and Julius Turner, "Responsible Parties: A Dissent from the Floor," *American Political Science Review,* XLV (March 1951), 143–52. For recent analyses of the report, see the papers of Evron M. Kirkpatrick, "Toward a More Responsible Two-Party System: Political Science, Policy Science, or Pseudo-Science?" and Gerald M. Pomper, "After Twenty Years: The Report of the APSA Committee on Political Parties," both delivered at the Annual Meeting of the American Political Science Association, Los Angeles, September 8–12, 1970.

328 reform on the order of the "responsibility" model.[88] But there are two trends that may contribute to the development of a more responsible party system.[89] The first is found in the increasing *nationalization* of American politics. Evidence of this trend appears on many fronts: nationality politics is clearly on the wane; changes in technology, communications, population patterns, and voting behavior have made major inroads on sectionalism; one-party constituencies in the South have declined sharply; black voting power in the South has contributed to the rationalization of southern politics and reduced the number of campaigns tied closely to the racial issue; prospects for the development of a national electorate and a national majority have increased as sectionalism, parochialism, and one-party political systems have dwindled; and, finally, there has been a sharp growth of interest in party and governmental reform.

In the second place, new breezes of *legislative* reform have been blowing through Congress and the state legislatures. Traditional arrangements of power and privilege increasingly have come under review and attack. The struggle for fair apportionment has been largely won. Congressional reorganization, most recently fashioned in 1970, has contributed to the development of a more effective and responsible legislature. The seniority system in the U.S. House of Representatives recently has undergone revision; under the new rules the selection of committee chairmen will be subject to approval by party caucuses. The sectional bias in committee and subcommittee chairmanships which so often has militated against responsible party performance in Congress is less pronounced today than at any time in recent decades. Finally, it is clear that a great many national and state legislators today are concerned to discover ways by which their legislatures can be made more effective and responsible.

There are, in sum, too many straws in the wind to go unnoticed. Yet it will be some time before we know how these developments will affect the party system, particularly the performance of the legislative parties. A decision-making system characterized by responsible parties is not around the corner by any means, but neither should it be considered an impossibility. Major change in the American political system, it is worth remembering, is fashioned out of small and occasional developments. Under the right circumstances, it is clear, the deadlocks of American politics can be broken.

---

[88] Although it does not involve the legislative party system directly, the current drive for reform in the Democratic party is worth noting. Largely as a result of the rancor generated in the 1968 Democratic National Convention, two commissions were formed to study party processes with a view to fostering a greater measure of intraparty democracy. The Commission on Party Structure and Delegate Selection was given the responsibility of developing guidelines for reform of the delegate-selection process as a means of stimulating citizen participation and of making the party more representative of grass roots sentiment. The Rules Commission was created primarily for the purpose of developing proposals for the reform of the national nominating convention. What the long-run impact of these commissions will be remains to be seen; at the least they are a good indication of the current interest of some party politicians in bringing new vigor to the party system.

[89] Morton Grodzins has noted that "it is remarkable how many of those who believe in the desirability of disciplined parties which will focus power, see trends and social forces moving in that direction; while those who believe not, see not." "American Political Parties and the American System," *Western Political Quarterly,* XIII (December 1960), 997.

Supported by powerful Democratic majorities in both houses of the 89th Congress, President Johnson was remarkably successful in securing the passage of his legislative program—a program which, in many ways, represented a sharp departure from the past.[90] One example, of course, neither completes an argument nor establishes a trend. Government through presidential leadership and responsible parties is not likely to be a continuing pattern in American politics, but it may be less an anomaly than we have come to suppose.

[90] Stephen K. Bailey writes: "[The lessons of the 89th Congress] proved that vigorous presidential leadership and sizeable partisan majorities in both houses of the same partisan persuasion as the President, could act in reasonable consonance, and with dispatch, in fashioning creative answers to major problems. The nation's voters could pin responsibility upon a national party for the legislative output. If that partisan majority erred in judgment, it could at least be held accountable in ensuing congressional and presidential elections." *Congress in the Seventies* (New York: St. Martin's Press, 1970), p. 103.

10

INTEREST GROUPS AND
THE LEGISLATIVE PROCESS

The legislature is the natural habitat of political interest groups. Because interest groups are "usually engaged in getting exceptions made to established policies or in breaking down policies or preventing the creation of general policies,"[1] they are attracted to the legislature, with its many stages where legislation can be resisted, obstructed, or sandbagged permanently. Of all groups, those concerned with defense of the *status quo*—as distinguished from those attempting to change governmental policies or to promote new ones—have found the legislative process most likely to serve their ends.[2]

Legislative politics often center in the struggle between groups. There are two principal interpretations of the nature and significance of group conflict in the legislature. Earl Latham, for example, writes:

> The legislature referees the group struggle, ratifies the victories of the successful coalitions, and records the terms of the surrenders, compromises, and conquests in the form of statutes. Every statute tends to represent compromises because the process of accommodating conflicts of group interest is one of deliberation and consent. The legislative vote on any issue tends to represent the composition of strength, i.e., the balance of power, among the contending groups at the moment of voting. What may be called public policy is the equilibrium reached in this struggle at any given moment....[3]

[1] E. E. Schattschneider, "Pressure Groups Versus Political Parties," *Annals of the American Academy of Political and Social Science,* CCLIX (September 1948), 23.

[2] David B. Truman, *The Governmental Process* (New York: Alfred A. Knopf, Inc., 1951), p. 353. The generalization that "defensive organizations"—interest groups devoted to maintaining the *status quo*—are more successful than "offensive organizations" has long been accepted by most political scientists. Whether this is altogether true is open to question. Lester Milbrath's interview study of Washington lobbyists indicates that, in the estimations of lobbyists themselves, organizational success is not associated with defensive or offensive orientation. For one reason, "the legislative process is not so neatly arranged that defensive organizations will nearly always attempt to defeat bills while offensive organizations will nearly always attempt to pass them. Both types of organizations attempt to pass some bills and to defeat others." *The Washington Lobbyists* (Chicago: Rand McNally & Company, 1963), pp. 349–50, quotation on p. 350.

[3] "The Group Basis of Politics: Notes for a Theory," *American Political Science Review,* XLVI (June 1952), 390.

On the other hand, E. E. Schattschneider argued that Latham's "referee" concept is too restrictive, since it suggests that Congress "has no mind or force of its own" and hence is unable to affect the outcome of conflict between groups:

> Actually the outcome of political conflict is not like the "resultant" of opposing forces in physics. To assume that the forces in a political situation could be diagrammed as a physicist might diagram the resultant of opposing physical forces is to wipe the slate clean of all remote, general and public considerations for the protection of which civil societies have been instituted. ...*Private conflicts are taken into the public arena precisely because someone wants to make certain that the power ratio among the private interests most immediately involved shall not prevail.*[4]

It would be wholly arbitrary to say that one interpretation is correct and that the other is not. Many factors—including circumstance, the subject matter of legislation, and party position—help determine the impact of interest groups on public policy. At times, to be sure, group influence is decisive; at other times, and just as plainly, the legislature is master of its own house.

Interest-Group Politics in America

Neither the proliferation nor the importance of groups in American politics can be explained by recourse to a single factor, even though, at bottom, one condition is essential to their development: freedom of association. Madison put it succinctly: "Liberty is to faction what air is to fire, an aliment without which it instantly expires."[5] Given conditions which foster free association, what immediate factors serve to augment the power of private groups and to encourage their participation in politics? In the case of the United States, several reasons, associated to some degree, may be advanced.

These reasons, presumptive and familiar, may be sorted into three categories: legal-structural, political, and ideological. The structure of American government invites vigorous group action. *Decentralization* is a hallmark of the system: federalism serves to parcel out authority and responsibility to the fifty states and a national government, while the system of separated powers has a similar impact within each level of government. Nowhere is power concentrated. The value of these structural arrangements apart, it seems obvious that they contribute to conditions under which interest groups can exert considerable influence. Battles can be fought on a variety of terrains, and one lost or hopeless on the national level, for example, may be waged vigorously in the states, as in the case of management-sponsored right-to-work laws which were steered through about one-third of the legislatures when a national law had no chance of passage. Dispersal

---

[4] *The Semisovereign People* (New York: Holt, Rinehart & Winston, Inc., 1960), p. 38.
[5] *The Federalist*, ed. Benjamin Fletcher Wright (Cambridge, Mass.: Belknap Press of Harvard University Press, 1961), p. 130.

332 of power within and between branches of government carries a similar invitation to group activity. "Nothing about the system is direct and simple. Authority is perplexingly subdivided and distributed, and responsibility has to be hunted down in out-of-the-way corners."[6] Under such circumstances, it would be surprising indeed if groups were less attuned to the possibilities for gaining access to critical centers of power. From the vantage point of groups (with some exceptions), governmental decentralization is reason for celebration.

The American political milieu, reinforced by historic customs and outlook, also helps account for the primacy of groups in national and state politics. A principal result of our decentralized governmental system is a decentralized party system,[7] one with considerably more "*pluribus* than *unum*," in Bailey's choice phrase. Arguing that policy is "frequently developed by an infinitely intricate system of barter and legerdemain," Bailey holds that:

> The real issue is that the government, in a generation of prolific services and equally prolific regulation, has become a vast arena in which group interests and personalities struggle for power without sufficient reference to questions of the long-range public interest. These groups and personalities use the pressure points and divergent party roles and constituencies of the President, the bureaucracy, the national committees, and the two Houses of Congress as instruments of access and finagle. This produces a politics of "boodle" and accommodation, but not a politics of responsible power and clear national purpose.[8]

The absence of a unified and responsible party system magnifies the opportunities for effective interest-group action, especially in the legislative process. Organized pressures are not easily resisted by weak and undisciplined legislative parties, and it is not excessive generalization to suggest that where parties count for little of what is done, groups count for much. Writing of Congress, Schattschneider observed that "the parties do very little to discipline or defend their members," thus permitting pressure groups to "trade on the fears and the confusion of individual members of Congress." The consequences are predictable: "In the struggle for survival in a highly chaotic political situation, the Congressman is thrown very much on his own resources, seeking support wherever he can find it and tending strongly to yield to *all* demands made on him. Any reasonably convincing demonstration of an organized demand for anything is likely to impress him out

---

6 Woodrow Wilson, *Congressional Government* (New York: Meridian Books, 1956 [first published 1885]), p. 214.

7 The typical interpretation is that one result of a federal system of government is a decentralized party system, but the argument may also be made that in some ways the party acts to foster decentralization in *government*. For a consideration of the role of party in the sharing of legislation between federal and state governments, the impact of undisciplined parties on the relations between legislators and administrative agencies, and the consequences of the party's inability to control administrators in their negotiations with legislators, see Morton Grodzins, "American Political Parties and the American System," *Western Political Quarterly*, XIII (December 1960), 974–98.

8 Stephen K. Bailey, *The Condition of Our National Political Parties* (New York: Fund for the Republic, 1959), p. 10.

of all proportion to the real weight or influence of the pressure group."[9]
The system of district representation makes the congressman especially
susceptible to appeals from groups powerful within his home constituency,
from which he must win reelection.

The vulnerability of governments to the sorties of pressure groups
poses a thorny question concerning responsibility. Who is to be held accountable for a course of governmental action, a policy, a matter handled badly,
a matter left undone? It becomes more and more difficult to gauge where
effective power lies, where blame should be fastened, where merit should be
recognized. Interest groups, states the report of the Committee on Political
Parties of the American Political Science Association, "cannot attempt to
define public policy democratically. Coherent public policies do not emerge
as the mathematical result of the claims of all of the pressure groups."[10]
Consider the matter of national health: "It is one thing to insist that those
who have responsibility for the nation's health have some knowledge of
medical science," wrote Peter Odegard. "It is something else, again, to say
that decisions as to whether the government should do anything at all about
the nation's health, ought to be left to the medical profession."[11]

Finally, the virility of groups is related to the low ideological content
of American politics. That American voters as a whole are not moved to
act on stern ideological or programmatic grounds has been well documented.
What perhaps is not so well known is that the same can be said for their
lawmakers. How have legislators come to acquire their political beliefs?
What forces converge to shape their views of public matters? A study of
California, New Jersey, Ohio, and Tennessee legislators opens up this question. Out of several hundred legislators interviewed, only a handful contended that they became interested in politics and motivated to participate
as a result of socio-economic beliefs which they had acquired. Ideological
commitments, in brief, had little to do with impelling them toward a career
in politics. Far more important in their political socialization (the process
by which they acquired their political values, attitudes, interests, or knowledge) were primary-group influences, major events, personal predispositions
(e.g., a sense of obligation, admiration for politicians), and their participation in certain forms of political action.[12]

The barrenness of ideology in political socialization—shown in Table
10.1, borrowed from the four-state study—is suggestive regarding legislators'
relations with political interest groups. Loosely or briefly linked to ideology,
legislators may be particularly responsive to the demands of interest groups.
Political outlook, it may be hypothesized, is something to be worked out
pragmatically, as a part of the process of determining the relative weight
to be assigned factors bearing on one's career as a legislator. Under such
circumstances, and in the absence of disciplined legislative party organiza-

9 "Pressure Groups," 18–19.
10 American Political Science Association, *Toward a More Responsible Two-
Party System* (New York: Holt, Rinehart & Winston, Inc., 1950), p. 19.
11 Peter H. Odegard, *Politics and Politicians in a Democratic State* (Pittsburgh: United Steelworkers of America, Department of Education, 1958), p. 13.
12 See H. Eulau, W. Buchanan, L. Ferguson, J. Wahlke, "The Political
Socialization of American State Legislators," *Midwest Journal of Political Science,* III
(May 1959), 188–206, especially pp. 204–6, and also their book, *The Legislative
System* (New York: John Wiley & Sons, Inc., 1962), pp. 77–94.

TABLE 10.1
Major Sources of Political Interest

	Calif. $N = 113$	*N.J.* $N = 79$	*Ohio* $N = 162$	*Tenn.* $N = 120$
Primary groups	34%	47%	43%	42%
Political or civic participation	70	60	49	43
Particular events or conditions	42	25	21	18
Personal predispositions	52	53	52	33
Socio-economic beliefs	16	10	6	3

SOURCE: Wahlke, Eulau, Buchanan, and Ferguson, *The Legislative System* (New York: John Wiley & Sons, Inc., 1962), p. 79.
NOTE: Percentages total more than 100 since some respondents gave more than one answer.

tions, it is plausible to suppose that pressure groups are the principal beneficiaries of the low ideological content in the typical legislator's outlook. Bargains may be struck more easily—and retained as long as expedient. This interpretation, if speculative, is also consonant with Schattschneider's contention that a congressman "is in no good position to assess accurately the influence of minorities which make demands on him. In an extremely irresponsible political system a vote for anything looks like a cheap price to pay for the privilege of being friendly to everyone."[13]

The Lobbyists

There are many ways by which a group may communicate its views on policy matters to government officials. Since not all organizations are of equal size or possess equal resources, not all use the same techniques for advancing their claims in the lobby process. Small organizations are often forced to wage their campaigns at a distance—through telephone calls, telegrams, and the mails. Powerful interest groups, on the other hand, invariably include in their pressure arsenal one or more professional lobbyists (or legislative agents) to represent their views personally to government officials. Moreover, all the main lobby groups have a headquarters in Washington and an impressive retinue of research and clerical workers. As a rule, there is nothing imposing about lobbies' headquarters in the capital cities of the states. In fact, only a few organizations have anything more than a lobbyist's hotel room to serve as a staging point for their "raids" on the legislature. Short legislative sessions (and short work weeks) make it impractical to maintain and staff a permanent headquarters.

Lobbying is a professional matter, and a full-time, experienced lobbyist is regarded by *major* interest groups as indispensable for the effective representation of their views. Groups deem it especially important to have a lobbyist who not only is personally engaging and who has the requisite skills in negotiation, but one who knows the legislators and has their confidence—in a word, who has "access." Although these specifications for the

13 "Pressure Groups," 19.

effective lobbyist are easily drawn, they are not easily met, and hence the major organizations tend to be represented year after year by the same individuals. Old hands among the lobbyists have a "door-opening" power not often equaled by the newcomer to their ranks.

A fairly sizable literature on lobbies and lobbying has been produced, but only limited attention has been given to the lobbyists themselves—their backgrounds, personal characteristics, careers, and role in the lobby process. A study by Lester Milbrath helps to answer some questions regarding the political party activity of Washington lobbyists.

Lobbyists, the study discloses, are not as a rule active participants in party politics. In the same way that most pressure groups strive to avoid identification with either political party, believing this would imperil their access to the other party, so also most lobbyists attempt to steer clear of entangling partisan commitments. Moreover, their personal histories are notably free from partisan ties: only about one-half of them participate in politics in any active way and less than one-third have held elective or appointive public office. About three-fourths of the lobbyists have received legal training, many having worked previously for the federal government. Despite a popular myth to the contrary, only a handful of the lobbyists are former members of Congress; in fact, former congressional staff assistants turn up in far greater number than former legislators. The principal way by which lobbyists participate in politics is by making financial contributions to campaigns. Plainly, the study concludes, Washington lobbyists do not feel that their role compels them to participate actively in party politics; on the contrary, most of them scrupulously avoid it in the belief that involvement cuts down their effectiveness. "Party control of the Congress shifts frequently enough to give pause to any lobbyist who might contemplate putting all his eggs in one basket and becoming closely identified with one of the parties."[14]

State lobbyists are difficult to bring into articulate focus, for only a few studies have been made of them. There isn't much doubt, however, that they differ from Washington lobbyists in several respects. They are less likely to be professionals at their job. Many will be newcomers—perhaps as many as half in some states. Not many state lobbyists are engaged full time in lobbying, and about one-fourth of those registered represent more than one client. Lobbyists with law backgrounds are much less common in the states than they are in Washington. Lobbyists with records of active participation in party politics are common in some states and rare in others, but why this should be so is not at all apparent. The evidence of a scattering of studies shows that there are not a great many ex-legislators in the ranks of state lobbyists, although where they are found they appear to be more effective than other lobbyists.[15]

Former legislators who seek positions as lobbyists are likely to find their talents in demand, since in hiring an ex-legislator to represent its claims an organization acquires a certain amount of "built-in" access to the legislature.

---

[14] Lester Milbrath, "The Political Party Activity of Washington Lobbyists," *Journal of Politics,* **XX** (May 1958), 339–52, quotation on p. 351.

[15] This sketch of state lobbyists is drawn from Harmon Zeigler, "Interest Groups in the States," in *Politics in the American States,* ed. Herbert Jacob and Kenneth N. Vines (Boston: Little, Brown & Company, 1965), pp. 129–31.

336 Such lobbyists will know most of the legislators, their idiosyncrasies and preferences, and normally be accepted as a member of the club. Not the least of the advantages which accrue to a former member (especially at the state legislature level) is that often he will have the privilege of going on the floor while the chamber is in session. Committee doors are sometimes left ajar for him even in executive sessions.

Some indication of the value of an ex-legislator as lobbyist is shown in the experience of the Petroleum Industries Committee, whose legislative agent in the Colorado legislature was a former Republican floor leader. His approach to lobbying is instructive:

> I keep close watch on the legislature on oil matters. I make it my business to visit at home each elected state legislator—or perhaps even before he is elected—to get to know him. I want to do this before he comes to Denver where my face is just one of a hundred new ones he'll have to know. If I can get him on a first name calling basis that means a lot. When he comes up to Denver, he'll be lonely, but he'll see a friendly face. I'll help him around, find out what committee he wants, explain about them, and help him get set on the committee if I possibly can.[16]

The former member's familiarity with the subtleties of the legislative process, coupled with his intimate friendships among the lawmakers, gives him an advantage sometimes resented by other lobbyists. Occasionally efforts are made to restrict the rights of former legislators functioning as lobbyists. One proposal which has been made would prevent former members of Congress from engaging as lobbyists for a period of two years following the termination of legislative service; this "cooling-off" period presumably would serve to diminish their influence among former confreres.[17] Actually, there is no evidence on which to judge whether ex-members of Congress are more effective than other lobbyists.

Legislators linked in a fixed or steady relationship with a particular interest group have come to be termed, somewhat pejoratively, "inside lobbyists." It is not unusual to find interest groups which have special influence, a lien of sorts, upon individual legislators, causing them to respond sympathetically and predictably on certain types of legislation.[18] Customarily

16 Robert Engler, "Oil and Politics," *New Republic,* September 5, 1955, p. 14.
17 See John F. Kennedy, "Congressional Lobbies: A Chronic Problem Re-Examined," *Georgetown Law Journal,* XLV (Summer 1957), 564.
18 "Inside lobbyists" can have any of a variety of relationships with the organizations they "represent." A man may have spent much of his adult life as a labor union official before coming to the legislature, another may have substantial holdings in oil or simply represent a state in which oil is a predominant industry, and so on—their ties may be psychological, ideological, economic. What would seem to stretch the bounds of propriety, beyond any typical question of conflict of interest, is a case in which state legislators are placed on the payroll of an organization in order to advance its interests in the legislature. Robert Bendiner's study of the clash between the Pennsylvania Railroad and the Pennsylvania Motor Truck Association over a bill to liberalize the weight limits for trucks using the state's highways disclosed that, at the time the bill was considered, five members of the state legislature—four of them members of the strategic Senate Highway Committee—were on the payroll of the Pennsylvania Railroad. This is about as far inside as it is possible to go. "The 'Engineering of Consent'—A Case Study," *The Reporter,* August 11, 1955, p. 22. A further example of the seamy side of this form of lobbying appears in many states where there

the sponsors of legislation of concern to the group, they lobby their fellow members, smooth the way for favorable bills or hamstring those which are hostile, and vote according to the best interests of their affiliation. When farm legislation is at stake, for example, the agricultural lobby sometimes seems fully as evident within Congress as without. Representatives and senators openly regarded as "farm bloc" spokesmen, "oil" men, "labor" men, and the like, are easily found.[19]

A principal characteristic of an effective pressure group and the stock in trade of a competent lobbyist is a large reservoir of expert knowledge concerning the legislative process, its labyrinths as well as its main paths, its vulnerability to penetration. Knowledge of the process, however, may be of little avail unless a group has access to the principal decision-makers. Although procedure varies from legislature to legislature and from state to nation, the principal junctures in the legislative process where group influence can be brought to bear are everywhere the same.

Major Access Points in the Legislative Process

THE INTRODUCTION OF BILLS

Although the number of bills whose origins stem from interest groups cannot be reckoned with precision, it obviously is great. Many ideas for new bills or for transformations of old ones are born in the offices of pressure groups and later drafted there for submission in the legislature; on other occasions groups contribute their ideas to friendly members who rely on legislative agencies or staffs for the actual drafting. Bills occasionally bear the notation, "by request," which means that the sponsor has agreed to introduce the measure for some group or individual but that he either has reservations about it or else does not intend to work actively on its behalf; bills thus disfigured rarely survive for long.

Who introduces an organization's bill is likely to have considerable bearing on the eventual outcome. The director of the national legislative commission of the American Legion testified before a congressional committee investigating lobbying:

---

are tie-ups between state legislators and race tracks. The tracks are, of course, regulated by the legislature. In Rhode Island, for example, "many legislators have been in the employ of the race tracks in such jobs as clerk at a betting window. Often it has been shown that these legislators and other paid staff members of the legislature were recorded as 'present' in the House of Representatives while in fact they were working at the tracks. When on one occasion a reporter found fourteen state legislators working at the tracks while being reported as 'present' in the General Assembly, there was no great outcry." Duane Lockard, *New England State Politics* (Princeton: Princeton University Press, 1959), p. 210.

[19] See a study of "labor legislators" at the state legislative level by Jay S. Goodman, "A Note on Legislative Research: Labor Representation in Rhode Island," *American Political Science Review*, LXI (June 1967), 468–73. Goodman finds that the most significant service which labor legislators provide labor is that of transmitting information concerning the group's legislative interests to rank and file Democratic legislators. An increase in the number of labor legislators in that state (between 1934 and 1962) was not accompanied by an increase in the number of labor bills passed.

I attempt to get the bill introduced by the chairman of the committee. If I can't get him to introduce it I try some other member of the committee. If I can't get any member of the committee to introduce it, then we try some other Congressman or Senator, whichever the case may be.[20]

Groups strive to have their proposals introduced early in the session, hoping thereby to avoid losing them in the hectic closing days when the calendars may be cleared imprudently. To guard against detrimental legislation, a continuing danger, large and well-staffed organizations customarily examine all bills and resolutions introduced, in order to chart a course of action; hostile bills are followed through the legislative mill as assiduously as the group's own proposals.

THE COMMITTEE STAGE

The life of a bill is always tenuous, but at no time is it more vulnerable than in committee. Victory here augurs well for final passage, while a major setback at this point is rarely undone. Accordingly, groups concentrate their heaviest fire on the committees,[21] often on their chairmen. Their task is less formidable when sympathetic legislators are there to shepherd their interests—hence groups show keen interest in committee appointments, occasionally being able to influence them. Committee hearings afford groups an opportunity to record their positions on legislation and to submit opinions and data in support of them. Ordinarily the officers of organizations, rather than their legislative agents, are used to testify when major bills are under consideration, in the belief that their views will swing greater influence among committee members.

Committee decisions tend to foreshadow the final outcome of legislation. Alterations made in bills on the floor often are minor in scope, involving details rather than major purposes. The upshot of this is that hearings are treated as serious business by pressure groups hopeful of securing favorable provisions from committee members or of vitiating legislation judged harmful. "Great ingenuity has therefore been shown in attempts to influence committee opinion," writes Dayton McKean. "The crippled victims of industrial accidents and diseases have been paraded before committees; specimens of adulterated or misbranded foods and drugs have been displayed; where committees have consented, moving pictures of poor schools, of slums, of

[20] Quoted in *Final Report* of the Special Committee to Investigate Political Activities, Lobbying, and Campaign Contributions, 85th Cong., 1st sess., 1957, p. 43.

[21] Legislators often contend that record votes make them vulnerable to interest groups. When legislative reorganization was debated in the 90th Congress, opposition appeared to a provision that would require a public announcement of the results of roll-call votes taken in all committee meetings. The case for not making committee votes public was made by a senior senator: "It may be politically advantageous for a Senator to vote in support of [a powerful interest group]; however, it may be in the public interest for him to vote the other way. He can cast a vote in the people's interest much more easily if he knows the vote will not be made public, but if the vote is to be announced he is more likely to cast the vote where he knows it will do him no harm politically, even though it may do severe damage to the general public." *Congressional Record*, 90th Cong., 1st sess., February 3, 1967, p. S1487. (Daily edition.) For similar testimony concerning secret committee votes at the state level, see Robert Karsch, *The Standing Committees of the Missouri General Assembly* (Columbia: University of Missouri, Bureau of Governmental Research, 1959), p. 3.

conditions in prisons, have been shown."[22] Veterans' groups have no qualms about producing a Medal of Honor winner for testimony and trading upon his wartime valor to advance the interests of the organization. "Average" housewives, "average" businessmen, "average" workers, "average" druggists, and "little people" are sometimes used by organizations to testify on legislation; the "plain folks" approach is more common on the state than on the national level.[23]

FLOOR ACTION

Even though pressure groups customarily expend their greatest efforts attempting to win their way in committee,[24] they are by no means powerless on the floor. Because floor action invites public scrutiny, legislators are sometimes more vulnerable to groups there than in committee. Every roll-call vote on an amendment or major bill is potentially dangerous to the legislator, since his decision, preserved in the records of pressure groups, may cost him campaign funds and election support. Particularly hazardous is a record vote on an amendment whose purpose is to favor a certain interest by bringing it within the scope of a bill or by excluding it: the issue is sharply drawn, and to vote against the amendment is perhaps to make new enemies. Not surprisingly, in search of a measure of protection from pressure groups, legislators often prefer voice votes and, as in the case of the U.S. House of Representatives, "gag rules" that limit the opportunity to offer amendments to pending measures.

THE CONFERENCE COMMITTEE

Because House and Senate frequently disagree on legislation, the conference committee has become a conventional hurdle in the life of many bills. Major

---

[22] *Party and Pressure Politics* (Boston: Houghton Mifflin Company, 1949), p. 617.

[23] Karl Schriftgiesser recounts a similar "plain folks" technique considered by the real estate lobby but later rejected. The sponsor of the idea, a realtor, put it this way: "I believe our case opposing the extension of rent control would be helped tremendously if we could parade in a few small property owners from around the country, a little bedraggled and run-down-at-the-heels-looking, who could get their story over to Congress that the small man who owns property is taking one hell of a beating." *The Lobbyists* (Boston: Little, Brown & Company, 1951), p. 217.

[24] In committee or elsewhere, legislators are not simply the pawns of interest groups; relations between the two cut both ways. Stanley Surrey provides an interesting sketch of the relationship in formulating tax policies: "The desire—sometimes the need—of a congressman to be useful often places a congressman who sits on one of the tax committees, the House Committee on Ways and Means or the Senate Committee on Finance, in a difficult position. A fellow congressman who sits on the Public Works Committee, for example, can respond to constituency pressure by approving the project involved; a member of the Appropriations Committee can respond by a favorable vote on a specific appropriation. But a congressman on a tax committee can respond only by pushing through a special tax provision. His legislative stock in trade, so to speak, is special tax treatment. This difficulty is especially acute in the case of those congressmen who come to sit on a tax committee only after they have been members of other committees and have become so accustomed to using their committee powers in helpful ways that the habit persists." "The Congress and the Tax Lobbyist—How Special Tax Provisions Get Enacted," *Harvard Law Review*, LXX (May 1957), 1155–56.

340   bills in Congress invariably are conference products. The reports of these committees not only carry high priority but also are closed to amendment on the floor; conference committee decisions thus tend to represent the last word of the legislature. An organization able to influence the choice of conference committee members or otherwise able to inject its outlook into committee deliberations is in a strategic position to gain its ends. The element of conference secrecy presumably works to the advantage of interest groups.

Special Techniques Used by Lobbies

INSPIRED COMMUNICATIONS

A lobby technique occasionally employed rests on appeals to the public at large—through newspapers, magazines, television, and radio—or to members of the organization to contact their representatives regarding legislation. All large organizations have thousands of active members who, on short notice, can be rallied to send telegrams and letters or to make telephone calls to legislators. At a decisive juncture in the legislative battle, Washington or the state capital can be rapidly flooded with communications from "the folks back home." A narrow-gauge communications campaign may be based on telegrams and calls from a select group of powerful constituents. The following paragraphs taken from a letter by the secretary of the General Gas Committee to the president of a Texas refining company, a member of the committee, illustrate how and where pressure is to be applied:

> Because this threat is so real, so immediate, we in the industry must rally to complete a legislative victory now only half won. We must carry the truth to our Senators on a ground swell of public opinion. The alternative is concession by default to an opposition that is as well organized and active as it is misguided in its affection for regimentation.
>
> Those Senators who are already favorable to our cause deserve the reassurance of support from their constituents. Those who are presently undecided must be given all the facts. *Those who favor keeping controls must be convinced by a flood of opinion that the ground they are on is not only fallacious but unpopular as well.*[25]

The efficacy of inspired communications is probably not great.[26] A deluge of identical or "stock" telegrams, postal cards, letters, or telephone

[25] *Hearings on Oil and Gas Lobby* before the Special Senate Committee to Investigate Political Activities, Lobbying and Campaign Contributions, 84th Cong., 2d sess., 1956, p. 545. (Emphasis added.)

[26] With a modicum of ingenuity the whole process can be made automatic; effective citizenship can be as near as the stenographers' pool of one's favorite organization. At one time the State Council of the California CIO sent out a letter to several hundred citizens holding "pro-liberal-labor views," enclosing a business card which said: "I hereby authorize the CIO State Council to act as my Legislative Secretary on any State and National legislation endorsed or opposed by CIO. I understand I will receive an original and carbon copy of *my* correspondence typed for me by the Council. I will mail my original copy to my legislator." *The Reporter,* June 16, 1955, p. 4. (Emphasis added.)

calls is next to worthless as a means of influencing legislators. Moreover, signatures are sometimes found to be fraudulent, and occasionally letters and telegrams are sent on behalf of individuals without their consent.[27] Even when different types of messages, variations on a theme, are used—in an attempt to suggest spontaneity—standard clauses, repetitive and shopworn expressions, and the tendency of the messages to arrive in batches ordinarily give clues that the "voice of the people" has in fact been organized by someone. A Wisconsin state legislator gives an account of such a campaign:

> There was an episode a couple of years back when the firemen were pushing through a so-called heart and lung bill. They had their lobbyists here and it looked like the bill wasn't going to go through one house. So, a lobbyist put a call back home to certain other people, who in turn put in certain other calls. Pretty soon the telephones were jammed. The firemen back home were calling their legislators and there was a constant stream of legislators to the telephone answering long-distance phone calls from constituents telling them to vote in favor of this bill. Well, when it became obvious that this was a pressure movement, I contacted the lobbyist I knew had charge of this and said, "Now look, you'd better cut those phone calls off. I'm not interested in talking to them. I know what your position is. I've already indicated that I will support this bill and I don't want to be bothered." Boom, those phone calls stopped just like that.[28]

Although campaigns to rally the public are often unsuccessful, on occasion they produce dramatic results. Casting about for a way to secure new revenue, the Pennsylvania legislature recently passed a bill to levy a 6 per cent tax on insurance premiums. The response of the insurance industry was to launch a massive public opinion campaign designed to generate opposition to the tax. In a matter of days, the legislature and the governor received more than 100,000 letters, some 10,000 telegrams, and countless telephone calls. Breaking all records for dispatch, the legislature frantically adopted a "repealer" by overwhelming majorities in both houses. Explaining the debacle, the House Democratic majority leader said: "The insurance industry spent a million dollars in advertising. The industry did it very cleverly. They stirred up public indignation and scared the pants off all of us."[29]

---

[27] Suggested reading on this score is testimony in the 1956 hearings on the oil and gas lobby. In an incredibly clumsy effort, hundreds of more or less uniform telegrams concerning the Harris-Fulbright bill were sent to Minnesota Senator Thye from towns and cities around his state. To launch the telegram barrage, each Standard Oil salesman was expected to contact bulk station agents in his territory and to have them contact three prominent people to wire the Senator urging him to support the bill. As it turned out, some of the salesmen were tired, others had sick children at home, still others had enormous districts to cover: they simply went to the telegraph office and fired off batches of unauthorized telegrams using the names of prominent citizens. In a further burst of enthusiasm, company funds, $1,500 in all, were used to cover the tab for the telegrams. *Hearings on Oil and Gas Lobby,* especially pp. 309–73.

[28] Quoted in Ronald D. Hedlund and Wilder Crane, Jr., *The Job of the Wisconsin Legislator* (Washington, D.C.: American Political Science Association, 1971), pp. 86–87.

[29] *Pittsburgh Press,* March 12, 1970. p. 10.

THE SOCIAL LOBBY, CAMPAIGN CONTRIBUTIONS, AND BRIBERY

Three other forms of lobby activity clustered around the edge of the legislative process may be noted. These are the social lobby, the use of campaign contributions and campaign work, and outright bribery. The social lobby refers to a practice employed by many interest groups of providing entertainment for legislators—cocktail parties, dinners, a night on the town, to mention some common forms. The impact of the social lobby on legislation is probably exaggerated; nevertheless, its wide use suggests it may bear fruitful results.[30] "In its sophisticated form," writes Congressman Emanuel Celler, "this activity never includes *request* for a favor, but limits itself to the extension of amenities and courtesies in the form of free transportation, hospitality, and adjuncts to 'gracious living.' "[31]

Direct political action in the shape of political funds and assistance in campaigns may be held out to legislators by interest groups with sufficient financial or manpower resources. Since parties or candidates rarely judge their campaign larders to be adequate, they find it difficult to ignore an opened treasury or a group of volunteer workers. There are, to be sure, various federal and state laws designed to limit campaign spending by organizations (e.g., corporations and unions are forbidden to contribute money in connection with any federal election, and similar enjoiners are present in a number of states), but the most that can be said for restrictions of this sort is that they may temper spending; they do not prevent it. With a little ingenuity the laws can be evaded. Labor unions have formed separate political arms, such as the Committee on Political Education (COPE) of the AFL-CIO, which raise and spend money with unabashed vigor. Corporations may and do enter the political thicket by contributing the time and skills of their employees to campaigns and by aiding the cause through sustained propaganda efforts. And, of course, corporation officers may make contributions in their individual capacities. Because these possibilities for campaign support are generally available, to be tapped by the candidate whose voting record and outlook meet the proper tests of orthodoxy, legislators are constrained to give careful thought to the claims of groups whose wherewithal may prove useful at election time.

Lobbyists do not have to be especially diligent to ferret out those candidates in need of campaign funds. Few candidates enjoy a surfeit of reelection money. Perhaps legislators from competitive districts attach a special urgency to gathering a campaign "kitty." What is gained by lobbies that make contributions to legislators' campaigns? James Deakin reports:

---

30 There are no bounds to the social lobby—even academe is aware of its potential for influencing legislation. With choice football tickets and assorted hospitality looming in the background, state universities have been known to invite state legislators for a weekend visit to the campus, and if it happens that members of the appropriations committees are among those attending to inspect the institution and its plant, so much the better.

31 Emanuel Celler, "Pressure Groups in Congress," *Annals of the American Academy of Political and Social Science,* CCCXIX (September 1958), 4 (emphasis in original).

When the lobbyists themselves are asked to define the chief value of campaign contributions in their work, they frequently reply with one word: access. The campaign donation, they say, helps them obtain access to the legislator so they can present their case.... Since it would be unrealistic to expect the lobbyist to describe his campaign contributions as attempts at influence, the "access" explanation may be, in some cases, a cover story. In the majority of instances, however, it is probably the truth or close to it. Senators and Representatives are busy men, and the competition for their attention is keen. The lobbyist who makes a campaign donation—or arranges for one to be made by his client—frequently is doing nothing more than meeting the competition and creating good will, to insure that he, too, will be heard.[32]

The legislator who accepts electoral support from an interest group cannot avoid some measure of obligation to the group. The nature of the obligation undoubtedly varies from group to group and from legislator to legislator. It may involve merely the obligation to give the lobbyist a hearing as to his group's interests, or it may, of course, involve much more. The observations of a lobbyist whose organization makes it a practice to contribute to state legislative campaigns show something of the character of the exchange:

If it is an important bill, one that we just about have to get passed, usually I'll go to somebody and say "Look, this is one I have to have and I want you to vote on this bill." I am calling in a debt. However, I don't use this very often because you can only use it once in a while. And you can only use it on a legislator once during a session. It is best to avoid an overt feeling of obligation, but every lobbyist does have certain legislators that he can go to if he really needs a vote. I'll probably do this two or three times during a normal session. You just don't put on the pressure every day. You save it until you need it.

I will also ask a legislator to get a vote that I can't get. This is the kind of pressure that you use, but you just don't go to a legislator and say "You do it or else." That is the poorest tactic you can use. Remember that we know most of these people very well, and in some cases have gotten them to run for office. We have worked with them in their campaigns. Even so, if I go to him and he says "I can't do it," then I'll say, "Okay, I'll get somebody else," and forget it. You don't do it by using threats or being cute. You do not campaign against them. If they are consistently against you, they know that we would like to see them defeated, and they know that we will try to get somebody to run against them, but that is as far as it goes. I would never say to a legislator that I will try to find a candidate to oppose him, but the feeling is there.[33]

[32] James Deakin, *The Lobbyists* (Washington, D.C.: Public Affairs Press, 1966), p. 101.

[33] Quoted in Harmon Zeigler and Michael Baer, *Lobbying: Interaction and Influence in American State Legislatures* (Belmont, California: Wadsworth Publishing Company, 1969), p. 116.

344   The power which interest groups come to wield as a result of contributing campaign money may be exaggerated. It is tempting to speculate on the impact which the giving or withholding of campaign funds may have on candidates, parties, and policy, but there is no hard evidence to prove a case. Does money "buy" access? If so, how much access does "x" quantity of money secure? A study of campaign finance in Michigan, where the automobile companies long have been identified with the Republican party and labor unions with the Democrats, raises a doubt or two about the power of money. Although labor unions provide an important source of funds for the Democrats and the manufacturing interests (especially automotive) a similar source for the Republicans, both parties secure a considerably greater share of their revenues from other quarters. "If these interest groups exercise control over party policy," the authors state, "they have purchased it at a relatively low price."[34]

A popular theory of interest-group influence holds that some legislators are venal men, easily swayed under the proper conditions. If women and wine are held to be occasional factors in their fall from grace, money is thought to be a constant. With a pragmatic concern for results, lobbyists may bribe legislators and buy their votes—so runs this cynical interpretation of legislative life. Corrupt legislators have made their way through the pages of a good many novels and, in real life, infamous cases of venality dot the annals of Congress and the state legislatures. But it is unlikely that the bribery theory explains much about legislative behavior today. As the former Speaker of the California Assembly, Jess Unruh, has argued:

> Today it is rare for a legislator's vote to be corrupted by the exchange of money. Far more often the integrity of the vote is shattered by a commitment to a particular interest group, resulting from a lack of independence on the part of the legislator for a variety of nonfinancial reasons. For example, a vote may be influenced for reasons of ideology or fear of antagonizing the voting strength of a particular group. One who is overly committed to labor or to management, or to any other interest group, whatever his reasons, can be charged with being as guilty of selling out the public interest as the man who takes money for his vote. Yet how can one search a man's mind to determine what prompted his vote?[35]

The nature of bribery diminishes its utility as a means for influencing legislators. Very simply, it is risky business, for legislator as well as lobbyist; it is costly; it is hard to conceal, for to be effective it must involve a number of law-makers. Dark rumors about "money" or "Mae West" bills ("Come up and see me sometime") continue to float around the corridors of state

34 John P. White and John R. Owens, *Parties, Group Interests and Campaign Finance: Michigan '56* (Princeton: Citizens' Research Foundation, 1960), p. 35. Dwynal B. Pettengill provides corroborative data regarding the tenuous ties between contributors, candidates, and access. His investigation of campaign contributions in Maryland disclosed that candidates and party officials did not know personally or could not even identify a large proportion of the most prominent contributors to state campaigns, including their *own*. "Campaign Finance in Maryland" (Ph.D. dissertation, Johns Hopkins University, 1959).

35 Donald G. Herzberg and Jess Unruh, *Essays on the State Legislative Process* (New York: Holt, Rinehart & Winston, Inc., 1970), p. 82.

capitols, and while undoubtedly such bills do crop up occasionally, their importance, indeed the prevalence of bribery in any form, is grossly exaggerated.[36]

Nevertheless, political affairs are not easily preserved in a pristine state. No more than a fine line sometimes separates a campaign contribution from an outright bribe. In 1956 a full-scale congressional investigation of the gas and oil lobby was touched off after a senator from a western state reported that he had been offered $2,500 in campaign funds by a lobbyist at a time when the principal item of business before Congress was a bill to exempt gas producers from federal regulation. Apart from the surface implications of such an offer, which are ugly at best, it poses special problems for the legislator. He is forced to wonder "to what extent he owes a campaign contribution to recognition of his qualities of statesmanship and to what extent it reflects approval of his particular past or anticipated action on a matter close to the contributor's heart. It begs the question to say that such contributions are proper when the purpose for which they are given is the election of the candidate and not the purpose of influencing his vote."[37] It is a short and simple step to conclude they serve both ends.

SANCTIONS

Lobby groups are wary in threatening the use of sanctions against legislators who refuse their demands. The threat to oppose a legislator at the polls is, of course, the most severe sanction available in the pressure arsenal. And although groups resort occasionally to this crude form, they prefer to communicate their power in subtle ways, through intermediaries, stimulated letter writing, and alliances. A pledge of support in the next election is a more circumspect way of reminding legislators of group power.[38] Yet communications which convey a vague hint of sanction, of the presence of group power, are fairly common. Thus, for instance, the chairman of the Legislative Committee of the National Editorial Association, in testifying against an increase in the minimum wage, noted that his trade association spoke for 6,000 weekly, semiweekly, and small daily newspapers, and went on to discuss the geography and operations of his clientele in what amounted to "pressure" terminology: "It is a fact," he said, "that more than 90 per cent of these publications serve communities of less than 10,000 population. One or more is published in practically every congressional district and most, I think you will agree, are particularly sensitive to the needs, the demands,

---

[36] Some congressmen, however, seem to believe that attempts to bribe state legislators may occur with some frequency. Lester Milbrath quotes a congressman who had once served as a legislator: "Bribery and such things never happen in Congress; members of Congress are much too smart to get mixed up in that kind of thing. It does happen fairly often, however, before state legislatures. I never engage in bribery, and I resent it very much when members of state legislatures come up and ask, almost straightforwardly, for a bribe in order to back a certain bill." *The Washington Lobbyists* (Chicago: Rand McNally & Company, 1963), p. 277. Nevertheless, isolated testimony of this kind is thin evidence on which to develop a general indictment of state legislatures.

[37] Celler, *op. cit.*, p. 4.

[38] Lester W. Milbrath, "Lobbying as a Communications Process," *Public Opinion Quarterly*, XXIV (Spring 1960), 36.

346   the habits of thinking of the people who send more than one-half of the members of both branches of this Congress to Washington."[39]

Several studies have sought to determine whether there is a relationship between crucial votes cast by legislators and their fortunes when running for reelection. V. O. Key's early inquiry into the fate of congressmen who opposed bonus legislation favored by the American Legion is relevant to this question. Congressmen who had voted against Legion policies were about as successful in their campaigns for reelection as those who had supported the Legion's side. The pivotal factor was not their voting record but rather the success of their party.[40] A study by Thomas Gilpatrick of the 1954 and 1956 congressional farm votes in relation to the voting records of congressmen on price support legislation offers additional evidence on the importance of party. Republican congressmen who had voted in favor of flexible price supports lost in about equal number with their party colleagues who had voted for 90 percent supports. The study concludes that "the generally unfavorable image created by the national Administration in the eyes of farm constituents overrode the particular stands of individual Republicans."[41]

A recent study of the way that congressmen evaluate interest groups discloses that very few members perceive these groups as applying pressure on them:

> Interest groups rarely have the capacity to coerce legislators. They know this and the congressmen know it. Therefore, the rules of the game have been defined, informally, so as to preclude this sort of effort. Congressmen see interest groups as having a helpful and legitimate role in the legislative process, and they appear to have no quarrel with groups so long as they do not step out of that role. When this does occur and it appears to encroach on the territory of the congressman, then the reaction on the part of that individual is apt to be negative and sharp. "When a man comes in here," one congressman said, "pounds on my desk, and tries to exact a commitment from me, I'm just liable to tell him to go to hell."[42]

DEMONSTRATIVE LOBBYING

Lobby techniques which tend to the bizarre and sensational are worth a few lines, since they are not uncommon, particularly in the state legislatures. For example, a bill under consideration in the New York legislature to provide for the regulation of airways was protested by one hundred pilots who flew their planes to Albany and put them through maneuvers over the capitol; later, in pilot's garb, they appeared at public hearings.[43] Humane

[39] *Hearings on Various Bills Regarding Minimum Wage Legislation* before the Subcommittee on Labor Standards of the Committee on Education and Labor, U.S. House of Representatives, 86th Cong., 2d sess., 1960, p. 278.

[40] "The Veterans and the House of Representatives: A Study of a Pressure Group and Electoral Mortality," *Journal of Politics*, V (February 1943), 27–40.

[41] "Price Support Policy and the Midwest Farm Vote," *Midwest Journal of Political Science*, III (November 1959), 319–35 (quotation on 321).

[42] Andrew M. Scott and Margaret A. Hunt, *Congress and Lobbies: Image and Reality* (Chapel Hill: University of North Carolina Press, 1966), pp. 58–59.

[43] Belle Zeller, *Pressure Politics in New York* (Englewood Cliffs, N.J.: Prentice-Hall, Inc., 1937), p. 245.

societies and those who travel with them can be expected to put on a flamboyant performance when a vivisection bill is before the legislature. To protest the adoption of strip-mine legislation in Pennsylvania in 1963, the wives and children of several hundred strip miners marched on the capitol, bearing signs such as "Save our daddy's job." When a bill was before the Illinois legislature to regulate the interior height of taxi cabs, 150 "jitney" drivers from Chicago descended on Springfield, the state capital, and spent the better part of a day driving in and out of the capitol grounds, honking, blocking traffic, and otherwise making a nuisance of themselves. Their appeal, as fantastic as it was ill conceived, aroused small sympathy among exasperated legislators seeking a place to park their own cars. The net result of extravagant behavior in lobbying is usually failure.[44] Examples of this type confirm the judgment of S. E. Finer that "often the more demonstrative the lobbying, the weaker and poorer in repute the organization concerned. The best equipped lobbies tend to work silently."[45]

LOBBY ALLIANCES

Pressure groups are habitually alert to possibilities for increasing and widening support for their legislative objectives, in the knowledge that backing by an additional group or two strengthens their position. Legislative combinations may be formed because groups share a common ideology and a complementary set of goals or because they are willing to engage in logrolling. Logrolling alliances are linked by *quid pro quo* agreements. Some of these alliances are more or less continuous, others are sporadic or spontaneous, and some are gained only with difficulty and are easily dissolved.

One of the most durable alliances found in Congress and in the state legislatures involves the major farm organizations, the Farm Bureau and the National Grange in particular, and their "city cousins," business organizations such as the Chamber of Commerce and the NAM. As McCune makes clear, "not all who sport the farm label are in overalls." The farm organization–business alliance was forged out of their common conservatism and their abiding dislike for organized labor.[46] Business organizations sponsor a variety of activities to keep the alliance firm. For example, the Chamber of Commerce, through its agricultural department, helps to develop farm forums and institutes, promotes the development of local study groups which bring farmers and businessmen together, and arranges such events as "farm-city week" celebrations. Among its principal publications is the

---

44 Possibly under the right circumstances the blunt use of political pressure is effective. In the 86th Congress, for example, a pay-increase bill for 1,500,000 federal employees was passed without difficulty over President Eisenhower's veto. Senators and representatives were under heavy pressure from federal employees. Postal workers, attired in their blue uniforms, roamed the halls of Congress and packed the galleries; others buttonholed lawmakers, urging them to override the veto. Part of the veto message was devoted to upbraiding the postal workers for their "intensive and unconcealed political pressure." *New York Times,* July 1 and 2, 1960.

45 S. E. Finer, "Interest Groups and the Political Process in Great Britain," in *Interest Groups on Four Continents,* ed. Henry W. Ehrmann (Pittsburgh: University of Pittsburgh Press, 1958), p. 136.

46 Wesley McCune, *The Farm Bloc* (Garden City, N.Y.: Doubleday & Company, Inc., 1943), pp. 8–11.

348   *Agricultural Bulletin,* a monthly publication for the nation's farmers. Solidarity achieved at the grass roots works to strengthen the alliance in legislative chambers, contributing to the result that the major farm and business organizations tend to have a common outlook on public policy questions. A comparable alliance has been developing in recent years between the most liberal of the agricultural organizations, the National Farmers' Union, and organized labor.

Similar camaraderie and mutual helpfulness typically permeate relations between farm and business organizations on the state level. Marian Irish notes that in southern states there is "considerable ideological coincidence between the industrial and agricultural groups—a general predilection for private enterprise, public subsidies, and 'least government.' "[47] A controversy in the North Dakota legislature further illustrates this point. When a gross production tax on oil was being debated in the legislature, a large caravan of citizen-lobbyists descended upon Bismarck, the state capital, to protest the imposition of a high tax; it turned out that many of the "lobbyists" were farmers, not oilmen, and that the protest had in fact been organized by a local Chamber of Commerce.[48]

The strategy of alliances warrants further illustration. Among veterans' organizations, for example, the American Legion has long been linked with the viewpoint of business organizations and the Republican party. Teachers' associations have been known to undergo a quickening of interest in the objectives of other groups when teachers stand to profit in return. Thus state teacher lobbies frequently have supported the oil industry in "oil states" because revenues from that source contribute heavily to public education; similarly, the oil holdings and investments of some universities may cause them to look with kindly eye upon the oil industry.[49] No organization has practiced intergroup lobbying more faithfully or effectively than the American Medical Association. In its campaign against compulsory health insurance in the late forties and early fifties, the AMA—via the California public relations firm of Whitaker and Baxter—eventually obtained endorsement of its position by some eight thousand assorted organizations.[50]

Richard Neuberger, who served in the Oregon legislature before becoming a U.S. senator, records his bout with an impromptu and transient alliance when he introduced a bill in the state legislature to limit the number of billboards on state highways:

> Although I had a perfect voting record on the A.F. of L. scoresheet, the head of the Signpainters' Union called me an "enemy of labor," and claimed that I wanted to throw hundreds of men out of work. Then the "widows and orphans" began to appear: forlorn families which would become public charges if they no longer could rent their roadside property to the signboard companies. The state advertising club sent an impressive delegation, which accused me of being a foe of the Bill of Rights: The advertising men would

---

[47] "Political Thought and Political Behavior in the South," *Western Political Quarterly,* XIII (June 1960), 411.
[48] Robert Engler, *New Republic,* September 12, 1955, pp. 12–13.
[49] Robert Engler, *New Republic,* September 26, 1955, p. 25.
[50] Stanley Kelley, *Professional Public Relations and Political Power* (Baltimore: Johns Hokpins Press, 1956), p. 81.

lose their "freedom of speech" if their billboards were barred from the countryside. Although the bill had been suggested to me by a wealthy old woman who loved the outdoors and did not like to see it defaced, my proposal was denounced by these delegations as being of Communist origin. ...Put to a public referendum, I imagine the bill would have passed by at least 5 to 1. These few small pressure groups were able to induce the legislature to reject it overwhelmingly. I still marvel at the fact that the billboard owners themselves never once appeared during the entire operation.[51]

Finally, administrative agencies have learned that they can make a greater mark on the legislature if their program is supported concurrently by pressure groups; hence continuing, if sometimes subterranean, alliances between agencies and groups within their clientele have come to be common in Washington and the states. Administrative agency–interest group linkage is particularly strong on matters involving veterans' affairs. Leiper Freeman has observed: "The Veterans' Administration counts heavily on the American Legion and to a lesser extent on other veterans' organizations to support its recommendations to Congress. In fact, it seldom tends to make a recommendation to Congress that is not reasonably acceptable to these organizations, so strong is their partnership in all pressure politics dealing with veterans' affairs."[52]

Grass Roots Lobbying

Group strategies for influencing public decisions take many forms. Recently a new emphasis in lobbying has developed, that of seeking to mold public opinion as well as to exert immediate influence on decision-makers in government. Operating on the assumption that the development and execution of public policy may be influenced by indirect ("long-distance") techniques as well as by direct methods, groups now "lobby" the public as vigorously as they lobby office holders. They seek a favorable public attitude toward their organizations and goals; techniques for gaining public acceptance center in problems of "merchandising." Although the formal lobby organization is not ignored, its importance may be diminished. "Manipulation replaces domination or outright demands."[53] The following colloquy in a congressional investigation of the oil and gas lobby suggests how a group's "educational" program (not regulated by lobby law) may be used to influence public policy.

Mr. Fay (Chief Counsel to the Special Committee to Investigate Political Activities, Lobbying, and Campaign Contributions). Would you say it was correct or...incorrect to conclude that one of the ultimate aims [of your

[51] *Adventures in Politics: We Go To The Legislature* (New York: Oxford University Press, 1954), pp. 102–3.

[52] "The Bureaucracy in Pressure Politics," *Annals of the American Academy of Political and Social Science,* CCCXIX (September 1958), 17.

[53] Samuel J. Eldersveld, "American Interest Groups: A Survey of Research and Some Implications for Theory and Method," in Ehrmann, *op. cit.,* p. 193.

organization] was to influence legislation which would exempt gas producers from regulation or control?

Mr. McCollum (Chairman, Natural Gas and Oil Resources Committee). You said one of the ultimate aims. Now I can answer your question this way. In the record is a statement of the Natural Gas and Oil Resources Committee [which indicated] that the purpose of this committee...was a long-range information and education committee....

Certainly if the public were informed on a subject as we understood it... one thing ultimately could be legislation of some form or the other. Another thing was that if we had to live under regulation, we realized full well regulation would be less onerous if we had an informed public than otherwise.... To answer your question, yes; it is conceivable that one of the results would be legislation.

The Chairman (Senator McClellan). And one of its purposes was, in fact primarily its chief purpose was, to influence legislation by informing the public and trying to persuade the public of your point of view; isn't that correct?

Mr. McCollum. One of its purposes.

The Chairman. But just be frank. Wasn't that the real reason for it, to inform the public and get public sentiment built up behind the character of legislation that the industry desired?

Mr. McCollum. The principal purpose was to have an educated and informed public, so that the public would act, and one of the results could be legislation, not only against this Federal regulation but also that it would be an informed public, that we are under the threat of price controls, and they think we are making too much money and we don't think so.[54]

Because it was not engaged in conventional lobbying activities, rather only in an "information and education" program, the National Gas and Oil Resources Committee did not register under the Federal Regulation of Lobbying Act.

Public relations has come a long way in politics. Formerly of small consequence among the activities of organizations, it is now recognized as a central, sometimes predominant, means by which groups seek to obtain their goals; indeed, no major organization would feel at all secure without a broadly based program for influencing public opinion. Major organizations have found it advisable to organize both short- and long-range public relations programs, the former focused to gain immediate public support in skirmishes with other groups and government, the latter aimed at molding a climate of opinion friendly to the organization and its aims. At bottom, the purpose of each "is to make the program of the group appear synonymous with the general welfare."[55] Groups have come to recognize that, over the long haul, success is likely to depend on their having accumulated a reservoir of public goodwill, which in turn will have been shaped partially

---

54 *Hearings on Oil and Gas Lobby, pp. 124–26, passim.* Parts of this testimony also appear in the *Final Report,* pp. 11–12.

55 Henry A. Turner, "How Pressure Groups Operate," *Annals of the American Academy of Political and Social Science,* CCCXIX (September 1958), 69.

by widespread acceptance of their ideological positions. Merchandising an ideology or educating the public, whatever the process may be termed, is the continuing function of interest-group public relations.

Of all the groups that engage in the dissemination of propaganda and the cultivation of favorable attitudes, none is more persistent or formidable in its efforts than business: "Business was, and is still, the public relations man's most important patron."[56] Holding a view which has since become common among all types of groups, a spokesman for public utility interests put the matter bluntly in the 1920s:

> I am fairly familiar with legislative practice and procedure and have not many illusions in that quarter. Sometimes the political road has to be traveled. When a destructive bill is pending in a legislature it has to be dealt with in a way to get results. I am not debating that. But to depend, year after year, upon the usual political expedients for stopping hostile legislation is shortsightedness. In the long run isn't it better and surer to lay a groundwork with the people back home who have the votes, so that proposals of this character are not popular with them, rather than depend upon stopping such proposals when they get up to the legislature or commission?[57]

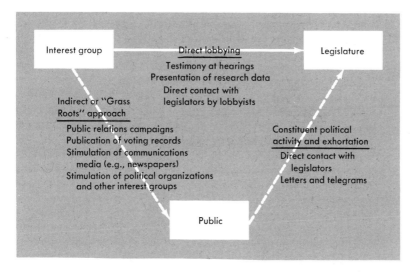

FIGURE 13 *Forms of communication between interest groups and legislators.*

A grass roots campaign to influence public attitudes on an issue is most effective when it is successful in enlisting support from other powerful organizations. A cardinal precept followed by Whitaker and Baxter, public relations specialists, calls for mobilization of "natural allies" in campaigns. Natural allies, Stanley Kelley points out, are those organizations and associa-

---

[56] Kelley, *op. cit.,* p. 13.
[57] Senate Document 92, part 71A, 70th Congress, 1st sess., p. 17, quoted by Kelley, *op. cit.,* p. 13.

352 tions which have a financial interest at stake, an ideological bent which coincides with the campaign's objectives, or a financial or psychological relationship to the client which impels them to join forces. "Organizations are approached not only because they represent blocs of voters but also because they can be made channels in a general system for the distribution of ideas."[58]

Properly instructed by the professional public relations team of an interest group, the public instinctively should favor the "right" side of an issue and do the organization's bidding. This consists of communicating with its representatives in order to promote or impede the progress of legislation relevant to the group's interest. Such, at least, is the assumption upon which political public relations rests.

Putting together a public relations campaign on a legislative issue is an intricate matter, and it calls for financial and manpower resources in large quantity. A Senate report on the activities of the Natural Gas and Oil Resources Committee (NGO) on behalf of the Harris-Fulbright bill to amend the Natural Gas Act furnishes clues as to how it is done. The pressure-group activities in the story of this bill—one of the most controversial of its or any other decade—began when:

> NGO retained the public relations firm of Hill & Knowlton, Inc., to furnish an outline of a complete program of operations. One of the first steps taken under the guidance of Hill & Knowlton was the retention of Opinion Research Corp. to conduct a survey of thought leaders (editors, teachers, clergymen, professional people, businessmen, and farm leaders) on matters pertaining to the gas industry, at a cost of $10,000. . . .
>
> Under the broad program outlined by Hill & Knowlton, NGO set up fifteen regional districts throughout the country, with a regional chairman for each district. A chairman was also selected for each State. In addition, chairmen were also chosen for county areas and other local levels, personnel for which were furnished by the oil and gas companies.
>
> The campaign to mold public opinion involved all media of communication, including newspaper and magazine advertisements, radio and television programs, film, speeches, and wide dissemination of numerous pieces of literature. Elaborate kits were prepared by NGO for distribution to its representatives throughout the country, containing, among other things, material for newspaper editors, press releases, speeches tailored to various types of audiences, interviews, and scripts for radio-television broadcasts.
>
> By September 1, 1955, it was estimated by NGO that it had distributed over 5,000,000 pieces of literature; that its representatives had delivered thousands of talks and made thousands of contacts with editors of daily and weekly newspapers and organizations such as chambers of commerce; that about 500 radio broadcasts had been made by its representatives; and that extensive exhibition had been made around the country of a film distributed by NGO entitled "You, the People."
>
> The manpower which enabled NGO to carry out its extensive program nationally was furnished by various firms in the industry without charge. The part-time services of approximately 3,000 men were thus donated to NGO.

[58] Kelley, *op. cit.*, pp. 58–59.

Such services were rendered while these men were engaged in their regular employment in the industry.

The expenses of NGO from October 1954 until March 31, 1956 amounted to $1,753,513.70.

One of the perplexing problems before the committee was whether to recommend that activities such as were conducted by NGO should be brought within provisions of any legislative activity disclosure act.[59]

Pressures on the Parties

Relations between pressure groups and political parties are highly variable. Generally, the nexus between groups and parties is weaker in the United States than in Britain, where, for example, trade unions are formally attached to a major party. Moreover, since parties count for less in the United States than they do in Britain, pressure groups customarily have not addressed their main energies to establishing beachheads within the parties. "Where the power is, there the pressure will be applied."[60] In Britain this means that pressure groups concentrate on the administration and the parliamentary party; in the United States, on the other hand, pressure group efforts of great variety have been developed. Grass roots or public relations campaigns, virtually unknown in Britain, are joined in the United States with attempts to influence legislative committees, legislative party organs, individual legislators, the administration, and all other centers of independent or of relatively independent power. A realignment of the parties in the United States—resulting in a sharpening of their policy differences— would probably affect the behavior of pressure groups in the legislature. Instead of massing their attack upon committees, powerful committee chairmen, or individual members, pressure groups would be encouraged to seek their ends through influencing the decisions of legislative party organs.

In those states where legislative parties are strong and cohesive, lobby groups concentrate their energies on winning party support. Though the individual member remains important, the party caucus is the center of things. Concerning Connecticut, Lockard states: "The customary volume of pleading communications, hallway conversation, and other forms of entreaty are involved, but instances of specific effort to get legislators to ignore the caucus and the party leadership to ram a bill through are rare indeed."[61]

Most interest groups strive to walk a line between the two parties, doing business with both if circumstances permit and avoiding deep involvement with only one. This approach gained currency in labor circles as the Gompers policy—a nonpartisan doctrine of rewarding friends and punishing enemies without regard to party affiliation. Groups continue to pay lip service to the principle today, though some have come to ignore it in practice. Several major pressure groups now identify their welfare with a single

[59] *Final Report,* pp. 14–15 (emphasis added).

[60] Samuel Beer, "Group Representation in Britain and the United States," *Annals of the American Academy of Political and Social Science,* CCCXIX (September 1958), 138.

[61] Lockard, *op. cit.,* p. 288.

354 party and its program. The "alliances" formed may involve nothing more than an occasional joining of forces or perhaps a kindred feeling; in other cases, however, the development has progressed to the point of "infiltration." Examples of state party organizations heavily influenced, if not controlled, by certain interest groups are not difficult to uncover: the Non-Partisan League in North Dakota and the Pennsylvania Manufacturers' Association (PMA) have enormous influence in the state Republican organizations; the United Automobile Workers union in Michigan has comparable influence in the state Democratic party. In states in which no one group holds a commanding place in party councils, a cluster of like-minded groups may carry great weight. In the Massachusetts legislature, for example:

> Closely allied with the Republican party are the public-utility interests, the real-estate lobby, the Associated Industries of Massachusetts (the local version of the NAM), the Chamber of Commerce, the insurance companies, and the Massachusetts Federation of Taxpayer's Associations. All these groups have easy access to the leaders of the Republican party. Through shared opinions, campaign contributions, and at times common business connections, the lobbyists for these groups know they can present their arguments to attentive ears within "their" party, even as labor has similar access to the Democrats.[62]

The Effectiveness of Interest-Group Tactics

No more than a rough measure can be taken of the effectiveness of given tactics upon governmental decision-making.[63] An interview study by Milbrath of over one hundred Washington lobbyists, however, affords good evidence concerning the tactics and techniques that lobbyists *perceive* to be most and least efficacious in communicating with government officials. The study reports: (1) Nearly two-thirds of the lobbyists believe that the most effective tactic involves the personal presentation of their case. Testifying before hearings, included in this category, is ranked somewhat lower than personal contact with a single person. (2) An increasingly important tactic used by lobbyists, and ranked high in effectiveness, is to arrange for intermediaries—close personal friends of the legislator or a constituent—to plead the group's point of view. Lobbyists placed constituent contacts markedly higher on the scale (i.e., more effective) than contact by a friend. (3) Public relations campaigns rank somewhat higher than letter and telegram campaigns; lobbyists for mass-membership organizations such as farm and labor view both approaches more favorably than lobbyists from other groups. Labor and farm group lobbyists also contend that the publicizing of legisla-

---

[62] *Ibid.*, p. 165.

[63] A related question involves the personal qualities and background factors which make a *lobbyist effective.* A study based on the opinions of Indiana state legislators sheds light on this. In the view of about 70% of the legislators, the most important qualities a lobbyist should have are honesty and integrity. Next came knowledge of the subject matter (53%), an agreeable personality (38%), helpfulness in conducting research and providing information (16%), and previous legislative experience (12%). Only 5% of the legislators thought formal education was important in the background of lobbyists. See Kenneth Janda, Henry Teune, Melvin Kahn, and Wayne Francis, *Legislative Politics in Indiana* (Bloomington: Indiana University, Bureau of Governmental Research, 1961), p. 19.

tors' voting records is moderately effective, while many other lobbyists view this method as worthless, even dangerous, since it may antagonize members whose records emerge unfavorable. (4) Of all the techniques for opening communication channels between lobbyists and legislators (entertaining, giving a party, bribery, contributing money, campaign work, collaboration with other groups), the tactic of collaborating with other groups is most valued; campaign work and campaign contributions rank next; bribery is dismissed as both impractical and ineffective.[64]

The effectiveness of interest-group contacts with legislators can also be examined from the standpoint of the legislators, as a recent study by Scott and Hunt has done. Among members of Congress, the interest-group techniques judged to be most effective in securing favorable congressional action are *indirect personal contacts* (individual letters, form letters, petitions, telegrams, telephone calls) and *direct personal contacts* (office call, committee hearing, use of a personal friend as an intermediary, conversation with a constituent). Ranked most effective among the indirect personal contacts by this sample of congressmen were individual letters and telephone calls; form letters and petitions, on the other hand, were held to be ineffective. In the category of direct personal contacts, testifying at committee hearings and office calls were cited as most effective, followed by contacts through friends and conversation with a constituent. *Collective personal contacts* (e.g., social engagements, speeches at organization meetings) and *campaign contacts* (campaign work, campaign contributions) do not appear to most congressmen to have a significant effect on legislation.[65] On the evidence of these studies, members of Congress and lobbyists do not view lobbying techniques in altogether the same light. One notable difference is that lobbyists see the personal presentation of their case as their most effective tactic while congressmen believe that committee testimony ranks above all other interest-group techniques in influencing the attitudes of members and the decisions of Congress.

Although evidence on the effectiveness of various interest-group techniques at the state legislative level is available for only a few states, the broad picture appears to be similar to that of Congress. Table 10.2, the work of Harmon Zeigler and Michael Baer, reports on the effectiveness of different methods of communication as perceived by legislators and lobbyists in the states of Massachusetts, North Carolina, Oregon, and Utah. Both legislators and lobbyists rank direct, personal communication (personal presentation of arguments, presenting research results, testifying at hearings) as the most productive lobbying technique. Interestingly, in nearly all categories lobbyists regard their techniques as more effective than legislators regard them.[66]

Factors in the Effectiveness of Interest Groups

It is one thing to seek to influence decisions and quite another to succeed in doing it. A group may have extensive access to members of the legislature, including its key leaders, and yet have relatively meager influ-

64 Milbrath, "Lobbying," 32–53.
65 Scott and Hunt, *op. cit.,* pp. 70–85.
66 Zeigler and Baer, *op. cit.,* pp. 174–75.

TABLE 10.2

Effectiveness of Lobbying Techniques, as Perceived by Legislators and Lobbyists, in Four States

	Degree of Effectiveness*							
	Massachusetts		North Carolina		Oregon		Utah	
Method	Legislators	Lobbyists	Legislators	Lobbyists	Legislators	Lobbyists	Legislators	Lobbyists
Direct, Personal Communication								
Personal presentation of arguments	5.8	6.6	4.7	6.7	6.7	6.9	5.3	6.4
Presenting research results	6.0	5.8	5.4	5.4	6.8	6.0	6.3	5.5
Testifying at hearings	5.2	5.6	4.8	5.3	6.1	5.7	5.1	5.0
Communication Through an Intermediary								
Contact by constituent	2.5	3.2	3.0	5.4	2.7	4.3	3.6	5.0
Contact by friend	2.0	2.5	3.0	4.2	2.4	3.7	3.4	4.0
Contact by other lobbyists	2.4	4.3	2.5	4.2	3.2	4.5	3.0	4.8
Indirect, Impersonal Communication								
Letter-writing campaign	2.0	3.4	1.7	4.0	1.6	4.0	2.8	4.0
Publication of voting records	2.0	2.2	1.3	1.4	1.5	2.0	2.0	2.4
Public relations campaign	3.5	3.7	3.5	4.6	3.5	4.0	4.1	4.6
Keeping Communication Channels Open								
Entertaining legislators	1.0	1.3	2.0	2.5	1.7	2.2	2.8	3.0
Giving a party	1.0	1.0	2.0	1.8	1.4	1.6	2.4	2.3
Campaign contributions	1.0	2.0	1.6	2.4	1.5	2.5	2.1	3.3
Withholding campaign contributions	0.3	0.1	0.3	0.4	0.1	0.1	1.0	1.0
Bribery	0.2	0.1	0.1	1.2	0.03	0.2	0.2	0.3
Mean for all Techniques	2.5	3.0	2.6	3.5	2.8	3.5	3.2	3.7

SOURCE: Harmon Zeigler and Michael Baer, *Lobbying: Interaction and Influence in American State Legislatures* (Belmont, California: Wadsworth Publishing Company, 1969), p. 176.
*Ratings of effectiveness on a scale from 0 (ineffective) to 8 (effective).

ence upon policy formation. In other words, there is a difference between the "door-opening power" of groups and the "decision-making power."[67] Plainly, not all groups share equally in access or in influence.

Theoretical tools for appraising the influence of political interest groups in the legislative process are not yet fully developed. At this point we must content ourselves with a general statement of the factors which appear, in one measure or another, to affect the influence of groups. They are: (1) the size of the group, (2) its prestige, (3) the cohesion of its membership, (4) the skills of its leadership,[68] (5) the distribution of its membership, (6) its ability to rally both widespread popular support and the assistance of other groups, and (7) its resources, especially financial. In addition, the structural peculiarities of the government[69] and of the political parties will tend to affect the access of certain groups to centers of power. Furthermore, though it would be difficult to prove, a group's effectiveness may hinge on whether the views of its leadership are judged to represent the outlook of its rank-and-file members—that organizational spokesmen invariably make this claim is not altogether persuasive among skeptical legislators. Finally, groups whose objectives do not trigger the opposition of other major groups hold a decided advantage.

One index to the power of lobbies is the judgment of the lobbyists themselves. Not surprisingly, they are not solidly in agreement. Yet, among Washington lobbyists, at any rate, there is general agreement as to the profile of interest group power: those groups with large memberships—e.g., certain farm, veterans', and labor organizations—are rated as the most successful in securing their objectives. The specialized groups singled out most frequently for their power are the American Medical Association and the oil and gas lobbies. Interestingly, a noticeable number of lobbyists pick a major antagonist as the most powerful interest group.[70]

The overall effectiveness of interest groups in the political system appears to be related to certain economic and political variables. Table 10.3,

---

[67] Eldersveld in Ehrmann, *op. cit.*, p. 187.

[68] See Truman, *op. cit.*, Chapters 6 and 7, for analysis of the problems of cohesion and of the bearing that leadership skills have upon group effectiveness. Harmon Zeigler concludes that "the influence of interest groups in the legislative process depends more on the harmony of values between the group and the legislators than it does on the ability of a group to wield its 'power' either through skillful techniques or presumed electoral influence." *Interest Groups in American Society* (Englewood Cliffs, N.J.: Prentice-Hall, Inc., 1964), p. 274. See also Oliver Garceau, "Interest Group Theory in Political Research," *Annals of the American Academy of Political and Social Science*, CCCXIX (September 1958), 108–9; and Janda *et al.*, *op. cit.*, pp. 10–19. For a study of the effectiveness of interest groups in the Tennessee legislature, see Lawrence D. Longley, "Interest Group Interaction in a Legislative System, *Journal of Politics* (August 1967), 637–58.

[69] The structure of government imposed by federalism, for example, often has proved to be a boon to business groups. While they have lost some battles in Congress, they have been enormously successful in the state legislatures, due in some degree to the overrepresentation of rural conservative interests whose outlook is roughly parallel to urban business. The doctrine of "states' rights," whatever its theoretical validity, is highly compatible with the advancement of business interests and the protection of the *status quo*.

[70] Milbrath, *The Washington Lobbyists*, pp. 347–51. Also see the analysis of conflict between two bank factions in the Wisconsin Assembly by Wilder Crane, Jr., "A Test of Effectiveness of Interest-Group Pressures on Legislators," *Southwestern Social Science Quarterly*, XLI (December 1960), 335–40.

TABLE 10.3
The Strength of Pressure Groups in Varying Political and Economic Situations

Condition	Types of Pressure System*		
	Strong (24 states†)	Moderate (14 states‡)	Weak (7 states§)
Party Competition			
One-Party	33.3%	0%	0%
Modified One-Party	37.5%	42.8%	0%
Two-Party	29.1%	57.1%	100.0%
Cohesion of Parties in Legislature			
Weak Cohesion	75.0%	14.2%	0%
Moderate Cohesion	12.5%	35.7%	14.2%
Strong Cohesion	12.5%	50.0%	85.7%
Socio-Economic Variables			
Urban	58.6%	65.1%	73.3%
Per Capita Income	$1,900	$2,335	$2,450
Industrialization Index	88.8	92.8	94.0

SOURCE: Harmon Zeigler, "Interest Groups in the States," in *Politics in the American States,* ed. Herbert Jacob and Kenneth N. Vines. Copyright © 1965 by Little, Brown & Company, p. 114. Reprinted by permission.
* Alaska, Hawaii, Idaho, New Hampshire, and North Dakota are not classified or included.
† Alabama, Arizona, Arkansas, California, Florida, Georgia, Iowa, Kentucky, Louisiana, Maine, Michigan, Minnesota, Mississippi, Montana, Nebraska, New Mexico, North Carolina, Oklahoma, Oregon, South Carolina, Tennessee, Texas, Washington, Wisconsin.
‡ Delaware, Illinois, Kansas, Maryland, Massachusetts, Nevada, New York, Ohio, Pennsylvania, South Dakota, Utah, Vermont, Virginia, West Virginia.
§ Colorado, Connecticut, Indiana, Missouri, New Jersey, Rhode Island, Wyoming.

the work of Harmon Zeigler, relates the strength of pressure groups to party competitiveness, party cohesion in the legislature, and several socio-economic variables. A profile of the data shows that pressure groups are likely to be strongest in states with these characteristics: (1) one-party political system, (2) weak party cohesion in the legislature, (3) low urban population, (4) low per capita income, and (5) low index of industrialization. While there are exceptions to this pattern, the evidence is persuasive that pressure group strength, party politics, and the socio-economic environment are closely related. In general, the data of this study support the hypothesis that urbanism and industrialization serve to increase group membership while at the same time decreasing group effectiveness. "The greater participation in organizations in the urban states means that more group-anchored conflicts will come to the attention of the governmental decision-makers. The greater the number of demands which come to the attention of any single decision-making agency, the less likely will be the probability that any one set of demands will be able to maintain control over the content of policy."[71]

71 "Interest Groups in the States," in *Politics in the American States,* ed. Herbert Jacob and Kenneth N. Vines (Boston: Little, Brown & Company, 1965), pp. 113–17, quotation on p. 113. Two notable exceptions to the pattern disclosed are California and Michigan; both are urban, industrial states with strong pressure groups. Note that every southern state is classified as having strong pressure groups. For additional support of the hypothesis concerning party strength and interest-group

Finally, the capacity of the legislature to resist the pressures of organized interests is likely to depend on its ability to gather and analyze information independently of other sources. Jess Unruh, former Speaker of the California Assembly, contends:

> [Lobbyists] have influence in inverse ratio to legislative competence. It is common for a special interest to be the only source of legislative information about itself. The information that a lobbyist presents may or may not be prejudiced in favor of his client, but if it is the only information the legislature has, no one can really be sure. A special interest monopoly of information seems much more sinister than the outright buying of votes that has been excessively imputed to lobbyists.[72]

FARM GROUPS

By any reckoning, farm groups wield considerable influence in national and state politics. The legislative branch in particular has been receptive to the claims made by farm organizations—more so than the executive, which farm politicians tend to view with suspicion.[73] The roots of farm power in American politics are not difficult to uncover. In the first place, equal representation of the states in the Senate very likely augments the political influence of the less populous farm states. Prior to the reapportionment decisions, the overrepresentation of rural areas in the House served the same purpose. Second, the traditional conception of agriculture as the "backbone of the nation," steadfast and indispensable, predisposes legislators to view the claims of farm groups favorably. Third, no powerful countervailing interest groups are present to oppose legislation backed by farm organizations. Finally, farm groups are heavily represented in Congress and in the legislatures by "inside lobbyists"—legislators directly and closely attuned to the needs of the agricultural community. In some state legislatures, in fact, it is still common to find as many as one out of every four or five members who list "farming" as their occupation.

Although the above interpretation of farm power is generally correct, it is not the whole story. The influence of groups changes as conditions change, and this is especially applicable to agrarian interest groups today. Two factors appear to be altering their influence. One is the steady increase in urban population; from a numerical standpoint, farmers are much less important today than they were in the past. "A farm bill must now meet approval of consumers as well as farmers," as an Iowa congressman from a rural district puts it. Second, the ideological split in the farm organizations, notably between the American Farm Bureau Federation and the National Farmers' Union, has taken its toll. It has become increasingly difficult to

---

activity and influence, see a study by Bernard D. Kolasa, "Lobbying in the Nonpartisan Environment: The Case of Nebraska," *Western Political Quarterly,* XXIV (March 1971), 65–78.

72 Herzberg and Unruh, *op. cit.,* pp. 17–18.

73 Charles M. Hardin, "Congressional Farm Policies and Economic Foreign Policy," *Annals of the American Academy of Political and Social Science,* CCCXXXI (September 1960), 99.

develop a farm program that has significant appeal to all farm groups.[74] To some extent at least, declining numbers and waning cohesiveness have begun to chip away the influence of farm pressure groups.

BUSINESS GROUPS

That business interest groups occupy the highest ground in American politics is scarcely arguable. It is not so easy, however, to depict precisely how their superiority in the political process was secured or how it has been sustained. A minimum interpretation of business power would take account of such broad factors as the role of wealth in politics, the high prestige of business groups, and the business ethic deeply imbedded in the public mind. Add to these advantages generally skillful leadership, massive and continuing public relations programs, an ideological unity among all kinds of business organizations (notwithstanding their particularistic goals), a steady success in forming legislative alliances, and the outline of business power becomes evident. Taken together, these factors make business groups consistently the most powerful of all private organizations.

LABOR GROUPS

A similar success story cannot be sketched of labor in politics. There have been occasions when labor has scored conspicuous legislative victories—during the early New Deal period, for example—but more frequently labor has been disillusioned by the treatment accorded its views and proposals. In comparison with business and farm interests in politics, labor appears much the weakest. How is its relative weakness *vis-à-vis* other major groups to be explained? A number of hypotheses may be suggested: (1) limited unionization; (2) uneven distribution of union membership—in some areas of the country, notably the South, unions are not highly developed; (3) absence of class consciousness; (4) lack of cohesion within organized labor; (5) relatively low prestige of labor in comparison with high-status business and professional groups;[75] (6) the tendency for labor activity to generate powerful counterpressures by conservative alliances, customarily led by the NAM; and (7) the existence of widespread public hostility toward labor unions and their objectives.

While labor has achieved moderate, if sporadic, success in Congress, its gains at the state level have been slight. Virtually without exception, even in heavily unionized northern states, labor proposals face strong opposition in the legislatures, dominated as they often are by small-town businessmen, farmers, and lawyers. Organized labor has a long list of the baneful effects of federalism.

---

[74] The quoted remark is by Representative Charles Hoeven of Iowa, cited in Charles O. Jones, "The Relationship of Congressional Committee Action to a Theory of Representation" (Ph.D. Thesis, University of Wisconsin, 1959).

[75] David Truman speculates that "the most basic factor affecting access is the position of the group or its spokesman in the social structure.... Even where flattery is not an influence, the high-status group is aided by the large proportion of key officials...whose class backgrounds are such that they have similar values, manners, and preconceptions" (*op. cit.,* p. 265).

The objectives of veterans' organizations such as the American Legion often are highly controversial. For example, John F. Kennedy remarked during his tenure in the Senate that "the leadership of the American Legion has not had a constructive thought for the benefit of this country since 1918."[76] There is no way of knowing how widely this judgment is shared by others, but what seems beyond dispute is that the Legion ranks among the most influential interest groups in American political life. How are its numerous victories in state and national politics to be explained? In the first place, it meets handily the basic determinants of group power: a large membership (dispersed throughout the country), high prestige, cohesiveness, and adequate financial resources. In addition, the Legion is not often opposed by other powerful combinations; an exception to this is an occasional squabble with the American Medical Association over veterans' medical benefits. Finally, as the late Professor Key pointed out, "The big guns of big business do not go into action effectively against Legion forays on the Treasury, a circumstance that gives plausibility to the hypothesis that a tacit alliance prevails between business and Legion leadership. For business the *quid pro quo* is the generally conservative position of the Legion."[77]

Legislator-Lobbyist Relations

Much of the writing on political interest groups, at least until recently, has served more to adumbrate relations between lobbyists and legislators than to illuminate them. The lobbyist is commonly portrayed as a genius at dissimulation, a person virtually untouched by ethical standards, and an agent of rapacious demands. In the usual treatment, lobbies are described as extraordinarily effective in getting their way in the legislature. Legislators fit into this interpretation more as victims or as hostages than as individuals with power in their own right. All in all, this is the "theory" of the omnipotent interest group, the passive legislature, and the defenseless and harried legislator. In one form or another this theory has been transmitted tirelessly down through the years, its durability in the folklore of American politics due in part to its frequent surfacing in the popular journals and newspapers.[78]

To set store by this thesis is to adopt a highly popular interpretation of American legislatures. One reason this is such a seductive thesis is that it exposes rather than muffles what are thought to be the ugly realities of the legislative process. The theory offers fascination for those who look for pathology in American public life and defense for those who must account for their own powerlessness in the system. Moreover, popular accounts of certain lobby machinations help to support the stereotype and to make

[76] Quoted in James M. Burns, *John Kennedy: A Political Profile* (New York: Harcourt, Brace & World, Inc., 1959), p. 75.

[77] *Politics, Parties, and Pressure Groups* (New York: Thomas Y. Crowell Company, 1964), p. 110.

[78] For a vastly amusing if exaggerated account along these lines, see Larry L. King, "Washington's Money Birds," *Harper's Magazine*, August 1965, pp. 45–54.

362 interest-group power credible. Despite its popularity, however, this thesis of legislative subordination to lobbies does not square comfortably with reality. It inflates the power of interest groups and deflates the independence of legislators. Put baldly, it tends to make the legislature nothing more than an arena for the joustings of interest groups, and public policy merely the expression of a dominant interest or a combination of interests.

Empirical studies in recent years have shown that relationships between legislators and lobbyists are highly complex and that legislators are at least as likely to influence lobbyists as lobbyists are to influence legislators. What emerges clearly in these studies is that most of the political resources that shape these relationships rest on the legislators' side. The study of the U.S. Senate by Donald Matthews points out that there are at least four ways by which senators may influence lobbyists. The most important of these is a threat of noncooperation. "The senators have what the lobbyists want— a vote, prestige, access to national publicity, and the legislative 'inside dope.' Moreover, the lobbyist wants this not just once but many times over a number of years. The senators are in a position to bargain. They need not give these things away." The need for cooperation from senators thus tempers the actions of lobbyists. A second technique is "the friendship ploy." A senator's friendship with a lobbyist gives him a measure of insulation: "it makes the lobbyist indebted to him, more sensitive to his political problems, less willing to apply 'pressure,' a more trustworthy ally." "Building up credit" is a third technique open to legislators. Senators can pass on inside information to lobbyists, help publicize a group's position by delivering a speech on the floor or by inserting favorable material in the *Record,* or schedule committee hearings in order to let a lobbyist make his case—in a word, senators can help a lobbyist to "look good." A lobbyist who is indebted to a senator for favors of this kind is not in the best position to apply pressure. Finally, senators can influence lobbyists by launching or threatening to launch a public attack on them. Legislative investigations of lobbies are especially damaging; the possibility of an investigation serves to inhibit lobbyists who might otherwise be inclined "to pull out all the stops" in their efforts to influence legislative behavior.[79] There is, in sum, far more reciprocity in relations between lobbies and legislators than has ordinarily been suggested in the literature on legislatures.

Research on congressmen's perceptions of organized interests offers scant support for the proposition that the legislative process in Congress is dominated by interest groups. Scott and Hunt have shown that, by and large, the visibility of interest groups to congressmen is low, that even in their fields of specialization congressmen have few contacts with any one interest group, that members rarely feel that groups are applying pressure on them, that members are more likely to attribute significance to groups when they are discussing them generally than when they are discussing their influence on a specific measure, that such influence as groups wield is nearly always confined to a special sphere of interest, and that only a few congressmen are vulnerable to any one group. The proper role of the interest group, as congressmen see it, is the provision of information, opinion, and

[79] Donald Matthews, *U.S. Senators and Their World* (Chapel Hill: University of North Carolina Press, 1960), pp. 188–90.

support. A group that ignores these limits is likely to alienate members and damage its cause. Interestingly, freshmen congressmen are much more likely than senior members to categorize interest groups as powerful agents in the legislative process.[80]

Finally, a preoccupation with the view that lobbies control the legislative process contributes to a misunderstanding of the effects of lobbying. Lobbying may reinforce, activate, or convert legislators; plainly the most important effect is reinforcement. Lobbyists know that few votes are ever changed as a result of their efforts, and accordingly they concentrate their resources on "backstopping" or reinforcing those members who are known to be favorable to their position. A lobbyist for the private electric-power industry explains:

> There is no point in me going in and trying to change an out-and-out public-power advocate. I might try to help a person make up his mind, but there is no point in trying to convert a person who already has a strong opinion. I would be wasting my time in trying to change their minds, especially in the limited time available during a [state] legislative session. And if you've been around very long you can be pretty sure who your friends are, judging from what they have done in the past. You know who the people are who voted for your legislation. You can go down through the legislative calendar and pretty well identify individuals who will, or should, support your legislation, and you work more closely with them.[81]

The activation of members also carries high priority for lobbies—here their effort is to persuade members to work even harder on behalf of the group's interests. Hence, strange as it may appear to outsiders, most lobbyists spend most of their time lobbying members who are already friendly to their cause or else leaning in that direction. As Bauer, Pool, and Dexter point out in their study of the impact of interest groups on the formation of foreign-trade policy:

> Lobbyists fear to enter where they may find a hostile reception. Since uncertainty is greatest precisely regarding those who are undecided, the lobbyist is apt to neglect contact with those very persons whom he might be able to influence. . . . It is so much easier to carry on activities within the circle of those who agree and encourage you than it is to break out and find potential proselytes, that the day-to-day routine and pressure of business tend to shunt

---

[80] Scott and Hunt, *op. cit.,* pp. 37–59. The authors make the point that "the area of freedom of action varies from congressman to congressman. If Congressman A listens when the Fruitgrowers Association speaks, Congressman B, C, D, E, and F are indifferent to the pleas of the association. Congressman B, in turn, might be vulnerable to a second group to which his colleagues A, C, D, E, and F are indifferent. When the patterns of individual vulnerability are overlaid on one another, so to speak, it is clear that relatively few congressmen are vulnerable to any given group. Individual vulnerabilities cancel each other out to a considerable extent and are lost in the indifference, inertia, and invulnerability of Congress as a whole. Advocates of the group interpretation of politics are led astray in dealing with Congress because they do not allow for this canceling-out process, and, instead, assume that Congress is a single, vulnerable congressman writ large" (pp. 95–96).

[81] Quoted in Zeigler and Baer, *op. cit.,* p. 130.

those more painful activities aside. The result is that *the lobbyist becomes in effect a service bureau for those congressmen already agreeing with him, rather than an agent of direct persuasion.*[82]

Interest groups are functionally important to legislatures. They contribute to the definition of policy alternatives, illuminate issues, marshal evidence and support, promote bargaining, and aid legislators in numerous ways that will affect legislative decisions. Some groups appear to have extraordinary influence on certain legislators. At times groups may appear to be the beneficiaries of misplaced power. On occasion their victories have been spectacular. But it is unrealistic to contend that they steadily dominate the legislative process. Legislators have minds of their own. Not all share the same orientation toward interest-group activity.[83] They are conscious of the "mandate" under which they came into office, often zealous in achieving consistency in their voting records, and fearful of being labeled as a captive of any interest group. Moreover, they are heavily influenced by the multiple ties of party, bureaucracy, executive, and constituency. Interest groups are but one element in the bargaining process from which policies emerge.

Regulation of Lobbying

CONGRESSIONAL HISTORY

The right of citizens to communicate their views to government officials is firmly protected by the First Amendment to the Constitution: "Congress shall make no law...abridging the ...right of the people...to petition the Government for a redress of grievances." Since the earliest days of the republic, lobbies have been active in attempting to secure the passage or defeat of legislation, and occasionally their zeal has culminated in corruption and other serious abuses of the constitutional right of petition. At other times the sheer volume of lobbying has called attention to the role of interest groups in policy-making. Prompted by disclosures of venality or by uneasiness

---

[82] Raymond A. Bauer, Ithiel de Sola Pool, and Lewis A. Dexter, *American Business and Public Policy* (New York: Atherton Press, 1963), pp. 352–53.

[83] The four-state study (California, New Jersey, Ohio, and Tennessee) indicates that, by and large, state legislators see interest group activity as legitimate. The study identifies three role-orientations of legislators toward interest groups: Facilitators (members who are both friendly toward interest groups and knowledgeable about them), Resisters (members who are hostile toward interest groups and knowledgeable about them), and Neutrals (members who have no strong attitude toward interest groups and little knowledge about them). Taking the four states as a group, Facilitators rank most numerous, followed by Neutrals in second place, and Resisters in last. Interestingly, legislators with the role-orientation of Facilitator tend to be members with substantial tenure and a strong sense of personal efficacy. The authors observe: "[Evidence] from several directions points to the conclusion that a central function of the American state legislature is the accommodation of interest-group demands in the legislative process. Experience in the legislature tends to produce in individual legislators, whatever their previous background and experience, the attitudes most appropriate to this function; individuals who possess those attitudes feel themselves to be more effective as legislators than their colleagues who do not." J. Wahlke, H. Eulau, W. Buchanan, and L. Ferguson, *The Legislative System* (New York: John Wiley & Sons, Inc., 1962), p. 342.

over heightened lobbying activity, Congress from time to time has investigated lobbies and lobbyists and drafted statutes to check improper or excessive activities.

Congressional regulation of lobbying has grown slowly; the steps taken
invariably have been tentative, often ineffective. Initial regulation came in
1852 when the House of Representatives adopted a rule providing that
House newspapermen employed as agents to prosecute claims pending before
Congress were not entitled to seats on the House floor.[84] In 1854 a select
committee to investigate the lobbying activities of Samuel Colt was formed;
its principal contribution apparently was to enhance public awareness of
the nature of lobby operations. An amendment to the House rules in 1867
stipulated that former members of Congress with an interest in the outcome
of any claim before Congress were to be excluded from the House floor.
Further experimentation with lobby regulation occurred during the next
decade when Congress passed its first law requiring lobbyists to register;
adopted in 1876, the law was in effect only during that Congress, the 44th.

Increasing awareness of lobby abuses developed early in the twentieth
century, chiefly as an outgrowth of a major investigation of the insurance
lobby in the state of New York in 1905 and 1906. In 1913 intensive investigations were made of the tariff lobby in the Senate and of the National
Association of Manufacturers in the House. Another intensive investigation
of the tariff lobby by the Senate occurred in 1929, and in 1935 the lobbying
methods of utility companies were examined. As a result of the latter investigation, a provision was inserted in the Public Utilities Holding Act of 1935
which required the registration of lobbyists representing holding companies
before Congress, the Federal Power Commission, or the Securities Exchange
Commission. Lobbyists involved with matters covered by the Merchant
Marine Act of 1936 were placed under a similar enjoiner. These efforts set
the stage for a more general law.

Congress passed its first comprehensive lobbying law in 1946: it was
adopted as Title III of the Legislative Reorganization Act. Had it appeared
as a separate bill, one authority observes, Congress may well have refused
to approve it, for there had been no outcry over lobby abuses at the time.
With members' attention riveted on other features of congressional reorganization, however, the lobbying regulations were accepted without serious
challenge.

THE 1946 REGULATION OF LOBBYING ACT

The 1946 act regulating lobbying contains four principal provisions: (1)
Every person (individual, partnership, committee, association, corporation,
and any other organization or group of persons) who solicits or receives
contributions for the *principal purpose* of influencing legislation is required

---

[84] This historical review leans on Kennedy, *op. cit.,* 539–45; Edgar Lane,
"Some Lessons from Past Congressional Investigations," *Public Opinion Quarterly,*
XIV (Spring 1950), 14–32; and Edgar Lane, *Lobbying and the Law* (Berkeley: University of California Press, 1964). For a summary of national and state laws dealing
with lobbying and a review of the relevant literature, see John W. Smith, "Regulation of National and State Legislative Lobbying," *University of Detroit Law Journal,*
XLIII (1966), 663.

366 to keep a record of all contributions and expenditures, including the name and address of each person making a contribution of $500 or more and to whom an expenditure of $10 or more is made. (2) Detailed quarterly statements listing this information along with the purposes of the expenditures are to be filed with the clerk of the House of Representatives. (3) Any person who solicits, collects, or receives money for the principal purpose of influencing the passage or defeat of legislation is required to register with the clerk of the House or the secretary of the Senate. Furthermore, he is expected to provide information, on a quarterly basis, regarding his employer, his salary and expenses, his receipts and expenditures, a listing of articles and editorials he has caused to be published, and an enumeration of the proposed legislation he is employed to support or oppose.[85] (4) Information collected as a result of the act shall be published quarterly in the *Congressional Record.*

Government cannot become the captive of narrow private interests if adequate information regarding their activities is available to officials and to the public—such is the assumption of the national lobby law. *Identification, disclosure,* and *publicity* are the principal controls which the law makes available. The arguments adduced by the Supreme Court in support of the 1946 act are worth quoting:

> Present day legislative complexities are such that individual members of Congress cannot be expected to explore the myriad pressures to which they are regularly subjected. Yet full realization of the American ideal of government by elected representatives depends to no small extent on their ability to properly evaluate such pressures. Otherwise the voice of the people may all too easily be drowned out by the voice of special interest groups seeking favored treatment while masquerading as proponents of the public weal. This is the evil which the Lobbying Act was designed to help prevent.
>
> Toward that end, Congress has not sought to prohibit these pressures. It has merely provided for a modicum of information from those who for hire attempt to influence legislation or who collect or spend funds for that purpose. It wants only to know who is being hired, who is putting up the money, and how much.[86]

SHORTCOMINGS OF THE LOBBYING ACT

Although recognizing the gains brought about by the 1946 lobbying act, critics continue to have second thoughts about the wisdom of many of its provisions. In the first place, critics say, the act is undermined by ambiguities and loopholes. It has all sorts of loose ends. To whom does it apply? In *U.S.* v. *Harriss,* a 1954 case involving failure of the National Farm Committee to report receipts and expenditures connected with its lobbying activities, the Supreme Court held that the reporting requirements apply only to those persons or organizations which solicit, collect, or receive money which is used *principally* to influence legislation. This interpretation has

---

[85] The registration requirement was not made applicable to any person who merely appears before a congressional committee to express his views on legislation, to a public official acting in an official capacity, or to newspapers in their newsgathering functions.

[86] *U.S.* v. *Harriss et al.,* 347 U.S. 612 (1954).

served to sustain doubts regarding the applicability of the law, since groups whose funds are not expended for the "principal purpose" of securing the passage or defeat of legislation are exempted from the requirement. In addition, the Court emphasized that the act applies only to those persons and organizations which engage in "direct" communication with Congress. "Indirect" or "grass roots" appeals, to which groups have increasingly devoted large sums of money, do not fall within the compass of the lobbying act.

In the second place, control through publicity—the arch principle of the 1946 lobbying act—has not proved exceptionally effective. Lodging financial and other data with the clerk of the House and reproducing it in the *Congressional Record* offers no assurance that publicity will attend the revelations. Moreover, data collected are simply filed, not analyzed. Third, no agency was given the task of "policing" the act for compliance and no specific appropriations have been authorized for its enforcement. Fourth, individuals who engage in lobbying government agencies are not required to register. Fifth, information which might prove most useful is not collected, such as the number of members who belong to the organization and the manner in which its decisions on legislation are taken. In addition, students of the law are generally agreed that certain lobbying practices, such as contingent fee contracts (fees paid lobbyists are contingent upon their efforts being successful), not mentioned in the 1946 act, should be specifically prohibited.[87]

PROPOSALS FOR CHANGING THE LOBBYING ACT

Dissatisfaction with the 1946 lobby law has led to a number of proposals for revision. A bill reported by the House Committee on Standards of Official Conduct in late 1971 helps to illustrate the scope and direction of legislative efforts to reform the 1946 act. Entitled the Legislative Activities Disclosure Act, the bill, if adopted, would increase substantially the reporting and registration requirements for lobby groups and legislative agents (lobbyists).

Under the terms of the bill, which would eliminate the "principal purpose" definition of lobbying, all legislative agents and their employers would be required to file comprehensive semi-annual reports with the comptroller general showing income received and expended for the purpose of influencing legislation. To increase the probability of rigorous enforcement, administration of the law would be transferred from the clerk of the House and secretary of the Senate (the administrative agents in the 1946 act) to the comptroller general; his duties would include the enforcement of registration and reporting requirements for lobbyists and their employers (perhaps to the point of having the attorney general seek a U.S. district court order requiring compliance with the act) and the analysis of data on lobbying activities for publication in the *Congressional Record*. Of leading importance, grass roots lobbyists who solicit others to influence legislation

[87] Whether valid or not, a widespread belief exists that the contingent-fee lobbyist, spurred by the possibility of receiving exceptional compensation for his efforts if he is successful, is prone to use unreasonable or illegal means to gain his objective. Contingent-fee contracting is outlawed by the lobby laws of a number of states.

368 by direct communication would be required to comply with the provisions of the law.[88]

Should Congress eventually adopt this bill, or one with similarly broad disclosure requirements, several results are fairly predictable. One is that the bookkeeping, accounting, and reporting requirements for lobbies would be greatly augmented. Second, many individuals and their employers who have ignored the 1946 act would feel compelled to register and file accurate reports of their receipts and expenditures. Third, it is likely that a greater visibility of lobbying efforts, particularly at the grass roots level, would result. And finally, the new law, like Title III of the 1946 Legislative Reorganization Act, almost certainly would be challenged in the courts on the grounds that it contravened rights protected by the First Amendment.

In the opinion of many observers outside of Congress, as well as some members within, the adoption of a comprehensive lobbying disclosure act is necessary for the promotion of legislative independence and increased public awareness of interest group activity. Nonetheless, there is no evidence to suggest that such an act, even if vigorously administered, would have important consequences for the legislative process.

LOBBY REGULATION IN THE STATES

Lobby regulation in the states, like that in Congress, has had a checkered, generally unsatisfactory history. Its dim beginnings apparently trace to the Georgia Constitution of 1877, in which the practice of lobbying was held to be a crime. A survey in the early 1960s showed that thirty-three states require the registration of legislative agents and legislative counsel employed for compensation. Twenty-one of the thirty-three states stipulate that financial reports must be submitted. The total number of states with some form of lobby regulation is brought to forty-three by the addition of ten states which have statutes relating to improper lobbying activities. Seven states have no provisions whatsoever concerning registration or improper lobbying activities.[89]

In general, state laws are aimed at increasing the visibility of groups by disclosing the identity of lobbyists and by gathering information about their activities. Typically these laws relate only to direct communications with the legislature. Going beyond the federal statute, twenty-six states outlaw contingent fee contracts between lobbyists and clients. As with the federal lobbying laws, lobbying laws of the states prove better in theory than in practice: with but an occasional exception, a general malaise has settled over their administration and enforcement.

Interest Groups and Democratic Government

The arguments on behalf of interest groups (lobbies and lobbyists) do not circulate as widely as those which are hostile to them. Nevertheless a case can be made for pressure groups.

---

[88] For further analysis of this proposal, see *Congressional Quarterly Weekly Report,* November 13, 1971, pp. 2348–52.

[89] Belle Zeller, "The State Lobby Laws," *Book of the States, 1962–63* (Chicago: Council of State Governments, 1962), pp. 80–86.

American folklore to the contrary, pressure politics is not a one-way street. National and state legislators are not simply the inert victims of powerful lobbies. The truth is rather that legislators call for the support of lobby groups about as often as groups make claims upon them. David Truman puts it this way:

> The popular view is that the political interest group uses the legislator to its end, induces him to function as its spokesman and to vote as it wishes. [Although] this is not an inaccurate view...it is incomplete. . . . When a legislator arouses organized groups in connection with a proposal that he knows will involve them or when he solicits their support for a measure which he is promoting, the relationship becomes reciprocal. Even in connection with the development of a single bill from conception to enactment, the initiative may lie alternately with legislator and with group, including other outside influences.[90]

Political interest groups may be viewed, without stretch of the imagination, as supplementary instruments in the formal system of representation. The most equitable form of representation, certain political theorists have argued, is "functional" or "occupational"—a system which accords direct representation to the various economic interests and functions within society. The criteria of geography and residence are abandoned in favor of a system which represents discernible economic and vocational activities—farmers, businessmen, laborers, physicians, lawyers, and others. Occasional experiments with functional representation have occurred, as in the case of Germany and Italy, but success has proved slight. Today there is little interest in the idea. Yet with a broader interpretation of functional representation, one which centers in the interests represented rather than in the means by which the system is organized, it can be argued that we already possess a strong measure of functional representation. That our conventional organization of governmental power does not include a scheme for *formal* representation of groups has not diminished their opportunity to press demands upon government or restricted their access to the principal centers of political power. The representative function of groups may take on special significance where it involves communication of the aspirations of the weakest voices within society—ethnic, for example—perhaps ordinarily drowned out by the noise of powerful and insistent associations.

Pressure groups have come to be indispensable sources of information in the legislative process. No lawmaker brings to his job the technical knowledge requisite to an intelligent evaluation of all legislation; neither is the legislature as a whole geared to supply the necessary quantity of expert help. Accordingly, legislators turn to pressure groups and executive agencies for pertinent opinions, data, and analysis—and the information they provide may not be available anywhere else. The view that information conveyed by lobbyists is biased and not to be trusted is popular but probably misleading.

[90] Truman, *op. cit.,* p. 342.

370 "If the information should later prove to be false, or biased to the point of serious distortion, the decision maker is publicly embarrassed and is likely to retaliate by cutting off further access sought by the delinquent lobbyist."[91]

Policy ideas, rooted quite naturally in self-interest, are the standard equipment of interest groups. But the group contribution is not limited to advocacy of ideas nor to funneling information into the legislature. They also contribute essential energy to assembling and sustaining support for programs. Concerning their role in shaping school aid programs in eight northeastern states, one study reports:

> [Private] interest groups perform a variety of functions beyond the support of intellectual leadership. They mobilize consent within their own organizations; they develop linkages with each other in an attempt to build a common political front; they fertilize grass roots; they exploit mass media, and develop mass media of their own; they build fires under lethargic officialdom; they lobby and cajole legislators and governors; they provide a continuity of energy and concern in the face of temporary defeats and set-backs. Sometimes they work at cross purposes, but when they work together under strong and coherent leadership, they perform an indispensable function in the political process. State teachers' associations, teachers' unions, school boards' associations, PTA's, associations of educational administrators, other civic and professional societies—separately and as amalgams—have played essential roles in the politics of state aid to education.[92]

Finally, there is the view that not only is our anti-interest ideology fruitless, since there is no way by which a democratic society may stifle the organization of groups, but it also overlooks the vast potential of groups and their contributions to the transformation of politics: the language of politics today is the language of groups, not of individuals. We encourage groups on the one hand, suppress them on the other. "In pluralism and a national organization of interests," writes Alfred de Grazia, "can be discovered a new kind of democracy upon which a superior society may be founded.... It would teach groups to view themselves not as outlaws...but as integral parts of a whole in which they pursue their useful and dignified way. So long as we suppress rather than educate the group formations of American life, we lower the quality of their membership and activities."[93]

---

[91] Milbrath, "Lobbying," 47.

[92] Stephen K. Bailey, Richard T. Frost, Paul E. Marsh, and Robert C. Wood, *Schoolmen and Politics: A Study of State Aid to Education in the Northeast* (Syracuse: Syracuse University Press, 1962), pp. 106–7. In order not to be misleading, it should be noted that the authors are chary of placing too much emphasis on groups as "prime political movers." Although not ruling out the significance of group analysis, they regard their essay as reaffirming "the power of key individuals and of group-transcending politics in determining the range and effectiveness of group interaction.... One cannot understand the development of state policies for aid to education by establishing a model of feudal warfare among clearly articulated group interests or constitutional functions. The winds of change that have swirled around state capitols have been inconstant" (pp. xiii–xiv).

[93] "Nature and Prospects of Political Interest Groups," *Annals of the American Academy of Political and Social Science,* CCCXIX (September 1958), 120.

A POLITICAL SYSTEM RESISTANT TO PRESSURE

Current controversy over pressure groups is part of a continuing debate over the proper role of private associations in the American political process. Reasonable alternatives for integrating interest groups into the social order obviously cannot include their elimination as political agencies or their regulation in such a way as to encroach upon the constitutional right of petition. If difficult to resolve, the issue is easily enough stated: How can an adequate system of representation be insured, while at the same time preventing groups from gaining undue influence in decision-making processes? What steps can be taken to check the impulse to "government by pressure group"?

By resort to the theory of "countervailing power," one may be tempted to conclude there is little reason for apprehension over the growth of interest-group power. In short, this theory holds that groups tend to restrain and offset each other, inhibiting impulses present in organizations to seek total domination over society. Thus agricultural, business, labor, veterans', professional, ethnic, and other groups in quest of particularistic goals vie with one another, thereby preventing any one interest from gaining overwhelming advantage. One group's gain imperils the position of other groups, serving to set in motion countervailing forces. In effect, then, a "check-and-balance" process regulates political forces as well as the governmental system itself.

The countervailing theory is helpful in unraveling the threads of group struggle in the legislature and elsewhere, but it has certain limitations. Most important, it neglects to make allowance for the tendency of interests to form alliances whereby logrolling substitutes for checks, permitting powerful combinations to press vigorously for special advantage. "In the legislative consideration of many economic measures," Walter Adams points out, "the absence of countervailing power is painfully apparent. In the enactment of tariff laws, for example, equal stakes rarely elicit equal pressures."[94] Similarly, William Cary writes, in the matter of shaping tax laws in congressional hearings:

> There is practically no one, except perhaps the Treasury, available to represent the public. Perhaps the reason is that all of the pressure group proposals are of such character that no one of them would have a large adverse effect on the tax bill of any individual. Hence counterpressure groups seldom develop. . . . A second reason why the public is not more frequently represented is the difficulty of forming pressure groups around general interests. The concentration of business organizations on appeals brought to Congress and the emphasis placed on specific and often very technical information makes it difficult even for the members of the tax committees to secure a balanced view of what is in the general interest,

[94] "Competition, Monopoly and Countervailing Power," *Quarterly Journal of Economics,* LXVII (November 1953), 481.

what the public wants or, indeed, what the public would want if it were informed as to the facts.[95]

Given the inertia of the mass of citizens and the difficulty of discovering what the public wants, it is not surprising when legislators shape their views on issues with one eye on what is most appropriate and the other on what is most expedient. Sometimes the expedient side is simply that position held by powerful and militant interest groups. A public passive or oblivious to concessions made to pressure groups is not likely to find its interest, to the extent that it can be identified at all, zealously guarded by the legislature. Countervailance demands awareness, involvement, and comparable power. A prominent congressman sounds a recurrent lament: "It is disturbing to sit through legislative hearings at which the conflicting interests who should be heard are unequally represented in the presentation of their views. Worst of all...are those situations in which only the proponents of the suggested legislation are heard from.... [The congressman] is faced with a dilemma as to how far he can or should go to supply the omission."[96]

Interest groups may be kept within reasonable bounds, runs a common argument, by an effective lobby law. The argument is that politicians and the public have a right to know who is seeking what from government and how they are going about it. The most that can be said for even the best law, however, is that it may alert legislators and the citizenry to what is going on around them. Lobby law is an instrument, one of several, and it is difficult to think of it as a panacea.

Another school of thought holds that legislators can be moved to higher ground where they will be better able to withstand the blandishments or pressures of interest groups. The vehicle is the legislature itself. Under this heading come recommendations that more substantial staff services be made available to members and to committees; that legislative reference, research, and bill-drafting services be enlarged and improved; and that salaries and retirement benefits for legislators be increased. This is the formula of legislative improvement, of making it increasingly self-sufficient, of equipping it to do many of the things for which it now looks to outside agencies.

Another answer appears in the chorus of voices which instructs us that what is needed is "a party system with greater resistance to pressure." This school places upon groups the onus "for the deterioration and confusion of purposes which sometimes passes for compromise" in governmental policy. It states that "compromise among interests is compatible with the aims of a free society only when the terms of reference reflect an openly acknowledged concept of the public interest." It warns that the accountability of public men for their acts can only be enforced when running the political system is the responsibility of political parties.[97] In his classic study,

[95] Pressure Groups and the Revenue Code: A Requiem in Honor of the Departing Uniformity of the Tax Laws," *Harvard Law Review*, LXVIII (March 1955), 778.

[96] Celler, *op. cit.*, p. 7.

[97] Committee on Political Parties, *Toward a More Responsible Two-Party System* (New York: Holt, Rinehart & Winston, Inc., 1950), pp. 19–20.

Party Government, Professor E. E. Schattschneider made the point this way:

> In one way or another every government worthy of the name manages interests in formulating public policy. The difficulty is not that the parties have been overwhelmed by the interests, but that the political institutions for an adequate national party leadership able to deal with the situation have not been created. For want of this kind of leadership the parties are unable to take advantage of their natural superiority. Thus they let themselves be harried by pressure groups as a timid whale might be pursued by a school of minnows. The potentialities of adequate national party leadership in this connection have not yet been well explored in the United States, but it is a waste of time to talk about controlling the depredations of the pressure groups by other means. A well-centralized party system has nothing to fear from the pressure groups. On the other hand, aside from a strong party system there is no democratic way of protecting the public against the disintegrating tactics of the pressure groups.[98]

A final view holds that legal controls are not the best answer to controlling the lobby process. Lester Milbrath argues that "interdependence, rules of the game, power relationships, and threat of sanction against offenders that characterize the Washington policy-making system operate rather effectively" to control lobbying. Standards for the behavior of lobbyists (e.g., that the legislator should be able to rely on the accuracy of information communicated to him) are understood by legislators and lobbyists alike. The lobbyist who treats the norms casually, who raises doubts and anxieties among legislators, endangers his access and damages his cause. The lobbyist has no real immunity against political sanctions. Above and beyond the controls built into the legislative system, writes Milbrath, "the most effective control of lobbying, and perhaps all that is really needed, is the election of highly qualified responsible persons to public office. . . . Officials have so much power over lobbying and lobbyists that they can determine how the lobby system shall work."[99]

Virtually all writers who embark on a discussion of legislative reform feel it obligatory to tackle the lobby question—some seeing it as a nagging problem, others regarding it as a threat to representative government. It seems safe to say that in the public mind no political institution carries a more sinister image than the lobby. Because information about lobbies is partial, the case against them seems complete. There is, for example, scarcely any public awareness of the interactions between lobbyist and legislator initiated by the legislator in order to strengthen his hand. Overall, doubts and uncertainties over lobbying apparently trouble the public far more than they do the legislators themselves—this, of course, may be due as much to the legislators' insensitivity as to the public's neuroses.

The fact is that "solutions" to span all the problems thrust up by lobbies are not likely to be forthcoming. Each proposal for making the

---

[98] *Party Government* (New York: Holt, Rinehart & Winston, Inc., 1942), p. 197.

[99] Milbrath, *The Washington Lobbyists,* p. 326.

374 political system more resistant to pressure promises something, but none is likely to settle the matter for any significant stretch of time. The option of party control can be tested only when the parties are substantially more viable and cohesive than they are today. In the short run, the best, if unspectacular, answer may be simply to expose and highlight specific abuses by lobbies and to fashion piecemeal solutions to combat them. Added to this is the continuing possibility that elections can help to instruct and discipline parties or legislators that have fallen under the thumb of organized interests and have permitted them to appropriate governmental power for narrow and selfish purposes.

part four

Interaction with the Executive and the Courts

11

THE CHIEF EXECUTIVE
AS LEGISLATOR

Legislatures do not create public policy in a vacuum. Pressure groups and political parties can be influential in the legislative process. The president and the governor are regular and vital participants. In many basic ways, the behavior of the legislator and of the chief executive is shaped by common factors. Both take account of public pressures, both hear the demands of party, both are frequently concerned with compromise, and both vote on the substance of proposals for legislation.

The chief executive contributes to the legislative process in ways somewhat different from those of most legislators. The executive's functions in the legislative process are mainly three. First, he serves as one source of ideas for the programs which legislative bodies consider. Although the extent of this inspiration varies among the states and certainly between the state and national levels, political environments are rare where executive recommendations are not the principal items on the legislature's agenda.[1]

Second, the executive functions as a catalytic agent in the legislative process. Chief executives not only offer programs but also strive to structure support both directly within legislative bodies and indirectly through interest groups, party leaders, and other political activists. Occasionally, chief executives attempt to ignite the rarely flammable timbers of public opinion.

Finally, the legislative process seldom comes to a halt when the executive has signed a bill into law. In many cases, the obstacle course from bill to law is not even the most important step in the making of public policy. Much legislation is phrased in general terms to apply to a diversity of concrete situations. Law is interpreted and given new dimensions as it is applied under the direction of the executive. The need for change is sometimes crystallized as laws are applied. Implementation of law constitutes,

---

[1] Duane Lockard, in discussing the politics of Massachusetts, notes that "the governor's legislative program...is the base point for all major legislative operations." *New England State Politics* (Princeton: Princeton University Press, 1959), p. 159. For statistics in Ohio, see Harvey Walker, *The Legislative Process* (New York: Ronald Press Company, 1948), pp. 71–75. For Illinois, see Arthur F. Bentley, *The Process of Government* (Chicago: University of Chicago Press, 1908), p. 493. See also Neil MacNeil, *Forge of Democracy* (New York: David McKay Co., Inc., 1963), Chapter 10.

378 then, a third executive contribution to the legislative process. An awareness of the propinquity of law implementation to lawmaking is reflected in legislative eagerness to oversee administrative behavior, a topic analyzed in Chapter 12.

Thus far the terms *executive* and *chief executive* have been used interchangeably. The executive branch consists, however, of far more than the president or governor. The executive branch seldom speaks or acts with one voice, but, in order to bring a sharper focus to this chapter, emphasis is placed on the role of the president and the governor in the legislative process. At a few appropriate points the impact of the bureaucracy on the legislative process is considered as well. Chief executive behavior is sufficiently varied and complex to pose major problems of analysis; an attempt to deal comprehensively with participation of entire executive branches in the legislative process is all but impossible.

Presidential and gubernatorial influence rests on several bases. Despite vast variations in the roots of this influence among the fifty states and in the nation, the identification of several common factors renders order to an attempt at analysis. The influence of the chief executive on the legislative process is affected by four factors. In the first place, the societal environment sets boundaries within which the political system functions; second, the legal powers of chief executives channel and restrain their influence; third, partisan political factors condition executive efforts; fourth, personal considerations and role conceptions influence behavior. The scope, objectives, and limits of executive influence become more evident as these four factors are examined.

The Societal Base for Executive Influence

The societal environment within which the political system functions does not predetermine precisely what the government will do, but it does condition that determination. In the 1970s, the governor of Mississippi and the governor of Michigan, whatever their legal powers, electoral majorities, or personal status, will face different problems if they bring proposals to the legislature for changes in policy concerning labor-management relations or civil rights.

The societal environment for political decision-making is a vast and complex web. Several aspects of that environment will be singled out for illustrative purposes. The first of these is the homogeneity of the society. The greater the degree of homogeneity in public attitudes within a society, the greater the tendency toward executive-legislative cooperation in lawmaking. The development of an industrial, urban order means diversification, which in turn provides a socioeconomic breeding ground for political conflict between executives and their legislative branches. The typical system of representation in the United States (statewide or nationwide election for the chief executive and district elections for the legislative assembly) reinforces a proclivity for conflict. Industrialization and urbanization provide an environment for conflict but, at the same time, lead to additional pressures for governmental action in both the nation and the states. Such pressures can be translated into added executive influence as the nation or state focuses on the president or governor for action. One of President Kennedy's few major legislative victories on a question of domestic policy during his term involved the passage of legislation providing aid to economically depressed areas. Economic decline in many localities was the important factor making this victory possible.[2]

Executive influence, however, does not automatically increase as governmental units face increasingly difficult problems. Although the severe fiscal crisis in Michigan in 1959 resulted in missed paychecks for state employees, cutbacks in services, and reductions in expenditures for state universities, it did not immediately augment executive influence. Partisan political factors, among others, seemed more critical in the Michigan decision-making arena than pressing fiscal problems. Severe crisis, such as a full-scale depression, dramatically increases the executive's influence on the legislature. Compare the famous first hundred days of the Roosevelt administration in 1933 with those of the Kennedy administration in 1961. Each president was a Democrat succeeding a Republican chief executive. Each was a vigorous and astute politician. Each was elected with a substantial majority of his own political party in control of both houses of Congress. Yet one president was far more successful than the other in securing favorable congressional action on his program. Perhaps the basic explanation for the legislative successes of President Roosevelt and the legislative failures of President Kennedy is to be found in the public's perceptions of the crises at the time—one was deep and unmistakable, the other alleged and uncertain.

The relevance of the international political environment for policymaking is seen as the record of President Harry S. Truman is examined. President Truman had relatively modest success in persuading Congress to adopt his domestic programs but yet had exceptional success in foreign policy programs where Congress frequently deferred to his leadership, passing the necessary legislation to bring dramatically the new policies into being.[3]

Presidential influence upon the legislative branch approaches its zenith in time of war. At the onset of the Civil War, President Lincoln moved beyond his constitutional powers. Congress vindicated some of his actions, however, when it met in special session some six weeks later.[4] During World War I and World War II, Presidents Wilson and Roosevelt generally secured legislative compliance, or at least legislative acquiescence, to their requests for emergency powers. Environmental factors, in general, and the

2 Louis W. Koenig, "Kennedy and the 87th Congress," in *American Government Annual, 1962–1963,* ed. Ivan Hinderaker (New York: Holt, Rinehart & Winston, Inc., 1962), p. 74.

3 Richard Neustadt calls this success extraordinary and unprecedented in "Congress and the Fair Deal: A Legislative Balance Sheet," in *Public Policy, 1954,* ed. Carl J. Friedrich and J. Kenneth Galbraith (Cambridge: Harvard University, Graduate School of Public Administration, 1954), p. 352. Alton Frye suggests that the role of Congress in foreign policy has been less passive than is frequently assumed in "Congress: The Virtues of its Vices," *Foreign Policy,* III (Summer 1971), 108–25.

4 For examples of President Lincoln's extraconstitutional actions, see Wilfred Binkley, *President and Congress* (New York: Alfred A. Knopf, Inc., 1947), pp. 110–15ff.

380 presence or absence of war, depression, or other national disasters, in particular, provide one key to the understanding of executive influence in the legislative process.

The Legal Base for Executive Influence

Legal powers and limits also condition the performance of executive functions and the exercise of executive influence in the legislative process. Governors and presidents share many similar formal legal powers, e.g., to deliver messages, to prepare budgets, to veto acts of representative assemblies, and to call special sessions of legislative bodies. The mask of legal similarity, however, hides equally significant variations in practice.

THE BUDGET

Presidents and almost all governors are assigned the responsibility for preparation and presentation of the budget. Lynton K. Caldwell calls the governor's authority in budget-making the most important of his executive powers in the legislative process.[5] Leslie Lipson in his analysis of the evolution of the governorship asserts that "the executive budget, perhaps more than any other single factor, has strengthened his executive authority."[6] It the budget is conceived only as a mass exercise in arithmetic, then its importance cannot be understood. The budget is much more. It represents the most authoritative single measure of what the executive's program actually is. The loose, highly generalized language of the campaign—e.g., "I favor an equitable tax system," "I will build adequate highways"— provides a less than precise basis for predicting the executive's program. The generalization of the campaign promise translated into a hard, cold budgetary item provides the real measure of the executive's attitude.[7] One wag who had difficulty reconciling President Eisenhower's highly abstract pronouncements on national security with his actual budget requests concluded that his program consisted of "spiritual values and no ground troops."

When the president or the governor (or, more accurately, their executive subordinates and associates) prepares a budget, he is in effect presenting to the legislative assembly a blueprint for public policy. Legislators realize that the black print of columns of statistics in the budget document are the real tests of policy. Accordingly, the executive budget occupies the

[5] *The Government and Administration of New York* (New York: Thomas Y. Crowell Company, 1954), pp. 86–87.

[6] Leslie Lipson, *The American Governor from Figurehead to Leader* (Chicago: University of Chicago Press, 1939), p. 243.

[7] A comprehensive survey of the budgetary process is Arthur Smithies, *The Budgetary Process in the United States* (New York: McGraw-Hill Book Company, Inc., 1955). See also Robert Ash Wallace, *Congressional Control of Federal Spending* (Detroit: Wayne State University Press, 1960). For a political analysis, see Aaron Wildavsky, *The Politics of the Budgetary Process* (Boston: Little, Brown & Company, 1964). See also Murray L. Weidenbaum and John S. Saloma, *Congress and the Federal Budget* (Washington: American Enterprise Institute for Public Policy Research, 1965).

central position on the agenda of all legislatures. As a rule, sessions of the state legislature are unable to achieve any momentum until the governor's budget has been received; by the same token, when the critical budget decisions have been made, the legislators ordinarily are ready to return home.

The budget proposed by the executive provides not only the best single statement of the administration program, but usually the only comprehensive plan for action put before legislative assemblies. Availability and acceptability are hardly the same thing, but the executive does gain initiative by formulating a budgetary program. By and large, the fiscal document provides a focus for deliberation that legislative bodies are unable to provide for themselves. In the twenty states where earmarked funds constitute more than 50 per cent of the taxes collected, both executive and legislative discretion are sorely limited. Ransone asserts that "the most serious single weakness in the budgetary process at the state level at present is the fact that in far too many states, the governor's budget covers only a fraction of the state's total expenditures."[8] At the national level, fixed payments, such as interest on the national debt, grants to the states under existing programs, and agricultural subsidies, constitute firm limits on presidential discretion in budget-making.

The familiar response of legislatures to executive budgets is to look for ways to make changes. Congress and almost all state legislatures have unlimited legal authority to alter the executive budget. How this authority is used, with what purposes in mind, and with what skill varies with political environments. Arthur Smithies maintains that "in terms of aggregate figures, the Congress makes small rather than large changes in the President's figures. A *bona fide* cut in the President's appropriation requests of as much as 5 per cent, even by a hostile Congress, is the exception rather than the rule."[9] A president finding his requests for funds for a high priority program slashed by Congress might not be as sanguine as Smithies appears to be. There are few studies that appraise executive-legislative relations in budget-making in the states. Yet the argument "cannot be too strongly made that in the American states today the governor holds the initiative; he proposes and the legislature disposes." Continuing, Malcolm Jewell writes:

> In some states the governor's budget usually passes with little difficulty, but in others it is the most hotly contested issue in a legislative session. In these latter states the budget may frequently be cut, but it is much less likely to be raised appreciably and in a few states the legislature is not permitted to increase appropriations.[10]

---

[8] Coleman B. Ransone, Jr., *The Office of Governor in the United States* (University: University of Alabama Press, 1956), p. 291. See also, Belle Zeller, ed., *American State Legislatures* (New York: Thomas Y. Crowell Company, 1954), pp. 177–78, and Tax Foundation, *Earmarked State Taxes* (New York: Tax Foundation, Inc., 1965).

[9] Smithies, *op. cit.*, p. 140. For examples of more substantial cuts, see Holbert N. Carroll, *The House of Representatives and Foreign Affairs* (Pittsburgh: University of Pittsburgh Press, 1958), pp. 174, 178, 186. The incremental nature of budget making is stressed in Wildavsky, *op. cit.*, pp. 15–16.

[10] Malcolm Jewell, *The State Legislature* (New York: Random House, Inc., 1962), p. 108.

382   Legislative bodies not only reduce items in the executive budget but also increase appropriations beyond executive desires and add programs that the executive opposes. Almost annually from 1957 to 1962, leaders in the Department of Health, Education and Welfare went before Congress to do battle over increases in appropriations for medical research beyond what the department felt could be spent reasonably. In 1958 Nevada Senator George W. Malone was quoted as saying, "We've been building reclamation projects for fifty-five years. No one is going to pay a damn bit of attention to the budget. We're going to continue to build the projects."[11]

A president who thinks that Congress has appropriated too much money may simply refuse to spend it. Presidents have impounded funds for the Air Force, for supercarriers, for flood control as well as for other projects.[12] While disputes arise over whether the president can legally do this, the fact is that he does and frequently gets away with it. Congress itself cannot spend the money to carry out the programs it has authorized.

In budget consideration as in other policy situations, executive influence in legislative assemblies is seldom exerted on legislative bodies as a whole. The complexity of budgetary decision-making usually requires that the budget be considered in parts by committees and subcommittees.[13] In Congress, not only the appropriations committee of each house, but also subcommittees within them, consider the budget. Thus the House Appropriations Committee has divided in recent years into as few as nine and as many as fifteen subcommittees—e.g., Department of Agriculture, Department of Interior, Department of Defense—to consider the relevant portions of the budget. Except under highly unusual circumstances, the work of committees and subcommittees, each concerned with a relatively narrow segment of the total budget, receives the stamp of approval of the full legislative body.[14]

The impact of these subgroups, which can be substantial, is illustrated frequently. President Kennedy found this truth impressed on him in 1962 when, for all intents and purposes, he was forced to negotiate a "treaty" with Congressman Rooney (D., N.Y.), chairman of the Appropriations Sub-Committee for the State Department, when he wanted an increase in representation allowances for the American ambassador to France.[15]

The influence of congressional subcommittees, committees, and their chairmen serves as a substantial limitation on executive influence in budget-

11 Robert Bendiner, "Pennsylvania Avenue Gets Longer and Longer," *The Reporter,* February 20, 1958, p. 25.

12 For examples and analysis see J. D. Williams, *The Impounding of Funds by the Bureau of the Budget,* ICP Case Series no. 28 (University: University of Alabama Press, 1955). See also two articles by Louis Fisher: "Funds Impounded By The President: The Constitutional Issue," *George Washington Law Review,* XXXVIII (October 1969), 124–37, and "The Politics of Impounded Funds," *Administrative Science Quarterly,* XV (September 1970), 361–77.

13 The budget presented by the president to Congress compares in size to a large city's telephone directory and weighs more than five pounds. President Eisenhower's budget for fiscal 1958 (July 1957 to June 1958) involved the proposed expenditure of over $70 billion. President Kennedy's proposed budget for fiscal 1964 called for an expenditure of about $100 billion.

14 This process is best described in Richard F. Fenno, Jr., *The Power of the Purse* (Boston: Little, Brown & Company, 1966), especially Chapter 9.

15 *Pittsburgh Press,* August 15, 1962, p. 23.

making. That this pattern at the national level is not universal is seen in an analysis of the appropriation process in Illinois, where the standing committees do not appear to play a significant role in consideration of the budget:

> In the appropriations process, hearings before the standing committees of House and Senate are in the nature of necessary obstacles that must be overcome. They are not obstacles in the sense of dangers...the need for a committee hearing on appropriations bills is a nuisance requirement to be acknowledged and disposed of before proceeding to focus attention on other problems.[16]

In another analysis of Illinois, Thomas Anton concludes:

> The combination of decisions made by the Governor on all major and some routine matters entitles him to be described as the single most powerful actor in the system in 1963.[17]

After an extended analysis of the experience in the states, Ira Sharkansky concludes:

> The executive's recommendations provide the most well-informed advice that is consistently available about every agency. Legislators feel that they need help in reviewing agency budgets. In most cases, the executive's budget is the best assistance available.[18]

The complexity of contemporary public policy which provides the basic rationale for committee consideration enhances as well as limits executive influence, as legislators, at times, feel unable to cope with the problems at hand. Commentator Eric Sevareid exaggerates only slightly when he describes budget-making for national security: "In darkness, Congress will decide on these executive decisions, themselves made in a very thick fog."[19] Legislative inadequacy is seen most clearly on matters of foreign policy and national security, when the complexity of problems is compounded by a necessity for secrecy.[20]

THE VETO

The executive's budget-making authority provides a broad base for the exercise of executive influence in the legislative process. In contrast, the

[16] Gilbert Y. Steiner and Samuel K. Gove, *Legislative Politics in Illinois* (Urbana: University of Illinois Press, 1960), p. 78.

[17] *The Politics of State Expenditure in Illinois* (Urbana: University of Illinois Press, 1966), p. 247.

[18] *The Routines of Politics* (New York: Van Nostrand Reinhold Company, 1970), p. 83.

[19] "The Budget Mystery," *Reporter*, February 10, 1955, p. 32. Copyright © 1955 by Fortnightly Publishing Co., Inc., reprinted by permission by Harold Matson Co.

[20] For excellent examples see W. R. Schilling, P. Y. Hammond, and G. H. Snyder, *Strategy, Politics, And Defense Budgets* (New York: Columbia University Press, 1962).

384 veto is a tool for specific tasks. Essentially, the veto is a defensive weapon for the chief executive. Yet it also should be seen as one of the most powerful weapons in the arsenal of presidents and governors as they attempt to influence legislative behavior. In one respect, the exercise of the veto may be interpreted as a phase of an institutional struggle for power between the executive and legislative branches—but this lessens its significance. A more appropriate interpretation describes the veto as a weapon in the making of public policy; its use, in the main, reflects the fact that the legislative and executive branches often act for strikingly dissimilar constituencies. The power to veto acts of the legislature is held by the president and forty-nine of fifty governors (North Carolina is the exception) throughout the twentieth century. The details of the veto power vary with each constitutional document. The president must accept or reject bills as a whole. Some 80 per cent of the governors hold the power to veto items in appropriation bills.[21] The president and many governors have the power of "pocket veto," that is, to withhold their signatures from bills passed until after the legislature adjourns and hence to kill the bill.

Executives have used the veto power much more frequently in the twentieth century than earlier in American history. Among nineteenth-century presidents, President Grover Cleveland used the veto most frequently. During his long tenure in office, President Franklin Roosevelt used the veto 631 times; in a much shorter period of time, President Truman used it 250 times. President Eisenhower resorted to vetoes less frequently, 181 times in all, but used the power with great effectiveness to offset Democratic majorities in Congress.[22] In the states, between one-half and three-fourths of all vetoes registered by governors have occurred in the twentieth century.[23]

Several reasons account for the growth in use of this power: (1) the multitude of problems faced by the American political system under the impact of industrialization, urbanization, and international crisis; (2) the increase in public demands for governmental action to deal with matters formerly regarded as lying within the private sector of society; (3) the added intensity of political conflict resulting from the realization that governmental policies have serious consequences for many sectors of society; (4) the divergent interests represented by the executive and legislative branches, due in some part to rural overrepresentation in the legislature.

Still, few bills are victims of the executive ax. From George Washington through Lyndon Johnson in 1966, presidents used the regular veto only 2,238 times.[24] The average percentage of legislation vetoed by fourteen presidents from 1889 to 1968 was 2.5; President Truman used the veto

---

21 Nothing of great importance can be inferred from the presence or absence of the item veto without an examination of the context within which this device might be used. Whether appropriations are lump-sum or highly detailed is a critical factor related to the importance of the item veto.

22 President Eisenhower's veto of the usually sacrosanct public works bill in 1959 drove one commentator to exclaim "Ike vetoed Santa Claus."

23 Ransone, *op. cit.,* p. 181.

24 Data compiled from Joseph E. Kallenbach, *The American Chief Executive* (New York: Harper & Row, Publishers, 1966), as supplemented by *Congressional Quarterly Almanacs* for 1964, 1965, 1966 (Washington, D.C.: Congressional Quarterly, Inc.).

more heavily than other presidents since 1945, but yet he vetoed only 3.7 per cent of the legislation presented to him.[25]

In the states, the data is scattered and varied. In New York, from 1927 to 1951, about 26 per cent of the bills passed by the legislature were vetoed; in Pennsylvania from 1939 to 1946, 10.5 per cent of the bills passed by the legislature were given a full veto.[26] In thirteen southern states from 1937 to 1947, some 3.5 per cent of bills introduced were vetoed.[27] In 1923, 7 per cent of the measures enacted by forty-four state legislatures were vetoed; in 1937 the figure was 6.7 per cent; in 1945, 5.1 per cent; in 1947, 5.0 per cent.[28] In Arizona, from 1912 to 1963, the veto was used 182 times.[29] The full veto is not then a power used routinely. As to the pocket veto, there is considerable variation in its use among the states. Prescott asserts that it is used regularly in about one-half of the states that have it.[30] Not susceptible to precise measurement but assuredly of significance is the threat of a president or governor to veto a forthcoming bill unless it is revised.

Messages to accompany vetoes may be required by the constitution; at other times they are sent simply because it suits the chief executive's inclinations. Such messages range from terse, one-sentence rejections to more elaborate and colorful statements, e.g., these by Governors Sam Jones of Louisiana and Adlai Stevenson of Illinois.

The dictator of the lower coast spends 60 days fighting the poor, the sick, the schools and roads. But he wants the salary of his henchman raised at the expense of the public.... "Consistency thou art a jewel."

I cannot agree that it should be the declared public policy of Illinois that a cat visiting a neighbor's yard or crossing the highway is a public nuisance. It is in the nature of cats to do a certain amount of unescorted roaming.... Also consider the owner's dilemma: To escort a cat abroad on a leash is against the nature of the cat, and to permit it to venture forth for exercise unattended into a night of new dangers is against the nature of the owner. Moreover, cats perform useful service particularly in rural areas, in combating rodents—work they necessarily perform alone and without regard for property lines. We are all interested in protecting certain varieties of birds. That cats destroy some birds, I well know, but I believe this legislation would further but little the worthy cause to which its proponents give such unselfish effort. The problem of the cat versus bird is as old as time. If we

---

[25] John Carl Metz, *The President's Veto Power, 1889–1968* (Ph. D. Dissertation, University of Pittsburgh, 1971), pp. 413–14.

[26] Samuel R. Solomon, "The Governor as Legislator," *National Municipal Review,* XL (November 1951), 515; M. Nelson McGeary, "The Governor's Veto in Pennsylvania," *American Political Science Review,* XLI (October 1947), 942.

[27] Frank Prescott, "The Executive Veto in the Southern States," *Journal of Politics,* X (November 1948), 666.

[28] Frank Prescott, "The Executive Veto in the American States," *Western Political Quarterly,* III (March 1950), 102.

[29] Roy D. Morey, *Politics and Legislation: The Office of Governor in Arizona* (Tucson: University of Arizona Press, 1965), p. 33. Additional data on the experience in Iowa and Kansas can be found in *Midwest Legislative Politics,* ed. Samuel C. Patterson (n.p.: Institute of Public Affairs, University of Iowa, 1967), pp. 12, 41–42.

[30] Prescott, "The Executive Veto in the American States," 105.

attempt to resolve it by legislation who knows but that we may be called upon to take sides as well in the age-old problems of dog versus cat, bird versus bird, or even bird versus worm. In my opinion, the State of Illinois and its local governing bodies already have enough to do without trying to control feline delinquency. For these reasons, and not because I love birds the less or cats the more, I veto and withhold my approval from Senate Bill No. 93.[31]

Not all vetoes are based on executive-legislative conflict over vital questions of public policy. At the national level, vetoes based on constitutional grounds and policy differences are the norm. In the states, the veto is used, in addition, because bills duplicate one another, because acts of legislatures are vague and incapable of enforcement, or because technical flaws have occurred in drafting. The use of the veto is not an altogether accurate barometer of executive-legislative policy conflict. An attempt to assess the significance of the veto as a tool of executive influence will be deferred until we have discussed the other factors that bear on the executive's role as chief legislator.

MESSAGES

The obligation of the presidents and governors to deliver messages to their respective legislative bodies is a less obvious basis for influence. A chief executive, well endowed with prerequisites for influence, can translate the duty to deliver messages into a means for focusing both legislative and public attention on his program.[32] The chief executive less well endowed may find the duty to deliver messages to be little more than a burdensome chore. The executive message, then, may be an important element in executive influence or simply something of a formality. Messages may be filled with familiar civic platitudes, requests of exceptional modesty, or bold new programs. How seriously the legislators treat executive messages depends largely on how serious they think the chief executive is in making them. In brief, it depends on how they size him up—how they evaluate the lengths to which he will go to get what he says he wants. When the executive message is part of an effective process, its delivery is merely symbolic of what legislators already have reason to anticipate—that an administration bill with administration support will soon be before the legislature.[33]

Legislative reaction to executive messages is not likely to represent an unbiased verdict; neither is it necessarily proportional to the inherent logic of the chief executive's requests or arguments. Thus, Democratic Senate majority leader Mike Mansfield could view a message from President Kennedy as bearing "the authentic earmark of greatness," while his Republican counterpart, minority leader Everett McKinley Dirksen, could describe

31 The Louisiana message is quoted in Prescott, *ibid.*, 111. For Illinois, see *Journal of the Senate,* 66th General Assembly, p. 540.

32 See Lockard's comment on Massachusetts politics, *supra,* Note 1.

33 The practice of accompanying a message with a draft bill was refined to an art by FDR. Hallie Farmer notes that this is standard procedure in Alabama. *The Legislative Process in Alabama* (University: University of Alabama, Bureau of Government, 1949), p. 170.

the same message as "a Sears & Roebuck catalogue with the prices marked up."

Professor Corwin is quite correct in describing the sending of messages as a duty rather than a power,[34] but to abort the analysis at this point is to substitute formality for reality. Professor Richard Neustadt describes the potential of messages in these terms:

> Congress can gain from the outside what comes hard from within: a handy and official guide to the wants of its biggest customer; an advance formulation of main issues at each session; a work-load ready-to-hand for every legislative committee; an indication, more or less, of what may risk the veto; a borrowing of presidential prestige for most major bills. . . .[35]

SPECIAL SESSIONS

Of the constitutional powers which place the chief executive directly into the legislative process, the power to call special sessions is usually of least importance. The president can call a special session but, having done so, must risk legislative defiance and policy disaster. Congress is under no obligation to act on or even to discuss the subject about which the president calls the special session. In contrast, in many states the governor not only summons the legislature into special session but indicates the session agenda as well. Despite the relative advantage of the governor, experience demonstrates that the power to call special sessions cannot be considered a critical tool for chief executives as they attempt to influence legislative behavior.[36]

The power to prepare and submit budgets, to veto legislative acts, to send messages, and to call for special sessions provides a firm legal basis for executive influence in the legislative process. Each of these powers directly involves the chief executive in the lawmaking process. Other aspects of his legal environment which do not thrust him directly into legislative affairs do, however, both enhance and restrict his efforts in shaping the course of public policy. The chief executive's legal relationship with the bureaucracy, his legal relationship with the electorate, and the length of his term are all related to his leadership in the legislative process.

ADMINISTRATIVE LEADER

To the extent that the chief executive is, in fact, the chief of administration, he gains three basic assets for legislative leadership: (1) competent professional and technical assistance in formulating programs to meet felt needs; (2) control over the appointment of personnel and over the selection and allocation of programs; (3) an awareness of imperfections in existing programs through the experience gained in implementing legislative acts.

[34] Edward S. Corwin, *The President: Office and Powers* (New York: Columbia University Press, 1957), p. 265.

[35] "Presidency and Legislation: Planning the President's Program," *American Political Science Review*, XLIX (December 1955), 1014.

[36] For concurring judgments see Jewell, *op. cit.*, p. 109; Coleman B. Ransone, Jr., *The Office of Governor in the South* (University: University of Alabama, Bureau of Public Administration, 1951), p. 85. For an apparent exception, see Farmer, *op. cit.*, p. 175.

388   In the absence of large numbers of skilled staff persons and other resources, the legislative branch is forced to rely at times on information gathered by the executive. To some extent, the information which the legislature secures from pressure groups and other constituency interests serves to offset the information dominance of the executive. But in the realm of international relations and national security, Congress is forced to rely primarily on executive-supplied information. James Robinson writes:

> Owing to rapid means of communication, owing to improved facilities for procuring and storing information about a wide variety of subjects, policy making now involves consideration of larger amounts of more technical information about the objective conditions being considered. For reasons which are not altogether clear, bureaucracies associated with executive offices have more efficiently collected and processed information than have legislatures. Not only is Congress unprepared to collect independent information about the world through its own resources, but it must rely on data collected by the executive.[37]

Control over the bureaucracy provides the chief executive with certain controls over personnel. The president appoints the heads of the executive departments and can remove them at his discretion. Most governors, to the contrary, do not have these extensive powers of appointment for the heads of executive departments. What sometimes results is that men not in sympathy with the governor's programs win these positions; at times they are not even of the same party affiliation as the governor. Hence it is not an unusual state in which the top leadership of the executive branch is split both ideologically and politically, making coherent program formulation difficult.

Unlike many governors, the president is legally free to select the heads of his executive departments; in practice, the range of his choice is circumscribed. Certain appointments will be made with the view of unifying his political party; others will be designed to provide representation and to win support of groups and factions to which the president feels it necessary to appeal. Such appointees are political strangers thrust into top executive positions. When President Eisenhower selected Martin Durkin, a Democrat and a labor leader, to be his first secretary of labor, Senator Taft could only utter: "an incredible appointment."[38] There seems to be no doubt that certain appointments serve to weaken executive unity.

Disunity in the executive branch poses difficulties for executive influence. For example, executive departments may offer legislators alternative sets of data and conflicting analyses; legislative leaders may enter into alliances with particular executive subunits; and the chief executive's efforts may be blunted by prestigious subordinates who administer semiautonomous agencies.

One example illustrates the problem. On January 16, 1958, President Eisenhower submitted a $71.8 billion budget proposal to Congress. His

---

[37] James A. Robinson, *Congress and Foreign Policy-Making* (Homewood, Ill.: Dorsey Press, Inc., 1962), p. 192. A revised edition of this study appeared in 1967.
[38] Quoted in Richard Fenno, *The President's Cabinet* (Cambridge: Harvard University Press, 1959), p. 81.

subordinate, Secretary of the Treasury George Humphrey, ventured an opinion at a subsequent press conference that the budget could be cut in many places. New doubts were raised in Congress concerning what the president really wanted. In analyzing similar administration budget problems in May 1957, *New York Times* columnist James Reston argued: "The contradictory [budget] estimates of members of the cabinet, plus the failure of the President to support his budget effectively when it was first presented, have created a new and critical psychology among many influential legislators. . . ."[39]

Chief executives may also win support for their programs through the judicious use of patronage. President Theodore Roosevelt put it as bluntly as possible when he stated about members of Congress: "if they'll vote for my measures, I'll appoint their nominees to federal jobs. . . . I'll play the game, appoint their men for their support of my bills. . . ."[40] The extent of patronage in appointments available to the chief executive will vary with time and environment. The rise of civil service and other merit systems for selecting personnel has slowly narrowed the patronage potential of the president to a relatively restricted portion of national governmental employees. At the state level, the number of patronage appointees varies tremendously. In Michigan and Wisconsin, the governor has very few patronage positions at his disposal. In Pennsylvania, by contrast, thousands of positions are available to the governor for patronage purposes.

The "loaves and fishes" of personnel are not the only tools of patronage available to chief executives. Support for a legislator's pet program, contracts for constituents, allocation of money for roads, and issuance of pardons remain as possible levers for executive influence. The essence of the patronage process was captured in a statement attributed to "an observer" by E. Pendleton Herring: "his [President Franklin D. Roosevelt's] relations to Congress were to the very end of the session tinged with a shade of expectancy which is the best part of young love."[41]

The reciprocal relationships between the chief executive's legislative role and his administrative role are unmistakable. As legislative leader, the chief executive attempts to promote programs in the legislature which his administration can implement. As administrative leader, to the extent that he is one, the chief executive holds certain controls over personnel, programs, and information, which in turn enhance his efforts at legislative leadership.

REPRESENTATIVE CHARACTER

The chief executive is more than a spokesman for his administrative departments. He possesses by law a popular constituency, the state or nation, which

39 *New York Times,* May 14, 1957, p. 46. Copyright © 1957 by the New York Times Company. Reprinted by permission. The process by which executives coordinate programs for presentation to Congress is studied in classic articles by Richard Neustadt: "Presidency and Legislation: Planning the President's Program," *op. cit.,* and "Presidency and Legislation: The Growth of Central Clearance," *American Political Science Review,* XLVIII (September 1954), 641–71.

40 Quoted in *The Autobiography of Lincoln Steffens* (New York: Harcourt, Brace & World, Inc., 1931), p. 505.

41 "First Session of the Seventy-Third Congress," *American Political Science Review,* XXVIII (February 1934), 82.

390 differs from that of any legislator.[42] The chief executive's representative character both abets and limits his potential as a legislative leader. The statewide electoral base of the governor and the nationwide electoral base of the president provide logical and political grounds for the claim that the chief executive holds a superior position in interpreting public needs and public opinion. Elected by larger numbers of people than the legislator and viewing the policy process from the heights of his broad constituency, the chief executive generally sees himself as pursuing the state or national interest as opposed to the more parochial orientation of the typical legislator. His unique electoral position, added to his constitutionally and legally derived powers, help the chief executive to draw public attention to his program; these advantages, however, do not lead necessarily to the generation of effective political support for his program.[43]

Symbolically, the chief executive may claim to speak for the state or the nation, but political necessity leads him to speak with special vigor for those groups who contributed most significantly to his election. A brief glance at the pattern of presidential elections provides a clear illustration. To gain election, the president must receive a majority of the electoral votes—270 of 538.[44] The electoral votes of seven states—New York, Pennsylvania, California, Ohio, Michigan, Illinois, and Texas—provide about 80 per cent of this required total. When majorities in these states have similar problems that they wish resolved through public policy, the direction of a president's programmatic appeals is fairly clearly channeled.

Opposed to the executive's more generalized orientation lies the more specific and more easily identifiable orientation of the legislator, the interests of whose district are comparatively clear and concrete. The legislator's concerns may contradict, or at least fail to match, the interests of the supporters of the president or governor. Constitutionally specified differences in constituency are often, in turn, exaggerated by gerrymandering. The necessity for some cooperation tends to bridge this gap. At the center of the problem is the fact that the legislator's roots are deep in the constituency.

The broad base of the chief executive's constituency gives him an advantage in making news and winning public attention. But the advantage is of an uncertain quality. The heterogeneity of his electorate is such that the executive's attempt to translate his electoral majority into popular support for a specific program inevitably leads to antagonizing certain groups or segments of the population. To those that are antagonized we must also add those who are indifferent to the words and requests of the chief execu-

---

42 Richard Neustadt makes the point that the president has five "constituencies" toward whom he has responsibilities—the bureaucracy, the voters, his political party, Congress, nations and peoples abroad. *Presidential Power* (New York: John Wiley & Sons, Inc., 1960), p. 7.

43 In May 1962 President Kennedy gave a speech at Madison Square Garden in New York in support of his proposal for legislation providing medical care for the aged under the Social Security system. The American Medical Association felt compelled to rent this same arena so that its spokesman could speak to the nation before empty seats in symbolic protest.

44 The number of electoral votes is constitutionally based on the number of senators plus the number of representatives, i.e., $100 + 435$. The adoption of the Twenty-Third Amendment which, in effect, provides three electoral votes for the District of Columbia, increases the total to 538.

tive. "The weaker his apparent popular support," Neustadt observes of the president, "the more his cause in Congress may depend on negatives at his disposal like the veto. . . . He may not be left helpless, but his options are reduced, his opportunities diminished, his freedom for maneuver checked in the degree that Washington conceives him unimpressive to the public."[45]

TERM OF OFFICE

A final aspect of the chief executive's legal environment is his term of office. In about one-half of the states, the governor's term and reeligibility are strictly limited by law. Custom promotes the same end in other states. The president, of course, serves a four-year term and can be reelected once. Many observers assume that executive influence over legislation diminishes near the end of his final term. Malcolm Jewell, for example, states that "The consequence of his limitation [on years of service] is that during the second half of his administration the governor has declining influence in the legislature."[46] Similar assertions reverberated during debates over the Twenty-Second Amendment to the United States Constitution. At the national level, only President Eisenhower has been affected to date by the Twenty-Second Amendment. Here the facts trouble the generalization, for a good argument can be made that President Eisenhower exerted more influence on legislation in 1959 and 1960, his last two years in office, than in any previous two-year period.

A catalog of the chief executive's formal powers does not serve as a reliable index of his influence in the legislative process. Formal power is potential power. Its translation into actual power is a function of other elements.[47]

Executive Influence and Legislative Structure

The executive's influence is conditioned not only by his own legal environment but also by the legal environment within which legislators act. To the extent that these formal powers are shared or overlap, a potential for conflict is present.

Probably the most obvious characteristic of the legal structure within which legislators act is the dispersion of power and authority among the two houses, within the committee system, and among a number of offices such as the Speaker of the House. The argument is usually made that the

[45] Neustadt, *Presidential Power,* p. 90. Lipson points out that an appeal to the people is most likely to be effective where the issue is dramatic and the strategy is not used too often, *op. cit.,* p. 240. See also, E. E. Schattschneider, *The Semi-sovereign People* (New York: Holt, Rinehart & Winston, Inc., 1960), pp. 97–113; and V. O. Key, Jr., *Public Opinion and American Democracy* (New York: Alfred A. Knopf, Inc., 1961), pp. 284–87 and *passim.*

[46] Jewell, *op. cit.,* p. 111. See also Ransone, *The Office of Governor in the United States,* p. 295.

[47] Joseph Schlesinger, in Chapter 6 of *Politics in the American States,* ed. H. Jacob and K. N. Vines (Boston: Little, Brown & Company, 1965), constructs a "General Index of the Governor's Formal Powers," but is careful not to confuse his index with actual power.

392 presence of multiple centers of power in the legislative branch makes it difficult for the executive to mobilize support for his programs.

BICAMERALISM

The clearest example of dispersion of power and authority is found in the provision for a bicameral legislature, found in Congress and in forty-nine of the fifty states. How bicameralism affects the chief executive's ability to influence the legislature is uncertain. Of the governor's power in Nebraska, the only state with a unicameral legislature, Belle Zeller writes: "His influence is important but not decisive." Much the same observation would be accurate for other states.[48]

Although the presence of two houses instead of one tends to complicate the executive's political life, it is probable that the characteristics of the two bodies do more to determine his influence than does the mere fact of their existence. To the extent that one house differs from the other in respect to length of term or nature of constituency, legislative bicameralism may inhibit executive influence. Another possibility, however, is that the existence of multiple access points within the legislature may enable the executive to build support initially within one house; having won it there, he may be able to increase his leverage on the second house. Steiner and Gove indicate that in Illinois interhouse rivalry is not common.[49]

To some observers the most serious drawback to bicameralism is that it opens up the possibility of divided party control between the houses and between the executive and at least one house of the legislature. In a great many northern states it is common to find the Democratic party in control of the governor's office and the lower house while the Republican party is dominant in the upper house. Bicameralism may affect legislative-executive relations quite apart from party battles. President Kennedy's major legislative proposals ordinarily were treated more sympathetically in the Senate than in the House. What this means is not so clear. Does it indicate that bicameralism obstructs executive influence or that it enables the chief executive to seek support in more places?

COMMITTEE SYSTEMS

The dispersion of power and authority is reflected as well in the committee system. Whether committees impede or augment executive influence depends upon such things as the methods used in selection of members, the rules and traditions about reporting bills in each environment, and on the prestige possessed by particular committees within the legislative system. Committee independence of executive influence seems to be directly related to the means by which members receive committee posts. Where procedures for selecting committee members, promoting them within committees, and selecting the chairman are either semiautomatic or not firmly governed by the leadership, as in Congress, committees are most likely to constitute barriers to executive influence. In almost all of the lower houses in the states,

---

48 Zeller, *op. cit.,* p. 250.
49 Steiner and Gove, *op. cit.,* p. 19.

the Speaker formally appoints members of committees; the critical fact in this circumstance is the relationship between the chief executive and the Speaker. There are other states in which the governor picks the members of the crucial committees, thus usually assuring a favorable response to the major items in his program.[50]

In Congress the accident of succession to the chairmanship of a committee or subcommittee can be critical. When Graham Barden, a conservative Democrat from South Carolina, chaired the House Committee on Education and Labor, this committee acted at times as a veritable graveyard for administration measures. In the 87th Congress, when Congressman Adam Clayton Powell succeeded Barden, who had retired at the end of the previous Congress, the committee became much more receptive to executive proposals. Several of the major bills passed during that Congress had in earlier sessions been bottled up in the Education and Labor Committee.

The method of selection of committee members and of the chairman sets the pattern for executive-committee cooperation and conflict. The legal apparatus encompassing committee work reinforces or weakens that pattern. In Congress, committee independence is a fact. Most bills, administration as well as any other, die in committee. In the Senate, during the 89th Congress, for example, of 4,567 bills introduced, 2,151 were reported by committees; in the House for the same period, 21,999 bills were introduced and 2,049 were reported by committees.[51] In those states where committees are important, their decisive role seems to be that of killing bills. In about 25 per cent of the states, committees are required to report all bills, but this rule does not automatically augment executive influence. Discharge petitions are possible in Congress and in many states, but they are rarely used and even more rarely effective.[52]

More elusive but still relevant in assessing committee impact on legislation is the status and prestige of each committee. Donald Matthews has shown that the cohesiveness and prestige of committees in the Senate help to determine their ability to achieve their purposes on the floor.[53] The united high-prestige committees often generate favorable decisions in the Senate as a whole. Legislative committees may constitute "feudal baronies" or may be subordinate dependents to other forces. Whatever their degree of freedom, they may be tools of executive leadership or impediments to it.

SIZE OF LEGISLATIVE BODIES

Several less critical aspects of the legal life of legislative bodies are relevant to the analysis of executive influence. The size of legislative bodies is one of these. Students of organizations and groups are in general agreement that

---

50 See, for example, Farmer, *op. cit.*, pp. 138–39.

51 Floyd M. Riddick and Murray Zweben, "The Eighty-Ninth Congress: Second Session," *Western Political Quarterly*, XX (March 1967), 176.

52 In April 1962 the senate in the state of Michigan discharged a committee from further consideration of a tax bill. Such an event had last occurred some fifty years previously. For a more general statement, see Zeller, *op. cit.*, p. 198.

53 Donald Matthews, *U.S. Senators and Their World* (Chapel Hill: University of North Carolina Press, 1960), pp. 168–69. This point is spectacularly confirmed for the House in a more recent study by Richard Fenno, *The Power of the Purse* (Boston: Little, Brown & Company, 1966).

394   any sizeable body of individuals united in common tasks seldom acts spontaneously without direction. The necessity for leadership is now widely recognized. Legislative bodies in the United States vary in membership from eighteen in the Delaware state senate to 435 in the U.S. House of Representatives. The necessity for leadership in legislative bodies can be predicted; the source of that leadership is not equally apparent.[54] Whether the chief executive can perform this function cannot be predicted on the basis of the size of the legislature.

LENGTH OF SESSIONS

The length and frequency of legislative sessions may also have a bearing on executive influence in the legislature. In many states, biennial sessions and severe time limits almost guarantee a last-minute rush. Much the same thing occurs in Congress. Whether executive programs will be pushed quickly to passage or quietly buried in the struggle of the closing days will vary from political environment to political environment.

Partisan Politics and Executive Influence

Executive influence is registered within a partisan political as well as a socio-economic and legal environment. As noted in Chapter 9, the idea that competitive two-party politics characterizes the American political scene and that the majority party runs the government has only the status of mythology in many political environments.[55] The arena of political party conflict in one-party states is typically within the dominant party. To the extent that the governor leads he does so by molding personal, ideological, and regional support into majority factions.[56] In states where competitive party politics is the rule and where the governor and the legislative majority wear different party labels, party often serves to hinder executive influence.[57]

The president and the majority in each house of Congress usually wear the identical party label. From 1901 until 1972 the party in control of the presidency produced a majority in both houses of Congress about 75 per cent of the time. The Eisenhower presidency was unique in that the Democrats controlled Congress for six of eight years. President Eisenhower put it well in his 1960 State of the Union message: "I am not unique as a

---

[54] The necessity for leadership is heightened by rapid turnover in the personnel of the state legislative branches. No available research demonstrates any connection between the effectiveness of executive leadership, in general, and legislative turnover. In Alabama, turnover does seem to enhance executive leadership. Farmer, *op. cit.,* p. 189.

[55] See Ransone, *The Office of Governor in the United States,* p. 94; Jewell, *op. cit.,* Chapter 2.

[56] One useful index of executive influence in one-party states is the ability of the governor to place legislators who will cooperate with him in leadership positions. Ransone, *The Office of Governor in the South,* pp. 99–100; Jewell, *op. cit.,* p. 115; Farmer, *op. cit.,* pp. 168, 185.

[57] Norman C. Thomas, "Michigan's Party System: Blessing or Curse," in *Parties and Politics in Michigan, A Symposium* (Ann Arbor: Michigan Citizenship Clearinghouse, 1961), pp. 3–14.

President in having worked with a Congress controlled by the opposition party—except that no other President ever did it for quite so long!" But, as demonstrated in Chapter 9, sharing the cloak of a party label is in no sense the same thing as sleeping in the same ideological bed. Party lines are crossed in Congress with monotonous regularity as coalitions are formed in support of legislation.

The president takes votes for his program from any quarter where they can be found. Not infrequently he looks for supporters among the opposition party, even though this poses problems for his other role as party leader. Thus in May 1962, President Kennedy campaigned throughout Wisconsin for Democratic senatorial candidate Gaylord Nelson who was running against Republican incumbent Alexander Wiley. What made this troublesome was that Wiley was the ranking minority member of the Senate Foreign Relations Committee, and the president needed his support.[58]

Given the decentralized nature of power and authority in Congress, sympathy and support from key committee chairmen can sometimes be more significant than several votes from the rank-and-file party members. In 1962, of the eight Democratic senators whose records of support for the Democratic administration were lowest, five held committee chairmanships; in 1967, of the four Democratic senators whose records of support for the Democratic administration were lowest, three held committee chairmanships.[59] The importance of a chairman to the president is illustrated by this story concerning President Kennedy and Congressman Wilbur Mills (D., Ark.), chairman of the House Ways and Means Committee: "I read in *The New York Times* this morning," the president said in a visit to Arkansas to dedicate a new federal dam, "that if Wilbur Mills requested it, I'd be glad to come down here and sing *Down by the Old Mill Stream*. I want to say that I am delighted."[60] The impact on policy of key personnel in state legislatures can be equally potent. Lockard, discussing New Hampshire, distinguishes the influence of veterans and novices: "Those who do stay achieve considerable influence over the others who are passing through on their way from oblivion to oblivion."[61]

In the states, as might be expected, the pattern of party control is less distinct. After the November 1970 elections, almost 50 per cent of the governors confronted a state legislature with the opposition party in control of one or both of the houses.[62]

The appeal to party meets a ready response when it reinforces other pressures on the legislator. The legislator caught in cross pressures is more likely to pursue an independent course. Psychological pressure toward party

58 *New York Times,* May 21, 1962, p. 26.

59 For the statistics on the support of the administration, see *Congressional Quarterly Almanac, 1962,* p. 707, and the *Almanac, 1965,* p. 1110 (Washington, D.C.: Congressional Quarterly, Inc.). The *Congressional Quarterly Almanac* each year lists the administration-support records of congressmen. The impact of these statistics is tempered by David B. Truman's finding for the 81st Congress that floor leaders and seniority leaders on particular committees tended to agree on votes concerning issues arising from that committee. *The Congressional Party* (New York: John Wiley & Sons, Inc., 1959), p. 282.

60 *Time,* October 11, 1963, p. 26.

61 Lockard, *op. cit.,* p. 78.

62 Samuel R. Solomon, "Governors: 1960–1970," *National Civic Review,* LX (March 1971), 133.

396 regularity exists; its impact is not always decisive.[63] The pull of party is illustrated in these remarks by a Republican senator:

> If the Republican party is going to stay in power it must support the President. As a result, I sometimes "hold my nose" as the saying goes—and go along with the administration, though I might personally prefer to vote the other way.[64]

The chief executive uses his party as best he can. The ultimate test of his effectiveness rests on the extent to which his interests, those of legislative party leaders, and those of party members in the legislature become functionally interdependent.[65]

The Personal Dimension of Executive Leadership

If the influence of chief executives is enhanced or hindered by societal factors, legal rules and procedures, and the status and condition of political parties, it is not always established by them. A missing link is the chief executive himself. His prospects for influencing the legislature are in part a function of his personality, his conception of his office, his policy desires, and his own political skill along with that of his associates. The context of political conflict does not always predetermine the results. Who the participants are is frequently relevant.

The weight of analysis on the links between personality and political behavior is far from overwhelming. Yet few would deny the importance of trying to establish these relationships. Fred Greenstein links the potential personal impact with such factors as the ambiguity of the situation, the sanctions related to alternative acts, the active investment of effort required, and the extent of fixed expectations attached to a position.[66] Only the edges

---

[63] Truman, *op. cit.*, p. 285. Two articles by Mark Kesselman indicate a change in congressional voting patterns on foreign policy questions when there is a party turnover in the presidency. "Presidential Leadership in Congress on Foreign policy," *Midwest Journal of Political Science,* V (August 1961), 284–89; "Presidential Leadership in Congress on Foreign Policy: A Replication of a Hypothesis," *Midwest Journal of Political Science,* IX (November 1965), 401–6. For the states, a useful discussion of the relationships between the governor and his party is Sarah P. McCally, "The Governor and his Legislative Party," *American Political Science Review,* LX (December 1966), 923–42.

[64] Quoted in Matthews, *op. cit.*, p. 140.

[65] See Truman, *op. cit.,* Chapter 16, for an elaboration of this theme. An illustration of functional interdependence came after the landslide Democratic presidential victory in 1964, which swept many new Democrats into Congress. These freshmen, in turn, supported the administration vigorously. As House Democratic majority leader Carl Albert put it: "They're the reason we're doing so well." *Time,* July 30, 1965, p. 12. See also Lewis A. Froman, Jr., and Randall B. Ripley, "Conditions for Party Leadership: The Case of the House Democrats," *American Political Science Review,* LIX (March 1965), 52–63.

[66] *Personality and Politics* (Chicago: Markham Publishing Company, 1969), pp. 50–57. Not many efforts have been made to mine this subject matter in a presidential context. For some examples see James D. Barber, "Classifying and Predicting Presidential Styles: Two Weak Presidents," *Journal of Social Issues,* XXIV (July 1968), 51–80; James D. Barber, "Adult Identity and Presidential Style: The Rhetorical Emphasis," *Daedalus,* XCVII (Summer 1968), 938–68; Alexander and Juliette George, *Woodrow Wilson and Colonel House* (New York: John Day, 1956).

of these problems have been scratched, but most students of leadership do agree that leadership is a function both of environmental factors and of personal qualities and behavior.

It is difficult to establish a direct connection between personal relationships and political leadership. President Roosevelt at times resorted to condemnation of Congress. On the other hand, President Eisenhower seemed to believe, at least during the early part of his first administration, that the road to executive influence was paved with bacon and eggs for visiting congressmen who attended White House breakfasts. It would be rash to state that either of these patterns is more effective in all situations.

However attractive his personality and however great his popularity, a president finds it difficult to translate these assets into favorable votes for his legislative program.[67] Although the public opinion polls demonstrated with monotonous regularity that the people of the United States liked President Eisenhower, Congress demonstrated with comparable regularity that it was not anxious to support all of his programs. President Eisenhower's personal popularity may have convinced congressional Democrats to tone down their opposition.

The chief executive's influence is also related to his conception of his office.[68] The president or governor who sees his role essentially as that of a faithful executor of legislative policies is unlikely to ignite much opposition among legislators. It may even be true that within this narrowly defined conception of his office, he may compile an impressive statistical record of accomplishment. The chief executive who sees his role as that of an initiator or catalyst may not fare so well. Nothing is so likely to stir the legislature as a chief executive who takes an openly active role in the legislative process. Chief executives who define their office as Theodore Roosevelt did—"a bully pulpit"—or as Franklin D. Roosevelt did—"a place of moral leadership"— are not necessarily more successful in securing legislative responses. Since the chief executive commonly represents a set of interests different from those of the typical legislator, his programs frequently encounter vigorous legislative opposition. Executive vigor and executive effectiveness are far from interchangeable terms.

Each chief executive defines his own concept of what behavior is appropriate to the office he holds. In addition, chief executives bring their personal policy preferences into office with them. To the extent that a president or governor is oriented to the *status quo,* or no more than marginal modification of it, he is more likely to be successful with his legislature than if he brings vigorous reformist programs with him into office.[69] By and large, legislatures are more inclined to prevent action than to promote it; accordingly, a politically activist chief executive, except under circumstances of

[67] An unusually interesting piece of research on presidential popularity is John E. Mueller, "Presidential Popularity From Truman to Johnson," *American Political Science Review,* LXIV (March 1970), 18–34.

[68] For examples of differing presidential conceptions of the office, see Corwin, *op. cit.,* Chapter 1; Norman Small, *Some Presidential Interpretations of the Presidency* (Baltimore: Johns Hopkins Press, 1932). For the governor, see Ransone, *The Office of Governor in the United States,* pp. 140–43.

[69] Farmer, *op. cit.,* p. 185. March and Simon note as a general principle of organizational behavior that the costs of innovation often are such as to produce continuity in program. James G. March and Herbert A. Simon, *Organizations* (New York: John Wiley & Sons, Inc., 1958), p. 173.

398 unusual duress, such as war, may expect to meet towering legislative road-blocks.

The attributes of political skill are not always easy to pinpoint, but the importance of having it is agreed upon. Richard Neustadt argues persuasively that a president can muster extra margins of effectiveness through the diligent exercise of political skills. To make his colleagues in his administration and his associates in Congress see that what he wants them to do is in their own interests is the crucial task for the president. Neustadt's conclusions for the presidency are reinforced by more generalized analysis of organizations. James March and Herbert Simon argue that individuals see problems from a selective frame of reference.[70] To enlist support sometimes means to alter their frames of reference.

Presidential efforts at persuasion can be augmented or harmed by the political skills of his top assistants. Lawrence F. O'Brien, a master of legislative liaison, provided massive boosts to administration programs during the presidencies of John F. Kennedy and Lyndon B. Johnson.[71] Failures and deficiencies in political skill on the part of the president or his aids can also account for legislative setbacks. Some examples are instructive. Concerning the Kennedy administration's efforts to pass a federal aid-to-education bill, Senator Monroney (D., Okla.) observed that the administration, through its ineptness, had "snatched defeat from the jaws of victory."[72] In 1957, during the struggle over a civil rights bill, President Eisenhower stated at a press conference, when questioned about one part of the bill: "Well I would not want to answer this in detail, because I was reading part of that bill this morning and—there were certain phrases I didn't completely understand.... I would want to talk to the Attorney General and see exactly what they mean."[73] In 1970 and again in 1971 the Nixon administration blundered in lobbying Senator Margaret Chase Smith (R., Maine) thus contributing to the defeat of a nominee to the Supreme Court and of a proposal for continuing work on a supersonic aircraft.

The Effectiveness of Executive Influence: Overview

The executive's influence in the legislative process is, then, related to a series of environmental factors which set boundaries within which his own personality, role conceptions, ideology, and political skills can be relevant.[74]

[70] March and Simon, *op. cit.,* p. 152.

[71] Talented liaison persons are useful not only for persuading congressmen but also for bringing information from "the Hill" which can be turned to strategic and tactical uses. The most thorough study of legislative liaison is Abraham Holtzman, *Legislative Liaison* (Chicago: Rand McNally & Company, 1970). See also Thomas E. Cronin, "Everyone Believes in Democracy Until He Gets to the White House," *Law and Contemporary Problems,* XXXV (Summer 1970), 601–2.

[72] Quoted in National Committee for an Effective Congress, *Congressional Report,* X, no. 3 (December 20, 1961), 1.

[73] Quoted in Douglass Cater, "How the Senate Passed the Civil Rights Bill," *The Reporter,* September 5, 1957, p. 10.

[74] Such boundaries may be rather confining, as in Wisconsin, where David Carley quotes a veteran Wisconsin assemblyman as stating: "a good governor can do some good and a bad governor can't do much harm." "Legal and Extra-Legal Powers of Wisconsin Governors In Legislative Relations—I," *Wisconsin Law Review* (January 1962), 3.

To what extent do attempts at executive influence merely constitute energy expended fruitlessly?

On balance, when assets, liabilities, and experience are blended, most students agree—some with satisfaction, some with dissatisfaction—that presidents and governors are very likely to be significant elements in their respective legislative processes. Malcolm Jewell notes, for example, that "the chief executive is frequently, though not always in the states, the most powerful single force in the legislative process."[75] Hallie Farmer agrees, citing the governor as "the most powerful single factor in the legislative process in Alabama."[76] Ransone is only slightly more restrained when he notes that "the average governor in the United States in the past fifty years has proved to be a legislative policy maker of no mean stature."[77] As to southern governors, Ransone writes: "The governors of the Southern states, with the exception of South Carolina and Texas, are traditionally very effective in their legislative leadership."[78] For Illinois, Steiner and Gove find that "the most effective of these non-member influences [on the legislature] is surely the governor, and this tends to be true whether or not the legislative majority and the governor are of the same political party."[79]

A powerful chief executive is not a universal pattern in American states. Duane Lockard points out that in New Hampshire organized interests have a more significant impact on the legislative process than does the governor.[80] Of Maine, he writes: "A Democratic governor's hands are tied so firmly by the governmental and political structure that his accomplishments are at best limited."[81]

The president's influence with Congress, commentators agree, tends to be significant despite frequent legislative rebuffs. At question is whether the growth of this influence is desirable. Most analysts note, with approval, the necessity for presidential leadership in the legislative process. Professor Corwin fears the enlargement of presidential power. He sees the possibility of such power becoming "dangerously personalized."[82]

The Effectiveness of Executive Influence: The Problem of Measurement

Few observers doubt that the influence of the chief executive on the legislative process is significant. Why they think so is not always as clear. What are the standards for judging? How is influence measured? How can we tell if a president is influential? The difficulties in measuring executive success are aptly illustrated in President Kennedy's experience in 1962. His top priority legislation, the Trade Expansion Act, emerged from Congress to become public law. Overall, however, of 298 specific requests only 132 (44.3 per cent) became law. Defeated were proposals for aid to education,

[75] Jewell, *op. cit.,* p. 105.

[76] Farmer, *op. cit.,* p. 167.

[77] Ransone, *The Office of Governor in the United States,* p. 184.

[78] Ransone, *The Office of Governor in the South,* p. 72, *The Office of Governor in the United States,* p. 178.

[79] Steiner and Gove, *op. cit.,* p .32.

[80] Lockard, *op. cit.,* p. 70.

[81] *Ibid.,* p. 118.

[82] Corwin, *op. cit.,* p. 312. See also, MacNeil, *op. cit.,* pp. 268–69.

400 medical care for the aged, tax revision, and other such high-priority items. The assessment of President Kennedy's impact on Congress ultimately will depend on which measures of success are applied.

If one accepts the executive's own priority list as the standard by which to judge his success, then adoption of the leading item on that list is significant. But what test is to be made of the executive with modest ambitions? Those who ask for little of consequence may in fact be quite successful—on their terms of measurement. An alternative standard for gauging executive influence lies in assessing the urgency of existing problems for the system and in comparing such lists with executive accomplishments. But this, too, is troublesome. What is an urgent priority for one man may be of no more than casual importance for another. Which is most important: civil rights, reciprocal trade, or a tax cut?

Some conceivable measures of executive influence are easily quantifiable. How many proposals does he make? How many messages does he send to the legislature? How many television and radio speeches does he make to build support or to pacify opposition? How many conferences does he hold with legislative leaders? The difficulty is that answers to these questions provide measures of activity rather than indices of influence.

PROPOSALS MADE AND LEGISLATION PASSED

A more fruitful statistical measure of influence involves analysis of the ratio of proposals made to legislation passed. Statistics appear to be on the governor's side, judging from an assortment of studies. Hallie Farmer found that between 1903 and 1943 the Alabama legislature enacted 50 per cent or more of executive recommendations overall.[83] During Governor La Follette's three terms in Wisconsin, the legislature adopted seventy-three of 117 administration proposals; between 1951 and 1955, the Wisconsin legislature enacted over 60 per cent of the recommendations made by Governor Kohler.[84] In the 1948 session of the Kentucky General Assembly, over 90 per cent of Governor Clement's program was enacted; the record of Virginia governors from 1934 to 1941, as reported by George Spicer, has been equally impressive: over 80 per cent of their proposals were passed.[85]

Evidence supporting an alternative conclusion is found in Arizona, where an average of 23 per cent of the governor's proposals to regular sessions of the legislature from 1912 to 1963 were enacted.[86]

The statistical record of presidential success is easier to compile; its significance is not necessarily easier to fathom. Table 11.1 provides data covering the eight years of the Eisenhower administration. The table reveals the decisive change brought on when the Democrats regained control of Congress in 1955.

Since 1953, *Congressional Quarterly* has compiled, using several meas-

83 Farmer, *op. cit.*, p. 172.
84 David Carley, "Legal and Extra-Legal Powers of Wisconsin Governors—II," *Wisconsin Law Review* (March 1962), 307, 327.
85 Ransone, *The Office of Governor in the South*, p. 74; Spicer, "Gubernatorial Leadership in Virginia," *Public Administration Review*, I (Autumn 1941), 441.
86 Morey, *op. cit.*, p. 58.

TABLE 11.1

Eisenhower Support in Congress

Year	Proposals	Number Passed	Percentage Passed
1953	44	32	72.7
1954	232	150	64.7
1955	207	96	46.3
1956	225	103	45.7
1957	206	76	36.9
1958	234	110	47.0
1959	228	93	40.8
1960	183	56	30.6

SOURCE: *Congressional Quarterly Almanac, 1960* (Washington, D.C.: Congressional Quarterly, Inc., 1960), p. 93.

ures and its independent judgment, a "presidential support score." Figure 14 shows how this measure compares with a related but more focused and clearer measure, the ratio of proposals passed to proposals made.

Variation occurs not only from year to year but from president to president. Moreover, a president may have greater influence on some kinds of policy questions than on others. This is shown in Table 11.2, which

TABLE 11.2

Truman Support in Congress

Congress	% of Requests Approved	
	Overall	Foreign Policy
80th (1947–48)	46.7	50.0
81st (1949–50)	44.1	61.25
82d (1951–52)	37.0	88.3

SOURCE: *Congressional Quarterly Almanac, 1952* (Washington, D. C.: Congressional Quarterly, Inc., 1952), p. 58.

contrasts congressional support given all of President Truman's requests between 1947 and 1952 and support given his foreign policy programs. The difference is marked. Although this evidence provides hints as to executive influence, it is far from conclusive. The reason is that no bill equals precisely any other in significance; the omission of a qualitative dimension is a serious impediment to any study of legislative voting behavior.

Vetoes Overridden

Another measure of influence may be found in the number of vetoes overridden. The extent to which a chief executive can muster sufficient support to defeat legislative attempts to surmount his vetoes gives some indication of his influence among legislators. Here the governors' record is extra-

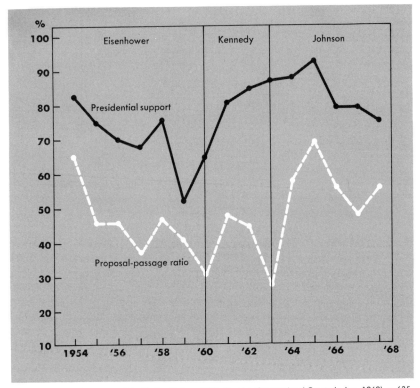

*Source: Data from Congress and the Nation, Volume II (Washington: Congressional Quarterly, Inc., 1969), p. 625. CQ Weekly Report, January 29, 1971, p. 222.

FIGURE 14   *Two ways of viewing presidential success, 1953–1968.**

ordinarily impressive.[87] In Pennsylvania, Michigan, Iowa, Alabama, and Illinois the veto is almost never challenged successfully.[88] From 1900 to 1947, only one veto by a Pennsylvania governor was overridden.[89] In New York, no full veto was overridden from 1870 to 1957.[90] In the South, from 1937 to 1947, of 1,501 vetoes, only 101 were overridden; about half of these were in Florida alone.[91] In Arizona, from 1912 to 1963, 12 per cent of the vetoes were overridden.[92] In Illinois, Gove and Carlson state, only four vetoes have been overridden since 1870.[93]

Very few presidential vetoes are overridden in Congress. The experience after World War II is detailed in Table 11.3.

87 Ransone, *The Office of the Governor in the United States,* p. 182.
88 Prescott, "The Executive Veto in the American States," 104.
89 McGeary, *op. cit.,* p. 944.
90 Solomon, "The Governor as Legislator," 516.
91 Prescott, "The Executive Veto in the Southern States," 666.
92 Morey, *op. cit.,* p. 33.
93 *An Introduction to the Illinois General Assembly,* rev. ed. (n.p.: Institute of Government and Public Affairs, University of Illinois, 1970), p. 20.

TABLE 11.3

The Presidential Veto Record In Congress, 1945–70

Years	Presidents	Vetoes	Vetoes Overridden
1945–53	Truman	250	12
1953–61	Eisenhower	181	2
1961–63	Kennedy	21	0
1963–69	Johnson	30	0
1969–70	Nixon	11	2

SOURCE: Data from the *Congressional Record's* "Daily Digest" for the appropriate years.

Conclusions and Tendencies

Any of the statistics for the success or failure of the chief executive must be treated with caution. What they hide may be as important as what they show. Short-range failure, for example, may pave the path to long-range success. In his evaluation of the legislative record of the Truman administration, Richard Neustadt cites domestic programs that fell before congressional attack like tenpins. But by vigorously advocating proposals that were doomed then, Truman set the stage for future successes.[94] Innovations in policy eventually became orthodoxies in politics. On this count, the ultimate judgment concerning the influence of the chief executive has to be made many years later.

Whatever their actual influence, presidents and governors claim to be superior to congressmen or state legislators as agents of representation, citing the breadth of their constituency and their greater resources in information and expertise. The president or governor, however, cannot be presented as a spokesman for the public interest while the legislator is marked as simply the agent of narrow parochialism. Executive-legislative conflict is not necessarily a battle between heroes and villains; rather, it is a battle of spokesmen for different elements within the political system. Just as the legislator cannot speak for all of his district, so the executive cannot speak for all of the state or the nation. His electoral base, his party affiliation, and his personal background contribute to the pressure to which all representatives, both executive and legislative, attempt to respond.

To the extent that chief executives and legislators respond to different sets of political pressures, political conflict becomes inevitable. Conflict between the branches of government contributes to the articulation of the many voices of society, but it makes it difficult to reach authoritative decisions, especially if the decisions represent a noticeable departure from past policy. Yet conflict is hardly an inherent evil. The extent to which executive-legislative conflict resolution is desirable and necessary is a function both of objective needs (such as a successful prosecution of war) and of the analyst's own ideological predispositions (Is a system of government-run national health insurance desirable or not?).

The phenomenon of executive influence does not lend itself easily to

[94] Neustadt, *Public Policy,* 1954, pp. 380–81.

404 generalization. But there are several tendencies for which some evidence is available: (1) Crisis does tend to increase executive influence but not always so. (2) Executive influence is not confined to suggesting ideas to legislators and to receiving bills from legislative bodies. It can be and often is exerted at all stages of that process.[95] (3) Executive influence varies with legal and other environmental factors as well as with changes in personnel or in party majorities. (4) The presence or absence of many legal and institutional features such as the item veto or the power to call special sessions is probably not in and of itself critical in determining executive influence. Still, Bennett Rich is probably correct when he argues that constitutional reform is a prerequisite for improved leadership.[96] (5) Successful exercise of executive influence often requires appeals based both on the inherent logic of the executive's case and on bargaining and accommodation. Societal conflict as to what is "good policy" is commonplace. The merits of the executive's program often are far from self-evident to the conscientious legislator. "It avails nothing to have good programs if you cannot persuade people they are good and rally support for them. And that is rarely done by abstract arguments. It requires a combination of personal contact, persuasion, cajolery, returning support for support given, rewards where available and sometimes retribution where possible. In short, politics."[97] (6) Executives can and do exert considerable influence over legislatures but seldom are able to guarantee any given result.

The executive becomes a legislator because his environment and formal power provide both opportunity and rationale, while his representative capacity imposes on him the obligation to do so. Representation in a democracy involves speaking for the represented, blending their disparate viewpoints, suggesting effective solutions for the problems of society, and seeking support for appropriate policies. Promoting the second and fourth functions may be the indispensable contribution of the chief executive to the legislative process.

95 Clinton Rossiter, "President and Congress in the 1960's," in *Continuing Crisis in American Government,* ed. Marian Irish (Englewood Cliffs, N.J.: Prentice-Hall, Inc., 1963), p. 100.

96 *State Constitutions: The Governor* (New York: National Municipal League, 1960), p. 33. For a discussion of the significance of the absence of the veto in North Carolina, see Ransone, *The Office of the Governor in the United States,* p. 214. For a study of the relationships between the formal powers of the governor and public policy outputs, see Thomas R. Dye, "Executive Power and Public Policy in the States," *Western Political Quarterly,* XXII (December 1969), 926–39.

97 Quoted from the *Wall Street Journal* in National Committee for an Effective Congress, *Congressional Report,* vol. 7, no. 2, May 29, 1958, p. 2.

12

LEGISLATIVE OVERSIGHT
OF BUREAUCRACY

Contemporary legislatures confront extraordinary difficulties as they attempt to perform their traditional functions. This pattern is dramatized most spectacularly when Congress, and at times a state legislature, attempt fitfully to provide a measure of external control over governmental bureaucracies. Such episodes represent a continuing scene in the drama of responsible government where legislative assemblies seek to impose effective restraints on executive branches. The rise of democratic government, some thought, marked the triumph of the people and their representatives over encrusted officialdom; government would now simply speak for all, not just for the few most powerful. Experience reveals the democratic process to be more complex.

As the modern democratic state evolved, the impact of two forces, industrialization and world strife, was to raise perplexing questions about the capacity of legislative bodies to meaningfully supervise enlarged and complex governmental structures. Events have translated nagging doubts into clearer conclusions. Just as an inexorable logic had thrust chief executives into energizing and coordinating roles in the legislative process, so similar forces were at work in lessening the ability of legislatures to supervise and control chief executives and the governmental bureaucracies which they directed. The basic explanation for these developments lay not in rapacious seizures of power by chief executives nor in the adoption of the ideology of big government, but rather in the changing nature of modern society itself.[1]

The Evolution of Bureaucracy

Bureaucracy is not a function of modern life. Vast bureaucracies functioned in ancient Egypt and in fourteenth-century China. And to the American colonist, the collector of the tea tax was part of an apparatus of king's agents sent to the colonies to extract the hard-earned money of

[1] See Peter Woll, *American Bureaucracy* (New York: W. W. Norton & Company, Inc., 1963), Chapter 2. For a conflicting interpretation, see James Burnham, *Congress and the American Tradition* (Chicago: Henry Regnery Co., 1959).

thrifty and industrious citizens. Bureaucracies have persisted and grown in modern society. Bureaucratic structures seem universal in modern Western industrial society, regardless of each country's political traditions, its contemporary ideological leanings, or the form of its governmental institutions.[2] Whatever the differences implied in labeling modern industrial societies— oligarchic, democratic, totalitarian, socialist, Communist, capitalist, two-party, one-party—such distinctions conceal one fundamental similarity, i.e., the common characteristic of extensive and powerful governmental bureaucracy.[3]

The evolution of modern industrial society taxed not only the energy and capabilities of entrepreneurs but also the capacity of governmental systems to function. The increasing complexity of industrial society calls for no particular pattern of governmental response, but the emergence of new problems rooted in technological developments, adaptations in social relationships, and the pressure of external events does provide an environment within which pressure for governmental response is characteristic.

Richard Fenno cites four "great transformations" in American history, each of which opened up new demands and new opportunities for governmental action: (1) westward expansion, (2) industrialization, (3) world responsibility, (4) concern for social justice.[4] Governmental response in each case was variable, partly as a result of differing patterns of pressure.[5] Whatever the time lag in each instance, societal demands were eventually translated into governmental action; governmental action did not precede societal awareness and demands.

Fenno's suggestions provide a broad sketch of the environments within which governmental structures expanded. What specific manifestations emerge from these societal transformations? First, the limits of individual human capacity to handle volume become self-evident. The secretary of state and a few clerks could handle the business of a State Department in 1795. The sheer volume of increased business alone has forced some increase in governmental personnel. Problems of volume were compounded by problems of complexity. A clerk could transcribe the messages which Thomas Jefferson had composed without assistance. A contemporary secretary of state could hardly feel as confident when called upon to decide complex technical matters of international trade involving balance of payments, gold outflows, devaluations of currency, and equally obscure questions.[6]

2 James G. March and Herbert Simon trace the necessity for organization simply to the finite limits of rational intellectual capacity. *Organizations* (New York: John Wiley & Sons, Inc., 1958), Chapter 6.

3 C. Wright Mills, *The Power Elite* (New York: Oxford University Press, 1959); James Burnham, *The Managerial Revolution* (New York: The John Day Co., Inc., 1941); Reinhard Bendix, *Max Weber, An Intellectual Portrait* (Garden City, N.Y.: Doubleday & Company, Inc., 1962), Chapter 13 and the citations therein.

4 *The President's Cabinet* (Cambridge: Harvard University Press, 1959), p. 21.

5. *Ibid.,* p. 22.

6 The evolution of the Department of State can be traced in Graham H. Stuart, *The Department of State* (New York: The Macmillan Company, 1949). See also Leonard D. White, *The Federalists* (New York: The Macmillan Company, 1956), Chapter 11. White asserts that the early work of the Department of State was "not organizational" but personal (p. 128).

A second manifestation of the societal transformations which marked the late nineteenth and early twentieth centuries was a need for specialists to advise and support top-level decision-makers. Out of volume, complexity, and specialization grew the need for order and consistency. The order imposed by one intelligent human being reacting to situations was hardly sufficient when thousands of governmental officials had to make decisions many times each day about distributing seeds, examining applications for visas, prosecuting crimes, and allowing or not allowing tax deductions. Complex government, then, usually means organized government, i.e., individuals grouped so as to gain the advantage of orderly human cooperation and to minimize the effects of individual human lack of capacity. That organization is an all-pervasive response to volume and complexity is illustrated in the corporate world of industrial giants as well as in government, the universities, the military, and almost every other major aspect of American institutional life.

Intimately bound up with the roots of the evolution of modern bureaucracy is the inability of legislative bodies alone to meet the challenges of complex society. If the generalist in an executive department could not manage a pyramiding volume of work, the legislator concerned with all aspects of policy and all departments could hardly be expected to do so. Hence, a fundamental reason for the growth in size and potency of the governmental bureaucracy lay in the inability of legislatures to face the complexities and challenges of modern society without help.

Under the banner of efficiency, rationality, and the need for expertise, governmental bureaucracies have made spectacular gains in the twentieth century. In the popular image, legislative bodies are staffed by amateurs—men who lack the time and expertise to do much more than bicker over the details of executive proposals, men who usually find it necessary to defer to the wishes of the executive bureaucracy. Such phrases as "the age of the experts," "the need for technical competence," and "facing the technical revolution of our times" are the slogans of modern society. Such symbols are rarely descriptive of legislative branches; in some ways they provide the very definition of bureaucracy. Whether more recent pleas from some for more "humanization" and for less concern for efficiency will have more than a marginal impact on bureaucracy is yet to be demonstrated.

Bureaucratic expansion in size and expenditures is self-evident. In 1970 nearly 3 million persons were employed in an executive branch, spending a budget of approximately $198 billion. Consensus on the extent of bureaucratic power is more elusive. Writers such as James Burnham and C. Wright Mills see the growth of powerful bureaucracy as a critical fact in modern social organization. Mills asserts:

> The executive bureaucracy becomes not only the center of power but also the arena within which and in terms of which all conflicts of power are resolved or denied resolution. Administration replaces electoral politics; the maneuvering of cliques replaces the clash of parties.[7]

Burnham argues essentially that all aspects of society are governed today by "managers" rather than by owners, consumers, or workers. "The state...

---

[7] Mills, *op. cit.*, p. 267.

408 will, if we wish to put it that way, be the 'property' of the managers and that will be quite enough to place them in the position of the ruling class."[8]

The implication of these distinctions is that, as the problems of society become more complicated and technical, their resolution becomes more the task of trained experts rather than the responsibility of "amateur" political leaders.

Politics and Administration

Lurking beneath the surface of this argument is a rather precise, easily identifiable demarcation between politics and administration—politics is the process by which the general rules that govern society are formulated; administration is the process by which these general rules are applied to specific cases. Politics is the province of the elected representative; administration is the province of the technically trained expert. Whatever its contemporary validity for a theory of politics, such a distinction did serve a useful purpose historically: to provide the rationale for the creation and development of a trained and competent civil service selected on the basis of merit. With due recognition for its ideological value, the policy-administration distinction is best laid to rest—with minimal regret. Few analysts would argue, as did President Andrew Jackson, that any citizen could fill any governmental job. Recognition of the technical skill of lawyers, accountants, engineers, and others like them is appropriate, but it is inaccurate to equate technical tasks with the whole process of law implementation. Recognition that the world of politics and that of administration are linked came easily as governmental bureaucracies expanded their powers.

The basic proposition to be remembered is that the evolution of complex societies and the development of a core of trained specialists in governmental bureaucracies does not render the political process obsolete. Quite the contrary; as bureaucracy expands in size, scope of activities, and power, it is inevitably drawn into the political process.

The expansion of bureaucratic power means that more and more people are affected to a greater degree by the decisions of bureaucrats. Because the interests of individuals and groups are promoted or retarded by such decision-making, efforts are made either to support the *status quo* or to modify unfavorable decisions. Thus a setting natural for politics is created. As David Truman points out in his book, *The Governmental Process,* organized groups seek to gain access and exert their influence wherever they can gain advantage;[9] the expansion of bureaucratic power amounts to a standing invitation to organized interests to address their pleas and demands to executive units. As sensitivity develops throughout society to the far-flung consequences of bureaucratic action, political pressures are increasingly exerted on bureaucrats.

An awareness of the importance of bureaucratic decision-making leads to concern with bureaucratic structure and personnel as well as with

---

8 Burnham, *The Managerial Revolution,* p. 72. Copyright 1941 by James Burnham. Reprinted from *The Managerial Revolution* by James Burnham by permission of the John Day Company, Inc., publisher.

9 David B. Truman, *The Governmental Process* (New York: Alfred A. Knopf, Inc., 1951), p. 264 and *passim.*

policies. Groups and individuals thwarted by executive departments seek to gain support in the legislature, since that branch often can alter the rules about structure, personnel, and policy which political interests seek to have adjusted. The realization that bureaucratic structures and procedures have consequences for politics is the birth of attempts at merging the realms of politics and administration.

The extent to which bureaucrats are involved in the allocation of values in society provides one explanation for attempts at political influence. A second basis emerges from the realization that key decisions in the bureaucracy inevitably involve political as well as technical considerations. While technical experts can determine which design for interceptor planes offers least wind resistance and which model will cost less money to build, a decision whether the increased cost of one plane is offset by sufficient added utility involves the weighing of alternatives. Technical specifications are not automatically translated into policy. Recognition that experts differ and that the top bureaucrats must weigh alternatives and make political judgments stimulates some legislators to conclude that they, too, are capable of making rational political decisions. Their decisions will not necessarily coincide with those made by top bureaucrats. The position of the top-level bureaucrats *vis-à-vis* their departmental technical experts is related to the relationship of the legislator to these experts. In each instance, a nonexpert is attempting to weigh the merits of technical proposals, the details of which he may not completely comprehend.[10] Department heads are asked to weigh the judgments of competing experts. Understandably, the legislator sometimes feels that it is appropriate for him to second-guess the department head.

The vast power of contemporary governmental bureaucracy is challenged, then, because administration (law implementation) is viewed as an integral and important part of the processes by which the benefits and burdens of society are authoritatively allocated. Administration is not a set of value-free tasks. Norton Long points out that administration problems cannot be solved "in isolation from the structure of power and purpose in the polity."[11] In other words, goal attainment is a concern of both legislators and bureaucrats.[12]

If politics provides the motivation for legislative oversight, law provides the opportunity. Constitutional mandates to the legislature to create executive departments, to provide revenue for their operation, and to set personnel practices constitute legal levers which legislative branches, in quest of influence, can substitute for their relative lack of proficiency in subject matter.

[10] The relationships between top administrators and subject matter specialists are explored in Victor A. Thompson, *Modern Organization* (New York: Alfred A. Knopf, Inc., 1961).

[11] Norton E. Long. "Power and Administration," *Public Administration Review*, IX (Autumn 1949), 264. See also his article, "Public Policy and Administration: The Goals of Rationality and Responsibility," *Public Administration Review*, XIV (Winter 1954), 22–31, and Herbert Simon, *Administrative Behavior* (New York: The Macmillan Company, 1947), Chapter 3.

[12] William C. Mitchell, *The American Polity* (New York: Free Press of Glencoe, Inc., 1962), pp. 239ff. For insightful comments on the representative character of bureaucracy, see Anthony Downs, *Inside Bureaucracy* (Boston: Little, Brown & Company, 1967), pp. 231–33.

Because they see a connection between their own political lives and bureaucratic activity, legislators have a compelling reason to oversee the bureaucracy. Reelection, advancement to higher office, and the general prestige of legislators may depend as much on the announcing of contracts, the awarding of defense plants, the building of veterans' hospitals, or the successful intervention on behalf of constituents as on their voting records. The political lives of the legislator and of the bureaucrat are far from isolated. Yet the legislature finds it difficult to compete with the bureaucracy. Available time, limited experience, and a lack of expertise stand in the way.

Legislative oversight of administration takes many forms in practice. Although the legislature finds it difficult to create programs, it can debate, amend, and criticize programs suggested by the executive. Although the legislature is usually unable to implement the programs which it approves, it can find ways to affect that implementation. Although Congress, as a body, seems unable to understand the details of missile policy, a few of its members can, and all of them see the impact of awarding contracts to their home districts.[13] Although the legislature cannot understand the details of complex scientific research, it can keep bureaucracy on the defensive by publicizing expenditures for research on such superficially trivial topics as senility in salmon. Although the legislature seems unlikely to solve problems of employment, it can irritate the bureaucrats through investigations.

The inadequacies of legislators are often those of top executives as well. Hence both groups stress the high relevance to decision-making of intelligence, diligence, and that elusive quality labeled political skill. On these revised grounds, legislators feel, rightly or wrongly, that they possess the necessary credentials for oversight of the bureaucracy.

Techniques of Legislative Oversight: An Overview

With rare exception, legislative oversight of administration, at least in Congress, follows well-established patterns: a myriad of potential controls over policy, personnel, structure, and expenditures exists. Legislators make decisions about using these controls in the context of the same factors that shape executive involvement in the legislative process. Societal factors, legal structures and procedures, partisan relationships, and personal and interpersonal aspects define the environment. These factors emerge in concrete questions. Is the country at war? Does the same political party control both Congress and the presidency? Are the president and the Speaker of the House at personal and political logger-heads?

In law, the techniques for oversight apply potentially to all executive acts. In fact, bureaucratic activity is too vast for total legislative control. Choices have to be made concerning which techniques of control will be applied to which executive agencies, how often, with how much perseverance, and by whom. As Roland Young so trenchantly observes, "the impor-

---

13 In 1963, during the dispute over the awarding of the contract for the so-called TFX warplane, Secretary of the Air Force Eugene Zuckert listed twelve members of Congress who had contacted him about the contract during the negotiations. *New York Times,* August 8, 1963, p. 2.

tant question concerns the issues which are decided and the best procedure for raising these issues."[14] Congress is not organized to provide a coordinated mechanism of choice. In effect, then, such decisions will come from committees, their chairmen, and individual congressmen.[15] Accordingly, the accident and luck of politics, personality, and seniority are crucial in the process of choice. Oversight inevitably will be partial and selective. How and in what areas is it carried out? What techniques are available? How do they work in practice? What circumstances seem central in determining whether techniques are successfully applied? To these questions we now turn our attention.

Ultimately, legislative oversight is linked to the legislature's concern with public policy. More specifically, however, oversight manifests itself in four related but identifiable areas: (1) direct concern with the substance of policy itself, (2) the personnel who implement policy, (3) the structure through which policy is applied, and (4) the expenditure of public funds.

Oversight and Policy

The complexity of the issues to be resolved sometimes forces legislatures to draft bills in highly generalized language. Legislators presume that when more specific rules are needed, they can be formulated within the bureaucracy. Accordingly, legislation is regularly fashioned around such terms as "the public interest," "fair standards," and "reasonable regulations."[16] The frequent use of such imprecise standards suggests that when legislative bodies confront complex and difficult policy conflicts, they shift the burden of more precise definition to bureaucrats who are confronted by concrete problems. Legislatures thus escape the problem of definition but, at the same time, create opportunities for the exercise of administrative discretion. Since such rule-making involves heavy policy overtones, legislative interest in its substance should not be too surprising.

Although Congress has been involved in policy oversight from early in American history, its concern was mainly intermittent. Joseph Cooper records the change:

> The emergence and acceptance of the notion of continuous oversight in the 1940's represented a distinct break with past tradition, though this was

[14] Roland Young, *The American Congress* (New York: Harper & Row, Publishers, 1958), p. 227.

[15] See Seymour Scher, "Conditions For Legislative Control," *Journal of Politics,* XXV (August 1963), 526–51; Ira Sharkansky, "An Appropriations Subcommittee and Its Client Agencies," *American Political Science Review,* LIX (September 1965), 622–28; John Bibby, "Committee Characteristics and Legislative Oversight of Administration," *Midwest Journal of Political Science,* X, (February 1966), 78–98.

[16] For excellent examples, see Charles A. Reich, *Bureaucracy and the Forests* (Santa Barbara, Calif.: Center for the Study of Democratic Institutions, 1962), pp. 3ff. For striking examples in the area of defense policy, see Bernard K. Gordon, "The Military Budget: Congressional Phase," *Journal of Politics,* XXIII (November 1961), 691–92.

largely obscured by the plasticity of doctrine and a century of erosion in strict interpretation of the separation of powers principle.[17]

Formal, legal recognition of such interest in Congress came as a part of the Legislative Reorganization Act of 1946, which stipulated that each committee should exercise "continuous watchfulness" over the activities of those administrative units acting within the subject matter jurisdiction of that committee.

The Legislative Reorganization Act of 1970 reiterated this concern:

> Each standing committee shall review and study, on a continuing basis, the application, administration, and execution of those laws, or parts of laws, the subject matter of which is within the jurisdiction of that committee.

The complaints of individuals and groups may stir the legislature to a concern over the application of administrative policy. The legislature may hear that a law is too harsh, that it is being improperly interpreted, or simply that constituents need relief from the demands of the law. Such complaints arise from organized interests as described in Chapter 10, but also from individuals. In February 1963 an airman wrote to Senator Jacob Javits (R., N.Y.) protesting against an air force questionnaire which, among other questions, asked, "Are you a member of an interracial marriage?" The Air Force dropped the question from the form after several protests from Senator Javits.[18]

Congressional oversight is sometimes exercised as a part of a desire to note and record deficiencies in current policy and to recommend appropriate corrective legislation. Oversight is also used from time to time to propose that the executive branch reconsider and perhaps redraw its policies. Samuel P. Huntington generalizes that "congressional challenges to policy . . . at least force the Administration to confront the issue again and to articulate a defense of its course."[19] An apt illustration came when President Truman fired General MacArthur during the Korean War. The Senate Committees on Armed Services and Foreign Relations held joint hearings to air the accompanying dispute.[20] No mere fact-finding effort, these hearings, impressive in their bulk, were viewed by some senators as a vehicle for putting pressure on the executive branch to defend its foreign policy.

More recently, partly as a result of perceived disasters arising from United States involvement in Vietnam in the 1960s, congressional commit-

---

[17] Joseph Cooper, *The Origins of the Standing Committees and the Development of the Modern House of Representatives* (Houston: Rice University Monographs in Political Science, 1970), p. 107.

[18] This incident is reported in the *New York Times,* July 3, 1963, p. 12. For a discussion of some relationships between casework and oversight, see Kenneth G. Olson, "The Service Function of the United States Congress," in *Congress: The First Branch of Government,* ed. Alfred de Grazia (Washington: American Enterprise Institute for Public Policy Research, 1966), pp. 369–71. See also, Dale Vinyard, "Congressmen as Washington Agents for Constituents," *Business and Government Review,* VIII (September–October 1967), 19–25.

[19] *The Common Defense* (New York: Columbia University Press, 1961), p. 146.

[20] *The Military Situation in the Far East,* 82d Cong., 1st sess., 1951.

tees have probed government policies in Southeast Asia and have extended their surveillance to defense policy areas seldom investigated previously with such seriousness. The desire for oversight is increased as bureaucrats make decisions unpopular with segments of Congress.

Overall, the record of expenditures for congressional investigations indicates that the trend is upward. In 1955–56, standing committees in Congress spent over $6 million for investigations; by 1967–68, the figure was near $21 million.

Finally, legislative bodies can exercise a sort of policy "preoversight" by writing detailed prescriptions into the statutes themselves. It is not always possible to predict when Congress will write extensively detailed statutes. In this respect, Professor Hyneman offers the suggestion:

> In the initial period of regulation, Congress is forced to abdicate to the administrator for the extension of policy beyond the statement of general purposes. As time passes and administrative experience is examined, Congress is able to incorporate into statute the policies formulated and pursued by the administrative department.[21]

Controls Over Personnel: Selection, Conduct, Removal

Legislative oversight is exercised secondly through controls over personnel. From a constitutional standpoint, legislative interest in the personnel of government and their conduct stems from the requirement that certain executive appointees be confirmed by the Senate, that the House shall impeach and the Senate shall try civil officers of the United States.[22] More immediately, from the political standpoint, legislative interest derives from the realization that, while the words "personnel" and "policy" may be etymologically separate, they are politically inseparable. Who applies a policy may be just as significant as what the policy provides, especially when policy is set down in general terms. Legislative anxiety over the personnel of the executive branch centers on three aspects of personnel policy—the appointment, conduct, and removal of office holders.

SELECTION

National and state government bureaucrats are selected in accordance with statutory provisions which sometimes detail large parts of the selection process.[23] A substantial proportion of national bureaucrats are chosen in accordance with the examination and rating practices charted in the rules of merit systems. But wherever the "rule of three" operates—selections are made from among the top three scorers on a roster of eligibles—choices

---

[21] Charles S. Hyneman, *Bureaucracy in a Democracy* (New York: Harper & Row, Publishers, 1950), pp. 88–89.

[22] Article I, Sections 2, 3; Article II, Section 4.

[23] For example, veterans are awarded special advantages. See the Veterans' Preference Act of 1944. On veterans' preference generally see O. Glenn Stahl, *Public Personnel Administration,* 5th ed. (New York: Harper & Row, Publishers, 1962), pp. 90–100. On loyalty oaths, see Ralph S. Brown, Jr., *Loyalty and Security* (New Haven: Yale University Press, 1958).

414   must be made, and the doors to legislative influence are at least ajar if not wide open.

More formally, the U.S. Senate each year is called upon to give its advice and consent to thousands of executive nominations and candidates for promotion. Almost all such nominees are approved in routine fashion.[24] That so few are considered at length and that even fewer are rejected masks as much as it reveals. Quantitatively, most of these cases involve military and foreign-service appointments and promotions. Except for an occasional squabble over whether a movie star should receive a military promotion, such proceedings personify the perfunctory. Data on the experience with nominations from 1946 to 1970 is provided in Table 12.1.

More attention is usually given to the appointment of ambassadors and members of the president's cabinet, but here also confirmation is generally the rule. Only eight presidential nominees for cabinet positions have been rejected outright by the Senate—only two of these in the twentieth century.[25] The price of confirmation is sometimes high: the Reconstruction Finance Commission, for example, was removed from the jurisdiction of the Department of Commerce before former Vice-President Henry A. Wallace, considered by some senators to be a fuzzy-thinking radical, was confirmed for the post of secretary. At times in American history the Senate has confused the words *advise and consent* with the word *control*. Professor Binkley reports: "To the amazement of these senators [President] Hayes prepared his own list of Cabinet nominations in utter disregard of their wishes.... President Hayes had embarrassed these senators by the sheer fitness of his nominees."[26]

The nomination of an ambassador may produce acrimonious debate, often with partisan and ideological overtones.[27] In 1959, when President Eisenhower nominated Clare Boothe Luce to be ambassador to Brazil, the Democratic members of the Senate Foreign Relations Committee questioned her intensively concerning statements which she had allegedly made. One such statement was: "For twenty years mortal enemies of ours [the U.S.] have been growing and thriving in the organism of the Democratic Party."[28] Eventually Mrs. Luce was confirmed, but partly as a result of these hearings she resigned from office.

American history is only speckled with instances when ambassadorial nominees have not been confirmed.[29] But Senate reactions to nominees

---

24 Senator Monroney (D., Okla.) noted in June 1952, that 100 appointments to postmasterships has been approved in committee in thirty seconds. Joseph P. Harris, *The Advice and Consent of the Senate* (Berkeley: University of California Press, 1953), p. 355.

25 *Ibid.,* p. 259, notes seven rejections. Subsequent to the publication of the Harris study, the Senate in 1958 disapproved the nomination of Lewis L. Strauss to be secretary of commerce.

26 Wilfred E. Binkley, *President and Congress* (New York: Vintage Books, 1962), p. 188.

27 Harris, *op. cit.,* Chapter 16. See also James N. Rosenau, *The Nomination of "Chip" Bohlen* (New York: McGraw-Hill Book Company, Inc., Eagleton Institute Case Studies in Practical Politics, 1962).

28 U.S. Senate, Committee on Foreign Relations, *Nomination of Clare Booth Luce,* Hearings, 86th Cong., 1st sess., April 15, 1959, p. 6. For similar statements, see p. 24 and *passim.*

29 For a brief sketch, see Richard W. Leopold, *The Growth of American Foreign Policy* (New York: Alfred A. Knopf, Inc., 1962), pp. 69–71.

TABLE 12.1

The Record of Presidential Nominations, 1947–70

	Total Nominations	Rejected	Withdrawn	Unconfirmed	Confirmed
1947	40,557	0	132	570	39,855
1948	26,084	0	21	11,122	14,941
1949	55,311	2	39	401	54,869
1950	31,955	4	6	252	31,693
1951	26,284	2	40	173	26,069
1952	20,636	0	5	196	20,435
Truman	200,827	8	243	12,714	187,862
1953	23,542	0	31	91	23,420
1954	45,916	0	12	761	45,143
1955	40,686	3	15	771	39,897
1956	43,487	0	23	667	42,797
1957	45,114	0	33	461	44,620
1958	59,079	0	21	367	58,691
1959	46,934	1	8	553	46,372
1960	44,542	0	22	992	43,528
Eisenhower	349,300	4	165	4,663	344,468
1961	50,770	0	1,271	538	48,961
1962	52,079	0	8	291	51,780
1963	67,456	0	21	832	66,603
Kennedy	170,305	0	1,300	1,661	167,344
1964	54,734	0	15	1,121	53,598
1965	55,765	0	13	1,176	54,576
1966	67,254	0	160	805	66,289
1967	69,254	0	19	153	69,082
1968	50,977	0	15	1,813	49,149
Johnson	297,984	0	222	5,068	292,694
1969	73,159	1	477	46	72,635
1970	61,305	1	10	132	61,162
Nixon	134,464	2	487	178	133,797

SOURCES: *Congress and the Nation* (Washington: Congressional Quarterly, Inc., 1965), p. 102a, as supplemented by the *Congressional Record*'s "Daily Digest" for the appropriate years.

are a good warning to the administration that it should heed the quality of its future appointments. In 1957 President Eisenhower nominated businessman Maxwell Gluck to be ambassador to Ceylon; superficially, his only major qualification seemed to be that he had donated more than $26,000 to Republican campaign efforts.[30] The confirmation proceedings demonstrated that, whatever Mr. Gluck's other talents, he was far from knowledgeable about Ceylon. The hearings fortified the view of some senators that ambassadors should be appointed from the ranks of professional foreign-service officers.

If proceedings in the Senate on ambassadorial and cabinet appointees

---

[30] Alexander Heard, *The Costs of Democracy* (Garden City, N.Y.: Doubleday & Company, Inc., Anchor Books, 1962), pp. 128–29.

416 sometimes seem tinted with partisan or ideological conflict, confirmation proceedings involving a job to be filled within a state can provide an occasion for truly fierce political struggles. Senators try to bolster their own political fortunes by influencing nominations to such positions, e.g., judgeships for the federal district courts. Here the practice of senatorial courtesy —nowhere mentioned in the Constitution but enshrined in U.S. Senate practice—comes into play.[31] Briefly, senatorial courtesy may be defined as the practice of the U.S. Senate in accepting the veto of the senators of the same political party as the president for an appointment in the senator's home state. When an appointment is made to such a position and sent to the Senate to be confirmed, if a senator of the president's party rises and objects to the nomination, the Senate, as a whole, will usually vote it down, regardless of the experience and competence of the nominee. Realizing this, an astute president will clear relevant appointments with appropriate senators. The record of few Senate rejections is primarily evidence not of senatorial submission to executive choice but rather of an extensive system of prior clearance.[32]

Legislative influence over appointments in the states is so varied as almost to defy description. Statutory restrictions, confirmation requirements, and investigations are the relevant techniques. Over half of the states have extensive systems of merit appointments, which serve to limit direct legislative influence on appointments. A few states use merit systems only because they take part in federal grant-in-aid programs in which this is required. The particular pattern through which patronage is dispensed in each state will determine the extent to which legislators can influence the job-selection process.

Legislative influence in the appointment process is partly a matter of interest in policy and partly a matter of political promotion and survival. Perhaps the most obvious and spectacular examples in the twentieth century of legislators taking an interest in personnel appointments came during the escapades in the early 1950s of Senator Joseph McCarthy, who extended his influence to the point described by analyst Richard Rovere:

> The President shared with McCarthy the command of many parts of the government.... In the first few months of 1953, three heads of the International Information Administration came and went because McCarthy wished it so.... McCarthy [in fact] appointed Scott McLeod as the State Department's Personnel and Security Officer; and in the early days it was

---

31 Congressman Leonard Farbstein (D., N.Y.) attempted in 1965 to extend this doctrine to one of "congressional courtesy": "One would think that when people were appointed from my district, I'd be given the courtesy of awareness so I wouldn't have to learn about it from the grapevine. It's simple congressional courtesy." *New York Times,* June 17, 1965, p. 21.

32 For an interesting and detailed history, see D. G. Fowler, "Congressional Dictation of Local Appointments," *Journal of Politics,* VII (February 1945), 25–57. Leonard White (*op. cit.,* p. 83) asserts that at the close of John Adams's administration consultation with members of Congress over appointments was a well-established pattern. A fascinating account of the informal dimension of congressional influence on appointments is Rowland Evans and Robert Novak, "The Yarmolinsky Affair," *Esquire* (February 1945), pp. 80ff. For a similar analysis see "The Olsen Affair," *Time,* September 14, 1970, p. 17.

pretty much of a tossup as to whether Dulles [the Secretary of State] or McLeod...had more influence in departmental affairs.[33]

Whatever the technique of oversight, the recurring question remains: Does legislative participation in the appointment process stimulate administrative responsibility? John D. Millett asserts somewhat ruefully, "No reliable information is available on this subject."[34]

CONTROL OF ADMINISTRATIVE CONDUCT

Legislative bodies are concerned with the rules under which bureaucrats are appointed as well as with the individuals who gain these posts. Once men are appointed, legislative attention comes to focus on the conduct of bureaucrats. Laws and resolutions are passed regarding advancement and promotions, creating codes of ethics, formulating rules about disclosure of information, and delegating power to executive agencies to prescribe rules of administrative conduct. Beyond such everyday statutes, legislative bodies attempt to regulate subversive activities, to limit partisan political activity of bureaucrats, and to guard against conflicts of interest. If such statutes are the staples of legislative oversight of bureaucratic conduct, investigations, routine and spectacular, provide the spice of the legislative diet. Legislative forays in quest of peculations and the peculators, inefficiency and the inefficient, subversion and the subversives are characteristic aspects of legislative oversight.

Political participation. Beyond efficiency and general honesty, several aspects of the conduct of personnel have received unusual attention among legislators. One problem has concerned the political participation of bureaucrats. Restrictions on the political activity of some federal officials preceded the famous Pendleton Civil Service Act of 1883. The continuing congressional concern with political activity is a concomitant of the extension of merit systems in the federal bureaucracy.[35]

Early legislative ventures in this area were aimed at prohibiting political assessment of bureaucrats.[36] As the idea became well established that more and more federal bureaucrats should be fired, hired, and promoted through civil service or other merit procedures, legislators took a greater interest in shielding bureaucrats against political pressures. In 1939 the Hatch act extended the restrictions on political activity to include all federal employees except top policy-making officials; previously, only classified employees were subject to such restrictions. The Hatch act of the following year specifically adopted the political activity rules of the Civil Service Commission. The second Hatch act also applied these rules to state employees working in agencies financed wholly or in part by federal funds.[37]

[33] Richard H. Rovere, *Senator Joe McCarthy* (New York: Harcourt, Brace & World, Inc., 1960), p. 32.

[34] *Government and Public Administration* (New York: McGraw-Hill Book Company, Inc., 1959), p. 223.

[35] Herbert W. Cornell, "Legal Restraints on Political Activity of Public Employees," *Public Management*, XXIX (July 1947), 190.

[36] H. Eliot Kaplan, "Political Neutrality of the Civil Service," *Public Personnel Review*, I (April 1940), 12.

[37] Stahl, *op. cit.*, p. 368.

The passage of the Hatch acts by Congress provides an excellent example of the link between politics and administration in legislative oversight. In part, of course, these acts represent a sincere desire to protect government employees from being coerced by the party in power to contribute their energy and money to that party's campaign efforts. However, the fact that state and local political machines would be strengthened because of the removal of federal employees from politics was not lost on members of Congress.[38]

Conflict of interest. Restrictions on the political activities of bureaucrats are designed in part to separate partisan politics from administration. Other statutes, commonly called conflict-of-interest laws, are designed to separate the private economic gain of the bureaucrat from his administrative duties.[39]

Concern over the possible confusion of public and private interests is as old as political science itself. For Plato, the solution was to remove the possibility of such conflict by withdrawing private wives, children, and property from his philosopher-kings. In our society, less extreme measures have been adopted. At the national level, seven leading statutes on this subject cover the following areas of conduct:

> Five of the seven provisions forbid officials to assist outsiders in their dealings with the government; one requires officials to disqualify themselves from acting in government matters in which they have a conflicting personal economic interest; and one prohibits outside pay for government work.[40]

Most of this legislation was conceived not as part of a theoretical, rational attempt to deal with the problems but in specific response to the abuses mentioned therein:

> It was an environment [1850s–1860s] of actual fraudulent claims, sale of information. . ., overt sale of influence, improper diversion of public funds, corruption in public office, and wartime contract frauds and favoritism.[41]

Earlier in American history, when government did fewer things, spent less money, and reached fewer sectors of society, a public-private distinction evidenced a modicum of realism. In mid-twentieth century, when the impact of government is so pervasive, this distinction becomes far less clear. The profundity of this problem, as well as contemporary congressional difficulties in dealing with it, is exemplified clearly in the circumstances surrounding the appointment and confirmation of Charles E. Wilson as secretary of defense by President Eisenhower.

In 1953, when Eisenhower assumed the presidency, his intention was to seek the best business talent of the country to advise him. Viewing the

---

[38] V. O. Key, Jr., "The Hatch Act Extension and Federal-State Relations," *Public Personnel Review,* I (October 1940), 31.

[39] An excellent study of the problem of conflict of interest is the Association of the Bar of the City of New York, *Conflict of Interest and Federal Service* (Cambridge: Harvard University Press, 1960). The following section leans heavily on this work.

[40] *Ibid.,* pp. 28–29.

[41] *Ibid.,* p. 36.

Department of Defense as a citadel of complexity, President Eisenhower nominated as secretary Charles E. Wilson, president of General Motors, the country's largest corporation. A disturbing fact to many was that General Motors was the government's largest single defense contractor. Would Wilson, then, as secretary of defense, function in the public interest or in the interest of General Motors? Rejecting Wilson's equation of these two interests—"what was good for our country was good for General Motors, and vice versa"[42]—a majority of the Senate Armed Services Committee, in the course of confirmation hearings, assumed the position that Wilson must divest himself of his General Motors stock before the committee could recommend his confirmation. Somehow, the committee apparently thought, Wilson's life's labor in General Motors would be set aside if he sold his stock. What is admittedly a profound problem was settled by a simple and superficially satisfactory example of congressional diligence. C. Wright Mills calls this performance "a purifying ritual,"[43] implying that the congressional action made people feel good but that not much had really been accomplished. Mills' judgment is one that is widely shared.[44]

Legislative oversight of conflict of interest is more productive in simpler cases. When Harold Talbott was discovered in 1955 to be seeking business for his firm in letters written while he was secretary of the air force, he resigned. Despite a few obvious cases, the problem of conflict of interest seems destined to become more intense. By and large, top governmental executives are recruited from selected segments of the business and professional communities. As government becomes more and more involved in defense and research contracts and associated with universities and research associations, the task of attracting suitable top-level administrators not affected by conflict-of-interest problems becomes ever more difficult.[45]

At the national level the problems of conflict of interest are profound, and solutions have been scarce. At the state level, conflict of interest is rarely even recognized as a problem serious enough to require legislative attention. Only a few states have adopted conflict-of-interest laws.[46] In many states, funeral directors enforce legislation for themselves, as do doctors, dentists, beauticians, and many others.

Loyalty. A third area of executive conduct, which at times has been of intense interest to legislators involves loyalty or disloyalty of bureaucrats. This is an old problem, going back at least as far as the Civil War. In

[42] *Hearings Before the Senate Committee on Armed Services on the Nomination of Charles E. Wilson et al.,* 83d Cong., 1st sess., 1953, p. 26.

[43] Mills, *op. cit.,* p. 285. A useful work on symbols in politics is Murray Edelman, *The Symbolic Uses of Politics* (Urbana: University of Illinois Press, 1964).

[44] NYC Bar Association, *op. cit.,* p. 108. For additional case studies on this problem see *ibid.,* Chapter 5.

[45] On the recruitment of officials for the executive branch, see W. L. Warner, P. P. VanRiper, W. H. Martin, and O. F. Collins, *The American Federal Executive* (New Haven: Yale University Press, 1963). See also Dean Mann and Jameson Doig, *The Assistant Secretaries* (Washington: The Brookings Institution, 1965); David T. Stanley, with Dean Mann and Jameson Doig, *Men Who Govern* (Washington: The Brookings Institution, 1967).

[46] Ralph Eisenberg, "Conflicts of Interest Situations and Remedies," *Rutgers Law Review,* XIII (Summer 1959), 677. Modest evidence of increased concern in the states is found in the actions of state legislatures in 1967. See *State Legislatures Progress Reporter,* June–July, 1967, p. 3.

general, periods of major international crisis produce legislative agitation over the loyalty of bureaucrats. With normalcy, such interest tends to recede.

Harold Hyman records the adventures of Congressman John Fox Potter, who, in July of 1861, convinced the House of Representatives to create an investigating committee to unearth disloyal bureaucrats.[47] After being named chairman, Potter roamed far and wide collecting hearsay evidence, planting informers in executive departments, and forwarding such information as he received to executive officials, expecting that they would discharge employees cited as disloyal. Potter's informers delivered choice items—e.g., the wife of a revenue officer was addicted to embroidering her lingerie with Jefferson Davis's image. Not only did Potter search out disloyalty, but he sometimes followed up his reports with recommendations for worthy replacements.

In recent years, legislatures have attempted to meet the problem of disloyalty by adopting laws to require loyalty oaths of bureaucrats and by granting extensive power to the chief executive or the Civil Service Commission to set rules of conduct. Some states have conducted vigorous investigations of "subversive activities."

If legislative investigations rarely uncover disloyal bureaucrats, they do, at times, stimulate executive action. President Truman's executive order no. 9835 of March 21, 1947, creating a comprehensive loyalty program, was surely prompted in part by the work of congressional committees as well as by the threat of harsher legislative action.[48] In a speech in 1963, Congressman Willis, chairman of the House Un-American Activities Committee, reported that as a result of his committee's labors, the National Security Agency had made twenty-two reforms in security personnel practices.[49]

Legislative investigations of bureaucratic loyalty have produced much publicity, occasional corrective legislation, and a variety of actions by the executive. There is no doubt that, at times, they have also disrupted bureaucratic efficiency. Richard Rovere, for example, writes of the work in the early 1950s of Senator Joseph McCarthy's Permanent Investigations Subcommittee of the Government Operations Committee and of its then famous staff members, Roy Cohn and G. David Schine:

> By the time Cohn and Schine and McCarthy and the television cameras were through, they had toppled most of the Voice [of America] leadership, forced the administration to disown it, sown despair and confusion throughout the ranks, and scandalized a good many foreigners who had been in the habit of listening to it.[50]

Legislative investigations for executive disloyalty do not provide the best examples of diligent, productive legislative oversight; they do, however,

---

[47] Harold Hyman, *To Try Men's Souls* (Berkeley: University of California Press, 1959), pp. 156–64.

[48] Alan Barth, *The Loyalty of Free Men* (New York: Pocket Books, Inc., 1952), p. 106; Stahl, *op. cit.,* p. 352.

[49] "The Committee and National Security," Speech reprinted in *Congressional Record—Appendix,* 88th Cong., 1st sess., July 31, 1963, p. A4884. (Daily edition.)

[50] Rovere, *op. cit.,* p. 198.

provide fascinating case studies of the strengths and weaknesses of legislative oversight.

REMOVAL OF BUREAUCRATS

Legislative concern with the conduct of executive officials leads in extreme cases to questions of removal. Here, as in other areas of legislative oversight, the impact of legislative bodies has both a formal and informal aspect.

The most potent legal power of removal that Congress possesses is that of impeachment. Article I of the Constitution provides that the House "shall have the sole power of impeachment," and that the Senate "shall have the sole power to try all impeachments." A two-thirds vote of those senators present is required to convict. Subject to impeachment, according to Article II, are the president, vice-president, and all civil officers of the United States. Impeachment proceedings may be brought only on charges of "treason, bribery, or other high crimes and misdemeanors." This powerful tool has been used only twelve times in American history and only twice in cases involving the executive branch. President Andrew Johnson was acquitted; President Grant's secretary of war, William Belknap, resigned after formal charges had been brought against him. Despite his resignation, the Senate placed him on trial, but a two-thirds vote could not be mustered for conviction.[51] The impeachment weapon is simply too strong to use in the everyday process of legislative oversight; its regular use might be equated with dropping atomic bombs to erase the daily traffic snarls so characteristic of contemporary urban life.

The excessive power of impeachment is seen at the state level as well. "In all of the states except Oregon the Governor may be removed from office by a procedure which is generally similar in form to that used in the national government."[52] Despite the widespread availability of this power in the states, Ransone reports that only four governors have been convicted through the impeachment process in approximately the last ninety years.[53] Ransone speculates that impeachment may be most significant for its deterrent effects—it may give pause to a governor.[54]

Legislation itself may be a vehicle for removing unwanted bureaucrats. A staple provision in legislative statutes is that removals are to "promote the efficiency of the service."[55] Laws may make it especially difficult to remove bureaucrats who are also veterans.[56] If these provisions about removal have been sanctified by tradition, other types of statutory enactments, while used, seem less strongly supported. One technique, described by John Millett, is for the legislature to "reduce the appropriation of an agency and let it be known that the reason is the presence of a disliked administrative officer."

[51] For details, see White, *The Republican Era* (New York: The Macmillan Company, 1958), pp. 368–69.

[52] Coleman B. Ransone, Jr., *The Office of the Governor in the United States* (University: University of Alabama Press, 1956), p. 369.

[53] *Ibid.,* lists these instances on p. 369, footnote 2.

[54] *Ibid.,* p. 370.

[55] Stahl, *op. cit.,* p. 376, provides examples of the phraseology in various states.

[56] *Ibid.*

422 Another technique is to "pass a law abolishing a particular bureau or office."[57]

Probably the most direct effort to remove executive officials through statute came in 1943 when "Congress named three...individuals in an appropriation bill and specified that the money appropriated should not be used to pay any part of their salaries."[58] In a subsequent legal proceeding, the Supreme Court ruled in the case of *U.S.* v. *Lovett* (1946) that such legislative action constituted a bill of attainder (direct legislative punishment of individuals), and hence was contrary to Article I, Section 9, of the United States Constitution.[59]

The constitutional power to impeach provides Congress with the legal justification to seek out wrongdoing. Partisan and policy differences, as well as personal clashes, also stimulate such congressional activity. To be effective, Congress does not need to act directly. Thus, Senate pressure on President Grant led him to ask his attorney general to resign.[60] Congressional committees during the Eisenhower administration had similar successes when their investigations spotlighted evidence that forced the resignation of officials such as Harold Talbott, secretary of the air force; Hugh Cross, chairman of the Interstate Commerce Commission; Peter Strobel, public buildings commissioner; Robert Ross, assistant secretary of defense; and Sherman Adams, assistant to the president.[61]

Controlling the Decision-Making Structure

Legislative oversight is promoted through determining the administrative structure as well as through concern with personnel and policy. Proponents of a combined Department of Health, Education and Welfare believed that creating this department would heighten attention to problems within its jurisdiction. Congress was intensely concerned in 1962 about creating a Department of Urban Affairs. Arguments about whether a separate department should exist masked clear policy differences among the protagonists. Warner R. Schilling captures the intimate links between policy and structure:

The "best" organization is that which distributes power and responsibility in

---

57 John D. Millett, *Government and Public Administration* (New York: McGraw-Hill Book Company, Inc.), p. 226.

58 Hyneman, *op. cit.,* p. 199. Equally blatant was the Tenure of Office Act of 1867, which provided that appointments subject to Senate confirmation could only be terminated with the approval of the Senate.

59 For a detailed description and analysis, see Robert E. Cushman, "The Purge of Federal Employees Accused of Disloyalty," *Public Administration Review,* III (Autumn 1943), 297–316, and F. L. Schuman, "Bill of Attainder in the Seventy-Eighth Congress," *American Political Science Review,* XXXVII (October 1943), 819–37.

60 Binkley, *op. cit.,* p. 183.

61 For excellent capsule accounts see NYC Bar Association, *op. cit.,* pp. 125–29.

such a fashion as to facilitate the policies you favor and make difficult the policies you oppose.[62]

The concern of Congress ultimately is with policy, not structure, so congressional attention tends to stray from formal structure to the actual structures through which decisions are made. Increasingly, Congress tries to insert itself or its committees into the decision-making structure by requiring regular reports and by use of the legislative veto. Congress seldom acts so directly as in 1962, when it passed the Trade Expansion Act with a provision requiring that two members of the House Ways and Means Committee and two members of the Senate Finance Committee participate in tariff bargaining sessions.[63]

REPORTS

Requiring a report is hardly identical to direct legislative intrusion in the decision-making process. Yet, indirectly, this requirement confers a meaningful addition to legislative oversight.[64] The traditional annual reports from the executive departments are now supplemented by literally hundreds of reports each year. Many of these documents remain undigested and perhaps even unread by members of Congress, but they do provide a potential source of information for congressmen, as well as an opportunity for legislative oversight. The regular written reports which form the grist of the governmental process are supplemented by scores of executive officials trooping before congressional committees to testify.[65] Apparently the barrage of information aimed at congressmen is not deemed sufficient by some, since proposals arise from time to time to schedule formal question periods, at which time members of the president's cabinet would appear before Congress to be questioned about the activities of their departments. Hundreds of such proposals have been made but none implemented at the national level.[66] This fact speaks as loudly, perhaps, as reams of analysis about the desirability of such a plan.[67]

[62] Warner R. Shilling, Paul Y. Hammond, and Glenn H. Snyder, *Strategy, Politics, and Defense Budgets* (New York: Columbia University Press, 1962), p. 230.

[63] See the analysis by Harry G. Brainard, "The Trade Expansion Act—1962," *Business Topics,* XI (Winter 1963), 7–19.

[64] J. Malcolm Smith and Cornelius P. Cotter, "Administrative Accountability: Reporting to Congress," *Western Political Quarterly,* X (June 1957), 405–15.

[65] The question should be raised as to whether some of this time might be more appropriately spent in supervising subordinates, etc. In 1961 Secretary of State Dean Rusk made twenty-nine appearances before congressional committees. In 1962 he made twenty-five. Secretary of Defense Robert McNamara spent nearly ninety hours in 1961 testifying before congressional committees. In 1962 he spent over 114 hours. Hubert Humphrey, "To Move Congress Out of Its Ruts," *New York Times Magazine,* April 7, 1963, p. 132. Dean Acheson estimates that, in four years as secretary of state, he met 214 times with bipartisan groups of congressmen. *A Citizen Looks at Congress* (New York: Harper & Row, Publishers, 1957), p. 65.

[66] In Pennsylvania, the House of Representatives adopted the question period procedure. For details and rules, see *Legislative Research Checklist,* III (June 1961), 2.

[67] For a history of such proposals at the national level, see Stephen Horn, *The Cabinet and Congress* (New York: Columbia University Press, 1960).

TABLE 12.2

Personnel and Total Costs for Congressional Activities, Fiscal Year 1963

Executive Department	Personnel Directly Involved in Congressional Information	Total Congressional Information Costs
State	68	$ 711,373
Treasury	16	155,901
Defense	230	2,409,900
Justice	39	269,987
Post Office	28	374,440
Interior	17	291,079
Agriculture	13	113,685
Commerce	29	280,781
Labor	23	289,500
HEW	37	536,292
Total	500	$5,432,938
Independent Agencies Total	233	$2,336,251
Executive Office of the President Total	4	$ 35,000
Grand Total	737	$7,834,189

SOURCE: Russell Pipe, "Congressional Liaison: The Executive Branch Consolidates its Relations with Congress," *Public Administration Review*, XXVI (March 1966), 17.

An index of activity for the executive branch in responding to congressional requests, both formal and informal, is seen in Table 12.2.

LEGISLATIVE VETO

The "legislative veto" is one of the newer techniques of legislative oversight. Essentially, Congress provides, depending on the situation, for one of the following:

1. Executive proposals lie before Congress for a specific time, e.g., sixty days. If one or both houses of Congress disapprove, the proposal dies. The absence of congressional action signifies that the executive can proceed. The handling of plans to reorganize the executive branch illustrates this technique.
2. The executive presents a proposal which must sit before Congress for a fixed time. The executive can implement the plan after that time period expires. Presumably, if Congress is sufficiently upset in the interim, new legislation can be pushed through or informal pressures can be applied. Requirements regarding the closing of military installations fit this pattern.
3. Executive action proposed to Congress must have the approval of one or both houses of Congress or one or several congressional committees before implementation is possible. Presidents Eisenhower and Johnson

both objected to a congressional committee having this power. President Johnson vetoed several bills containing a provision for a "veto by committee."

What occurs when these or similar devices are used is that Congress projects itself or one of its committees into the administrative decision-making process. Instead of exercising oversight by setting conditions for action in legislation, by checking on past executive activity, or by investigating conduct, Congress assumes a direct role in the process. The necessity for speed, the burdens of complexity, and the barriers of secrecy have contributed to Congress's use of the legislative veto to control the executive.[68]

In his testimony in 1965 before the Joint Committee on the Organization of the Congress, Arthur Maass stated:

> The veto [legislative] is in the Atomic Energy Act, it is in the National Aeronautics and Space Act, in the Small Watershed Act, and one could name another 25 acts in which Congress has used the veto as a new technique of congressional control.[69]

The experience with presidential reorganization plans for the executive branch shows that the legislative veto is more than a potential weapon.

TABLE 12.3

Presidential Reorganization Plans in Congress, 1946–68

Years	President	Total Plans	Plans Rejected
1946–52	Truman	47	14
1953–60	Eisenhower	17	3
1961–63	Kennedy	10	4
1964–68	Johnson	17	1

SOURCES: *Congress And The Nation* (Washington: Congressional Quarterly, Inc., 1965), pp. 1458–70; *Congressional Quarterly Almanac, 1968,* p. 797.

The Power of the Purse: Control over Expenditures

The fourth and final broad area in which legislative bodies exercise oversight is through setting appropriations and then checking on the expenditure of money. Historically, the first wedge that consultative assemblies

[68] For details and analyses of the use of the legislative veto in specific areas, see Cornelius P. Cotter and J. Malcolm Smith, "Administrative Accountability to Congress: The Concurrent Resolution," *Western Political Quarterly,* IX (December 1956), 955–66; Harvey Mansfield, "The Legislative Veto and the Deportation of Aliens," *Public Administration Review,* I (Summer 1941), 281–86; John D. Millett and Lindsay Rogers, "The Legislative Veto and the Reorganization Act of 1939," *Public Administration Review,* I (Winter 1941), 176–89; Joseph Cooper, "The Legislative Veto: Its Promise and Its Perils," in *Public Policy, 1956,* ed. Carl J. Friedrich and Seymour Harris (Cambridge: Harvard University Press, 1957), pp. 128–74; Peter Schauffler, "The Legislative Veto Revisited," in *Public Policy, 1958,* ed. Friedrich and Harris, pp. 296–327; Joseph Cooper, "Schauffler and the Veto," *Public Policy, 1958,* ed. Friedrich and Harris, pp. 328–35.

[69] *Hearings before the Joint Committee on the Organization of the Congress,* June, 1965 (89th Congress, 1st Session), p. 944.

426 used in developing bargaining status with kings was in refusing to assent to new taxes until grievances were settled.[70] The maturing of legislative control over appropriations provides an opportunity, not necessarily used diligently and wisely, to oversee executive activity.[71]

At the state level, review of the budget is "the chief instrument for oversight of the executive branch."[72] Legislative concern with the finances of government manifests itself at two different stages: (1) where a program is formulated and money provided to the executive; (2) after funds are provided, in attempting to ascertain whether appropriated funds are disbursed according to legislative intent. Zeller indicates that "too' often legislative involvement in the budget process ends with the approval of the appropriation bills."[73]

Regarding Congress, the constitutional mandate is clearly established in Article I, Section 9: "No money shall be drawn from the Treasury, but in Consequence of Appropriations made by Law." Congress has, throughout American history, attempted to build a structure of power on this constitutional foundation. The net result often has been dissatisfaction and anxiety concerning control of expenditure, for, as Roland Young points out, policies that are most difficult to control by law are equally difficult to control through appropriations.[74]

Congress has used a variety of structural devices in an attempt to set and control expenditures. The number of standing committees devoted to this task has gone up and down as alternative theories of oversight were adopted.[75]

The post-World War II pattern of legislative oversight emerges from the Legislative Reorganization Act of 1946. In brief, programs arc formulated with amounts of money specified to carry them out. The authorization stage, dominated by the substantive standing committees, sets a ceiling for expenditure. The actual money is provided through appropriations, at which stage the appropriations committees and subcommittees dominate. Thus, four stages are involved: authorization in each house of Congress, and appropriations in each house of Congress. The absence of an overall mechanism for coordination in this multistage process complicates efforts at legislative oversight.

The authorization stage is more important than may be commonly realized. "To a large extent control of expenditures over the long run lies in the area of authorizing legislation, for it is here that new activities get

[70] Herman Finer, *Theory and Practice of Modern Government,* rev. ed. (New York: Holt, Rinehart & Winston, Inc., 1949), pp. 508ff.; Albert F. Pollard, *The Evolution of Parliament* (London: Longmans, Green and Co., Ltd., 1926).

[71] For an example from early American history, see White, *The Federalists,* p. 81. Two fine introductory analyses are found in Arthur W. Macmahon, "Congressional Oversight of Administration: The Power of the Purse," *Political Science Quarterly,* LVIII (June, September 1943).

[72] Belle Zeller, ed., *American State Legislatures* (New York: Thomas Y. Crowell Company, 1954), p. 174.

[73] *Ibid.,* p. 180.

[74] Young, *op. cit.,* p. 234.

[75] For a brief history, see Robert Ash Wallace, *Congressional Control of Federal Spending* (Detroit: Wayne State University Press, 1960), pp. 7–12. For a more extended analysis, see Lucius Wilmerding, Jr., *The Spending Power* (New Haven: Yale University Press, 1943).

their start."[76] Programs once established in legislation create fixed demands over a period of years. As part of an effort at more legislative control, Congress in recent years has moved toward more authorizations limited to one year and hence subject to new inspection annually. Michael W. Kirst indicates the extent of this movement:

> Since World War II there has been a remarkable trend toward short-term authorizations. Indeed over 35 per cent of the money in the President's budget for fiscal 1967 cannot be appropriated until Congress passes authorization bills that last for one year only.[77]

Control efforts at the appropriations stage are somewhat limited since many of the basic decisions have already been made. The authorization, however, is a ceiling and not a mandate. Thus many decisions of consequence remain to be made at the appropriations stage. Foreign-aid appropriations, for example, rarely reach the ceilings authorized.

Congressional control over appropriations is furnished almost entirely by the appropriations committees in each house, and especially by their subcommittees. Subcommittee recommendations are generally accepted quickly by the entire committee, whose recommendations are, in turn, usually accepted by the entire house. Richard Fenno, for example, found that "of the 443 separate case histories of bureau appropriations examined, the House accepted Committee recommendations in 387, or 87.4 per cent of them. . . ."[78]

The overall quality of such oversight varies, of course, from issue to issue, but there is at least sound evidence that as far as the defense budget is concerned, such oversight focuses on assorted details rather than on general priorities and problems. Warner Schilling's analysis of the defense budget for 1950 reaches these conclusions:

> The 3,000 pages of the committee's record not only failed to add anything to the information already developed in the press about the major policy issues

[76] Committee for Economic Development, *Control of Federal Government Expenditures* (1955), p. 6. The relationships between annual authorizations and oversight are probed in Ralph K. Huitt, "Congress, The Durable Partner," in *Lawmakers in a Changing World*, ed. Elke Frank (Englewood Cliffs, N.J.: Prentice-Hall, Inc., 1966), pp. 16–20. For an article indicating the importance of authorizations for oversight see Herbert W. Stephens, "The Role of the Legislative Committees in the Appropriations Process: A Study Focused on the Armed Services Committees," *Western Political Quarterly*, XXIV (March 1971), 146–62.

[77] *Government Without Passing Laws* (Chapel Hill: University of North Carolina Press, 1969), p. 162.

[78] Richard Fenno, "The House Appropriations Committee," *American Political Science Review*, LVI (June 1962), 323. Individual members of Congress can use their key positions in the appropriations process to seek specific gains for their states or districts. Senator McCarran, for example, was able to persuade the executive branch to release funds during World War II for the construction of two small airports in Nevada. The fact that McCarran was chairman of the Senate Appropriations Subcommittee dealing with money for the Civil Aeronautics Administration was not lost on the executive branch. See J. D. Williams, *The Impounding of Funds by the Bureau of the Budget*, Inter-University Case Program Case Series, no. 28 (University: University of Alabama Press, 1955), pp. 21–23. For a more extended discussion of subcommittee-committee-House relations, see Richard Fenno, *The Power of the Purse* (Boston: Little, Brown & Company, 1966).

involved in the budget; the committee's record actually fell far short of containing even that much information.[79]

Schilling writes of the "intellectual poverty of the committee's record." He found that decisions in Congress are made "without any real understanding of the alternatives involved." Committee work did however excel in "development of the alternatives involved in the financial trivia of the budget."[80]

Like other students of the problem, Schilling argues that the inherent complexity of modern defense policy places formidable if not insurmountable barriers in the path of legislative oversight.[81] Immediate and overwhelming crisis diminishes the role of Congress even more. According to former Speaker Sam Rayburn, the House of Representatives appropriated $800 million to develop the atom bomb without even being aware of where the money was going.[82]

According to John C. Donovan, experience in the 1960s confirmed this pattern of modest congressional attention to profound problems and massive expenditures in the defense area.

> Both Houses of Congress failed in their important function of providing an independent review of Executive policies in the 1960's. Congress failed most conspicuously to develop a responsible critique of the nation's military programs. Congress did not evaluate critically the assumptions and concepts of our national security programs largely because the senior men who dominated the Armed Services and Appropriations Committees in both Houses did not see the need to do so. Armed with the power of the purse and the power of investigation, Congress, more than any other national legislature of which I am aware, has the inherent power to provide the independent critique of Executive policies which we must have. What is lacking, thus far, is a political force in the Congress which *perceives* this as a vital Congressional function and which is strong enough to undertake the task.[83]

There was some evidence in the early 1970s of a resurgence of congressional willingness to challenge administration defense programs. The vitality and durability of this challenge is yet to be established.

The record of legislative oversight is somewhat more impressive in matters of domestic policy; this is due partly to the fact that issues are less complex and partly to the greater availability of information. Yet even on domestic policy, one writer asserts with only slight exaggeration that "any bureaucrat worth his salt can win over Congress when it comes to justifying

79 Schilling *et al., op. cit.,* p. 60.

80 *Ibid.,* pp. 60, 79, 92. The long-standing congressional concern with budgetary trivia is reflected in the plaintive appeal of Congressman Sherley, made in 1918 and reprinted in Wilmerding, *op. cit.,* pp. 152–53.

81 For a more complete elaboration of this point, see Schilling *et al., op. cit.,* pp. 10–14ff. For a less pessimistic view, see Edward A. Kolodziej, *The Uncommon Defense and Congress, 1945–1963* (Columbus : Ohio State University Press, 1966).

82 W. B. Ragsdale, "An Old Friend Writes of Sam Rayburn," *U.S. News and World Report,* October 23, 1961, pp. 70 and 72. For a second version of this incident and another example, see Douglass Cater, "The Secret Life of the A-11," *The Reporter,* April 23, 1964, pp. 16–17.

83 *The PolicyMakers* (New York: Pegasus, 1970), pp. 166–67.

his budget."[84] The inherent difficulty of the legislative task is compounded by a fundamental role conflict for some legislators who desire rationality, efficiency, and economy in the abstract, but more expenditures and projects for their state or district in concrete situations.

Congressional oversight through appropriations may be the best that Congress does, but it is not always impressive.[85] All congressional committees have a great deal of help available to them when they want to use it. For example, the General Accounting Office, created by Congress to monitor executive expenditures, has a vast array of personnel and skills for Congress to rely on. Originally concerned largely with technical financial matters, the GAO has shifted its emphasis toward more general review of executive programs.

Here again policy helps shape process. The GAO attempts to be very responsive to congressional requests for help. The unrest in segments of Congress in the late 1960s and early 1970s over defense spending has led to heavier reliance on the GAO for data and analysis that congressmen need to be more effective in oversight activity.[86]

Even this brief analysis suggests that as problems of policy become more complex, especially in that half of the budget that goes for defense, the likelihood of close, effective legislative oversight decreases. Congressmen may become irritated at executive reprograming and shifting of funds from one project to another; they may chafe at the size of emergency and contingent funds over which the executive has sole control, but focusing this frustration in terms of carefully conceived alternatives seems much more difficult for them.[87] Congressman Clarence Brown (R., Ohio) succinctly stated the problem when he noted in May 1963, during congressional discussion of the National Aeronautics and Space Administration budget, that "there seemingly are few Members of the House—and I suspect very few citizens of this country—who know for a certainty whether the amount contained in this bill is the proper one."[88]

Informal Techniques of Oversight

Formal techniques of oversight receive more attention because they are more readily observed. More difficult to assess are the daily informal

[84] Robert Novak, "The Eighty-Eighth: Will It Be Called A Do-Nothing Congress?" *The Reporter,* January 31, 1963, p. 26. Copyright © 1963 The Reporter Magazine Company.

[85] See, for example, the charges made by Congressman Hale Boggs (D., La.) in 1971 about oversight of the FBI. Reprinted in *Congressional Quarterly Weekly Report,* April 30, 1971, p. 963.

[86] The complex status and functions of the General Accounting Office will be clarified with the publication of the thorough and insightful study by Joseph Pois tentatively entitled, "Watchdog on the Potomac."

[87] See Bernard K. Gordon, *Journal of Politics* (November 1961), p. 708. Richard Leopold traces the origin of executive contingent funds apart from the regular diplomatic budget to 1806 (*op. cit.,* p. 72). During a congressional investigation of the awarding of a defense contract in 1963, Secretary of Defense Robert McNamara and Attorney General Robert Kennedy are alleged to have given Senator McClellan a list of questions to ask military leaders. Evidently executive department help is necessary at times to help focus congressional inquiries. Details of this incident are reported in *Time,* April 5, 1963, p. 27.

[88] Quoted in *Congressional Record—Appendix,* 88th Cong., 1st sess., August 6, 1963, p. A5007. (Daily edition.)

430 interactions between executive and legislator which may, in fact, constitute the bulk of oversight activity. In addition, oversight occurs during legislative hearings on bills, in the processing of casework, through comments in committee reports on bills and in other activities not actually called oversight.

What these activities add to the oversight product is not precisely known, but students of Congress generally agree that they do add quite a bit. If the techniques of oversight seem frequently ineffective and often unused, that may be in part because other less visible acts are promoting at least some of the same ends.

The Quest for Rationality and Responsibility

The ostensible goals of legislative oversight are to promote rationality, efficiency, and responsibility in the bureaucracy. Although some legislators have high regard for these goals, they are also concerned with promoting their own careers and causes. Legislators oversee not in terms of abstract functions but in concrete situations where personal motives and broader goals may become hopelessly intermingled. In situations where the inherent complexity of the subject matter tends to frustrate legislative attempts at oversight, the ambivalence of the legislator may manifest itself in ways not dreamed of by dispassionate observers. The end product of oversight is usually a mixture of asset and liability. Legislative scrutiny may serve merely to frustrate conscientious officials, to seek special favors, to promote political careers, and to disrupt carefully conceived executive programs.

Despite the discomforting aspects of legislative oversight, most observers continue rightly to stress the importance of this legislative function. Typical of such opinion is this statement appearing in a metropolitan newspaper: "unless there is a congressional check on the executive branch, executive agencies frequently go hog wild."[89] The empirical evidence in support of such assertions is slim. Their primary value is to raise the fundamental question of how responsibility is to be enforced. Contrary to the editorial, a more reasonable hypothesis is that alternative means to promote responsibility are both possible and practicable.[90] Although writers assign varying importance to specific techniques for promoting responsibility, there is wide consensus that responsibility may be promoted by adhering to organizational rules, by obeying organizational superiors, by following the standards of one's profession, by legislative diligence in lawmaking and oversight, and by acting in accordance with the common values of society.

Legislative bodies, in creating executive structures, personnel policies, and financial policies, provide relevant standards for bureaucratic activity. It is equally clear that alternative means for achieving responsibility may be useful. Far from self-evident, however, is what patterns of legislative behavior can most effectively promote executive responsibility.

Two broad models of executive-legislative relations provide a focus for analysis. The first may be sketched as follows. Legislative bodies should set

[89] *Pittsburgh Press,* February 24, 1963, Section 2, p. 2.
[90] For an inventory of how political scientists have used the word *responsibility,* see Charles E. Gilbert, "The Framework of Administrative Responsibility," *Journal of Politics,* XXI (August 1959), 373–407. See also *Responsibility,* ed., Carl J. Friedrich, *Nomos III* (New York: Liberal Arts Press, 1960).

only broad policy and not interfere with the details of administration. Legislative bodies can represent the interests of society, but neither their structure, organization, personnel, nor practices seem conducive to effective control over details. The chief executive and his top subordinates are viewed, on the other hand, as possessing more potential for success in supervising the bureaucracy. The implications of these propositions are that legislative bodies should set structure, personnel, and fiscal policies only in the broadest sense. Their objective should be to promote centralization of control through the top echelons of the executive branch.[91] Bureaucratic breaches then become the primary responsibility of the chief executive, who can be controlled through elections, impeachment, statutes, or investigations. Other control is exercised through top subordinates, and for their actions the chief executive assumes responsibility. Proponents allege that such a pattern stimulates efficiency and rationality and pinpoints responsibility.

An alternative model looks as follows.[92] A primary task of legislative bodies is to further bureaucratic responsibility. The legislative body must be concerned with all policy—both broad and detailed. Despite the claim of chief executives to superior representative character, the heterogeneity of the nation is best reflected in Congress, that of the state in the state legislature. Accordingly, lines of responsibility ultimately run to the people; since the people are best represented by legislative assemblies, the chief executive cannot be as effective as the legislature in controlling the bureaucracy in the public interest. Indeed, legislative bodies must watch the chief executive himself to insure that responsible government is achieved.

These models place in sharp focus some critical questions: Should Congress or the president be given the responsibility of creating executive units and altering executive structures? Should legislative grants of authority go to the chief executive to be distributed among many subordinates or should such grants go directly to subordinate executive departments, agencies, or even bureaus? Should statutes embodying personnel policy be written in minute detail or should the top executives be allowed to fill in details? Should there be precise, rigidly allocated appropriations for the executive branch or should the executive be empowered with discretion in spending? Should legislators investigate the smallest details of administrative behavior or should investigations generally be directed at broader questions of fundamental policy?

Each of these two approaches can be supported in theory. In practice, this dichotomous approach to the problem of achieving responsibility highlights some crucial problems but obscures others. Circumstances determine which approach to administrative responsibility is used. A continuing bargaining and accommodation process is at work. In legislative-executive struggles, Congress as a whole seldom engages the executive branch as a whole. The more common pattern is for congressional committees and executive bureaus to form alliances against other such combinations or against their respective branches of government as a whole.[93]

---

[91] Stahl, *op. cit.,* pp. 424ff.; Zeller, *op. cit.,* pp. 185–86.

[92] This approach is developed fully in Hyneman, *op. cit.*

[93] The importance of subsystem coalitions and conflicts is now generally acknowledged in studies of executive-legislative relations. For an early analysis and documentation of this theme, see J. Leiper Freeman, *The Political Process* (Garden City, N.Y.: Doubleday & Company, Inc., 1955).

432   The forms that executive-legislative conflicts take can be illustrated briefly through the examination of two of the perennial problems of legislative oversight. The first is executive secrecy. The second concerns which officials of the executive division should testify in congressional hearings and investigations.

EXECUTIVE SECRECY

Problems of executive secrecy arise when Congress asks the executive branch for files and other data which it deems useful in reaching policy decisions. Although the executive branch sends reams of routine data to congressmen and to congressional committees, there are times when, for reasons of administrative efficiency, national security, or even political survival, it declines to comply with congressional requests. The conflicts that arise are usually settled by bargaining and accommodation. In the Washington administration, executive papers were turned over to Congress to satisfy its demands for information on General St. Claire's military defeat, but the executive branch declined to provide information to the House of Representatives concerning the Jay treaty. Thomas Jefferson and John Tyler were among the early presidents who refused to send information to Congress.[94] All of these disputes seem to produce the same charges—one of legislative meddling, the other of executive cover-ups. No conclusive determination seems to result.[95] Each case opens up the problem anew.

The problems became especially acute in the post-World War II era when Congress instituted loyalty-security programs. To increase its effectiveness, Congress steadily sought information presumed to be lodged in executive files; time after time it met rebuff and defeat. In 1948, for example, President Truman ordered all confidential loyalty reports of the FBI and other investigating agencies to be released only on his authority. Again in 1954, President Eisenhower ordered certain types of intraagency documents to be withheld from congressional investigators. Executive explanations for these actions did little to diminish the irritation felt by congressmen. Accommodations continued to be worked out piecemeal. In the dispute over the confirmation of Ambassador Bohlen, Congress was first denied access to Bohlen's personnel files; later, helping to salve matters, Senators Taft and Sparkman were permitted to study these materials.[96] Compromise, rather than the deductive application of pure doctrine, seems to be the governing rule. Such disputes are muddled further by the fact that much executive secrecy is authorized by Congress itself in statutes.[97]

In the 1960s disputes flared over executive secrecy regarding U.S.

---

[94] For more detailed accounts, see Francis E. Rourke, *Secrecy and Publicity* (Baltimore: Johns Hopkins Press, 1961); and Clark Mollenhoff, *Washington Cover-Up* (New York: Popular Library, 1963).

[95] Mollenhoff points out that both individuals and political parties seem to shift their attitudes about governmental secrecy in the context of particular disputes. See *op. cit.,* pp. 75ff. for examples.

[96] Robert J. Donovan, *Eisenhower: The Inside Story* (New York: Harper and Row, Publishers, 1956), p. 88. See also, Rosenau, *op. cit.,* p. 9.

[97] For a listing of such statutes, see Rourke, *op. cit.,* pp. 57–62. A useful analysis is Raoul Berger, "Executive Privilege v. Congressional Inquiry," *UCLA Law Review,* XII (1964–1965), 1043–120, 1287–364.

foreign-aid programs in Vietnam, the Cuban Bay of Pigs invasion, defense weapons systems, and assorted activities of the Central Intelligence Agency. Those in Congress who thought that executive policies were wrong and that fundamental errors were being concealed were the most vocal critics of executive secrecy. Yet the complexity of the problem continued to be widely understood. Pragmatic accommodation rather than absolute showdown continued to be the norm.

EXECUTIVE TESTIMONY

The problem of selecting spokesmen from the executive branch to testify before congressional committees also helps to focus alternative notions of responsibility. Committees themselves have difficulty in deciding what they want. At times, committees are mainly interested in hearing department heads; at other times they want to hear from lower-level employees, on the grounds that they are the persons who know what is going on and how and why decisions are made. In the model which calls for centralizing responsibility in the executive branch, it would be appropriate for Congress to hear only a department's top political officials. If Congress is the primary agent for promoting a responsible bureaucracy, then it is presumably appropriate for it to hear any officials that it thinks can supply it with the information it wants.

The conflict over who shall testify frequently occurs in debates over military budgets. Representatives of all the armed services are invited to appear before committees and to air their differences with the top political leadership in the Department of Defense.

In a spectacular episode in 1954, Senator Joseph McCarthy made famous the question, "Who promoted Peress?" Dissatisfied with Secretary of the Army Robert Stevens's replies to his inquiries about the promotion and discharge of an army dentist, Irving Peress, Senator McCarthy called General Ralph Zwicker, the commanding officer of the base where Peress was stationed, to testify. Under the theory of centralized executive responsibility, Congress should not call subordinate officers and career civil servants to testify, but rather should center its concern on top political officials.[98] On the other hand, if Congress is to be held responsible for bureaucratic performance, summoning Zwicker was perfectly reasonable and, in fact, necessary.

The central example of the early 1970s came as congressional critics sought official testimony from Henry A. Kissinger, national security adviser to President Nixon. Kissinger declined to appear claiming confidentiality in his advisory status; key senators pressed for his appearance before a Senate committee on the grounds that Kissinger was the decisive foreign policy voice in the executive branch. Both sides had good reasons for what they wanted to do. Each placed different weights on the values involved.

The problems involved in legislative oversight probably have no ultimate solution. Recurring conflict between the executive and legislature is to be expected; settlements are never more than temporary. The shortcom-

[98] This position was supported in *the New York Times,* February 26, 1954, p. 18.

434 ings of legislative oversight are captured in this analysis by Leonard D. White in his presidential address to the American Political Science Association over twenty-five years ago:

> It is basically control over details, not over essentials. It is negative and repressive rather than positive and constructive. It reflects fear rather than confidence. It is sometimes irresponsible. It is based on no rational plan, but is an accumulation of particulars whose consequences are seldom seen in perspective. Congress has done both too much and too little in trying to discharge this phase of its responsibilities.[99]

Events since 1945 have only somewhat eroded his indictment. Yet in actual application, legislative oversight, though not matching Professor White's expectations, does at times contribute something of utility to the American political system. Congressional inquiries have, from time to time, focused attention on significant problems.[100] They have provoked executive reexamination of some policies and procedures. They have broadened the scope of alternatives considered by the executive. In short, legislative oversight has sometimes been an effective agent of innovation and change.

Even on foreign policy and defense problems, where congressional oversight is allegedly at its weakest, there are examples of congressional efforts having significant consequences.[101]

Fragmentary evidence points in one direction concerning legislative oversight in the states: the job is not being done well. Alan Rosenthal in a survey of legislators in six states found that few rated their performance in exercising oversight as "excellent" or "good."[102] A group of experts and informed citizens meeting as the "Southern Assembly" concurred:

> The Assembly views legislative oversight of the operations of the executive branch as a difficult but important responsibility. In general, it was conceded this responsibility has not been performed with desirable effectiveness and is in need of renewed attention.[103]

More directly, the Citizens Conference on State Legislatures, after surveying activity in the states, asserted:

[99] "Congressional Control over the Public Service," *American Political Science Review,* XXXIX (February 1945), 2–3. A more balanced set of conclusions based on extensive personal observations is supplied by Ralph K. Huitt, *op. cit.*

[100] For example, the work of the Constitutional Rights Subcommittee of the Senate Judiciary Committee and the efforts of the Special Subcommittee on the Invasion of Privacy of the House Government Operations Committee in the general field of invasion of privacy.

[101] Louis Fisher, "Delegating Power To The President," *Journal of Public Law,* XIX (1970), especially 278–80. See also Alton Frye, "Congress: The Virtues of Its Vices," *Foreign Policy,* III (Summer 1971), 108–25.

[102] "Legislative Review and Evaluation," paper prepared for The Sixth Annual State Legislator Conference, Palm Beach Shores, Florida, July 25–31, 1971; p. 3.

[103] *Power in American State Legislatures,* ed. Alex B. Lacy, Jr. (New Orleans: Tulane Studies in Political Science, 1967), p. 176.

With the exception of California, no state legislature is equipped to carry out its "oversight" function with any degree of adequacy.[104]

Finally, John Pittinger, legislative assistant to Governor Shapp of Pennsylvania and a former member of the legislature himself, put it most pungently in describing the Pennsylvania state legislature:

> If I were grading the legislature, I'd give them a B-plus on constituent homework, a C-plus on the quality of legislation, and a D on legislative oversight.[105]

Whatever the realities of legislative control, the perceptions of officials in state executive branches lends weight to discussions of legislative impact. In a survey of 933 state executive-branch officials, Deil S. Wright found that 44 per cent of them thought that the legislature exercised greater control over their agencies, while only 32 per cent thought that the governor's control was greater. Twenty-two per cent thought that their control was about the same.[106]

In his study *Dynamics of Bureaucracy,* Peter Blau contends that "to extend these [democratic] institutions by developing democratic methods for governing bureaucracies is, perhaps the crucial problem of our age."[107] Legislative oversight is far from the sole democratic method for governing bureaucracies. It is, however, the primary means of restraint by legally constituted bodies. As such, the potential power of the legislature is substantial. How it exercises that power becomes a relevant and perhaps crucial question.

[104] Citizens Conference on State Legislatures *The Sometime Governments,* ed. John Burns, (New York: Bantam Books, Inc., 1971), 127.

[105] *Wall Street Journal,* June 28, 1971, p. 1.

[106] "Executive Leadership in State Administration," *Midwest Journal of Political Science,* XI (February 1967), 4.

[107] *The Dynamics of Bureaucracy* (Chicago: University of Chicago Press, 1955), p. 216. Samuel P. Huntington sees legislative oversight as possibly the primary function of legislatures in the future. "Congressional Responses to the Twentieth Century," in *The Congress and America's Future,* ed. David B. Truman (Englewood Cliffs, N.J.: Prentice-Hall, Inc.; 1965), pp. 30–31.

13

LEGISLATIVE-JUDICIAL RELATIONS

Creating and interpreting law is the task not only of legislative assemblies but also of the courts. Both legislators and judges speak for the state or nation; both translate the pressures of society into the language of law. From the standpoint of function, courts too are an integral part of the legislative process. This description of the relationship between legislatures and courts contradicts the more common stereotype: politics is the domain of the legislature; law, the domain of the courts. Despite many similarities, subtle yet significant differences distinguish these two institutions.

Legislatures differ from courts in their constitutional mandates. Congress and state legislatures, according to their constitutions, create public policy by making law and determining expenditures. The basic constitutional task of courts is to settle particular disputes in cases that properly come before them. In legislating, representative assemblies inevitably interpret their respective constitutional documents; in deciding cases, courts unavoidably read meaning into both legislative acts and constitutional phrases.

The members of legislative bodies are selected through the mechanisms of the political process. Federal judges, appointed rather than elected, gain office on the basis of extralegal as well as legal considerations. In the states, judges, like legislators, most often run for election on partisan slates; the difference typically lies in the longer terms of judges and in their less overt partisanship. Legislators face the possibility of removal each time they encounter the electorate. Federal judges serve during "good behavior"; most state judges face the electorate less frequently than do legislators. Judges work within the boundaries of the political process but are more insulated from its operations than are legislators.

Legislators and judges carry on their activities in much different environments. The legislator is forced to work out his roles and to provide for his security within a highly political environment. The judge, in contrast, has markedly greater freedom, due in some part to continuing public respect for the law. Possibly the difference in circumstance is less today than in the past, since one impact of modern legal theory has been to separate the voice of the judge from that of God. That judges are engaged steadily in making political decisions has come to be recognized by sectors of the public as well as by political action groups and scholars.

Pressure groups seek access to both legislator and judge. They supply the legislator with campaign funds, but also provide money for individuals pressing cases before the courts. They offer top legal talent in court cases just as they send lobbyists to testify before Congress. They seek out support to pressure legislatures just as they search for cases which may goad the courts into action. Money, energy and skills are the resources allocated to influence both legislatures and courts.[1] The manner of access rather than the attempt at influence distinguishes pressure-group efforts in the legislative and judicial arenas. Buttonholing the legislator is commonplace; contacting judges for unofficial sessions seems beyond the pale. Both legislator and judge receive reams of information from organized interests, but the judge has a greater role in determining the form in which the data are presented. The federal judge is immune from the threat of retaliation in the next election, and the lengthy terms of some state judges may create a similar effect. The legislator is more fearful about interest-group opposition in the next election. Pressure groups attempt to influence judges, but when they do, they act not only under more formal procedures but under the taboos imposed by a society which views its judges as defenders of the purity of the Constitution.

Legislative and judicial bodies share a dependence on the executive branch to implement their decisions. In turn, each has an identifiable, if somewhat different, impact on the behavior of the executive. Both institutions act mainly outside the public gaze, but public concern focuses on legislative activity more regularly than on judicial decision-making.

The basis of legislative power is found in its representative character as fortified by its legal authority; the ultimate strength of the courts rests on its public status as guardian of the Constitution. In the words of Robert McCloskey: "If the public should ever become convinced that the Court is merely another legislature...the Court's future as a constitutional tribunal would be cast in grave doubt."[2] In sum, the similarities between the judicial and the legislative processes are substantial. The differences are often those characteristic in political analysis: matters of degree rather than of kind. At times these differences do become crucial. In 1965 the United States Supreme Court overturned Connecticut's birth control laws. A participant in the struggle explained: "We went to Hartford a number of times trying to get the laws changed through the legislature, but it never worked. Finally... [her husband insisted] the court is the only way."[3]

Functioning in related but poorly defined spheres, legislatures and courts inevitably clash at critical intersections of the political process. Whether legislatures and courts will quarrel or cooperate is determined in some degree by constitutional provisions. Constitutions either settle questions about the size of courts, their structure, their procedures, and their powers, or grant legislative bodies the authority to do so. The net result often is to cast legislative-judicial conflict over policy in the form of technical differences over personnel, structures, and procedures.

[1] See Henry J. Abraham, *The Judicial Process,* 2d ed. (New York: Oxford University Press, 1968), pp. 235–40; Clement E. Vose, *Caucasians Only* (Berkeley: University of California Press, 1959).

[2] "Foreword: The Reapportionment Case," *Harvard Law Review,* LXXVI (November 1962), 67. Copyright © 1962 by the Harvard Law Review Association.

[3] *New York Times,* June 8, 1965, p. 34.

Judicial Personnel

SELECTION

Congress plays a key role in the selection of most federal judges. The constitutional mandate, Article II, Section 2, gives the president the power to appoint judges to the Supreme Court with the advice and consent of the Senate. Congress determines the method of appointment for judges of "inferior courts"; the procedure adopted matches that for the Supreme Court.[4] Nearly 80 per cent of the nominees for the Supreme Court sent to the Senate have been confirmed. Most of the rejections came before 1900. Nominees were rejected most often because of political controversies, senatorial opposition to the president, or personal vendettas; rejection rarely has been based on a holding that the nominee lacked technical qualifications or integrity.[5] Three nominees have been rejected since 1900: John J. Parker in 1930, Clement F. Haynsworth, Jr., in 1969, and G. Harrold Carswell in 1970.[6]

Congress places firmer limits on the appointment of judges to district courts. The selection process which is specified in law tends to be reversed in fact. Senatorial courtesy dominates the selection process. The senator of the president's party from the state concerned tends to "nominate" and the president tends to "confirm" the appointee. Once selection is settled through such informal procedures, the president can with confidence submit the name of "his" appointee to the Senate for formal confirmation. Senate control is so iron-clad that conflict is most often resolved through negotiations which rarely reach the pages of daily newspapers. Practice is somewhat different if there is no senator of the president's political party from the state concerned. Then, members of the state's House delegation and other state political leaders are consulted. If the rules of the political game have been followed, rejections are few. A miscalculation can upset prevailing practice. In 1965 President Johnson, with the endorsement of Senator Edward Kennedy of Massachusetts, nominated Francis X. Morrissey for the position of federal district judge. The instant outcry based on questions of competence, personality, and partisanship led Senator Kennedy to ask that the nomination be set aside. Later, President Johnson withdrew the nomination. If nominations are rarely rejected, senators can still delay confirmations to gain bargaining advantages.[7]

[4] This discussion applies only to the so-called constitutional courts. Legislative courts—those created by Congress on the basis of its authority granted in Article I—tend to be more specialized. For discussion, see Abraham, *op. cit.,* pp. 146–51.

[5] Abraham, *op. cit.,* pp. 78–87. See also William F. Swindler, "The Politics of 'Advice and Consent,'" *American Bar Association Journal,* LVI (June 1970), 533–42. An excellent analysis of the process by which G. Harrold Carswell was rejected is Richard Harris, *Decision* (New York: E. P. Dutton, 1971).

[6] Details of earlier rejections can be found in Joseph P. Harris, *The Advice and Consent of the Senate* (Berkeley: University of California Press, 1953), pp. 305–9 and *passim.*

[7] For examples, see Walter F. Murphy and C. Herman Pritchett, *Courts, Judges, and Politics* (New York: Random House, Inc., 1961), p. 71. The informal dimensions of judicial selection, especially the role of the American Bar Association, are treated in Joel B. Grossman, *Lawyers and Judges* (New York: John Wiley & Sons, Inc., 1965).

In law, the selection of federal judges has remained relatively constant. The legal pattern in the states has been more variable. In seven of the original states, legislative selection of judges was the pattern; the legislature played a lesser role in the six other states.[8] A marked shift toward the election of judges was characteristic of the Jacksonian revolution. By 1860, about two-thirds of the states were selecting their judges through direct popular election.[9] Each state admitted to the Union since 1846 has provided for popular election of all or most of its judges.[10] Today, most of the states elect a majority of their judges; judges are appointed by a number of different procedures in the remaining states.

Disputes over whether judges should be elected or appointed have raged throughout the legal journals. Evidence of a relationship between selection procedures and judicial behavior is scarce but seemingly points to the conclusion that "the circumstance that judges have been elected or that they have been appointed cannot be shown to have had any appreciable direct bearing upon their decision of questions of constitutional policy."[11]

The term of federal judges is for "good behavior," thus diminishing a potential opportunity for exerting political pressure on them. In the states, terms of judges vary tremendously; only New Hampshire and Massachusetts match the federal example.[12] The terms of many state judges are long enough to provide some measure of political insulation.

Congress sets the salaries of federal judges, but judicial independence is promoted by the constitutional provision, Article III, Section 1, that their salaries "shall not be diminished during their Continuance in Office." Legislatures usually determine judicial salaries in the states, but most states also protect judges against reduction in salary while in office. This safeguard may have been more meaningful years ago; Lewis Mayers asserts that this form of guarantee usually has "purely symbolic" significance today.[13] Earlier in American history, one legislature in anger over a state supreme court decision reportedly reduced the salary of the judges to 25 cents per year.[14]

REMOVAL

Congress plays a vital role in the removal of federal judges since impeachment is the only method available. The House of Representatives has formally impeached nine judges; five were acquitted and four were convicted by the Senate.[15] The last federal judge to be impeached and convicted was

[8] Shelden D. Elliott, *Improving Our Courts* (New York: Oceana Publications, Inc., 1959), p. 163.

[9] *Ibid.,* p. 164. For a table providing data on constitutional and statutory aspects of judicial selection and tenure in the states from 1776 to the early 1940s, see Evan Haynes, *The Selection and Tenure of Judges* (National Conference of Judicial Councils, 1944, n.p.), pp. 101–35.

[10] Murphy and Pritchett, *op. cit.,* p. 69.

[11] Speech made by James Parker Hall and cited in Haynes, *op. cit.,* p. 189.

[12] John W. Wood, "State Judicial Selection: Realities v. Legalities," *State Government,* XXXI (January 1958), 17.

[13] Lewis Mayers, *The American Legal System* (New York: Harper & Row, Publishers, 1955), p. 372.

[14] Haynes, *op. cit.,* p. 195.

[15] Abraham, *op. cit.,* pp. 43–45.

440 Halsted L. Ritter in 1936.[16] Impeachment is such an ultimate weapon that it is rarely used. Congress continues to wrestle with the problem of how to establish removal procedures short of impeachment but without success.

Most states follow the federal pattern in providing for removal of judges through impeachment; like the national government, most states use the device sparingly. A 1960 survey discovered recollections of fifty-two instances of impeachment of judges in seventeen states; nineteen removals and three resignations resulted.[17] More recently, from 1928 to 1948, only three impeachments were recorded; in each case the accused was acquitted.[18] The impeachment and conviction of Judge Napoleon Bonaparte Johnson of Oklahoma in 1965 was an event unusual enough to merit extensive national coverage by the media.

Legislatures also use more subtle techniques to ease judges from office. Murphy and Pritchett state: "The first retirement act, that of 1869...was designed to ease Justices Grier and Nelson off the bench."[19] The equivalent logic prevailed in 1937 when Congress attempted to stimulate the retirement of Justice VanDevanter, among others, through the attractiveness of retirement benefits.

The Structure of the Courts

The United States Constitution directly creates only the Supreme Court. Congress is assigned the task of creating "inferior courts." In addition, Congress determines the number of judges for all federal courts. The Judiciary Act of 1789 generally set the pattern of lower court organization. A study of congressional juggling of the number of federal court judges demonstrates the close relationships between politics and law. The size of the Supreme Court was set at six judges in 1789. The Federalist party lost control of the presidency and Congress in 1800. Before the Jeffersonian majority could take office, Federalists pushed through the Judiciary Act of 1801 which provided that the next Supreme Court vacancy was not to be filled. The new majority in Congress promptly repealed this legislation. The size of the Court was subsequently altered four more times until it was stabilized at nine members in 1869. The most recent episode in these pseudostructural battles occurred in 1937 during President Roosevelt's ill-fated plan to increase the size of the Supreme Court by adding a new justice for each one over seventy years of age who refused to retire. President Roosevelt spoke of bringing "young blood" into the Court and of "more rapid justice"; few people failed to recognize the policy implications of this proposal, and Congress refused to accept it.

The growth in size and complexity of the political system provides a

[16] *Ibid.,* p. 45. Congress has investigated the conduct of nearly sixty federal judges. In most cases, the judges were absolved of impeachable conduct and formal proceedings were not undertaken. See Carl L. Shipley, "Legislative Control of Judicial Behavior," *Law and Contemporary Problems,* XXXV (Winter 1970), 192.

[17] George Brand, "Discipline of Judges," *American Bar Association Journal,* XLVI (December 1960), 1315.

[18] *Ibid.*

[19] Murphy and Pritchett, *op. cit.,* p. 553.

basic explanation for the addition of new federal judges. Jack W. Peltason finds, however, that increases in the number of judgeships are related to partisan politics; ordinarily the number of judges is increased after a political party which has long been out of power regains power.[20]

It is difficult to generalize about the relationships between court structure and state legislative processes for two reasons. The first is that there is a great variety of structures in the states; the second, that the subject has simply not received much attention from scholars.[21] In almost all states, the court of last appeal is created in the state constitution. Inferior courts are a product either of the constitution itself or of a constitutional grant of authority to the legislature. Constitutions typically are phrased to allow legislative bodies to establish courts other than those named therein.[22]

Judicial Procedures and Jurisdiction

Judicial procedures and jurisdictions sometimes are prescribed in constitutions. Legislatures fill in constitutional gaps. Only the original jurisdiction of the Supreme Court is spelled out in the United States Constitution. The appellate jurisdiction of the Supreme Court is exercised "with such exceptions and under such regulations as the Congress shall make." Few cases come to the Supreme Court under its original jurisdiction; Congress can wield a powerful weapon over the court through control of appellate jurisdiction. In fact, C. Herman Pritchett concludes, "perhaps the most drastic congressional authority over the Court [is] the control of its appellate jurisdiction."[23] Congress has attempted to exert this authority only under exceptional circumstances. Perhaps the most blatant example was in the case of *Ex Parte McCardle*.[24] After the Supreme Court had heard argument on the case but before a decision was announced, Congress acted. In 1868, concerned over the possibility that the Court would declare the Reconstruction acts unconstitutional, Congress passed a law removing appellate jurisdiction in this case. The Court then dismissed the case, stating that its decisions could only be rendered in instances where the Court had jurisdiction. Robert Harris argues: "The Court wilted—as it must always wilt—in the heat generated by a serious and determined congressional majority...."[25]

Lower federal courts are wholly dependent on Congress for their jurisdiction. Beginning with the Judiciary Act of 1789, Congress at irregular

---

[20] Jack W. Peltason, *Federal Courts in the Judicial Process* (New York: Random House, Inc., 1955), pp. 40–41. In 1961, reinforcing the Peltason thesis, Congress created seventy-three new judgeships.

[21] But see Donald P. Kommers, "Judicial Politics in Wisconsin, A Case Study in Court Reorganization," paper presented at the Sixty-first Annual Meeting of the American Political Science Association, 1965.

[22] Legislative Drafting Research Fund of Columbia University, *Index Digest of State Constitutions*, rev. ed. (New York: Oceana Press, Inc., 1959), p. 216.

[23] C. Herman Pritchett, *Congress Versus The Supreme Court* (Minneapolis: University of Minnesota Press, 1961), p. 122.

[24] The discussion of this case is reconstructed from the description in Robert Harris, *The Judicial Power Of The United States* (University: Louisiana State University Press, 1940), pp. 83–85.

[25] *Ibid.*, p. 84.

442   intervals has adopted statutes to modify the jurisdiction of the lower courts. The federal courts of appeals, for example, have been given the duty of reviewing the actions of many executive agencies that exercise quasi-judicial functions. Among the agencies whose actions come under review are the National Labor Relations Board, the Federal Communications Commission, and the Civil Aeronautics Board. In 1958 Congress stipulated that cases involving citizens of different states could come before the federal courts only if the money involved were over $10,000.

Predictably, one can assert that attempts to amend or alter the jurisdiction of the courts are exerted in response to new problems or in reaction to unfriendly court decisions. Clarence Manion, formerly chairman of the Commission on Intergovernmental Relations and Dean of the Notre Dame Law School, charged: "The record reveals that the chief, if not the only, beneficiaries of the Warren Court's constitutional constructions have been convicted criminals, Communists, atheists, and clients of the NAACP." His remedy was to "strip the Supreme Court of its appellate jurisdiction which it now exercises so prodigally to reverse the sound judgments of all the inferior courts in the country. . . ."[26] In 1958, Senator Jenner (R., Ind.) submitted a bill proposing to withdraw five areas from the appellate jurisdiction of the Supreme Court where it had rendered controversial decisions.[27]

Congressional prescription of judicial procedure extends beyond the subject of jurisdiction. In the Judiciary Act of 1789, Congress determined the time and place for court sessions and the ability of the courts to issue writs. Congress provided that the courts could "make all the necessary rules for the orderly conduct of their business."[28] Congress was quick to use these powers for political purposes. In its 1802 repeal act, Congress postponed, in effect, the next session of the Supreme Court, thus prohibiting the judges from ruling on other sections of this piece of legislation.[29]

Congress has authorized the Supreme Court to establish rules for the operation of the federal courts. It has also withdrawn and restored such authority. In general, Congress now authorizes the Supreme Court, with few restrictions, to make rules for the federal constitutional courts.[30] In 1958, Congress authorized the Judicial Conference to adopt rules of procedure for submission to the Supreme Court for approval. These rules, if approved, become effective in ninety days unless specifically rejected by Congress.[31] An equivalent movement toward allowing state supreme courts to set rules for their systems has gathered some momentum.[32]

The impact of courts on congressional procedure has been less substantial. The Constitution authorizes Congress to make its own rules and to judge the election and conduct of its own members. In many states, the identical rule obtains. Where rules of procedure are created by the legislative assembly and no constitutional questions are at issue, courts generally refuse

---

[26] *Manion Forum,* July 14, 1963, p. 3.
[27] Pritchett, *op. cit.,* pp. 31ff.
[28] Robert Harris, *op. cit.,* pp. 81–90.
[29] *Ibid.,* p. 79.
[30] Elliott, *op. cit.,* pp. 19ff.
[31] Abraham, *op. cit.,* p. 169.
[32] Elliott, *op. cit.,* p. 19; *The Book of the States, 1966–1967* (Chicago: Council of State Governments, 1966), pp. 109–10.

to review these legislative acts. In *United States* v. *Ballin* (1892), the Supreme Court stated:

> The constitution empowers each house to determine its rules of proceedings. It may not by its own rules ignore constitutional restraints or violate fundamental rights, and there should be a reasonable relation between the mode or method of proceeding established by the rule and the result which is sought to be attained. But within these limitations all matters of method are open to the determination of the house. . . .[33]

The exceptions to this generalization are few. Perhaps the most spectacular in recent years came in 1969 when the Supreme Court ruled that the U.S. House of Representatives had acted unconstitutionally in excluding Congressman Adam Clayton Powell. The Court argued that Powell was duly elected and met the constitutional qualifications for membership: age, citizenship, and residence. The House could not therefore exclude him, but could punish or expel him if charges were brought and if he were convicted of them. State courts are much more active in hearing cases concerning legislative procedures since so many state constitutions spell out in minute detail how their legislatures should conduct their business.

Legislatures, Courts, and Policy Formulation

Legislative-judicial conflicts are often verbalized in procedural terms. In many cases these procedural disputes simply disguise policy battles. Problems of personnel, jurisdiction, and structure are often problems of power:

> The mechanism of law . . . cannot be dissociated from the ends that law subserves. So-called jurisdictional questions treated in isolation from the purposes of the legal system to which they relate become barren pedantry. After all, procedure is instrumental; it is the means of effectuating policy.[34]

Spectacular battles between the Supreme Court and Congress catch the public eye; less eventful interaction is the more characteristic relationship. Day after day, the courts decide cases involving the application of public policy reflected in constitutions and legislative acts. The issues involved, while undoubtedly of great consequence to the participants, often have little relevance in the broader forum of the political system. The decision in many cases adds increments of meaning to public law but in such small doses that they escape attention. The great bulk of court decisions pass largely unnoticed into the volumes of court reports. Statistically, it is highly unusual for a court decision to make a lasting impact on the political process. Precisely for that reason, legislative bodies rarely concern themselves with the activities of the courts. Record of discussion and debate over the courts and their activities is seldom found in legislative journals; court structure

[33] 144 U.S. 1. See Frank E. Horack, Jr., *Statutes and Statutory Construction,* 3d ed. (Chicago: Callaghan and Company, 1943) I, 126–28.

[34] Felix Frankfurter and James M. Landis, *The Business of the Supreme Court* (New York: The Macmillan Company, 1928), p. 2.

444 and procedure is the subject of very few bills. Examples of legislative-judicial conflict should be examined against this background of peaceful cooperation and mutual indifference. Legislative-judicial interaction takes place in the few situations when courts significantly interpret legislative acts or subject them to judgments about constitutionality and when legislators in turn respond to judicial decisions.

Policy Formulation—Judicial Interpretation

Each judicial decision involves some interpretation of law. Judges are required to match the phrases of law with the facts of concrete cases which come before them. This task is neither simple nor scientific. This task is least difficult in the lower courts, where most cases are decided. Law and fact often match, without the judge exerting great effort. In the appeals courts, and especially in the supreme courts, where the more complex cases inevitably end up, the judge must extend more effort and creativity to reconcile law and fact. In his decision-making, the judge is forced to read precise meaning into legislative acts. This judicial creativity is a necessity for several reasons. First, the words in statutes are merely "symbols of meaning" phrased with only "approximate precision." Second, the ambiguity in statutes reflects the doubts and compromises of legislative accommodations— the legislature is not always certain of its goals. Third, draftsmanship in statutes is not always characterized by care and creativity. Fourth, the inherent complexity of some subjects defies exhaustive statutory treatment— legislatures cannot anticipate all possible situations. Fifth, "provisions at times embody purposeful ambiguity."[35]

Faced with an obligation to interpret statutes, the judge cannot pretend that he is merely supplying the intent of the legislature as he reads meaning into statutes.

> The [Supreme] Court no doubt must listen to the voice of Congress. But often Congress cannot be heard clearly because its speech is muffled. Even when it has spoken...what is said is what the listener hears.... One listens with what is already in one's head.[36]

Day-to-day judicial interpretation rarely elicits legislative concern. Even more fundamental interpretations may not provoke a legislative response. How and why legislators react can be illustrated through examples involving lobbying, regulation of commerce and trusts, and subversion.

L O B B Y I N G

In 1946 Congress passed the Federal Regulation of Lobbying Act. The provisions of the statute applied to persons or organizations attempting "to influence, directly or indirectly, the passage or defeat of any legislation by

---

[35] Felix Frankfurter, "Some Reflections on the Reading of Statutes," *The Record*, II (June 1947), 213–15.

[36] *Ibid.*, p. 224.

the Congress of the United States." In 1950 a House committee created to investigate "all lobbying activities" subpoenaed the Committee for Constitutional Government, a private group, to provide specified information about some of its contributors. When Edward Rumely, representing this committee, refused to provide the information requested, he was cited and convicted for contempt of Congress. On appeal, the Supreme Court set aside the conviction on the grounds that the House committee was to investigate "lobbying," a term which the Court defined as excluding indirect efforts at persuasion through such techniques as distributing literature to members of the community. In essence, the Court defined lobbying as only direct activity to influence Congress. The efforts of the Committee for Constitutional Government to "educate the public" could not be regulated as lobbying, and Rumely, therefore, could not be in contempt of Congress for refusing to answer questions about indirect activities.[37] The Rumely decision seemed to modify substantially the Federal Regulation of Lobbying Act. Yet it made no great impact on Congress. The explanation is perhaps threefold: (1) Congress itself was strongly divided on the definition of lobbying and how to regulate lobbies; (2) no immediate, organized, and substantial interests pressured Congress to act; (3) no self-evident threat to the integrity of the political system was posed by this decision.

COMMERCE AND TRUSTS

In its first major exercise of the power to regulate interstate commerce, Congress passed the Interstate Commerce Act in 1887. Within a few years, the Supreme Court had interpreted this statute so restrictively that "by 1896 the agency [ICC] was practically out of business."[38] However, "a series of new statutes and a change in judicial attitudes" altered the Court's judgments[39] In a second major exercise of the commerce power, Congress passed the Sherman Anti-Trust Act of 1890. The Sherman act made illegal "every contract, combination...or conspiracy in restraint of trade or commerce among the several States...." A question temporarily left unanswered was whether manufacturing trusts were part of interstate commerce and hence subject to the restrictions in the act. In *United States* v. *E. C. Knight Company* (1895), the Supreme Court distinguished "manufacturing" from "commerce," the effect of which was to exclude manufacturing from the regulation of the act. The impact of this decision, as viewed by Kelly and Harbison, was to vitiate "in very large degree federal control of trusts and monopolies."[40] Only nine years later, the Court again defined "commerce" in the case of *Northern Securities Company* v. *United States*, but this time the effect of their decision was to breathe new life into the Sherman act.[41]

[37] This episode is detailed in Telford Taylor, *Grand Inquest* (New York: Simon and Schuster, Inc., 1955), pp. 140–47.

[38] Murphy and Pritchett, *op. cit.*, p. 400.

[39] Pritchett, *op. cit.*, pp. 7–8.

[40] Alfred H. Kelly and Winfred Harbison, *The American Constitution* (New York: W. W. Norton & Company, Inc., 1963), p. 560.

[41] *Ibid.*, p. 597. For a brief review of the Court's interpretation of the meaning of commerce, see Robert Carr, *The Supreme Court and Judicial Review* (New York: Holt, Rinehart & Winston, Inc., 1942), pp. 99–138.

Whatever the policy result, the importance of judicial interpretation was dramatized. Congress need not wait for court interpretations. In 1914 Congress passed two statutes, the Clayton act and the Federal Trade Commission act; both were designed to expand and reinforce the antitrust laws.

In the interim between the restrictive Court interpretation and the passage of new legislation, Congress tried to counter Court decisions in other ways. A proposal for a constitutional amendment to strengthen regulation of trusts failed to pass the House.[42] Legislation to accomplish similar purposes passed the House but was not voted on in the Senate. In all, from 1889 to 1913, eighteen constitutional amendments on the subject of regulation of trusts were proposed; none received congressional approval.[43] In sum, Congress recognized the importance of Court interpretations but did not move directly to limit Court powers. Instead, Congress achieved its objectives through writing its own interpretations of policy into law.

SUBVERSION

In 1940 Congress passed the Smith act, making it unlawful to teach or to advocate the overthrow of the government by force or violence, to print and distribute materials so advocating, to organize for these purposes, or to conspire to commit these acts.[44] Eleven top Communist leaders were prosecuted successfully under the Smith act in 1951. In the case of *Yates* v. *United States* (1957), the Supreme Court reversed the convictions of lesser Communist party leaders and ordered retrials for others. The Court strictly construed the term "organize" and seemingly placed firmer boundaries on government prosecutions under the Smith act. On the day of the *Yates* decision, the Supreme Court decided two other highly controversial cases, *Sweezy* v. *New Hampshire* and *Watkins* v. *United States*. Both decisions seemed to impose restrictions on the procedures of legislative investigating committees. Antagonism in Congress toward the "Red Monday" decisions blended with hostility to the school segregation decisions and enmity based on alleged denials of states' rights. As a result of these decisions, numerous attempts were made by members of Congress between 1957 and 1959 to limit the power of the Supreme Court; few were successful. Proposals were made to require Supreme Court judges to have previous judicial experience. Some attempted to limit the appellate jurisdiction of the Supreme Court. Constitutional amendments were proposed to limit federal judges to specific terms, for example, ten years. Table 13.1 quantifies congressional efforts to reverse selected Supreme Court interpretations of law and the Constitution. Impeachment of judges was about the only legislative weapon which was not actually used.

Pritchett asserts: "The most direct and serious attack on the Court as an institution was the bill introduced by Senator William E. Jenner (R., Ind.) on July 26, 1957, about a month after the Yates and Watkins deci-

---

42 M. A. Musmanno, *Proposed Amendments to the Constitution,* 70th Congress, 2d sess., H. Doc. 551 (Washington, D.C.: Government Printing Office, 1929), pp. 116–18.

43 *Ibid.,* p. 119.

44 The following discussion leans heavily on Pritchett, *op. cit.,* pp. 59–69.

TABLE 13.1

Congressional Efforts to Revise, Clarify, or Modify Selected Supreme Court Decisions

Case	Issue	Number of Bills Introduced
Brown v. *Board of Education* (1954)	School segregation	53
Pennsylvania v. *Nelson* (1956)	State sedition laws	66
Mallory v. *United States* (1957)	Criminal procedure	30
Jencks v. *United States* (1957)	Criminal procedure	10
Watkins v. *United States* (1957)	Congressional investigations	7

SOURCE: Clifford M. Lytle, Jr., "The Warren Court and Its Political Critics" (University of Pittsburgh, Ph.D. dissertation, 1963).

sions."[45] The proposal sought to remove five types of cases from the appellate jurisdiction of the Supreme Court: (1) admission of lawyers to practice before the state courts; (2) procedures of congressional investigating committees; (3) administration of the loyalty-security program; (4) state statutes controlling subversion; (5) rules about subversive activities among teachers. The Court had rendered controversial decisions in each of these five areas. After complex maneuvering, the revised bill, called the Jenner-Butler bill, was tabled.[46]

Congressional response from 1957 to 1959 to this series of Supreme Court decisions was loud and emphatic; its legislative product was slight. Why was Congress unable to act more successfully? Pritchett presents a four-point explanation. First, there is widespread respect for judicial institutions both in and out of Congress; second, the character and motives of the attackers were suspect; third, many of the charges leveled against the Court represented gross exaggerations; fourth, the Court was able to dampen attacks by subsequently pursuing a moderate course in its decisions.[47]

Legislative response to court interpretations varies from inattention to flurries of proposals to alter the structure and procedures of the courts or to change their substantive rulings. Legislative reaction to exercises of judicial review of legislation follows similar patterns.

Judicial Review

The most spirited interaction between legislative and judicial bodies occurs when courts exercise the power of judicial review to determine the constitutionality of governmental actions. Courts make these judgments even when there is no constitutional mandate to do so. Whatever its origins, judicial review has become so accepted in the American tradition that its existence and its future must be presumed. A brief survey of the practice of judicial review yields insights that are useful in understanding contemporary legislative-judicial relationships.

[45] *Ibid.*, p. 31.
[46] *Ibid.*, pp. 31–40.
[47] *Ibid.*, pp. 119–121.

448   Judicial review was an accepted practice in the colonies. After the American Revolution, several states adopted the practice. From 1788 to 1802, state courts held state legislation invalid in more than twenty instances in eleven of fifteen states.[48] By 1803, the date of *Marbury* v. *Madison,* judicial review was well established in eight states.[49] In 1798 the Supreme Court had sustained a state legislative act in the case of *Calder* v. *Bull*; in 1796 it had upheld an act of Congress in *Ware* v. *Hylton.* The presumption that the courts could exercise judicial review existed before 1803, but in that year the Supreme Court for the first time declared part of an act of Congress unconstitutional, in *Marbury* v. *Madison.* Seven years later, the Supreme Court for the first time declared a state legislative act unconstitutional in *Fletcher* v. *Peck.*[50]

The significance of John Marshall's decision in *Marbury* v. *Madison* apparently was lost to most observers. Some described the decision as "a perfectly calculated audacity"; others saw it as "a partisan coup." In the heat of the partisan furor over Marshall's oral rebuke to President Jefferson, few people were concerned with the impact of Marshall's pronouncement on judicial review. In particular, congressional reaction was slight. Perhaps part of the sting of *Marbury* v. *Madison* had been removed by the Court's decision six days later, in *Stuart* v. *Laird,* upholding an act of Congress.[51]

The Supreme Court did not declare an act of Congress unconstitutional again until the ill-famed case of *Dred Scott* v. *Sanford* in 1857. Justice Taney went out of his way in that case to invalidate a section of the Missouri Compromise of 1820. What was especially perplexing about the Taney decision was that the section declared unconstitutional had been repealed before the Supreme Court had made its decision.[52]

The Supreme Court declared few acts of Congress unconstitutional until after the Civil War. The subsequent increase in judicial activity can be traced in part to disputes arising out of the war. The most intensive exercise of judicial review occurred, however, during the period between 1890 and 1937 when the Court, applying the doctrine of substantive due process, substituted its collective judgment of the reasonableness of legislation for the judgment of Congress. Constitutional guarantees of due process had been regarded previously as insuring that government would use fair *procedures* in dealing with the citizenry. Now the courts used this constitutional phrase to assess the substantive merits of state and national legislation. Such merits came to be evaluated in terms of the judges' own social and economic philosophies; for most judges this meant laissez faire and the protection of private property would be given primacy. Robert Carr demon-

---

[48] Kelly and Harbison, *op. cit.,* p. 229; Charles Warren, *The Supreme Court in United States History* (Boston: Little, Brown & Company, 1926), I, 263.

[49] W. Brook Graves, *American State Government* (Boston: D. C. Heath & Company, 1953), p. 586.

[50] Charles Grove Haines, *The American Doctrine of Judicial Supremacy* (Berkeley: University of California Press, 1932), pp. 193–204. Previously, circuit courts had declared state acts unconstitutional. *The Constitution of the United States: Analysis and Interpretation,* 82d Cong., 2d sess., S. Doc. 170 (Washington, D.C.: Government Printing Office, 1953), p. 560.

[51] Warren, *op. cit.,* I, 269.

[52] Walter F. Murphy, *Congress and the Court* (Chicago: University of Chicago Press, 1962), pp. 29–31.

states the importance of a "personal as well as a legal motivation on the part of the justices":

> Where legislation directed against such admitted social evils as the theft of automobiles or kidnaping has been in question, judges have not been at all inclined to erect any constitutional barriers in the way of federal action.... Where a social practice was not quite so recognizably evil, and some opinion has opposed governmental "meddling," as was perhaps true of the lottery traffic, judges have begun to entertain constitutional doubts about the validity of federal legislation. Finally, when Congress endeavored to employ its commerce power against a highly controversial evil touching the field of business enterprise, and encountered the opposition of a vociferous, although perhaps minority, faction of the American people, a Supreme Court dominated by a conservative majority interposed a legal objection.[53]

Under the Court's interpretation, the due process clause came to be associated with "reasonable legislation." The Court, rather than Congress, became the arbiter of what was "reasonable."

Specifically, the courts found an act of Congress outlawing "yellow-dog contracts" to be unconstitutional in *Adair* v. *United States* (1908). A statute setting minimum wages for the District of Columbia was found to be an unconstitutional deprivation of liberty in *Adkins* v. *Children's Hospital* (1923). The high point in the history of Court reversals of Congress came in 1935 when seven statutes were voided. In 1936 four additional decisions upset acts of Congress. Congress and the president had entered into a new era in policymaking, but the Court was still holding fast to nineteenth-century doctrines. Since the 1930s, as indicated in Table 13.2, the Supreme

TABLE 13.2

Number of Cases in Which Acts of Congress Were Declared Unconstitutional by the Supreme Court

Years	Number of Cases
1789–1864	2
1865–69	4
1870–79	9
1880–89	5
1890–99	6
1900–1909	9
1910–19	7
1920–29	19
1930–39	16
1940–49	2
1950–59	4
1960–69	14

SOURCES: Data from Henry J. Abraham, *The Judicial Process*, 2d ed. (New York: Oxford University Press, 1968), pp. 285–94. More recent data from relevant issues of the *Supreme Court Reporter* (St. Paul, Minn.: West Publishing Company).

[53] Carr, *op. cit.*, p. 114.

450   Court has declared fewer acts of Congress unconstitutional. The broad interpretation rendered to the "commerce clause" has eased the close control by the Court as Congress proceeds to regulate segments of the economic life of the nation.[54]

The Supreme Court seldom challenges Congress lightly:

> What seems clear—and clearly recognized by both bodies [the Supreme Court and Congress]—is that if the plain legislative intent is plainly distorted by a zealous Court, the reaction of a proud Congress will be plainer still. It is with this understanding that the Court proceeds, where it deems it appropriate, to make, or to shape, or at least to refine, public policy.[55]

FEDERAL COURTS AND JUDICIAL REVIEW OF STATE ACTS

Federal courts became concerned with the constitutionality of state legislative acts early in American history. Before 1800, a circuit court judge had found a state act to be contrary to the Constitution; another state act was declared unconstitutional because of conflict with a treaty.[56] The Supreme Court first voided an act of a state legislature for reasons of unconstitutionality in *Fletcher* v. *Peck* (1810). In the 1820s state statutes were declared unconstitutional in almost every session of the Court. Up to the Civil War the Supreme Court had declared state legislation void in some sixty cases.[57] With industrialization came an increase in judicial review of the acts of state legislatures. In the last quarter of the nineteenth century, well over one hundred state acts were declared unconstitutional.[58] Of the 125 state laws invalidated by federal courts before 1888, fifty concerned commerce, fifty involved the obligation of contracts, and only one was related to due process; in the era when judges most often applied substantive due process, from the 1890's to 1937, some 400 acts of state legislatures were declared unconstitutional.[59] The explanation for this increased activity is threefold: an increase in the volume of cases, the attitudes of judges applying the "rule of reason," and many legislative experiments aimed at meeting the challenge of industrialization provided a target for judges concerned with maintaining laissez faire and property rights.

In recent years, a shift in emphasis is detectable. At both national and state levels, judges are more reluctant to apply their judgments about social legislation instead of accepting those of legislators. The contemporary court attitude was captured by Justice Black in *Ferguson* v. *Skrupa*:

> The doctrine that prevailed in Lochner, Coppage, Adkins, Burns and like cases—that due process authorizes courts to hold laws unconstitutional when

---

[54] The post-1937 experience of the Court is analyzed by Bernard Schwartz, *The Supreme Court* (New York: Ronald Press Company, 1957), pp. 34–42.

[55] Stephen P. Strickland, "Congress, The Supreme Court and Public Policy," *American University Law Review*, XVIII (March 1969), 298.

[56] Haines, *op. cit.*, pp. 179, 181–83.

[57] Kelly and Harbison, *op. cit.*, p. 541, citing Benjamin Wright, *The Growth of American Constitutional Law* (Boston: Houghton Mifflin Company, 1942), Chap. 4. For somewhat conflicting statistics, see Arthur Holcombe, *State Government in the United States* (New York: The Macmillan Company, 1926), p. 431.

[58] Kelly and Harbison, *op. cit.*, p. 541.

[59] *Ibid.*, p. 541.

they believe the legislature has acted unwisely—has long since been discharged.... Courts do not substitute their social and economic beliefs for the judgment of legislative bodies.... We refuse to sit as a "superlegislature to weigh the wisdom of legislation.".... [60]

JUDICIAL REVIEW IN THE STATES

By 1818 judicial review was recognized as legitimate in all states but Rhode Island. Yet its exercise was infrequent and restricted to relatively few states. [61] In Indiana, few legislative acts were declared unconstitutional between 1816 and 1852; in Pennsylvania, no act of the legislature was held invalid for some fifty years after the adoption of the constitution of 1790; in Massachusetts, one legislative act was voided in 1813, after which none was overruled for thirty-four years; in Ohio, from 1802 to 1851, seven state laws were declared unconstitutional; in Virginia, from 1789 to 1861, two laws were declared invalid on constitutional grounds. [62] From 1776 to 1819 there were only some eighteen cases in which state legislative acts were declared unconstitutional. [63] Such statistics have led Arthur Bromage to conclude: "Early judicial review was not a very decisive check on state power." [64]

In the post–Civil War era, and especially near the end of the nineteenth century, judicial review in the states was on the upswing. Several factors help explain this trend: (1) many of the state constitutions drafted in the late nineteenth and early twentieth centuries, reflecting a distrust of legislatures, spelled out the structures and procedures of government in minute detail; (2) legislative discretion was circumscribed by a detailed listing of powers; (3) the rise of industrialization and urbanization led to an increased volume of governmental activity. According to Holcombe, nearly 400 state laws were declared unconstitutional by state courts between 1903 and 1908. [65] Of these 400 decisions, only thirty-two related to interference with the judiciary, which in earlier years had been a common cause for judicial review. Most related to "defective legislative procedure" or alleged violations of due process of law. [66] In Virginia, from 1902 to 1928, Nelson describes a vast increase in the use of judicial review; in New York, from 1906 to 1938, some 136 state statutes were declared unconstitutional; in Ohio, from 1912 to 1936, forty-four state legislative acts were declared void; in Nebraska, from 1920 to 1936, twenty-five statutes were held unconstitutional. [67]

[60] 83 S. Ct. 1028.
[61] Holcombe, *op. cit.*, p. 431.
[62] Oliver P. Field, "Unconstitutional Legislation in Indiana," *Indiana Law Journal,* XVII (December 1941), 102; Arthur W. Bromage, *State Government and Administration in the United States* (New York: Harper & Row, Publishers, 1936), p. 321; Margaret Virginia Nelson, *A Study of Judicial Review in Virginia* (New York: Columbia University Press, 1947), pp. 204–5.
[63] Holcombe, *op. cit.*, p. 431.
[64] Bromage, *op. cit.*, p. 321.
[65] Holcombe, *op. cit.*, p. 431.
[66] *Ibid.*, p. 434.
[67] Nelson, *op. cit.*, p. 204; Franklin A. Smith, *Judicial Review of Legislation in New York, 1906–1938* (New York: Columbia University Press, 1952), p. 223; Katherine B. Fite and Louis B. Rubenstein, "Curbing The Supreme Court—State Experiences and Federal Proposals," *Michigan Law Review,* XXXV (March 1937), 774–80.

452   Despite this increase in the use of judicial review, its overall application in the states still seems slight. In a study of judicial review in ten states, Oliver P. Field found that about 1,400 statutes had been declared unconstitutional until 1940.[68] Of the cases involving constitutionality which reached the courts, over four-fifths of the statutes questioned were upheld. In these ten states, the courts declared legislation unconstitutional most often between 1890 and 1910 as new constitutions were drawn and interpreted by the courts in cases brought before them.

Overall, judicial review in the states tends to focus on procedural details and technical formalities rather than on the grand issues of public policy.[69] Martin Hickman concludes that the impact of judicial review on policy-making has been slight in Utah; for Indiana, Oliver P. Field found that most unconstitutional legislation has dealt not with great socio-economic issues but with "squabbles."[70] After examining the history of judicial review in Virginia, Margaret Nelson concluded:

> The exercise of judicial review in Virginia from 1789 to 1928 was, generally speaking, of little practical significance in that it exerted slight tangible influence upon the course of legislative enactment and played an unimportant role in the shaping of vital public policies. . . .[71]

In the few cases when statutes were declared unconstitutional, "the decisions were of no great importance except to the persons immediately concerned." She suggests further that judicial review generally has not been significant in one-party southern states where court and legislature tend to be in harmony on basic issues of public policy.[72]

In his study of the American legal system, Lewis Mayers only slightly overstates the case:

> State judicial review has become a humdrum institution, indubitably useful in enforcing observance by legislative and executive branches alike of the multiplicity of detailed regulations of their activities in which the typical state constitution of today abounds.[73]

Legislative Reaction to Judicial Behavior

REVERSAL THROUGH CONSTITUTIONAL AMENDMENT

The most direct method of response to judicial declarations of unconstitutionality is to alter these decisions through proposing and passing constitutional amendments. Only a few such attempts have been successful; there

---

[68] *Judicial Review of Legislation in Ten Selected States* (Bloomington: Indiana University, Bureau of Government Research, 1943). The states are listed on p. 5. A chronological table of statutes declared unconstitutional in each state is provided on p. 14.

[69] Frankfurter and Landis, *op. cit.,* p. 306.

[70] "Judicial Review of Legislation in Utah," *Utah Law Review,* IV (Spring, 1954), 61; Field, *Indiana Law Journal,* XVII, 104.

[71] Nelson, *op. cit.,* p. 202.

[72] *Ibid.,* p. 202.

[73] Mayers, *op. cit.,* p. 322.

are only four examples for the United States Constitution. In 1793 in the case of *Chisholm* v. *Georgia*, the Supreme Court ruled that states could be sued by citizens of other states without the consent of the state. This ruling, seemingly in contradiction to widespread understandings of the Constitution, was quickly overruled by the passage of the Eleventh Amendment in 1798.[74] The Eleventh Amendment provides the only instance in United States history of the curtailment of the jurisdiction of federal courts through a constitutional amendment.

The Thirteenth and Fourteenth Amendments reversed, in part, aspects of Taney's decision in *Dred Scott* v. *Sanford*. The ending of slavery and the establishing of specific criteria for citizenship for all persons had the effect of overruling Taney's assertion that Negroes were not eligible for citizenship and that Congress could not prohibit slavery in the territories.

A third example of an amendment reversing a Supreme Court decision came after the decision in *Pollock* v. *Farmer's Loan and Trust Company* in 1895. The Court had ruled unconstitutional an act of Congress setting a uniform income tax. Constitutional amendments to offset the impact of this decision were introduced in 1895, 1898, 1907, and 1912. From 1897 to 1909, thirty-three amendments were introduced to override the *Pollock* decision.[75] These efforts were finally successful with the passing of the Sixteenth Amendment in 1913.

The fourth example involves lowering the minimum voting age for state and local elections. In 1970, Congress lowered the minimum voting age to 18. The Supreme Court in December of that year upheld this action for national elections but ruled that the change was unconstitutional when applied to state and local elections. Early in 1971 a constitutional amendment to lower the voting age in national, state, and local elections was introduced in Congress. The proposal passed both houses with unusual haste and was ratified by the states in the record time of slightly over three months, as the Twenty-sixth Amendment.

More typical were the unsuccessful attempts to overturn decisions by the Supreme Court in the 1960s dealing with criminal procedures, school prayers and Bible reading, and reapportionment.[76]

REVERSAL THROUGH NEW LEGISLATION

Congress quite regularly offsets the impact of Court decisions by the adoption of new legislation. Nearly one hundred provisions of federal laws have been declared unconstitutional by the Supreme Court. Henry J. Abraham suggests: "No fewer than twenty-nine times has Congress passed legislation that had the effect of reversing the Court either totally or in substantial measure...."[77] Table 13.3 demonstrates the congressional response. Where the courts have restricted law through interpretation, Congress can act to redraw the statute. This has been the experience since 1937, when the federal

---

[74] Haines, *op. cit.*, pp. 287ff.

[75] Musmanno, *op. cit.*, p. 212.

[76] In 1964 the House Judiciary Committee held hearings on 147 proposals aimed at the Court's decisions on school prayers and Bible reading. *Congressional Quarterly Weekly Report,* May 1, 1964, p. 881.

[77] Abraham, *op. cit.*, p. 334.

TABLE 13.3
Type of Congressional Action after Supreme Court Decisions
Holding Legislation Unconstitutional within Four Years
after Enactment (Including New Deal Legislation), 1803–1955

Congressional Action	Major Policy	Minor Policy	Total
Reverse Court's policy	17	2	19
None	0	12	12
Other	6	1	7
Total	23	15	38

SOURCE: Adapted from Robert Dahl, "Decision-Making in a Democracy: The Supreme Court as National Policy-Maker," *Journal of Public Law,* VI (Fall 1957), 290.

courts began to restrict their overseer's role. From 1945 to 1957, Supreme Court interpretations of statutes had been reversed, in effect, by subsequent statutes in twenty-one instances. In nearly all of these instances, Congress acted to restore a widespread consensus which had been upset by a court decision. Reversal was most predictable when the groups affected by the Court's decisions were politically articulate and united in support of action by Congress. Court decisions that met with less opposition were very rarely upset by Congress.[78]

ATTACKS ON THE COURTS

Legislative reaction to judicial decisions also takes the form of attacks on the courts themselves. Many controversial court decisions are followed by legislative attempts to restrict the activities of the courts. A common proposal would require the courts to have more than a simple majority vote before they could declare legislative acts unconstitutional. Several such amendments were proposed in the 1820s.[79] From 1900 to 1936, thirty-seven proposals were introduced in Congress to limit the power of the courts to declare legislative acts unconstitutional; of these, twenty-five required more than a simple majority to invalidate legislative acts.[80] Proposals to restrict judicial review reached their apogee during the crisis over New Deal legislation. Table 13.4 shows something of the dimensions of congressional antagonism toward the Court in the mid-1930s. Other proposals involving alteration of selection and removal procedures, as well as the jurisdiction of the courts, are sprinkled throughout the nineteenth century. Recently, a rash of congressional attacks have taken such forms as bills proposing to revoke the jurisdiction of the federal courts over cases dealing with the apportionment of state legislatures. One such bill passed the House in 1964. However, few of these proposals received serious attention in Congress. The history of

[78] "Congressional Reversal of Supreme Court Decisions, 1945–1957," *Harvard Law Review,* LXXI (May 1958), 1326–36. Congressional reaction in 1967 and 1968 to Supreme Court decisions on the rights of accused persons is detailed in Adam Carlyle Breckenridge, *Congress Against The Court* (Lincoln: University of Nebraska Press, 1970).

[79] Haines, *op. cit.,* p. 469.

[80] Fite and Rubenstein, *op. cit.,* pp. 763–64; Musmanno, *op. cit.,* p. 94.

TABLE 13.4

Proposed Constitutional Amendments Designed to Limit or Deny the Court's Power to Declare Acts of Congress Unconstitutional, 1935–39

Year	Number of Amendments Proposed
1935	3
1936	3
1937	15
1939	1

SOURCE: Data from U.S., Congress, Senate, *Proposed Amendments to the Constitution of the United States of America*, 87th Cong., 2nd sess., Doc. 163 (1963).

legislative attacks on the courts in the states is about the same. Criticism of the courts is sometimes intense, but it seldom results in any direct action being taken. Altering the selection process in the states is the major exception.[81]

The record of legislative response to judicial decision-making can be spelled out, but analyses of why these reactions occur and explanations of their success or failure are more difficult. Each major judicial decision is likely to produce new controversy—both inside and outside legislative assemblies. Yet the response is seldom translated into effective action. One basic explanation for this is that courts are able to temper their controversial decisions by more restricted action in subsequent cases. In this manner, criticism may be deflected. For example, the Supreme Court's decision in *Stuart* v. *Laird* helped soften the impact of *Marbury* v. *Madison*. In the late 1820s and early 1830s, the Supreme Court rendered decisions modifying earlier and stronger statements on the subjects of impairing obligation of contract and federal control of commerce.[82] Much the same thing occurred in the so-called New Deal cases when the famous "switch in time that saved nine" took place. In four months in 1937, the Supreme Court upheld the validity of several key statutes and thus apparently saved itself from a successful executive and legislative attack.[83] Controversy over the school segregation cases was somewhat diminished by the behavior of the courts in applying these rulings to specific situations. Other good examples are available in judicial decisions on legislative investigations. In the late 1950s, the Court seemed to modify the highly controversial *Watkins* decision in the *Barenblatt* case, just as it seemed to modify the *Sweezy* decision in *Uphaus* v. *Wyman*.[84]

A second explanation for the failure of most attacks on the courts is found in the fact that key provisions of the Constitution often have no self-evident meaning. Reasonable men will differ in their interpretations.

[81] Haines, *op. cit.*, p. 428–29. See his Chapter 17 for a discussion of proposals for reform.

[82] Murphy, *op. cit.*, p. 27. For a related analysis, see Stuart S. Nagel, *The Legal Process From A Behavorial Perspective* (Homewood, Ill.: Dorsey Press, 1969), p. 278.

[83] Kelly and Harbison, *op. cit.*, pp. 759–64.

[84] Pritchett, *op. cit.*, p. 121.

456 Moreover, court decisions rarely antagonize all segments of society. Decisions which offend some groups will please others. Generally, when agreement is lacking in society, successful opposition to the courts is less likely. The absence of a "unified enemy" is seen most clearly when the courts have declared state legislative acts unconstitutional. Attacks on the Marshall Court were blunted in part for this reason. The same reasoning helps to explain the failures of the Populists and Progressives in the early twentieth century in their efforts to attack the courts.

Third, legislative bodies are generally organized more to prevent action than to promote it. A successful attack on the courts depends on the ability of legislatures to transcend their typical patterns of behavior. This action is unlikely unless legislative authority is challenged directly or unless powerful organized groups are prodding the legislature to act.[85]

In a sweeping survey of experience in American history, Stuart Nagel finds:

> The factors that have an affirmative correlation with the success of Court-curbing bills...[are] as follows: (1) sponsored by the majority party in Congress, (2) party split between the Court and Congress, (3) crisis present and allegedly made more severe by the Court's decisions, (4) public and pressure group support, (5) northern sponsored attack, (6) introduced in Senate, (7) limited in purpose, and (8) has Presidential support and cohesive congressional leadership.[86]

These correlations carry us beyond mere conjecture, but in terms of causal analysis, Walter Murphy's general conclusion must probably suffice:

> Recognizing the potential threat to their own policy aims which the authority of the High Bench poses, members of Congress and executive officials will continue to view judicial power with a suspicion which will turn to hostility whenever they themselves or articulate segments of their constituencies disapprove of specific decisions, or when these officials fear that their own policy-making prerogatives are being threatened.[87]

Legislatures, Courts, and the Political Process

Legislative-judicial relations in the United States are ordinarily marked by harmony and mutual indifference. Such comity is hardly surprising since both legislative and judicial institutions tend to reflect the dominant attitudes and policies in society at a given time. When conflict does occur, the courts tend to be least successful against enduring, cohesive political majorities and most successful "against a 'weak' majority; e.g., a dead one, a transient one, a fragile one, or one weakly united upon a policy of sub-

---

[85] For a related analysis, see Murphy, *op. cit.*, Chapter 11. The danger in accepting easy explanations of the defeat of anti-Court proposals in Congress is stressed by Harry P. Stumpf, "Congressional Response to Supreme Court Rulings: The Interaction of Law and Politics," *Journal of Public Law,* XIV (1966), 381.

[86] Nagel, *op. cit.*, p. 279. More generally, see pp. 260–79.

[87] Murphy, *op. cit.*, p. 268.

ordinate importance."[88] The judiciary is most likely to be successful when it avoids the critical, highly charged political controversies and deals with less substantial issues.[89] Judges demonstrate an awareness of their position in the limitations that they impose upon themselves. Henry J. Abraham records sixteen types of self-limitations.[90] These range from a judicial presumption of the constitutionality of statutes to a practice of hearing only cases properly brought before them. Judges avoid "political questions"—that is, questions which they feel are more appropriately resolved by the executive and legislative branches. If possible, they decide cases on other than constitutional grounds.

If the courts generally choose to avoid conflict with the legislative branch, it is likely that the judiciary will frequently hold a subordinate position among political institutions. One impressionistic study of the relative strength of the president, Congress, and the courts discovered a tendency, with some overlap, toward judicial supremacy over about fifty years, a tendency toward legislative supremacy over about seventy-five years, and a tendency toward presidential supremacy over some sixty-four years.[91]

Ultimately, the political influence of the courts rests primarily on their "unique legitimacy"—on an attitude bordering on veneration among the people. If popular support of the courts is insufficient to permit them to challenge the legislatures steadily, that attitude is nevertheless useful in helping the courts to defend themselves against legislative onslaught. Despite an overwhelming victory in 1936 and the presence of a Democratic majority in Congress, President Roosevelt failed in his attempt to "pack" the Supreme Court in 1937. One explanation for his defeat rests on the "magic of the courts."[92] This "unique legitimacy" serves other functions besides insulating the courts. Courts in upholding legislative acts can assist legislatures by bestowing this legitimacy on the compromises and practical decisions of the political process.[93]

Judges interpret the generalizations of legislative statutes outside the gaze of the public. Only rarely do the courts challenge legislative bodies and even more rarely do they do so successfully. Unusual instances—as in the school segregation decisions—sometimes place the courts at the center of the lawmaking process. The courts then can act as more than a moral stimulus to the legislature in particular and the nation in general. But the role of the courts should be put in perspective. Although they can at times restrict legislative activity, "as an administrative means of preventing legislative tyranny, judicial review of national policy appears to have marginal value."[94]

[88] Robert Dahl, "Decision-Making in a Democracy," *Journal of Public Law*, VI (Fall 1957), 286.

[89] Robert McCloskey, *The American Supreme Court* (Chicago: University of Chicago Press, 1960), p. 229.

[90] Abraham, *op. cit.*, pp. 355–77.

[91] *Ibid.*, pp. 342–43.

[92] In assessing the relevance of judicial prestige to explaining the defeat of congressional attempts to counter Court decisions, Stumpf distinguishes between anti-Court and antidecision proposals. *Op. cit.*, pp. 390–91.

[93] Murphy and Pritchett, *op. cit.*, p. 555.

[94] S. Sidney Ulmer, "Judicial Review as Political Behavior: A Temporary Check on Congress," *Administrative Science Quarterly*, IV (1959–1960), 445.

part five

Conclusion

14

THE LEGISLATIVE PROCESS:
PROBLEMS AND PERSPECTIVES

The blueprint for an effective and responsible legislature is not hard to draw —the difficulties and intricacies lie in converting the design into reality. A number of writers have argued that the legislatures fall far short of their potential and have suggested a variety of reforms. There is, in fact, a general restiveness among students of government concerning the performance and viability of legislative institutions, though it cannot be said that this has led to a lively public debate. No more, indeed, than a handful of publications maintain a steady interest in appraising the work and effectiveness of Congress, and fewer still engage in exploring in depth the behavior of state legislatures. Popular reporting on the legislature is preoccupied with issues, politics, and personalities; the institution, with its system of power and priorities, is not often placed in focus. There is nothing unusual in this finding, of course, for the reportorial media have an investment in conflict and gear themselves to gathering and circulating accounts of it. Ordinarily the "system" is not easily visible, and should it lie exposed, it seems not to qualify as "good" news.

The controversy over legislative performance occurs for the most part outside legislative halls, occasionally in the newspapers and more regularly in the professional literature. In the world of politics there is nothing resembling a persistent demand for an overhaul of the legislative institution. Nor is such a demand to be found among the public. Quite the contrary, it seems probable that most people are not troubled in the slightest by the performance of American legislatures or apprehensive over their loss of vitality.

Who finds the legislature satisfactory? Subject, we suppose, to exceptions and modifications, the answer is clear: first, those legislators who enjoy preeminence under existing arrangements; second, those interest groups whose influence would be imperiled by new forms and practices; third, those who prefer that political power be located in nooks and crannies rather than in central agencies; fourth, those who have an ingrained aversion to centralized power in any form; fifth, those devoted to advancing local rather than state or national priorities; sixth, those who laud the customary and traditional in American political life.

Those who look with equanimity on the legislature and its devices for containing the flow of power are not without argument. The key to their position is the belief that legislatures perform about as well as can be expected in a pluralistic political system which values accommodation, compromise, and decentralization. If the legislature is weak, it cannot easily advance arbitrary and pernicious innovations. If the diffusion of legislative power makes it perplexing to fix responsibility, it also makes it difficult to undo the accumulation of traditional habits and arrangements. If legislative procedure makes it difficult for the majority to work its will, it also assures the minority of its right to be heard. If legislators subordinate broad interests to provincial ones, they nonetheless make government responsive to local needs and viewpoints. And finally, if the legislature is often slow to respond to impulses for change, it is likewise less apt to act capriciously.

Not all the strictures lodged against the legislature and its procedures are either valid or moderate. It is altogether easy to see the legislature in the light of continuing exaggeration and just as easy to ignore the limitations under which it conducts its business. Great size alone makes it difficult for the legislature to operate with the alacrity its critics would prefer. What passes as somnolence is often no more than the inertia inevitably linked to the involvement of large numbers in decision-making.

Second thoughts are also in order concerning the petty quarreling and garrulous debate which at times make the legislature its own worst enemy. We come closer to a realistic appraisal of legislative behavior if we recognize that bickering and factionalism are unavoidable in a democratic society. Unlike judges and administrators, who have their quarrels and make their decisions in relative privacy, legislators live in glass houses where anyone may observe their foibles and disputes.[1] It is about the same with "partisanship," oftentimes strident and disquieting. However unseemly it may appear and whatever its cost to the legislature in public esteem, it cannot be excised without impairing the free function of party. Moreover, what appears as blatant and ugly partisanship to one man is no more than simple justice to another. No small amount of the criticism visited upon the legislature, we are saying, comes from a misunderstanding of its functions in a democratic political system.

The newspaper view of the legislature, frequently uncomplimentary (especially in the case of state legislatures), is not necessarily a faithful reproduction. Newspapers, as has been said of pressure groups, live by exaggeration. Harmony and quiet accomplishment, as items of news, are steadily subordinated to suspense, excitement, controversy, and a variety of nickel crusades that include pillorying the legislature. Moreover, political news is shaped to some extent by those who report it:

---

[1] The image of the legislature is difficult to protect. A single incident is likely to trigger a vast amount of public criticism. Consider these observations by a state legislator in Wisconsin: "We're all tarred with the same brush. What one legislator does affects all 133 of us. I can give you an illustration of that. A few years ago, some of the boys were whooping it up over in the Belmont Hotel and they amused themselves at night by throwing beer cans out of the window where they clattered musically down on the pavement below and the police were called and it was headlines in the paper. When I returned that weekend, as other legislators did, although I personally was not involved in the beer can throwing incident, we became the beer can throwing legislature. My constitutents were saying to me: 'Is that all you've got to do down there is throw beer cans around?' " Quoted in Ronald D. Hedlund and Wilder Crane, Jr., *The Job of the Wisconsin Legislator* (Washington, D.C.: American Political Science Association, 1971), p. 69.

The reporter is the recorder of government but he is also a participant. He operates in a system in which power is divided. He as much as anyone, and more than a great many, helps to shape the course of government. He is the indispensable broker and middleman among the subgovernments of Washington. He can choose from among the myriad events that seethe beneath the surface of government which to describe, which to ignore. He can illumine policy and notably assist in giving it sharpness and clarity; just as easily, he can prematurely expose policy and, as with undeveloped film, cause its destruction. At his worst, operating with arbitrary and faulty standards, he can be an agent of disorder and confusion. At his best, he can exert a creative influence on Washington politics.[2]

Finally, the issues thrust before the legislature are extraordinarily complex. A few originate in the legislature; most are handed over to it because they cannot be resolved to the satisfaction of all interested parties anywhere else. "The flight to government," Schattschneider remarks, "is perpetual." It occurs because the losing contestants in *private* conflicts seek relief, new and more favorable settlements, from a *public* authority.[3] Conflict is not easily managed in the legislature, for on every major issue there are clashing opinions of powerful and insistent pressure groups. Our expectations concerning the legislature are unreasonable if they include the notion that the resolution of issues, or lawmaking, can be handled with dispatch or that the complex of threads which compose any issue can be unraveled and rewoven without strife and acrimony.

In sum, though it is easy enough to criticize the legislature for ineptitude and occasional gross behavior, it is not altogether fitting to assay its performance apart from the environment in which it functions. In a word, defining what the legislature ought to be, like defining the "public interest," is a troublesome task. Much of the remainder of this chapter is concerned with identifying and evaluating the principal weaknesses of the American legislature. At this point, however, it may be well to point out that some observers view American legislatures in about the same light as Clinton Rossiter viewed American political parties: that what is needed is not a major overhaul but rather "another three tablespoons of discipline and five pinches of responsibility."[4]

Efforts to Reform the Legislature

CONGRESS

Every now and again Congress turns introspective, seeking ways of improving its organization and better methods for handling persistent problems. Numerous changes have been made since the first Congress assembled in Washington in 1789, but only a few have had any more lasting impact than a stone

[2] Douglass Cater, *The Fourth Branch of Government* (Boston: Houghton Mifflin Company, 1959), p. 7.

[3] *The Semisovereign People* (New York: Holt, Rinehart & Winston, Inc., 1961), p. 40.

[4] *Parties and Politics in America* (Ithaca, N.Y.: Cornell University Press, 1960), p. 180.

464 dropped in the water. Congress, like other social institutions, is wary of innovations that might do violence to traditional values.

The principal object of reform has been the committee system. Change has taken two forms. The first, occurring in the early nineteenth century, saw Congress abandon its preoccupation with creating numerous special committees and move to a more orderly system of standing committees. The second has involved a continuing struggle to streamline the committee structure by eliminating those no longer useful. Until recently, battles to cut out committees were more often lost than won. Early in the twentieth century, well over one hundred standing committees were found in the House and Senate. A good many had lost their reason for existence and others plainly were moribund; ambiguous and conflicting jurisdictions compounded the problem. A number of committees were erased in the 1920s, but it was not until 1946 that a significant paring down took place. The Legislative Reorganization Act of that year reduced the number of standing committees in the House from forty-eight to nineteen and in the Senate from thirty-three to fifteen. Currently there are twenty-one standing committees in the House and seventeen in the Senate. Obviously the consolidation of committees does not of itself assure greater effectiveness in the legislature, but, in the opinion of most observers, Congress is better off now than before.

Many changes in congressional organization and practices in the nineteenth century had the function of centralizing authority. The Rules Committee of the House, for example, began its rise to power in 1841, when it was given the power to report at any time. Later on, in 1858, its position was enhanced further when the Speaker was installed as its chairman. Its sphere of influence was widened again in 1883 when it was given the power to report special orders fixing the terms of floor debate. During the tenure of Speakers Reed and Cannon, the Committee on Rules became the principal agency for controlling the House.

Another change in congressional organization worth noting occurred in 1865, when a separate Appropriations Committee was formed in the House; responsibility for appropriations formerly had been entrusted to the Committee on Ways and Means. Conflict over the authority of the Appropriations Committee soon developed, however, and in 1885 the House chose to vest the power to report appropriations bills in a number of committees, one for each of the executive departments. Not until the passage of the Budget and Accounting Act of 1921 was the appropriations function again consolidated in a single committee.[5]

---

[5] The House decision in 1885 to manipulate the Appropriations Committee's jurisdiction, removing nearly one-half of the total federal budget from its control, occurred because of growing House dissatisfaction over the independence and imperialism of the committee, along with its excessive "economy-mindedness." The move to strip the committee of its jurisdiction was led by members of the most powerful committees of the House, including Ways and Means, Rules, Judiciary, Banking and Currency, and Commerce. Members of those committees which would assume some portion of the Appropriations Committee's jurisdiction heavily supported the change. When this decision was reversed decades later, members from those committees which would lose jurisdiction were the principal opponents of consolidating the appropriations function. See Richard F. Fenno, Jr., *The Power of the Purse: Appropriations Politics in Congress* (Boston: Little, Brown & Company, 1966), pp. 42–46.

Although the houses of Congress frequently have made organizational and procedural alterations, the record suggests that in only two cases, both in the twentieth century, has the overhauling been of major proportions. The first occurred in 1910–11 when the autocratic Speaker of the House, Joseph G. Cannon, was stripped of his most important powers. A "reorganization" in the broadest sense, a political revolution in the strictest sense, the changes found the Speaker shorn of his right to appoint standing committee members and of his membership on the Rules Committee; in addition, his power over recognition was curtailed. Probably no other action in the history of Congress has altered so fundamentally the internal distribution of power.

The second major attempt to transform Congress took place in 1946 when, following lengthy study and substantial bargaining, the Legislative Reorganization Act was passed. Unlike the 1910—11 episode, this one was "bloodless," and in its final form the act contained little of *political* significance. As we have noted, the historic gambit of eliminating and revamping committees was invoked. A number of housekeeping provisions involving committee organization, records, and meetings were introduced. Staff assistance for legislators and committees was augmented and the Legislative Reference Service and the Office of Legislative Counsel were strengthened. To enhance congressional control over spending, the act provided for a legislative budget which would set a ceiling on appropriations for each fiscal year; this was tried once in 1948 and promptly abandoned. Another feature of this legislation was Title III, requiring lobbyists to register and file financial reports. Rounding out the modernization effort in pleasant style were provisions which increased legislative salaries and expense accounts and made legislators eligible for a retirement plan.

Nearly twenty years after the Legislative Reorganization Act of 1946 was passed, Congress decided to reexamine its legislative machinery. A Joint Committee on the Organization of Congress was established, and Senator A. S. Mike Monroney (D., Okla.) and Representative Ray J. Madden (D., Ind.) were selected as co-chairmen of the twelve-member committee. Although the joint committee issued its report in 1966, it required four years for Congress to pass a reorganization bill. By no means a major reform of Congress, the Legislative Reorganization Act of 1970 nevertheless contains provisions which, if implemented, are likely to improve congressional procedures and eliminate certain abuses in the legislative process.

The most important provisions of the 1970 act concern the committee system. Among other things, the act provides that committees may sit while the House is in session (unless a bill is being read for amendment), opens committee meetings and hearings to the public (unless a committee majority votes to close them), requires committees to provide a week's notice of hearings to be held except in unusual circumstances, empowers a committee majority to provide for broadcasting or televising of hearings subject to certain conditions, eliminates proxy voting (unless otherwise provided by a committee), permits minority party members to have at least one day during the course of any committee hearing to call witnesses of their choosing, requires that a committee report on a bill be filed within seven days after a committee majority makes such a request, and brings the Senate into agreement with the House by permitting a committee majority to call a special meeting if the chairman fails to call a meeting on request.

466   The main thrust of these procedural changes is to diminish arbitrary rule by the chairman. Nevertheless, whether these changes will contribute significantly to the democratization of the committee system will depend on the willingness of committee members to insist on their implementation— and perhaps in the process to risk alienating the chairman. If it chooses, a committee majority can set aside most of these provisions.

Still other provisions of the 1970 act permit teller votes to be recorded if demanded by twenty members,[6] permit ten minutes of debate on any amendment printed in the *Congressional Record,* provide for ten minutes of debate on any motion to return a bill to committee with instructions, and divide time for debate on a conference report between the majority and minority.[7] These changes, like those involving the committee system, not only help to "open up" the legislative process but also provide safeguards for the individual member. Linked to the recent (if modest) changes in the House seniority rule,[8] they hold some promise for a Congress more in tune with democratic tenets.

Comprehensive reform of Congress has never been an easy goal to achieve. Reasonable men differ not only on the need for congressional reform, but also on the objectives and consequences of it. How Congress is seen depends on where the viewer stands. Critics who see Congress through "executive" eyes, classifying the institution as an obstacle to be overcome by the president, are not interested in exactly the same reforms as those men who desire to strengthen legislative independence and autonomy. Moreover, legislators who occupy key positions are chary of reforms that may seem to threaten their power or the power of their party, friends, state delegations, or regions. Proposals for legislative change often fail outright, or are re-shaped to the point of innocuousness, because they cannot meet the critical test of political feasibility—a test set by legislators rather than by outsiders.

STATE LEGISLATURES

The impulse for reorganization of the state legislature is not to be found in the public at large. Such concern as exists is chiefly centered in a handful of groups and private organizations. "Good government" organizations of one sort or another are dedicated advocates of change, as are some newspapers. Academicians of all stripes similarly see the need. Some labor unions offer instruction for their memberships concerning the difficulties labor faces in the legislative process, and spokesmen for the cities come together regularly to

---

6 On the early evidence, the change in teller voting ranks among the principal features of the 1970 act. For example, in the judgment of both opponents and proponents of the supersonic transport plane (SST), the successful effort in 1971 to delete funds for the plane from a Department of Transportation funding bill was due to the use of a recorded teller vote. With teller votes now likely to be recorded on crucial amendments, members will be unable to hide their voting record from constituents. See an account of the SST vote in the *New York Times,* March 19, 1971, p. 24.

7 A convenient summary of the central provisions of the Reorganization Act of 1970 can be found in the *1970 Congressional Quarterly Almanac,* pp. 447–61. Also see an analysis of the act by Bruce R. Hopkins, "Congressional Reform: A Little, but Possible, Bit," *American Bar Association Journal,* LVII (January 1971), 62–65.

8 See the discussion of the revised seniority rule in Chapter 6, pp. 183–84.

complain of ill treatment by the legislature. Bar associations at times become exercised over the legislative function, but usually only when the judiciary is somehow implicated. Even some legislators here and there put themselves on record for reform. In general, it is those individuals and groups on the outside looking in—whose influence ordinarily is slight or shrinking—who seek to break the legislature out of its conventional mold.

In a majority of states, modernization of the legislature has taken place so gradually as to be imperceptible to all but close observers. Dropping a committee at one point, adding one at another point has been a standard prescription for remedying the ills of legislative organization. Clearly, the response of many legislatures to proposals for profound change has been to cling even more tenaciously to the *status quo.* And in the absence of public interest in the legislature and steady concern over how well it does its job, the lawmakers' passivity toward significant reform should not be astonishing.

Nevertheless, some genuine reorganization has occurred, some experimental action has been attempted, some hurdles to effective lawmaking have been surmounted. The principal efforts to renovate the legislature have concerned the committee system, sessions, salaries, staff, information systems, and the introduction of machine voting.

With some exceptions, the states have made noticeable progress in recent years in streamlining cumbersome committee systems. Emulating Congress, they have cut out a vast potpourri of bogus and extraneous standing committees. The typical lower house today has less than twenty standing committees, about half the number it had in the 1940s; in the typical senate the number is even less. Be that as it may, there are still some legislatures with an extraordinary number of committees: at last count the Mississippi legislature had over eighty standing committees. A few New England states have adopted and found effective a system of joint committees; elsewhere this arrangement has been used sparingly. And despite improvements, it is still not unusual to find legislative houses where members serve on half a dozen committees during a session. The record of committee modernization, in sum, is good but somewhat spotty.

Trends in legislative sessions are also worth recalling at this point. More states (thirty-six) now have annual sessions than at any time since the era of disillusionment set in late in the nineteenth century. The newest states, Hawaii and Alaska, both began with annual-session provisions. It continues to be true in a majority of states that the legislature is only partly master of its chambers, and whether its work is finished or not it must end its session by a certain date. Given the extraordinary problems now thrust upon the states, sessional limitations appear unwise, even foolish, in the opinion of many commentators.

The most significant contribution to legislative renewal in this century is found in the creation and development of service agencies to provide legislators with information and assistance. The principal agencies are legislative reference services and legislative councils, but increased use is also made of various kinds of interim (between-session) legislative commissions. Research staffs have been augmented, and in some states one or more universities have assisted the legislature in its quest for reliable information. In state after state a new urgency has become associated with "fact-finding"

468 and expert research—occasioned by the novel and increasingly technical problems that make their way to the legislature.

The service agencies engage in a number of related activities, including research and reference assistance, bill-drafting, statutory revision, codification, preparation of recommendations for legislation, and review of state revenues and appropriations. A few states empower their legislative councils to screen administrative proposals and even to take the testimony of interested citizens concerning proposals. At one time radical innovations, reference services and councils have become indispensable units in the legislative process.

Over one-half of the states now use electric voting machines in one or both houses to record and tabulate roll-call votes. This has resulted in conserving considerable time, of which there is seldom enough in the usual legislature. Presumably the legislatures using this mechanical aid have been improved as a result, but this claim must be accepted on faith alone. The only certainty about it is that it speeds up the process of counting votes. As with automation generally, there are subtle as well as manifest consequences. In this case, the trouble is that many legislators seem to believe that legislative "reform" consists of putting in voting machines (or raising salaries or expense accounts, or increasing the stenographic pool, or adding a full-time staff member to the appropriations committee). There may be nothing wrong with any of these ideas, as there is nothing wrong with taking aspirin for pneumonia. Fundamental disorders, however, are not so easily remedied.

Not dramatically visible, but worth noting, is a miscellany of other legislative improvements which have been made in recent years. For example, bill-drafting has been improved; more states now have provisions for presession filing of bills; presession orientation conferences for freshman legislators are becoming increasingly common; committee research staffs are being developed; local and special legislation have declined markedly; expeditious ways of handling noncontroversial bills are being sought and developed; new concern over redistributing committee work loads is in evidence; and legislative salaries in many states have been raised to more realistic levels (on an hourly basis it is still more remunerative to collect garbage than to legislate in some states).

From an overall perspective, however, most state legislatures still have a long way to go before becoming genuinely effective institutions. Figure 15, drawn from a 1970 study by the Citizens Conference on State Legislatures, shows the relative ranking of the fifty state legislatures in terms of their decision-making capabilities. The ranking does not indicate, necessarily, how well these legislatures perform; rather it depicts their capacity for effective performance.

A state legislature ranking high in capability, for example, would have unrestricted annual sessions, competent staff support for members, well-developed information systems, individual offices for members, rules of procedure that foster individual and collective accountability, substantial budget and subpoena powers, oversight and audit capabilities, and comprehensive public records. In addition, it would have a membership of modest size, a limited number of committees, and a high salary level for members. By and large, state legislatures that rank high in one respect rank high in all respects, while those at the bottom show a similar consistency. The California and New York legislatures rank near the top in virtually all categories. Southern legislatures tend to be clustered among those states that rank low in legislative capability. Florida is a conspicuous exception among southern states.[9]

The state legislatures of the 1970s are not *au courant* with the ways of Congress, but to some extent they have shaken off their lethargy. There are a number of state legislatures today that are characterized by a growing professionalism, a rising concern for standards of performance, and a heightened sensitivity to the need to free the legislature from traditional— and not altogether legitimate—opprobrium. The prospects for reforming state legislatures are better now than at any time in the past.

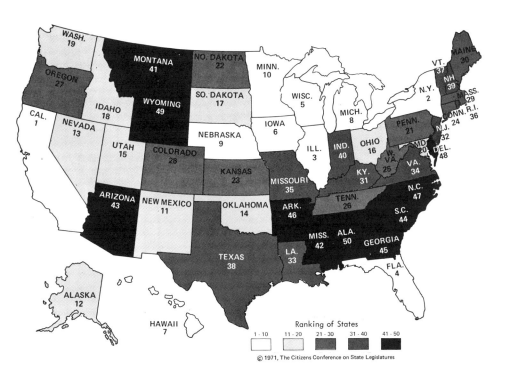

FIGURE 15　*The functional capabilities of the fifty state legislatures.*

The Real Dilemmas

In the matter of legislative reorganization it is easy to mistake shadows for substance, modernization for reform. The chief fact about past congressional and state legislative reorganizations is that in all but rare instances

---

9 *Report on an Evaluation of the 50 State Legislatures* (Kansas City, Mo.: Citizens Conference on State Legislatures, 1971).

470 they have centered on streamlining the institutions rather than on eliminating the fundamental causes of malaise. A major reason that change is difficult to bring about is that existing arrangements inevitably are entangled with basic allocations of power and privilege. Consequently, reorganization efforts, unless produced by new political settlements, scarcely touch the underlying conditions of the legislature. Reorganization ordinarily is not the culmination of a reshuffling of political power in which new men with new loyalties gain control of the legislative machinery. Changes are brought about periodically, but the fundamental, business-as-usual arrangements are seldom disturbed.

The interest of American legislatures in examining their organization, rules, and procedures crops up on only the rarest of occasions and is difficult to sustain; when it does develop it is perhaps as likely to have been induced by pressure from outside as from pressure by members. The evanescence of the reform spirit among both legislators and outsiders is not hard to understand. It is not simply a case of reform being effectively resisted by a legislative "establishment" that feels itself threatened—however attractive such a simple thesis may be to some legislators or to the press. An equally sound explanation is that support for change is hard to generate because legislatures tend to be evaluated on the basis of their current performance:

> Much reform energy is wasted because agitation among members (and outsiders) tends to be greatest when policy conflicts are most intense. When the issues are resolved (with or without institutional change), the concern over modifying the structure abates. Thus, at a time when there is consensus within the legislature there is little pressure to effectuate change.[10]

INORDINATE MINORITY POWER

In the judgment of many observers, the first and most significant problem ignored in reorganizations is "minority power." Sometimes decisive and sometimes not, it is a prominent factor in most legislatures. As in the case of power generally, it is not often put on public display—one feels it even if he does not always see it. But whatever mystery may surround minority power in the legislature, there is no problem knowing where to look for traces. We find them in the seniority system, in the committee system, and in the network of intricate rules and practices that govern legislative behavior.

Let us take Congress, for example, as the critics see it—especially those concerned about minority rule. They may begin by saying that although the weak deserve some protection from the strong, and certainly deserve to be heard, it strains democratic theory to the breaking point when a minority is able to resist whatever displeases it. On occasion only a fine line distinguishes minority rights from minority vetoes. It is true, of course, in theory that there are no *formal* barriers to majority rule and that a persistent majority can *eventually* win its way.

What troubles critics is that in practice the delays seem interminable: a committee chairman opposes a bill and it is not brought up for consider-

---

[10] Roger H. Davidson, David Kovenock, and Michael O'Leary, *Congress in Crisis: Politics and Congressional Reform* (Belmont, California: Wadsworth Publishing Company, 1966), p. 169.

ation; a committee unrepresentative of the chamber as a whole refuses to let important legislation come to the floor after a reasonable time or under ordinary procedures; a committee holds prolonged hearings on a bill as a means of delaying (and perhaps preventing) its consideration by the chamber as a whole; a Rules Committee majority in the House refuses to give a bill a green light to the floor, though it has already been passed by a substantive committee, and it is lost for the session; a conference committee is selected and members hostile to the legislation are appointed conferees; a House Rules Committee majority objects quietly to the Senate's inclusion of a particular provision in a bill and the provision is dropped for fear that it would doom the bill; a highly controversial issue looms, its opponents threaten or launch a filibuster, and the bill is lost without a vote; a party wins a broad electoral victory but a majority of the committee chairmanships are awarded, by the seniority rule, to members from one region of the country; vacancies occur on key committees and the new members appointed are unrepresentative of the party and out of step with its program.[11] The result, too frequently, is impasse—irritating and deadening.[12]

An explanation often singled out to account for minority power in the legislature centers on the committee system and the way in which chairmen are chosen. Congress stirs when the committees come to life, and if the committees dawdle and delay, Congress follows suit. The key issue, however, is not committee work but committee power. When committees (or their chairmen) have what amounts to the final word, as they do some of the time, one wants to be sure, say critics, they speak for the chamber's majority. Plainly, this is not always the case. And although means exist for bringing a committee down (e.g., discharge petitions, Calendar Wednesday), the hard fact is that these devices are cumbersome and exceedingly difficult to employ. As a result, on many a major issue majority rule is diluted, held in check, or emasculated by powerful committees dominated by organized minorities. Woodrow Wilson's judgment in 1885 that the House and Senate function according to a "scheme of distributed power and disintegrated rule" is, in the main, as appropriate today as it was then.[13]

The seniority rule for picking committee chairmen long has had a

---

[11] Numerous examples of the kind mentioned here can be flushed out of the literature on the legislative process. As a starter, see Robert Bendiner, *Obstacle Course on Capitol Hill* (New York: McGraw-Hill Book Company, Inc., 1964); Richard Bolling, *House Out of Order* (New York: E. P. Dutton & Co., Inc., 1965); and Joseph S. Clark, *Congress: The Sapless Branch* (New York: Harper & Row, Publishers, 1964). Of a different order (sans indignation), see Lewis A. Froman, *The Congressional Process: Strategies, Rules, and Procedures* (Boston: Little, Brown & Company, 1967).

[12] In Congress in recent years the House of Representatives has been singled out as the principal culprit in the obstruction of majority rule. It is easy enough to locate arrangements in the lower house that serve to impede majority action. Nonetheless, there is more than a ripple of suspicion that at times the inability of an apparent House majority to act is illusory. One can never be quite sure, as Douglass Cater has suggested, whether a viable majority has been thwarted by the "system" or whether in fact a "silent" majority is having its way, shielded by institutional forms and procedures that make it difficult to pinpoint responsibility. See "Spotlight on the House," *The Reporter*, September 28, 1961, pp. 27–29.

[13] *Congressional Government* (New York: Meridian Books, 1956 [originally published 1885]), p. 76.

472 corrosive effect on majority rule in Congress.[14] Because it favors those legislators who have the longest *continuous* service, it favors those predominantly one-party areas which return the same men to office election after election. As it works out, southern Democrats, midwestern Republicans, and representatives of rural areas in general have been its principal beneficiaries.[15] The irony is not lost on critics: the two-party areas of the country provide the votes for a congressional majority, but, having won it, receive less than their share of leadership positions. In the case of Democrats, states like California, Michigan, and Pennsylvania contribute the congressional majorities that make committee chairmen out of fellow party members from North Carolina, South Carolina, Georgia, and Tennessee.

It is perhaps true, as many observers contend, that no better system for selecting chairmen is available. The seniority method contributes to stability, insures experience in office, and by making investiture automatic, eliminates confusion and bickering. But it may also bring mediocrities to the top—age, circumstance, and electoral success become the critical variables in the rise to power. "In the long run," observes Roland Young, "the problems raised by the seniority method of selecting committee chairmen may perhaps best be met by modifying the functions of the chairman, making him simply the presiding officer of a collegiate body and not an official having independent authority by virtue of his title."[16] If the chairman's role were that of administrator and moderator, thus permitting a committee majority to act more freely, much of the criticism of the seniority device would vanish. Yet, though a chairman could no longer run his committee like a feudal barony, the fundamental powers of the committee itself would be unimpaired. This is the rub for critics who chafe under committee rule: there is no guarantee that the decisions of a committee majority will mirror the sentiments of a majority of the chamber.

---

[14] Another perspective on the issue of seniority may be found in the argument of Theodore J. Lowi. He contends that the problem is not one of seniority, of the regional distribution of chairmanships, or of the advancement of junior members in the congressional system. The real question is rather "how to loosen up the structures of Congress so that it can more effectively govern in a time of complexity and crisis." He offers two proposals for changes in the committee system. First, there should be an expansion in the number of committees in the Senate and House. "Twenty-five years under the 1946 reforms should prove that reduction of the number of committees merely increases the power of the remaining committees and their chairmen. Adding committees would first increase the available chairmanships, and that would mean an increase in the proportion of these important posts held by representatives from competitive districts and states. The increase would offer valuable patronage opportunities to the party leadership." Second, a chairmanship should be granted "to any congressman, regardless of seniority, whose drafting or floor leadership of a bill leads to the establishment of a new committee or subcommittee. Nothing is more likely to provide incentives for creative leadership in Congress; yet in no way does it attempt to revolutionize the seniority criterion." See his article, "How to Make Congress Work," *New York Times*, May 27, 1971, p. 39.

[15] The seniority issue would be eased by the development of competitive two-party politics in the South and in northern one-party Republican states and districts. The seniority rule has become a problem *chiefly* because it has become linked with one-partyism.

[16] Roland Young, *The American Congress* (New York: Harper & Row, Publishers, 1958), p. 72.

Though the committee system frequently is seized upon to explain a loss of legislative initiative, the matter is more fundamental. Committees have won a license to perform as "disintegrate ministries" because there is no central authority sufficiently powerful to control them. A vigorous legislative party is, of course, an agency of central control. But party rule in Congress has not been a dependable alternative to committee rule for a great many years.

The ultimate weapon of minority control is the privilege of talk; carried to an extreme, when the purpose is to prevent a vote from being taken—which the minority would surely lose—the practice becomes a fiilibuster. Filibustering is often successful because it is based on the sure intelligence that the unorganized majority will grow impatient to move on to other proposals crowding the calendar. A filibuster or the *threat* of one works at any time: at the beginning of a session because the members are anxious to get things rolling (especially the administration forces, who are concerned that their program not be imperiled), at the end because of the inevitable closing rush of business. The threat of a filibuster is far more common than the filibuster itself.

Two central principles are at stake in the dispute over unlimited debate: the right to be heard and the right to govern. Democratic theory insists that the minority have the right to be heard. Can an assembly place limits on this right without retreating from the basic principle of free expression? The answer, most political scientists would claim, is "yes." There is nothing illegitimate in lengthy, even belabored exposition held necessary to inform the assembly or to arouse the public—the latter in particular takes time. But there are limits to free debate: the task of the legislature is to balance the opposing pulls of the right to talk and the right to decide. The signal that debate has become promiscuous, that the right to talk has exceeded its bounds, is not simply the time it consumes but rather the presence of a plan to keep the assembly from ever voting on the question. Though the minority's right to be heard is broad and incontestable, requiring considerable forbearance by the majority, the minority has no right to govern. This right belongs to the majority, in whatever way it may constitute itself. Governing, it is well to remember, is fully as much a matter of vetoes as it is of adopting policies.

Minority control, the *bête noire* of most critics of Congress, is present in many state assemblies as well. But two of the principal strictures involving Congress—the seniority method and filibustering—are of only minor importance in the usual state legislature. Most states follow the seniority rule only casually in selecting committee chairmen, and in a number of states seniority counts for nothing at all. Although state legislative committees ordinarily do not have as great a measure of independence as the committees of Congress, they nevertheless are powerful agencies.[17] In some one-party states the standing committees constitute the principal device available to a dominant faction for controlling the legislature. As a general rule, where neither parties nor factions are able to control their members, committees tend to play a

---

[17] See Malcolm Jewell, *The State Legislature,* 2d ed. (New York: Random House, Inc., 1969), pp. 51–61.

474   significantly independent role. The committee position is strengthened by a widespread reluctance to invoke discharge rules. Independent committee power is minimal in those states which require all bills and resolutions to be reported. In at least some of the states the powers of committee chairmen appear to be as fully developed as in the most unreconstructed committee of Congress.

At bottom, the major shortcomings of the legislatures seem to be due more to fundamental weaknesses in institutional design and to traditional practices than to the quality of legislators or to the absence of legislative vision. The legislative system often makes the rule of majorities transient or precarious. As for the legislators, no matter how tarnished their public image is at times, they are neither simple-minded nor scoundrels. They live with conventional arrangements—partly because the *status quo* is comfortable and partly because it is hospitable to an established hierarchy of power.

UNREPRESENTATIVENESS

A remarkable fact about American legislatures, perhaps especially state legislatures, is the absence of genuine ferment over the major social problems that come before government—so contend critics in general and the press in particular. Cool and detached as a rule, state legislators, the argument holds, easily become embroiled over proposals to provide for pari-mutuel betting or to abolish "blue laws," but ignore long-run goals in public education or pressing metropolitan problems. A traditional explanation for the failure of legislatures to come to grips with important problems has centered on their unrepresentativeness, as reflected either in the overrepresentation of certain areas (usually rural) in the membership as a whole or in the overrepresentation of certain elements in the "power structure" of the institution.

Over the years no fact of daily civics has been more familiar to legislative observers than malapportionment. Prior to *Baker* v. *Carr,* equitable apportionment, like the legislature itself, remained largely unexamined and surely unvisited in most states. It scarcely exaggerates the situation to remark that in certain states the equal-population doctrine enunciated by the Supreme Court appeared to many legislators as a totally new concept, so accustomed were they to old apportionments and inherited arrangements. Rural power in virtually all legislatures was inflated. Typically, critics pointed out, major shifts in American social and economic life had not been accompanied by shifts in the locus of legislative power. The world had changed, but many of those who sat in the legislatures and manned the key positions saw it as it used to be. The inevitable result, in this interpretation, was that unrepresentative legislatures had not only failed to address themselves to many important questions of public policy, but also had neglected or directly damaged the interests of the nation's urban populations. Beyond that, of course, malapportioned legislatures were out of harmony with the idea that one person's vote should be equal to any other person's vote.

Malapportioned, unrepresentative legislatures are not yet out of style, but they are on the way out. Within the next few years legislative unrepresentativeness induced by malapportionment is likely to be of slight significance, so great has been the impact of the Supreme Court's reapportionment rulings. Although gerrymandering (within the equal-population doctrine) will doubtless continue to excite controversy, it is hard to imagine that it will ever produce grossly unrepresentative assemblies.

Unrepresentativeness in the "power structure" of legislatures is another matter. Virtually all legislatures at one time or another are criticized for the existence of inequities in the distribution of power among members. Typically, neither individual members nor regions share equally in legislatve power— as reflected in the selection of party leaders, the choice of committee chairmen, or in the assignment of members to key committees. Congress provides evidence for this point. Southern Democrats, for example, customarily hold a disproportionate number of committee chairmanships when the Democrats are in a majority in Congress, a fact that undoubtedly enhances southern influence within the system. Indeed, there is good evidence throughout both houses of a "conservative bias" that results from skewed representation. One way to measure this is to calculate the extent to which committees represent a cross section of the entire membership as shown by the voting behavior of their members. Research by Lewis A. Froman has shown that, for the 89th Congress, the seven most important Senate committees ranked lowest (aggregating the votes of Democratic members) in support of legislation that made up the president's legislative program. In contrast, the highest "presidential support" scores were achieved by the least important committees.[18] Although the extent of its impact is difficult to measure, skewed representation undoubtedly affects certain legislative outcomes, especially at the committee stage. Not surprisingly, it is also a chronic source of dissatisfaction with legislatures.[19]

Although the argument is persuasive that power has not been widely dispersed in Congress in recent decades, there are ample signs that changes in the pattern of power distribution are under way. The dominant institutional position held by southern Democrats since the middle 1940s is now showing evidence of decline. In both the House and Senate, the number of Democrats elected from northern states has been growing steadily. In 1970, for example, a clear majority of the congressmen elected from *nonsouthern* states were Democrats; this has occurred in only six off-year elections during this century.[20] As the proportion of northern Democrats elected to Congress increases, the prospects for new distributions of power similarly increase. Although Table 14.1, drawn from a study by Randall Ripley, shows that southern Democrats in the Senate continue to be overrepresented in critical institutional positions, it also discloses evidence of considerable northern power, as reflected by the growing number of northern Democrats serving as subcommittee chairmen, their presence among the top three positions on all standing committees, and their assignment to major committees. It is also apparent that the proportion of southerners in the Senate Democratic

18 Froman, *op. cit.*, pp. 196–208. The central point of this paragraph is also illustrated in the scattergrams of Chapter 6, which show the voting behavior of committee chairmen in the 91st Congress on legislation of interest to the "conservative coalition." See Figures 7 and 8, pp. 189 and 190.

19 See Clark, *op. cit.*, especially pp. 111–45.

20 Ross K. Baker and Michael A. Rappeport, "Liberals are Infiltrating the House," *Washington Post,* January 3, 1971.

TABLE 14.1

**Southern Democratic Representation on Senate Committees
and Subcommittees, 1941–71**

Congress (Year)	All Democratic Senators	Committee Chairmen	Three Highest Ranking Democrats on All Committees	All Democrats on Four Choice Committees[†]	Three Highest Ranking Democrats on Four Choice Committees[†]	Subcommittee Chairmen[‡]
			% of Southerners* Among:			
77th (1941)	33	62	48	36	67	—
79th (1945)	39	50	44	35	50	—
81st (1949)	41	40	42	54	67	—
83d (1953)	47	47§	56	56	67	—
85th (1957)	45	53	44	58	58	45
87th (1961)	34	56	48	46	67	41
89th (1965)	29	62	52	43	83	35
90th (1968)	30	56	46	37	67	31
92d (1971)	31	53	37	38	58	28

SOURCE: Randall B. Ripley, "Power in the Post–World War II Senate," *Journal of Politics,*
XXXI (May 1969), 475 (as updated).
* Those from the eleven states of the Confederacy.
† Appropriations, Armed Services, Finance, and Foreign Relations.
‡ Accurate data on subcommittees are difficult to obtain before 1955.
§ Ranking minority members (Republican Senate).

party has been declining.[21] The trends shown in Table 14.1 point clearly to
the erosion of the institutional base on which southern power in Congress
has been erected.

It remains to be mentioned that legislatures come under strictures for
their failure to accommodate sufficiently all elements of the population.
Legislatures are far from being microcosms of the population. The Negro
community, for example, is starkly underrepresented (in terms of Negroes
who serve as legislators) in the great majority of states as well as in Congress. How soon this grim fact will change is problematical, though there is
little doubt that it will change.

[21] "Power in the Post-World War II Senate," *Journal of Politics,* XXXI (May
1969), 465–92. Deficiencies in institutional power may be neutralized or perhaps
overcome by the adroit use of personal power. Ripley argues that by the late 1960s
institutional power in the Senate was not only in the process of dispersal but that
the personal power of individual senators had grown significantly. He writes: "There
are few obstacles to any senator of either party who has the requisite personal skills
to develop legislative power and chooses to use those skills. Virtually all senators can
acquire substantial legislative influence. Those who do not have it usually have disqualified themselves by violating the Senate's code of acceptable conduct that is
understood by most members. The code is not highly restrictive; and only repeated
violations bring sanctions. The sometime violator may retain all or most of his power.
Only a few senators have ignored the code altogether and thus forfeited most of
their legislative impact" (p. 492). Also see his book, *Power in the Senate* (New
York: St. Martin's Press, 1969).

INEFFICIENCY AND TRIVIALISM

Still another weakness of the American legislature is that, with no one tending the shop of public priorities, the machinery tends to become clogged by trivia. Great quantities of time are consumed on questions of slight moment, or on routine chores, or on matters but distantly related to major legislative functions. Whether power shrivels for want of use may or may not be true, but in any case it is difficult to see how legislatures can be strengthened if the energies of their members are dissipated on minor matters. There are several reasons why legislatures are harassed by minutiae and why lawmakers find it difficult to concentrate their attention on big problems. One reason is found in the two-year term of office for members of the lower house.[22] Affecting Congress and the states alike, the two-year term compels many legislators to campaign continually during their terms of office, with the result that there is never enough time for the public's business.

A second reason is that legislative tenure is tenuous or, more commonly, perceived as tenuous by legislators. This fact impels legislators to cater to their constituents—to run frequent errands for them, to intercede with administrative agencies for them, to entertain them when they visit the capital. Any delegation of consequence that visits Washington or the state capital can see the local representative, as can the single constituent if he is at all persistent. The legislator's time is seldom his own.

Veterans' claims, immigration and deportation cases, and a variety of personal and local problems find their way to congressional offices. A good staff can take care of many of these problems, but there is still a heavy drain on the lawmaker's time. Thus a New York congressman reports, "In my district, one half of my time is taken up running errands." A southern congressman complains: "I would say that answering correspondence (we average more than 100 letters a day from our district) and doing favors for constituents, totally unrelated to the business of legislating (arguing veterans' cases, handling Social Security matters and the like), take up the greater part of my time."[23] Errand-running has become so onerous that a proposal has been made that each district elect two congressmen, one to tend to the lawmaking tasks and one to manage constituents' requests involving government agencies. Interest has also developed in a plan used by Scandinavian countries in which complaints and requests of constituents are handled by an *ombudsman* (a Swedish word for "representative") and his staff rather than by legislators.[24] However attractive plans such as these are in theory,

---

[22] A survey of congressmen in the 88th Congress disclosed that the two factors most closely associated with attitudes toward the four-year term were *ideology* and *party affiliation*. Liberals were strongly in favor of the proposal while conservatives were strongly opposed to it. A disproportionate number of the very conservative members who opposed the proposal were Republicans. Surprisingly, whether a member was elected from a marginal or safe district made very little difference in his attitude. See Davidson, Kovenock, and O'Leary, *op. cit.,* pp. 106–9.

[23] *U.S. News and World Report,* September 12, 1960, p. 60.

[24] See Walter Gellhorn, *When Americans Complain* (Cambridge: Harvard University Press, 1966).

478 they may be deficient in political terms, since legislators are inclined to believe that errand-running is critical to their reelection.[25]

A third reason why much time is lost traces to the weakness of the legislative party organizations. Concerted party action leading to the adoption of party policies is infrequent; the party neither originates most legislation nor sees it through the legislature. In the void created by party failure, legislators clutch at all straws. Sensitive to the entreaties of pressure groups and apprehensive over their security in the assembly, legislators attend to all manner of narrow requests in the belief that out of such service emerges new or strengthened political support.

And fourth, time is squandered because efficiency is subordinated to other considerations. Although the U.S. Senate once followed a rule that debate must be germane to the subject matter at hand ("No one is to speak impertinently or beside the question, superfluously, or tediously"), it no longer does. Countless hours are consumed on matters irrelevant or of low urgency, as anyone who glances at the *Congressional Record* knows. Reluctance to limit the length of speeches takes a further toll on efficiency. Considerable time could be saved in Congress and the states by holding joint hearings on legislation, and installation of electric voting machines would also help to expedite decisions.

The legislative burden of Congress could be eased by relieving it of the responsibility of legislating for the District of Columbia. As it is, Congress functions as the city council of the nation's capital. Quite apart from the fact that most members of Congress are not greatly interested in the affairs of the District, it makes little sense for the national legislature to devote innumerable hours to questions of local government. A grant of home rule to Washington, permitting the residents to handle their own affairs, would be a useful step toward trimming the volume of legislation and freeing the time of Congress for more significant undertakings.[26] And were the states to confer home-rule powers upon their cities or otherwise to relinquish their hold over local initiative, the task of the legislature would shrink to

---

[25] Some members, doubtless a goodly number, thrive on servicing their constituents and would not want any other arrangement. Concerning Congress's absorption in minor matters, Robert Luce wrote: "Those members who care only for the little things of life and those who love petty power might deplore such a change, but the great mass of men elected to Congress would prefer dealing with only big problems." *Congress: An Explanation* (Cambridge: Harvard University Press, 1926), pp. 150–51. For an interpretation that errand-running "may be a more noble form of representation than has heretofore been recognized," see Norman C. Thomas and Karl A. Lamb, *Congress: Politics and Practice* (New York: Random House, Inc., 1964), pp. 41–46. A recent survey of a sample of congressmen discloses that over three-fourths of the members believe that "casework" for constituents is a legitimate part of their job. See *Hearings* on S. Con. Res. 2 before the Joint Committee on the Organization of Congress, 89th Cong., 1st sess., 1965, p. 775. The survey was conducted by Professors Roger Davidson, David Kovenock, and Michael O'Leary.

[26] In managing District affairs, Congress becomes involved in such matters as authorizing construction of roads, acquisition of land, street closings, purchase of meals for members of the metropolitan police force serving on special details, and regulation of the manufacture, renovation, and sale of mattresses. For testimony that such questions rank as something less than quintessential, see the remarks of former Representative John Schmidhauser (D., Iowa) in *Hearings* on S. Con. Res. 2 before the Joint Committee on the Organization of Congress, 89th Cong., 1st sess., 1965, pp. 254–57.

more manageable proportions. The devotion of the typical state legislature to writing legislation for municipalities is so great as to cause wonder over what is left for city councils to decide.

State legislatures sometimes come under critical review for the improbable, bizarre behavior of their members. The following account of a session of the Texas legislature is far from novel; indeed, such unrehearsed if not entirely spontaneous antics very likely have occurred in most state legislatures:

> One night, in a bitter floor debate in the lower house, one legislator pulled the cord out of the amplifier system, another hit him from the blindside with a tackle; there was mass pushing, hitting, clawing, and exchanges about one another's wives, mistresses, and forebears. Sweethearts and wives, who were allowed on the floor with friends and secretaries cowered near the desks. In the middle of the brawl, a barbershop quartet of legislators quickly formed at the front of the chamber and, like a dance band during a saloon fight, sang "I Had a Dream, Dear."[27]

It is a nagging fact of life in the state legislature that members occasionally become engrossed in matters only a notch above absurdity. Should the term describing the study of foot disorders be changed from chiropody to podiatry? Should the citizenry be permitted to drink beer in taverns while standing up? Should the state permit women to serve as bartenders? Should the great dane or cocker spaniel or possibly the beagle be designated as the official state dog? Should the bed bug, "which has left marks of distinction on the people of this great state for generations," be designated as the official state bug? Should insectivorous birds be protected by a state law requiring cats to be strolled on a leash? Should individuals be permitted to advertise for matrimonial purposes? Should drum majorettes be permitted to parade their talents at the state university? Should the state permit one- or two-line fishing? Would it be sound public policy to make it unlawful to shoot a deer that is "albino or predominantly white"?

> Mr. McCormack: Mr. Speaker, I would like one of the sponsors of the bill to clarify for me...the word "predominantly."
>
> Mr. Breth: Mr. Speaker.... If you would see enough white or if there were enough white on a deer to be seen clearly, you would know that you were shooting either an albino or a part albino.
>
> Mr. Filo: Mr. Speaker.... [How] can you see both sides of a deer at the same time?
>
> Mr. Breth: To my mind, Mr. Speaker, that would be decided by the magistrate or by the arresting officer. If the deer had his brown side toward me, the bullet that killed it would enter the brown side; if the white side were toward me, the bullet would enter the white side....
>
> Mr. Adams: Mr. Speaker.... You have enough trouble finding a deer in the woods that has legal horns on it and being able to shoot it without having to go out and measure how much of it is white and how much of it is

27 Willie Morris, "Legislating in Texas," *Commentary,* November, 1964, p. 43.

brown. . . . You kill it thinking it is a brown deer, you go over and pick it up and find that one side of it is white and then the man is nailed. . . .

Mr. Hartley: Mr. Speaker. . . . When you find an albino, you have certainly found a rare specimen and a freak of nature. Therefore, you would want to have it mounted. . . .

Mr. Maxwell: Mr. Speaker, the gentleman made a statement that these white deer are freaks.

Mr. Gramlich: In my opinion, they are. In all the history of it, the albino deer is a freak.

Mr. Maxwell: Mr. Gramlich, what color are you?

Mr. Gramlich: Well, I do not know. I might be a freak, but I did not know anybody was concerned about it. And, Mr. Speaker, I only have two legs and pink skin.

Mr. Maxwell: Mr. Speaker, I did not hear the gentleman's answer but I suppose he said he was white.

The Speaker *pro tem:* The gentleman says he is pink.

Mr. Maxwell: Well then, the gentleman has called himself what he calls the deer, because there are more brown, yellow and black people in this world than there are white. . . . Now, ladies and gentlemen, in closing, practically every country in the world respects the color of white. We have the sacred white cow, we have the sacred white elephant, we have the sacred white cat. Even the American Indians have the white buffalo as their most powerful and their most sacred medicine. Now can we do any less in Pennsylvania except to pass the white deer bill?

Mr. Adams: Mr. Speaker. . . . [The] gentleman who just spoke would lead us to believe that an albino buck would go out and hunt an albino doe in order to propagate the white species. I think it is very unlikely that that thing would happen out in the woods. . . . I have been hunting in the woods for about 24 years and I only saw one partial albino deer and that did not have any horns, so I just had to watch it walk away.[28]

No state legislature spends most of its time weighing the merits of white-deer bills or considering the dangers which bounding majorettes pose for university propriety and public morality. There is little likelihood that silly or minor bills will collapse the fifty republics. The astonishing fact about these occasional sorties into the world of trivia, however, is the public response. We have the word of the late Richard L. Neuberger, a state legislator in Oregon and later a U.S. senator, that "the legislative mail pouch frequently gets its biggest bulge . . . from some bill that may appear irresponsibly frivolous to the detached observer."[29]

It is easier to raise questions concerning the style and habits of legislatures and to identify their arcane arrangements than to prescribe acceptable methods of improving operations. Reform proposals invariably clash with

[28] *Pennsylvania Legislative Journal,* March 13, 1961, pp. 742–44. The bill failed.

[29] *Adventures in Politics* (New York: Oxford University Press, 1954), p. 84.

other values. Moreover, it is no more than a guess—perhaps a good one—that a legislature bent on increasing its efficiency will, if successful, provide better representation, write better laws, or otherwise help to restore institutional vitality. Will the time saved legislators by eliminating certain minor but burdensome tasks and anachronistic practices be spent in useful ways? What could result, of course, is simply more and improved errand-running.

PAROCHIALISM

Each legislator "belongs" to a number of groups. The member of Congress, for example, belongs to a political organization in his home constituency, to one or more interest groups in his constituency (veterans', business, church, etc.), to several different legislative groups (committees, blocs), to the national party, and to the government of the United States. He is a formal and participating member of some of these groups; he may simply sympathize with the objectives of other groups. One and all press demands upon him: "A Congressman's behavior may be conceived of as a resultant of the claims operating upon him through his affiliations with these organized and potential groups."[30]

This leads us to the problem: Much of the dissatisfaction with the legislature traces to its excessive parochialism—the tendency of legislators to look only to their home districts for guidance, to defer to the claims made by individuals and organizations which help comprise their individual constituencies, and to treat indifferently matters of national (or statewide) significance. Thus among the groups to which the legislator belongs or to which he defers, those which are based at home (interest groups and the constituency political organization, especially the former) have first claim on him. Theirs may be the only claims which are heard.

Parochialism is a problem because it concentrates the attention of legislators on narrow, often special-interest politics. For reasons we shall enumerate later, lawmakers come to Washington lacking a national viewpoint or to Albany or Austin lacking a state viewpoint. Elected by radically different constituencies, they bring with them a concern for local problems and local advantage. Critics of localism contend that in the process of ministering to localized demands, legislators overlook the most obvious statewide or national needs.

In the constituencies, as in the parties, no single interest is apt to be dominant. A legislator soon learns, if he does not already know when elected, which groups comprise the dominant combination in his district. He seeks to stay in office by faithful representation of these groups; much of the time, to be sure, constituency aims and his own convictions or "conscience" mesh harmoniously. Just as certainly, there are occasions when he follows constituency directives because he is fearful of reprisals which might result from his apostasy.

The legislator's orientation toward his locality—the constituency comes first—is a major fact about Congress and the state legislators. Localism and

---

[30] "The Roles of Congressional Leaders: National Party vs. Constituency," *American Political Science Review*, XLVI (December 1952), 1026. (This is one of several papers produced by an SSRC seminar in 1951.)

482 logrolling are joined when decisions are made to build highways, hospitals, post offices, flood control projects, airports, and to locate military installations. Few policy questions are more likely to alert the typical legislator than the allocation of funds for public works projects. Consider the observations of a member of the House Public Works Committee:

> If you're going to stay around here, you've got to take care of the folks back home. And, if you're not, you don't belong here. You're supposed to be representing them and if you don't, somebody else will. We are all national legislators in a sense and we have to be but the national issues don't mean a damn thing back home—oh, sure, they read about it in the newspapers but it doesn't mean much to them. They've got to see something; it's the bread and butter issues that count—the dams, the post offices and the other buildings, the highways. They want to know what you've been doing. You can point to all these things you've done and all of them go through my committee.[31]

There are not many major pieces of legislation which pass through Congress without being shaped to confer special advantage on certain interests. Foreign economic policy is especially vulnerable to attacks by local and regional interests. When trade-agreement legislation is before Congress, pressures are massed to protect the domestic oil industry from foreign imports, to restrict the importation of cheese, to require the labeling of alien trout, to unload farm surpluses through foreign trade policy, to require a certain share of foreign-aid cargoes to be shipped in American vessels, *ad infinitum*. In the consideration of foreign economic policy, Holbert Carroll observes, the House "mirrors the varying approaches...of the diverse components of the executive branch. What the House adds to this confusion is the babble of more localized pressures applied to wool, textile, coal, soybean, shipping, and scores of other interests."[32]

Another good example of the necessity to tailor legislation to serve local and regional concerns is available in the act setting up the Area Redevelopment Administration in the Department of Commerce. Originally and explicitly designed to provide federal loans and grants for distressed industrial and commercial areas, the bill could not be passed until rural areas with low per capita income were included under its provisions. This change in the accent and scope of the bill eventually led to the certification for rehabilitation of many more agricultural than urban-industrial counties—such is the

---

[31] Quoted in James T. Murphy, "Partisanship, Party Conflict and Cooperation in House Public Works Committee Decision-Making," Annual Meeting of the American Political Science Association, Washington, D.C., 1968 (as revised in 1971). Although committee members on Public Works share an interest in bringing federal projects into their districts, the decision-making pattern in the committee is not simply one of favor-trading. Indeed, the dominant characteristic in decision-making in this committee is party conflict. Democrats and Republicans on the committee have different perspectives on public works issues, especially when their individual districts are not affected by the proposed allocation. Cooperation between committee Democrats and Republicans occurs when the allocative decision to be made affects the constituencies of virtually all members.

[32] *The House of Representatives and Foreign Affairs* (Pittsburgh: University of Pittsburgh Press, 1966), p. 73.

price of passage in a Congress in which representatives from rural and semirural constituencies are in ascendancy.

The Burkean notion that "Parliament is a deliberative assembly of one nation, with one interest, that of the whole" does not have wide acceptance among American legislators. Save in times of national crisis, the predominant loyalty of many members is to the state or district. The essence of this commitment is caught in these remarks by the late U.S. Senator Harry F. Byrd:

> My allegiance is to Virginia where the people have elected me six times to the United States Senate. I have what is to me the supreme honor of having served in the Senate longer than any other Virginian in history. I recognize no control over my votes in the Senate from any outside influence including the national Democratic convention and a caucus of my Democratic colleagues in the Senate. ... As a Member of the Senate, I am under oath to support the Constitution of the United States. This I have done. Every President of my time has had my full support when there was need for strong national defense and when there was need for national unity in international crises. Beyond this, my unqualified allegiance to the people of Virginia has been preserved, and it will be. I know their principles. I have confidence in their judgment as to what is good for the country. I have followed their will as I understood it in the past, and I shall conform to it in the future.[33]

The unflagging parochialism of legislatures, easily visible on all sides, is not difficult either to account for or to understand. To sum up a long story, it traces to the decentralization of American politics, to the influence of interest groups resulting from the inability of the parties to generate legislation or to hold their lines intact, to the custom that legislators must reside in the districts they represent, to the insecurity of short-term legislators loosely linked to party, to the dispersal of power within the legislature, to the weakness of party organizations at *all* levels of government, and to the heterogeneous quality of American life. In addition, the parochial spirit is at the root of much of the buffeting between the executive and the legisla-

---

[33] These statements appear in a letter from Senator Byrd to Senator Joseph S. Clark who, following the 1960 presidential election, had questioned whether a senator who had not endorsed his party's presidential candidate or supported the party platform should have the privilege of serving as a committee chairman. Senator Byrd would not have qualified on either count.

In his reply to Senator Byrd, Senator Clark stated: "I agree with you that each Senator owes allegiance to the people of his state whom he has been elected to represent (I would add that he has a higher allegiance to the people of the United States). But in his capacity as a committee chairman, a Senator is chosen not by the people of any one state but by his colleagues in his party in the Senate. ... I respect the integrity of your views ... [but] I also respect the right of the majority of the Democratic members of the Senate to decline, if they so choose, to nominate for a committee chairmanship a Senator who has issued an open declaration of war against important measures which will come before his committee with the backing of the Democratic convention, the Democratic President, and a majority of Democratic Senators. ... This is not a question of 'purging,' because a chairmanship is a *privilege* conferred by the Party members in the Senate subject to the approval of the Senate as a whole, not a *right* conferred by a Senator's constituents." Press release from the office of Senator Clark, December 9, 1960.

484 ture—their constituencies dissimilar, one sees the need for a broad plan of action, the other the need to keep things at home in repair.

The congressman who yields to local pressures and who spends his time satisfying constituents' requests is following the surest route to reelection. If, in the course of supporting local claims, he opposes national party positions, there is not much the party can do about it. He wears the party label whether the party likes him or not, and he can rise to power in Congress without the party's blessing.[34] On the other hand, if he supports his party and the president at the expense of his district, he has gained virtually nothing and may have lost his bid for reelection. The national party will be of little direct assistance to him in his campaign, and possibly his identification with it may hurt his chances. Hence the cards are stacked in favor of the congressman who is sensitive to the interests of his district and accords priority to its claims. Under the circumstances, it may be surprising that any congressman will risk the wrath of his constituents (or organized groups) to support a position unpopular at home. Yet many do. A majority, it would seem, play it safe.

A description by James Burns of the behavior of a "safe-district" congressman (over one-half of all congressional districts ordinarily are safe for one party) shows the nature of a congressional party system whose roots are deep in the constituencies:

> [Rather than seek a statewide office] the congressman from a safe seat usually follows the easy alternative: he stays put. He placates the dominant social forces in the district; "protects" his district against hostile outside forces; does a great many individual favors; lobbies for benefits for the district; maintains a friends-and-neighbors political organization that scares would-be opponents out of the primary or trounces them if they come in; and comfortably overwhelms the opposition party's candidate—if there is one—on election day. His main commitment politically is to the *status quo.* He wishes nothing to disrupt his easy relationships with the public officials and private interests that rule the area. He views with alarm the great issues that sweep the nation and threaten to disrupt the familiar and comfortable politics of his district. He does not want to broaden the franchise or encourage more voting, because this might disturb existing arrangements.[35]

Though it supplies no broad or national vision, localism in moderation is neither harmful nor undesirable. Local interests require representation in national (or statewide) legislation, and there are obvious values to keeping "distant" government responsive to the people at home. The grounds for

---

[34] There are exceptions to this large generalization, but they occur only rarely. In the 89th Congress (1965–66), the House Democratic caucus stripped two southerners of their seniority rights for having publicly endorsed the Republican presidential candidate, Barry M. Goldwater. Discipline may also touch the constituency interests of a member. Congressman L. Mendel Rivers of South Carolina bolted from the Democratic party in 1948 to support the Dixiecrat ticket. When he was criticized in 1964 for failing to bolt again, this time to support Senator Goldwater, he replied, "I had my bolt, and all it got me was that my navy yard (in Charleston) was desegregated." *Congressional Quarterly Weekly Report,* February 5, 1965, p. 185.

[35] *The Deadlock of Democracy* (Englewood Cliffs, N.J.: Prentice-Hall, Inc., 1963), pp. 243–44.

criticizing localism are more circumscribed than might appear at first glance. They become relevant as parochialism becomes rampant, as broad purposes become blighted or vitiated through obsessive concern for local advantage.

FRAGMENTATION OF POWER AND EROSION OF AUTONOMY

Each legislature has a profile of its own. But though no legislature is precisely the same as any other, all have certain features in common. In greater or lesser degree, all are troubled by problems of minority control, unrepresentativeness, inefficiency, and localism. Another factor, the fragmentation of party and legislative power, is linked to the severity of these problems and magnifies it. Localism, for example, gets out of hand because legislators lack strong attachments to institutions which transcend their constituencies, notably party. Minority power, in similar sweep, often turns to minority domination because the majority is unable to organize its power by consolidating its forces and by ordering the ground rules of the legislature in such a way as to make majority control a distinct and continuing possibility.

All this is familiar ground by now; we need come back to only a few points. The key for understanding American legislatures lies in the absence of party rule and party discipline. "The party in Congress is like a Mexican army," Schattschneider observed. "Everyone in it takes care of himself. When the enemy appears he may fight, or parley as he thinks best. This is the kind of army that can be overwhelmed by one man assisted by a boy beating a dishpan."[36] Because the party is not equipped to mass persistent majorities, responsible rule goes by default. Effective power comes to rest with transient bipartisan majorities—sometimes brought into being through the pressure of a vigorous executive, sometimes the product of careful engineering by a perennial bipartisan coalition (e.g., southern Democrats and Republicans), sometimes no more than the deft concoction of an alliance of logrollers, and sometimes purely accidentally.

Whatever may be the advantages of coalition rule and majority-by-logrolling—and it is difficult to attribute more to them than unadorned expediency—they are not consonant with the idea of responsible party government. At no point in the political process are these combinations accountable for their behavior. Never required to produce a platform, or to campaign on a collective program, or to submit their record to the voters, coalitions can work their extravagancies without significant restraint. In only the vaguest sense can it be said that the public is able to take account of what they do, approving or rejecting it. With each election campaign, coalition members find their way back to the same old parties for a short stay. Once the election is out of the way, the air cleared of programs and promises, and members returned to the legislature, the process begins anew.

The weakness of the parties is accompanied by a dispersal of power in the legislature. The latter owes its existence to the former. Were the parties strong agencies of majority rule the legislature would function much differently. Committee power would be linked to party power, committee chairmen to party leaders, and rules of procedure to party requirements.

---

[36] E. E. Schattschneider, *Party Government* (New York: Holt, Rinehart & Winston, Inc., 1942), p. 196.

486   Such is not the case in most American legislatures and most certainly not in Congress.

The failure of party is the principal explanation for the erosion of legislative autonomy. Its inability to integrate power and to control (or to back up) the individual members lays the legislature open to manipulation by interest groups. Where private organizations have unhampered access to the centers of power, where the response of the legislature is simply to "referee" group struggles, where private actions in public establishments are withdrawn from public review—the initiative and self-sufficiency of the government is endangered. To a notable extent, by any reckoning, pressure groups have moved to fill the void created by the abdication of party.

The integrity of government is inherently vulnerable to outside groups and private connivance. Its vulnerability derives from the separation of power and responsibility. If policy belongs simply to those who exert the most influence, whether in dark corners or on the public stage, the autonomy of the legislature is narrowed, its claim to speak for the people as a whole is vacated. The business of the legislature is more than the total of all private business brought before it. The legislature's role is both creative and regulatory—creative in the sense of enlarging opportunities for popular direction and review of the goals of society, and regulatory in that any government worthy of its name is required to prevent interests from trampling each other, or any one interest from gaining ascendancy over all others. Neither task can be discharged by a legislature which is the captive of those it seeks to regulate. The legislature "can't be everybody's friend, all the time," Roland Young observes.

> If a legislature is subjected to such rigorous external pressures that it cannot maintain its own identity, if rules having the sanction of government are in effect made by private groups, society may shortly find itself deprived of the benefit of a stable and effective political authority. Government would be up for grabs, with individuals and groups appropriating indiscriminately the symbols of government for their own purposes.[37]

THE FAILURE TO REPRESENT THE UNORGANIZED PUBLIC

"All power is organization and all organization is power. . . . A man who has no share in any form of organized power is not independent of organized power. He is at the mercy of it. . . ."[38]

The proposition that legislators listen only to those who make the loudest noises is not wholly true. But there is little doubt that it is mainly true. Legislators seldom constitute an audience attentive for sounds coming from the unorganized public. If they listen at all, and some do, they hear very little; and it could hardly be otherwise amid the noisy clamor of organized voices. This is a problem of representation not to be solved by any apportionment formula or any reorganization—it will remain at least so

---

[37] Young, *op. cit.,* p. 267. See pp. 267–69 for further discussion regarding the need for legislative autonomy.

[38] Harvey Fergusson, *People and Power* (New York: William Morrow & Company, Inc., 1947), pp. 101–2.

long as political interest groups are strong and political parties are weak. And perhaps, of course, the problem of representing the unorganized is unsolvable. Its essence is caught in these remarks made in the U.S. Senate when legislation to remove federal control over the natural gas industry was under consideration:

> Mr. Aiken (R., Vt.): The final and deciding conclusion I have reached is that if we take the line of least resistance and yield now to the pressure exerted upon us, we will in truth have lent color to the charge that the special interests are running the country. Never, since I have been in Washington, have I seen such intensive, varied, and ingenious types of lobbying used to promote legislation. If the pending bill were good for the whole country, its promoters would not have to resort to [these] methods to secure its enactment. . . . I have been badly overlobbied.
>
> Mr. Pastore (D., R. I.): Let me ask the distinguished Senator from Vermont if he has been approached at all by any consumers' lobby?
>
> Mr. Aiken: No.
>
> Mr. Pastore: As a matter of fact, in this whole business the only person who has not been heard from has been the consumer. Is that correct?
>
> Mr. Aiken: The consumer seems to be unaware of the import of this legislation.[39]

In the last few years Congress has come under especially critical review for its failure to represent adequately the "have-nots" in American society. Duane Lockard argues:

> Whatever else may be said of congressional power, this much is true: it is exercised so as to render difficult or impossible the task of developing policies addressed to the needs of those in the most desperate straits. It is not especially difficult to get a huge defense budget through Congress with relatively little examination and not much dissent. Defense budgets have formidable support: they are endorsed by the President, they have the awesome backing of the military-industrial complex, they are difficult to oppose for to do so may appear to be failing the troops in battle or "endangering" the safety of society, and they are, after all, a test of the national power, which arouses nationalistic feelings in the patriot. . . . To get through the needle's eye of Congress a law to protect farm workers attempting to form unions or to feed the starving is another matter. For there are almost limitless ways in which an intensely interested minority can block such laws. In this respect Congress perverts the priorities of the nation; it responds to money, to organized power, to vested interests of various kinds, but it has little sympathy for migrant farm workers, the poor, or the prisoner.[40]

[39] *Congressional Record,* 84th Cong., 2d sess., January 31, 1956, pp. 1667–68. For an analysis which suggests that "urban interests" are essentially "consumer interests," see Frederick N. Cleaveland, "Congress and Urban Problems: Legislating for Urban Areas," *Journal of Politics,* XXVIII (May 1966), 304–7.

[40] *The Perverted Priorities of American Politics* (New York: The Macmillan Company, 1971), pp. 125–26.

The notion that Congress and the state legislatures are not functioning properly is a central theme in much of the contemporary literature on American politics. Plainly, there is nothing prosaic in the problems that confront the legislature. To the extent that the foregoing evaluations reflect accurate appraisals, they help to explain why most observers contend that the legislature today is not at the creative center of the political system. Yet there is another side to the evaluation. The legislature may also be seen as a bargaining institution whose merit is that it is able to develop successful compromises among a variety of antagonistic interests in a diverse society.[41] From this standpoint, certain of the deficiencies of the legislature may appear as virtues.

A Defense of the System

The defense of Congress, as well as the defense of American legislatures generally, consists of a composite of several ideas. Defenders may say, in the first place, that the shortcomings of the legislature have been exaggerated; second, that in exposing faults one should not overlook virtues; third, that some suggested reforms would exacerbate rather than assuage problems; fourth, that basic legislative reforms are contingent on the introduction of other basic changes in the external political system; fifth, that the legislature could not be vastly different since it mirrors the values and conflicts in American society; sixth, that the legislature is not the only social institution to resist change and that the pace by which it moves has advantages as well as disadvantages; seventh, that a legislature in which power is dispersed is more compatible with a pluralistic society than is a legislature in which power is centralized. Some may say, finally, that American legislatures, like American democracy, have stood the test of time, and that other styles and practices might be not only inappropriate but injurious. Since these assertions tend to run together, we shall limit our comments to the broad justifications of existing arrangements.

The principal desiderata in the summons for reform are a stricter brand of majority rule and a more responsible two-party system—one which brings executive and legislative powers into steady and effective harmony. At present, it is argued, the national government is unable to respond vigorously to crises or to develop broad and comprehensive programs for meeting increasingly difficult problems. The requirement is for a system that can withstand or harness the pressures of special interests in such a way that advances toward general or national priorities can be made. Finally, the call is made for a party system with a new capacity for presenting voters with meaningful alternatives in public policy.

---

[41] See Robert L. Peabody, "Organization Theory and Legislative Behavior: Bargaining, Hierarchy and Change in the U. S. House of Representatives," a paper delivered at the 1963 annual meeting of the American Political Science Association, New York City, September 4–7, 1963. See also Thomas and Lamb, *op. cit.,* pp. 128–35; Froman, *op. cit.,* pp. 16–33; and Richard F. Fenno, Jr., "The Internal Distribution of Influence: The House," in *The Congress and America's Future,* ed. David B. Truman (Englewood Cliffs, N.J.: Prentice-Hall, Inc., 1965), pp. 73–76.

Those who make a case for the present system recognize its deficiencies **489** in at least a general way, though they add that the failings are not as great as are usually made out. And other distinctions, they contend, need to be borne in mind. In the first place, advocates of strict "majority rule–party responsibility" have not weighed carefully enough certain basic characteristics of the American community and its political traditions. Second, the "responsibility" school has lost sight of the benefits of the present system. Third, the cure which the "responsibility" advocates prescribe may be worse than the disease.

ARGUMENT 1: A HETEROGENEOUS NATION

The American community is dynamic, enormously complex, and vastly heterogeneous. It contains all manner of economic interests, social classes, ethnic and religious groups, regional political loyalties, and assorted values, beliefs, and sentiments. Though agreed on some broad goals and able to submerge their differences at certain times, these diverse groups normally respond to stimuli by going their separate ways when their particular interests are at stake. No government can win universal acceptance for any policy, since invariably the parochial values and interests of one section (area, district, state) or group collide with those of another section or group or with a majority of the country. In a word, American society is too heterogeneous to permit the emergence of a single majority, including party, able to speak steadily and authoritatively for the American people.

American diversity, remarks Herbert Agar, requires acceptance of the fact that

> most politics will be parochial, most politicians will have small horizons, seeking the good of the state or the district rather than of the Union; yet by diplomacy and compromise, never by force, the government must water down the selfish demands of regions, races, classes, business associations, into a national policy which will alienate no major group and which will contain at least a small plum for everybody. This is the price of unity in a continentwide federation.[42]

ARGUMENT 2: THE BENEFITS

The second argument, anchored to the first, states that although the present system is loose and untidy in many respects, the problems it creates do not substantially negate or diminish its benefits. This "traditionalist" school contends that the requirements of harmony, compromise, and consensus have a higher priority than the requirements of clarity, responsiveness, and accountability sought by the "majority rule-party responsibility" advocates.

The underlying problem of government is to find means by which diverse and antagonistic groups can be held together and conflict over policy kept within tolerable dimensions. The United States has succeeded in doing this, writers like Peter F. Drucker and John Fischer conclude, by adapting

[42] *The Price of Union* (Boston: Houghton Mifflin Company, 1950), p. xiv.

490 John Calhoun's mid-nineteenth-century doctrine of "concurrent majority" to modern negotiations over policy.[43] Congress serves as an example. Now imbedded in our "unwritten rules of politics," the "concurrent majority" principle holds that major policies must be adopted under circumstances in which every significant interest group has a "veto power" when and if its *vital* interests are threatened. The "veto"—informal, subtle, and implied— must be exercised with great toleration and discretion; a negative power, it is a "last resort" weapon, available to any bloc when all efforts at compromise have failed.[44]

The presence of this tacit "veto"—the filibuster is perhaps the best example—serves to foster accommodation and compromise in Congress. Because any major group normally can block a proposal it finds wholly repugnant, legislators are forced to search for a halfway house, a settlement which, though it is located in the direction the majority wants to move, is not at so extreme a distance that it leaves the minority bitter and irreconcilable. The various civil rights acts passed in the 1950s and 1960s provide good examples of the workings of the principle; by and large they were too weak to suit the northern majority and too strong to suit the southern minority. Much of the labor-management and social welfare legislation of the last two decades has been written in a way which has tempered the demand for change with a reasonable deference to those unalterably opposed to new directions.

The essence, then, of the "concurrent majority" principle is accommodation and compromise; it argues that the purpose of politics is to unite rather than to divide. It survives, indeed, flourishes, by certain congressional usages which defy majority rule—unlimited debate, bloc politics, logrolling, independent committee power, and rules which amplify minority voices.

The style of the American party and legislative system—loose, decentralized, fragmented—engenders several values, say its supporters. In the first place, by bending extreme positions toward the middle or simply by isolating them, the system narrows the scope of conflict. Second, it makes it difficult for a majority (some of whose members may feel *indifferently* about the issue) to force its policy upon a vigorous minority (whose members are likely to feel *intensely* about the issue).[45] Third, it diminishes the probability of major and persistent class or party conflict. Fourth, it makes it possible for the vanquished minority to accept the majority verdict with some grace, since, as a rule, the final decision is rarely if ever as obnoxious as it might have been—the majority seldom wins completely, the minority seldom loses completely. Finally, as we noted earlier, those who prefer the present system to proposed alternatives contend that a persistent lawmaking majority eventually will gain its ends.

---

[43] Peter F. Drucker, "A Key to American Politics: Calhoun's Pluralism," *Review of Politics,* X (October 1948), 412–26; John Fischer, "Unwritten Rules of American Politics," *Harper's Magazine,* November 1948, pp. 27–36.

[44] Fischer, *op. cit.,* p. 30.

[45] But, majoritarians may ask, what of the case in which the "system" impedes an altogether *intense majority* from working its will? See Robert Dahl's analysis of the majority principle and the intensity factor in *A Preface to Democratic Theory* (Chicago: University of Chicago Press, 1956), Chapter 4, and Froman, *op. cit.,* pp. 188–93.

ARGUMENT 3: THE CONSEQUENCES
LATENT IN RESOLUTE PARTY RULE

The advantages of majority rule through the instrument of party are canceled out, some writers have held, by developments that likely would follow in the wake. One result might be the emergence of a multiple-party system. It seems to be implicit in the majority rule–party responsibility theory that new party alignments would be required, in which "liberals" would be grouped in one party, "conservatives" in the other. But, as Austin Ranney and Willmoore Kendall point out, "political conflict in the United States is enormously more multifarious and complicated than a simple division between pro–New Dealers and anti–New Dealers; and a great many groups could find their home in neither party."[46] Unless members chose to defy their leadership, and possibly suffer sanctions, they would have no option but to launch a new party. Rigorous party rule, then, if superimposed upon a community of disparate and conflicting interests, might lead ultimately to the disintegration of the two-party system.

Another possibility is that in quickening the pulse of party and in clarifying party tenets—"rationalizing" the system—overall consensus would be jeopardized. As party appeals became increasingly dissimilar, interest groups would be forced to choose sides. Eventually, this interpretation holds, group would be arrayed against group, and class against class. The decisions of government would become less and less tolerable for the losing side, placing new and heavy strains on the bonds of community. Finally, there is no guarantee that the party responsibility system could elude a major dilemma of the existing system: legislative deadlock. Should the centralized system contribute to the formation of multiple or splinter parties, each disciplined and rooted in ideology, the likelihood of jarring and irreconcilable conflict would be heightened.

GOVERNMENT BY COMPROMISE: WEAK BUT WORKABLE

Government by "concurrent majority" has, its advocates admit, glaring weaknesses: (1) It cannot invariably act vigorously in a time of crisis, for power is ranged at all points of the system. (2) Since it requires the acquiescence of all major groups whose interests are touched, it is easier to block a policy than to adopt one. (3) It devolves great power upon an interest group which is able to influence a decision at a crucial stage in the process, say, in committee. (4) It leads to legislation which stresses local purposes at the expense of broad plans.

Were it not for another factor, executive leadership, legislative obeisance to the "concurrent majority" principle would result in endless snarls over policy-making. In this century the chief executive has assumed increasing responsibility for the development of general legislative programs. "Laws and customs," Richard E. Neustadt observes, "now reflect acceptance of [the president] as the Great Initiator, an acceptance quite as widespread at

---

[46] *Democracy and the American Party System* (New York: Harcourt, Brace & World, Inc., 1956), p. 530. The argument in this section leans partially on the Ranney and Kendall book; see especially pp. 530–32.

492   the Capitol as at his end of Pennsylvania Avenue."[47] Today, administration bills are the key items on the legislative agenda, and though sensitive lawmakers may chafe over this fact, they nevertheless await their arrival. Voters also "sense intuitively the patent realities of the legislative function of the President. . . ."[48] Presidential election campaigns, emphasizing policy questions rather than executive talents, are another reminder that the president is in fact the "chief legislator." The same is of course true in the case of the governor.

Legislative leadership by the chief executive and his administrative officials does not end with providing ideas for a legislative program or with the actual drafting of bills. This is no more than the beginning. The chief executive is expected to mobilize the forces necessary to pass his program. Some of the time he is able to do this by the skillful use of party machinery. Or he may seek to gain support outside the system by arousing the public or by marshaling political forces in the constituencies, which in turn leads to pressures on the legislature for action. Often he must rely on his ability to splice together temporary (and ever-changing) coalitions for his "must" bills. Hard bargaining and persuasion are the keys to getting the Congress to back his program. In dealing with congressmen, writes Neustadt, the president's task "is to induce them to believe that what he wants of them is what their own appraisal of their own responsibilities requires them to do in their interest, not his."[49]

Faith in the ability of the chief executive in times of crisis to chart a course and to manage the necessary legislative majorities, party or otherwise, is at the root of the argument in support of the traditional system. This view recognizes that the legislature functions most effectively when the chief executive takes the lead, furnishing the program and the initiative for its passage. This obviously does not call for a legislature with a creative energy of its own, but rather one which will submerge its parochial moods and loyalties and its historic distaste for executive leadership in order to meet emergencies.

The Party Government Response

Assuming it possible, could coherent and effective party machinery be introduced in Congress without subjecting the political system to the consequences critics have forecast? Specifically, would a responsible party system impair national consensus, promote class antagonism, and undermine the two-party system? The answer, if unsatisfactory, is that there is no answer. The writers who hold these views may or may not be right. The American political system is inordinately complicated. There is no way of assigning relative weights to the factors that help to stabilize the two-party system or to the factors that help to foster consensus; neither are there means for

---

[47] Richard E. Neustadt, *Presidential Power: The Politics of Leadership* (New York: John Wiley & Sons, Inc., 1960), p. 6.

[48] Wilfred E. Binkley, *The Man in the White House: His Powers and Duties* (Baltimore: Johns Hopkins Press, 1958), p. 162.

[49] Neustadt, *op. cit.,* p. 46 (emphasis omitted).

calculating the impact of forces that threaten stability and unity. There is no evidence on which to predict that the rigorous majority rule of disciplined parties would generate an intolerable conflict between classes or, for that matter, that it would not. Would class conflict be enlarged greatly if, under "party government," the ideological gap between two *cohesive* parties were no greater than it is today between *majorities* in the two parties? We cannot be sure.

There are some things, however, that can be said with greater certainty. One is that, insofar as the legislature is concerned, internal reform of any significance must either await, or go hand in hand with, external reform—the party system as a whole must be strengthened if party rule in the legislature is to become a possibility. The chief requirements for the recrudescence of the parties are an expansion of party competition into many more legislative districts, a heightened concern within the party organizations for the recruitment of legislative candidates, and the development of broadly based party financing. At least one constitutional change would seem to be required, an amendment to increase the term of office of members of the lower house from two years to four. This longer term might ease the pressures of campaigning, diminish parochialism, and narrow the possibility of party division between executive and legislature. Finally, to continue this point, a healthy party link between president and Congress is not likely to be forged until presidential and congressional electorates behave regularly in the same way.[50]

Advocates of "party discipline" recognize that the traditional system unites rather than divides the political community—the "catch" is that the uniting is often done on minority rather than majority terms. Government by compromise has perhaps worked well enough in periods of normalcy, but is it equal to the task ahead? If crisis is to be perpetual, as it seems, is government machinery adequate if it responds only in "fits and starts," or if it can be put in motion only after agreement is reached to tailor broad purposes to local and regional demands? Using executive spurs and relying on crisis occasions in order to gain legislative action and a greater measure of coherence and consistency in public policy appears not only insufficient but nothing short of perilous to many critics. The techniques for releasing power are incommensurate with the difficulties of the age; they fail to provide a reliable means for generating sustained attacks on pressing problems.

Political reorganization, in this view, does not require the parties to become more distinct ideologically, as the argument is sometimes presented. Significant differences between the parties already exist. What is now required is a political organization (in and out of the legislature) which is able to keep the power of private groups within tolerable limits and to act decisively for a majority of the people. The ability of either party to do this depends in great part on its ability to expand cooperation between the executive and legislative branches.

Advocates of basic reform set great store in two ideas. The first insists that the nation is more than the sum of its parts, and that in the present ordering of political power the parts (some of them at least) have gained

[50] *Ibid.,* p. 191.

494 ascendancy to a degree that threatens national goals. The second holds that the key to the development of national perspectives and orderly politics is a strengthened party system. The party, as James M. Burns has observed, "is the institutionalization of majority action."[51]

The Outlook

Writing in the early twentieth century, James Bryce observed that "Congress does not receive the attention and enjoy the confidence which ought to belong to a central organ of national life."[52] State legislatures ranked even lower in public esteem. Moreover, Bryce reported in *Modern Democracies,* a decline in the prestige and authority of the legislature was occurring in country after country.

Why had the legislatures lost ground? In the case of Congress, Bryce remarked, the fault lay in a failure to meet the great problems: "It fumbles with them, does not get to the root of the matter, seems to be moved rather by considerations of temporary expediency and the wish to catch every passing breeze of popular demand than by a settled purpose to meet the larger national needs." The "intellectual power" of Congress was not impressive, and the institution had failed to attract the outstanding political talent of the nation. Debates, especially in the House, were seldom enlightening and the proceedings seldom of interest, even to the educated classes. State legislatures suffered similar maladies, differing only in that logrolling, jobbery, and domination by selfish interests were more prevalent.[53]

Legislatures everywhere, Lord Bryce found, had failed to live up to expectations. Their principal ailments, varying in degree from country to country, were filibustering, the rise of class antagonisms and multiple parties, the disproportionate power wielded by organized minority groups, the sacrifice of national aims to constituency imperatives, and the development of majority party rule that undermined the legislature's deliberative function and made it a "mere voting machine." These internal deficiencies were compounded by the indisposition of the most qualified citizens to run for legislative office.[54]

Is the situation improved today? Do legislatures enjoy a greater measure of respect? Are they closer to representing the best wisdom of the country now than in the past? Obviously, there is no possibility of answering these questions with any degree of exactitude—no evidence exists for gauging fundamental legislative "improvement" or, for that matter, the intensity of public dissatisfaction with legislatures. It is plain to anyone, however, that the twentieth century, in Bryce's time and ours, has taken an enormous toll of legislative vitality and self-sufficiency. Totalitarian regimes have all but put legislatures out of business, converting them, as in the USSR, into

---

[51] *Congress on Trial* (New York: Harper & Row, Publishers, 1949), p. 195.
[52] *Modern Democracies* (New York: The Macmillan Company, 1921), II, 62.
[53] *Ibid.,* pp. 63–66, Congress (quotation on p. 63); pp. 141–42, state legislatures.
[54] *Ibid.,* pp. 345–57.

"transmission belts" for directives from a ruling oligarchy that is above and beyond the law and the constitution. Serving ideological and propaganda purposes, and bearing only a superficial resemblance to Western parliaments, they have been shorn of the function of representing a free electorate. The fiction of legislative independence and function is of course everywhere retained and advertised.

The atrophy of the legislature in democratic regimes, albeit less pronounced, is hardly less discernible. Here the loss has not been functional *independence,* as in totalitarian states, but rather *parity* with the executive power. Many observations in Woodrow Wilson's *Congressional Government* are as accurate today as in 1885—especially those which describe the internal distribution of congressional power—and they will doubtless remain so for some time to come. But the main thesis that marks his early book—that Congress is the crucial power in the American political system—is no longer fully applicable, for at times we have "presidential government" as surely as ever we had "congressional government." Legislative parity with the executive is always in flux. At times it is grasped, even exceeded, at other times lost, virtually beyond recall. In the usual relationship, crisis produces an interval of executive ascendancy, tranquility an interlude of relative parity, perhaps legislative dominance.

This is a generation of perpetual crisis, but this fact alone does not account for the diminished significance of legislatures or for the rise of executive power. Another factor is of comparable importance. The problems of modern government now have become so technical and complex that the legislature has found it increasingly necessary to defer to the executive for answers and recommendations. No matter how hard the legislature tries to inform itself (and Congress tries very hard indeed), its store of information and its access to necessary knowledge are rarely if ever as developed as that of the executive authority. The committees, to be sure, are specialized agencies, but by and large they cannot produce swiftly and surely the kinds of information needed to *initiate* policy; they are better geared to review it and reshape it.[55] Moreover, each committee's view is constricted by the specialty it serves, so that the legislature finds it difficult to weigh one general priority against another and to shape a larger plan of action.[56] The diversity and complexity of the materials with which legislatures work today are such as bear only a dim resemblance to the problems of nineteenth-century assemblies.

The loss of initiative does not make the legislature idle, it makes it

[55] This observation requires refinement. John F. Manley makes this point: "Granting the power of initiation to the president, however, is not equivalent to granting him a preponderant share of influence on policy: it is often possible for Congress to be secondary in time but primary in influence. Congress responds to the executive but sometimes it responds with a flat 'no'; more frequently, it amends the executive proposal; less frequently, it so amends proposals that there is a qualitative change in the original and Congress, in effect, becomes the most important policy-making body." *The Politics of Finance: The House Committee on Ways and Means* (Boston: Little, Brown & Company, 1970), p. 327.

[56] See an article by Edward Schneier, "The Intelligence of Congress: Information and Public-Policy Patterns," *Annals of the American Academy of Political and Social Science,* CCCLXXXVIII (March 1970), 14–24.

496 dependent.[57] It begins work after hearing the chief executive's statement of the problems and his recommendations for policies to meet them. The key bills of a session are administration bills; the key testimony in hearings is ordinarily the testimony of executive spokesmen; the key items on the legislative agenda are born in the offices of administration officials; support for proposals is often mobilized by administration agents; even the pace of the legislature is affected by executive preference. This is not to say the administration outlook is invariably accepted—the legislature has a mind of its own and shows it. What we are rather saying is that everywhere today the legislature leans on the executive branch for a program and for the momentum to see it through. That the legislature may frame its own alternatives to executive requests (or perhaps take no action at all) is less revealing about the relationship than the fact that the executive significantly influences the legislature's agenda and defines the areas within which policy is to be negotiated.

To a remarkable extent, the modern chief executive gives the legislature its job, checks over its shoulder to be sure it is doing it, and dangles carrots or brandishes sticks to spur it along. It goes without saying that he must be discreet in his approach. Yet, if he is substantially successful (or vigorous) in his efforts, the law of political historians will require his name to be entered as a "strong" executive; if he allows the legislature to dominate the scene, he will just as surely enter their narratives as a "weak" executive.

Legislatures have lost vitality partially for intrinsic reasons and partially for external happenings. What may be broadly described as "structural" defects account for the former, crisis and the complexity of the times for the latter. In general, structural barriers to centralized decision-making have resulted in a loss of power to pressure groups, while the increasing complexity of issues has led to a loss (or "delegation") of power to executive authority. But the diminished significance of the legislature, if this description is correct, should be seen in perspective. It does not include an erosion of constitutional powers—these are as fully intact today as ever in the past. The loss has been more subtle and shadowy. It consists of the legislature's holding its powers in reserve, being unable to release them in a way that produces a regular and even flow of energy. Legislative action tends to come in spurts,

---

[57] James A. Robinson describes the transformation of Congress in this way: "The role of Congress in the U.S. system of government has been shifting gradually away from the *initiation* of public policies toward the *legitimation* and sometimes *amendation* of policies originally devised in the executive branch. The change in the major function of the legislative process has been especially notable with respect to foreign affairs. . . . Foreign policy-making today is characterized by the need for large amounts of technical *information,* short decision *time,* and by great financial *cost.* Only the fact that Congress controls the purse makes it relevant to these three policy needs, but even its power to appropriate (or not to appropriate) can hardly be employed for positive or initiating purposes. In short, the nature of foreign policy-making requirements stands as an obstacle to Congressional initiative." *Congress and Foreign Policy-Making* (Homewood, Ill.: Dorsey Press, 1962), pp. 191–92. See a similar argument by Thomas R. Dye concerning state legislatures—that is, that legislatures are more likely to function as "arbiters" of public policy than as "initiators." "State Legislative Politics," in *Politics in the American States,* ed. Herbert Jacob and Kenneth N. Vines (Boston: Little, Brown & Company, 1965), pp. 200–201.

more in the nature of assertiveness than in a steady application of legislative intelligence to persistent and critical problems.

If it is true that the legislature has mislaid or abandoned its initiative, or had it wrenched away, the further question arises: Can it be restored? In the first place, let us rule out the possibility that times will become less critical or that issues will lose their complexity. This leaves the possibility of eliminating "structural" defects as a means of revitalizing the legislature. Is there reason to believe that legislatures can or will make basic changes in organization? Does it make any difference whether they do?

Reform is the doctrine of restive observers. To many scholars and commentators it has seemed that the more legislatures have sought to reform themselves, the more they have resembled their old selves and conventional ways. The fundamental problems are scarcely touched in legislative reorganizations, and there is small reason to believe that comprehensive reform will soon be initiated by the legislature. If this is not to be explained as simply a case of submissive adherence to traditional arrangements nor charged to the absence of exceptionally able men in legislative office, how is it to be accounted for?

Legislators are pragmatic and skeptical men. They are occupied by practical affairs, with settled and predictable relations, and are little disposed to try the new and experimental. They are, moreover, realists. They have an acute sense for the snares that can trap the unwary. Change makes them uneasy, as it does most other men; they doubt its necessity. As well as anyone, they know that neither traditional arrangements nor formal rules are neutral—some interests are benefited and others are disadvantaged.[58] Their welfare or that of their friends may be at stake.[59] This is perhaps the crux of the matter: Legislative reform culminating in steady majority rule would threaten established legislative ways; it would upset the traditional balance of power within the legislature; almost certainly, it would strengthen the chief executive's influence upon legislation. Major reform, in short, would bring down the barriers that now prevent a national (or state) majority from securing effective, continuing power in the assembly. Vigorous majority rule would mean the abandonment of the old language of politics.

We said earlier that we cannot be sure that the new language of politics—majority rule–party responsibility—would have an altogether salu-

---

[58] Heinz Eulau has put the argument this way: "[At times] 'reform' comes to have a very particular meaning. It comes to mean the creation of temporary devices designed to serve the temporary advantage of partisan groupings, ideological factions, interest-group combinations, or the President. The long-range role of the Congress in the system of balanced powers is ignored, or else the Congress is assigned a secondary role in the scheme of governmental things." "The Committees in a Revitalized Congress," in *Congress: The First Branch of Government* (Washington, D.C.: American Enterprise Institute for Public Policy Research, 1966), p. 214.

[59] Note this comment by a member of the U.S. House of Representatives: "One of the problems here is that of cronyism. All kinds of strange alliances develop and people just don't like to hurt one another. Part of the problem is that the men who might well bring about reform in our system are so much a part of the cronyism that you really cannot count on them. They are the kind who say, 'yes, I agree with everything you say, something should be done, but so far as I am concerned. . . .' " Charles L. Clapp, *The Congressman: His Work as He Sees It* (Washington: The Brookings Institution, 1963), p. 17.

498   tary impact on the political system. One school of writers is convinced that the drawbacks would outweigh the advantages, and their assessment could be correct. To the persistent critics, however, it appears plain that legislative prestige and inventiveness cannot be regained in the face of, or coexist with, customs and practices, such as those of Congress, which drain the energy of legislators and smother effective majority power: the filibuster, independent committee power, unchecked seniority, antediluvian rules, malapportionment, immoderate errand-running, and the pervasive parochial spirit.

The state legislatures, by the same token, cannot regain a place in the sun if they are shackled by outmoded constitutions, if their structures are inflexible or weak and rickety, if they are unable to induce outstanding citizens to stand for office, if they are not given powers commensurate with their responsibilities, if they are run by factions that cannot be held accountable for their actions, if they have as many leaders as followers, if their dynamic areas are subordinated to their countryside—if, in sum, power cannot be coordinated to transform majority preferences in the electorate into the public policy of the legislature. Political majorities in the United States, to bend a phrase of T. S. Matthews, have been kept standing on their tiptoes a long time without being kissed. It is no wonder that they are becoming tired of waiting.

The American people are not without a choice concerning their political systems and the role legislatures are to play. On the one hand, they can preserve (or acquiesce in) the present system in which "the making of governmental decisions is not a majestic march of great majorities united on certain matters of basic policy." In this they gain a "relatively efficient system for reinforcing agreement, encouraging moderation, and maintaining social peace in a restless and immoderate people operating a gigantic, powerful, diversified and incredibly complex society."[60] This option is clear enough; it has the superiority of convenience, and the values are not inconsiderable.

The principal alternative is perhaps not so clear; it has the disadvantage of all innovation—uncertainty—and its values may appear mixed. The alternative hinges on the reinvigoration of the party system—the institutionalization of majority rule—as a means of integrating legislative and executive purposes and consolidating power now diffused. It promises a government with the capacity to act steadily and responsibly, one better able to meet unremitting crisis.

The design of a disciplined party system is, of course, neither simple nor one-dimensional. There is no way by which the idea can be translated into a concrete question to place before the people or their representatives— in other words, a deliberate decision on the total option can never be made. The alternative thus is relevant only insofar as it involves *increments* of party rule, or *tendencies* toward party rule. In this sense, decisions can be made at almost any time to strengthen majority rule and party institutions. Congress could decide to institute majority cloture or to liberalize the House discharge rule. The Constitution could be amended to provide four-year terms for House members. A seniority formula could be devised that would link committee chairmanships more firmly to party loyalty. Committee power

---

60 Dahl, *op. cit.*, pp. 146 and 151.

could be vested more securely in committee majorities. New life could be breathed into legislative party organs. Ways could be found to cut the risk for the legislator who accepts party goals rather than pressure group or constituency demands. Ways could be found to attract some of the most talented persons to party and legislative careers.

In practical terms, then, the substitute for a legislative system that acts by "concurrent majority" is not immediate, full-blown party government, a parliamentary system, or a plan for the massive upheaval of established political institutions—the obstacles to wholesale revision of constitutional and conventional forms are much too formidable. The alternative turns out to be a series of alternatives, each distinct yet related to the others, each able to be judged as a single item.

Whether Americans ever will become sufficiently frustrated to insist that something be done about their legislatures is far from certain. "The cares of politics," Tocqueville wrote, "engross a prominent place in the occupations of a citizen of the United States."[61] Possibly this generalization holds true today. If it does, it describes the citizens' interests in the current issues of politics rather than in the institutions which give them form and meaning. By and large, the public is not so much skeptical of its political institutions as it is indifferent to them—whether any significant portion of the public ever looks beyond the ways in which legislatures function to the ways in which they might function is doubtful at the least.

Public sensitivity and interest sharpen the cutting edge of change. Where these are lacking, change comes hard or not at all. The critical point is unavoidable: Given the public's mild interest in the legislative system, its instinct for the preservation of established institutions, its aversion to the claims of party, and the inability of majorities to assert themselves in the election process, no one should expect legislatures to abandon easily their traditional arrangements and procedures. Major reform would place power and advantage in jeopardy and open up old policies to new settlements. All this suggests that such basic reform as comes to Congress or to the state legislatures will arrive in small and uncertain increments. Future chief executives and legislative party leaders cannot count on having available more potent resources for influencing legislative behavior and shaping public policy than those now at hand. Legislative politics for some years to come is likely to be strikingly similar to the legislative politics of today. Whether the response and contributions of American legislatures will be adequate to fulfill the tasks required of them will be tested repeatedly.

[61] *Democracy in America* (New York: New American Library of World Literature, Inc., 1956), p. 109.

INDEX

Abernethy, Byron R., 38
Abraham, Henry J., 437, 438, 439, 442, 449, 453, 457
Acheson, Dean, 196–97, 226, 423
Adair v. *United States,* 449
Adams, John, 416
Adams, John Quincy, 29
Adams, Sherman, 422
Adams, Walter, 371
Adkins v. *Children's Hospital,* 449
Adrian, Charles R., 28, 40
AFL-CIO, 303, 321, 340, 342, 348
Agar, Herbert, 489
Aiken, George, 487
Alabama, 48, 51, 81, 182, 216, 394, 399, 400, 402
Alaska, 48, 181, 467
Albert, Carl, 43, 246, 396
American Farm Bureau Federation, 87, 347, 359
American Legion, 337–38, 346, 348, 349, 361
American Medical Association, 348, 357, 361, 390
American Political Science Association, Committee on American Legislatures, 166, 250–51
American Political Science Association, Committee on Political Parties, 96, 192, 198, 325–27, 333, 372
Americans for Constitutional Action, 306, 307
Americans for Democratic Action, 306, 307
Andrews, Hiram, 296
Anton, Thomas J., 317, 383
Appointment process, 18–20
Apportionment (*see also* Representation):
  constitutional and statutory provisions, 70–73
  criteria for, 69–70
  gerrymander, 27, 72, 76–77, 83–84, 88, 474–75

Apportionment (*cont.*)
  malapportionment, consequences of, 75–77, 324
  malapportionment, dimensions of, 73–79, 474
  multimember districts, 71–72, 83, 88
  reapportionment, 79–88
  rural-urban conflict, 27, 74–76, 84–86
Appropriations process, 18, 39, 57–58, 158–59, 167, 168–69, 175, 178, 208, 235–36, 240, 242, 255, 380–83, 384, 388–89, 426, 427–29, 464
Arizona, 85, 164, 385, 400, 402
Arkansas, 58, 117, 272
Atkins, Burton M., 93

Baer, Michael A., 93, 343, 355, 363
Bagehot, Walter, 20
Bailey, Stephen K., 23, 185, 247, 329, 332, 370
Baker, Bobby, 10
Baker, Gordon E., 73
Baker, Ross K., 475
Baker, Russell, 286
Baker v. *Carr,* 70, 72, 73, 80–81, 87
Barber, James D., 91–92, 123, 136–40, 287, 396
Barden, Graham, 393
Barenblatt, Lloyd, 221
Barenblatt v. *United States,* 221, 455
Barkley, Alben, 257
Barth, Alan, 219, 223–24, 420
Bauer, Raymond, 62, 363–64
Bayh, Birch, 134
Becker, Robert W., 317
Beckett, Paul, 117
Beer, Samuel H., 26, 353
Behling, Burton N., 173
Belknap, William, 421
Bell, Charles G., 65, 143

NOTES